LITHIC LANGUAGE

THE DISCOVERY OF STONE AGE MEANINGS

LORD WALSINGHAM

Published by New Generation Publishing in 2013

Copyright © Lord Walsingham 2013

First Edition

The author asserts the moral right under the Copyright, Designs and Patents Act 1988 to be identified as the author of this work.

All Rights reserved. No part of this publication may be reproduced, stored in a retrieval system or transmitted, in any form or by any means without the prior consent of the author, nor be otherwise circulated in any form of binding or cover other than that which it is published and without a similar condition being imposed on the subsequent purchaser.

www.newgeneration-publishing.com

Paperback ISBN: 978-1-909878-43-3
Hardback ISBN: 978-1-909878-44-0

 New Generation **Publishing**

CONTENTS

	PAGE
Preface	5
Chapter 1 Introduction	9
Chapter 2 Lithic	19
Chapter 3 BA	49
Chapter 4 KA	68
Chapter 5 TA	83
Chapter 6 FA	97
Chapter 7 HA	120
Chapter 8 LA	142
Chapter 9 MA	163
Chapter 10 NA	183
Chapter 11 PA	213
Chapter 12 RA	228
Chapter 13 ISH	253
Chapter 14 The Phonemes WA and VA and the Vowels	303
Chapter 15 On Thinking	322
Chapter 16 Conclusions	348
Appendix A The Philosophy of Language	370
Bibliography	393

FIGURES

		PAGE
1 & 2	The Dialectic	44
3	Sketches for Chapter 15	326

TREES

1	Psychosemantic Tree for BA	61-63
2	Psychosemantic Tree for KA and GA	75
3	Psychosemantic Tree for TA and DA	89
4	Psychosemantic Tree for FA	103
5	Psychosemantic Tree for HA	124
6	Psychosemantic Tree for LA	146
7	Psychosemantic Tree for MA	166-167
8	Psychosemantic Tree for NA	186
9	Psychosemantic Tree for PA	216
10	Psychosemantic Tree for RA	234
11	Psychosemantic Tree for ISH	260
12	Psychosemantic Tree for WA, VA and the Vowels	306

PREFACE

This is a popular short version of a much larger (624 large pages) volume published in 2006, "On the Origins of Speaking" (ISBN 1-4120-7697-8). The present volume can be read on its own, and it has the benefit of being half the size, and still covers all the same discoveries. Comments on the first volume made it clear more emphasis should have been given to the thinking which lies behind the burgeoning of meanings over the millennia. Both books change the way we look at the development of language, and claim to discover the way it was first spoken in the old Stone Age when first we learned to speak - hitherto treated as impossible. There will be some surprises.

The message of both books is thus powerful, as well as highly controversial. They claim to get behind words, as we understand them, that is as meaningful items with their meanings just given them, their construction secondary and only traceable as far back as to their 'roots', which turn out to be their core syllables, supposedly randomly selected. Instead it is argued here that words are really comparatively late inventions, and have been made up of strings of individually meaningful phonemes (effectively letters), in terms of which we conversed for hundreds of thousands of years before deciding to forget the past and learn words parrot fashion, without any longer following through the meanings of the elements of which they were - and are - composed. We made it all up; and now we still live with the way we did it; but it is all forgotten by the waking mind. In fact we are still making it up, along with everything else we discover. Even science itself is not how the world actually works. It is how we represent the way it works to ourselves. You may think that is much the same but it is not. Nature meanwhile is not a mathematician; it does not need to do the sums as we do - unless perhaps it has a subconscious mind too? But I doubt it. The subconscious is part of our minds, and sometimes shows up. The fully unconscious never does. It comprises the brain functions automatically controlling our physical behaviour like breathing, digestion, etc.

Freud and Jung, both psychics and Freud on drugs, had some pretty wild ideas. They patterned the subconscious quite deliberately and elaborately with their own perceptions, for which the empirical evidence was and is abstruse, and ultimately lacking. But it appealed to some folk wanting escape from conventional thinking, who have generated a scientific domain for psychology. But these are not the types to study linguistics, because they posit meta-physical patterns of thinking which are ultimately magical, while linguists are traditionally tied to empirical study and shun the arcane. They claim to be entirely scientific.

By contrast with the psychologists, the Lithic Hypotheses only require we have a subconscious. There is no need to stock it with patterns of anybody's choosing. The evidence for the subconscious is actually widespread. Even the ancients acknowledged a disembodied muse, which prompted perceptions, arising apparently from nowhere in particular, personal spiritual entities which could provide valuable insights.

The ages down which Sapiens Sapiens has sauntered have yielded slurring and slovening enough to blur the original configurations in many cases, which is why Lithic language has been concealed for so long a time, and has to be laboured over to demonstrate it today. What is needed is to get back to the original habit (before the Tower or Tao of Babel, when human conceit got us into a muddle) of thinking in semantic terms, that is in the first place with the meanings; instead of thinking in words learned by heart and only secondarily in terms of the meanings they vouchsafe us. That may not sound all that different, but it is. Thinking in words is thinking in minted pieces, making a world of rigid bits we can only just shuffle in our minds, like stepping stones in a stream. The real world is much more fluid than that. At one stage it is said Einstein abandoned language altogether as a basket case, and indeed we all notice as much when we have an idea we have difficulty putting into words. It becomes necessary to break the mould to free the mind to follow the real world as nearly as possible. For this we need to work in accordance with the original ground plan of our mind, now presented in this book, with all its fallacies and fuddled thinking, instead of starting half way through the word game when many messes have already been made. It sounds alarming; but it can be made simple. Well if not all that simple, anyway pretty simple. You should get a few laughs as well.

I would like to thank my literary agents for banging my head until I understood the requirement, when writing a book for the personal fun of it, to remember the readers too, and tailor my vapourings so as to hold some appeal for the reader as well. That is why the original tome laying out what had been gleaned over forty years in over 600 much larger pages has been cut to half its original size; as well as jargon eliminated and a whole lot of additional explication put in where the logic had, all unawares, been skimped. If you know what you have written means it can easily escape you that that is an entirely private state of affairs.

I must also acknowledge my even greater debt to those who have gone before. Foremost is the late Eric Partridge, "The Word King" and author of many dictionaries; but his life work was his large 972 page book "Origins. A Short Etymological Dictionary of Modern English" published in 1958. He was a New Zealander who polished a seat in the British Museum Library for forty years like Karl Marx before him, but by how much more profitably engaged, passing his wisdom to his successors in place of the legacy of economic error and poisonous malice left behind by Karl Marx, most likely prompted by the boils he had on his bottom, due to his bad feeding and unhealthy living. He never had a proper job. However he was an accomplished intellectual - yet he believed in Hegel's dialectic. In his day you could, but not now. However you can read Partridge every day, and I do.

Partridge's Origins, in a single volume grouping all the words with a common derivation together, packs for etymologists a punch comparable to the thirty five volumes of the Oxford English Dictionary (OED); and at the same time is much more convenient to carry and consult. The OED is historical rather than principally etymological, and the history is mostly of English, and goes back three thousand years at most, seldom behind the Latin and Greek. Partridge, on the other hand, quite often attempts Ancient Egyptian, and sometimes even Akkadian (a proto Semitic language) and Sumerian (Adam's language,up to now on its own), 5000 (plus) years ago. The Akkadians, after defeating the Sumerians, appear to have copied the more civilised Sumerians a lot, including their myth and religion. Adam was a Sumerian and not originally a Semite at all, just borrowed for Genesis from Sumerian myth (where it just means the First-born), by the Akkadians. They were just desert goat herds in those days. There is a Semitic lobby amongst linguists trying to turn Sumerians into Semites.

More superficially I should also acknowledge the encouragement I got from Alfred Kallir's "Sign and Design" of 1961. Almost entirely unrecognised, it examined the messages carried by the letters of the alphabet, though not their meanings as such. He found their shapes significant. B for instance looks like bubs or a bum and so suggested curvaceous things. The Lithic explanation, per contra, is semantic: ba meant the fleshy bits because pronounced by the lips, the fleshy bits surrounding the mouth, and so flesh. Kallir had a hang up with what he called "acrophony", his made up word: the importance of the first letter at the head of a word for its meaning. Heads were important for him. Glancing in his book recently, it left me cold; but it originally challenged me to try to make sense of it. The other book that nudged me into Lithic (Stone Age) language, when otherwise I might have given it up as too difficult, or too absurd, was a two hundred page paper back "The Key", published in 1971 by an Irish journalist John Phillip Cohane, which I came upon second hand quite by chance. He thought he could detect the passage of two great waves of linguistic influence, supposedly carried by prehistoric world wide migrations, and gave examples of the same sequences of phonemes in place names he had found on maps. He did not attempt any analysis of meanings but suggested they were to do with religious beliefs. I still much admire the way Kallir and Cohane both stuck their necks out. So far as I know, nobody but me paid any attention whatever to either of them, and they can both now be forgotten.

After a lifetime abjuring schematic thinking and ideology, the philosophical addiction to consistency, the worst case the dialectic, I am now finally forced to concede the historical validity of finding the original patterns of our thinking. Moreover in point of fact the historical evidence, if slender, does now seem to point to a global migration with the ice's final melt 8,000 to 10,000 years ago, which may have been relatively sudden, when a large block of ice slid into Hudson's Bay and the seas rose and the Garden of Eden (Eastern Malaya, Malaya means Garden Land) disappeared, now three hundred and fifty feet below the South China Sea, drowning Adamite (the original Sumerian?) civilisation.

Finally I must thank once again Miss Alison Lambert who painted the picture on the front cover, just as for the earlier work. A busy civil servant from Norwich, England, she nevertheless found time to do over and over again and again the specification for the scene outside the cave, in order to present in a small space both the crucial central hearth itself and the bare bottomed naming committee hunkered around it, with hominids looking not nearly as savage as academia thinks, but not too clever either. With continued study I think I can detect a certain similarity in the face of the principal hominid on the front cover to Ludwig Wittgenstein. The picture represents the birth of language and civilisation.

Once again, of course, I must gratefully acknowledge here the stoicism of my wife and family who, over more than forty years, have endured my absence of mind at meal times and the paper trails around the house as my scribblings, along with the supporting paperworks, continued to accumulate on top of my business substrate brought home from the office.

Lord Walsingham, Hassocks, Merton,
Thetford, Norfolk, IP25 6QP, UK
hassocks@lineone.net

CHAPTER 1

INTRODUCTION

Little Red Books and Black Books abound. This is a White Book. It means nobody any harm. It can be read without any discomfort by those of all religions or none, as well as of any skin colour or none. That is because its subject matter precedes religions, way back in the Pleistocene, before Sapiens Sapiens was around, when our hominid forebears first began to speak; before too, any of us had decided to change our skin colour from its original tone - nobody knows what it was anyway, and probably nobody ever will, nor indeed whether changing it ever did anybody any good, unless perhaps as a badge - but of what? Nice, really, to be able to shuck off our current cares and dwell for a spell in a time when none of the present world mattered in the slightest bit; especially when what we discover turns out to have profound significance for the way we think today. It took forty years to put this book together – the author is now heading for ninety; and although there may be those who will wish to airbrush out again some or even all of what it says, it is going to take them just as long, and with no guarantee of success at the end of their endeavours; because once folk see the light they see the light; and with the mind you can't rub out what has been rubbed in.

There surely can be no harm in trying to find out how it was we first learned to speak, and what we can learn from the way we did it. Indeed it kept me sane in business crises, and it could do as much for others. Just living can be traumatic today, as neo-Fascism seems to be winning all around the world. But compared with the hundreds of thousands of years since first we spoke, today's problems are put in proper perspective. The really odd thing is nobody before me has ever sat down and tried to think how we managed the business of learning to speak. Of course before Charles Darwin put Homo Sapiens Sapiens (us) back into our proper place in Nature in 1859 it was supposed we were kitted out with speech ab initio (from the beginning) by God; so it would have been cheeky to enquire how He set about it. But even after Darwin folk concluded it would be impossible – after all there was no record to examine – so they did not think about it any more. But now here we go. Let us see what we can discover. I can promise some surprises in store.

The whole book is written as a history of meanings, how they were first fitted to the stop sounds (consonants) as we first learned to utter them and identify them, and how the semantics have been built since then ever since, over tens of thousands of generations, with never a break in the tradition. It alters the mindscape of humanity. It is a word game, and the longest game of Chinese Whispers ever conceived or anywhere to be found. It is obvious that since we learned to speak we have never stopped speaking. So it is not possible to argue such a tradition is impossible, although this is the common position in academia. It is however by no means an easy exercise – one Professor Chomsky has indeed declared too difficult to be worth attempting. We shall see. The key to unlock this conundrum is the recognition that, long before we composed our very first word, we very easily made do with meaningful single phonemes; and since there were only about a dozen easily identifiable ones, they soon became very meaningful indeed. That polysemy in turn was what led to Babel, when we abandoned Bab-El, the original Speech of the Gods, as originally taught to us, or strictly as first worked out by us, latterly supposed with divine guidance.

Chapter 1 Introduction

It is not intended to suggest we all learned to speak as one, passing the tricks needed around, all across the world. Obviously we did not, since our primitive dumb forebears have left their bones lying about all round the world; and there was no internet or any kind of communication straddling great distances for the passage of information in those days. But there are two things almost as incredible which can be seen nevertheless to have been the case, when the evidence is sufficiently examined. First, whenever and wherever our forebears embarked upon giving meanings to the sounds they uttered, they went for what they supposed must be their actual natural meanings; and – Surprise, Surprise! – they matched up what they took to be natural meanings with their own experiences, of themselves and of the world around them, as they saw it; particularly those experiences they wanted to share, so they could be shared. After all, how else? [1] We may not readily accept any sound has any actual natural meaning; but if you were trying to get young Tarzan hunkered beside you around the hearth to understand, how else would you, without speech to help you, find a meaning that he could find too? Only if there were something prompting him that was prompting you already, and that could surely only be the true and actual meaning of the sound.

For starters we are obviously just talking about echoism here. But pointing and articulating would sometimes do. Even here we will have to be a bit careful. It could not have been easy. But it could have been done. Cuckoo for the cuckoo young Tarzan surely would have twigged straight away. "Grrrr!" for the sabre toothed tiger should have worked immediately, and was probably well understood by those brainy enough and fit enough to survive, even before much speaking was around. It meant for Homo Erectus, when still at the shrieks and howls stage: "I spy a sabre toothed tiger! Jump for the tall trees!", and it may well have meant about as much even before we could frame that whole sequence with any precision in our minds at all. Fear is a great teacher. It is obvious we did not start to speak in heroic couplets, or even making much in the way of sentences at all; that came aeons later. Ter-wit-ter-woo would probably have been a failure. Whoo-oo-oo'ooh in a whistling tone would have been much better for an owl. When we did learn to speak, however, Ti-grrr, Mistress-growler, meant the tiger, just as in France they still pronounce it today, long after her original namesake with sabre teeth is extinct; while the English make a pretty good mess of it today (our tiger), and our children are even encouraged to go for tigger instead.

Piling Ossa upon Pelion, the second incredible fact is that, as we squatted around our hearths (in our birthday suits) all around the world, what we took to be the actual natural meanings of the sounds were all virtually the same. This is going to need some explanation. How could it possibly have happened? First of all it has to be understood a good deal of our thinking has piggy-backed upon our talking. No talk, not much thinking, in other words. So there were thin pickings to choose from, when it came to guessing the meanings of sounds. In modern linguistics it is all about symbolism, roughly how we related meanings to their phenomenal correspondences, how the idea which the word represented was related to what was meant. Or perhaps more accurately how did the thing represented get handed out the word for it which it got? Now we must cut down our modern fanciful ideas to basics. In what terms did dumb hominids think? Obviously in pictures, what they had seen, because impossible in words when there were none. Still, there may well have been a few unsung Einsteins about, capable of following a sequence of consequences in their minds without any medium of record to keep the mind on track and able to go over the same sequence time after time, to burn it into the mind so to speak.

Chapter 1 Introduction

But they will not have been many, any more than they are today – mathematicians mostly these days.

So now, thirdly, we move to looking at the subject matter of what they were capable of thinking of, when they were starting to speak. It surely will have been the things holding the most importance and appeal for them, and surely they will have been food and shelter and sex, with all their contributory domains: hunting, fishing, grubbing for roots, picking berries, caves and shelters, wood for the fire, courting and seduction, keeping face with other members of your tribe, confronting competition, fighting when necessary. All that will have been much the same the world over. If speaking came with the taming of fire – as, more or less, it did – everyone had hearths and flaked flints for cutting and pounding and scraping. Indeed it could be argued we are just overgrown lemmings, and so capable of breaking stones and breaking fire to our will: that is what it has taken to finish up talking our way to civilisation.

Now all that remains necessary is to derive our initial meanings from the flaking of flints, from making shelters, from the chase and gathering, and from life around the hearth, which was cooking and sex; and of course the preparedness to try to do it.

Before we spoke, just howling and yowling and waving our arms about, making faces and drumming on our chests, along perhaps with other rude gestures that nature had equipped us with, best left to the imagination (with just the prompt that at the time in question we weren't wearing any pants), can hardly have contributed much to theorising of any kind. This is when we were flaking flints (latest estimates are they were getting flaked, if not very well, as long ago as one and a half million years before the present, but nobody knows if man or monkey was doing the job at that time) and learning from echoism the way to start thinking in symbolic terms. "Cuckoo" symbolised the cuckoo; and "Grrrr" symbolised the sabre toothed tiger; and there were a lot more symbols, echoic or something like it, as we shall see in the following pages, which have left a mark on the way we still think today. That surely is surprise number one. The trick is to guess as far as possible what echoisms struck these primitive jolly boys and girls (see the front cover) as the right ones – for which purpose we have to be guided by the composition of the languages in use today, which still have traces of these original patterns of composition.

This is the time consuming bit. There are between six and seven thousand languages around today, and you need a decent sample. I have been chewing on the dictionaries of just over a hundred. The test of all the guesses, like the rest of science, is how they fit together with the rest of what we know. But with language this is really schoolboy stuff. You hardly need to have passed any examination at eleven years old, or have a bunch of GCSEs, even less to have graduated at a university. So, whoever you are, you can sit back and enjoy what is to come. It isn't SciFi, but it is rather more fun, and no more taxing; and when you are done, you will be able to think for yourself with the best of them. You will have broken free from the mental trammels of conventional thinking – schooling if you like. You will be off on your own whenever you want, perhaps for the first time in your life, cutting your own path through the mental jungle, using the insights discovered here.

It is argued that when first we learned to utter as separate syllables the sounds like those which now make up the alphabet, we hunted down the natural meanings for them immediately, probably even urgently as soon as a committee – a quorum will have been two - could agree on a pronunciation. We did not wait to form an alphabet and spell out words with them (just talking that is, not writing) before identifying and utilising their semantic potentials. To think we did because we do is an anachronistic way of looking at it. As each phoneme (uttered sound) was identified we gave it its natural meaning as we

Chapter 1 Introduction

imagined it at the time to be. You can see them at it on the front cover. Now you just need the trick of looking at letters (phonemes) and their meanings in the same way. Then the way they inter-relate and pick up from each other begins to become clearer. In an earlier volume, a six hundred and twenty four large page monster designed to provide sufficient evidence to prove the case to academia (while still attracting folk) there were "psychosemantic trees" for each letter in turn, showing how letters (single phonemes) were assumed to have natural meanings when we first learned to utter them and began to speak, hundreds of thousands of years ago; the how and why also explained, but all too briefly; and then tracing the development and elaboration of meanings attached to single phonemes (letters, more or less) over the millennia, from a first fifteen phonemes (counting the vowels) with meanings to the hundreds of thousands of words in English alone today – actually hitting one million while this book was being prepared for print. These trees of meanings, critical for understanding, are repeated and more simply explained in the present book. Properly understood they completely replace the conventional word 'roots', like the Reverend William Skeat's list of three hundred and sixty five, published in 1879 to 1882, still conventionally believed to underlie our lexicon. It can now be seen that they are misconceived and misleading rubbish. It isn't that the roots do not carry the meanings Skeat claims, but that reducing words to a core element when they are really sentences made up of strings of constituent meanings (which are in reality carried by all the individual phonemes or letters) is a nonsense. Paring down words to a fraction of their original phonetic (and semantic) composition, as if to get at a kernel within, which carries the meaning (and never mind why), merely mutilates the original composition, ipso facto destroying part of the original meaning, so that "never mind why" is the only solution left. But we should mind why; because that is the key to understanding language, how it came about and what it has done to our minds, both of utmost importance quite apart from the fascination any scientific revelation carries.

In spite of Professor Noam Chomsky's best efforts, by means of his "Universal Transformational Grammar", at MIT (Massachussets Institute of Technology), on the far side of the pond, with his brain structure co-workers over a number of decades, to identify language as essentially a system of symbolic logic, the fact is we are still parroting many of our original guesses, and their progenies, as we learn the meanings of our words by rote.

Not only all that, but my original "On the Origins of Speaking", of which the present book is merely a more popular resumé, (to bring the public up to date with the linguistic hanky-panky), also claimed to get back behind words, as we understand them, that is as meaningful items with the use meanings just given them, their construction secondary and only traceable to the aforesaid 'roots'. Instead the earlier book defined words as comparatively late inventions made up of strings of meaningful elements (phonemes: now since alphabetic writing was invented called letters and taken to be meaningless), in terms of which we conversed for hundreds of millennia before deciding to forget the past and learn words parrot fashion without any longer following through the meanings of the elements of which they were - and are - composed. This decisive turnover (or tao or tower) of Babel (Bab-El, Speech of the Gods) has proved to be a peculiarly fertile one, leading on to a great deal more ratiocination than occurred when we were speaking slowly in sentences made up of individual meaningful sounds in turn. But it also follows that we have increasingly become parrots, so that it now requires considerable intellectual effort to break free from conventional thinking, and start to examine the make-up of meanings again, and how we strung them together into words. Even science, using words, is not free

Chapter 1 Introduction

from this rote thinking. We are perhaps not only the only featherless bipeds but also the only scientific parrots.

None of this means that, before the turnover from Bab-El, (literally Mouth-of The Lord [God]) we could only speak in single phonemes, because we quickly learned to put them together and work out meanings for the combinations (strings of phonemes), in the way the Chinese language, for instance, still can be seen to be doing today. It makes for a lot of extra learning - the mandarin syndrome - which leads to elitism; but it keeps mandarins' minds supple. The phonemes actually were uttered one by one, and individual meanings worked out for each of them when first we learnt to utter them. Language built from there. The point is it involved reasoning of a sort. It was not a process to which we were subjected, willy-nilly and all unawares like genetic evolution. We made it up; and now we live with the way we did it. In fact we are still making it up, along with everything else we discover. There is more on this ("The Wall Paper Theory") in chapter 15, which deals with how we developed our thinking along with our speaking.

The ultimate historian finds himself working back down the bean stalk of the human record, remarking as he does so the way-stations in human thinking, a history of ideas, which have exhibited a volatility quite unknown to the man in the street, and even unbelievable to hodge, steeped in a bunch of the common thinking patterns of the day. The big bang for humanity, which separates us from ingenious monkeys, was learning to speak, which has shaped our minds - which are philosophic entities, the nature of which has nothing directly to do with the structure of our brains, any more than the structuring of our legs has anything to do with the particular walks we may take. Our brain is an organism. Our thinking is an activity, and our minds are just shorthand for our thinking, meta-physical entities not to be confused withany kind of physicality.

The whole of this book is of course highly controversial, since the conventional wisdom espoused by academic experts in the study of language for generations is that words just have randomly chosen original 'roots' (apart, that is, from a few quite exceptionally chosen for echoism) and have simply come to mean what they mean effectively by chance. Now they have to learn they haven't. Furthermore it is also now widely believed in academic circles attempts to trace phonetic forms or meanings over very many millennia is impossible, and therefore should not be attempted, because of the volatility of language and the speed and inconsequence with which it changes. There comes a time, it is argued, when there is not enough left behind leading to our present expression for a trace further back to be possible. This snap judgment also now turns out to be wrong. It was made up before linguists had heard of our subconscious minds, capable of retention when our conscious minds are blank. Now we all have to take them into account. Nevertheless working back through earlier and earlier forms in the Indo European language family, a proto language (of the Indo-European family) has been given the name "Nostratic" (from the Latin noster, nostra, our) and has been derived for a few words to guessed probable originals from say five thousand years ago at most. This has nothing to do with Lithic, some six hundred thousand years before the present or more, when hominids (before Sapiens Sapiens, the reader's race, had come into existence) first began to speak. In other words it now appears Homo Sapiens Sapiens who is you, gentle reader, did not invent language after all. We got it from our hominid predecessors who had already worked out a (rather modest) linguistic modus operandi. Or else you could argue it was Homo Sapiens slowly putting the second Sapiens in place, who actually began speaking. That is merely a matter of names and definitions. There aren't enough bones left, nor are they sufficiently understood as yet, to settle the point. But whoever did it, it was "Brill", since it has

Chapter 1 Introduction

informed our accelerated mental development ever since that time. Still, whatever you call the first speakers, it was pretty basic stuff he and she first spoke, as will transpire in the following chapters. Then as now, it was probably she who did most of the talking – in those days in fact probably setting the pace and launching progress leading to civilisation, while her chauvinistic spouses were still locked into their traditional skills based upon their musculature, and out hunting in the hinterland. But before we start on the language there should perhaps be a mental health warning on the cover: not to be sold to anyone under twenty one years of age. We do not want impressionable youth on a copycat track back to the Stone Age.

What is still incredibly difficult is to determine exactly what it is that goes on, all unawares, in the subconscious thinking we apparently all enjoy. We have to bring the subconscious into the conscious mind. The less of this it proves necessary to require of course the better, because the easier to accept. Well, we all dream. The conscious mind is at rest. All sorts of ideas which we would not countenance when wide awake can and do arise. They may be silly stories with changes in the factual grounds as we go along, as if the world were not consistent with what just went before. Characters can flip from one personality to another, as the mood of the dream changes. Composite characters can be accommodated, perhaps with added features to make them more appealing or more like the dreamer or more like the dreamer would like to be, or all of these together. There is also a poverty of vision: the scene is a small spot compared with our waking thinking and vision, such as a hibernating mind might well slip into. But sometimes we may wake up with genuine new insights into matters which had been teasing us. So there must be a capacity to think to some purpose in there somewhere, however confused it may generally be. It is certainly fuzzy thinking. But as well there is often considerable subtlety, of a sort, as anyone who for one reason or another tries to recollect and study his or her dreaming state will discover. It is a classic de-inhibitioner. We can sometimes come upon truths concealed from us in the waking state by our self imposed denials. There is a Mrs Grundy tucked away somewhere in every waking mind, protecting our pride if not our virtue. We are not entirely masters of our souls, as the poet fancied. We just like to think we are.

One school of thought believes there is a revealing capacity for the subconscious to speak true when traumas overtake us in waking life. You can pay large sums to these folk for their analyses, because if they are right their observations clearly may resolve your problems. All this proves to me we must at least have a subconscious mind, as well as the conscious one we all enjoy. With diligence and insight the promptings from the subconscious can to some extent be identified, even though not directly experienced. They are of course of a different class from the totally unconscious (autonomic) processes of the brain which control our physical life processes like heartbeat, digestion, etc. The Lithic hypotheses require the subconscious mind to host meaningful perceptions, not necessarily correct or even helpful, but sufficient to build semantic connections between linguistic inputs, and spot their components, and then go on to build a memory bank associating the meanings underlying language, in spite of their disregard recently up above in our conscious minds. The result is that, for every language, the original elemental meanings are read afresh in the subconscious mind of every child born alive when he or she learns the language developed from them. It may seem that is asking a lot, but the idea isn't actually all that difficult; and the consequence is that, for every language, for every child who learns to speak, the Lithic keel of original phonemic meanings are derived afresh and imprinted afresh in the subconscious mind, because they were and are actually all implicit as components in the words as they are learned. That is how the refresh rate, the repeated access to Stone Age thinking, has kept pace with the generations, without any need for inherited ideas (individual actions of the brain) somehow to be locked into the genes, as is quite widely fancied at the Massachusetts Institute of Technology, where Noam Chomsky is their linguistic guru. Nor is there any need for Jung's group soul, situate in limbo, yet to which our individual minds are (absurdly) supposed to have magic access as offshoots of it, (if well tuned in Jung's spiritual dimension), and from which we may be advised of quite complex constellations of images (Jung's archetypes). These archetypes were really just peculiar to Jung; but at the same time not a mile away from those peculiar to each of us, if we try hard enough to compile them from our own subconscious strata. But there is no mental internet: that is the point.

So, with Lithic, even if we have, since Babel, consciously tried to invent meanings and their phonetic expression from scratch we have in fact been prompted by our subconscious store of original phonemic meanings, so even now we pick meanings which, to some degree at least, derive from our original understanding. Only prompted, mark you, not compelled. We are not being lived by our subconscious minds, which in fact we configured ourselves, (much of it some time ago), and even less by any of Professor Dawkins' selfish genes, which of course have no minds (or thinking) at all.

However, discovery of one hundred percent Lithic derivations of all the words in any or every language is asking too much. The slovening and slurring over the millennia can indeed rub out the possibility of tracing original forms, but not universally as the critics maintain. It is moot how often it happens that way. Moreover there is no guarantee all branches of the species picked exactly the same idioms for attaching meanings to sounds in the first place. The surprise is the extent to which they apparently did all think the same way, which is what enables us to trace the semantics all the way back to the Stone Age.

In fact the wonder is that to an extent which is quite astonishing it turns out we all opted to speak with the same original Lithic meaningful roots for the sounds as we learned to utter them. We all gave the sounds the same "natural" meanings as we learned to speak. Of course you can argue that is something we would not have done; so we could not have done it. The matter is only settled when you discover that in fact we did. It is bound to come as a bit of a surprise. But surprises are fun unless you are mentally a stick-in-the-mud. It in no way impugns anybody's lifestyle or beliefs. It just shows whence they grew up the way they did. It is an under-layer of our current modern thinking, which is of special interest because of what it adds to our understanding of the human mind and its behaviour. In particular it trumps the single plank brigade who fancy we are being lived – by tyrannical genes (as if genes could plan, which Darwinism says they didn't) - or by fancy dialectics of one kind or another (eg Marx). We are not. To an astonishing extent we are the captains of our souls and free to think about them, and everything else, as we please. How else could we have gone to the moon? Our genes determine our legs but not the walks we may take; and in a precisely similar manner our genes determine our brains but not the thoughts we may think. Our genes merely determine our capacities. This is because genetics is the science of organisms and how they develop, by sexual procreation involving random mutation (variation of the genetic constitution of the cells), followed by selection in accordance with the fitness of the phenotype in its environmental role, the less fit (efficient) slowly losing out. It is of course the changing environmental role which determines the fitness or efficiency, not the virtue of the phenotype, which in any case had no say in its own genetics. So social Darwinism is bunk. It has nothing whatever to do with our thinking, which is an activity and not an organism at all. Neo-Darwinists in their enthusiasm have slipped into what is known in philosophy as a category error which

Chapter 1 Introduction

Charles Darwin himself never made, and never would have made. They treat activities as the same as organisms. Any man in the street can correct them, once the error is put to him: the bigger the thinking, the vainer the thinker and the bigger the mistakes.

It is a matter of personal pain to me that in Oxford University, my alma mater, there is a young geneticist with professorial tenure who when it comes to thinking can not match the man in the street. But then until the other day there was a guitar player in Downing Street, and after that an autistic bumble with a single plank Scottish Presbyterian mind, and yet not entirely honest with it. It did not use to be like that, at least not unless you go back hundreds of years. Second-raters riding in Darwin's train misprise his message as a preaching system. That does not impugn science, which is the best thinking we have managed so far; but it is a clear identification of 'scientism' which is a bogus use of scientific theory to discredit adversaries. Scientists are human too. Indeed they are human first and only scientists by adoption. A course of semantic analysis is highly illuminating here, and is what will be attempted in the following chapters. It is in effect an appeal to the man in the street – the majority of us – over the heads of the academics with tenures to defend, should they insist on defending them regardless. It also seeks to level the playing field between academic wrangling and common sense. Darwin (and his followers) have nothing to say about thinking at all, how and when it popped up, any more than how organic chemicals could and did come alive in the first place. These are two unexplained jumps, apparent discontinuities in nature, their track records endlessly charted; but their provenance wholly unexplained – most often as if no explanations were necessary. In philosophic terms, if such be allowed, these are ontological mysteries hard to explain away as merely epistemological ones. It may not indicate divinity, but it must surely give single plank thinkers pause. It makes a powerful case for good manners in debate. Nobody knows it all; and it certainly appears (see Chapter 15) that nobody ever will!

There is one further political issue the book addresses when it comes to how we think. It eliminates dialectical thinking once and for all (much of it of course left wing, and all of it recently emanating from Germany). Young Georg Hegel (1770-1831) had no time for the old Jewish God, since He had been adumbrated in a historical period at too early a date for an enlightened age. But he reproduced a secular "iauai" (Jaweh or Jehovah) nevertheless, by means of his dialectical hypothesis, which he gradually firmed up as the backbone and explanation of everything. With the dialectical process - and it was effectively a process with a life of its own in antithesis to the natural process - thought and understanding both progressed historically in parallel zigzags, each as in a discussion between two academic disputants each presenting conflicting positions and then reconciling them - in a thoroughly liberal democratic manner. This was his Thesis, Antithesis, Synthesis, a mental spirit world leading the natural one, revealed to him by a study of classical history (comically borrowing from Gibbon's Decline and Fall. The author, we may imagine, would have fallen over laughing). Hegel then added his own German gloss Gibbon would certainly have laughed out of court. His dialectic produced a mental space curiously made up of coat-hangers, two opposite facing arms coming together in a node or synthesis with a hook on it to join on and do duty as the first arm of the next coat-hanger and the confrontation it in turn carried, each thesis evoking its contrary doppelganger and rewarded by an automatic resolution in a higher synthesis. Each synthesis in turn acted as the thesis for the next stitch. The rest was just verbage. It was, Hegel supposed, the way the spirit was working out the world through this spiritual science. It was packaged as logic, in several volumes. It was German logic, far divorced from the usual meaning of the term. The wide gap made it easier to live in the new

Chapter 1 Introduction

territory. Karl Marx was immediately at home in this world of miasmas. It is all drawn out in Figure 2 on page 44.

German idealism was thereupon headed for a totalitarian world view which would accommodate, as well as Marx and Communism, Oswald Spengler, Joseph Goebels, Nazism, Marshal Petain and Existentialism, with Jung watching fascinated from the gods. A space entirely filled with these coat-hangers, hooked up to each other to make a texture filling the whole universe, makes a memorable picture (in Figure 2); and this scheme of arrangement as a historical process has largely satisfied the majority of mankind (particularly those with intellectual pretensions for which they were barely equipped) since it was adopted by Karl Marx - with only modest adjustments in order to extract it from its lodgement by its author as the prop of conservative society and convert it instead to a revolutionary totalitarianism, by (as Marx himself put it) standing it on its head. Now this determinist and unattractive dialectical materialism was to lead human mentality; instead of Hegel's world with his logical and scientific spirit leading nature. Both schemes were and are equally absurd. Both attracted maniacal leaders to impose its teachings by force, killing even fancifully imagined challengers en masse. They gave us Stalin's Russian Gulag Archipelago and Hitler's genocides. This is why Kruschev could bang his shoe with such confidence in the United Nations chamber. Nobody could step outside their predetermined natural position presented by their economic and social classification because they were being lived by the materialistic dialectic. Independent thought was impossible. History itself was predetermined (by all those coathangers), so that all those riding the wrong arm of one were doomed. Revolution was nevertheless needed to achieve the predetermined outcome and wise men should work for it, by means of every skulduggery they could dream up in total defiance of truth, although it was inevitable. It probably accounts too for Arthur Scargill's comparatively minor intransigences, but ideologically almost a match for Kruschev's. The dialectic can get you in a headlock, but once it is seen through it evokes the most extreme disgust. While he lives Mr Scargill will probably be puzzling his brain over history's contradictions. Pooh bear would probably do better. Sapiens Sapiens does not score highly in these encounters: "Could do better". He certainly can, having already mastered iteration, counting from three towards infinity, with scientists even at home with a mathematical infinitesimal calculus Hegel ignored, so busy was he with his world-shaking coathanger technique. Even Klaus Fuchs, an atomic scientist, put the coathangers first, because they were prelinguistic – you simply intuited them directly. Effectively he swopped places with Tarzan; betraying his tennis club, his family, and his country – apparently in that order. The black humour of it all, as his only reward, like the other traitorous inadequates with minds capable only of shallow ratiocination along patterned lines picked up from others, was a reduced standard of living. It calls for a revision of what it is to be clever. It is not a single track affair but rather its opposite. It is not a magpie philately: a good, even a master memory is no guide, and may well conceal an inability to think for yourself. Thinking constructively is more like gnawing a bone, scraping away the existing tissue to get at the mental marrow.

It still has to strike academia that this dialectical process has no warrant in reality whatever. Nothing goes that way. The coathangers are figments. Their only virtue is to provide a route for resuming everything under one simple rubric which is so general and ill-defined that its total irrelevance, and indeed its ludicrous absurdity, is not immediately apparent. In the Marxian redefinition it has proved an excellent selector for an apostolic succession of operators incapable of running a party in a brewery other than by butchering any possible opposition even before it shows its head. The inevitable outcome is the

Chapter 1 Introduction

brewers eventually step in and take their premises back again, and it then proves their brains too have no upper storey. The world is set back five hundred years by these sotisseries, emerging at the stage at which it was set back; and can only recover in its own time. Only a genuine historian can rubbish these stupidities which have their latest origin in German intransigence marrying history with philosophy, and alas genuine historians are now in very short supply thanks to the bad odours of the Hegelian school of history which even reached old Henry Ford's nostrils. He spotted at once Hegelianism was bunk. It is the gulf still keeping the Anglo Saxons out of Hitler's Thousand Year European Reich (resurrected as the EU), with only some young ahistorical characters (including until recently a young and wholly naive prime minister with only a legalistic training and some work with a guitar to sustain him, keen to jump through the hoop and dissolve the United Kingdom in the European mess of Fascist establishment pottage). His name is Anthony Blair.

NOTES

1. Of course Noam Chomsky has declared this impossible without genetic inheritance of linguistic rules, but thinking is an activity, and inheritance is of predispositions and facilities only. Moreover Luc Steels and others at the Sony Computer Science Laboratory in Paris have got computers to do it and even invent proto grammar, all without any genetic guidance whatever.

CHAPTER 2

LEARNING TO SPEAK LITHIC

To start with the easy bits first, every schoolboy knows words are made up of letters of the alphabet, even if unsure which bits to use; while schoolgirls nowadays apparently know it all much better. Admittedly alphabets vary, and in China boys and girls alike are made to work to a rather different system of picture writing far freer from any restrictive grammar. But in reality words are only represented (symbolised) by strings of letters. The word is the utterance, the way we say it. That is perhaps the easiest demonstration of what it is that a symbol means, which flummoxes many people. It is just anything picked on to represent something else. There does not need to be any rhyme or reason to it, although of course it helps. A picture of a cat, or the word cat, "symbolises" a cat. The actual cat is just a cat. There is no surprise in that. The picture is a symbol, the meaning of which is rather more than hinted at in the picture: a cat. Children soon pick up the trick of recognising pictures, although some aboriginal folk are said to have difficulty at first. All those I have known found it a pushover. Words themselves however are actually made up of uttered sounds, and the words as they are uttered are symbols of something else. Of what? Well, of their meanings, their semantic contents, which are quite a different kettle of fish. It amounts to an extra layer of meanings between the word and the symbolised.

What this book is about is how the uttered words come to have the semantic contents they do. Why does do mean do, for instance? Or any other word for that matter mean what it does? Contrary to popular belief there are perfectly good reasons, but you do not find them lying about. There is a code of a kind, and it has to be cracked. The code is just the way we thought when first we learned to speak, which was different from the way we think today. Words are actually made up out of meaningful elements, the sounds that we make, but the individual meanings of these elements, roughly the letters, have been forgotten - probably about four or five thousand years ago if we go by the Bible, which is not always reliable as a historical work but in this case appears to be the best evidence we have. I will guess the loss of the original babel actually came as long ago as some ten thousand years ago. Meanwhile the conventional belief we are all taught is that there is no reason why words originally got picked from the sounds that we make, they are just built up from conventional roots which were chosen at random, or anyway for reasons long ago lost, so it is a waste of time to try to discover why these word roots sound as they do; and anyway, even if they were originally picked for any reason or other they will have got altered so much over the aeons that it is a waste of time to try to work out what they originally meant or why.

So it is argued it is better to devote our efforts to understanding how we built up our grammar, and look at languages as repositories of grammatical thinking. There we can really stretch our intellects and discover patterns of thinking. The superficiality of human understanding is compiled of confusing mistakes like this: alphabets treated as meaningless rigmaroles in aid of a common alphabetic recording system. It takes a poet to get to grips with language and even begin to understand its diversity and composition. For the rest of us, words tend now to be simples, atomic. They mean what they mean what they mean, just as a rose is a rose is a rose (or a cat a cat). We shall in fact see later precisely why a rose is a rose and why a cat is a cat, by discovering the original thinking which went into the naming. Worse still, the philologists have persuaded themselves that this random thinking is a good definition of meaning. In this Alice in Wonderland world, word roots have been worked out as if a particular basic meaning actually started out clothed in particular random basic sounds – another rigmarole without reason. So we have the Reverend Walter Skeat's three hundred and sixty five phonetically random proto-Indo-European roots of 1879-82[1] for the most part represented by two or three letters to provide a pronounceable syllable; and we have Ancient Egyptian word roots without any vowels at all, often handing us a totally unpronounceable syllable. The proto-Egyptian was evidently a pretty tongue tied fellow. We must then suppose such word roots to have grown into fully fledged and articulated words, not much different from the way Oswald Spengler's cultures were supposed to have grown from primitive roots, to burgeon, flourish and finally die – and all by rote, like clockwork oranges, or indeed like cabbages and kings. Spengler's philosophy was adopted by the Nazis, because he found civilised culture "decadent" and preached action. He was a post first world war disgruntled German secondary school teacher. As an undergraduate in the nineteen forties, after war service, I named him "the Butcher of Blankenberg" (where he taught - am Rhein, on the Rhine). My contemporaries mistook me for a Nazi for reading him, so they never learned his significance; and by now most will have died still ignorant of this quite important matter.

To make a comparison between any two things it is necessary to hold in the mind simultaneously or in close succession the two cases, compared in sufficient detail to identify the similarities. If the comparison is of two objects obviously similar, like two shoes for instance, this hardly taxes the mind. But if the similarities for perception are hidden, remote, largely semantic, or unrecognised before, and particularly if they are all four, the mental task can be quite severe, and even beyond a great many people too busy to really bother. To resume a galaxy of such arcane cases and then inter-relate them similarly, disclosing a network or matrix, in order to establish a systematic explanation of linguistic relationships must surely take much time and effort and be hard to follow through. This, by the way, is what this book is about. One is conscious of cutting across the grain, because what is proposed is new and contra-indicated by the common sense of the majority. Others have not thought the same way, and there is commonly the comfortable presumption that the solid core of what most people think is sound, with error only at the edges, so that a proposal which seeks to radically alter the perception of how languages have been formed must surely be wrong. If the correlations proposed are veridical, why were they not perceived before? Surely they would have been.

But would they? History is the dismal record of human error, spiritual, moral and intellectual, as the human mind has come down out of the trees, falling it has to be said at most of its fences, and learning painfully slowly to contradict presumption and accept the advancement of science. Science is of course here used accurately with a small s, in its quite general sense of knowledge, from the Latin scire to know, so scientia is quite literally just knowledge; and that ultimately from the Lithic phonemes ish-kai, bright-making, illuminating or clarifying so that we can see how something works or what it means. The -ire stuck on the end of scire is from -are or -ire, verb indicators. The advancement of knowledge has generally been fiercely opposed by its keepers, as a derogation of their status. All intellectuals are apt to suffer from Jowettism[2] or hubris in the Greek: if they don't already know it they think it can hardly be knowledge. Jowettism is alive and well and institutionalised these days as peer review. Bolder spirits on the wilder shores of knowledge know they shall not easily pass. Regrettably, serving up an oxymoron like

Chapter 2 Lithic

prehistoric linguistics is tantamount to taunting the intellectual establishment. That is what of course provides a certain spice, but it does not help at all with the publication.

Readers may like to reflect on the remarkable similarity between our modern English word sun and the Ancient Egyptian word Aton. Phonetically s and t are not that far apart. It was reflecting upon this remarkable apparent persistence of nomenclature over thousands of generations and several times as many miles which first led me to look for and research the other linguistic traces I have come to call Lithic Language. The aton-sun match is by no means perfect, but much better than one could expect to achieve in a few hundred throws of a dice with the whole gamut of possible sound combinations on it – unless of course the things were weighted so as to land sunny side up. Ancient Egyptian is not even recognised as in the Indo-European pipe line; although I now know it is, through Greek. Aryan (Indo-European) languages owe a good deal to Semitic tongues.

As a matter of fact I have come to the conclusion by now aton and sun have very different origins and I was wholly misled, when I started out, by the t/s and n/n similarities in thinking otherwise. The Hittite (early Indo European) version of sun meanwhile was Tun Akalas. The Greeks and Latins thought it meant World Eye, and so adopted oculos for eye, which is why we use binoculars, binary oculars, for our two eyed viewers. But this Hittite tun was actually from aton in Ancient Egyptian, which came from Lithic aa-ta-oon and meant the everlasting-birth-canal, birthing light into the world each day. If tun was from taun, world, of course the akalas must be the eye, making tun akalas world eye, up there in the sky. Actually it is the orbiting birth canal, with a-ka-la-s, that goes loop-action, an orbiting one. However Tun we can usually identify as from the Egyptian Taun and even the Mayan Tan on the other side of the Atlantic Ocean, which both mean world. Meanwhile my initial foray into spotting similarities between words in different languages was about as confused as it is at all easy to get. Sun, from sunne, and the Lithic Sa-u-nai, with the meaning Fire-what-shows, actually has nothing whatever to do with Egyptian Aton which is also sun and is from the Lithic aa-ta-un, the everlasting-birth-canal. The Egyptians started out thinking of the sun as birthing the light into the world anew each day. Sir Wallis Budge, in his 1921 dictionary, translated aton, the fully frontal sun as the disc of the sun. Of course he knew it wasn't a hole with light pouring out of it; and anyway he wasn't into birth canals, and of course he had no Lithic. He thought in 1921 English.

The polysemy involved in taun meaning the vulva and also the world, depending on context, took me some time to work out, since they seem to the modern mind worlds apart - from recollection it took me some twenty years. But Ta started out as the echoic sound of a breaking stick. It wasn't an obvious choice of meaning (semantic content) unless you had already adopted ka as the sharper and more effortful sound of flint on flint as you knapped your hand axe, your personal tenderiser and eating tool. Stone tools go back a million and a half years. Breaking a stick, you finished up with two sticks, twins, one in each hand – which is why we say two, from tau or broken in two, and so two.

The Tau is one of the oldest symbols known to mankind, with two lines in a T, a symbol of two bits, whence two dimensions. It means two, slovened around the world to deux, dos, duo, tweo, zwei, tsvei, duak, dua, dwa, to, do, dol, di'o, etc. It moved too into the active sense of to divide; and so a divide, a slit or slot, and quite soon the slit for parturition, prompted by the dual symmetry of the human body with two mirror images on either side of a centre line, and the vagina neatly on the centre line. (With the discovery of the twin helix we are perhaps lucky not to have turned out helical, as well as twin, ourselves). Parturition is then the separation into two, hence to be born, birth, and so coming into being, to become; events; but also the birth canal, and even geological channels like the river Don, and London (from the Lithic Lau-en-don, which meant originally the sloping down or estuary of the river). But in Ancient Egypt the changes the world enjoys were regarded as a sequence of births or events, a bit like the individual pictures which go to make up a film today, because to be born was to become, to begin your being. (Ba first meant flesh because the sound is made by the two fleshy lips: fancifully "Lips speaking!"; whence to be came from to be flesh or fleshed). Ta-un meant births-all or all the becomings in Egyptian, which together made up their world: a historical description of all the events as opposed to the spatial description we favour. U is pronounced oo, an o made with the mouth, an orifice or rounded hole. Such a round could be taken as the symbol of wholeness as well: an enclosure but alternatively as an abyss, the inclusive unity and the exclusive unity.

The polysemy of the oo allowed it to stand for a hole or the whole, the inclusive unity as well as the exclusive. It now becomes possible to regularise and confirm the Hittite Tun Akalas with Tun like the Egyptian Aton, a birth canal and not a universe like the Egyptian Taun and the Mayan Tan; followed by a-ka-la-sai with the meanings eternally-go/make-loop-action/movement, or in other words the birth canal-that-makes-loop-action: the orbing vagina in the sky. For the Hittites the sun was the eternal birth canal that went round the earth. Of course they were wrong, but we only just spotted it, and we have piled Ossa on Pelion (confusion on confusion) by imagining the Hittite sun was the world eye like the Egyptian Ra, which does mean eye and replaced the vagina, which the Egyptian priests felt rather left them out, the boys finding their self confidence to dump their mothers. So we twitchers watch birds looking through twin orbiters all unawares. The bi-, as in binoculars, got its meaning of two (and beside besides) via the fleshy bits, because of the bilateral symmetry of the hominid body and bum. Bum came later, but ba has always meant flesh (because it was perceived as the lips speaking, and that is why the haunch is nicknamed the bum, it is the two main fleshy bits, the haunches which drives the legs. So legging it and going is ba too. The next chapter enlarges on the sound (phoneme) Ba, so that is more than enough for now.

Compare the Greek Apollo, from A-pau-lau, That-travel/flight-round in a loop. Pa has another complex semantic tree (in chapter 11). Legging it is usually ba, from the muscular movement of the haunches, the bum, and pa is saved for small legs or other small bits (including the penis, from the Lithic pa-nai, which means piece-protruding, and so could, as well as man's pride and joy, as neatly refer to the tail of a dog in the original Latin), and particularly those other limbs used for flying, because pa was not only a small shoot or bud but also, as the thinned diminutive of ba (which meant flesh in chief), meant skin, a surface, and a wing (anyway in Greek: pteron, was a pai-ta-rau'n, in Lithic a surface-become-rayed/raised/drawn up'one. Wings were seen as sky hooks which lifted birds in flight). So Apollo flies round in a loop or orbit, and the Greeks mistook the Hittite world orbiter, akalas (from the Lithic a-ka-la-sai, that-makes-loop-action) for a world eye, understandable enough when you consider by the time the Greeks came along the Egyptians too had abandoned the idea of an eternal world vulva in the sky and renamed the sun Ra, or The Eye. It is not altogether fanciful to see this as a reflection of a sea change in the balance of power in the sex war going on down below in Egypt, the boys feeling a bit left out with a vulva (clearly it must have belonged to a goddess) in the sky and counter proposing an Eye instead - surprise surprise, with a male god behind it. The eye was first of all taken to be on the look out for impious behaviour down below with a view to punishing it; and the way the punishment was handed out made religious folk concerned to find out what was taken as mischievous and to show their subservience in the hopes of

Chapter 2 Lithic

avoiding afflictions. But eventually it occurred to folk to think the watching from above might show concern even for sparrows' falls below, and the idea of a loving god was born. To love in Egyptian was from mai, the earthing or planting of seed. In Egyptian mai meant penis, the planter, but amai meant loving, from a-mai, as-[when] earthing, that is when planting your seed, when even the most chauvinist of pigs is inclined to feel affection for his mate, (from ma-tai, the planted-become). The Egyptians' One God, Amun-Ra was the Aa-ma'un-Ra, The Ever-Loving'one-the Eye. Not many people know this. The Ever Loving Eye is traditionally just regarded as the apposition of two gods, Messrs Amun and Ra, and never mind why. The Latin amare to love has the same ever so slightly indelicate derivation, and our own marriage and amatory exploits also come from the earthing up of the Egyptian seed, using the Egyptian seeder/planter, his mai. Is the maypole in the same tradition? It is. The girls dancing round it with attachments is a mischievous reminder of primitive psychological perceptions. Sorry girls. There is more in the same vein to follow - as a matter of record, not of admiration.

The identification of the real male role as merely pollination took another few thousand years, and is little regarded even today. The Latin semen for seed perpetuates the misconception, the Lithic from which it comes is sai-mai'n, alive-planted'one. Well you earth the seed up and it comes to life. The switch away from the vagina in the sky to the eye was indeed a highly significant move, connected with the shift away from the original mother goddesses to father gods, as well as from water holes and springs to eggs and beans, and indeed triggering the move from mothers to fathers as principal parents. It must surely have enlightened many an early philosophical debate in councils hunkered around the hearth, the pros and cons of either perception mulled over interminably with emotions rising as evenings wore on. It would be unfair to suggest the ladies lost the argument. More likely they were silenced by the threat of no more meat; in spite of which they appear to have kept their end up for a few hundred thousand years, and Isis (Isis is the Greek mispronunciation, the original Egyptian was Au-Si-ti, World-Life-Source, that term precisely in use today in Malay for the Blessed Virgin Mary, Our Lady, Au Siti) and the Catholic Mary, the Mother of God, still carry the torch as gestators.

When confronted with the task of resurrecting the meanings of the prehistoric vocabulary of the Old Stone Age, whatever it was when men first began to speak, about the only prompt to rely on is psychosemantics, the meanings prompted by the psyche, our own guesswork according to what seemed good to us at the time. It is necessary to leave far behind Professor Chomsky's transformational grammar as way in the future, and virtually the whole, certainly the core of modern linguistics with it. Away with its mathematical structure derived from Boolean logic which is obviously a modern figment. Forget Frege, Russell, Wittgenstein and the other somewhat lesser writers luxuriating in their wakes. It must surely be moot if the grammatical figment is inherited hard wired in the subconscious of the race at large, or merely loose in the private lucubrations of the professor. Many theories can be devised which touch reality at a number of points and yet have room for arabesques at the whim of the inventor, and the Lithic hypotheses stand or fall by the same criterion. Do the points of contact in the case of the Lithic hypotheses justify belief?

Psychosemantics is the study of those meanings which naturally commended themselves to the simple untutored minds of our still inarticulate forebears. If they fit at all with the meanings in the languages that have come down to us, that is a bonus. These hominids were deriving their meanings for their uttered sounds from what has been called sound symbolism. I am endebted to Jarvis Nicholls for this term in his book "Sounds like

Chapter 2 Lithic

Life", Oxford Studies in Linguistics, A Study of the Pasteza Quechua Language of Ecuador: it is fascinating, if not exactly a mainstream study. The attachment of meanings to simple sounds chimes with Lithic, but the Quechua meanings are not carried far into the expanding lexicon as breeders of metaphors, but are kept clinging close to their original senses by the Quechua speakers. It is as if they were stuck in phase one of linguistic development. They probably are rather slow coaches intellectually; jungles don't encourage wrangling. Your nose is down finding food.

Sound symbolism includes most obviously the echoic. Straight echoism like cuckoo or miaow or moo is simple. Quechua echoism is more fanciful and complex, shading into whimsy. So for instance "Tsak" is apparently taken as the sound of an arrow entering the body of a monkey or a bird or some other small game, the smack as it goes in. Then from the meaning of perhaps "Bullseye!" it is developed semantically until it comes to mean just a specificity in time "precisely then" and so, as Nicholls has it, to an adverb "making it clear that there was a definite point in time when the action took place". I rather like this, although initially I reserved judgment whether to believe it or not. It makes my semantic identifications seem comparatively or even excessively sober. But on the other hand it must be remembered my psychosemantic identifications claim to be universals, not just Quechua whimsy. On reflection "Tsak" is in fact not so far from the Lithic phonemes Sa-ka, Action-strike. Similarly "Tsuk" which is said to be derived from the sound of plucking something from a mass (like an arrow from the monkey's flesh), as an adverb qualifying the verb to pull renders it to pluck out. The u (oo) in place of the a as a vowel is of course a Lithic pointer to the rounded lips and so to a sucking sound; and u is the dual determinative vowel so that tsuk is the second sound which finishes the job – tsak as the arrow goes in and tsuk the second sound as it is pulled out again. We must just hope the unfortunate animal was dead before it heard the tsuk, since no doubt the arrows were barbed as well as poisoned. The scheme is fanciful but believable. The layman may find it far fetched but the etymologist versed in the byways of semantic derivations will, I think, recognise the pattern.

The novelty is the starting with sound symbolism. Linguistic roots have been generally assumed to be phonetically random, perhaps just as an admission that if they have any rational bases they are too remote to be recovered. But with no vocabulary to cover the case, a quite sensible ploy was to mimic the sound accompanying the action to be captured. Of course to work well it needs to be a readily recognisable sound known to the hearer. It helps in such a case if he is first and foremost a hunter with bow and arrow so that his mind readily refers to the repertoire of hunting sounds. It will be less obvious to a pop mind today, more accustomed to noises like "brm-brm" and raucous thumping music out of Africa.

In Malay and a number of other languages there is no verb to be, and indeed the semantic content of the verb is not much, probably derived from being fleshed (bai) and so, as an animal, to be around, to be. "Him angry" tells us almost as much as "He is angry". There is a problem with "Man angry" because it could be merely adjectival, the angry man, or else an observation drawing attention to a novelty, the man is angry, he has become angry. In Quechua it is even worse "Him angry" can also mean the man being angry or when angry. So "Tsak"-him angry-ashka, tsak-him angry-agent suffix, followed by wife strike is the Quechua idiom, if I have it right. The proper nuanced translation into the English idiom would be "He flew into a rage and struck his wife", an action, it should be mentioned, as socially disapproved in the jungles of Ecuador as in the streets of London – or probably more so. Simple it ain't unless you are reared in Quechua speak. Computer

Chapter 2 Lithic

aided translation has some way to go before it can accommodate this kind of paradigm shift. Malay has other tricks. Orang amok itu, Man angry that, is that angry man, whereas Orang itu amok, Man that angry is that man is angry, not so far from the angry man and the man is angry where the position of the adjective is before or after the verb. In Malay with no verb to be you just don't have any 'the'. Using the same word for the and that does very well and saves learning another.

What we are learning is that some of our grammatical distinctions are second thoughts. Earlier you could get away with only a few and very general and inconclusive terms by our standards, after a few hundred thousand years of mature consideration sifting out additional distinctions. The interesting business is how from a few rather literal ideas attached to a dozen or so stop phonemes (consonants), originally of an ostensive nature merely identifying aspects of the objective world, pointing things out, drawing attention to them, indicative terms, we were able to develop the more abstract ones needed for logic, like for instance the ifs and buts, whereases and whys, the causes and becauses. It appears that from an original rather undiscriminating adjectival mind, whilst learning discrimination we first progressed to recognition of the substantive, items, things, (as things in themselves, or things for themselves as Kant would say) rather than as merely exemplars of universal adjectival qualities, as previously supposed. Things are still made up of bundles of qualities but at a stroke now permanently itemised. Itemising the phoneme strings that described them was bound to follow.

The door was thereupon opened for grammatical concepts; but enormous leaps of imagination have been involved in grasping the abstract thinking on which syntax fundamentally depends. It is easy to see that the starting out on this intellectual odyssey will have been with the easier ideas, where the original phenomenal concept of a thing fairly readily translates into the phenomenal type and then into a more general type, from flitting seen to be an aspect of a fly perhaps, and then a flyer, and finally the fully abstracted concept of flight. A relative pronoun or adverb, which or where for instance, is only a small remove from him or it, or place, from the perception of direction in vision. If place itself seems to involve a degree of abstraction already it will have come from the idea of ground or even via group from loop, looped or grouped. A loop on the ground is a location. I think a loop, an actual one like the horizon or skyline at sea (which was a line when seen from the shore as well as a loop at sea) was an early perception, and from it in time came the geometrical circle or cycle as well as the line (and of course the Ls in our words). We can list the terms of symbolic logic and look at their provenance in turn shortly.

Helpful meanwhile for the break-in to the primitive mindset of our hominid forebears' adjectival minds when first they began to speak is the realisation that their identifications of meanings were nasty brutish and short. They were often low brow and rude, as I suppose should be expected. None of them had been to school. Every sensation conveyd to their minds came via their own bodies, just as today; but they accepted them all without discrimination, whereas we are expected to filter ours. What really got their minds racing was hunting for the two gratifications, food and sex, and their respective consummations around the women's hearth. Here are the twelve presumed original phonemic lexical identifications, with their 'natural' meanings and their derivations, from perhaps six hundred thousand years ago, which can astonishingly be discovered still operative in the lexicon of languages all round the world today. They are explained in the following alphabetical chapters. In brief here they are.

Chapter 2 Lithic

1. Ba, chapter 3. Echoic. The sound made by lip on lip, of flesh on flesh, flesh-speak, and so meaning flesh (and also mouth); the bungey bulging bits, breasts, bubs, bellies, bums, bumming (using the haunches), legging it, going. Bungs, bunds, buoys, boys, burgeoning, covering the bones, fleshed, alive, in being, bio, the bilateral symmetry of the flesh, binary, and so on. Ba and la (lip and tongue) mean speaking, or bellowing if you are a bull. For further examples and derivations see any good etymological dictionary, in any language, and pick them out for yourself. They are there.

2. Ka, chapter 4. Echoic. The sound of striking stone on flint. Strike, effort, force, flake, cut, sharp, hard, shape, structure, skeleton, solidity, rock, ground, location. Spark, kindle, make, beget, and so on.

3. Ta, chapter 5. Echoic. The sound of snapping and tapping, a doublet with Ka but without the effort of the blow. Break into two, do (any other handiwork), broken in two, two, a break, to cut in two, to slit, a slit, the sexual slit, the birth canal, source, parturition, to give birth, birth, becoming, becomings, natural events, and so on. Ta-un, all the becomings, was the world in Ancient Egyptian and in Aztec. Da was a slovened Ta.

4. Fa, chapter 6. Echoic, but also logical later as well. Originally the pronunciation Ph suggested expectoration. This is a difficult one to follow because of the shifts in pronunciation to b, bh, p, v, etc. Ph was at the time of the birth of the Egyptian language, prehistorically but quite recently as languages go, pahei rather than ph. (Their h glyph was actually pronounced ahi). Pa-hei meant joy piece, or as we say penis, from pa-nai, which is protruding or witness piece – which it is in the bare buff. Egyptian nefer (as in Princess Nefertiti), is from nai-pahei-rai-titi, [when] presented-the pahei-rises-titi. The titi needs no translation. She was Princess Pretty Tits. Nefer meant pretty, fair, fine, fun, and so on; including nefarious.

5. Ha, chapter 7. Echoic. The sound of any sudden shocked expulsion of breath, as in picking up a "hot" stone in mistake for a piece of wood to throw back into the fire; but then also a gasp at orgasm. Hot, horror, orgasm, high emotion, happy, joy, rejoice, hosannah, welcome, greet, hi, and so on. But also a cockney h, protecting two vowels from eliding, usually unsuccessfully in the long term, leaving just the h in place of the first one. H was originally pronounced Ahai or Ahi in Ancient Egyptian, whence our Aich, rather than Ha or He.

6. La, chapter 8. Echoic, and soon logical as well, with a curled tongue and so "Nasty taste!" as with brackish water; whence flavour and liquids, whence the instincts of liquids to leak and slope off down into the lows and to become nastier to taste as they do so; finishing up brackish at the estuaries and then briney in the ocean (Laut in Malay, fully low and fully lye, both); lye, lime, pickle, piccalilli, sly, lie (in your teeth); taster, tongue (langue), lick, slobber; language, loud, laud, bellow, bolna (Hindustani to speak, lip and tongue), bal (from Djeribal, a Queensland aboriginal tongue, meaning speech); go la, gala, gale, gull, nightingale, call, lyric, libretto, flute; leak, slip, slide, slope, slink, slack, lack, limp, lie (down), lazy, lizard, low, flow, slow, flop, slop, fail, lame, leech, lava, blue, shalom, lieber (Gott); the skyline at sea (the only straight line in nature), and so line, long, lean, lanky, flank, lead, bill; the skyline at sea (out of sight of land), and so loop, circle, cycle, orbit, Apollo, loose, pommel, pill, glans, phallus, lanyard, leap, link, lieu, pelt,

Chapter 2 Lithic

volume, liber (book), ball, bell, lease, release, unleash, allow; fly, flea, flee, flick, fling, sling, slap, lance, flip, flap; and so on. It may seem odd all these words can make use of a prehistoric sense of nasty taste, but by means of multi-metaphors they can, with many more besides. Once you have followed through one of these many faceted catenas, you are half way to speaking Lithic.

7. Ma, chapter 9. Echoic. The sound of a hungry baby crying for mother, to be fed (when comfortable they just babble), and so mother, mammal, drink, eat, meat, mess, mass. The opposite of Ish (hisses breathing out, hums not, a push-me-pull-you oppositional pair appealing to the primitive dialectical mind, see paragraph 11, Ish, below): and so dark, down, heavy, mass, matter, hurtful, harm, mortality, earth, to earth seed, impregnate, propagate, gestate, concealed, mind (mental gestation), and so on.

8. Na, chapter10. Echoic. The sound of holding your breath and then gasping on letting it out; and so orgasm, ejaculating, copulating, erection, protrusion, pushing, presenting, the present (nau, now), show, witness, explain, advise, minister; but also gaping open, to be open, be wanting, be empty, without, negative, and so on.

9. Pa, chapter 11. Echoic. A puff or spit (including one of rejection like Pah!, Pooh! or Pish!) or cheep or peep; but also from echoic Ba: a thinned and less substantial (unvoiced) Ba, and so thin or small flesh, viz skin or a small shoot or bud, whence surface or piece, skin roof, roof, cover, lid, top, patch, pie, pan, panorama (the visible surfaces); also petals and penises, etc. Also a peep (cheep), a pan pipe, pipes galore, pipit, spit, spray, spring, and so on. At one remove papa, I think actually from the Egyptian pata, to go with mama (the mammalian sex).

10. Ra, chapter 12. Echoic. The sound of a rapid succession of raps (of the tongue, like Peter Ustinov's internal combustion engine. As a boy he drove himself everywhere around the house with different speeds and volumes of "rrrrrrr", with gear changes superimposed, driving his parents to despair). Then uncountable multiplicity, fur, hair, prickles, myriad sunbeams (rays), Ra (sun) who rai or rays, and a whole spectrum of fanciful rays and their effects of acting at a distance, eg fire rays, eye rays, audible rays, growing rays, sexual rays, brain rays, anger rays, rage, heroic rays, raising rays, raise, ba raised (berry), rise, rouse; fire rayed and warm, braise, roast, fry (rayed by the fire, see Ish below), and so on.

11. Ish, chapter 13. Echoic. The sound of a burning brand when dunked (Ishshsh!). The dying cry of fire killed by water, fire, flame, sun (a fire hole), shine, show, see, the visible, the existent; the hearth, warm around the hearth, comfortable, at ease, pleasant; sedentary around the hearth, alive (animals are warm, have ish), active (animals are active, plants rooted), animal, active, action, actual, moving, movement; up (the flame springs upwards), a vertical line, whence one, also the super-material, or in Greek meta-physical (you can pass your hand through the flame), whence spirit, spiritual, sanctity, saints and so on.

12. Wa, chapter 14. Echoic. The sound of shivering, whence cold, cold water, water, but also vibration, change of tack, turn; and of course fear, woe, wail, and so on. Also a semi vowel and with different connotations when pronounced oo or read as oo-a in place of wa, when it takes its place in the vowel sequence.

Chapter 2 Lithic

It certainly sounds a radical plan to seek to ground the whole of human language meanings over some six hundred thousand years of thinking on these twelve original motifs, or perhaps a few more if you take into account the meanings that have been extracted from the vowels; and then to claim they have all survived (refreshed subconsciously) over all of this time. I certainly never intended it. It must be the longest game of Chinese whispers conceivable, and indeed the longest game of any sort in the universe. The fact is that is how it has worked out. The chances of these budding semantic trees, subject to slovening and recombination, and erosion and recombination again and again, over so many years, but still presenting themselves today, so that language appears to be based on these semantic grounds, whilst not in reality being so, must surely be of the same order as the chances of a team of monkeys on a computer typing the Bible a randon (at random). Well, come to think of it, actually even less likely with millions of hominids and billions of humans at it. Linguistic change itself is like a gigantic rope with twisted skeins of astonishing complexity but nevertheless woven with an underlying semantic simplicity - almost poverty. When we learn a language we are presented with a cross-section of the part of the rope concerned cut across at the relevant stage of development; and the weave of the skeins is semantic, and firstly the semantics which make up the word, which is apt to be ignored by the grammarians having intellectual fun playing with sentences and their grammar as if they occupied the whole linguistic court to play on.

The ten initial conclusions, arrived at as part of an introductory chapter in the earlier work, are repeated here because they are fun. They are relevant to linguistics in one way or another.

1. Our reasoning now is an offshoot of our language, but speech was first an offshoot of the mind (our thinking) before speaking.

2. Our identifications are subjective affectations, a bi-blow of our speaking, by which we paper over the world with the entities which catch our attention and allow us to caricature them.

3. Thinking is an independent mystery, something which is now mostly done with the aid of language: a use of it. Language is originally the first differential of thinking; the thinking is an independent calculus. It has nothing to do directly with the heritage of the brain. It is a use of it. A hundred Einsteins in descent one from another, a hundred lifetimes scribbling, would not advance brain power one iota. For that the hundred would have to gain access to sufficient descendants to skew the gene pool, a business in itself, and with so little influence that it probably takes nearly as long as we have been speaking, never mind doing math. Math would not improve our genes, merely replace inferior genes – for math! To improve our genes we have to wait for random influences to make the changes which turn out to be improvements. Darwin said so. But it goes very slowly. It was Charles Lyell, who established the slow evolution of the rocks as scientifically proven in 1831, which gave Darwin the idea of the time scales available for species evolution by (mostly minuscule) natural selection over vast expanses of time. We should always remember the vast expanses of time necessary. The progress of our thinking is nimbler by far, although still dismally slow.

Chapter 2 Lithic

4. Math is an independent mystery, something which is now done with the aid of thinking, a use of it. It is the second differential of thinking after language, it is another independent calculus.

5. Each one of us lives in a self blown bubble provided by our senses, like a subjective wall paper covering the real wall, and the bubble then turns out to be papered on the inside of our own heads. For druggies it can appear as if we were all yellow submarines (urine colour, with headaches on surfacing). For the rest of us it is an intellectual cocoon which druggies miss out on entirely, alas. We read and write on its inner surface to guide our surmises as to what is going on outside us in the real world, of which we only ever access the wallpaper of our subjective senses. This in no way impugns the surmises, viz. science and human knowledge, only its direct applicability to reality. Our knowledge is and always will be at one remove from reality because of the subjectivity of its empirical sources, via our senses. Empiricism rules, OK.

6. The world is what it is and not another thing: Wittgenstein's 'the case,' at every turn.

7. Analogy fails to describe the mind because it is like nothing else in our experience. It is an abstraction from the activity of the brain, and just entifies our thinking. Our genes determine our limbs but not the walks we may take. Our genes determine our brains but not the thoughts we may think, which are meta-physical, not mystical at all but just outside the laws of physics including neurobiology.

8. Mental events are therefore properly treated as sui generis and meta-physical. They have a history, which nature doesn't – only the course of nature. History has to cater for human psychology and whimsy. It is the history of our mental interactions with reality with consequences.

9. William of Occam presented a true bill (unfortunately in Latin) widely known as Occam's Razor: "Res non multiplicanda". It may be loosely translated as "Check your baubles before relying on them", ie go for the simplest explanation. Get rid of the elephant standing on a tortoise on which at one time it was suggested (as aspects of inertia?) the earth rested, to explain how it stood still in space, (which of course it doesn't) rather than falling. And shun Ptolemy's coggery to account for the movements of the heavenly bodies; and so on: the philosophic cobwebs left by the self-appointed cognoscenti of yesteryear. Even watch out for still more cobwebs today's cognoscenti are still busily accumulating.

10. Science is partial and never conclusive. It does not approach reality, well or badly. It merely works with the doodles on the wall paper, see 5 above. However they have got us to the moon and back, giving us a feel for reality.

Based on no more than the above, the reader may now, if he or she is so disposed, try his or her own hand at playing the Lithic word game for himself or herself. When my sisters and I were children in the 1930s, between the wars, our mother taught us to play a game of free composition to exercise the imagination, for which the rules were very simple. It was a kind of Chinese whispers out loud, for any number of players but with an additional semantic element. The opening player announced any substantive thing at all – for younger players it was usually a visible entity, res vista, say a wheelbarrow. The next player had to say "A wheelbarrow reminds me of......"; and the next player taking it on from whatever was reminded; and so on ad nauseam. The (unspoken) aim of the game was to produce opening and closing terms as far apart as possible, on a scale also unspoken but pleasing to the players, Skill was displayed in thinking of way-out semantic connections nevertheless capable of being followed by the other players when confronted with the new idea, If any player could not follow the catena, often my youngest sister, a challenge would be made, whereat the players would immediately go into umpire committee and agree on the validity or otherwise of the intellectual catena. The game became known, inelegantly as it now appears to me, as "The Wheelbarrow-Cow Game" from the outcome of an early session. The relatively close similarity of the two end terms which so satisfied us as worlds apart owed some of its fame, I have now come to suspect, to the unspoken and perhaps barely perceptible element of cheekiness to the cow, large horned beasts we knew to steer clear of in the home pasture, by deriving its status from a mere wheelbarrow, a two legged dumb gardening tool. We can now see the naivety in the choice, with two farm yard phenomena regarded as miles apart. Academia is not represented, nor is there so much as a shadow of originality in it.

The rules for the game of Lithic are somewhat similar but there are, alas, some additional restrictive rules born of some further eighty years of ratiocination. With Lithic the Challenge Committee is permanently in session in the background and each move is open to inspection by it. However, so as to keep the game in play as far as possible, you can co-opt yourself to your own committee, and even allow yourself alone to be a quorum for the time being if playing on your own. Indeed it is the solitaire version of the game which is the most enjoyable as well as the most rewarding. The other rules are just the rules of reason. Only it is not the reason of the scholiasts or Boolean logic, just Lithic reasoning. Fancy is OK provided it is Lithic fancy, the thinking is OK provided it is Lithic thinking and fits in with the rest of hominid thinking in their ignorant Lithic posture, squatting bare bottomed around the hearth six hundred thousand years ago. None of these cheery folk, it must be remembered, had been to school. They could not have had the slightest idea of what any grammar might be. They just went by what seemed to work naturally, what was for them common sense. So we should just do the same if we want to recover their thinking.

The aim of the game is to derive as many words as possible, in any languages the players may know, from the prescribed list of original Lithic elementary phonemes (letters) and their derived original psychosemantic contents or meanings. You can of course add additional meanings yourself to these listed meanings if you can make them fit. Drop me a line if they are good ones. Lithic meanings were expansive and covered a great deal of ground, many of them originally so general as to be virtually useless by today's standards, but nevertheless matching the thinking of the day. It is a game for any number of players with or without the aid of sources such as etymological dictionaries[1,] and can be played silently by oneself in the train, or when ostensibly listening to sermons, or in class, or even engaged in idle conversation. It is not particularly addictive for any reasonably balanced person, though others, myself included, should perhaps beware. The skill lies in awareness of the rules of Lithic which are the ways our hominid ancestors were thinking hundreds of thousands of years ago, together with those rules required to cater for the erosions and elisions, the additions and subtractions over the same period of time. That allows for a deal of expansions of the elements of words to get back to the original meanings and the phonemes carrying them. It sounds alarming but the rules are in fact relatively easily

Chapter 2 Lithic

stated. The original phonemes and their psychosemantic contents are as already laid out in the twelve paragraphs above, and in much greater detail in the psychosemantic trees and in the following chapters. Their justifications, the evidence so far accumulated for them, are in the following chapters, which sketch them in far greater detail and provide some practice in their combinations. There is however a good deal more in the original work from which this shorter book has been culled[2]. The simple rules of Lithic grammar - nothing to do with Boole or Chomsky, you don't need to know about them and if you do it is a disadvantage – are laid out below. Nobody welcomes a lesson in grammar. This chapter aims to dispose of it once and for all on the grounds the origins of speaking preceded its invention.

The rules of Lithic grammar – grammar just means writing - or better syntax (sun means all the instances of the Greek taxis, putting ideas together), were few indeed; since like Simple Simon our dumb ancestors they had not any – or anyway they had not adumbrated any. What was going on in their minds before they spoke is another matter and a hard one to crack since all the direct evidence is, by definition, missing. "Cognitive Archaeologists" (sic) are simply reduced to guessing, by how they handled their tool making, etc. But anyway here are the rules of Lithic grammar.

1. <u>Apposition</u>. What we find in the earliest language use extant is adjectival apposition, putting one adjectival idea next to another and treating them as connected together – not so much like "black hat" where there is an obvious pecking order, the hat, a noun, leads and the black qualifies it; but more like "high green", where it just means both high and green and may refer to a bowling green on a hill or alternatively a green hill or even just bright green. We do not need to distinguish between adjectives and nouns because nouns will have only come much later; in fact we ought not to do so. Our first mental world was an adjectival universe, so think just in adjectives. That is rule one.

2. <u>The Idiom of Pairs</u>. Apposition puts ideas (later perhaps distincta and then categories) in adjectival pairs, and the Lithic idiom was then to put these pairs in turn in pairs. So we often find our words originally composed of two or four Lithic elements, though subject to elision since. So we should be looking to open them back out, as far as possible into pairs.

3. <u>Vowelisation.</u> The rest of Lithic syntax was vowelisation. Most of the virtue was in the new consonantal elements, the leading elements when speaking, and with an articulation you could set your mind on. The vowels were therefore markers superadded. In fact they actually were the grammar, what has since got lumbered with the name of "The Vowel Oon", because they formed a unity, a triune one as it happened because there were only three vowels, Tarzan's mouth parts being a whole lot less nimble than ours are today. They were a, i and u, (pronounced aaa, eee and ooo). No e or o.

4. <u>Aaa</u> was the middling general vowel, the one that comes most easily, and so the first and leading one in the vowel oon, unmarked. Because you can go on saying aa as long as you have breath, which you can't with consonants, aaa conveyed continuity, extension, the ongoing, even just plain going, so long as it was smooth and not thought of as articulated with consecutive haunchings which needed a ba in it from the bum, the fleshiest bit or ham (ha-mai in Lithic is a joy (ha) when eating (mai), but also a joy when earthing (mai) seed, including of course planting your own: the flavour or the functions, take your pick. My guess is Tarzan read both together and smiled. He may even have thought they belonged

together. The hip (from hai-pai) has a similar derivation, picked up by hippies who waggle their hips in a suggestive manner, while masturbating their ukuleles (whether they know why hips are hippy or not).

5. <u>Eee</u> was the thinned diminutive, and so a pointer (like that other thinned diminutive the pa phoneme) and so the indicative and reduplicative vowel, including becoming the genitive in Latin and –ing in English, the singular individual, as well as a plethora of them (the plural), and then the temporally shrinking, and so the past tense; and then also the second term in the vowel oon, which fathered a dialectic (hundreds of thousands of years later rediscovered by Hegel in Germany and disastrously borrowed by Marx).

6. <u>Ooo</u> was the completive vowel, the whole, all, in a loop or group, like the lips when it is spoken, and then the substantive (and so eventually the noun form), also the dual vowel (because it resumed the other two), and the third and completive term in the vowel oon, the Lithic dialectic. Unsurprisingly they still come in the same order in the alphabet today. It can be noted here why it was so, as we may take it those bare bottomed naming committees similarly spotted, all those years ago: the lips are protruded sequentially from aa through ee to oo, while the tongue is flat and relaxed for aa, curled and raised for ee, and in a middle position for oo, resuming the other two vowel positions; so that we have a thoroughly dialectical vowel u which is sequentially third as evidenced by the lips, whilst at the same time in the middle as far as tongue position is concerned. This is probably the best and strongest evidence for dialectics, and it turns out to be neither a mental nor a physical process at all, but in origin no more than a Stone Age whimsy, based on nothing more than the physiological functioning of the human mouth parts: very early science, laughably percolating to academia even today, via Marx.

The slovening and slurring, erosion and elision which have occurred over many millennia are from the lazy tongues and absent minds of common speakers, taking the exquisite formulations of the elites of the day, sitting and working over the imagined evidences in those bare bottomed naming committees; and then massacring them with careless abandon so as to be able to romp through simple phrases with the minimum of effort. I have described this dichotomy elsewhere as the dialogue of Scrimshaw Man with Wayland Smith. Consequently, it is argued, there can now be nothing left of original speech to discover. But this is not borne out by the evidence. What mechanism has survived the depredations of time and ensured the survival of Lithic language idioms is secondary; but survive them it has. Without rubbing out the whole lexicon at a stroke and replacing it piecemeal with a new lexicon, based on a different linguistic plan altogether, surely an impossibility, it is fairly obvious as one word is spoiled – rendered incomprehensible in terms of its original Lithic elements by slovening – it can be reconstructed with its original elements intact, simply by analogy with all the rest of the lexicon. So it is a fair presumption there has never been a total break since the origins of speaking. After all, since we learned to speak we have never stopped speaking. That means language has in effect a self repairing mechanism, which has proved sufficient to reinvent Lithic sufficiently, regardless of the relative mindlessness of the great majority of speakers, over the past few hundred millennia. Language is by now buried deep in the human psyche, sufficiently established therein to be attended to without conscious attention. It is, it would appear, the subconscious workings of the human mind which have assumed responsibility for the refreshment – in computer speak the refresh rate – of age old Lithic protocols, quite

Chapter 2 Lithic

regardless of surface erosion and elision, so that now it is not too fanciful to borrow from Chomsky's jargon and talk of a deep structure within the subconscious, which is the Lithic language underlying all the languages of the globe – but not hard wired at all, just transitory neuronal electronic configurations, the softest and most ephemeral software, with no hard disk. Switch off the brain and the programmes and the work in progress are lost for ever. Almost as astonishing as Chomsky's ideas, (but more scientifically based), how it actually happens is each infant individually recomposes the underlying information inbuilt in the lexicon as it learns to speak, while uttering only the surface layer of current verbage required for conversation. Whether such a subconscious substrate of language learning can cohabit in the subconscious with a late Boolean universal grammar, such as Chomsky provides, I leave to others to debate. Be that as it may, all we have to do to attend to the surface presentations is to undo the damage done by the slovening. Here are the six rules for that.

1. <u>Expansion.</u> Primitive languages are built from short bits with wide usages. The phonetics were short. A whole sentence in Lithic language would fit into a word these days; we can sometimes find it doing so. Where developed words have generally been bunched up from comparatively long original strings the rewarding technique is to expand them, giving each single phoneme (letter) its full value as originally conceived.

2. <u>Final Consonants.</u> Final consonants, copying the glottal stop, came late. Many or perhaps most result from the first modifier -i, converting the initial -a form to the modified form -ai, then fading to the dipthong -e, and so to just -y, and then being lost altogether. It is therefore a fair first rule to think in terms of reading final consonants such as -k as originally -kai, and in that case with the principal or head Lithic meaning striking off [a flint], and so making, shaping, shape, kindling, etc, that is all the meanings that can be derived from striking a flint in a few hundred thousand years. See all chapter 4 for this case.

3. <u>The Dipthong Vowels.</u> The vowels e and o are to be read as in origin ai and au respectively. Of course the u in this latter expression is the symbol for the sound made with the lips pushed forward and rounded as in the final position when we say o precisely, the final vocalisation of ooo; as commonly in Chimpish, which - to a chimp - probably carries the psychosemantic content "Ooh!", "Attention!", "My Goodness!" or something like that; even "I have something I am trying to communicate to you, and you don't seem to understand any Chimpish".

4. <u>Repetition.</u> Repetitive phonemes are used in primitive languages as plurals. With usage they may nevertheless elide so that a double letter results. They may also come together as back and front end terms of two elements put together in apposition. In this case also they may have elided. A case in point is the Australian aboriginal budgerigar, which is made up from the three aboriginal words baji-djeri-gara, which means bird-bright-colour. The use of the -gara for colour makes it clear in what sense the djeri is to be understood, since we find it elsewhere in use as clear [in sense] and loud [in tone]. To that extent the gara comes close to what the Ancient Egyptians would append as an unpronounced 'determinant' in their glyphs. A budgerigar is a bright bird or a bright coloured bird, a bird of bright colour. Fanciers have reverted to the original Lithic Ba-ji or Go-up for bird, though quite unaware of what they were doing, just finding the aboriginal

term a mouthful. It is only sad they do not allow them to baji much any longer, to fully be birds. The gara we translate as colour really means make-ray, or make-see, the substantive which we think in terms of being represented as a happening, keeping the thinking fluid – or perhaps better put as using the available fluid idiom which springs to the aboriginal mind. Anyway an occasional double use of consonants elided over time as in budgerigar to discover baji jeri gara is permissible. It is irresistible here, while we are thinking of a bird as a go-up, to reflect upon the aboriginal turn of mind which framed our bird as a go-up as well. Lithic Ba-rai-dai, is go-raised-does, just another go up in fact. Eric Partridge derives it from the word breeding, but that is hardly an avian peculiarity. Breeding is semantically a form of warming, a brooder is a warmer, the rai in this case being the relatively innocent and original rays which come from the fire, and not the other rather naughty rays which raise things up, which the birds were supposed to be using to get airborne. The Spanish bird, a pajaro, is yet another go up from the same stable as the passer or sparrow, and I have long thought the parrot is just another go-up from some jungley native tongue in South America, with pa, surfaces [wings] rayed and drawn up become, rather than a Pierot or cousin to peruques and periwigs as in the established etymology. Whitey, pointing to a parrot: "What do you call that one then?" "We call 'em birds". "Birds is it?" "Yes". "Many thanks, Goodbye!"

5. <u>Consonant Change.</u> This is the contentious area of Lithic research. In different languages there have been different consonant exchanges, though some are common to many. The French can be found changing their Bs to Vs, for example, with the pronunciation following. The Spanish can be found writing their Bs as Vs but retaining the original pronunciation as Bs. Sanskrit has a fancy for writing sh where kh or even k originated. Greeks have traded s for h in many places: both, after all, are made with forced expulsion of breath, the sibilant with the tongue pressed tightly against the palate, the ha just more loosely (idly) pronounced. Ks have become Gs all over, and Ps Bs, and Ts Ds, and so on, the voiced forms exchanging readily with the unvoiced. The result of these changes has generally been to ease pronunciation, the lazy mouth-parts syndrome, but some are reasoned – grammarians' kind of reasoning only – which suggests they have been given a fair wind by the grammarians tidying up and uniformitising the language from time to time. Anyway the result has been to afford a good deal of flexibility in interpreting the original Lithic consonants which went to make up a word. This is unfortunate because it invites criticism as taking liberties to preserve the thesis, and is what makes me describe the grammarians, the systematisers, as the villains of the piece. But they have to be lived with.

6. <u>Ostensives.</u> What was our first speech about? It is an anachronism to suggest it was an expression of a poetic urge to declaim, since that came aeons later. It may have been prompted in part by a less than poetic urge to express emotion; plain hunger for instance, or "Phoaw!" But to judge by the chimp, communication of some matter of urgent import such as the advance of a predator or the location of food open to predation was the principal spur; and this was because it required a degree of specification unneeded for simple emotional expression; and the lack must have been apparent to all parties. The voice was originally for warning of danger. Indeed "voice" actually meant danger. The Sanskrit "vac" for voice, pronounced in its pristine form "Wa-ka" says "Fear-make", ie a panic signal: Raise the alarm! And it certainly can be so read in elementary Lithic phonemes, just like the schoolboys' "KV" today, or is it yesterday with now no Latin

Chapter 2 Lithic

taught, (from the Latin "cave" [pronounced in Latin kar-wey or kar-vey], the imperative of cavere to beware, just waka the other way about), used in school dormitories throughout the land to warn of the approach of a roving beak or other inspector (or inspectress) looking for any infringements of the rules after lights out, or indeed at any other time that mischief was afoot. Lack of any such warning once got me a good beating when the boy in the next bed was talking after lights out and the headmaster's torch beam fell on me; so I remember it well from 80 years ago: at the fourth stroke of his slipper on my bare bottom bent over a desk I pissed, it stung so; but I still got the full six. I believe the headmaster would have waded through Jordan to complete his mission.

Meanwhile the Old Persian or Avestan "Wackis" pronounced "Wa! Kais!", a battle cry, was also a fear-make, but this time putting the frighteners on the enemy. Soldiers will still do it when closing to close quarters: an undifferentiated "Haaarrr!" is often fancied. It is not entirely clear whether it is principally to alarm the enemy or to embolden the screamer. It is not so far from the Maori "Hakka!" where the "Ha!" is variously used around the world for sudden emotional responses, when burnt for instance ("Ha!" for "Hot!"), from the horrendous or the hideous to the hooraying or the hilarious (Ha! Ha!). In the Maori case it appears to be a rejoicing in their own Ka and the burning of yours, but it probably also is designed to help summon up their own Ka. Compare Japanese Karate, the Ka-Roused-Becoming: practice of the techniques supposedly emboldens the practitioner by preparing him for ritualised combat (otherwise why bother?).

As a starter for Lithic gaming it is probably best to think in terms of the total absence of any grammatical sense when language was born. It is hard to see how it might have enjoyed a prior development for some extraneous utility with evolutionary survival potential, to be handy to be prayed in aid when language needed a bit of structuring. Nor is the time scale helpful. Our progress in speaking has been far too fast for Darwin's formulaic evolution, and whimsical with it. Nor is it any real answer to allege it is hard wired as part of the human brain structure and function, which is merely another way of proposing the preceding hypothesis that it assembled itself in advance for some other beneficial purpose. Name one possibility! Reason, which is what makes semantics, is the ability to think half way straight, and it goes back a long way. It must be prior to language, else how could we have dreamed up the idea of speaking; although in the more recent millennia, as language has developed the marriage of thinking and speaking, it has encouraged some people to think speech supports thought; and indeed most people to think solely in the terms in which they speak. The latter is of course an intellectual disaster, triggering every kind of obscurantism and vice, not excluding Nazism and the other totalitarian miasmas. It is thinking which from the outset supports, even informs speaking, and it is the thinking, the semantics, which unravels the development of language and now the etymological derivations. That is exactly what this book is about. Sounds do not develop. Thinking does.

Indeed our word elements appear to have come down to us in an unbroken semantic catena or chain all the way from our hominid ancestors hundreds of thousands of years ago. That may seem far fetched and an overly long time for a game of Chinese whispers, especially now when we rehearse it all without any recess for refreshments; but every link in the chain was a single one-to-one link in use between consenting adults, remember, thousands and then millions and then tens of millions and now hundreds, even thousands of millions of times, every single day. The shifts between repetitions do indeed show the degree of whimsy and wandering attention we might expect, revealed in the semantic

Chapter 2 Lithic

record. That is why a great deal of effort has been spent in trying to lay out semantic trees tracing the meanings linked to the phonetic utterances, and marking the semantic traces in step with the changing phonetics. This is quite different from the traditional derivation of nonsense language roots by a simple evolutionary process, like vegetable evolution, which is quite inappropriate for thought processes. The mind does not function as a potato grows, like cabbages and kings.

Skeat's 364 Indo European roots of 1879-1882, for instance, fascinating though these are, are roots with no reason for their being other than as termini from which the phonetic trains supposedly set out. But even if they set out from these buffers, phonetic language trains had semantic carriages attached from the outset, indeed it is better argued the semantics actually comprised the prime movers. Language did not spring from nonsense roots, nor proceed along similar lines. The naming committees – it is probably right to think of them as hominid elders, sex unknown, hunkered hirsute and bare bottomed around their hearths many hundreds of thousands of years ago – by a mixture of gesturing, mimicry and reason were trying to discover what was the "natural" meaning which brother Tarzan might hopefully twig from an utterance if he tried hard enough. It must have been desperately frustrating and claustrophobic work, reminiscent of the chimpanzee's desperate chirruping when trying to communicate – just better done.

We should next note what it is in Lithic which is to be grammaticised, that is worked up into a structure of thinking. It was single syllable phonemes already with semantic contents of their own which were the initial elements of speech, and not the words fancied by Skeat and all. Words were not yet composed. They were not yet on the thinkers' menu. Most likely the ideas which later were attached to the phoneme strings making up words were not yet being thought either. Or if they were it was only on an occasional basis, much as we think these days of a sentence, but with a sentence we do it by putting it together to suit the occasion and do not usually carry it in memory as a unit, for reuse on later occasions. No more did our hominid forebears with their phonemic sentences. A phoneme string will at first have been treated just as a sentence is now, worked over word by word today to pick up the overall sense of the sentence string, and phoneme by phoneme then to pick up the sense of the word string. We can hypothesise this already from the fact speakers of the smaller less developed languages with small vocabularies use shorter word elements and often single syllable phonemes with meanings. For them prestidigitation or hyperphosphorylation would be lengthy sentences. In Germany they would be completely at sea.

There is the case of Yosemite National Park in California. Yosemite (pronounced in American English Yo-zemm-ity, with the accents on the Yo and the -zemm- in the middle) is taken to be the local Navaho Indian Awani tribe's name - their language is Navaho - for the brown bear, which was their totem. But Grizzly Bear National Park turns out to be 'That is our Tribal Mother' National Park. How come? Miner Forty Niner to his local Man Friday, as he points a grubby finger at a retreating grizzly: "What do you call that one then?" Navaho Man Friday: "That is our Tribal Mother" (thinks: "and I'm not telling you Her name or you might conjure Her against us") Miner Forty Niner (later in the canteen): "It sure was a big one. Sounded like Yosemite in their lingo". What Man Friday actually said was "Ia-ushi-Ma'-i-Tai", readily translating from the Navaho tongue to "It that-our-mother-of-tribe". He spoke good Lithic too. His forebears had done their homework for his use of shi for my and ushi for our. The sibilant, stands first for the flame, which says ishshsh when extinguished, and which very unusually – most things if you drop them hit your toe - springs upwards as if it had a life of its own, and burns your hand instead. So it

Chapter 2 Lithic

came to mean up and upright, then an upright mark, then one, counted in scratched upright scores, then number one, and then the first person singular, me. The -i, as the diminutive reduplicative vowel is added to indicate me as a single individual (one of many). Shai is the first one, slovened to shi, the -i firing twice as it were and meaning both one and of, typical Lithic thinking. Yosemite's manager was informed and passed the information to UCALSF (The University of California in San Francisco) and was promised a response. None so far in the last 35 years.

The u vowel was the completive, plural, definitive one, so if shi meant my then it was obvious ushi meant a plurality of my, or as we would say our. Ma means mother in most tongues. It is the distressed cry of the infant wanting feeding. "The little darling is calling for me" many mothers around the globe imagined, as they put the little howler to the breast. The reduplicative vowel i can also indicate connection, which is all that "of" signifies. Tai is birthing, from ta, the slit or birth canal, ta being first of all the sound taken to signify breaking in two [a stick for the hearth for instance], and so two, twoing, parturition, the slit between the two sides of the body, the birth canal (and so on). The tongue takes sharp leave of the palate to say ta or two, too. Here, with ta-i we have the reduplicative -i in action again, indicating reduplicated births, whole generations of them in fact, making a tribe appear. It can even mean, in Navaho, tribal, and so customary and so good. Gap Year Student to a Navaho elder sitting at the entrance of her wigwam, as taught in the pamphlet on sale at Mariposa (Butterfly) Grove tourist shop in Yosemite: "Ia-te-shi-Ma!", "It is-good-my-Mother!", or as we might say "Good morning Ma'am!" Then they can probably get down to the ethnology in English. Whitey has shown willing. The good (from tai) is the traditional or tribal, and so good for the Awani. They felt safe there, faced with these Androids with guns.

When we come to look into the etymology of numerous languages, we soon start to pick up within present day words these semantic nuggets attached to the same phonemes across surprisingly wide fields of application and interpretation. Once the early semantic content of a phoneme is worked out, usually with a fair indication why the earliest meanings were picked, a whole range of primitive usages together with the early 'grammar' for word-making reveal themselves in use, under cover of conventional word construction. It builds like a crossword puzzle, with one usage supporting another like the letters down and across. We can finish up recognising almost as much of the original Lithic language as the modern languages we profess to speak. That is a bold claim, perhaps over bold; but the book has to be read before deciding against it. With a crossword when even just half filled, the chance all your entries are wrong is not a worry. Language development has an interlocking texture or matrix like a crossword, helping us recover it. Decoding dead languages uses the same tricks.

The first rule for reconstructing the first grammar concerns the order of speech. If the simplest elements are syllabic phonemes (they are: a consonant and a vowel in other words, the vowel to allow the utterance of the consonant), their ordering is the first concern which can rank as grammar. Originally we may surmise "Pa ka" (perhaps "A shelter let us make") and "Ka pa", ("let us make a shelter") were alternative usages: just "Cover make" or "Make cover". Think about it. You could not put it in either order unless the two bits took their meanings with them. A caper and a perca (a sea bass in Spanish), are just not the same, although they go quite well together on a plate. A caper is a berry, it is ka-pai-rai, shape-piece-rayed, ie a plumped up piece from the sun's rays, whilst a perca is a fish pairai-ka, a fat-body (easily filleted and tasty), like the bass, from ba-sai, flesh nice. So we should be on the look out for the transposition of elements which take their meanings with

Chapter 2 Lithic

them. They answer to metatheses in the linguistic jargon. Major metatheses, big changes in order, generally indicate the bits exchanged are taking their meanings with them. But a vowel slipping from one side of a consonant to the other may be just slovening to save moving the mouth parts promptly.

However with the inversion of consecutive substantive usages, for instance with 'ka-pa' (perhaps 'root [well core anyway] of the matter [well perspective anyway, since pa is skin and so surface, which is what is seen]') and 'pa-ka' (perhaps 'the surface of the earth'[earth here the ka or hard core of our world]), there could have been different semantic contents associated. The ones offered as examples are perhaps a trifle sophisticated for a hominid, but they are nevertheless illustrative of the differencing that can arise. So you can not simply treat them as the same just because they are the same pair of phonemes. There is likely a fancied reason at least for preferring one order or the other, which probably has to do with the ideas being passed in review. Certainly, the simpler the language, the more preponderant is the polysemy (one phoneme with lots of alternative meanings, numerous semantic contents for the same utterance), as well as the more general and undiscriminating each meaning. This is because as languages build the phoneme strings get longer, increasing vocabulary by discriminating meanings previously lumped together. The Australian aborigine djeri means bright as in budgerigar, a bird of bright colour, but it means clear as in the name of an extinct Queensland tribe, the Djiribal, Clear-speakers (as opposed to other tribes who irritatingly were speaking in code), and it means loud in didgeridoo, a di-djeri-doo, a tit or tube with a loud toot. The ordering is the birth of the idea of 'of'. The reasoning takes the form a-b, a > b, a leads to b, so a leads: that is all it takes to entail the subordination of b and then the consequential dependence of b upon a. Is-ka-nam is him-of-name: his name, in Hindi. We say his name, from he-of name, from he with the genitive ending –is. Compare the Latin third declension –is for the genitive, if you happen to know Latin, rare these days. "It is his": a nice string of i terms: it from i-tai, which-become, ie an existing thing; is from which-alive, and so in being (being is from bai, fleshed, and so alive). Of/from comes from hiss and so issue and so originating (from), and so from him and therefore still his. The i did not really mean which exactly. It is a single it or item, a thinking bit, but our nearest equivalent is probably it or which. Remember in the Stone Age they did not use our words. Our words just make do when representing Lithic thinking.

It is arguable all the other prepositional and postpositional helper words are conceptually merely glosses in elaboration of the initial apposition and then the dependence derived from it, as just indicated in the case of "of". Certainly the way symbolic logic has been used to portray tidy mathematical values as essential building blocks for language is a late fabrication. For our purposes, researching origins, it is simply wrong. Such values will hardly have troubled plain Sapiens, bent no doubt on adding the doubled sapience but struggling a bit with it. To and for, by, with and from for instance add greatly to the simple genitive 'of'. But they are not such great leaps away that they can not be judged to be from the same source. Pick any sentence with a preposition in it and substitute 'of' as if wrongly spoken by someone learning English as a foreign language, and the meaning will be identifiable with a sufficiently lively imagination. The meanings are different and distinct but they will have built gradually from a single origin. We even say "I should of done it" instead of "I should've done it" for "I should have done it", and it is understood. Indeed many folk are unaware of the absurdity of this wrong grammar. Not many will quarrel with "Yes, I suppose I should of" unless challenged. A good deal of articulation is actually redundant, the mind flits along leaving

Chapter 2 Lithic

the full official grammar far behind. There is no question of rehearsing it at all. That must mean it is all being resumed in the workshop down below in the subconscious, according to Chomsky[3]. Or else it is mostly redundant most of the time.

Grammar in its fullest sense appears to have first developed with the invention of surrogates: pronouns such as this and that, he and who; and adverbs where and whence, whereunto and wheretofore, etc: ostensive and inquisitive both. It reached its most dominating with the conjugation of verbs and the declension of nouns. None of this, mercifully enough, was within the hominid purview at all. It has all been invented as add-ons since. It is not clear if Chomsky is aware of this, since elements of his grammar are hard wired in our genes. If surrogates are really no more than ostensive nouns they are less obviously so than a mere name. They involve abstraction. 'This' abstracts from a potential plethora of items present at one time or another, their presentness when they were or are present; and 'that' does the same a little way off. 'He' abstracts from persons similarly, present or further off (and can be marked for gender - she).

It is perhaps an appropriate moment to remind readers of the richness of the notation (and analysis) available to be used here. Him refers to the person indicated, while "him" is the utterance, the word "him", eg he said "him!" and 'him' is the idea of the utterance "him", which lies behind the word, though often referred to as if it were the word. For most purposes of course the distinction between the word and its utterance is otiose, but it is sometimes relevant to the consideration of the way language has developed, for example which came first, the idea or the utterance. It is nowadays pretty clear the idea did. Philosophers, logicians and other pernickety modern folk with a knowledge of symbolic logic to guide them may like to inject further complicating levels of discourse. For instance as well as the utterance (sound) "him" also the word ""him"", written or otherwise symbolised, and then the ideas symbolic of that or those in turn. We then have apparently acquired a quiverful of words expressed one way or another. But these frills and fripperies are generally ignored in what follows, as superfluous to our purpose.

'And' is a specific (limited) case of 'more'; "more" often being used for both ideas. Hindi "aur" springs to mind: "aur us ke bad" (and that of after) for instance and "kuch aur chini" (some more sugar). So "and" is short for "What is more", "there is more to tell you", "moreover". The Lithic elements are a'an-da, with the vowel aaa the extensive vowel here: ongoing, and da which has amongst its semantic contents a meaning close to do. So 'and' means "It goes on", from literally 'extending does'. In French the ongoing is expressed ai (slovened to e, in Hindi au, in Arabic wa, in Malay dan lagi, the dan from ta-an, become ongoing, the lagi meaning more from la-kai, the looping-kindled (you can almost see the balloon getting blown up, adding more). The English words today may not capture the original semantic contents particularly well, but the original compositions make perfect (Lithic) sense.

The negative comes from the negative imperative 'don't'; but also from the open and empty category, the absence of anything, however illogical that may appear when confronted. An absence, after all, in no way negatives a presupposed presence, although if a question be asked "Is x present?" the answer may well be in the negative. This is a matter of presence. It has nothing to do with a category such as "Red" and the absence of red outside of the category, if we think of them as an enclosure you are either inside or outside of. If the category "Red" does not apply, the state is unqualified. Red is not negatived. That hasn't stopped some folk thinking quite differently and getting themselves tied up in some bad knots as a result. The late Mr Kruschev banging his shoe in the United Nations Council is a nice case in point, a mut showing off his mutton head. His dialectical

Chapter 2 Lithic

materialism allowed him to think the world develops opposites and then rubs them out with a superior term of thinking reserved for the dialectical materialist. So he thought in terms of his dialectic, with negatives with every thesis, and applied the logic to the deletion of the West, imagining he was making a telling contribution to political debate. Also Na can mean to gape open, and so openness or absence. That is the fanciful lead to the negative. It is based on falsehood. An absence is not a negative, but many millennia ago single Sapiens thought it was, and Mr Kruschev eagerly picked up on his thinking. There is more to say on true and false negatives when we come to finally demolish the dialectic (Hegelian and Marxian together) in chapter 15, exposing precisely its flawed thinking, a terminator - which has never been attempted before, only anecdotal chat disagreeing with some of the corollaries.

Equality is a specific limited case of (adjectival) apposition, and it goes with 'is'. With 'earth-surface' the surface does not equal the earth; but with 'tomato-red' the tomato does in a way equal 'red'. It really 'is' red. Equality is in origin simply essence (being) spelt differently; it comes from mere equivalence, equi-valence. The song has it: "One is one and all alone, and evermore shall be so". This perception is not entirely helpful for such as Gotlob Frege, looking to award a special stative function to the essential category which is elsewhere simply omitted.

There is more on the adjectival mind elsewhere. But "Tomato" and "Potato" can be regarded as adjectival, a bundle of qualities merely, rather than as nouns, although this might these days be taken as eccentric. But that is how the names started out. If it is wished to argue a bundle of qualities must be substantive because the bundle makes it so, a bundle of one should qualify, making "red" a noun too – one hand clapping to confound the critics! That is how the human mind works, wicked though it may be. In explanation Tomato is from the Nahuatl "tau-ma-tau, "birth-death-birth". You have to collect the seeds and replant them; whilst potato – they were originally the very same plant – is pau-tau-tau, tuber-birth-birth. You can plant the tubers and have them grow in turn again and again, abandoning seeds and their propagation. (You can even eat the potato and just cut out and plant the eyes in fact). Darwinists will be interested in the speciation of these plants from cultivation, at the hands of the Nahuatl speakers, who described their lingo as na-(h)u-a, the presenting-everything-one. The –tl is just their noun ending, I think from ta-lai, become-lasting, or even substantiated from long born or linear [adjectival descriptive elements]. The potato and tomato certainly do not interbreed readily any longer, although if you irrigate a crop of potatoes immediately after flowering you will get a crop of golf ball sized green and mildly poisonous tomatoes for your pains, instead of boosting tuber growth. I cooked them and can warn you: you should not eat them even cooked. They will give you a stomach ache. Think of the suffering of Nahua stomachs as they worked on and tested the plants for a thousand years, reducing the stomach aches by a judicious selection of the fruits and tubers year after year. Nowadays we do it by directly manipulating the genes rather more efficiently and with fewer stomach aches (to the loud discomfort of the green belly achers).

To add to the grammatical categories those of temporal discrimination, tenses may be derived from a lively sense of the here and now, those environmental stimuli actually being experienced which thus denote the time in question as the present time. Time is simply a matter of observing the course of events, the scenery changing, the procedures we appear to be in the midst of. "Time", from tai'm, is the process of becoming, which almost everything appears to encounter: originally - if the words used have anything to say (they do) - the process of being born and coming into being, tai-, the two-ing, parturition, birth

Chapter 2 Lithic

canal or birth. Partridge gives the Indo-European word root as te- or de-; which in Lithic is tai, with the very early semantic content of birthing or becoming. The pundits will argue one of the oldest words is tik for the digit or finger. The suspicion must be it was a very early word indeed because it appears to have been dreamed up by the girls hunkered around the hearth from ti-ka vagina-stimulator or tickler, whereas our finger is a boy's word from phai-en-kara, a pahei or penis-of-stimulator. These were mischievous slang words no doubt, but they seem to have caught on. It will be disturbing for many to find our primitive elders masturbating, and apparently with some glee – and without their eyesight in the least impaired. But it appears unavoidable. Of course you can dub the boys' fin-kara for finger as fine-worker because fine is from the same root anyway, its meaning was originally pleasurable, from the penis-pleasuring, and no doubt the finger was identified as useful for delicate (fine) work of all sorts, whether pleasurable or not. It is important to remember the original meanings mostly got drowned out long long ago by the ones derived from them piled on top. We have not gone along for millennia thinking so intrusively in sexual terms, although we have continued to build vocabulary from that base up, as can be demonstrated by triangulating meanings backwards from words in use today. In Spanish we have the word finca which means a property, often in the country and originally with land, to which one retired when able. A pleasure place is a reasonable definition of the Lithic phai'n-ka. Vegetables are often grown there. But a wealthy Spaniard of my acquaintance explained, with a mischievous leer, he had bought such a property for his son on coming of age to which he could take his girlfriends for weekend forays. The facility was an early identification. There is however also the Egyptian taun, meaning the world, from Lithic ta-u'n, becomings[ie events]-all'one, (like tan in Aztec on the other side of the pond, as in Wakan Tanka, Fear-making World-maker, their Creator God, the Awesome Creator). The Tau, the two or T (which is just two directions or dimensions, much revered by flat earthers) is even older than the tik or tick, meaning finger, pointer, pointer-outer, indicator of the correct, the correct, in Hindi tikh, with tikh hai, meaning that's correct or OK, usually followed by Sahib or in Lithic Sai-bai or Top-being: Oh Top Chap. It is also the Tao in China, by way of the born, the become, the becoming one, the route, the way, the indicated ethical way to be followed, and so on. Now Homo Erectus was already scratching Ts on rocks. A penny for his thoughts? Was it just the aesthetic appeal of the right angles involved? Surely not! He was writing! Indeed it was poetry, admittedly of a rather simple sort. It packed a lot of dense thinking into a succinct (Lithic) medium which could be read with a number of implications all at once: the two dimensions – of a surface, of space and time - parturition, the universe; all patterns emanating from the rich but whimsical vocabulary of the subconscious mind. Exactly how much he already had in mind before he began to speak I fear we shall never know; but clearly he had some of it.

The conditional 'if' comes from the expectational or suggestive sense: eg "stay on the ground and you get eaten": "I give you the meat and you sleep with me": If I give you the meat you sleep with me, OK?" If links two propositions, just like 'and'; but with 'if' the linkage extends to another proposition, namely that the two are also semantically linked. The difference is nicely caught by the rascal above, flirting in the first pair of propositions linked by and, and buying sex in the second linked by the conditional.

Primitive grammar – a late gloss on the original articulation - is much mixed up with the vowels; and the perception of the vowels is much mixed up too; so the primitive vowel dialectic is grammar too, as well as vice versa. The general vowel "aaa" features as the thesis in this dialectic, the initial posit. The thinned diminutive reduplicative vowel i (eee) features as implicit in but distinguished from the general vowel, budded off as it were, hanging off it, a natural offspring from it, a chip from the block, marked out from it and to that extent already antithetical. It is not intended to show that hominids were Hegelians of course. Hominid dialectics were not answerable to Hegelian categories. But their dialectical thinking was as compulsive and insidious as any kommissar's, or even more so. It was the human mind at its most vulnerable gyrating in a rut like a crazily cracked gramophone record. The "Vowel Oon" looked like a string of scratched beads, while the Marxian dialectic makes a world fabric more like a chain mail of coat hangers as in the diagram 1 on page 44 and is fully described in chapter 15. Needless to say neither of these patterns correctly represents the world, they are merely fanciful. The hominid version is made up of the "aaa" vowel which contributes the ongoing lateral scratches, while the contrary (vertical) lines were its individuations; and the beads, partly there merely to be scratched on, were the encompassing synthetic snapshots, the "ooo" or Os laid in a row like fish eggs or a television slowed down to individual frames. These are really primitive cosmological ideas, blundered into without further analysis (see the Tau-oon [Taun] added on the end of the hominid dialectic row in the sketches on page 327 in chapter 15). The wonder is these cosmological abstractions came to mind so early on and have left their marks in the intellectual ether still within the grasp of linguistics. This latter circumstance indeed calls for some justification, since it will otherwise be dismissed as at best a brilliant piece of extemporisation seeking to illustrate the kind of world that hominids lived in, but otherwise without any particular warrant.

Shortly, the pattern can be teased from the language, what there was of it. It is not to be expected that a point source of any of this early ratiocination can be uncovered; nor indeed what such a source might consist of. A longer answer is to be found throughout the length and breadth of the book. The origins of speaking presented are early origins, hopefully the earliest obtainable, and anyway sufficiently early to shed new light on the nature of our first speech as well as of thinking.

Finally, in order to clear the decks, it should perhaps be asked directly if language, like physical attributes, is properly subject to any kind of Darwinian scheme of evolution. We can guess Darwin probably thought so. He had read up linguistics, as far as the subject was understood in his day, which was not much. The young East India Company judge William Jones was learning Sanscrit and working out the links with Greek in the 1780s and the whole Indo European family of languages was already proposed in Darwin's day, though without the rich evidential working which has blocked out the relationships since his time. However it could be the question should really be put the other way around. Did Darwin really pick up his distinctive contribution to the evolution of species from the development of language families and their "speciation", so that slow changes in the various minutiae of pronunciation and borrowings from neighbouring languages etc gradually resulted in mutual incomprehensibility with new languages being born? For mutual incomprehensibility read inability to interbreed, and you have speciation. Language families no doubt seemed similar to animal families. What you needed in both cases was long periods of time, and Charles Lyell had provided this. Darwin, it is now known, already had the evolution of species from his mentor Charles Lyell whose 1831 book "The Principles of Geology", (which Darwin had with him on his five year world cruise on HMS Beagle, 1831-1836), had already established the evolution of microscopic shell forms included in the sedimentary rocks. Lyell had simply relied upon the negative entropy of life forms (their natural development is towards complexity and more energetic forms) to use the more developed shells included in the sedimentary rocks as markers for later formed rocks; and it had worked[4]. That put the evolution of species, since shells are formed by species, securely within the scientific corpus – although they were at once air brushed out again by the Victorian church, for which the evolution of rocks was unwelcome, but the evolution of species was inexcusable sacrilege. Yet Lyell's book, recently republished, has the evidence of the shells on every other page. So Darwin simply fibbed when 28 years later, after most of those years pestered by Lyell to publish, he finally did publish his own "On the Origin of Species", and pretended he had thought of species evolution himself from the evolution of the rocks in Lyell's book. Lyell was by then Sir Charles and received by good Queen Vic at court – she clearly had never read his book – and Darwin simply thought to spare his mentor the obloquy he knew his own contribution would condemn him to. Scientists world-wide preferred to accept what they read in the press in place of looking at the evidence, and the evolution of species from geological evolution is now treated as proven scientific history. But it is, quite simply, false. Anyone who disagrees should read Lyell's 1831 book which will wise him up at once.

Meanwhile language speciation actually owes nothing at all to Darwin. Having nothing to do with breeding or genetics, it proceeds under the guidance of human whimsy and happenstance which change at a variable but much faster speed than genetic evolution. There is no linguistic process. Language is an activity, not an organism, and as such just has a history, like all the human activities, arts and sciences alike. If Lithic is correct there is an element of oscillating about a norm, amounting to a wave form in time, since slovening allows the loss of original Lithic structure and then the subconscious mind restores it as new formations reflect the Lithic substrate; but it has no inevitability.

Looking further at the issue, there is a neat parallel in the origins and evolution of clothing, which can perhaps throw some light on the development of the art of speaking. It clears away the problem of the reflexivity between speaking and thinking. Clothes don't think. They are obviously unnatural and artificial, and (less obviously) like speech in this. The first hominid to furl a fur about their shoulders or about their waist was yet another example of the genius of the human race, their nearest rival perhaps the caddis fly lava or the hermit crab. Was such genius innate? And which came first, the fig leaf or the fur? Was it for warmth, or was it for shame as the Bible has it, that clothes were first worn? Already in Biblical times, say five thousand years ago, or at the absolute most ten thousand years BP, it was shame. But our earlier forebears were more pragmatic, and certainly much less shameful, as we can still determine from the shape they gave to language when first they began to speak, which was aeons before the Bible was written, perhaps around a hundred times as long ago. Shame came rather late; in fact we are still just riding the wave as it comes in. We ran stark naked like Barbary apes with no distinction between public and private parts or acts for hundreds of thousands of years before the first breech clout was invented. Instinctive inputs and outputs, after all, are not noted for their delicacy even today. We learn to moderate them as a pragmatic exercise known as civilisation. Body clothing at first was clearly pragmatic, to keep away the cold. It marked mankind's spread from the tropics and the hot climatic conditions inducing excess body heat which over millions of years had led to the descent in all mammalian species of the testes out of the body cavity in search of a cooler resting place. Imagine now the exploring Neanderthal's unadorned gonads confronted by the chill winds of a barely thawing Europe. Small wonder they called for the first pair of trews, whilst meanwhile retracing their precipitate descent. They still do the same when a chill wind blows in the kilted Scottish highlands, or immersion in cold water occurs. The fact is the body probably first acquired tabu areas

Chapter 2 Lithic

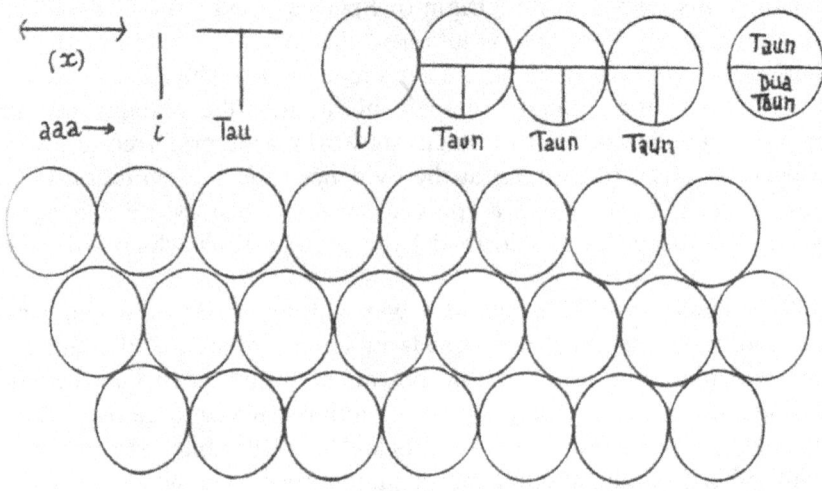

FIGURE 1

THE LITHIC VOWEL OON

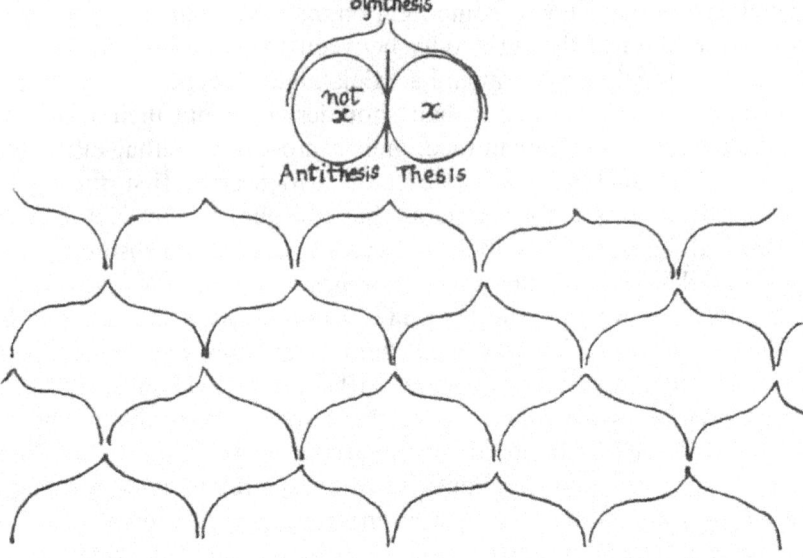

FIGURE 2

HEGEL'S AND MARX'S DIALECTIC

Chapter 2 Lithic

with the cold weather, but it was an after thought. Of course primitives did not think solely in terms of their sexual proclivities. But there can be no doubt they must have bulked largest in their repertoire of feelings and responses, if only because extraneous thinking in the absence of vocabulary to express it must have been peculiarly impoverished by comparison, whereas their emotional promptings were immediate and widely understood; and it has always been something to jabber about, it seems. Some of the best established lines of thinking were evidently in the tabu areas. Ab origine, the Devil has had the best themes, and that was because mankind readily conceded them to him. Any author writing on primitive language matters is confronted with this issue. If he is pilloried for undue fascination with these primitive patterns of thinking, even of having made them up, he can only retaliate by pointing out the neurosis, if neurosis it be, is not his but humankind's.

Without the acceptance of this human bias, progress in psychosemantics is likely to be scant. The box office spin-off must compensate for any little local embarrassments. When you think of the sensual and pornographic muck on display in bookshops and stationers around the world, this book ought not to be pilloried for dealing scientifically with the origins of thinking. The way it has been built up is by compiling linguistic relationships piecemeal from etymology; always bearing in mind the semantics as well as the phonology, the meanings along with the sounds, working in a double matrix of sounds and meanings, inescapably linked together in fact, over a theoretically limitless set of instances: the world lexicon from its first accumulation, of which of course only the merest smattering can be sampled in a single lifetime. Sex has two handy keys to unlocking the earliest meanings in human speech. First, it probably has not changed much over the time span in question, since changes in the flesh are glacial compared with the wagging of the tongue, so our prejudicial perceptions do not spoil our thinking much. Secondly, sex is conducted on a fairly narrow track compared to human experience in general. Not only are there these two handy keys but surprisingly enough hominids seem to have thought about the subject even more than the present generation, in a world where pleasurable indulgences were few – the warmth of the sun (which brought them to sexual reverie); a full belly (ditto); a smiling child (perhaps the same again); the excitement of the chase and the kill (well the boys at least may have been able to forge a connection with sex); and best of all a safe warm place around the fire in the hearth to lie at night, and the orgasm with a partner that would often follow. There was no television, no soaps, no sport to watch, no property or fashion or shopping to think about, not even much in the way of menu, and even less of mental abstraction to occupy the mind; only survival skills, with sex the unchallenged hobby for all, (and still remembered as the Garden of Eden, when even giving birth was easy).

Not only that, but thinking in itself is introversion, private and hidden. So you start by mulling over your own internal data rather than conceptualising the external world: that is left to be built subconsciously – just as it was before the mind got around to thinking about thinking, that is to say to conscious thought. Our mental world was thus built in the image of our own bodily design to a degree which now ranks as absurdity; but our first thinking forebears evidently could not see it. We just identified the working of our own bodies and then we sailed straight on to identify the rest of the world under those preconceived categories. We anthropomorphised the world as if it was the most natural thing to do – just more of the same as we experienced in effect. We can see now that there was an inbuilt egotistical streak in this, a natural autism every infant must start from, which has not yet entirely gone away. Moreover it was probably inevitable with this plan of attack that the bodily motifs that we most liked to think about were what mostly got hung on the scenery.

Chapter 2 Lithic

We have inherited a sexually charged lexicon which must leave Mrs Grundy incredulous and lightly stunned, and may even be providing the subconscious sexual pump leading to sexual recidivism in modern times. We have this sexual reservoir which we have stored away in our language, which the subconscious mind can read and find arousal from. It is really no more far fetched to believe so than to credit the direct visual and multimedia stimulation of television with a copycat effect for the weak willed and suggestible. We are after all what we think about to an astonishing degree. Or at least we were until we learned to prevaricate, or sublimate in Freud's rather Victorian terms, so as to switch course and go about on another emotional tack – making Sapiens Sapiens into Homo Fraudster instead, and incidentally filling the asylums with simpletons who have got knotted in the confusion and locked in to a posture unacceptable to them or to us, (or to both of us). There is still in our mental world a strong bodily and particularly sexual penumbra which invades and distorts our perception of reality. At one remove, Darwinism is about discovering and promoting the importance of breeding and sex in the world, which was probably another reason why it caused such a stir on publication, to add to the atheism it appeared at the time to imply. But we should perhaps first stop to ask who put sex there in the first place. Perhaps it was the First-born (A-dam) in us, and the chauvinism packaged with him. But we live in a made up world, we have developed everything in it in our own terms. Of course we have taken note of our spatial environment because when we have not we have been tripped up. But everything that has been recorded in all the encyclopaedias ever written, as well as everything that hasn't, has been spun like gossamers out of our own heads.

In Egypt, only some five thousand years ago they still retained some of the earliest ideas of physiology. The ka phoneme still stood for hard structure (ultimately from the sound of stone striking flint, a fanciful echoism), for instance the bones of the body, the skeleton which determined its shape and performance and gave the possessor his drive and his will power as well as his locomotive abilities; and it was all male. The ba was the fleshly matter clinging closely round and covering the bones and it was female. Every man and woman and every animal that found its way into the ark had both ka and ba, skeletal structure and flesh surrounding it; but the males had more ka and the females more ba. Women's job in life was to put the ba round the ka in the womb, a bit like getting a bun to rise in an oven. The ka was magically introduced, but at the same time rammed home at intercourse, the planting of the seed by the male, unaware his role is merely pollination and he has no seed at all. That is solely female. A full ka was double, one for this world and one for the next. The traces are just about universal. The Malays dub their aboriginal tribes still in the jungle 'Sakai', single Ka'd folk without any expectation in the hereafter, just animals really with no souls it was therefore not unjust to kill them at any time since they had no preparations to make for any future life. They don't even cut off their foreskins. In Hawaii the 'uku-lele', or 'two ka-singer', singing insects as we would say, grasshoppers, wear both ka in this world, having hatched from egg and larvae, born twice and with two bodies, thorax and body, a premature squandering of their assets, with no hereafter. Is that what makes them sit up and sing so? The musical instrument is called a grasshopper because it makes a somewhat similar stridulent sound. We just say insect, because its torso is nearly disected or cut in two. Meanwhile the Japanese seek to strengthen their ka by means of karate, getting it -ratai or -become raised or roused. It is a psychological activity in inspiration as well as a physical technique. The 'uku' of Easter Island were deposited by the islanders in caves as personal markers for burial space and the hereafter, and comprised personal nick-knacks, amulets representing the ka. Finding the

Chapter 2 Lithic

male soul or ka so widely spread, from Egypt to Malaya, Japan, Hawaii and Easter Island might suggest support for Lithic; and indeed the meanings can be traced to Lithic psychosemantic origins. The Pacific basin was perhaps colonised from the Garden of Eden when the final great glacial melt submerged it 360 feet beneath the South China Sea, when many Noahs will have set sail for higher ground in all directions, taking with them their gardening techniques. 'Malaya', the hilly hinterland still above the waves, means 'the garden land' and in the East (Eden) it was flat, where irrigated agriculture and the static living in large conurbations was first developed. Unfortunately it makes Adam a goy. The Akkadians (primitive Semites who conquered Sumer) borrowed from the Sumerians, Sumerum in Sumerian, which means the Westerners, the ones whose action was to travel West when the floods came, unlike those who went North towards China or into the Pacific ocean to the islands still above the water. They came by sea like Noah and his immigrants – noah means the sailors. It appears they still considered themselves Malayans forced to emigrate. These historical elaborations do nothing for the hypothesis that Lithic phonemes were at the origins of speaking, since that was hundreds of thousands of years earlier. But by the same token they do point up the pervasiveness of psychosemantic elements, if their original presence can be conceded on other grounds. It is these other grounds the remainder of the book will go in search of.

NOTES

1. Where Eric Partridge's "Origins, a Short Etymological Dictionary of Modern English", actually his magnum opus, the product of forty years' research in The British Museum Library (now the British Library) is an almost obligatory provision as a starter for those without many languages, and is about all they will need, by cause it already traces the origins of English words – if not into the ark as the mad poet William Cowper had it (your author is descended from his sister, who was relatively sane) at least as far back in some cases as Ancient Egyptian, and even Sumerian (such as was known in his day - not much, it is still a mess I hope to help to melt one day).

2. "On the Origins of Speaking", 624 pages, published POD in 2006 by Trafford Publishing Ltd of Canada and Oxford, UK, on the internet. See www.ontheoriginsofspeaking.com. POD stands for Printing on Demand, which holds the whole book on CD and prints and covers a copy when ordered and despatches usually within five days. It saves wasting paper and money on pre-publishing copies which need warehousing and many never get sold; and is rapidly being adopted (but without any publicity so they can continue to charge conventional prices and enjoy super profits) by the major publishers all over the world. A six hundred page book, with diagrams but no pictures, actually costs less than £2 to produce (2005 prices). Originally paperbacks only, but hardback copies are now available too at a modest additional cost. The considerable savings in cost have generally not been passed on to the purchaser or the author, who after all has done the most of it, including, with POD, even all the proof reading; but can get as little as 1.5 percent of the recommended retail price, after all the discounting due, as it passes down the retail chain. It keeps authors scribbling all their lives. There is nothing surprising in this when you consider daily newspapers are nowadays passed over the internet around the world and copies printed off locally. The economies just need to be

passed on there too, as the capital costs are covered. The actual production costs will be in pennies.

3. If I sometimes appear to be gunning for Professor Chomsky, and his hard wired universal grammarians (mostly unaware of their wiring) clustered around MIT, I can state positively I remain an admirer of his grammatical expertise, without espousing his overall linguistics, nor indeed his maverick (and wholly mischievous) dissident politics.

4. I only know this because my great grandfather (1804-1870) collaborated with Lyell, who used my great grandfather's shell collection – I remember it well, it occupied two double fronted glass cabinets which ran the whole length of the gallery occupying the top floor of Merton Hall (a hundred yards of closely packed and labelled shells) - to identify the shells in the rocks. They were fellow barristers in London, and week-ended on the shell collection by train. My great grandfather inherited the core of his collection from his father, (who had been Arch Deacon of Surrey and Prebendary of Winchester and must have been put out when he realised his son was using them to demolish the literal reading of Genesis).

CHAPTER 3

MISTRESS BA AND FRIENDS

Now the whole business of linguistic analysis must be tackled in detail. If when we first learned to utter the consonant sound Ba we gave it a meaning we can still discover, then how and why is this the case; and how can we know as much, considering it was hundreds of thousands of years ago and there is no record to consider? In this chapter it is intended to address the psychological backing for belief in Lithic, which requires that the subconscious mind is able to derive the original Lithic meanings of the phonemes from nothing more than their appearances in the lexicon of the language of the day, and so to have carried Lithic forward in the subconscious from generation to generation as it was learned afresh again and again subconsciously by everyone who has learned to speak. There was also of course the fact the syllabic meanings, when they were being strung together to make up words over the millennia from the combined semantic indications of the words' original component Lithic syllabic elements were exemplars all this time teaching the then current methodology. This was the case right up until Babel, as the Bible reports, marked the abandonment of logical word composition, adopting instead the way we have been thinking ever since, with words just with meanings in use, for no particular reason, learnt parrot fashion. It meant of course you only knew the words you had learnt the meanings of, and could not any longer read the meanings of the words in other languages you did not know, by transliterating each syllabic element in turn. You were in much the same pickle as the children recently taught in the United Kingdom, by benighted teachers, to read words without knowing the sounds even of the letters of which the words are made up: words without the alphabet. The alphabet has twenty six letters. English has just over a million words. The teachers were not in reality even practising themselves what they preached; they just knew a few hundred words by sight after learning to identify them by means of the alphabet. A significant proportion of the British public were soon illiterate under this treatment. A vocabulary of twenty six letters was one thing. A vocabulary of a million words was quite another. Our hominid forebears had much more sense than that. They started with just a dozen phonemes to master.

    You may not jump to accepting all of this. But the evidence builds; as you will see. First of all, the burgeoning of the phoneme Ba with its semantic contents skipping along (over the millennia, remember) will be examined in detail. Because when it is seen how the development fits in so well with the lexicons of so many languages today it will be easier to demonstrate how it occurred psychologically. Don't be put off, as your author was for years, before the weight of evidence convinced him.

    You must first of all put yourself in the position of an inarticulate hominid, such as you see on the cover, with no clothes on at all, hunkered around the hearth at the mouth of your cave at the end of the day. Throw away your clothes. Try to forget any civilisation you may have acquired – harder perhaps for some than others. Strip yourself mentally as well as physically bare. The game the men have caught has roasted in the red hot embers of the fire kept blazing in the hearth, and with full bellies warmed by the hearth, minds will soon be turning to the goodnight pleasures provided by sex. You are not now asked to join in, but only just to remember there were no other post-prandial entertainments available to divert attention from those provided by mother nature in those far off days so long ago.

Chapter 3 Ba

You have to imagine yourself a hominid as well, Homo Erectus, a single Sapiens. Hominids are generally taken to have been hairy hell-raisers with flat heads. But they were nothing of the sort. They were very much like you with your clothes off, slimmer and more wirey perhaps. They were quite capable of thinking things out, although of course they had no science as we understand it at all. So they were entirely free to think that the sun puts the fire out because the flame looks dimmer when the sun shines; and other simplistic muddles like that. You can surely believe that already the girls were wanting to gossip and the boys to have their say. Only they couldn't, because they had no language with which to share their thinking; or even to express it to themselves as any kind of personal memo.

Scientists have queried which prompted speech: to help in thinking for ourselves, or to communicate with others. The frustration on all sides must have been oppressive, squatting around the hearth, just gesturing. So how were you to get young Tarzan hunkered beside you, and probably by now making amorous noises, even pawing already and wanting to cuddle, and plainly exhibiting his readiness for sex without any trousers, to think the same as you, when it came to giving meanings to the new consonantal utterances you were all learning to make.

Surely you must have put your trust in finding out the natural meanings of sounds, because if they were natural he should be able to access them just as well as you could. So what were the natural meanings? Or rather what did they appear to be to our hominid forebears when first they began to learn how to pronounce the sounds, one after the other? We must now think about it. We are trying to relive the experiences of the Stone Age, way way back, and we can easily get it all wrong. Nobody has succeeded to date. But then nobody has really tried.

Well, hunting cries and waving your arms about and pointing had been used already to draw attention for aeons. "Grrr" has meant tiger and sent the tribe scampering up the trees already - ever since we first came down from them in fact. That is of course simple echoism, like the cuckoo. Think about it. Parrots can do it. The noise the tiger makes is taken to mean tiger, the noise the cuckoo makes is taken to mean cuckoo. "Grrr" is very soon practised and in use, symbolising the tiger naturally enough in the human mind because it echoes the tiger's growl, his signature tune as it were. The French is ti-grr or mistress growler today. The cat tribe were female because of their dainty walk. We can pick up the ti as feminine from the Ancient Egyptian with -ti the feminine suffix. (We mispronounce tee–grr as tai-ger because we say I for the first person singular and follow its pronunciation). It was just the same with "cuckoo" as the cuckoo's signature tune, although there was not quite the same urgency with cuckoos. You would have had to be a fool not to recognise echoism; but then even a fool would have learned it from his cohorts (his neighbours of the same age, brought up beside him). That is how meanings got established, just as - for the most part - they still do. The whole of civilisation can perhaps be derived originally from mimicry – only just rather slowly. The important point is it got the mind going on using uttered sounds to carry meanings. There is nothing new today in this idea. Nor was there in the Stone Age. Echoism has been a commonplace in linguistic studies for ever. Its central significance has perhaps been neglected. Philosophers have argued about symbolism as if it were difficult to understand, giving it a tertiary relationship: the symbol, they say, is the signifier of the significand to the signified for instance (or is it the signifier of the signified to the significand?), as well as other cat's cradles which get you doctorates of philosophy, and in turn signify you a senior wrangler to the rest of us. The reality is that way back in the Stone Age what actually happened was

Chapter 3 Ba

Tarzan (1) spotted "Grrr" (2) meant tiger (3). There is the tertiary relationship for you. History is hard to beat!

But now with Ba you were up against it, squatting there. Ba is not a sound you have come across in nature. In nature here just means in the world you live in. No good, by the way, suggesting sheep or goats were saying Baa in the Stone Age, because they weren't - and don't even today. What they actually say is more like Maa, and with good reason as we shall see when we come to examine Ma and its role in expressing the tensions of wanting something. The M just comes originally from a stressed stomach. Sheep and goats have been given a Baa as if it were what they said because Ba came to mean mouthing for our subconscious minds, and after that bellowing, etc, as well as "bal" for speak for aborigines in Oz – lip and tongue - and "Bolna" for Indo-Europeans in India and "bahasa" for Malays. Animals bay, dogs bark, (ba-ka, make with the mouth) or just bay (like deer), and in the Fon language gbe means to speak, from ka-bai (make mouthings again). There must surely have been some clue to the meaning of Ba for our forebears squatting around the hearth. "Grrr" means tiger because of the noise the tiger makes. So what Ba means must be because of what makes the noise; and that is more difficult because you are making the noise yourself, but you have no need for self identification, nor very possibly much idea of the self to identify. So it was not unreasonable to focus on the lips, in fact it was pretty well common sense, because Ba comes from pursing the lips and then letting them part with a puff of breath, letting the glottis go at the same time so the Ba was voiced as well. (Pa is of course virtually the same without the voicing). So the lips are saying Ba. Are the lips not expressing their nature with Ba just as the tiger was expressing its nature with grrr? This was radical thinking by the standards of the day for sure, because echoism only identified the phenotype (the individual being, like tiger or cuckoo) before; but now we are identifying the bits of the body responsible, as if humans had discriminatory powers beyond those appropriate for the animals: as indeed they have. It is a new level of analysis, a major discovery, though simple enough for us to pass it all by without comment today.

So now what is the nature of the lips? Are they not the fleshy bits around the mouth? Then Ba is saying "flesh here" just as Grrr is saying "tiger here". Ba is the signature sound of the flesh just as Grrr is the signature sound of the tiger. None of this thinking could we express in words at first. It was just private thinking, brain damage merely, for thinking is long prior to its expression. We have been thinking for aeons, but unable to express our thinking in words as we now can, which must have been a nightmare frustration at the time. You are entering a new world of succinct expression as you learn to make the different noises, instead of just the coarse expression you had managed until then using echoic cries and waving your arms about. – or (dare we say it) exposing your sex as an invitation. The new ideas were not wholly different but they were very much more precise, matching your thinking a mite better. Ba is the echo of the flesh. It has meaning. It is saying as much to you. The flesh is announcing its secret identity, its nature. If that is the case, surely Tarzan sitting beside you should be following through the very same thinking. If you can see that, surely he can too, if he stops pawing for a moment and gives the matter his attention. Keep saying it to gain his attention. He is bound to be following the same line of thought because he is your kith with the same responses to all the other inputs you both experienced. Bab meant two lips, the mouth, as it does still in Arabic. Their subconscious minds are clearly fully functioning, hanging on for ever.

He has a mouth the same as you. He should spot the same significance, the same symbolism. He can read "Grrr" the same as you. So he can read "Ba", the same as you can, too. Say Ba and point to the lips as you do so, to get him to pay attention to your gist. You can gather him to your way of thinking just as you did when you practiced how to make the growling sound for him in play. Learning is copying. Tarzan, the dumb coon, had probably learned flint making just by copying already. Now he can copy verbalism too. Surely he can. He has followed your thinking well enough when you have pointed at a scorpion or a snake in the grass, and he has given it a whack for you. So point to your lips when you say Ba. Keep at it until he does the same. He is learning to communicate just as he learned to flake flints (if not very well) just by copying. Bab, two Ba, one close beside the other, only separated by an undifferentiated vowel, which suggests a physical vacancy to anyone with any grasp of metaphor (it teaches it too): so even an orifice already; so with the two ba it surely must make a mouth. It makes babble in English too, an activity of the mouth this time, a natural enough development of the mouth idea in the first place: a mouthing. The -le which appears in babble is significant here as well, after the bab bit. Its significance will be spelt out in full as we go along. Here we may note that La has the semantic contents of slipping and sliding and slurring amongst others. Babbling is slurred mouthing.

Hey Presto! We have established the origin and nature of symbolism which philosophers are still arguing about. Ba symbolises the lips, the lips symbolise the flesh, and the flesh can be used as metaphor for every quality the flesh and the lips display in turn. We have lift off in this scene, as we squat outside the cave in the Old Stone Age, for the development of human speaking for the next few hundreds of thousands of years; and now likely to prove coterminous with the human race: with a bit of luck good for as long again, if Weapons of Mass Destruction (WMD)[1] can be controlled. On the front cover is the very scene as civilisation achieves lift off. We just had to keep thinking in this same old way and building on it, adding more symbols and then more metaphors as we went along. Our progress so far can be summed up with two little dickie-birds: the cuckoo and the seagull, the first marking echoism and the second our remarkable facility for transferring an idea derived from one symbol to another, which is generally referred to as metaphor. All we have to remember so far is a cuckoo says cuckoo and a seagull, the sea caller, bred a silent gull wing. A metaphor is a gull, because a gull wing is a metaphor. A gull wing neither squarks nor is coastal. It just has the shape of the seagull's wing. We have pulled that pattern off the bird.

However Ba has another role almost as important in linguistic outcome as its meaning discovered for flesh. It is the prime example of a meaning derived from the happenstances of the human body. We have been picking meanings off our anatomy ever since, almost as if there were no other tomorrow; just as we have learned to point with our fingers and even count with them, as well as to use them for every kind of manipulation for which they were evidently developed in the first place, as well as some for which they never were.

Not only that, but once the trick of relating sounds to how (and then also why) we utter them was discovered, the bits of human anatomy which fielded the most attention were, rather unsurprisingly, those bits we now are expected to ruminate upon in private or not at all, our reproductive facilities, and particularly the male genitalia, both penis and testicles, which do and did in fact offer a positively baroque and surprising range of appearances and performances for remark. Quite a significant proportion of the thinking which has informed human language to date appears indeed to have been originally hammered out on the anvil of our own genitalia - and of course assessment of animal performance as well. Whether this arose from the preternatural tendency of Ms Tarzan to gossip about whatever her fancy trawled up, or alternatively from the chauvinistic preoccupations of Tarzan himself, is one of the more difficult questions the student of prehistoric language development, and the psychology upon which it was based, has to face. It is probably best to assume a concordance of interests where sex was concerned, so that conversation was heavily laced from day one with sexual motifs, and then the thinking about thinking just followed along.

Hominids, like the Bonobo miniature Chimpanzees, (whose scandalous enthusiasm for sex is so pronounced they can not any longer be put on display in zoos), we know now spent a good deal of their time in the practice of sex, since humans are now (uniquely) sexually active all the time. It implies, according to Darwinian evolution, that in order to pass on your genes you had to be a top performer when it came to copulation, ready at the drop of a hat (had there been any hats around) to get in there, so that the race gradually weeded out the slow coaches and reproduced the genes of those with the most voracious sexual appetites. We have gradually become more and more sexually voracious, although it is of course likely that the more voracious organs will have largely belonged to those with the better built bodies all round, capable of warding off the competition. So it does not follow sex dominated evolution, just superior force.

All this sex is not the meliorists' position; and it is indeed alternatively possible our sexual voraciousness has piggy-backed on well developed bodies, the one bringing the other with it. However it has since been discovered that the artificial building of muscle, to excel at sport, etc, has a reverse or balancing effect, and the sexually greediest males are these days those relatively lazy and louche, preening themselves and liable to choose careers in personal display and political prestige. Our MPs can not be trusted; but in the Stone Age, while the hunters, the worker bees, were loping all day after game, Jacques was spreading his charms around the women's hearth perhaps. He would likely have got short shift with the hunters' return.

Laughably – but it is a black humour – human whimsy, the result of thinking, may have turned evolution around. Very probably Dr Arnold, headmaster of Rugby School (his boys invented rugby), had already spotted this, way back in the nineteenth century, since he prescribed plenty of exercise and cold showers for his pupils in order to get them to concentrate on learning and postpone any sexual practice. Well, it worked at the time. But unfortunately it has worn off – perhaps from better feeding and better thinking. In any case, the analysis of the thinking behind prehistoric language roots inevitably explores everything that we were thinking in our bad old hominid days about sex, and uses it to resolve much of the way language got built. There is no pornographic intent, but it is hard to review the way we have thought without sailing at times close to the line. So we should perhaps start out by politely saying sorry to Mrs Grundy. If there is an undue interest in sexuality it has been humanity's undue interest all along, and must by no means be fobbed off on the author, who has had to mug his way through it all.

The original meanings have been worked out from the meanings given words in many languages spoken today, using the meanngs of their words to break them down into their constituent single sounds or phonemes; and then to work out how the constituent strings of phonemes, when their meanings are put together, were used to indicate the meanings of the words. A pattern of meanings implicit in the phonemes emerges and is confirmed, picked out by comparing their common roles in many words. So for instance, to show what is implied, I am prompted as I write in Tenerife, with the windows closed, by a "kalima" blowing outside to indicate the Lithic constituents of the word. It is a hot wind off the Sahara desert which carries with it the finest of powdered sand - stifling in the Sahara where local folk have learned to cover their faces in cotton cloth to filter the dust, but

Chapter 3 Ba

having to suffer the heat - leaving everything covered in a coating of fine yellow dust – and bringing a few flies carried two hundred miles across the sea to Tenerife with it too.

The word comprises the phonemes ka-lai-ma. From the Psychosemantic trees for ka, la and ma it may be seen these phonemes can mean 'make, loop (and so fly), soil'. The Lithic meaning is 'makes the soil fly', not a bad name to give the kalima. In the desert it is a khamsin or a shinook, from ka-mai-sai'n or shai-en-au-kai, make-the soil-fly up, or the upping-of-that what-earth. To fly in turn comes from fa-lai, and moreover its original form was with a -ga on the end, which has slovened to ya, (the same phoneme pronounced lazily), omitting the contraction of the glottis; and then slovened again to a single -ly syllable. The psychosemantic trees for these phonemes fai-lai-kai make available for flying the meanings 'faring-looping-going' or 'faring-looping-making'. It is a gull. A loop was derived in turn from the sun's orbit which copied, so our forebears thought, the circle of the skyline at sea, but vertically up and down this time, and then round under the horizon to rise again at dawn. The skyline at sea is seen from the shore as a straight line (the only one in nature) but from a boat on the ocean as a perfect circle. Flight admittedly does not have to be in a loop, but the looping sun evidently flew; so loop became fly.

The Sahara is a very hot desert, from the constituent phonemes sa-ha-Ra, fire-hot-Sun. The sibilant was given the original meaning fire, because when in the Pleistocene age you dunked your burning brand in the nearest puddle at dawn it said "ishshsh". It still does. You can try it for yourself if you wish. The uniformity of nature over time does sometimes give us a glimpse of how our forebears thought over many millennia. Elsewhere it has been suggested that if by misfortune the burning brand had instead said "Rumpelstiltzkin" as it died, Tarzan might well have flown into a sulk and refused to take any more of this language lark for another few hundred thousand years. Big issues do sometimes hang on little ones, like the butterfly in Patagonia fluttering its wings and causing a storm over Europe – a mythical circumstance of course just like rumpelstiltzkin.

These meaning patterns are what is new and a challenge to conventional etymologists, who start out by just assuming the constituent phonemes (letters, more or less) never had and have no meanings of their own, and the constituencies of words follow from roots, the sounds of which are without any intrinsic meanings of their own and have just been picked by chance by random thinking. Lithic meanings disprove these assumptions by means of the patterns which work when giving phonemes original individual meanings, including the derivations of the meanings of these phonemes by way of catenas or strings of metaphor after metaphor. These patterns are demonstrated in the psychosemantic trees for each of the phonemes in turn, which are reprinted from the original major work in this short introduction to Lithic Language. The development of language by means of metaphors is currently 'intellectually correct' (IC), by the way. The Lithic hypotheses are fundamental and sound.

Carl von Linné (Linaeus) a biologist in Sweden towards the end of the eighteenth century brought shame upon his father, a pastor in the Swedish church, by identifying the family relationships between all vegetable species (plants, large and small) by way of their flowers, which he identified as their sexual organs. For destroying the innocence of the flowers he was told by the Swedish Church he would burn in Hell. The prospect drove him mad and he died in an asylum three years later. But his science survives. The young ladies in the following century pressing flowers to preserve them found them attractive, we must suppose, for their colours and delicacy alone. My great great grandfather, the 4th baron (Tom 4), a parson, 1778-1839, who wisely married his bishop's daughter, with equal wisdom shunned flowers and collected shells instead, quite evidently without any genitalia,

Chapter 3 Ba

long gone. It enabled his son, Tom 5, a lawyer, my great grandfather (1804-1870), to anticipate Charles Darwin by collaborating with Sir Charles Lyell, a fellow barrister in London, who used Tom 5's shell collection and established geology as a science, by publishing "The Principles of Geology" in 1831, identifying the sequence of the sedimentary rocks by means of the collections of microscopic shells contained within them, assuming they had evolved and the more developed shells came later. It was a guess based upon the principle now established as entropy, but it worked, and implied the bombshell that species evolved. Of course in 1831 the Victorian church airbrushed out the shells, the species, accepting reluctantly only the geological evolution. Lyell was Darwin's mentor and Darwin, as the geologist on HMS Beagle, took Lyell's book with him on his five year world cruise, 1831-1836. In 1859 when Darwin published his "On the Origin of Species" Lyell had been knighted and was received at Court – good Queen Vic had clearly not read his book – so Darwin pretended he was responsible for species evolution which he had deduced from Lyell's geological evolution, to save his mentor from the obloquy he knew his book would earn him. Lyell was still a Fellow of a Cambridge College where most of the dons wore dog collars. The truth was the other way about: species evolution had been used to establish geological evolution in 1831. But the press copied Darwin's pretence, and the historians of science copied the press. Darwin contributed the survival of the fittest, and the consequent gradual domination of their genes, in the environment encountered by the phenotypes, as the evolutionary process.

Lithic is a fascinating texture of original meanings from which all our languages have been built, which has all been forgotten, so that it takes a fair bit of working out, which most folk have not got the time, or perhaps the patience or the brains to do. But it makes better sense to assign the loss of understanding to Babel, the decision (whether by God or man) to learn words like parrots, thus saving following through their original compositions, a decision which has given us civilisation by freeing the mind to build on the meanings of words, building higher by starting higher up the level of meanings. It was not a punishment but a boon; and now learning the Lithic base for thinking is a bonus, because it is a much needed exercise in independent thinking, a semantic game of scrabble picking out the meanings which fit instead of just the letters. It is an intellectual exercise much needed to free the mind from intellectually correct rutted thinking just following along what is presented as intellectually correct. It in no way impugns science, knowledge which is the best way of thinking discovered to date. It amounts to "think of an idea and test it to destruction if you can".

Once you have fully hoist aboard how Ba has played its part in linguistics – it is not taught in any syllabus to date – you are already half way to understanding how the human mind works, and without the benefit of any academy at all, just using common sense and our innate brilliance and imagination when it comes to thinking, if only we give the mind free rein. Civilisation has added a great deal of useful information to the human curriculum, but it has inevitably resulted in a degree of mental sclerosis as well, as thinking the same as the rest of informed society has gradually become intellectually correct (IC). So if a mistake is made we all tend to make it, without challenge - until some maverick comes along and spits in the eye of the senators. It then becomes possible to see the long march from echoism to civilisation in our languages, from the traces the passage has left.

Apart from the original meanings of phonemes and their development, it only remains to show how thinking is mediated by that major part of the mind which as yet remains below the threshold of consciousness, and nevertheless enables us to recover our original thinking even after hundreds of thousands of years of neglect; an astonishing outcome

Chapter 3 Ba

which will be demonstrated later; but not now – see chapter fifteen. Before that we should review the meanings given to all the other phonemes (roughly letters) as we learned to utter them, as well as the dependent meanings developed from them over the millennia. This ground is covered in full in a previous book on the subject[2] which runs to over 620 large pages and carries with it what has been criticised as a surfeit of instances to illustrate the meanings in as many languages as could be fitted in. So the "Psychosemantic Trees" used in the earlier book are reprinted, but without repeating all of the chat.

There is a problem at once when it comes to illustrating the original phonemic meanings because the illustrations are to be found, as in the kalima, in words in use which are compiled of several phonemes (letters) each contributing their mickle to the overall muckle of the meaning of the words in use. Longer words amount to a string of individually meaningful elements, all of which have to be taken into account when deriving the overall composite meaning in use. So you really need to have been over the quiverful of meanings of all of the letters before you start putting together the meanings of words which use them.

All this is poison to the accepted ideas on linguistics which rule that word roots, the core bit arbitrarily cut out of the whole word, are random and arbitrary, a position not hard to justify once you have rendered them so by reducing them to a single syllable. In addition the Lithic elements with their individual meanings give only somewhat approximate indications of the precise meanings in use today. Back in the Stone Age they thought that way. You could write the tale of a Harry T (for Tarzan) far more amusing than a Harry P (for Potter), if you had the inclination and the time to spare. But you are not going to be able to rewrite any dictionary of today by means of Lithic meanings. All you are going to be able to do instead is to discover the secret of the way the human mind works, and has worked since we first began to speak, and to compile the sources of the meanings of words which now appear in dictionaries for yourself. It is moreover a measure of the ingenuity of the human mind, that we should have built a lexicon from basic semantic units in combinations, which far exceeds the precision possible with them on their own. We have done it by then simply picking more precise meanings and defining them more precisely in use. Such developments in use do not impugn the soundness of Lithic analysis, but on the contrary actually confirm it, showing which way the mind went on its way to continually more precise definitions. The wonder must surely be that Lithic works at all. Indeed the wonder is at times so great that for some folk a credibility gap opens and sets in, which of course saves further consideration. The author himself has more than once been round this course, but has always been forced back, by the sheer weight of instances which illustrate their Lithic substrates, into getting on with it.

So now, having cleared away some of the background orientations explaining what Lithic is about, if we turn to the psychosemantic tree for Ba on pages 61 to 63, there is first of all a note of the phonetic variations which occur, all the way from Fa to Wa. The variations are most often from slovening while ignorant of the significance of the sounds. The Spanish for instance are in a mess when it comes to pronouncing B and V. They generally pronounce B as virtually the same as V, leaving it only to be resolved whether they have altered the pronunciation in the first place or the spelling. Going by the rest of the Indo-European group, it is generally a maverick pronunciation, but there is still a need to be on guard for the spelling having jumped across the divide to match the pronunciation. The Welsh take pride of place for polluting their language by means of "Sindi", a shifting of the initial consonants depending on the grammar (which is a late invention, now treated as a branch of applied mathematics). When it comes to identifying original Lithic roots the

Chapter 3 Ba

Welsh are therefore probably best just left out, simply to save brain damage involved in first discovering whence their words first set out. With Irish, moreover, the spelling (like most else) has simply become a political statement, with little regard for the original history, in this case the pronunciation, and then the pronunciation made to follow the spelling. The original Celtic is nevertheless full of Lithic roots which deserve attention.

The sounds Ba and Pa that we utter are separated solely by the voicing which accompanies Ba. There may perhaps be some further distinction to be made in so far as Pa is spat out a bit more sharply than Ba, but that is simply because Pa is not encumbered by a simultaneous vocal accompaniment from down below in the throat. You don't need to be a senior wrangler to spot this. It stands out a mile, as soon as you think about it, although it has no academic recognition. The meanings follow along. That is the point. Pa is naturally perceived as the thinned diminutive of Ba, a piping sound compared with the bumbled Ba. So, if Ba, sounded by the lips, comes to mean flesh, Pa is (vocally) its thinned diminutive. So what, when we come to consider the meanings, is the thinned diminutive of flesh? It was, our forebears thought - with some perspicacity it must be said – the skin. The skin surrounds the flesh providing it with a surface which is its more or less impervious boundary. Vegetables were taken to be similarly composed of skeletons and flesh, as more or less they are. Their surfaces were their skins just like ours. Indeed by extension of the idea the skins or surfaces of everything were their visual appearances, what you see, as in reality they are, res vista, as in a panorama, (pa-en-au-ra-ma, the surface-of-all-the eye-devours), which gives pan its sense of all in Greek – as in turn in a bus, (the wrong bit used). Pa could also be a diminutive bit of flesh, as in chapter 11.

A psychosemantic tree is a novel coinage, unavoidable to get across the idea that language is based upon our original psychologically prompted perceptions of the natural meanings of the sounds as we learned to utter them, and from them have come all our very many meanings over the very many millennia. Sounds haven't all stayed the same; but they have not gone all over the place as some folk fancy. The lines in the phonetic trees on top are intended to show the directions in which, over the millennia, consonants have sometimes shifted their pronunciation to similar sounds, one way or another. There is no single reason why these changes should have occurred. The development of language is not a process but merely the result of human whimsy. We have processual minds and are apt to suppose the whole world is the same. Some of it is but some of it isn't. The brothers Grimm made processes of it all. When trying to read the original meanings of words in use today, it is necessary to be aware of the changes in pronunciation which may have occurred. Ba may have shifted left or right, all the way to Fa in one direction or Wa in the other. It can make finding the original ba in modern languages difficult. However there are also plenty of cases where it hasn't, and it shows up, and others where we can spot the shift.

The examples of the semantic tree for Ba provide a mere nine original meaning groups, from which it is proposed all the usages of the ba phoneme in languages around the world today are ultimately derived. The first meaning (1) is just echoism; and then (2) Babbling B from a kind of echoism, from babies' babbling, followed by (3) other Bs with meanings derived from the lips and mouth, and then (4) the meaning of flesh, which comes from the lips, the fleshy bits surrounding the mouth (which do the babbling).

All from so little? Yes; but over vast periods of time. That is what spooks folk. They can't imagine hundreds of thousands of years, nor what might happen in – on a human scale - such vast periods of time. A lot happened. Language developed. How did it do it? Better, how did we do it? A very primitive language went in one end of a time sequence, and a whole lot of highly developed languages came out the other end. Explain. Well, it was the exercise of the human mind. This is an attempt – the first – to explain the exercise; and it makes perfectly good sense.

Religionists without any judgment can continue to prefer a descent of language from on high, and we should wish them luck as we pass by, but we can not stay. God is not mocked, only the coons. Flesh effectively leads in to all the other meanings, and this is represented by 4 not being separately shown on pages 62 and 63. The rest all come from the attributes of flesh – which after all are legion, as well as easy on the hominid mind. So by now language, and the contents of the subconscious mind which derive from it, are stuffed with fleshy bits; and we have to face the fact it includes some naughty bits. Mistress Ba is more than just a dainty step. Columns 1 to 9 (4 is covered by 5 to 9) give the examples which spring to mind, or anyway sprang to mine. If the Lithic hypotheses are correct there will be many more in many languages. Most of those listed are in English, but salted with examples from other tongues. English speakers can judge the English ones. Without English much work remains to be done. There is no suggestion Lithic is mostly to be found in English, and indeed Malay is probably the richest seam to be mined as in origin closest to Adam's tongue; and before him nothing linguistic survives.

It is unfortunately necessary to mention in passing Adam did not speak a Semitic tongue because he was not a Semite. The Akkadians borrowed him from the Sumerians. The relationship between the Akkadian and the Sumerian languages is moot, but probably the borrowings were all from civilised Sumerians to relatively savage proto-Semite Akkadians, after they conquered the Sumerians. (There may have been return donations later). This is unwelcome to the Jewish intelligentsia working on the case, although it need not be. Adam's garden was a vegetable garden – no flowers at all. It was Eastern Malaya. Malaya actually means garden. It was padi, irrigated from the rivers in Eastern Malaya, now only detectable by sonar 360 feet down on the bottom of the South China Sea. When the circumpolar ice finally melted about 8000 BC Noah (it means the sailors from Nau-awa-ai, All those of-the water-ones), apparently fled West to the Gulf, where their colony was drowned simultaneously out of the Persian Gulf but had a back-up in Iraq with flat land at a higher level. Behind the South China Seas there were only hills, the present Malaya, no longer a garden land but still carrying the name after some 10,000 years or more. Sumerians means the Westerners, (from Su-mai-arai 'n, [to the]light-dying-going-ones, ie those that fled West. Others went in different directions, including round as well as over the Pacific Ocean, and north and inland to China. There is good history behind the Bible. It just needs to be understood properly. Not all of it is correct, because the original Semitic hinterland was up around Lake Van, and translating the Malayan story uphill and naming events there made a funny flood in the highlands. Ararat is really just the new shore line.

We do not know precisely why the circumpolar ice finally melted. The late Professor Velikovsky suggested it was due to Venus, originally a comet, as it adjusted its orbit on capture by the sun, tipping the earth and killing the mammoths. He was cruelly abused by the conventional scientists, principally the late rather arty conventional astronomer Professor Carl Sagan, who threatened publishers of Velikovsky with school books denied. The matter is still open, but it is not the most important thing. It certainly was not from carbon dioxide generated by human activities as the Greens assume must be the over-riding cause of the cold global warming today, happily ignorant of catastrophic world history to date. Anyone reluctant to consider Eastern Malaya as the true Garden of Eden should read Dr. Stephen Openheimer's 558 page book published in 1998 "Eden in the

Chapter 3 Ba

East", Weidenfield and Nicholson, ISBN 0 297 81816 3; and best of all write another one as detailed to disprove it, if they can.

So column 5 is Bulgy B, those meanings derived by metaphor from the propensity of the flesh to be softish and bulgy, and so to float and block free passage equally. But then of course you find these propensities leading to others - all over the millennia, remember. Column 6 picks up on the bulginess of column 5 in so far as what is bulgy is also bendy. Under this heading are those meanings close to bending the leg, for example when walking, which we manage with the muscles of the haunches.

But meanwhile, the proclivity of the flesh, animal and vegetable together, to burgeon results in Burgeoning B and forty examples, twenty four of them from foreign tongues.

Ba is to do with the buzzing of bees, big bangs, etc. Bees really just "zzzz". They get the B and the name too solely because B has become associated with lips and mouthing. Bangs are much the same. The B simply denotes a burst of sound – like an utterance. The aaa with a bit of nasalization in the –ng of the bang comes from the ongoing reverberating effect of the sound upon the human ear. Bang is echoic, but with a b in front because we utter one.

Bah! is an old fashioned expression of contemptuous dismissal. It gets its sense from the expulsion of breath indicating rejection, and indeed Pah, which is clearly closely akin, is a fair representation of a spit. If you spit something out it is because you want to get rid of it. You can say Pish! in much the same manner. You will be showing yourself an oldie, but you will be understood. If you say Bu in Chinese it means No! Perhaps in China, Ba started out as a negative imperative, a dismissive response, and later spread over to mean just the negative. Or else it started out as a reference to certain dual fleshy bits, used in the same way by the uninhibited moderns in English too, to express a radical disagreement. In Borneo for instance, where boars come from, the Bau were their balls: ba is fleshy bit, and –u is the dual, their dual fleshy bits, their testicles; and the r at the end is the relict of rai, which means both raised and visible. Boars have the remarkable peculiarity, as every farmer's boy soon learns, of wearing their testicles tucked up behind their rumps, out at the back with their tails in the air, whereas all other species, including mercifully Sapiens Sapiens, keep theirs rather more discreetly bagged between their legs. Otherwise sitting down would present an ever present hazard. Boars never sit. They wallow. We can work this out partly because the Malay, next door, for fruit is buah, and it also means testicles. The fruit are the fleshy bits of the plant. Testicles were originally taken to be the animal equivalents of vegetable fruit and were thought to contain seed like the fruit in the vegetable kingdom, whereas of course in reality they are the equivalents of the vegetable stamens carrying just the pollen. What is even odder is that the term buah has the dual vowel, meaning twin bits, which suggests that the fruit meaning originally identified them as vegetable testicles, rather than the similarity being noted the other way around, with testicles animal fruit. We built nature on ourselves. Moreover in Sumerian we have doburr for testicles, where they appear to be saying two fruits in Malay (do buah). That chimes with Adam's Sumerians sailing west from the Malayan garden land to Mesopotamia as their homeland, the Eastern or Eden plain, was flooded. Adam appears to have spoken Sumerian and Malay today is the nearest language to it, probably a provincial Sumerian spoken by the tribes up country (and slovened over ten thousand years).

The other thing about the pig soon learned was their remarkable fertility, a dozen piglets at a time in the wild – which is why you eat bacon. It was most available. It is said the need for copulation to induce fertility was first discovered when sows kept alone failed to breed. With humans adult virginity was at that time yet to occur, so sex was probably initially just instinctive and recreational. Male animals at least take pleasure in it; females are less sure. Apparently only the subconscious was aware of the Darwinian imperatives, if you go far enough back.

In an age when fertility was quite literally worshiped, the tribesmen in Borneo formed the habit of copying the boars, perhaps in a hopeful way, leaving their own testicles exposed to view and to the breezes, with just a penis sheath for social purposes as guarantee of good behaviour, and probably hoping the exposure of their dual fruiting bodies to the sun's rays like the boar would result in a truly porcine fertility. These sheaths became prized possessions with tall extensions and tufts of feathers on the end secured with a strip of liana around the waist, a decoration for the men's pride and joy. One was ceremonially presented to Prince Phillip when he visited. He received it with gravitas and appreciation, as royalty should. But you should not think the wild tribesmen who were the presenters were unaware of the element of humour in suggesting their prestigious visitor should disrobe, and at the same time shed any prejudices he might harbour about the manner of his attire, and decorate his person in the same way as they did. They could see the awkwardness for him just as well as he could, probably better, and they knew he could not show it. In Borneo a good deal is about not showing, with the occasional splendid fling when there is a chink in their reserve.

David Attenborough and his team, supposing they were ingratiating themselves, stripped off and ran out of a hut dressed only in a native 'chawat', a thin strip of cloth passed between the legs and around the waist, a crotch piece (chawat also means a branch or fork in Malay, like the crotch), David leading at the canter to break the ice and the others awkwardly following, with their little pale pink bums behind their ample bellies a mild comicality to the viewers for whom it was recorded on camera on TV in the West; but a huge source of amusement and delight at the time for their native viewers, who of course maintained a show of absolute gravitas, just like Prince Phillip with his penis sheath in hand, and without any of his extensive training, in their case simply from natural good manners; and also I think from a dawning concern as to what young David might be going to get up to. Whitey, they must have thought, is just like that: throwing away their elaborate tailoring and adopting the primitive. What next? Was it to suggest they would welcome feminine entertainment, perhaps? Had they any obligation to offer a few virgins to these extraordinary foreigners? Surely not. You didn't get the girls by just throwing off your clothes, least of all if you had a pale pink bottom. You had to prove your mettle in tribal wars, during which your bottom would get tanned and your muscles hardened as you roamed the wild wood bare at the back and spear in hand. It is doubtful if any of this registered with young Attenborough. He thought he was just showing a collaborative spirit by baring his bottom, but he had all the dignity of a hermit crab nipping between shells for cover. Interpretations are simply not the same in Borneo as they are with the lovies in the BBC, where it might indeed have been read as he imagined. Never mind. He had certainly made an impression in both places; and he was soon the director, if not of the Queen's Navee, at least of the BBC. Lest he should find himself left just a figure of fun for a single silly misunderstanding, it must be said the programmes on animal life he hosted over a lifetime were highly commendable, breaking new ground and even involving quite strenuous working on the ground as well, underviewing bats flying in caves, standing in piles of bat guano, and coaxing gorillas far too close for safety, had old Daddy Silverback taken him for a sexual threat, instead of dismissing him as a curious sexless and therefore harmless creature. Of course he was probably getting very well paid as well.

Chapter 3 Ba

THE PSYCHOSEMANTIC TREE FOR BA

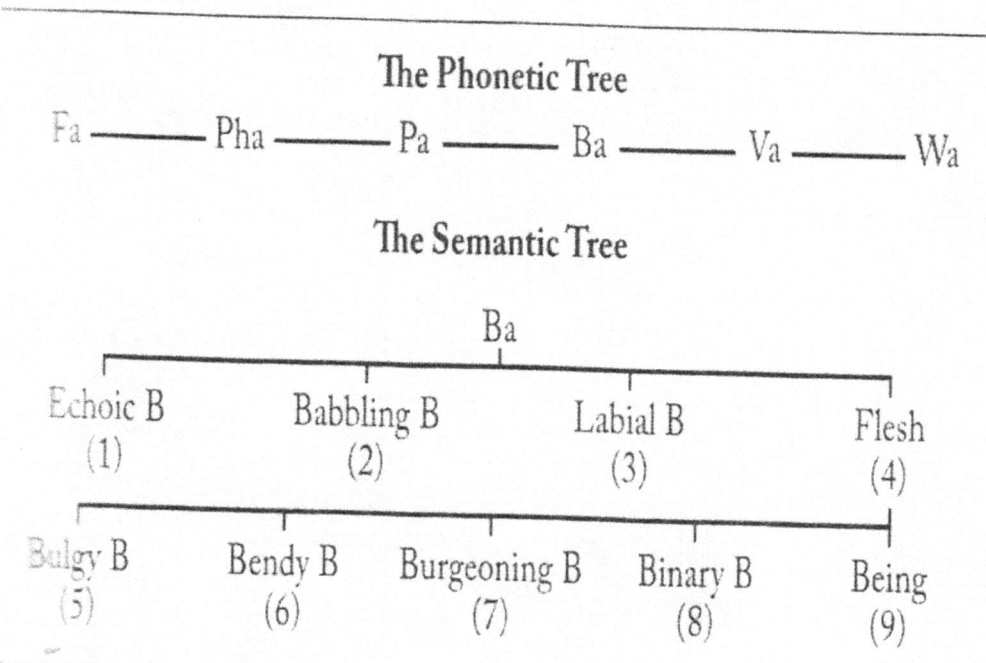

THE PSYCHOSEMANTIC TREE FOR BA

PAGE 2 EXAMPLES.

Column 1	Column 3	Column 5	Column 5 (cont)
BAH!	LABIAL B	BULGY B	
Bang	Bab (Arabic)	Bulgy	Belly
Banga (Old Norse)	Bouche (French)	Bungey	Banana
Boo!	Bucca (Latin)	Bung	Bar
Buzz	Ba'al Zebab (Hebrew)	Bum	Barbeque
Bee	Bab I Laun (Akkadian)	Bub	Barbakoa (Arawak)
Abeille (French)	Bite	Bust	Barang (Malay)
	Bait	Breast	Sumbat (Malay)
	Bit	Bosom	Lembu (Malay)
	Bibere (Latin)	Bottom	Gambar (Malay)
Column 2	Bay	Buttock	Brown
BABBLING B	Baa	Bone	Balkans
Baby	Bark	Boa (Latin)	Belang (Malay)
Baba	Gbe (Fon)	Bag	Belit (Malay)
Baba (Spanish)	Indaba (Zulu)	Bas (French)	Semblit (Malay)
Babador (Spanish)	Liber (Latin)	Buoy	Bongkah (Malay)
Bib	Bahasa (Malay)	Bwoid (Gaelic)	Kembang (Malay)
Babosa (Spanish)	Bugle	Boy	Labuan (Malay)
Bueh (Malay)	Book	Budak (Malay)	Bu (Chinese)
Bumbo (Italian)	Bab el Mandeb (Arabic)	Bobo (Spanish)	Tumboh (Malay)
	Sebab (Malay)	Bodoh (Malay)	Bakelos (Malay)
	Bacha (Malay)	Brain	Avocado (Quechoa)
	Bantai (Malay)	Bank	Bocado (Spanish)
	Blah	Bund (Hindi)	Bunga (Malay)
	Babuine (Old French)	Bund (German)	Bull
	Baboon	Bend	Abang (Malay)
	Bader (Provencal)	Bind	Bagus (Malay)
	Bacalar (Spanish)	Bahei (Egypt)	
	Ban	Bare	
	Batare (Latin)	Button	
	Beak	Babi (Malay)	
		Bor (Senoi)	
		Borbi (Senoi)	
		Buah (Malay)	

Chapter 3 Ba

THE PSYCHOSEMANTIC TREE FOR BA.

PAGE 3 EXAMPLES

Column 6	Column 7	Column 8	Column 9
BENDY B	BIOLOGICAL B	BINARY B	BEING
HAUNCH	BURGEONING		
LEG	LIFE	Body	Be
GO	Bion (Greek)	Bottom	Be-
Ba (Egyptian)	Verde (Spanish)	By	Ber- (Malay)
Bous (Greek)	Brer	Buttuc (Old English)	Become
Baino (Greek)	Bough	Balluc (Old English)	Behet (Albanian)
Bear	Bud	Butt	Liber (Latin)
Aber (Gaelic)	Bad	Bulrush	Seberang (Malay)
Nabi (Arabic)	Bor (Bornean)	Ambi (Latin)	
Naib (Arabic)	Barra (Hindi)	Bind	
Labalaba (Malay)	Besar (Malay)	Badhna (Hindi)	
Berbaling (Malay)	Labu (Malay)	Bashki (Albanian)	
Bilabong (Oz Abo)	Rambutan (Malay)	Bilanx (Latin)	
Baji (Oz Abo)	Bengala (Benali)	Bellum (Latin)	
Boomerang (Oz Abo)	Bawang (Malay)		
Burong (Malay)	Bulb		
Terbang (Malay)	Bamboo (Malay)		
Bangli (Hindi)	Buloh (Malay)		
Bangle	Kebun (Malay)		
Beliong (Malay)	Boabab (Hamitic)		
Bamboula (Creole)	Babul (Bengali)		
Lambat (Malay)	Babul (Bengali)	Column 7	
Bangsat (Malay)	Nave	Continued	
Bintang (Malay)	Navis (Latin)	Brank (Breton)	
Boleh (Malay)	Beam	Bhura (Sanskrit)	
Balek (Malay)	Board	Brinnan (Gothic)	
Belakang (Malay)	Barn	Bachelor	
Balalaika	Barm (Swedish)	Bhura (Sanskrit)	
	Bergen (Swedish)	Bachelor	
	Biarg (Old Norwegian)		
	Biargahei (Gothic)		
	Beorh (Old English)		
	Barrow		
	Burrow		
	Brand		
	Burning		
	Brank (Breton)		
	Brinnan (Gothic)		
	Burning		

Chapter 3 Ba

But we are supposed to be following through the various meanings of the phoneme Ba over the millennia, and have become sidelined by Prince Phillip and Mr. Attenborough and their comical encounters with antiquity. A mouth (bab) is not necessarily one admitting food to the body. By only a slight extension of meaning it can be taken as a river mouth or a sea channel. An estuary is not really much like a mouth, but the gull was taken from the fact it let the water into the sea, just as the mouth lets it into the stomach. Similarly paps, a plurality of diminutive mouths, feed babies; and by metaphor has the meaning of sustenance of the same nature.

The Akkadians who captured Sumer in Iraq some five thousand years ago called their city Bab-i-lai-un, which appears in the Bible tidied to Babylon. The Bible writer of the day, whoever he was, thought it was to do with psychobabble and had a story of the zigurrat there offending Jahweh who fixed it that all the languages of the world should from then on be incomprehensible the one to the other. We have to correct him (the scribe, of course, not the one God that all Christians as well as Jews and Moslems worship) because Bab had by then acquired the meaning of river mouth, and Babylon was just above the river mouth where the gulf had invaded a wide estuary where the land is very flat and salt sea water renders cropping impossible so that the marsh Arabs who have lived there - probably ever since the latest of the great circumpolar ice melts at times between eighteen thousand and eight thousand years ago - are forced to live on elevated platforms by fishing. In Lithic la meant both evil tasting and so salt, and then as well, by way of several metaphors or gulls, flat like the salt sea – just as in the lawn for lawn tennis which has no salt, so Bab-i-la-un is mouth-of- the lawn or flat salt marshes-one; and a ladang is a jungle clearing in which the Senoi tribesmen in the Malayan jungle grow their ubi-kayu, which means something like 'very-fleshy-grown', or tapioca in the language of the Brazilian Guarani tribe on the other side of the world, which is (in Lithic, as well as Guarani) tapai-a-u-kau, become fat-first-what-grown, ie the fat root. It is a plant with a hard white tuberous root, not unlike a Jerusalem artichoke (Jerusalem here a mispronunciation of girasole, sunflower in Italian, sun rotater!), which raw is a hard chew but roasted is tender and delicious, and boiled just pap.

Jerusalem the biblical city is Heiru- or Yeiru- or Ur- or Uru- or some such, the oldest (3450 BP) is the Egyptian Uru-, followed by Salaim (or in Old Assyrian Salai-immu), meaning peace. The Lithic can handle Salaim, it is from Sa meaning something like action or acting followed by lai meaning lowered or level, the blessed state of no more struggle, as in the Arab greeting Salaam alai ikum, Peace upon you. The front end is more difficult. Heiru looks quite like the heiro- in hieroglyphics, which means sacred or holy or some such. But the H is probably a false lead. In Egyptian it was pronounced ahi (not many people know this), and as the h could be a cockney one separating the a- from the -i, it can just yield ai. Lithic favours 'It that which' for Yei or that which for Ai or 'That one' for U; and roughly 'Raised' for Ru, from Rau; so 'That which raised' can be 'Built', and conventional etymologists actually favour the noun 'City'. If so it would conventionally mean City of Peace; but it could be read also as Built for Safety, in other words 'The Refuge', which makes better sense today as the religions fight for possession of it. It doesn't make it any less religious in origin. Religion itself is a refuge from the world. In Ancient Egypt Taun was The World. Set, the evil god, often taken to be the original form for Satan, was actually pronounced Sai-Taun in Egyptian, and not Set at all. Sai-Taun is the actions of the world, the way of the world, which the Egyptians – with some sagacity it has to be said - took to be the source of all evil.

Chapter 3 Ba

The Egyptian god "Set" arises from the inability of professional Egyptologists to discover the vowelisations, instead treating the glyphs as alphabetic, whereas most had vowels attached and were syllabic, even multi-syllabic, (except when spelling out the names of foreigners, which foreign names were the clues for cracking the Rosetta Stone to recover the language, after Moslem Wahabi Jihadists had killed off the language, along with most of the original speakers, after the death of the Prophet and the infiltration of Islam by unreformed Wahabis. Wahabi means Terrorists, the judgment of neighbouring tribes in prehistoric times, against whom, his tribal elders, The Prophet fought both of his own jihads - worshipers of the prehistoric black goddess of the night, Kali, who preached deceit and hostility to unbelievers and promised - thousands of years before the birth of Mohammed - seven virgins in the hereafter for any of her followers killing fifteen unbelievers. Mecca is from Mai-ka, Of the Fall-the Place. What fell? A black meteorite, taken at the time to be Kali's calling card, saying "These are my people". It was stuck in the wall of the shrine the Kaaba (from Ka-a-ba, it means 'Place [where]-it-went'). It was originally the splash shape where they dug the meteor out, but now rebuilt a rectangular box - and only aeons later reconsecrated by The Prophet, (may His soul rest in peace), as sacred to Allah al Lahi, Allah the All Merciful; so that all Moslems must kiss it once in their lifetime if they can. Osama of the Laden tribe, a died-in-the-wool terrorist, rejoicing in the killing in fact – his brothers had treated him and his mother with spite and it burnt into his psyche - was showing his many brothers (he told them), although he was by birth only on his father's side a pukkah Wahabi, (and was mocked by them as the son of the slave girl, a wifelet his father picked up to add to his already substantial harim on a business trip to Lebanon) he was a more authentic Wahabi than any of them. He certainly was. But as a Moslem he was guilty of a secret heresy, worshiping in the way that Kali the enemy of Islam requires, which has afflicted Islam for centuries and must now be confronted as heresy by the faithful. Prompted by Kali, in Baghdad today Islamists, influenced by the al Kaeda heresy, are torturing, killing and putting out the eyes of rival sects in the name of Islam, which means Peace. You can only conclude Sapiens Sapiens is basically mad, for which there is ample supporting evidence. It just takes different forms. For genuine Islamists Jesus is Nabbi Issus, which means the Prophet Jesus, who was really called Joshua anyway. He spoke Aramaic and his word for God was Ellieh, more like Allah than God. It means The Lord, the Merciful One. Kali's followers, after killing their fifteen, put out the eyes of their victims as an oblation to their Goddess whose worship was involved with deceiving all unbelievers: "We deceived them, they did not see us coming!" It is her signature, not The Prophet's at all. It was pagan Kali worship he waged his jihads against, for goodness' sake! When he finally captured Mecca with a surprise night occupation, he forgave her worshipers, his own Wahabi tribal elders, who had been trying to kill him, if they converted to Islam. Some clearly deceived him. Islamist jihadis who have been putting out the eyes of their victims in Iraq today, can only be doing it for Kali, whether they realise it or not. None of it is in the Holy Koran: of course not. It is an outrage. The Prophet must be turning in his grave. How could Islamists have let the pagan Black Goddess in? The fact is centuries of false Hadiths by these conspirators have fed Kali worship back in. Only the Holy Koran can validate belief. If it is not in The Koran, it is no part of Islam. Well, you won't find Kali worship in there; there are no virgins on the other side. There just aren't any virgins on offer in the next world. How could there be? The souls of the righteous are welcomed there: souls not bodies. In Heaven sex is over. Osama fooled the simpletons in pursuit of a political agenda. That is not Islam, it is Kalian paganism. Allah Al Akhbar just let an evil Osama go. He let the followers of Nabi Issus take him out.

Like Babylon, London is at the estuary of the river. Lau-en-don is Estuary-of-the river in Lithic. Moreover Wimbledon where the lawn tennis is played is from Wimblendon, U-im-ba-lai-en-don: in Lithic Where-him-belly(flesh-loopy or goes loopy)-of-river, where the course of the river goes round in a loop. Most of this matches pretty well the Ancient Egyptian, and there is some evidence they were colonists before the Celts arrived and killed them all – and probably ate them, or their brains at least, since it was their practice. It may have been the Egyptian colonists who built Stone Henge, being good with big stones in Egypt too. I doubt the Celts of the day could have done it. It was most likely a legacy from their victims, and they just dug an earth tump nearby, and used the site for worship.

A metaphor is a development of a meaning applied to another case taken to have a similar semantic content. A classic case is a gull, and the term is used in this book as more user friendly than the Greek meta-phor, a development-of the form (of the meaning, not the word). The sea gull is actually a sea caller, related to a gale, which whines and whistles in the trees, and a miners' gala, originally a sing-song, and Latin gallare to sing, and the gallery where the singing was done, and the nightingale which sings in the night, and even tralala and go la. The seagull calls, in Basque it is Kriaou, which is echoic, a cry-one; but a gull wing is silent and takes its title from the shape of the gull's wing, an incidental character borrowed by human whimsy to designate an aeroplane wing of the same shape that artists draw distant seagulls in seaside views. You will get this repeated yet again in chapter 8, for the phoneme La where it really belongs, but the derivation of the gull wing bears repetition as a mnemonic case of a major metaphor such as we find repeatedly in the development of language.

The flesh, ba, has many gulls taken from its characteristics. It is bulgy and bendy. It burgeons, it has a binary symmetry, two arms and two legs, etc, etc, two side by side images of the sides of the body, which is a dual burgeon with its bottom or buttocks (bulges-dual-mass and bulges-dual-shapes), which provide the muscle power for ambulatory movement. But only one brain (although, if you look within, the brain too has two sides to it). The brain is the ba-rai 'n, the rayed flesh one – rayed in from outside, because all thinking was at first supposed to be impregnated from outside the body by rays like sun rays, which similarly raised the plants, and roused the genitalia. Nowadays this idea is only to be found in lunatic asylums. But you can see how it found favour to start with. We still do not understand how it is we think, and ideas appear apparently unannounced as if born from nowhere, and sometimes prompt for actions we are reluctant to undertake, especially if it involves danger. A hero was hai-rau, in receipt of stimulating (rejoicing) rays so he ignored perils which would otherwise have caused him to quail (or chicken). Language and science were as yet undifferentiated.

A baboon has ultimate (prehensile) lips, but in Hindi a babu is a clerk or wordsmith, master of mouthing from an ultimate mouth. Nowadays he is apt to type letters in an office, but originally he gathered your scattered thoughts for you and after interrogating you presented your case in a well organised and convincing manner. He wrote your letters for you if you could not write. He can probably claim to have been the first solicitor. A ban in English is a verbal pronouncement and so a verbal prohibition, as well as an announcement of a forthcoming marriage; to give the public in turn the chance of banning it perhaps. A bung is a bungey bit, and so also a gentle push in the right direction with a bribe. The Gaelic bwoid, penis, is from Lithic bouai-dai, a bunged-become orifice, the

Chapter 3 Ba

boys' pride and joy, the penis, realistically defined, ruling out childbirth. English boys, it may be assumed, are all suffering the same constriction, although they are probably unaware of the definition. Kith of all sorts may have a ba, because they are all of the same parentage and flesh. Auda Abu Tai who fought with T E Lawrence in the desert was Auda the Father of his Tribe. He was first (a-) the one or single origin of all the fleshing out (-bu, from ba-u). Lithic just makes the point these words are composed of meaningful elements. Of course it could be just coincidence with no particular reason for the sounds. In a few cases, certainly. But the same meaning structure, woven together by metaphors worked out in advance for all the letters, applying to a wide spread of words in many languages? Surely not. The correspondences with the dictionaries are sometimes a bit rough. So were the minds which first derived the simple semantic structures from so few elements, and over the aeons imprinted them onto language so our subconscious minds can still pick them up when we send down our surface language as we learn it. It is not inherited. It is genuine rediscovery every time without any help at all from the genes, as thought necessary at MIT. Professor Chomsky is far cleverer than he thinks; and so are we.

Oh, and by the way the world lexicon is really just a single giant crossword puzzle, a single cobweb spun from humankind's mental spinnerets; and we can access its earliest threads best by running the threads through the very same spinnerets once more. These chapters on the phonemes, as they were originally discovered by our hominid forebears, aim to do exactly that.

NOTES

1. WMD are the Weapons of Mass Destruction which proved so elusive in Iraq. Saddam had disposed of them, probably because of the cost, but pretended he still had them by subtle deception plans in order to bolster his prestige and influence in the area, a strategy so successful it soon brought about as an unintended consequence he did not foresee his downfall, the destruction of Iraq and his own death by hanging. None of this has anything to do with Lithic, which indeed provides some solace in a world increasingly dominated by the prehistoric black goddess of the night, Kali. Kali means black in Hindustani and cheating in Lithic. In the night, undercover operating is the order of the day. A book could be written on Kali today, and her many followers - infiltrated heretics within an Islam all unawares. But it is not this one.

2. The book is "On the Origins of Speaking" published POD (Printing on Demand) by Trafford Publishing Ltd of Canada and Oxford, England, in May 2006, available on the internet at www.Trafford.com/05-2593, or else go to www.ontheoriginsofspeaking.com for a six page introduction and then click at the bottom on Trafford to get the Trafford internet page in turn, which gives you the gist of the book in a few pages. Both these internet pages can be downloaded and printed for free. Trafford hold the book on CD and print a copy and despatch within 5 days when ordered.

CHAPTER 4

KA AND GA. THE BIRTH OF WAYLAND SMITH

The phoneme Ka, with its meaning deriving from the fancied echoism of chipping stone on stone, was the start of the gradual discovery of Lithic language roots, the break-in to the idea of a trace reaching back to when we first learned to speak, with the original Lithic bedrock meanings we gave to the sounds as we learned to utter them. Nothing quite like this has been attempted before. For a million years and more, nowadays archaeologists are pushing it back to perhaps even four million years – in human terms that is a very long time indeed, perhaps the longest time we are capable of marking within the human or hominid span – we were breaking stones and making tools, later mostly the so called hand axes, actually meat choppers and tenderisers before the taming of fire, when everything we ate was raw and needed a good hammering to crush the tissue and make it easier to chew. Housewives still hammer steaks to tenderise them before cooking. That is why we say cook as well as make. Kaka, consecutive chops, were what you did before you ate your meat to make it tender. With the taming of fire it turned out the flame did it for you, as well as making it taste nicer for you too. (There was also the sterilisation by the flame, but you did not know about that). So it was kaka or tenderising, or better kuku, because the kaka was all done for you a myriad times and the u vowel was the compleative and conclusive one. The Latin to cook was coquere, with the -ere bit just the verbal suffix, a late grammatical concoction. The Greek verb was pessein, the -ssein meaning to fire, and the pai- were just pieces, to fire the pieces. The Sanscrit, which came in the historical sequence before the Greek, was pacami, I cook, where the –mi suffix was the first person singular marker (like me). They were still saying chopping pieces just as they had been before the hearth was invented hundreds of thousands of years before. To knap is to ka-na-pai, strike-present-flakes; while a canapé is a make-present-piece (toast with a savoury mounted on top).

    The late Eric Partridge, "The Word King", in his 1958 Etymological Dictionary "Origins", has the Italic root for cooking *kokw- or *kekw- and the root for the whole Indo European family *pekw- or *pokw-. So it was "chop-chop" in Italy and "chopping the pieces" across the continents. It meant tenderising and that is how it also meant cooking. Kaka could have been used too when Tarzan wanted Mum to put the meat he had brought home on the spit to cook. The slang "chop-chop" and "chop up" for "supper is served" is surely coming from the subconscious, reminding us of the simple kaka with hand axes which preceded eating, to tenderise the meat, before we got around to cooking it.

    Then again, by repetitively striking flakes off the core you made your artefact. So kaka could be used when you wanted Tarzan to make something for you too. The ma- in our making is the left-over from the mush or mass, anyway the solid you were pounding, such as the clay for a ceramic pot, or even just a cake. The Latin facere for to make gets the making from the fac-, too close to the four letter English word for coincidence, making babies originally, and by rather rough analogy thence anything else. You need to be a speaker of Ancient Egyptian to crack the fa- bit. The Greek phi (Φ), pronounced fai, came from the Egyptian pa-ahai, (their p-h), pronounced as spelt here. It meant the joy piece or the pleasuring piece, otherwise known as the mai in Egyptian: the earther, planter or impregnator. The glyph is an ejaculating penis, and it is hard to make it mean anything else. Our marriage comes from that, it celebrates the planting of the seed. We call the Egyptian pahei a pai-nai-s, or penis, the piece which presents or witnesses, copying the Latin idiom. Before trousers, its angle of attack gave the onlooker a fair indication of what was on young Tarzan's mind. It should not be thought the Romans knew their fac- had to do with our four letter word. Its earlier meaning had been long forgotten, although the knowledge still hung around in the subconscious mind of course. But it was the making with the pahai, the making of babies, which had caught the fancy of earlier Italians, just as it still does today. We turned our earlier perception into a naughty word, the Italians into daily use. It should not shame them. It is simply the Mediterranean climate is warmer. It was probably the warmth of the hearth once fire was tamed which originally developed human sexuality to the point where libido is perennial. Today the better class of prostitutes will offer their clients a hot bath. It makes them livelier lads as well as smelling sweeter (hearsay only).

When knapping flints we shall see how the other elements (na and pa) came to stand in for these meanings in due course. Briefly, Na had the original rather naughty meaning pushed forward and presented. You will find out what it was originally and why in chapter 11 for Pa if you can not guess meanwhile. In this case it was the well directed blow which struck off the flake, thus presenting it. Pai was taken to be the thinned diminutive (the slightly sharpened and unvoiced) Bai; which was then taken to mean the thinned version of what Ba meant; and Ba meant flesh because it was the sound of the two fleshy bits, the lips, uttering a buff or puff, as has already been explained in chapter 3. So Pa was taken to be the skin or surface of the flesh, or else just a thin diminutive piece of flesh; or – and here is the Lithic idiom for you – both at once if they fitted. The flakes the flint knappers struck off were thin pieces with flat surfaces. It fitted. The flake, a Lithic doublet with a plaque, is from the Lithic elements fa/pa-la-kai, piece-flat-struck off/made; which after all is precisely what a flint flake is. A flint meanwhile is, of course, from the Lithic fa-lai'n-tai, piece-flat'one-becoming, that is to say identified as suitable for flaking. In the next chapter we shall see precisely how the bare final t of the flint derives originally from tai, and why it means becoming, so the flint nodules found lying about, and later mined in sandy soils, as at Grimes' Graves in Norfolk over five thousand years ago, were identified as suitable for fine sharp flakes, as above.

Furthermore flaking flints leaves a lot of chippings, which modern flint workers call debetage, the waste from any stone tool manufacturing process. So kaka, repetitive strikes, was also the waste chips from all that chipping; so that in due course it came to mean waste - of any kind, including human waste, and so excrement. That is how flaking and making and cake and cooking and excrement turn out all to have the very same pedigree. One grave and reverend lexicologist (dictionary maker), whose blushes we will spare, thought the caca meaning excrement must have had a separate etymology altogether - and suggested it must have been echoic of our forebears straining as they passed the coarse fare they were accustomed to. Even the word king, Eric Partridge, under cack which he derives from "the Mediterranean root *ka", (the asterisk means it is a made up root just guessed, and not in any actual record as such) after referring to the Egyptian kai-ti (actually little, ti, strikings, kai) and so the chips again, whence excrement again, just as with kaka from the chippings. But then he adds "clearly echoic". But we will stick with the knapping debetage, which does not require nearly so costive a condition. With all the wild berries that they ate, as well as the meat past its best, that will have been the least of their worries.

Chapter 4 Ka

An axe is from the Lithic elements a-ka-sai, that-strike-action: these days the one you swing for chopping wood. For the derivation of the sibilant sai as meaning acting or action you must wait for chapter 13. Meanwhile in brief: the semantic catena went from fire – and flame – to flickering and hot; to nice and warm, and the hearth; and so then to alive (most animal life is warm); and the live forms in turn; animals to active and acting and action. And of course there is more in chapter 13. The important thing to notice is it was echoism which was everywhere in at the birth of language and consciousness. It could be said mimicry and analogy virtually on their own kick started civilisation. Ga, the softened voiced version of Ka, was apt to be treated as at one remove from the naked physical action, the first abstraction, perhaps indicating the equivalent intention merely. In cut and kill and kharma we can still count the echo of the crude conception of striking, making and acting on the world, all from the clack of flint on flint. In coming and going we can see, if we are alert, the same agency. In acid and acropolis, in pickle and cranium, horn (from cornu) and geography we can distinguish, if we are careful, the growing gamut of descendant meanings. Ka, in Egyptian, in Japanese and in Hindustani carries the same message, albeit in different idioms but always within the same range: to strike, to flake off, striking, force, impulsion, drive, action, structure, skeleton, form, hard, durable, sharp, rock, core, ground, land, place, a miscellany of divergent applications of the same original semantic content pregnant with many meanings as the human mind sophisticated itself up by its own bootstraps, as the linguistic idiom proliferated to describe more and better. This is not just high flown metaphor. It is literally what happened, spread over just a few hundred thousand years of thinking. But it is necessary to guard against anachronism. The original psychosemantic content was simple and general and therefore diffuse. Our modern meaning systems are clear cut and differential by comparison, precisely and solely because they are modern and benefit from aeons of slowly clearing the attic, replacing relative chaos with neater tidier (and wordier) word patterns.

The juxtaposition of two Lithic elements so that one modified or at least marked the other, supplying more than one pointer to the intended meaning by (grammarless) apposition, was the means by which early communication could expand and increase its utility. It was before grammar, and even longer before grammarians. Two elements in apposition amount to a word beyond a peradventure, even if of a form barely sufficient for us to recognise it on its own as such today. Single grunts were and are just grunts. But grouped differential and sequential grunts must already be words – or else just a tune. The art of wordification is already suggested; language as we choose to define it has already begun. As yet grammar is unrecognised, so the first and second elements in any sequence must have ranked pari passu so far as their meaning function was concerned. The second adjectival element was just as much a noun as the first, and the first as much an adjective as the second. Effectively the mind was quite simply and solely adjectival. The substantive was a much later arabesque, from an adjectival cluster, which will have suggested formal clustering, and so a substantial entity. That is how we got there.

Original semantic contents appear to have been so general as to be diffuse. This is not quite the same as to say so general as to be useless, but it is getting near it. The adjectival mind, when it picked up an idea, was ready to find it duplicated anywhere or even everywhere. Readers of Bertrand Russell in his lighter moments will recall his tale of the professor of philosophy who had a tooth pulled out under laughing gas and discovered the Secret of the Universe (Hawking's "Theory of Everything") as he was coming round. Methodical fellow, he scribbled it down as he emerged into consciousness. Later, under the cold eye of reason, he examined his script. It read "A smell of ether – everywhere

Chapter 4 Ka

pervades". Generations of other philosophers, alas, have formulated whole systems of their universally pervasive abstractions every bit as fatuous in the cold light of reason as the smell of ether, without the aid of laughing gas and for all one knows with all their teeth at their disposal. It is fair to ask if Professor Hawking has got a whiff of laughing gas between ratiocinating.

Ka, it may seem at first, is almost as pervasive as the smell of ether appeared to Russell's (invented) philosopher. We can look here at case histories most easily in English, the commonest Indo-European tongue, as well as the largest anywhere ever, chiefly because it is the most easily accessible – particularly to those with English as their mother tongue. The term Lithic element is used to refer to both the phoneme (roughly the letter) and its semantic contents; and if it is necessary to identify which, the expansions Lithic phonetic element and Lithic semantic content are available and easily understood. A psychosemantic content is one presented to the human mind initially out of the blue, the prompt for the meaning coming subconsciously from the psyche. It wll have simply appeared as common sense in the Stone Age. Our common sense is not reasoned, it is taken as a matter of course, and what makes us take that course rather than another thing is the preconditioned subconscious mind. We just need to bear in mind what the psyche tells us may not always be entirely welcome to what we are consciously wanting to think. We all have these two minds and potentially split personalities if we do not allow any adjustment or give and take between the two.

The phonetic element is traditionally described by etymologists as a phoneme, that is a single sound as uttered by the human mouth parts, and is contrasted with a morpheme which is defined as a combination of one or more phonemes sufficient to have a semantic content – which comically enough the traditional wisdom does not allow the phoneme; except apparently on those rare occasions when it combines with itself to gain promotion to the morphemic class. I is an example. Q and owe are others. See comes near it. Or car, or tar or far or tea? Ha counts as a phoneme, but it does not mean much. About now you should see the exercise is absurd. Or you can take diphthongs as having free tickets for picking up meanings, being two vowels combined. These upstarts are vowels. A consonant needs a vowel with it to be pronounceable and so you might think qualifies under the general rubric as a morpheme, but consonants are regarded as being single phonemes without meaning although they mostly have a vowel attached so they can be uttered, but do not thus escape the meaningless phoneme category . In practice the single sound turns out to be taken as a single syllable. The Lithic hypotheses take leave of the conventional rails at this point, never to rejoin them again, by positing original meanings for every single syllable, a consonant with a vowel attached to utter it. Two would make it a morpheme, with meaning conventionally attached. The meanings actually resided in the consonants - as well as the vowels of course, when separately treated. Why not? They have all just been forgotten in a few hundred thousand years, as after all they well might be. Not lost, but gone before.

What is most pernicious in this plan to only allow meanings to molecular morphemes of assembled atomic phonemes, and the canonisation of phonemic structure as morphemic, is that in practice it prejudges where meanings begin; and it is a slippery slope to the promotion of structure over meaning. We are already in danger of finishing up like Chomsky with a rival scheme of meanings as part of grammatical structure, which hardly concerns itself with meanings other than the grammatical parts of speech; and these are mathematicised as examples of Boolean symbolic logic. In reality this is only a single Inkster's patch in a meaning field which is virtually infinite, the most of which

Chapter 4 Ka

grammarians leave out of account. The grammatical logic provides the slots and the slots are usually filled with semantic cyphers only, just holding the slots open. As a result, language, which has started out and made its way for hundreds of thousands of years as a genuinely human whimsy, is turned into an analytical academic exercise, with the study of little known languages conducted on a grammatical grid which they never really fit. So use of the term Lithic element rides across the distinction between phonemes and morphemes rather as if it had never been. It is meant to. By putting meanings earlier in the developmental chain and by giving them a larger place we dismiss the meaningless phoneme, replacing it with one already meaningful. It is not disputed that assiduous critics may be able to generate a meaningless cry, a phoneme, and go on to distinguish it from a morpheme with meaning; but they should be left to the exercise on their own. Some of their meaningless cries they may even be mistaken in treating as meaningless in that vague meanings may be attached to them, as we shall see. No phoneme, or morpheme for that matter, has any objective semantic content of its own. That can only be acquired in the mind of man, when appointed there by human whimsy of one kind or another. That is what meaning is about. Semantic contents are functions of the living species and do not in reality of themselves inhabit either phonemes or morphemes – or any other noise for that matter. A tiger's growl contains no menace. The tiger imagines it there, and the hearer, if he is to survive, learns to imagine the same. But it is just a learned response. It is not in the genes, certainly not in ours anyway, but probably in our subconscious recollection of growls, before we have learned language, along with its subconscious keel (which includes growls). It is not in the sound. It is only in the mind.

In the major work from which this book has been culled the psychosemantic tree for Ka extended to fifty two derived meanings for the phoneme. It is included again here, and is an example of the scope and power of Lithic analysis, on page 75. Since the first and original psychosemantic meaning was echoic of the strike of stone on stone it is no surprise to find the first idea it gave rise to is the knapping of flints, and the second the idea of knocking two things together. The mental process was this: "think of what we have in mind when we say Ka (knapping flints). From there, there is the more general idea of the same action but not necessarily involving knapping stones: the essential meaning of the knapping, but by metaphor applied to similar action in a different context. The same phoneme can be taken as meaning the more general (abstracted) case of just "knocking together". Remember we are trying to reconstruct how the untutored mind first found its vocabulary. There was no word for knock but the idea was there, abstracted from the knapping. Nor could you make the presentation in inverted commas above because you had no language for the job. You just had to try it out in use and hope young Tarzan would cotton on. It will not have been an instant success, certainly not in all cases. But we know it worked in time because we have the vocabulary to prove it. This tree along with the others has apparently taken us a few hundred thousand years of hop scotch from one idea to the next, with the making up of vocabulary as we went along. Metaphor is a powerful intellectual tool, and it can be quite abstruse. Emblematic is the gull: a seagull is a sea gala or caller, cousin to the gale of wind which moans in the trees, and the miners' gala, originally a sing-song before the politics got in. But a gull wing is not a singer, it does not go la, it just follows the characteristic shape of the gull's wing, now often seen in seaside paintings providing a bit of diversity in the sky. It is a metaphor. It takes a particular aspect of the first phenomenon named, the bird, and not the one originally picked to name it at that, and carries it across to another wing. It is tempting to remind ourselves at this stage that one look is worth a thousand words. One picture in the mind of the wings of a

Chapter 4 Ka

gull in flight defines the shape precisely. So we use it to describe the aircraft wing. The "gulling" of ideas from one to another like this is how we have built our language out of very little. To remind ourselves of this, it makes sense to call a metaphor a gull. To remind ourselves of a metaphor we need a dictionary of Greek. It is shorter and simpler too, and we can easily remind ourselves of what it means whenever we see it used. Particularly we must remember that a gull, as we use it, picks on a single aspect of all the bird displays (viz the shape of its wing) and fastens that one bit as a label on the target picked (a wing shaped the same). It does not matter one bit the wing we describe has neither the webbed feet nor the rather bad manners of the bird. We are that clever we just help ourselves to the bit we want and everyone follows suit. Had we been obliged to take the rest of the bird on board at the same time we would soon have been in such a mess communication would have been lost – perhaps for ever! Certainly young Tarzan would probably have gone back to just picking his nose.

For flaking flints hard hitting is involved. That provides the ideas of hard, and so harden, as well as the force employed. The force involved leads us into the idea of strength, the source of force. The blows are sharp and harsh, and so are the flakes struck off. It is rough business. It is an active business too. It is all get up and go. Flints won't flake themselves – well, not the way you want them anyway. You impose your will upon them. There is a long apprenticeship as you master the way the flints respond. Remember we have been thinking about flints, in so far as we could think, for a million years; and now we are beginning to think about talking. Ka will come to express will, drive, the indomitable soul. Indeed it becomes the soul as will and actor, Kaiser, Duke, Il Duce and Al Kaida, (Duke and Duce just Kaida the other way round) eventually, and the Ka-that-raised becomes in the Japanese Ka-ra-te, the hardness we like to think is in all of us, as well as in the oak (a-u-kai, that-very-hard). Indeed we associate Ka with the bones and skeleton, and even with the world's bones, the rocks which give it form. A rock is a bit of the world's Ka which has been raised up, sticking out of the ground. The Lithic elements are rau-ka, roused and raised core. If you dig down anywhere you will sooner or later come to the mother lode. That makes the world a tortured place with its bones sticking up in places in the open air. When mankind was young the earth may well have been a tortured place, with volcanic action as it settled after a convulsion, most likely the shifting of weight with the melting of the circumpolar ice mountains in the relatively recent past[1]. Kara, on the other hand, was taken as the Ka's (skeleton's) Ra (sun) in Greek, that is to say our skull; and then of course the horns, in Latin cornu, from kara-nau, were the skull's nau, protrusions-dual, (na-u). In passing that made the cow, ka-u, holy, suggesting she had the dual ka (prompting two protruding horns, skeletal [Ka] protrusions) with the second provided for the next life: a nice case of religious science from linguistic analysis. Cows are still treated as holy in India, although they call them bhail with their flesh or body (bhai) liquid (lai). But it is the horns that have done it. The body lye is just drunk.

Already we have stretched the gulls we have used beyond any ordinary span, and we must recognise some of the jumps we have made are fanciful in the extreme (the historic we, not the personal one). That is because they were made in the subconscious mind where fancy reigns without the encumbrance of much in the way of reason. Sequiturs still obtain, but not the pulling back from what is not immediately confirmed by the senses when we engage in conscious thinking. It is a dream world without the restraints of consciousness. The psychosemantic tree is one attempt to present the way ideas spilled out of the mind and were given utterance. Or, to put it the other way around, it is an attempt to show how the ideas we have, to which we have given tongue, can be traced and related by

Chapter 4 Ka

means of their constituents, the phonemes of which all words are strings, to our original thinking.

Ka, as the strike of stone on flint, will sometimes produce a spark. It could have lit dry stalks or seed fluff if lying around. That will have suggested the idea of kindling to add to the straight fashioning of the flint. The Egyptian rays we will meet in chapter 12 for Ra could be kindled or themselves kindle (in imagination) – just like the sun's rays with a magnifying glass actually can today. Ray kindling was creating (in Lithic elements ka-rai-a-tai), ray-kindled-that-becomes, and it had a sexual connotation, amongst other rays, including those the brain experienced, Lithic ba-rai'n, the flesh-rayed'one, the thinking organ; and the ones the eye threw out and caught back in, with a picture of the scene the rays had encountered, brought back and painted on the irradiated iris. Sexual kindling was begetting. It was supposed the male contribution was merely to trigger a fleshing out process inherent in the female. Well, actualy it is precisely that; although few males even today care to be made aware they merely supply the pollen, which does the trick. A straw poll on the matter would be revealing: m for seed and n for pollen. The pollinators might spoil their papers, rather than put in an n?

So we have economics from ekoi-nomoi in Greek which means household management (household nominal laws for pernickety translators). Nomoi, Greek nominal law (legislated as opposed to natural law) is from the Lithic nau-maui, presentation of thinking/decisions. The ekoi for household is really just home, but its true Lithic analysis is as ai-kau-i, and that is 'as which-begotten-they', better "that where our forefathers were born", viz home. Egypt, similarly, is from Ho-iku-Ptah which is taken to mean Iha-u-i-kau-Ptah, It that-where-which-begotten-Ptah, and is further glossed 'Where born Ptah' or 'Home of Ptah', or 'Land of Ptah'. This is not quite right. Ptah was an ancient Egyptian god. The puzzle is his hieroglyphs had no neter before them like all the other gods of Egypt (of which there were hundreds), although he was one of the oldest. Academic Egyptologists stay puzzled. The neter is a sideways triangle at the top of a stick, which the professional Egyptologists allege is a pointed axe of divinity. However we are going to have to tell them it isn't. It is a pennant blown out in the breeze. Who wants a pointed axe anyway? So far as is known only primitive Celts who used them to peck open their enemies' heads in battle, killing them and simultaneously bringing them to table, since they were head hunters addicted to sucking out brains. The celtoi were the axe people, in Lithic kai-lai-taui, striking-looping-ones, axe folk. Properly pronounced, neter is nai-tura, which we have come to know as Latin natura and our nature. We have not however any idea why it means nature, but the Egyptians had, because they made up the word. Na means to protrude, present or show. What in the first instance was protruded, presented and shown in the old Stone Age must remain a secret (for those who can not guess) until chapter 10. Nai-tura in Ancient Egyptian is properly translated 'Showing the draw or pull' (just as in our chest of drawers, which we pull out and push back, and the apparel, the drawers, we pull up. A tray is a drawer kept on a table). Nai-tura was an emblem (a pennant blown out in the wind, exemplar of a natural force) for all the natural forces the Egyptians had identified; but the primitive Greeks of the day supposed they were the same as their mischievous godlings they kept upstairs. That is why Ptah has no neter. He is properly pronounced Pata ahi, or Paita-ahi, Father our, with a blocked (pai) eurethra (ta), the male sex; or Our Fathers: he was an ancestor god, and not a force of nature at all, but instead to be prayed to as an ally against those unkind forces of nature who were wearing their badges of natural forces (Natura) whenever written. Naturally he never wore the badge of his enemies! The Egyptology profs know nothing of this, and may even cling to

Chapter 4 Ka

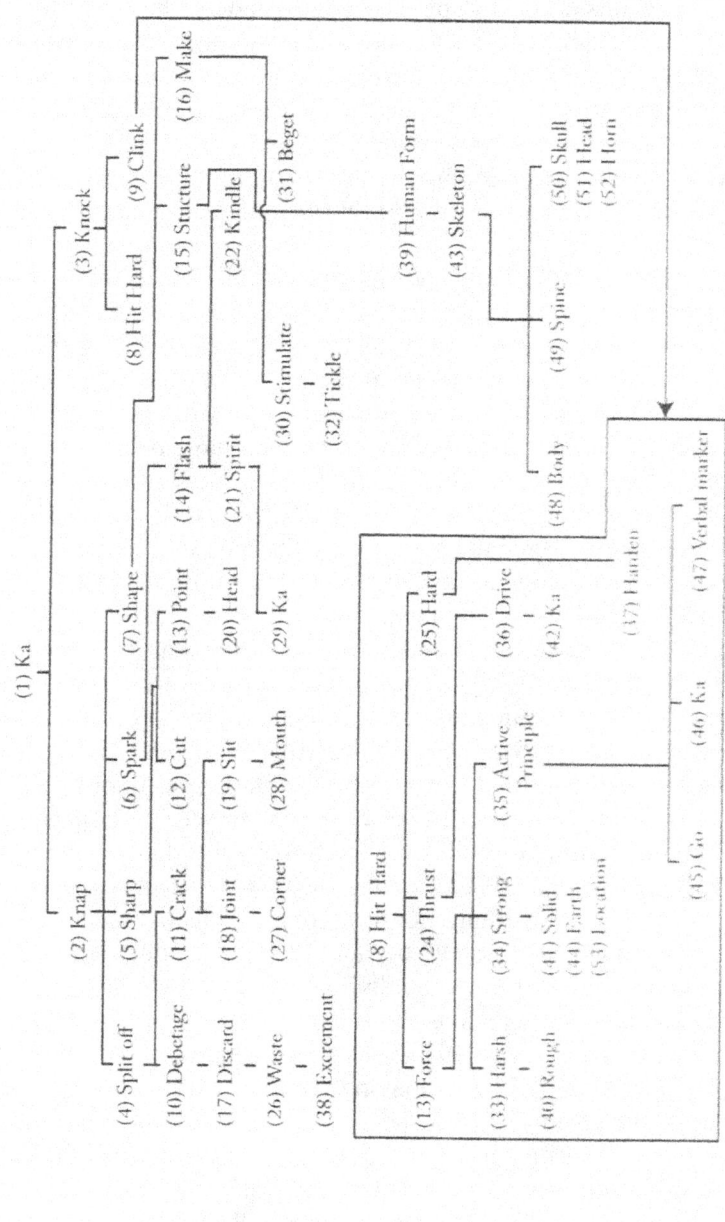

their pointed axes and seek to make out I am mistaken; but if so they will lose.

So what does this do for Egypt, now not the land of Ptah but the land of their ancestors, The Fatherland. It came quite late. For aeons the gods had all been goddesses, often very fat ones, mothers showing their fertility. The sun itself for the Egyptians started out female, the Aton, or better Aa-Ta-un, the Everlasting-Birth-Canal or Everlasting-Vulva in the sky, birthing light into the world each day – a busy lady! After how many aeons we shall never know, the boys, led by the priests of Amun-Ra, declared the sun not after all a Vulva at all (which was a girly thing), but the all-seeing and Ever-Loving (A-mau'n) Eye (Ra) of God the Father.

There was one backsliding when the sexually eccentric and physically deformed Pharaoh Akhenaton, who called himself Akhai-en-A-ton (That-born-of-the Everlasting-Vulva – a very grave heresy indeed for the priests who were selling the sun as the Eye of God) and tried to reinstate the image of the Mumsy in the Sky. Sure enough the priests of Amun-Ra eventually got him, and then erased him from the record, along with the city he had built away from them. Akhenaton may even have been the original Oedipus and had his eyes put out by the priests for not recognising the Eye in the sky and insisting it was a vagina – the punishment fitting the crime: "You won't have The Eye. OK. Well try living without them". Emanuel Velikovsky thought so. You can see the issue was bound to be a prime bone of contention. Certainly Akhenaton had fat malformed hips and thighs, and Oedi-pus means Fat-legs in Greek.

The Pharaohs were an incestuous lot. You had to start by sleeping with your mother to legitimate your inheritance. They were Akkadians (early Semites), farming the Africans. Since then it has been assumed by every monarch for the last four thousand years all gods in the West have been boys. The Hindus still have goddesses in their pantheon but they have to be properly married off to gods. Their matrimony presents problems, since marriage in Heaven is taken in India to be a marriage of similarities, so that for instance Shiva, the god of destruction, finds himself married to Durga and her avatar of prehistoric Wahabi origin, the black goddess of the night, Kali (it just means black), the goddess of darkness, deception and killing. Oppositional dualism, which lies behind the dialectic, probably came originally merely because the boys stick out where the girls stick in, making the sexes opposites where really they are complementary: the primitive mind looks deadpan at what it sees. "I am the slayer and the slain" has some of the same dualistic (one plus, one minus) vision. Ka + are is Make + verbal marker in Lithic phonemes, meaning making or maker, as in both Krishna and creation. With Krishna it can be seen that he is supposed to be the creator of ish, –ishna, which is life presenting; not the universe like the equally old Aztec creator god on the other side of the world, Wakan Tanka, who is Fear Making World Maker, or "The Awesome Creator". Krishna had quite a bit of the fertility goddess still with him. Wakan Tanka didn't. The Aztecs were away on a male killig spree, their mothers quite forgotten. We shall meet more of this same atavistic dualism later in an analysis of the dialectic, an ancient Stone Age mental stitch, fundamentally flawed (as will be explained in chapter 15) but nevertheless recognised in Ancient Egypt and resurrected by Hegel and borrowed disastrously by Karl Marx, as well as far too many of Western political cognoscenti even today for comfort. The dialectic is finally demolished in chapter 15 on thinkng, not done before: shown to result from the confusion of a boundary line and a continuum, also a line. Cabinets and high tables still feature addicts, nevertheless. We are a very foolish race, falling for anything smartly presented.

There are fifty two derived meanings for Ka in the psychosemantic tree. The derivations are not all obvious, and their demonstration occupied thirty three large pages in

Chapter 4 Ka

the original work. The present ones are tiddlers by comparison. They are left for private consideration here in order to save on pages. Perhaps the odd clue is called for. Flaking flints, they split off. If you put the flake against the core from which it had been struck it fitted cleanly. If you broke a stick, especially if it was green, it didn't. The flake marked the joint between the flake and core as well as the split (the primitive mind imagined the flake and its split lurking there within the stone before the well aimed strike revealed it). Think of the slayer and the slain again. Absurdly therefore the ka, which split the flake from the core, also marked where it joined. So Ka came to mean join as well as split. It went quite well with make too, of course. Be on your guard for this kind of flip with the same phoneme with completely opposite meanings. You just had to go by context to decide whether it was joining or splitting your interlocutor had in mind. You knew of course he was thinking of the flint job. As an intellectual habit it has nothing to commend it, but we have been at it for hundreds of millennia. In truth we are not all that sapient. You must remember that, and not get ideas above Sapiens' station when working on language roots.

You can practice linking words by their meanings, just like Lithic, even with everyday reading in any language. Take the Spanish ant for instance, known in Spain as a hormiga, a horma-maker. Horma is a form or mould, originally a wooden cobbler's last, the Lithic probably i(h)a-u-rai-ma, it that-orifice-roused-mass, a wood shaped to fit tightly in [the shoe] and hold it open while the cobbler finished the stitching - it seems inescapable the original naming committee was thinking in terms of a dildo, because of the ha phoneme beginning and the mai-ka ending. We are at a time hundreds of millennia in the past, and we can not be too surprised to find our ancient forebears a trifle on the vulgar side in their thinking, or even more so. It butters no parsnips to blame the messenger. Word origins were transient, original meanings no longer followed through with the passage of time. Ought we to hide our forebears' original thinking to save our own blushes? Surely not. We should expose them for what they were. That is where we all come from, like it or lump it. There is also in Spanish horno, a kiln or oven, which is hollow of course, and not holding anything open, but is itself held open to keep the flame off the viand. The common ground is the blocking of access.

The Lithic i(h)a-u-rai-ma can equally be read as it(h)that-one/what-orders-the mass, which fitted it for a mould just as well as a last (or indeed a dildo). Hormigon is concrete in Spanish, which you might think has little to do with ants. But concrete if put into a mould takes up its form. Hormigon is the moulded one. The same trick was followed with mud bricks which were made sun dried hard (berai-kai or bricks), just as you created ceramic pots from ray kindled earth, Lithic kai-rai-ma-i-kai (ceramic); and then there is a berry plumped up by the sun, ba-i-rai. English concrete is con-, that is joined together and -crete which is from the completive case of the Latin creare to produce, create, make to grow. Our concrete is described as growing or sticking together. Whereupon whatever is crete becomes (by metaphor) also solid and firm.

Indeed in Greek kara is the skull, which is solid and firm, hard bone; and in Latin credere is to believe, which is from the Lithic karai-dai + the verbal marker (-ere): firm-becoming + verbal marker. Belief is when your ideas become firm. Similarly Greek cephale (pronounced khepharley) is the head. Here ka, from the hard structure of the body, the boney skeleton, has become the main structure of the body and so then just the body. The head is defined as kai- (of the body) the phallus (-phale). That shows the phallus is properly the engorged glans or head, and not the whole erect membrum virile. Prudes will think these metaphors uncalled for. But the Latins were at it too. Their caput for head is

77

Chapter 4 Ka

from the Lithic ka-puti, body-penis-teat, the glans again. You can even compare prepuce from peri-puti, around-the penis teat. Magritte would probably say I told you so, but he is dead.

Numbers came later. Latin quinque for five is from the Lithic kau-en-kaui. Kau- is the plurality (u) of the hard structure (ka), all the hard, namely all the bones, the skeleton, and of that (en) the individual boney protrusions (kaui): which of course number five – two arms, two legs and one head. Eric Partridge takes two pages on this. The Greek pente, the natural points, the pieces born/become [of the body] make five too. The Sanskrit is panca, from pa-en-ka, the points of the body. It is panch in Hindi today (from pa-en-khai): whence the Punjab, from Panch awab, the five rivers. Note awab is from awa (water) bai (bumming or moving). A river is water on the move. You can compare the sharp valleys cut in the volcanic tuff in Tenerife. They are known as barancos in Guanche (which is actually just provincial Carthaginian), and subject to flash floods when it rains hard, from the Lithic ba-awa-en-kau, travellng-water-of-carved. So we have awa-bai in Old Indo European for river and ba-awa in Old Carthaginian. They do seem to be using the same semantic elements, don't they? Australian billabong for a bunged up river ox bow lake has bila for river (and fresh water). Here bai-la takes the place of ba-awa, travelling liquid in place of travelling water, leaving the modern Ozzie waiting for his billy (fresh water) to boil, and not his mug as many think.

Pushed for a sixth point these old fogeys were forced back onto the membrum virile, which is why six and sex have the same form. If you did not know that five was based on the points of the body you would not be able to crack the code for six. Sex is from Lithic sai-ka-sai, which carries the semantic contents acting-make-life, or pleasurable-make-life. Sai, from fire, could be warm and pleasurable, or active, because animals are both warm and active, unlike mere plants rooted to the ground. This is spelt out in more detail in chapter 13 for the sibilant, Ish. The male contribution was taken as a triggering one, a bit like a magic wand or verge. Even today few men realise they only carry the pollen. Many still wishfully think they have the seed, as they fancy in the Bible.

The Carthaginian occupation of the Canary Islands off the African coast - (Canary is from Carthaginian Kan-aria, Rocky lands, and not from Latin for dog at all, as Pliny the Elder pretended, which as a third declension Latin noun, canis, (like K9) would have yielded Canery Isles and not Canary) - heavily influenced whatever it was that passed for language there amongst the Guanche indigenous folk beforehand. Guanche, from Ga-u-en-kai, land-where-in-begotten, simply means native born, natives (in Carthaginian). The genuine aboriginal substrate of the language of the original Guanche people, now lost as a result of the Spanish conquistadors´ religious persecutions, will have been related to any one of the hundreds of Hamitic tongues spoken in the great African bight (Bai-kai-tai, Bulgy-land-become, three phonemes with matching vowelisations, the bit that sticks out).

In Tenerife the small hilly island of Gomera eighteen kilometers off Tenerife's Western coast, over which the prevailing trade winds sweeping up the African coast often produce a tuft of cloud which gives observers from Tenerife magnificent sunsets which the Carthagnian colonisers recognized perhaps as much as four or five thousand years ago. Gomera is from Ga-u-mai-Ra, Land-where-dies-the Sun, Sunset Island – certainly in Lithic, but also in Carthaginian. Watching these from the balcony of the apartment in which this book is largely written it is a thrill to think that, perhaps five thousand years before, somebody else was watching and naming the phenomenon. It follows as day follows night America is Carthaginian also. The Lithic phrasing Aa-ma-rai-ka is easily read as Far-death or sinking-of sun-land, the Far Western Land, a tradition passed down

Chapter 4 Ka

the millennia from the heyday of the Carthaginian Empire. The Carthaginians beat Christopher Columbus, as also Brendan the Celt, by thousands of years, and this is likely also the time which provided the link which explains the pyramids both sides of the pond. The myth America is simply the name of the cartographer Amerigo Vespuchi can be explained, since he must have been named at birth by parents well aware of the fabled land and keen to give him the stimulus to explore. That century the novelty of sailing to distant lands to discover the globe had the same fascination as space travel today, and there has been no count as yet of American boys named Buzz. In a few centuries it will probably be averred they were all named after the busy bee which generates so much sweetness. Meanwhile there are many hundreds of millions of folk on the far side of the pond who remain totally unaware they are talking Carthaginian and imagine the American continent is named after a sixteenth century European cartographer. Columbus could have disillusioned them but preferred not to do so. I have informed The New York Times as well, but they have not regarded it as newsworthy, perhaps waiting for one of their own Guanche or natives to break the news, instead of having it borne in on a haughty wind from the wicked old world across the water. Who would want to give them credit?

The Malay for a lighthouse is rumah api, house of fire. Note a Malay house is defined in terms of its function as a shelter from the sun: the Lithic ra-u-ma(h)i, sun-what-depressed/killed off It may sound far fetched. Just two phonemes are hard to be sure about. But then look at the Ancient Egyptian: hoiku, i(h)au-i-kau, it-that-where-one-begotten, birth place, home; and the Greek ekoi (in ekoi-nomoi, home laws, household management, economics. Ekoi may seem to anyone properly brought up rather a rough representation of "where we were begotten" and so our home. E is from the dipthong ai, and aa was where and i was we (well, anyway individualisations and their pluralisations). The original light houses did have a fire in them and a rotating screen so they could signal. A railway train is a kareta api, a cart or chariot of fire, with api from a-pai, the flame being un-surfaced, insubstantial, without a solid surface just like water in that sense. Compare pani, in Hindi, from pa-nahi, surface-none, which is their word for water. Nahi is no in Hindi. Water is sloppy, the flame flickers. You can push a finger into either if you don't mind getting burnt by the livelier element.

Nobody has cared to remark the similarity of cart and kareta in English and Malay to date, nor indeed the Ancient Egyptian akratu, a chariot. We have similar forms in Indo-European, Malay and Semitic, which must surely be a surprise. We can note at the same time the Malay kapal for ship, where ka- is go, and the –pal is probably the surface (pa) of the briney, the salt sea (lai). Laut is ocean in Malay. Lai was the instinct of liquids to run down into the lows in Lithic, see chapter 8. The ocean was altogether run down become (lau-tai). It couldn't get any lower, and its waves and storms suggested a certain dissatisfaction with this its fate. It could turn distinctly peevish. Anyway it all suggests the initial ka- meant go. But Partridge makes clear there may be a connection for cart with a crate, originally craet in Old English and wickerwork (like a cradle, Old English cradel) for lightness and manoeuvrability for a war chariot. In Old English there was also kratte, a wicker basket. But it appears nevertheless the -reta, -ratu and even the English -rt of cart all originally referred in the Lithic to wheeled transport, with the ratai or ratau meaning wheeled. A cart and a chariot was a rounded or rounding or a go-on-wheels. Ratu was Sun become and the sun was round. The discovery of the wheel was early and profound. Anyone with a wheelbarrow will know the power it gives, compared with shouldering a load; and to our simple forebears this power must have come from its similarity of configuration with the all powerful sun, also round. It all suggests to me a common Lithic

Chapter 4 Ka

origin, and those who won't see it seem to me just blind. Nowadays you can get a four wheeled barrow, much easier to pull when full.

Pan's pipes are not the only musical instruments to be called after the creature that makes a similar sound (the quail chic, pipi). The ukulele is named after the Hawaiian grasshopper which makes a stridulent sound by scraping its thighs together to attract the female. (But I am afraid you need specialised thighs for the job). Boys use their hips instead, which they gyrate hippy style, in ill concealed imitation of sexual intercourse, and the mood music has to be provided extraneously as an accompaniment. The hips are from the Lithic elements hai-pai, the ecstasy-pieces, and the hams (from Lithic hai-mai mean ecstatic-impregnaters, because they are needed for the movements of sexual intercourse, (or else just delicious eating, take your pick. The functional semantic is to be preferred). The bright scarlet hawthorn hips are ecstasy pieces as well, because fancifully they resemble the glans of the erect penis; and the haw with greater economy is just from a ha-u, the ecstasy-one. These are genuine traces of the way the words were originally compiled and the states of mind of folk at that time. Go back far enough and it looks as if we were all vulgarians all of the time, simple to a degree amounting to mania. In which case haven't we done well.

It has been widely believed from Egypt right across Asia and the Pacific Ocean that the Ka was the driving force or essential soul of the body, often thought to be the spine and skeleton. The Ka was hard, so the bones, the skeleton, the formative and so the controlling element, the driving force and the body structure. All of this was Ka, which they thought of in terms which we would describe as a magic force. Wicca words of power harked back to some of this. If you had any of these qualities or powers they led across to all of them. Ka could simultaneously be the hard element, the bones, the driving force, etc, all together. The phoneme covered all or any of the meanings in the psychosemantic tree to date, but usually just one or two.

In Egypt you had a Ba, resident in the fleshy bits, as well. The Ka and the Ba were respectively the boys' and the girls' contributions. Honest folk (anyway if they were male) had dual Kas, one half for this world and one for the next one, after death. Feminine claims to an immortal soul were less certain. Aristotle doubted it because Ba, flesh, decays. When I drew attention to Aristotle's view in a tutorial at Oxford (thinking his chauvinism should be exposed) sixty six years ago, a fellow undergraduate (male) walked out in disgust as if Aristotle's fault were mine. Some time later he committed suicide. He seems to have got Aristotle's message he at least would be all right, anyway, if he cut the discussion short.

Insects were taken to have deployed both of their Ka in the present world, many of them going in for dual births (from egg to larval form and then to final insect, as well as bearing the sign of their duality in their bodies, with thorax and belly both on display at the same time in the here and now. Their prospects after death were thus seriously compromised by their profligacy in this world. That may indeed have been why some of them rasped away so. The grasshopper or cricket in Hawaii is a ukulele. Uku is insect, with both dual kas, and the lele from lailai is sing-sing, singing all the time, like our gala or go-la, a sing song originally. The musical instrument, ukulele, is named after the insect, because fancifully it makes a somewhat similar stridulent note. Compare the pan pipes named after the quail chick. The aboriginals in the Malay jungle are unkindly called Sakai by their better dressed cousins living around the coasts. Sa is one in Malay. As single Ka folk they have no better prospects for an afterlife than grasshoppers. They are not Muslims and do not cut off their foreskins, as Semites and their converts do, taken, anyway in the

Chapter 4 Ka

old days, to be an essential prerequisite for survival in the next world . They do not bother with much in the way of clothes either – just like Adam and Eve in the padi Gardens in the East of Malaya, now since the last great ice melt between eight and ten thousand years ago three hundred and sixty feet under the South China Sea. The Malayan aboriginals prefer to be known as 'Orang Asal', Original Folk (the Lithic a-sa-lai is that-first-located). Orang we may surmise is from A-u-rai'n, that-ones-rayed/thinking. Compare Chinese rin, from Lithic rai'n, thinking folk, from the same Lithic. We thought ideas blew in on rays. The Pope still thinks the same and wears headgear to keep naughty thoughts out, as indeed do Jews too. (They cut their muzzle covers off to let their sex rays out, and put the muzzle covers on their heads to stop rays coming in). Both are fancies wholly ineffective, but so old they must be right you see.

The brain for Latins is cerebrum. Cerebrum is from Kai-rai-bai-rau-um, Of the body-the sun\[ie the head]-flesh-rayed-one. It illustrates the belief the head is the eye of the body and the brain within is the recipient of the thinking rays from outside, arriving without your intention. We can match the Greek kara- here again for the skull or head. So what is the –brum? In Lithic elements it is the ba-rau'm, the flesh-rayed'one: the Egyptian rays again, as with our own brains, ba-rai-'n, our rayed flesh. Ideas were supposed to light in from outside, borne in on invisible rays. Nowadays this belief is almost entirely confined to institutionalised maniacs (unless they have been let out as harmless, to kill at will). It made the brain the thinking element within the skull or head. So far, so good. But you were vulnerable to passing rays which could cause you to do things that were wrong, without incurring any personal blame. The pharaohs, who believed they were Ra's chosen penises on earth, had cut away (circumcised) their muzzle covers so that they could fire their seductive rays first. Orbs and tubes were ray guns according to Egyptian bio-science. The girls had the advantage while the boys muzzle covers were on. Their rays pulled the male member out and up towards the girl's shooter, only then enabling the boys to fire back. In this pickle the Pharaohs, expecting to inherit divinity, took a proactive view and grabbed the initiative. There is a clear male chauvinistic presumption that the girls were originally responsible for initiating every sexual encounter around the hearth. (Nor is it impossible that it was indeed the case. The girls were likely hunkered there longer than the boys, back late from hunting, so they will have warmed up first). Rape, under this rubric, was impossible. Pharaohs just wanted more personal prerogative, as befitted royalty. Faced with the same predicament, where their brains were exposed to any passing thought ray, they covered their heads with elaborate talismanic hats. Il Papa, to this day, wears a Pharaonic hat, and like the Semitic races, still wears a small prepuce or skull cap on his head to protect it from evil intrusions from without: different tactics in face of different predicaments, but all based originally on sex. You expose yourself when you want to let your own seductive rays out, but try to take cover when you want to stop other rays coming in. Could it be naughty thoughts il Papa shuns, like the naughty rays in the other case? The original thinking is long forgotten but the ritual still reigns supreme. That is what ritual is, leftovers from outmoded reasoning, bad science.

The paradigmatic Spanish ant can now be seen to have been a white ant or termite which makes a concrete nest with sand and spit. In Africa anthills often reach six or seven feet high, with a lot of ant spit from a lot of ants. The suffix –iga in hormiga for ant is from the Lithic ai-ka, that which-make. This is where the metaphors pick up and kick in. Hormiguear, which means to itch, is to be anted, that is experiencing the same sensation as when ants inject formic acid with their bite, a fine needling pricking stinging sensation, to ice the cake with a few more metaphors. But it also means to swarm or teem like ants; and a hormiguero is an anthill, where the ants live, an antery. But the antery can also mean any place with a lot of people, rather than ants, moving about. Latin termes, plural termites, however included wood worms. Here tere- is from the Lithic terere to rub or grind away, but the –rere can also mean round and round (as well as bristling), whence to drill [holes] as termites do. The growing motion is straight, not round, from the sun (Ra) raying and the rays pulling up the crops with them on their return journey to the sun. These were Egyptian rays which we shall encounter in their full panoply of meanings in chapter 12 for Ra. But grain in wood is round, from growing rings, (and round is what Ra-oo'n-dai, Rayed 'one-become) and only straight when cut lengthwise. The grain we eat has been ground, just like the ground, which is rock which has been ground to grains, soil or sand. Wood worms don't drill but the terere had come to mean to bore in, one way or another. The wood worms were wood borers and the Latin ants were ground borers. These must be the common or garden formica (ant in Latin), from fora-mai-ka: foramen (Latin hole-in-the-earth)-making (ka). They can be seen to have been up to the same –mai-ka as the Spanish hormiga, but in their case they were not making a concrete hive but fore-, pushing in, penetrating, f-o-r from the Lithic pahai-u-rai, penis-when raised/roused, which pushes itself in just as the ants push into the earth. Well, a bit like it, anyway, enough for single Sapiens to jump at it. Before we provided them with houses to infest they all lived in holes in the ground from which in the country green woodpeckers can be seen methodically removing them as they surface. In Spain hormiguear is to swarm - or to itch, both metaphors from the ant and not the concrete, but semantically directly relevant to neither. The swarming is clearly anting and the itching is from the formic acid they inject when they bite. A hormiguero is an anthill, and can also be used as a metaphor for a swarm of people. Now do you see how language has been built? By analogy and metaphor. If so, proceed to Ta and Da in the following chapter.

NOTES

1. Emanuel Velikovsky wrote a number of books about this, dismissed as fanciful by academia from jealousy and spite. But he got quite a lot of it right. His was a master spirit. He was a friend of Einstein's who sympathised with him when he was abused.

CHAPTER 5

TA AND DA. THE TWO WORLDS, INSIDE AND OUT.

We are trying to discover how we thought when first we began to speak, remember; and obviously because of the time scales involved it is not going to be easy. Whether we get it right will appear when it can be seen (or it can not) the meanings we have inherited can in fact be shown to follow through from the original thinking. The research worked the other way about: how we think today had to be parlayed by means of verbal comparisons, in order to discover the semantic links leading backwards to more and more previous meanings, all gravitating to and coalescing at the original individual semantic contents of the phonemes. It needed interlingual comparisons, with dozens of dictionaries, eventually of over a hundred languages. This was an exercise on its own. It was without the least consideration if such a pattern were possible. This is important because common sense suggests that it is not. But once confronted with the sequential patterns discovered, the next step is to see if there is any way they might be veridical after all. It is a temptation to appeal to genetic programming like Professor Chomsky and say the meanings (or at least some potential) are carried by the genes. But ideas are activities of the brain and not part of the organ itself. It therefore seems to be a category error to equate the activity of the brain with its genetic structure as Chomsky quite unblushingly does. Our legs are determined, no doubt, by our genes, but hardly the Sunday walks we may take. That degree of determinism does not make sense. Similarly our brains are determined by our genes but hardly the thoughts we may think. Our brains limit our ability but do not inform it. For that we provide our very own whimsy. How brains provide thought we wholly lack.

Darwinian evolution, strengthened as it has been by the monk's peas[1] and then by genetic discoveries resulting from the double helix and the cracking of DNA, has been so successful in informing biological research over the last century and a half that folk, including those educated in scientific method who perhaps should have been more discriminating, have come to see it as a cure-all not to be challenged or modified in any degree. This, as Henry Ford would have put it, is bunk. A linguistic study, taking in the thinking of which we have so far been capable, is needed to show that even the most illustrious scientific thinker – and Darwin was not the brain of Britain by any means, he was a comparatively slow coach but dogged with it – is unable to break out of the language medium he happens to inhabit. The same applies, and probably more so, to those who have come after, riding in Darwin's train. Darwin was for my great grandfather a junior, and for his son, my great uncle, a hero, and for me a constant thinking companion. But now it is time to put the boot in. Nothing should detract from what Darwin discovered and disclosed. But nothing should be added without careful thought. The whole of biological technology belongs to biology, and so far as linguistics is concerned may be left to MIT, The Massachussets Institute of Technology. But the philosophy of thinking does not and may not. Charles Darwin who is looking down on me as I write, as ever somewhat hesitant and intense, aged sixty five, courtesy of the London Natural History Museum who have added colour to an old photograph of 1874 in their library, evidently agrees with me. He favoured the birds nest style of beard, just like Karl Marx, but attached much greater importance to cleanliness and good manners. Consequently he has been adopted by

Chapter 5 Ta

scientists while Marx has mostly appealed to the scatter-brained, including scatter-brained intellectuals like Marx himself, still to be found sitting at high tables across Europe, in spite of the egregious failure of Marx's thinking everywhere it has in practice been tried. Dialectical thinking is bunk. It is demolished as a vulgar error in chapter 15 on thinking: the error closely and precisely described, which has not been done anywhere else to date. It should terminate dialectical thinking once and for all. It won't, becaue addicts can not shift position. But it should check recruitment, once it gets about.

This chapter deals with the third phoneme in the alphabet, Ta and Da. They sloven between the two forms so readily there is no point tearing them apart to treat them separately. The Tau is such an age old symbol the phoneme must rank high in the pecking order in the subconscious mind; being in the old days a feminine sex symbol, as well as a Tao or life path or way of life out East, and now with the alphabet just the letter T, stripped of any meaning in the West. Ta thus appears to be the original, and Da to be the marked version. Ta is and was originally a light tongue tap, or lingual plosive in linguistic jargon. Its original meaning was thus a light tap or snap, and in particular apparently the snap of a dry branch broken in two for the fire at the family hearth outside the family cave. It is in this sense a doublet with Ka, the more forceful and sharper clack of stone on stone which breaks off a flake, echoed by the more guttural and vigorous plosive from the glottis at the back of the throat. Both derived their original meanings from their fancied echoisms. As a matter of fact, allowing sufficient fancy, so does everything else. That was how language started out. The meanings came from echoisms, more or less fanciful. Since then language has expanded just by means of metaphor. These simple processes are only concealed, so that they can come as a simple surprise, simply because we have forgotten how to treat our single sounds as meaningful. Once the meanings implicit in the phonemes or letters (which are in the psychosemantic trees with the chapters treating each phoneme in turn) have been taken on board, there are only a few tricks to be learned to unravel most of the thinking since. So take courage. In each of the following chapters the attempt will be made to show how the words we use themselves provide the evidence for these Lithic hypotheses. The phonemes (letters) carry the meanings, and their use holds together in so many words that it can not be other than as a result of the letters originally meaning what they still do. It must also be shown how the meanings in the psychosemantic trees come about: that is to say how the meanings spread out as they do, how one leads to the other by gulling one from the other, in other words by metaphor[2]. You finish up with such a closely textured interlocking meaning field or matrix which holds together with so many linkages it is hard to know where to start and in which direction to go.

Once a branch is snapped you have two where before you had one; and quite likely one bit in each hand. That is why the snapped, the tau, where the -u added indicates a done job, in this case snapped in two, was used at once for two, as well as to break or cut in two. Maybe it was by means of a bus[3] here that the vowel -u got its own duality from tau too, whereas it really featured on its own just as the completive case and was wrongly picked from next door to the ta which alone carried the duality originally. Be that as it may, the vowel u was established as the dual vowel long before Ancient Egypt ever took up the tale some seven thousand years ago or more.

O and e are the dipthongs au and ai in origin, the original vowelisations were only three: a [aaa], i [eee] and u [ooo], the best Tarzan's mouth parts could manage. The ka won't do for two because although the flake if correctly struck can come off the core in a single piece and may well neatly match the core so that their joint is well preserved, and remarked as such, the knapping is for the most part a repetitive process with many chips

Chapter 5 Ta

produced as waste, and will have started out with the core [from kau-rai, the struck] itself gradually shaped, with many chips, to make a tool. So Ka can indicate a chopping stroke or thence a cut, but not cutting into two, for which we require the ta, as indeed in cut. With cut itself, from kai-ta the kai- is 'making'-two. The stoneware our forebears made for a million years and more was put together with a lot of chips; and ka, the sound it made, was taken for the meaning of make and even join as well as strike, but it never had anything to do with sequential numeration[4]. That at least is how a carpenter is made up, from Lithic kara-pai-en-tarai, joiner-pieces-of-cut [wood]. A carpenter is a cutter and joiner of planking, etc, with the plank, pa-la'n 'surface-flat' and 'shaped' by the -k (kai) at the end. We can note in passing the 'n after the pa-la, often from en meaning of the following phoneme, has the prior signification of acting as a linking marker of the second phoneme to the preceding one. Elsewhere it can link the preceding phoneme to the succeeding one. That is how its meaning turned into of, and anything a bit similar like in, or even -ing. Ka is the carpenter par excellence, not only chopping but also joining together, both meanings of the ka. Lithic meanings can be used to mean completely opposite things like this because there have been hundreds of thousands of years of usage in which to differentiate the meanings bit by bit. It can be a problem, since only the context will enable you to choose between chop apart and join together for instance.

This scenario is only possible if you come to accept the idea of each generation relearning Lithic with their subconscious minds (and so without knowing it) as they consciously learned to speak. Otherwise the common belief the Old Stone Age is too far away for any access today must prevail; and you probably would think that, unless you had found out Lithic worked, and had to make sense of it. Then you really need the repetitive refreshment rate. Does anyone want to deny there is a subconscious layer of the mind? Is there anyone out there who has never dreamed?

The psychosemantic tree for Ta and Da is on page 89. We are trying to follow the meanders of the primitive mind before it had all that much to think with, remember, aeons before the first mud brick was sun baked for the first building at Sumer some seven or eight thousand years ago or more. The mathematical school of linguistics started by Gottlob Frege (1848-1925) in the nineteenth century and now burgeoned quite beyond belief by Bertrand Russell and the early Wittgenstein, as well as many others, all the way to Noam Chomsky today, began with the concealed premises that language was informed by mathematics (symbolic logic); whereas the truth is it was the other way around and math developed out of language. Logic is thus informed by primitive grammar and not a transformational grammar by logic. It does not make any difference to the sums you can do; but it has a good deal of bearing on the status of the art and science of language.

With Ba and Ka already done – chapters three and four – we can afford to skim through the psychosemantic tree for Ta and Da. Little (13) is from li-ti-ti-li. Li-ti-ti were the titty little apertures in the teats of the breast, and to be little you were -li, from –lai, linked to them or like them. You tap a hole (14). To teach (25) is to become-make, but better to think-make. The thinking (21), the mental becoming is also to give birth to ideas. The totem pole deserves a mention, in Cree and Hawaiian ototoma (95), from au-tau-tau-ma, all-born-born-dead, all the dead generations: and there they are represented on the totem pole starting at the top with their totemic forebear, often a surprise package not even human. In Navaho ia-te-shi-ma is it is-good-my-mother, or as we would say good day ma'am. The te which is good is from tai, births or the birth line, the tribal, and therefore PC, that kind of good, socially correct behaviour. Yosemite National Park is Navaho too. It was really ia-ushi-ma-i-tai. The miner forty-niner who picked up this jewel thought it sounded like yozemmity, and was their name for the grizzly bear (the totem of the local Awani tribe). What his Man Friday actually said was that is-our-mother-of-the tribe. He preferred not to reveal the name of his totem. So the park is named after a whole sentence in Navaho. A town (39), originally a tun, is a collective and community, much like a taun in Egyptian.

The Tau was also what you got from the binary symmetry of the human body. The T has a central dividing line down the middle and two identical arms pointing in opposite directions, mirror images of each other, just like the virtual central line down the middle of human anatomy with two sides, mirror images, of the whole human body. That makes three directions, the upright of the T and the two arms; which is how the rays of the Tau, the tau-rai, or tres come to be three, while the Tau itself is really only two lines, and has been used for two. It depends whether you look at the Tau as one vertical line and one horizontal line on top, which makes two, or if you see it as three rays starting from a common origin where they meet. Animal flesh is formed two-sidedly, with bilateral symmetry. Body actually means ba-u-tai in Lithic, flesh-dual-become. It is an animal body. Plants grow all over the place. This is a peculiarly telling piece of Lithic.

Ra in A-maun-Ra is The Ever-Loving-Eye). The Ansate Cross is compiled from Lithic elements, a'n-sai-tai, and up to now has been a mystery within an enigma, but can now be read as the one-of the action-of birth' cross. The cross is here treated as another form of the original tau or T, as indeed it is – it has only the same two lines in the same relationship, but allowed to cross; and the upright (sai) is seen to be in the very act (-sai-) of giving birth, (-tai), the slit enlarging to admit the baby's head. The fact it is called a cross makes it clear the opening is part of the Tau, and so it is the tau which has been altered to show the opening shape. Ta-oo = Birth-hole.

The Ankh, A'n-khai can also be read as Everlasting-Ka, with Eternal Life; as well as The one-that kindles (impregnates). Today it is treasured as an amulet, and women all round the world are apt to hang it round their necks without quite knowing why. No doubt at one time they did. It records the fact that all belief began as recognition of feminine fertility, long before the boys were accepted even as pollinators at all. The Ankh amulet says quite subtly: "We come first, and at one time in the past it was recognised by all". Witchcraft got its cachet from the same perception, appealing particularly to old maids, and at one time men thought it a burning heresy, determined to eradicate it. I am guessing the ankh (well anakhai really) was the boys' name for the symbol, claiming it is their kindling of the tau which is shown, with their sexual rays triggering it, saying in effect, without any subtlety at all: "We come first and it must now be recognised by all". Human whimsy is like that. We are not very nice; but we can move on, and we do.

For the Egyptians the sun was at first the 'Aton', the Aa-taun, the everlasting birth canal, birthing light into the world afresh each day. It gave rise to further anthropomorphic musings about the cosmos. Isis, in Greek, was this female universal deity, in Egyptian correctly pronounced Au Siti, the World Light Source and Life Source (Sai can be both Light and Life, and Tai can be both Source and Term) and so the Sunset, when the sun died and was reborn into the Dua-Taun (conventionally the Duat! The academic Egyptologists have made no attempt to discover how Egyptians actually spoke and transliterate the glyphs as if they were simply consonants, whereas they were really syllabic and sometimes multi syllabic too), the Second World of the night, there to gestate as in the womb, with the Ka lai, the Ka or oomph of life laid low, like seeds in the ground, semen, from Lithic sai-mai'n, the living-planted'one, for propagating. For the Egyptians the goddess of the night was Nut, or in original Lithic extension Nau-tai, Exhibiting all-her

Chapter 5 Ta

orifices. The stars were, in this popular recension, all the nipples of the night, and the moon was her genital aperture varying from the merest slit to a fully engorged round shape with dirty marks on it, as if menstruating on a monthly basis. Admittedly not many ladies could boast a crescent shaped vagina, but the metaphor nevertheless served. The Heavens could not be expected to reveal a perfect match to us on earth. To fit this pattern Nut or Nautai was obliged to be bent over the world on tiptoe on one side of the world and supporting herself on her fingertips on the other side. That made her a rather elongated goddess, but it served. To mate with this perception the Egyptians had composed a god from Gaia, the earth, from Lithic Kai-a, the hard one, called Geb or Gebai, from gai-bai-a, the earth-burgeoning-one, who lay on his back on the ground and was required to perform gymnastic prodigies which left Nut's in the shade, since he struggled hopelessly with his phallus, though with a truly enormous erection, to reach the moon. The moon in turn, no doubt, was imposing her feminine guile or wiles upon the supine Geb below, using her ta rays to draw up his organ to her. This pantomime can only be seen in the night sky. The moon is from Mau-na, when dark and dead it shows, or else from luna, when the Ka is lau-na, laid low-it shows. It seems clear the Egyptian rays from the sun pulling up the crops could claim a kind of biological science, but the night time antics of these two were whimsys added, with poetic licence, to fill in the gaps. Chomsky's grammatical genes (sic) are very similar poetic whimsys, in his case taken from current evolutionary science.

 It would be wrong to think Egyptians took this modelling as a literal presentation, but they did take it as representing reality in metaphorical form. They were wrong again there of course. But Nut informed the language of the day and has fed through to the present day. The evidence for identifying these Lithic language roots must be found in the words we have used and use today, and nowhere else. The confirmation we have got them right comes from the fact they make sense (of a sort) – one meaning can be seen to follow on from another - and are consistent across the lexicon. In other words to carry the Lithic Hypotheses forward you have to use the same set of meanings for each letter world wide. Our night comes from the German nacht and that in turn from the Lithic na-kha-ti, or exhibiting-the body-orifices, Nut's many titi again. We say naked as well, similarly from the Lithic na-ka-ti, exposing the body's little orifices, and nude too from nau-di again, this time just with exposed orifices (the stars). Attempts to make naked the past participle of to nake, to throw off all your clothes in gay abandon (like the snake from si-na-ka, brer-bare-body: no limbs, see), have found no support from the lexicon; although Eric Partridge clings to a hypothetical lost Indo-European verbal root *nog- to bare, which he apparently gets from earlier lexical compilers' guesses. Lithic could accommodate it, were it to appear, as exposed body or the bare-making. Is this a common root with slang to snog, from sai-nog, the action of *noggin, which in Lithic can be read as nau-ka, exposure-of the body, or present-make? If so it is the subconscious mind informing slang; but the whole *nogging idea is made up. We can however find naughty, also from the same Lithic, which suggests the original naughtiness was nau-ka-ti, flashing, with exposed body orifices/teats, which even now still has for some a powerful subconscious appeal (usually the boys). Flashing is from phala-shai, first an ejaculation of light, but also phallus-showing these days. It has to be remembered before trousers we were accustomed for hundreds of thousands of years to exhibit ourselves fully exposed, when we were good and ready for sex - and wee boys at all times. These natural privileges die hard.

 The lowly snake, from the Lithic elements si-na-kai, brer-bare-bodied, has neither fur nor limbs to break the smooth outline of his torso. The older generation brought up on Kipling's stories will remember Kala Nag, Black Snake, the elephant, no doubt named for

Chapter 5 Ta

his trunk, with no Brer here. Elephant is o.o.o. of obscure origin according to Partridge, but the Lithic favours Ai-lai-pahei-en-tai, That which-long-pahei(penes)-of-two: ie with a formidable proboscis at both ends. Tarzan liked to talk smut. It can not be pinned on the author. The Latins lopped off the -of-two, probably unaware of what they were doing, so critics can argue the Lithic must be wrong – but their argument is specious.

Sai, from the active flickering of the flame and its heat, which animals had as well – some warmth and considerable activity – came to mean alive, live, and so life forms, which I have translated as brer. Sa in Malay is a single upright stroke, one in fact; and si is brer, as in Sungei Siput, River Snail, the river on which the capital city Kuala Lumpur, Muddy Estuary, sits. Si-puti, is Brer-Penis teat, (as with peri-puti or prepuce, around-the penis teat) a whimsical comparison since few folk, if indeed any, can boast a whorl in that department to match the snail's shell. In Malaya the Siamang ape is Si-a-mang, Brer-Un-heavy, or Brer Weightless. If you have known a tame one, capable of going twice round the room on the picture rails in half a dozen swings of its immensely elongated forelimbs, the name is etched in your memory. Si Plandok, the mouse deer, is Si pai-la'n-dok, Brer-feet-slippy-does, or Brer Slippy Stepper. He is the Brer Rabbit of Malayan folk lore, born and bred in the deep jungle. Lai can carry the meaning sly as well as slippery or light. Piscis the fish, virtually limbless like the snake also, is from pai-s-kai-s, feet of-movement-body of-movement. The movement of the body provides the locomotion which should properly, in our forebears' perception, be provided by the feet. He swims by wiggling his body, having no feet for the job, and is gone in a flash if you try to grab him. Perhaps the early Christians were drawn to the fish, their PX or vesica piscis, as a symbol for the church because of this mode of progression: the whole body of the church provided its own momentum regardless of its oppressors' attempts, often successful, to cut off its limbs by killing off its pilgrim teachers. If so, the symbol was one of subtle defiance in defence of belief, not much in evidence in the church any longer these days. The Malay for fish, which they share with the aboriginal tribes of New Guinea and beyond, which suggests it is genuinely ab-original, is ikan or ika. It means single-body (or sometimes it-of the body, when it is usually translated as flesh or meat). The ka, however, was not only the body structure but also its spiritual drive and source of its strength while alive, a catch-all term. The aboriginal perception, we can see now, was not only a single body, without any appendages (worth mentioning), but also a single driving force through the water, the very same idea the West presents with its piscis, Latin for fish, footing it with its body and achieving astonishing spurts of speed (fish, phai-shai, ejaculatory action) through the water. Was Hodge, in his own tongue, enlivening the Latin? Compare the frog, from phrau-gai, ejaculation-going, the leaper.

As a secondary fall out from this night time scenario with the sun Aa-taun and the sunlight from dawn to dusk, there is Isis, in the original Egyptian Au Siti, Au-Sitai, World-Life-source in Lithic. The source is her tai. She gave birth continuously to the light which sank with the sun at the end of the day, and managed to retain her throne in the light world above. A throne in English is from tarau-nau, a drawn up protruberant job, on which you could present yourself with your legs hanging down. Ordinary folk squatted a bit cramped on the floor. She was the white goddess of the day. She it was who set the scene for the various other goddesses who have been worshiped by the devout, extending even to the Mediterranean worship of the Virgin Mary, a virtual divinity. Her connection with the sea comes directly from the sun setting in the sea, le mer in French, from the Lithic mai-rai, the dying of the sun, as well as the name Mary, inherited from Au Siti, the world sunset as well as sun birth, in Ancient Egypt. In Malaya Siti Miriam is Our Lady Mary.

Chapter 5 Ta

THE PSYCHOSEMANTIC TREE FOR TA AND DA

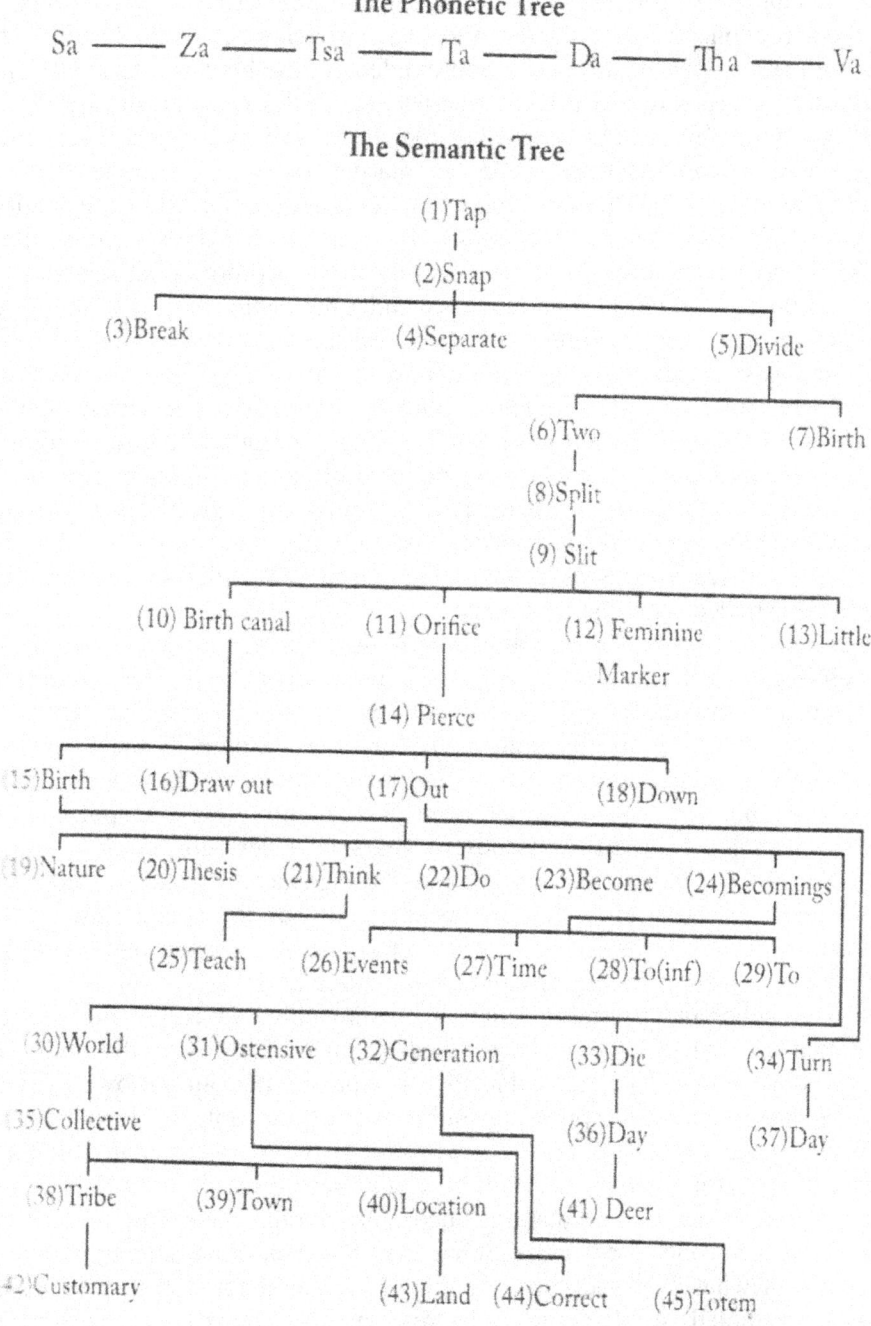

But siti is also a police whistle, from a hissing tube with a piercingly high note. In India, where the sun sets in glorious red sunsets over the Western Ghats, mai-Ra, the sunset, (merah) is used for red.

Kali, the Arabian black goddess of the night and death (kala is black in Sanskrit and Hindustani), became the negative of the goddess of the day. Ka-lai, as well as black and death, meant act slyly, and with lye, bitterness. In the Hindu pantheon she was introduced as another avatar of the goddess Durga of death and destruction, wife of Shiva, the god of death and destruction. It was Kali who, thousands of years before the birth of The Prophet (may his soul rest in peace), offered seven maidens in the hereafter to any of her Arabian followers who managed to kill fifteen unbelievers. In those far off days it was comically supposed the future life would be exactly like this one just with the nasty bits left out. Spirituality was still in the future. So her martyrs expected to arrive there with their wedding tackle intact. The Prophet Mahomed, per contra, believed in spirituality. He was a follower of Nabi Issus, the Prophet Jesus. There are no heavenly virgins on offer in the Koran. That was Kali's offer, in prehistoric times. It was more poetic infill just like Nut and Geb. As the second world (dua-taun) lay under the penny shaped solid world we lived on the upper surface of, everything down there was upside down and topsy turvy. So Kali the black goddesss, as goddess of the night, when the Ka of the world had been lai or lowered or had run down like liquids do into the lows, was everything opposite to the white goddess of the day. The primitive mind does nothing by halves. Consequently her worshipers were to do as you would NOT be done by, to lie and cheat, rob and harm, and best of all kill all unbelievers in her. It is uncommonly like Nazism, perhaps via the subconscious. Today it would count as devil worship, the opposite of religion. For all true Muslims the promised virgins as a reward for killing are quite simply a Kalian heresy, properly to be expelled with due ceremony.

Back to Ta. Ta in time became any becoming (tai'm for instance, time in English as here, which is simply the process of becoming, the temporal sequence, an abstraction and not a substance of any kind), and also any slit, and thence in particular natural waterways of one kind or another, with don, dhu or da for river. Sindhu is the Sanscrit for river, probably from the Lithic elements Sai-en-da(h)awa, moving-in-da-water, or as we would put it: water moving in a channel, which even Tarzan could probably spot was a river, and Sanskrit speakers hundreds of thousands of years later certainly could. Sindu was the Sanskrit name for the Indus river, and names the province of Sindh in India to this day. Putting the -s on the other end may have been to emphasise the fast flowing. The Indus had a riverine civilisation as old as or older than Sumer. It even had a sewage system. Everyone else was just fertilising the land on an ad hoc basis.

There were other gulls coming from the vagina too. In Egypt they concluded the world's actions at a distance were occasioned by rays. They were the raying of Ra, the sun, perceived as a world Eye, as well as the rays that came from our own puny eyes. The world Eye's rays were wide spreading and powerful and hot, and could be seen to be pulling back up the vegetation on their (presumed) return to the sun. So the Egyptian priests drew them with hands on the ends so Hodge would get the idea. It was long before priests and scientists came to be distinguished. Our similar but relatively feeble eyes sent out rays which were only cold; but they reached the panorama and returned to our eyes with a picture of what they had encountered, which could sometimes be seen painted on the iris (the irradiated) of the eye, to be read by the manikin behind waiting for the information. It may be it was the sun when perceived as the World Vulva birthing light into the world that was first awarded the retro rays which pulled up the crops, copying the human pattern where the boys blamed the girls for pulling them out with the retro rays from their vulvas. The pattern was simply assumed to be universal. The rays from the eyes were clearly retro-rays too, otherwise how did the picture of the local view reach the eye which had uttered its viewing ray to it.

In any case the first precedent was surely the one closest home. The rays which first revealed their power to draw things back to their sources by pulling their targets out and up, and thus demonstrated their retro action, were surely those that Tarzan registered personally around the hearth, when he found himself being drawn out and up by the girls squatting opposite him. There was nobody to tell him where is fancy bred. It is actually in the head; and the message is then sent down below via divers organelles, all of which have a role to play. The Pharaoh, from the Lithic Pha-Ra-a-u-hai, Penis in which Ra rejoices, or Ra's chosen penis, baulked at having to wait for the girls, and (wanting to fire first) cut off his own muzzle cover/foreskin. Wallis Budge, in his splendid Hieroglyphic Dictionary of 1921, with over a thousand pages of glyphs, thought the Pharaoh was a Paraoh, and so the roof or house in which Ra rejoiced, the Royal House. Perhaps the Pahai, the joy piece for penis, was unthinkable in 1921, and may still not be very welcome introduced into academic linguistics in 2013. The Pharaoh's organ was supposed to guarantee the fertility of the people and the harvest equally. The Pharaohs were Semites farming the Hamitic tribes. Circumcision later became a deal done with Jahweh. It is not clear why He had not designed the genitalia as he wanted them in the first place, so that his created people were reduced to modifying his design to suit. Now it is excused as a medical procedure to keep the penis clean; but the same query still applies, and the Pharaohs were not looking for superior hygiene but sexual dominance.

The T rays emanating from the birth canal are commonly found dotted all over the lexicon still today, meaning drawing or pulling out or up, but no longer consciously recognised as sexual in origin. A tree and its trunk and a chest of drawers, or even the trousers we males wear with draw up action each day testify as much. You only have to open an English dictionary at tr- or attr- or str- or dr- to see how many words have an element of pulling or drawing along. Trace, track, tract, trail, trailer, trawl, train (railway, bridal and horticultural kinds), trap, trip, trance, tray, trans-, tractor, trick, treacle, tremble, trend, truck, trouble, trauma, trigger, tribe, thrust, tribute, throw, intrude, troll, trolly, trundle, true, trick, strong, stress, strain, strap, straight, attract, attrition, true, drink, drain, drip, draw, drag, draught, dray, dredge, dreg, drench, dribble, drive, trickle, drizzle, droop: and so on. An Albanian dictionary does nearly as well, a language with a cosmopolitan etymology with borrowings from several language families. Torrit, to scatter, tork, a heavy wooden beam to exert pressure on an olive press, torua meaning track, trage meaning trace, tractorist meaning tractor driver, trakull to press, trellis to draw into a stupor, trand to quake, trap a furrow, trapa trapa staggering from side to side, trastar a purse snatcher or thief, trate a fishing net, trazone a mixing spoon, trino to harrow, troke a cow bell, trumhasu traumatised, trunggjat having a tall trunk, trys to press down or push down (close to the knuckle here, the action (sai) when ta-rai). Compare our press, from pa-rai-sai, the action of the rayed raised and roused piece). And so on.

The Egyptian neter, the supposed pointed axe of divinity which preceded all the names of 'gods', of which the Egyptians had hundreds, has been already mentioned out of turn. It was really pronounced naturai, like the Latin natura and our nature, from the Lithic na-tau-rai, displaying-the tau-rays, showing the tau's-rays, and so the pulls or draws [of nature]. It was a triangular pennant blown out in the wind, which is a natural force, and not a pointed axe at all; and not indicating divinity either, as the professional Egyptologists still imagine, but on the contrary an individualisation of one of the natural forces of the world. It would surely have been a matter of moment for all concerned long before anyone got around to working out the workings of the natural world, or the way the sun behaved at all. The World Vulva in the sky was thus most probably identified as such simply because of its similar powers with its rays showering all over the earth and drawing up the vegetation. The first world of our perception appears to have been built of feminine wiles. There is no record of whether the girls welcomed this or if it was forced upon them by the boys. My own guess is it was simply accepted by all and sundry, along with the power of the mothers to control the self confidence of their sons, as a matter of common sense. When the boys' intellectual rebellion eventually came, and they identified the sun as the world eye (Ra), it was no doubt long and fiercely fought, indignation building from the realisation the mothers had ruled the roost without any realistic warrant. In reality the boys had mostly put one over on themselves; but you should not expect the victim to do other than treasure his victimhood. These tau-rays emanating from the birth canal are commonly found dotted all over the lexicon still today, but no longer recognised consciously as such, they are simply built into the language, where they can still be discovered, embedded like flies in amber, stimulating the subconscious subconsciously.

 The Egyptian rays are one principal reason for believing our earliest thinking, and the meanings derived from it were hammered out, to a predominant extent, upon the anvil of our own genitalia. It was our own sexual performance which had the greatest appeal and attracted our keenest interest so long ago; and it naturally showed when we came to compile our first language and made use of our current thinking for the purpose. It may not be to everyone's taste to find our thinking was like this, nor to realise so much of our language is built, if not with four letter words then at least with an original kind of four letter thinking, and it was this which informed our first speaking – of course long forgotten. Nor is it everyone's cup of tea to realise the primitive gods and goddesses were mixed up in this, but they were. Religion started out as fertility religion, fertility being identified with survival; and the rebirth of the flowers of the field from the soil, as well as the sun arising, was what taught us to expect rebirth after death. Osiris (actually Au Sara in Egyptian), the World Sunrise, son but also spouse of Au Siti, the source of the sunlight, whose real son, Horus, the risen sun, was fathered by Au Sara, the sunrise, but mothered and nursed by Au Siti, from Au-Sai-Tai, the World-Life-Source, makes these metaphors a rich jumble too muddled for sorting out in full. Like fairy stories, they had numerous versions, not all compatible, and none of them entirely clearcut or understood. Digging up the ways we thought long ago, including the smut, is a necessary part of fitting together the meanings we have derived from it. Without the Aton and Ra, the sun, and the tau-rays around the hearth, and so the original meaning of nature, we would be taxed still further, perhaps beyond perception altogether, to trace the earliest meanings of our utterances, already prehistoric before the pyramids were begun.

 Tai, in so far as it was dividing into two, had more of a simple distinction about it, as a verb a parturition, than the first stage in numeration. As such, it was used for a day, which started with the birth of the new sun each dawning. Day, from the Lithic tai, is a doublet with time, from the Lithic elements tai-'m, which we would perhaps describe as the becomings, the sequence of events. It isn't very crisp thinking, but it surely carries conviction: breaking in two > division or separation > the tau pattern of the human anatomy > the female pudenda > birthing > coming into being > becoming > becomings > events > the flow of events > time > tau, all of them > all the events>the world, or later just a collective idea like a town, a collection of births and so blokes (in houses). The 'm in

Chapter 5 Ta

time, just like the –n in taun, can be virtually ignored because as a (rather meaningless) hum (see chapter 9), it really added no more than an indication Tarzan was mentally pausing there (just as we still say "um" while searching for the next word or phrase); he was pausing because he had reached a little local completion, he had finished defining the definand, so we should finish it off there as an individual thing. In other words it meant substantive or noun, except Tarzan had no grammar. With tau, with u the inclusive vowel so tau was all the divisions or becomings/events, instead of just the flow of time the Egyptians got all of it, with all that it carried along with it, all the events, the whole world, the totality (and totality is from tota, Lithic tau-ta, all things, but in this case just taken to be the whole - of things unspecified: the all). And the French say tout. But the Greeks say tito for the sun. It is from tai-tau, with the tai- the birth canal and the -tau -of the universe, like the Egyptian a-taun, the eternal birth canal, birthing light into the world each day.

The Latin dies, from which it is often claimed our day derives, is from the Lithic tai-sai, (the sai reduced in slow stages via –se to-s), the birth of the shine or light. It is a separated period of time marked by the sun rise, the birth of the light, which lasts until sunset when the day dies, with the descent of the sun into the sea (sea from sai-awa, the moving or live-water) often with a blood red sunset. Etymologists who have studied the word have been put off by the forms which have a g at the end. In German you say "Guten tag" to be polite. In Old Norse it is dagr; but they often use –r pronounced untrilled like an -a, which can be from –ai, just as we do in rugger and hugger-mugger, etc. Going further back to the Gothic we find dags, with the -s or daylight back in. G was not distinguished from Y a thousand or two years ago, as it is today. Y is often just a lazy G, in fact a G with the glottis not completely closed. Guard, garden and yard (the American English for garden) mark this ambiguity: nothing to do with flowers, but just a guarded area, usually with a fence. A Y can also come from ia of course, which G can't. With automobiles and supermarkets there is a tendency to concrete gardens or yards over. So the German tag comes from taya, birthing one; and the Gothic dags from tay-sai, from birthing-of the light. A day was the birth of the new sun and its life was a day. The dawn, when the sun was born, was in Danish, Norwegian and Swedish dagning, pronounced dayening, from Lithic day-ai-naing, the birth-that is-presenting or showing. To make it crystal clear the Old English was dagian and the middle English dawen, to become daeg, pronounced day, much as we still do today and lasting until the sun goes down.. It was at a time when the sun was still a fire well in the sky showing through a hole in the upper (stone) firmament (like the volcanos we knew on earth), which was rotating from East to West by day over the top, and rotating around the pole star by night, an echo of the day. The Aton of the Egyptians was the Aa-taun in Lithic terms, the Eternal birth canal birthing fire, and its light into the world. Tenerife (in Carthaginian – the Carthaginians were there in Tenerife some four thousand years BP) is from the Carthaginian Aa-aton-arai-pahai, The Everlasting-vulva-that rays-the ejaculater: in other words What-the Everlasting Vagina-rays [which was fire]-pahei, the ejacuater, The Fire Ejaculater, The Volcano. The whole of the island has been ejaculated from the crater of the volcano, El Teide, (The Titty, with a conical fumerole on one lip) and the Carthaginians knew it all about four or five thousand years ago.

That was a time when the sun was still regarded as a fire-well or volcano in the upper firmament or sky (sky from sai-kai, upper land or firmament, with the two vowel terminations originally the same, to show they were meant to match, sai rising or raised and kai just ka with ending to match), with fire shining through a hole in the upper rotating firmament made of rock; going from East to West by day and around the pole star by night when night's myriad teats were showing. It was not a picture entirely consistent all

Chapter 5 Ta

through, the rotations were contradictory, but the heavens were ineffable in any case so it was inappropriate to expect to be able to make sense of them altogether. You just picked up on any known patterns you could find, because it made you feel just that little bit more at home.

The gods in the sky were, sometimes at least, the planets visible at night. They made no match with human anatomy but they were firmly anchored in the upper firmament and could be seen to rotate with it, but wandering with wills of their own, out of control. At night you were vouchsafed a view of things not revealed by day, things of the mind, the inner world concealed from prying eyes, dazzled by day. Whereas the sun died each day and mortals did the same in their own time, so that their span was between the two terms, birth and death, tai and dai, two births if you believed at death you entered the dua taun, the second world of the dead. With the immortal gods on the contrary they remained immortal surviving both terms, indeed rejoicing in both lifes, tai-hei-u-sai, theus, the Greek for a god. This is why the Latin deus, god, and the Latin dies, day, are so similar to English death.

Next we should look at thinking, because it comes from tai too. Ideas simply popped up in the mind, concealed for the most part from other folk. Thinking is from ta(h)ai-'n-kai, birth-of-making The mind was the dark medium in which the ideas were born, created, even generated like by the Egyptian penis, mai, the planter or impregnater, literally the earther from planting seeds in the outside world. The mind, from Lithic mai'n-da, does the earthing or procreating so far as ideas are concerned, while the brain is the ba-rai'n, the flesh which is rayed. The idea here was that ideas were shot into the brain from outside by rays from whoever or whatever, just as the rays of the sun impinged on your flesh all over on the outside, and on the crops and pulled them up; and your eyes rayed out and saw the reflection that came back. Seeing (in the mind) was another metaphor. The Greek idein meant to see, compare videre in Latin, which persuades Eric Partridge at least that the Greek was originally from widein, so ideas were originally images as seen in the outside world used metaphorically for what was seen by the inner eye in the inner world of the mind. In somewhat similar vein, in Malaya mata meant eye, and mata hari the eye of the day, the sun, the eye in the sky. The eye as mata was the mind opening or entry to the mind, letting the world outside in picture into the mind inside, which with the eye shut of course was dark like in the world outside where in the womb of night the dead sun gestated in the dark to be born next day.

The Egyptians who had the sun the Aton or Aa-Ta-un, the Eternal-birth canal, birthing light into the world by day had the earliest version of fatherhood as well; pata was a covered (pa) birth canal (ta). Later folk preferred pa-terai, the piece-drawn out as in the Latin pater and our own paternity. The Ancient Egyptian usage is still a subject of some confusion. Sir Wallis Budge whose 1921 two volume dictionary of hieroglyphs is still without peer, has "ptah renpit" as apparently a title of God from a late Coptic text. The Copts were early Egyptian Christians who wrote in hieroglyphs. This is one of my minor triumphs in Egyptian. The academic Egyptologists are content with a stunted translation of the glyphs, because Champolion used the names of foreigners on the Rosetta Stone, the identical text inscribed in Greek and Egyptian, to discover the meaning of the glyphs; and when recording foreign names the Egyptians used the hieroglyphs as if they were just their first sounds, in other words as if they were letters. As an originally Semitic tongue Egyptian often did not include the vowels. So the values of the glyphs Champolion discovered were alphabetic. In reality the pronounciation was a great deal more complex, the glyphs being generally syllabic, and quite often multi-syllabic. The correct transliteration of Budge's ptah renpit is Pata ahi arai en Pai Taun, Father our around in roof of world, or Our father who art in Heaven, which Christians will immediately recognise as canonical. The arai conveys activity, which is slightly off centre for the deity today. Pai is skin or roof and Taun is the universe or world. The academic recension of the Egyptian for Heaven is Pet, but the glyphs were not primarily just alphabetic. They were really syllabic. P was pronounced like the Greek pi, which copied the Egyptian. The semicircle, identified as a bun (sic!) by academia, the glyph for T, was really the flat earth with overarching Heaven and was pronounced Tau – the Taw or Tao – or Taun, the Cut in Two, one or both hemispheres, generally the top one, since the underworld was the other half, called by the academics the Duat, but the Egyptians actually called it the Dua Taun, the Second World of the dead. The dead were reborn into it and lived there when they died out of number one. Death was like going through a doorway out of hemispheric world number one and into number two, just as Christian belief still copies. So much for the Duat. Tau meant for the Egyptians all the happenings, a temporal universe rather than our purely spatial one. These derivations have all been derived more fully in chapter 4. The Egyptian god Ptah, one of the oldest, nevertheless was not vouchsafed in front of his hieroglyph the neter or pointed axe of divinity like all the other "gods", however minor. Neter was really natura, na- meaning presenting or showing and -tura the draw or pull, showing the pull or natural force, the same word we use for nature (via Greek and Latin). The pointed axe of divinity was really a pennant blown out in the breeze, exhibiting a natural force, in this case the wind. It was the Greeks who made the Egyptian personifications of all the natural forces into godlings like their own mischief makers. It can now easily be spotted Ptah uniquely had no neter because he was really Pata-ahi (3), Our Fathers, the Egyptian ancestor god, and not a force of nature at all. Academic Egyptologists should be interested in this because until now they have been unable to solve the problem of Ptah's missing neter, and I have solved it for them by following up the meanings. That is why I keep repeating it all!

The Copts were early Egyptian Christians. Knowledge of Egyptian (Coptic) was lost when the Wahabi (6) marauders, masquerading as Muslims, killed or castrated every Egyptian who failed to speak Arabic and was caught speaking Egyptian. Reconstituted for religious purposes with the aid of Greek (which is half Egyptian) Coptic is now a mix of Egyptian and Greek, and now written in Greek letters. It is probably true both Christians and Jews had much greater connection with Egypt and owed much more of their thinking to Egyptian traditions than either religion now cares to remember. The Pharaohs (6) were pre-Jahweh (3) Semitic imperialists who brought the priceless gift of riverine irrigation technology with them to the African tribes, and then gradually went native. The cross-cultural influence of their native African subjects, darkening Semitic skins as they came to share Hamitic (6) genes, led to one of the greatest leaps forward in civilization the world has ever known, perhaps even to be compared to the taming of fire in the first place and the establishment of the first consensual civil societies around the hearth. It was an essential precursor of all modern religions which recognise a God with a personal relationship with individuals here on earth. Previously religions just preached resignation to a harsh natural order, while pagan (country bumpkin) beliefs remained immersed in primitive magic. The personal Egyptian god started out a harsh disciplinarian, although he was supposed to be Ever-Loving (A-maun), but the interpretation of His mind has become more liberal over the millennia. Nowadays His liberality is such He is thought by Christians to welcome even those sexual and marital malpractices He was previously declared to condemn. Egypt too is supposed to be the land of Ptah. It is really the land of our fathers, the father land. It all fits but it is still waitng to be accepted.

NOTES

1. Gregor Mendel an Augustinian monk and science teacher in Austria (1822-1884) bred peas and found they came in different varieties in accordance with a statistical regularity which demonstrated the segregation of individual inherited traits establishing independent inherited units, since identified as genes.

2. A metaphor is a gull. The seagull is a sea caller, like a gale of wind which wails and moans in the trees, and a miners' gala, originally a sing song. But the gull wing is shaped like the gull's, and neither wails nor moans. The mind can pick what it chooses to copy as a gull.

3. A bus is an inappropriate transfer of meaning germane to a word to an insignificant segment of it. A bus takes the case ending of an omnibus , which means for all in Latin, and calls the vehicle a for. It is a verbal convenience allowed to take precedence over reason. The mouth parts encompass bus more easily than omni and it is a neater bit. But it means that the meaning is transferred to a bit that does not really have that meaning. The reasoning which first dictated that the vowel u should be the dual vowel is obscure. Perhaps it was the inability to count at first, numeration starting out, before iteration, with just the division into two, so we sequenced the process one, and then its pair, and then both of them, instead of making the third term three. It seems pretty silly now, but it also seems it occurred. There were only three vowels to start with due to Tarzan's lazy mouth parts, aa with the mouth about middling and so the generic vowel, i (ee) as a diminutive reduplicative because that was the impression of the sound, a reduced thinner tone, and so a youngster pattern, leaving the third vowel u (oo) the inclusive with the mouth rounded, and so at the same time the dual as including the other two. You have to remember when we were learning to speak we were using naked thinking unclothed in words, so there were no safe pathways we trod repeatedly.

4. But multiplicity and multiplication from the waste (caca) is not an impossibility.

CHAPTER 6

THE PHONEME FA. FI, PHEI, FAU, FA'M

Rabbi Marc-Alain Ouaknin's "Mysteries of the Alphabet" [1] – as Professor and Director of The Aleph Center for Jewish Studies in Paris – provides a classic exposition of the aesthetic version of Lithic appreciation, which is without any of the hard graft putting real meaning into any of it, and instead indulging personal fantasy. Aleph, he declares, means ox in Semitic languages. "So in the beginning ox appeared". But did it? What actually appeared to his vulgar forebears far enough back was the animal's extraordinarily long dick. Cows were tamed early on for their milk, and the ox for his contribution to farming, treading out the corn and pulling the plough. His domestic performance therefore came under close scrutiny at an early date, and his sexual performance was at once a seven day wonder: just a whiff of a cow and the bull extrudes an astonishing length of verge swinging in the breeze. Aleph, from 'Aa-lai-pahei' is an 'Endlessly-long-wowing piece'. You do not stand in his way. Aleph can be variously interpreted of course: for instance (by the professor) as having lai-fai, smooth-puffing or breathing; but that has nothing to do with a bull, hardly notable for breathing gently. Moreover smooth breathing would leave out in the cold another seven days wonder, the elephant, from the Lithic elements ai-lai-pahei-en-tai, which is to say an animal 'with-long-cocks-of-two', one at each end, and the one at the front even more tiresomely inquisitive than the one at the rear.

Ouaknin's gloss continues: "The ox is the premier sign because it represents strength, the energy that is so important for living, for agriculture [ploughing], for transport [ox-carts], the elemental energy that sets everything in motion, which changes from being to existence". But it is not really that which appealed in the Stone Age, it was a much more earthbound dimension. He continues: "Some interpreters see the various directions [of the horns in the different developing scripts] as being symbolic as between man and the surrounding world. The horns are like antenna directed at the outside world, making it possible to capture energy and information". Further: "Where the horns point upward [Shem's original contribution!] this indicates the transcendental dimension in man's position in the world. It is the vitality of the finite, drawing his strength from the infinity of the creator, God, or the celestial powers. This relationship can be called vertical or theological. [It was the Jewish contribution]. The 90 degree turn directing the horns horizontally to the right or left indicate the change from theological to anthropological [some goy backsliding here]. Turning a full 180 degree circle [actually a half circle, Ouaknin is a rabbi not a mathematician, and a reversal is not a full circle] introduces an even more earthbound dimension" [i.e. a further vulgar one dreamed up by the goys]. Now this is certainly fanciful, making Lithic analyses by comparison look like bedrock science (which of course they are). When I look hard at Ouaknin's composition I have to say it seems to me to be interesting but ultimately all fanciful rubbish, however much I admire virtuosity.

You have to ask yourself what exactly is prompting these rabbinical whimsies. They are not wholly misguided, it is as if there were something guiding them though at one remove, and certainly not aiming for scientific rigour. This perception applies equally to Lithic language and to the Ouaknin fantasies of course. With the Lithic we can pin it down to a nascent logic with psychosemantic contents prompted for our hominid forebears by the phonemes, which they took to have natural meanings. Ouaknin's transcendental dimensions, theological vertices and anthropological horizons, per contra, hint at the hypothetical extravagances dredged up from the subconscious of the professional wrangler, rather than the word smith. It is free composition on a ground of psychic perception only: picking meanings out of the blue. Something is coming through from underneath in the subconscious, but it is by no means a full monty. The bull's formidable genitalia have disappeared completely, to be replaced by a theological fantasy of light breathing instead, so that the rabbi deserves in some ways high marks for his studied elevated sensibility, although his linguistics is ridiculous.

But it would be wrong to write him off entirely. Fossicking in the linguistic confabula there are symbolisms to be gathered. The original meanings of the Semitic Vav (our Fa) apparently for Ouaknin includes oar, hook and nail. An oar was first a rudder over the stern for steering a boat. Water in Lithic is often awa, and the agua group probably had a g smuggled in to replace a glotal stop, which then almost replaces the consonant in turn. The awa is water because water is without structure, which is consonantal; and also because if you immerse yourself in it for a time you find yourself saying Awawawa, shivering: so in a way it is the cold water speaking through you. I rather like the idea of a boy Tarzan in the Stone Age shivering when he stayed too long in the pond under a lowering sky just as I did 600,000 years later. It was he who was the hero, unable to retire to a dry towel and two squares of Cadbury's milk chocolate. Were there cow pats and duck lice in his pond too, I wonder? If he were still around I would hug him, whether or no he smelt sweet. Aua, from the Lithic elements a-u-a, can be "that-one[that]-go". Vav has the original phonemes awa-awa and the steering oar has to do with water travel surely. Hooks and nails suggest joining. A carpenter is a joiner. Carpenter in turn is perhaps from Kara-pai.en-terai, a joiner of precut pieces. But u is the dual as well as the completive substantive vowel, so Vav can perhaps be read as from the Lithic elements a-u-a-u-a "that-one-that-dual-one", in the same word family as juga, yoga and yoke, in spite of coming from different language families altogether. These are all vowel meanings and they are all in chapter 14. It is the meanings, the semántic contents, which provide the traces, (not the phonetics on their own, which academic etymologists think in terms of), one leading back to the other from the logic of the meaning descent, step after step, time after time. There is always a logic when meanings are involved.

Ouaknin's derivative meanings (which he leaves unexplained) include furthermore: phallus, pipe and finger, all three of which Lithic semantic analysis supports, as well as voice (think of Latin fari to speak, and a shower of words with meanings to match), and illuminate and shine (compare flame and pharos). He comments however "We have found no reference to these various meanings in the classic texts; neither the shape nor the etymology contain anything to justify this theory". But we have; though not in the Kabbalah, that mysterious jam pot to which he repeatedly refers, where the vertical line of vav is "the sign of the descent of divine energy downward, a meeting point between the transcendence of humans and the immanence of God". Ah well! Vav also, apparently "represents the various conduits by means of which the body can receive from the outside and exchange with the outside, thus the vav may represent the esophagus, the trachea, the artery [which one? There are several after all] or the spine in which nutritional and respiratory energy circulate [Oh! This is getting spooky!], as do the nerve pulses. It is also the male genitalia that permit coitus and build life based on the encounter". So is he (subconsciously?) on to the Egyptian wowing piece, pa hei, phi in Greek, at one remove?

Chapter 6 Fa

A phallus is a pahai which has got lau, roughly that is inflated into a loop shape as in chapter 8. It actually refers to the glans not the whole penis. A pipe is a pipi or quail chick in Egyptian because pan pipes peep like game chicks, and even a dumb drain pipe inherits the configuration as a gull. Finger can be read as Phai-en-kara, penis-of-the stimulater, a coarse description of its possible use certainly, but quite a good pointer to the primitive mind. It shows where the lewd and licencious soldiery when they get together get their lewdness and licenciousness from. The pahai carried across to the fair sex also, including their genital area too. Pa can be a pipe or a patch as well as a piece.

Of course nobody disputes the letter A started out as old long cock's head with the two horns sticking out of it. His original genital trademark at his rear end was a refractory glyph because of its shape and orientation. Horns were neater. An alphabet needs letters that occupy roughly similar spaces. In Egypt they had glyphed the human phallus, but then it was a comparatively neat job compared with the bovine version; and it was pronounced "mai" (the implanter) or "pahei" (the joy piece), the Greek phi (Φ), originally with the verge entering the circle rather than just laid across it, the symbolisation at the outset matching the phonetics and semantics and merely garbled later. This is yet one more case of the explicitness of Scrimshaw man followed up by Wayland's obfuscation. But alphabets represent a major advance in conventional thinking, dumping yesterday's mental pabulum and freeing the mind to attend to the job in hand, in the case of copyists an easy running hand, ignoring the original semantics in the pattern. It was speaking, we must remember, which first presented the possibility of this kind of public code. Finding meanings for sounds, propagating these meanings and carrying them forward in the public domain was the birth of convention, which has expanded unceasingly ever since. Now we call it culture and seek to trim up the convention wherever it pinches.

A glance at the psychosemantic tree for Fa on page 103 shows quite a complex and heterogeneous phonetic tree but a relatively simple semantic one. That is not to say there is not a lot of language using the Fa phoneme. On the contrary it gets more than its fair share of use, perhaps because of the subconscious psychic pull of the male genitalia. The Egyptian Pahei is in the top row of the psychosemantic tree at (3) because of its power. It meant originally the orgasmic piece (as laid out in chapter 7) quite like the joy stick world war one pilots grasped between their legs to keep their plane flying straight and level. The orgasm was always amongst the ephemera (17), from the Greek epi-hemera from the Lithic ai-pai-hei-mai-rai, as is-the penis-climaxing-impregnating-verbal. A Greek Ouaknin has tidied the ai-pahei-mai-rai to epi-mai-Ra, or ai-pai-mai-ra in Lithic, as it-goes-of [= to] death-of the sun, or perhaps better that which-covered or bounded-by the sinking-of the sun. So hemera is the day in Greek, noted for its ephemeral quality, a character originally cribbed from the orgasm.

Pharaoh, who evidently supposed the royal penis was of divine parentage, had his own cover cut off so as not to have his god Amun-Ra, the Eternally Planting or Ever Loving god Ra, the Eye in the sky, demeaned by having to wait for rays from any passing houri to start him off. The Egyptian rays are fully covered in chapter 12 for Ra. Or else he thought by exposing his phalus to Ra - the sun, the light, the ray source – He would come for his acorn and draw it out, just as He did for all the plants that grow. Pharaoh is conventionally translated House of Ra or Royal House. But that would not be a Pha-rau but a Pa-Rau, a roof or skin covering (5,8) against the sun's rays, a sun shade, originally a goat skin tent in the desert; whence the Greek polis, where the pa is still the skin roof as shade against the rays of Ra but the -lai is a loop indicating a collection of roofs, the city and thence the city state with police. We can not easily distinguish ray from raise since Egyptian rai meant

Chapter 6 Fa

both. Pahei (15) is unquestionably Egyptian for penis, the ecstacy piece, and "Pharaoh", from Pahei-Ra-au-hei, can also be translated as Royal Penis or Penis in which Ra rejoices, or even Penis-[of] Ra-Ever-Orgasmic, a Royal Super Stud, or all three. Anyway he wasn't waiting for his muzzle cover to be withdrawn by the ta-rays of any passing houri. The proactive monarch cut it off. He had no proper job to keep him out of mischief. The Semitic races have joined the party ever since, as if it were their divinity and not Ra with whom the original circumcision deal was done. Abraham from Aba-Ra-ham is a trimmed and tidied up translation of Ra-hai-em, Ra-rejoicing-in, with Aba as genetrix, father. The semantic pattern is virtually a doublet with John, from Johannes, from Iau-ha-nai, Jaweh-pleasure/grace-shows, but for Ra not Jaweh.

But first of all Fa is clearly a puff (1), half way to a sibilant. A continuous fff was originally more likely to be recognised as a hiss. It is also quite close to Ba and Bha which were identified ab initio as lip plosives. There is a lip plosive element in Fa but it uses the top teeth too. Its analysis as ph, made up of p h, is significant and at the same time quite difficult to understand. Pa and Ha put together phonetically do not make Fa or anything like it. But put together dialectically they do, since Pa is a stop and Ha its opposite: the breath is not stopped and may continue as an aaa ad nauseam. This may seem a silly analysis to us, based on a somewhat slender identification of the phonetics involved, but we are dealing with our silly hominid forebears remember, for whom this kind of ratiocination was taxing in the extreme. The dialectical synthesis Fa is a consonantal stop which at the same time is not a stop but a fine filter for the breath and thus a hybrid or synthesis of the two, retaining the semantic undertones of the two supposed prior constituents and a slice of the sibilant phoneme too. That is the dialectic for you.

Every utterance comes with a controlled expulsion of breath, every phoneme accompanied by a puff, variously modulated. So in a sense every puff may be thought of as a phoneme; and it is phonemes (7) (and their meanings) which have built into words. It is necessary to say this several times as it is no part of understanding current epistemology. In the same sense every puff may be thought of as a word. Speaking is uttering a sequence of puffs - think of spreche in German – admittedly quite variously modulated. If a sentence has too many words in it you run out of puff and have to pause for breath. So to puff is to speak and that is the meaning of fari in Latin, with the –ari suffix just the verbal marker. You spit out your utterances, a sudden cry is even an ejaculation, the same term used for down below. In English fate (from the Latin) (5) is what has been decreed for you, a divine statement of your curriculum vitae, like it or lump it. To date it has always included a fated fatality, as if the mortality of human kind were fatal, as indeed it is. The Greek is pheme (4), a saying, from the Doric phanai to speak (puff-presenting), with the Greek offering also phonein to utter, leading to phone (7) a sound, uttered or other, but mostly uttering, as with the telephone over a long distance, and of course a phoneme with the –eme probably just a mass or lump. When we come to look more closely at the phonemic structure of speak and spreche (4), s-pai-a-kai and s-pai-rai-khai respectively, we can see there is another sense in there as well as just puffing: action-pieces-that-[in a]row-joins or action-pieces-that-[in a]row-makes. Speech is the stringing of pieces in a row. It is the combinatorial novelty which makes the build up of meanings posible, and it is that which got our hominid forebears thinking to some purpose. The stop sounds (consonants) made this posible.

Partridge relates all these words to an original *Bhami, I speak. The asterisk means KV (cave! in Latin: watch out!) he may be just making it up, as it is not recorded. There is no doubt however that lip and tongue, Ba and La, go to make up the idea of speaking around

Chapter 6 Fa

the world while the ph phoneme means to ejaculate or throw out or spit or puff. Try Bal in Queensland, an aboriginal coinage for speaking, bolna in Hindi or lingua in Latin. The lips are really just fleshy and the tongue first of all the taster, both prior to any verbage. Phone, originally an utterance, is now used for any sound. The –nai phoneme has the very early meaning of to put forward or present, with no prizes for guessing it was the joy stick that was first perceived as pushing forward and presenting, as is fully explained in chapter 11. In English an infant (6) is an under aged person legally unqualified to testify, a non speaker, including the infantry joining as young boys, or anyway taught to just do and die without any right to speak. The Latin flare (1) to puff, where fari (2) is to speak, adds in the la phoneme bringing with it the notion of overflowing and flowing, the instinct of liquids to flow into the lows (chapter 8 on La), flatulence linking to that other puff the fart (1), and inflation to the Latin follis (1), the bellows; as Eric Partridge puts it all "ultimately echoic", like much of Lithic. A flavour too is from the old French flaar, an odour. A flare is a different ray (of light) – it has fa for the puff. Even the finch (4) or spink (2) is an utterer in its own way, and the humble puffball if you press it puffs its own kind of pollen just like the puffer we are now coming to in the following paragraph.

A puff can convey the sense be off, and you find it in flit and flee and fly and fleet of foot as well as in aerial flight. Birds fly when approached, they flit and take flight or fly away. The fly is fly and can fly so quickly you need to use a mesh to swat him, upsetting his response to the pressure wave so he leaves too late. Both flow and fly use la for the smooth kind of movement of liquids as their la instinct takes effect and they slip away into the lows: see chapter 8.

The rest of Fa is most readily treated principally under the Greek phi rubric, from the Ancient Egyptian pahei (3). Half the Greeks lived in Egypt in classical times, and most of the educated ones. Perhaps half Greek is closely related to Egyptian, a Semitic tongue. There must therefore be a suspicion Greek philosophy and thereafter Western civilisation received its first major input from these Egyptian Semites who had acquired an African colony – probably on the strength of their riverine agricultural skills which they had themselves learned from the Sumerians who came from Malaya and kept their foreskins (3) on, just as the Semitic Akkadians who captured Sumer probably did in those days before they got to Egypt. When they captured Sumer the Akkadians were still at the primitive beduin stage, bai-dau-in, travelling-born-ones, born on the hoof, goat herdsmen in fact on the light soils of what is today the Arabian desert. The Sumerians were refugees from the South China Sea, the Eden garden flooded 360 feet deep when the final big circumpolar ice melt raised sea levels that much, between eight and ten thousand years before the present. It means that Adam was not a Semite after all. The Akkadians borrowed him from the Sumerians after they captured Sumer, along with most else they knew. So for example ka in Sumerian meant mouth and the Sumerians called their cats ka-tse, mouth-spitters or spit-mouths. Akkadian for mouth was pu and they called their pussies spit mouths too, pu-tse in their language. I leave it to others to trace the etymologies of these 'pussy cats' as we call them over the intermediate five thousand years or so. The Latins picked up the same feline defiance with felis for cat, from phai-lai-sai in Lithic elements, spit-lye-acting, another spit mouth. The Egyptian term for their cat goddess, or natural essence of cat was Bast, properly pronounced Ba-Siti, girly bum or ladylike gait, a dainty stepper. They clearly entertained pet cats where the earlier barbarians thought of wild ones. The Egyptians indirectly emphasise the softness and gentleness of the feline paw, omitting to mention the sharp claws which enable it to tear

Chapter 6 Fa

the flesh. We may note the West has taken up the idioms of the barbarians though without understanding them at all.

Who the Adamites were perhaps we shall never know. There is a smidgeon of evidence that (like the Chinese) they spoke a language closer to Malay than any other. It was markedly different from Akkadian, the earliest Semitic tongue of which we have any record. Research may yet discover Chinese is now the nearest tongue to Adam's, and nigh on ten thousand years of Westward migrations, all prompted by the sea level changes which heavily punished the low lying Eastern (Eden) Garden land, has skewed our historical perspective and kept us looking towards the sunset, and heading that way, instead of towards our origins as speakers. The Garden of Eden was an irrigated paddi garden, not a flower garden at all.

It would be unkind to say the Chinese after starting out so promisingly have lagged behind a bit since then, but it is probably true. There is no royal road to progress, it is a haphazard affair which perhaps can not be planned for at all. A plan could help. But we are proven bad choosers, usually pressing forward firmly in the wrong direction. The Chinese uniquely retain the Lithic idiom of recognised word structure made up of strings of individual meaningful phonemes. The combinations often appear fanciful now due to meaning drift over the aeons, but the surprising thing is surely the degree they still fit together meaningfully. So long as the structure is recognised it holds the meaning in a headlock, retarding the semantic explosion which occurs when words are randomised. You even have to be something of a savant to have all the meanings at your finger tips. In China, when wrangling, you may even have to paint a meaning to make sure your interlocutor has picked the right elementary meanings available to string together correctly.

At the height of the Egyptian cultural dominance in the Mediterranean and Middle East their language was the Lingua Franca for the whole of the Mediterranean litoral. There may even have been colonial places in Britain with provincial Egyptian speakers. Some place names can be read in Egyptian. If so they did not survive the Celtic invasions. The Celts were head hunters with a yen for human brains for dinner, as well as some rather unhygienic habits when it came to displaying the heads they had cut in niches on either side of their front doors. They must have hummed a bit until the flesh had rotted off. You did not last long if they captured you. Your brains were for the pot. The heads were still outside their front doors when they reached Britain. Of course this was a very long time ago and there is very little trace left today of their former predisposition.

Hei as well as extreme pleasure could indicate extreme pain, shock or distress. Hot was a cry of pain on being burned. "Ho!" will convey to an infant, that is someone not yet speaking, the idea that touching something is painful. You put your hand towards the kettle and let out a "Ho!", and for good measure pull a face. For practical purposes you are back in the Stone Age. So it is of interest to us examining the origin of language to find it works. The phoneme really carries the psychosemantic content of sudden overwhelming shock, whether it is a nasty burn or an orgasm or any other shocking circumstance anywhere in between, like hurting or horror, or even humour which is another sudden surprise after being led up the garden path. But it is all fully covered in chapter 7 for Ha. Here we are solely concerned with the genitalia and the ecstasy or extreme pleasure to be obtained from that quarter. The Greek phuein (11) to engender may open the batting. It is related to the Greek phusis whence we get our physical, from Greek phusikos. Phusis is conventionally translated as nature, but it was a more proactive term than just the way natural events unfolded. It was the scheme by which natural, ie vegetable and animal, development took place. In the Stone Age when we were learning to speak there was no

Chapter 6 Fa

THE PSYCHOSEMANTIC TREE FOR FA

The Phonetic Tree

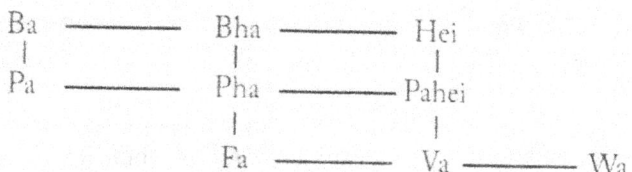

The Semantic Tree

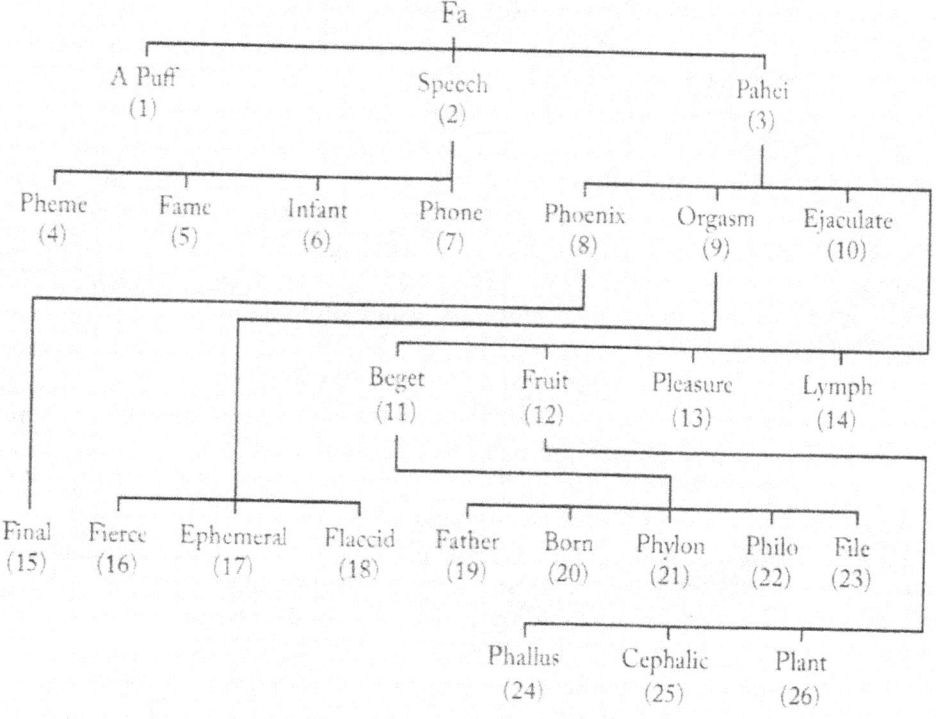

Chapter 6 Fa

separate nature that did not go the same way as we did. Plato and Aristotle debated the matter somewhat later at length. We can now follow them up. We can start by remarking once more the debt of Greek thinking to Ancient Egyptian. Phusis was from Phu-sai-s - in Egyptian, or indeed in Lithic. Sai can confidently be read as action, even as the system of action. We are well into the era of abstractions. The Egyptian pahei is in there, with a substantiating u vowel too. We can read phusis as the procreative scheme, animal and vegetative together. The final s is probably no more than a final Greek substantiating ending. The fact is it should really be translated as biology rather than physics today. We thought in our own terms. Separating out the basic physical substrate, electromagnetism, IT and all that, came thousands of years later, only the other day.

There is a well enough known four letter word in English which in Ancient Egyptian is to be read as making (perhaps literally striking as when flint knapping) with the pahei, pa-hai-kai in original Lithic elements, shortened to pha-k in English (10). So far as I know this is an entirely original etymology for this rather rude boys' word which has (until quite recently, long since I grew up), generally been ignored as impolite, which of course it is, since it covers an area with heightened emotional content with not so much as a nod to the emotional side, instead treating it as a crude physical phenomenon merely, just like making anything else. Folk have naturally dumbed down and fallen into the habit of using the word, almost as a badge of street cred, as they abandon any idea of emotional worth and treat our finest feeling as readily dismissed, mocking marriage as if they were just apes, or anyway all of them Wayland Smiths in person. Ka got its creative semantics indeed from the making of flint tools, since the phoneme Ka was first identified as echoic of the clink of flint on flint, as the shaping took place. The background is all in chapter 4. In Latin facere means to make, originally from making babies, a bit of penial knapping, but that is forgotten. The English make is a special case, originally pounding a mass into shape, like kneading dough, or more likely shaping clay. Homo faber (11) was a handy man or maker and a fabric is what has been made. Further off, a fact is what is composed, a statement put together to give a definite outline to belief rather than to a flint chipped to shape.

The Pharaoh of Egypt had a royal phallus (24), in fact Ra's, and Ra was the supreme god. It was also exposed and visible. The Egyptologists' idea that it was his house that was royal is the result of confusing pa with pahei; in Ancient Egyptian a parai, a skin of the sun, a parasol or sun shade parrying the sun's rays was a house, originally a goat skin tent named for the shelter it provided in the desert in the heat of the day rather than the warmth at night. But a pahei was the joy piece. Sir Wallis Budge apparently started this confusion between a Pharaoh and a Paraoh in 1921, with his splendid two volume dictionary of hieroglyphs, in two thousand pages of pictures, never again attempted afresh. Of course in 1921 you would have been putting yourself out of the running for a knighthood descanting on royal penises, however long ago. Ra was the World Eye, the sun looking down on His creation, bent at first on keeping everyone in order, but then actually seeding the idea Christianity adopted a few millennia later that even the sparrow's fall was of concern to Him in the sky, which kept him looking. In Egyptian ra meant eye at the same time as Ra meant the World Eye, and rai meant raying or being rayed, seeing or being seen, rising or being raised, growing or being grown. Latin res, translated as thing, is res vista, a phenomenon in our terms, from fancy which is from Greek phantazein, in turn from phanein to show. Na is to protrude and present, see chapter 9, where what was originally presented is derived. But here you are told anyway, Egypt's pahei once again. The sun sent out rays which returned to the sun, radar fashion, pulling up the plants with them. The animal eye similarly sent out rays which returned to the eye bringing back

104

Chapter 6 Fa

pictures only, which arrived on the iris (the irradiated), where they could be seen by the mannikin behind the eye.

The Pharaoh's royal phallus was visible because he had cut off his prepuce (from peri-pu-ti, which is 'around-the penis-teat' or glans). Peri, in Egyptian and then in Greek, is from pa-i-Ra-i in Lithic, skin-of-Ra-of, which is the sun's periphery, which goes around the sun in a circle, and so by metaphor it means anything that goes around the periphery of anything. The thinking is somethingg like this: "Hey! If you want to know how I'm thinking, think of the skin of the sun as you look at it, it runs all the way around the edge. Got it? Well my idea is the same: anything going all the way around something else is sun-skinning". Pharaoh's idea when he took a knife to his foreskin was probably to remove his muzzle cover so that he could project the rays supposedly emerging from his glans at the female and pull the ladies in his harem whenever he felt like it, instead of having to wait for the mood to arise and his piece be readied as a result of a feminine ray launched from a vagina confronting it, withdrawing his muzzle cover for him, and pulling out and up his glans, willy nilly, enabling it to respond by raying back. This science of the day was preached by the priests of Amun, Aa-Mau'n, The Ever Loving One, religion in those days being regarded as the same as science. So it would have been the priests who briefed Pharaoh on matters genital and will have advised him of the benefits of circumcision as an aphrodisiac measure, and even wielded the knife for him, much as religious practitioners with circumcising religions still do today, although the genital science has moved on, leaving the practice as just a symbolic mutilation by way of a contract with the deity, and now not Ra any more but Jahweh or Allah. Jesus was a Jew and will surely have lost his foreskin as a boy, but the Christian God does not require it. The raoh in Pharaoh is Lithic rai-au-ahi, raying everywhere and always, a dialectical verge befitting a supreme being, and a propensity only available if the essential modification of the commoner's pristine configuration of his genitalia has been effected with the knife. Rameses, from Ra-mai-sai, Ra-planted/impregnated-life, Ra's son, ought not to be kept waiting.

Who planted the life – seed is from sai-dai in Lithic, life-giver or life-giving - in the case of Moshe, the biblical Moses, is not made clear in the record. Probably it was Iauai or Jaweh, rather badly transliterated as Jehovah, first cousin of Jove and Jupiter or Jau-pater, Father Jahwe. Joseph, Iau-seph, with a sai-pahei, was evidently circumcised, sai-pahei is glans visible; and the –ai also hints at eternal as well, especially if we add it to the Iau-, making Iau-ai, Jehovah, with the circumcised penis right in the middle. By his day it appears to have been a badge of office at Pharaoh's court, like an order of nobility at court today, or anyway a cross between that and the Japanese Yakusa's pinky (severed top joint of one finger as badge of membership). The British Museum has a splendid statue of a pharaoh proudly showing off his circumcised and protruding penis. It is hard to think of his reasoning in any other way than as described. We do not know what relationship there was between him and Abraham, Aba-Ra-ham the biblical author of the foreskin trick, but now that it is known that the Pharaohs were Semites speaking a Semitic language, if much intermixed with the Hamitic tongues of their black subjects (as were their genes from concubinage), it is not so far fetched to have their Jewish cousins copying the pharaohs. But Aba is father and hai is rejoicing, so the biblical Abraham appears to have been in with Father Ra, just as somewhat later Johannes was Iau-ha-nai: Iauai (Jehovah the dialectical god now)-pleasure-showing, or shows pleasure (by vouchsafing a successful birth, the birth name acknowledging the obligation to Him).

Chapter 6 Fa

We can now deal with the Phoenician Phoenix group which Partridge was unable to crack. It involves Greek Phoinix, a date palm; and the Egyptian Pount, (really Pountai from Pau-u-nau-tai) "a collective name for the Semites of the Eastern Mediterranean hinterland", Latin Poeni, the Carthaginians, Carthaginian is Punic, the magic Phoenix bird, and the Greek phoinos for blood red or purple. For which Partridge says "The semantic succession and interaction are obscure. The date palm, the bird and the colour purple or scarlet senses of Greek Phoenix all follow naturally from Phoenix, a Phoenician; and Phoenix could be an –ix derivation of phoinos, blood red, purple if the Phoenicians were so named because they wore purple or scarlet robes. Probably, however Greek Phoenikes, Phoenicians represents, as Boisacq suggests, the influence of Greek phoenos, blood red, purple, on Egyptian Pount, a collective name for the Semites of the Eastern Mediterranean hinterland". The Queen of Sheba, it may be remembered, allied Sheba with the land of Punt. We have a Phoenician tree, a Phoenician bird, the Phoenicians themselves, and Semites labelled Pount, and some purple as yet unallocated; which we must now sort out.

The palm like the pine has a bare trunk, and the palm has the leaves in a bunch on top. Two very fine ones are only two hundred yards from where I write, believed some 80 years old and some seventy feet tall although their trunks are no more than eighteen inches in diameter. They tower to the leaf tufts on top which are quite small and neat. It was a Phoenician tree only in the sense that its growing habit matched the habit of the Pount, in Lithic analysis Pu-nai-tai, the Penes-exposed-cut ones, the circumcised tribes of the Eastern Mediterranean hinterland. The Lithic embedded in phoenix, a Phoenician is paha-u-ai-nai-kai (s), paha-one-that which-exposed-made (substantive ending). Pahai or pa-hei is the ecstacy or rapture piece, pleasure organ or penis in Egyptian, or otherwise in Egyptian mai, the earther/planter/inseminator. These tribes were not dressed in red or purple. Far from it! Phoinos, blood red or purple, was the colour of their pahai or glans when nai (orgasmic), which invited ever so slightly snide comment in their case because of their comical custom of cutting off their foreskins exposing the glans as if wanting to show it off. It may even have referred subtly to the belief behind the practice, borrowed from the Pharaohs, that it gave them an edge on the girls by enabling them, with muzzle covers off, to fire their imagined sexual attractant rays first, without having to wait for the girls to draw out their shooter, the glans. That would surely have raised a few smiles from amongst the powerful Jewish Momas. Indeed it may have been the conceit of the Pharaohs' belief that they were the divine penises on earth of their father the sun (Amun, aa-mau'n, for ever ejaculating [light] and so also for ever loving, and so with some claim to starting off the perception of an ever loving God who valued even the sparrow's fall), and which got them their phoinei sobriquet from the pagan goys: who themselves were happy with what nature provided them, and enjoyed orgiastic revels on a regular basis. It is hard not to side with acceptance and turn against mutilation, for whatever reason. The "circumcision" of women, which involves cutting out the clitoris or feminine penis altogether, rather than merely cutting round the male penis, and then stitching up the vagina to prevent penetration is a scandal like genocide but leading to longer torture, a savagery which can not be excused. It is atavistic pagan male savagery and in a modern civilised world must be stamped out and its proponents heavily punished. It has nothing to do with Allah the All Merciful or with Islam. As a subsequent pagan accretion it is not in the Koran. Punishment should perhaps fit the crime: the complete excision of the male penis for all those involved.

The word purple is of similar slightly off colour derivation since the l in the word started out an r. An r is just a trilled l, with the part of the tongue making contact with the

Chapter 6 Fa

palate only marginally further back. The Old English was purpure and the Old French purpre, with the earlier Latin purpura, a purple dye from a fish called unsurprisingly purpura, the purple fish. The derivation of the colour as well as of the fish is "of obscure origin" according to Partridge – as well he might fancy. The Lithic elements when identified say pu-rai-pu-rai, that is to say penis-roused-glans-raying, where the second rai can be read as indicating colour, since it was supposed to be conveyed to the eye by a ray. (It is). The glans of the male penis at this time is flushed red with blood and it is actually purple around the rim, as was probably common knowledge in the old unreformed uninhibited Old Stone Age when language first began, and we must assume close inspection of a neighbour's erect genitalia was as common as muck. Young Tarzan was probably showing it off in fact, as an advertisement to all comers. Moreover the fact is the rim remains light purple even when the penis is flaccid; and there were not any other purple coloured phenomena to direct Tarzan's attention to when the naming committees came to pick a name for purple. It can now be seen the metaphor was then applied to the fish with a tincture used as a dye that matched the purple colour; and the colour is not after all taken from the name of the fish, which had not actually already been named purple on a casual random basis, for no reason at all; but on the contrary from purpure, the color of the rim of the male glans, which was then applied to the fish which produced a colour which matched the rim of the glans in colour. The purple fish joins the sepia or cuttle fish which when pursued jets away behind a sepia cloud it squirts out and in this case is named for its performance, and the colour is gulled from that. The Lithic is si-pia or brer pisser, and it is the colour which is the gull from the colour of the fish's discharge. Fishermen enjoy a joke - the bawdier the better. They live their lives on the ocean wave, jockeying with an over powerful medium. It gives them a hearty appetite for life and a readiness to laugh at themselves, and their private parts and behaviours. The purple and sepia jokes must surely be very old ones indeed, going back hundreds of thousands of years. Well you would remember them. What about a Phoenix tree with a seventy foot penis?

The story of the magic phoenix bird is clearly an allegory, that is the story is otherwise than what it appears to be on the surface and has a concealed meaning, mutatis mutandis teaching a moral lesson or truth, or even being presented as a riddle to be solved. Chambers Dictionary of Etymology describes the phoenix as "the mythical bird that burns itself and rises from its own ashes. It is from the Greek phoinix......The Greek word can not be related with the unrelated word phoinos red with blood and phonos murder". What sense can be made of this?

Lithic suggests that the phoenix bird the ancients had in mind was the pippit or better the Egyptian quail chick pipi, which the Egyptians farmed for the table. They discovered the quail chicks always said pipi, and never a single peep. In point of fact the young of all game birds have this same habit, and though I have not followed chickens around to see if they do too, it appears they were anyway supposed to be sinmilarly habituated since in French they are known as pul (spelt poule). Shepherds playing their pan pipes (in Arcadia - "Et in Arcadia ego") - made a piping noise like a chick, so their pipes were known as chicks (pipi). The Egyptian genius fancied every animal and bird had as part of its heritage a knowledge, or was at least an illustration, of some natural principle – all their hundreds of animal headed 'gods' were really personifications of natural forces and had a 'natura' symbol before their glyphs, a triangular pennant blown out in the wind, Lithic na-tau-rai, showing the tau ray, the pull or natural - originally sexual - attractive force, in this case of the wind, which draws air and pennants out together, the pennant exhibiting the force, which for reasons never explained the academic Egyptologists have identified as a pointed

Chapter 6 Fa

axe of divinity (sic!), probably to illustrate their prior misconception these forces were godlings like the Greek mischief makers.

The chick, since it always cheeped in twin cheeps, was supposed to be equipped with one principle it acknowledged and displayed, namely that everything came in pairs. Really they don't. But this was already the belief of the Egyptians who had worked up a theory of a vowel dialectic presented in chapter 13 which comically enough, as we can nowadays see (since the collapse of the Marxist dialectic), they thought was a law of nature. Ideas came in pairs which combined in dual terms. Their original dialectic was an invention (misconceived as it happens) in the Ancient Egyptian mind, with the three vowels a, i and u (see chapter 13) the original vowel dialectic, later revised by Socrates, or else by Plato who attributed it to Socrates, as the Socratic Method. How far it actually went back before that is quite unknown, but perhaps hundreds of millennia to when you could get away with counting "one, two, both of them" in place of a legitimate one, two, three and so on. U was the third term in the series: a dialectical tria juncta in uno. Of the three vowels, a and i were the first and second, parents if you like; and u was the resultant completive, the child if you like, which grew up to out-top its parents as the dual or completive and substantiating vowel. Replicating this prehistoric (and pretty mad) pattern provides the Marxist pattern, like a chain mail of coat hangers, the proper pattern of the World, according to Marx, as well as of thinking. It was Hegel who was responsible for resurrecting this Lithic miasma, the dialectic, where opposition provides the link and the synthesis: unsupported whimsy in place of mathematics. (It is demolished and abolished for the first time in chapter 15 on thinking).

Much of these matters is in other chapters but it is brought together here to explain the phoenix group. This 'vowel oon' or dialectic was the reason for the quail chick which said pipi, the two peeps being named pu, the dual pi, and then used as the hieroglyph to stand for the vowel u. Pa meant 'that' or 'the' in Egyptian, and there was at the same time some uncertainty whether the second and third vowels, i and u, should be treated as new sounds on their own or as glosses on the 'original' and basic one, aaa, the daddy of the three; and so whether the i was really to be regarded as ai and the u as au, (now the dipthongs e and o). So pa-u said 'the u' in Egyptian, and consequently the quail chick glyph, from piping pipi, making pu or pau, was used as the hieroglyph for the vowel u. (Academic Egyptologists seem to think that the quail chick uttered "Wai!" rather than pipi and so was used for w). But it is most likely that since these academics saw no need for any reason for the use of any sound to represent any symbolisation, because the selection is supposed to be random, they just accepted what appeared without putting it to the torture to see what they could discover. Anyway it was a miss by a mile.

A pan pipe could be gulled for any similar sized and shaped item and it is not hard to guess the organ they immediately picked upon, which does not pipe or whistle at all, just as a gull wing is not a sea calling wing but just an aircraft wing the same shape as the caller's, and does not itself call at all. The Latin penis is from pai-nai-s (substantive), the protruding or presenting pipe (or witness piece). The Egyptian is pa-hei or ecstacy piece, the male phallus. (For substantiation of pa meanings see chapter 11, for hei meanings see chapter 7). The phallus referred originally to the glans on the top of the penis, supposedly the seat of orgasm. The double l may even be relict of an original pa-hei-la-lu, picking up both the linear (extending) and looping (swelling) of the engorged organ.

We are now in a position to explore the allegory of the phoenix. It reads in Lithic, still probably semi-conscious in Egyptian times, (and of course subconscious still even now) pa-hei-au-ai-nai-kai-(s), the penis-that one-that which-orgasmic-[when] kindled-

Chapter 6 Fa

(substantive suffix). To substantiate this you also need to know something of the Egyptian rays of chapter 12, based on the rays of the sun (Ra) which were taken to be emanations of fire. It is unfortunate this precedes the chapters in which the background of some of the elements involved are explained. It may well become clearer and less presumptive later. It really involves reading the whole book through twice; but that is asking rather a lot. Getting rayed could be from the flames of the hearth at night as well as from the greater flames of the sun by day. Sex rays were inflamation by the fire element in animals including man. It was not that the sexual experience was actually thought of as burning, but it was identified as an avatar of what it was to catch fire, flare up and burst into flame. It was a weak element of fire which also provided the normal warmth of the body; and orgasm was a flare up. It was that simple. From the ashes of last night's experience the pipi or pahei - the phoenix bird - was reborn, again and again, ready for another flare up. The flight of the Phoenix bird was an allegory for sexual intercourse. To fly up and flare up were akin. The etymology was supposed to be science.

The Pount, the Semites of the Eastern mediterranean hinterland were really pu-nai-tai, the glans-exposed-cut/become/tribe (see chapter 4 for tai). The Carthaginians were Poeni, their language Punic, they were Phoenicians, from the Lithic Pahai-au-ai-nai-kai or people with Phalluses-all-that which-exposed-[had been] made, the folk with the bared phalluses, circumcised folk, Semites bidding for imperial conquests based upon their undoubted skill as seamen. In Carthaginian also, Canary comes from Ka-en-aria, Land of rocks or Rocky islands. Petra, Greek, a rock is a piece (pai) -tai-arai, become-raised or drawn up. The idea of the kan-aria was of a piece of the rocky core of the earth which had been drawn up to the surface, where it was exposed[4]. It was Pliny the Elder (who foolishly insisted on stopping behind and was killed by poison gases when Etna erupted and buried Pompei, and his son fled by boat without him) who made up the tale about the Canary islands being the doggy isles, from Latin canis for dog. It was spin to conceal the Carthaginian achievement. But canis is third declension and doggy islands would have been Canery Isles. Moreover the pooches on the island are nondescript and insignificant in size and numbers. His fib lasted two thousand years until the Carthaginian origins of the topographical nomenclature of the islands was recognised. The canary bird was first found in the islands. It was a dull grey green but sang well. In the eighteenth century in Germany they were able to breed from a sport with yellow plumage, and now they are pale yellow to tangerine in colour. They still sing but after two centuries kept in small cages perhaps have lost some of their enthusiasm for life and now sing less than in the wild. Singing is often to let the nesting hen know all is well.

The phoenix (8) started out as the palm tree, as above. The adjectival mind saw the same patterns widely displayed in different circumstances, and some patterns appear to have been strongly imprinted on the primitive mind. The leaves when they die hang down in a dead brown mass (one outside my window as I write), where the birds nest, just as the animal manifestation, after its ejaculation, hangs down too. Planted close together and fired the trees flare up and burn off the leaves, leaving the trees otherwise unharmed. The nests of the birds nesting in the trees however are destroyed, including any young in their nests. The parent phoenix birds then lay another clutch – symbolising life after death, and that will do for an audience attuned to think at any opportunity in terms of sexual metaphor. They thought in terms of sex rather as water runs down hill. It helps if you have at one time been a schoolboy, however long ago, if you want to follow the vulgarity of our primitive forebears' minds. Our earliest aim was to master expletives as mischiefs rather than to understand, and even today the youth of the nation take sex to be an opportunity for mischief and blaspheming, rather than as any challenge for their understanding. How does psychology explain this? It surely betrays a tension brought on by sex. After all the survival of the species, fit and unfit together, has depended for many millions of years upon this sexual mischief, if mischief it is. Without it nobody survives.

The original idiom of the adjectival mind is explained in chapter 15 on thinking. There was a sense in which the penis and the palm tree had this commonality of character, expressed each in its own quite different way in their animal and vegetable kingdoms: the shared protocol an adjectival character to be found all over, intelligently picked up in the language. With pahei the priests were copying the mischief of the marketplace. It was the joy piece or ecstacy shoot. So the Phoenix which started out a tree became a bird and was then transmogrified into a penis, a rather more subtle string of connections than with the Phoenix tree which merely shared its erectile character and perhaps its efflorescence at the top with the male organ (if you wanted to think that way - as clearly we did). The fire it dies in and is then resurrected is the little death, the orgasm – with a sentient intensity like the flame but of opposite polarity, pleasurable not painful. Just as a tuft of palm leaves could emulate an ejaculation in the minds of our hominid forebears, so the sexual experience could be matched to a fire flaring up, flickering and then bursting into an all consuming blaze. Nobody ever imagined they were actually burning when they copulated. But they thought they were experiencing the same qualititive sequence as the flame, pleasure in a shared protocol with pain, a contrasting pair; a dialectical relationship in fact, thesis and antithesis, and that for them was science, spotting the common patterns in the world and coding them – much like today in fact. No doubt they picked on the motifs they liked to think about, much as (it is popularly argued) scientific research programmes today are environmentally determined, that is to say mediated by the social constraints present in the scientists' minds as they determine them.

The Latin for boy is puer, a piper, his voice unbroken. A pipi, two pi, made a pu, the u vowel was dual. The Malay for such a one's small penis is a sparrow, puzzling until you know the Malay for a sparrow is pipit from pipi-tai, or cheeper. The Finns from Finland however at first sight seem to destroy this Phoenix analysis. They live far too far North to be exposing their genitalia and they were not circumcised. Tacitus had them as Fenni and Ptolemy as Phinnoi. We must fall back on a reluctance to drop their trousers to urinate because of the cold, instead fitting themselves out with flapped codpieces, which struck Greeks and Romans, alike in more flowing garb, as highlighting their genitalia, so they called them exhibitionists when their instinct was in fact for minimum exposure because of the cold.

A fin is a pai-nai, a protruding piece on the back of a fish, which is from the Latin piscis, which in turn is from pais-kais, from pai-sai-kai-sai, foot-action-body-action: it gets along pretty well by just waggling its body without any proper limbs or feet for the job. Its fins are related to pins (protruding pieces) and Latin penna, a wing, an extended surface, made of feathers, which in turn matches quite well the Greek for wing, petera, from pai-tai-rai, a surface terai, drawn up and along by nature, as if it had a kind of sky hook, just as the boys at one time believed themselves drawn up and out by the ta-ray or T-ray the girls emitted. It supposedly had the propensity to call up the males in pursuit of sex by means of an invisible ray. The conventional derivations of vagina and vanilla are from the Latin meaning a sheath or a pod. The vanilla is a sheathed or podded seed like the pea, with a skin round a row of seeds. The vanilla appears to be from the Lithic elements u-a-nai-la, orifice-that-open-long, a sheath for a blade or a row of seeds. The vagina however can not be read as a sheath, although it may be thought of as a sheath for the male organ. It is

Chapter 6 Fa

described as u-a-kai-na, the 'orifice that kindled opens' - all very rude but exactly as we thought in those old days – but of course not now. Etymologists may not care for it but the simile actually works equally well both ways. It is not marked for the direction of the metaphor.

We get to finality (15) in quite a roundabout way, starting out with finis a land boundary, first of all a post stuck in the ground to mark the corners. It was a pai or phai which nai or stuck up, just as a post is a pa-u-s-tai, a piece-what-vertical-becomes [stands up]. Eric Partridge draws attention to its closeness to the Latin figere (11) to push or thrust in (to the ground in the case of a post) and so to fix. Finis transferred its meaning from the post to the boundary or limit it marked out, so far and no further, and so a terminus or ending. That way a boundary post achieved finality, but again courtesy of Tarzan's penis in origin, which was the original sticker upper and inner. That is language for you. Once Tarzan has the idea he sticks with it.

A fine is just an imposed payment, but one to achieve final settlement of a due, bounding the debt, putting a boundary to the debt. You pay and that is quits, it terminates the liability. Originally there was no blame involved. The meaning follows from the last paragraph, another further step away from Tarzan's penis, but still needing it to explain the thinking. A fine day is laughably derived conventionally from the same semantics, perhaps since a settlement may be regarded as satisfactory and so fine, so a satisfactory day is fine too. But pahai-nai was always pleasurable, as is a fine day. It just gets watered down over the aeons (inter alia) to merely any pleasurable sensation, or more precisely the pahai is the pleasurable sensation and the nai presents it. Fine is just about the same as nice, like nai-sai, feeling warm, at ease, from presenting-warmth. A fine day, incidentally, is probably a warm one. You can perfectly well have a nice day too. Finance, on the other hand, is back to the payments in final settlement, or indeed about the final settlements or sets of accounts they produce in turn. There is nothing about them which is nice, like feeling warm. There is no warm glow. Here is true polysemy. Partridge has fifty of these words listed as "derivations of Latin figere to thrust in", figere from Lithic pahei-kare, to strike with the pahei. The past participle is fixus, which does rather put the nay-sayers in a bit of a fix.

In Egypt Nefertiti has left us a fine sculpture of a beautiful princess. Nefer (13) meant pretty, while titi meant just that. So she was Princess Pretty Tits. Where I write this is under the lea of Mount Teide on the island of Tenerife, and the Carthaginian invaders, speaking a provincial Egyptian patois, named it Mount Titty. The volcano, the highest mountain in Spanish territory, has a conical fumerole on its lip. In Lithic nefer is nai-pahei-rai, presented-the penis-rises. Pretty is not so far away, pai-rai-tai-tai, the pai-rayed-by the titties, or in fact more likely by the single tai, the vagina, the same predicament entirely, but with the second –ti merely the feminine ending in Ancient Egyptian. That is not to say Nefertiti in her day was identified in quite such fundamental terms. She likely saw herself as of pleasant appearance, naiferai. The ending –ti was used as the feminine ending. The preceding -ti may well by then have become tacked onto the nefer and neferti meant just naturally become of pleasant appearance, even -ferai by then just easy on the eye – as well as feral, wild like wild animals which behave hysterically all the time as if with their cocks up. Tai meant birth from the birth canal and the diminutive ti meant many small orifices such as are found in the teats. Eric Partridge cites the Greek tit-the, for a nipple, and provides a suppositional *dhei to suck. Any *dhei would more likely come as a back formation from the nipple: if you are sucking you are nippling. Otherwise there is no backing for dhei for sucking. It is just one of the totally random and meaningless roots

111

Chapter 6 Fa

on which established etymology is based, dismissing the titi as if irrelevant, as well as the convention being randomly selected.

The English fair (13) appears to be allied to the Egyptian nefer. Its earliest form in English was faiger, which unmistakeably unravels as Lithic pahai-karai, making the penis aroused, penis kindling. The somewhat earlier Gothic was fagrs, (pronounced fayrs) with much the same Lithic constituency. Eric Partridge throws in Sanskrit pajras for good measure, which he has found, but meaning in good condition, fit and strong, which looks more like from pa-sh-rai, skin shining, a glossy coat indicating an animal in good condition, rather than the good looks of the girls. The Latin from which we get our pulchritude uses different phonemes but can quite easily be analysed from the Latin pulcher, beautiful, and the Lithic Pu-lai-kara, as a phallus kindler, making the pipi enlarged, much like nefer. Lai can mean loop, looped, and so bloated as well as line, linear, length, lengthened, etc; or even both together. These la meanings come via the horizon at sea, seen as the only straight line in nature from land and the only perfectly round one from mid ocean. See chapter 8 on La. Psychosemantics seem to rule.

The Arabic fakir (3) meaning poor is allied to the fakir who is a religious mendicant and may still sometimes be seen wandering the streets in India with no clothes on at all. Both the religious naturist and the abjectly poor with no money find themselves in the same position unclothed, with their genitals rendered visible, pahei-kerai, much as for the Australian aborigine gara is colour, what the (light) rays make visible. In 1902 in Durban my father reported the Zulu rickshaw pullers going naked. They fought earlier the same way. The Arabic for unbeliever, kafir, was perhaps one not ashamed to gaphirai, go naked, pahei visible; just like the fakir, the sage beyond worldly considerations. In Persian it becomes gabr, going with barai, the flesh visible, and in Turkish giaur, going au-rai, the whole lot visible. Unbelievers across all these languages were simply regarded as bare bottomed savages – or their like: reasoned disbelief was inconceivable. From that came the Arabic kfr root for disbelief, with a much more literal meaning in the West.

Friable (3) is such that it can be broken up into a grain (fractions) by rubbing with the hands. It is from the Latin friare to rub. Pahei-rai-are is to rouse the pahei. It can in fact be done by rubbing it. So rubbing is rudely defined as penis rousing and eventually applied even to polishing up the handles of the big front door. That is language for you. A finger, a pahai-en-kara, to do the rubbing, can be derived equally vulgarly. It has many other uses of course. But it is sexual metaphor which rules, look where we may. Mostly we have looked away.

Fat (3) is clearly a slovening of pahei. Why pai, originally the diminutive of bai, the flesh, and therefore skin or a diminutive piece of flesh, should come to mean to swell out and fatten is not obvious. But then the penis, one particular piece, is a classic as a diminutive shoot and also when it comes to swelling out and becoming fat. It is a classic gull. If there is any alternative derivation for this gull I have been unable to find it. That makes the shift from pa to fa- more understandable. A penguin is conventionally derived from the Welsh pen-guin, white headed. But a penguin is not white headed and there is no reason to imagine Welshmen to have ever entertained this misconception, nor indeed to have got to the bird first. It is folk etymology invented by the Welsh. Latin for fat bodied is pinguis. It seems obvious the penguin is properly a pinguin. A fatter waddler in the avian world is impossible to find. If ever there were a bird fit to be described as pinguis, plumped up, it must surely be the penguin, really a pinguin all the while. The French petite, pai-titi, just the teat, and perhaps the auriole surrounding it, pai, fattened, is another misunderstood Lithic link. Anything else little enlarged is petty by derivation. Partridge adds tone to these derivations by citing Sanskrit payate it swells or fattens. But he lists neither the penguin nor the pai titi. He does however include the Greek pion for the adjective fat and piar and pimele for the nouns, the former probably just the fat in situ and the latter the mailai or edible liquid after it has been fried. Fry, Lithic phrai, or phai rai (3), is therefore from the same source, phai, fat, which has been or is rai or roasted in the liquid fat which runs out. Roast is rau, altogether rayed, sai in the flame, and the tai is just become. Nowadays the literal technique is confined to chestnuts at Christmas or potatoes in boy scout camp fires, along with the twist, dough wound round a stick and offered to the flames to roast as a form of unleavened bread, thoroughly smoked and almost inedible even for a boy scout, but marginally less indigestible than eating the flour paste raw when it swells up inside you.

Frisky and fresh are doublets, although a frisky horse is not a pukkah term amongst the horsey sorority while a fresh one is. The actions (from the sibilants) are determined by the phrai, an erect penis. Fierce, freh for greedy, fuerte (Spanish for strong) and friend can be lumped in here. All these terms rely upon the male erection as explanation for their tensions. It is absurd, and maybe displeasing, but that is language for you. Greedy does the same, it is what being gerai or made roused does, the effect on the lower abdomen later transferred to feeding. The linguistic metaphor here plumps for the sexual connection even when it is obvious the eating frenzy has nothing directly to do with it – unless of course you prefer to posit a specific heroic eating ray to account for the greed like the bravery ray with which the brave, berani in Hindi, become berau, like the heroes in Greece. But were the Greek heroes (hei-rau-s) not hei too, their bravery from their erections perhaps, with only the brave deserving the fair. A bahadur is also a brave man in Hindi. Behai-durai, like the Malay durian, a fruit with a hard skin and prickles all over it from the Malay duri a thorn, just differently spelt in English. Both the bahadur and the durian appear to share the same durable hard on. Durability in general must be a gull from the hardness because the original erection is ephemeral.

A flagon, from which is derived a flask is a huge jug made of hide. It is related to ply which is to fold a skin (Latin pellis, any [flexible] surface, originally the skin, pai, of an animal surrounding, lai, the flesh) or any other pai. With its exaggerated spout for pouring it had fancifully the form or shape of the phallus, phalla-ka-un, an earlier form being flakon, related to the old French flascon, probably originally palais-ka´n, one made of lapped skin, which the French spotted could be seen as a phallic shape, flash shaped, a flash similarly an ejaculation of Light.

Franco (3), now free, was a spear originally, a prong kau, that is a sharpened one like the flaked flint. Any prong it seems was copying the rampant penis, pahai-rau, rayed, raised and roused by the feminine raying from the girls. Femina (3) is from pahei-mai-na, the penis-impregnation-presenting, the fair sex labelled the agressor and initiator of every sexual encounter since na meant drawn out and offering a rounded vagina equally. These spearmen were the Franks, and the army spear carriers were the only freemen of the day which puts a new gloss on freedom's roots. They were probably lancers fighting on horseback, the cavalry of the day, already the nobility able to afford two horses and a stable boy apiece and free to offer their allegiance to the military commander of their choice, not just fighting for their feudal masters on foot.

A brother or Latin frater was brau- or phrau -terai or born (20). Phrau has the dual vowel, indicating the same pahei in both cases. Brother is thus a doublet with boy, from the closely akin bwoid for penis in Celtic tongues. The Celtic bau-ai-dai is a bunged birth canal in Lithic, which indicates the strangler or penis on it makes it unfit for serving as a

Chapter 6 Fa

birth canal. Of course the internal plumbing arrangements provided further even more compelling reasons why the male could not give birth, but our hom**í**nid forebears knew nothing of them. A buoy is just the same bung, but in general use as a float. There is an alternative reading for brother, Sanskrit bhratr, Avestan brater, Tokharian A procar, Tokharian B procer with derivative old French fradre whence fredre and frere, Englished friar. Joel Chandler put Brer on the map, American slave slang for brother. Lithic barau-therai can be fleshed out both-womb raised or born, both raised in the same womb. Either the same father or the same mother marked you out as brothers. In Stone Age terms the brothers will have preceded recognition of fatherhood.

Fraud (3) is from the Latin fraus. The pahei is clearly rau, a cheeky chappie, but there is more, fraus is closely related to frustra, one of Eric Partridge's o.o.o. words (of obscure origin, ie he does not know what). Frustra, in vain, is in Lithic pahei-rau-ish-tai-ra. The penis, phai is rau, roused, ishterai, by [the warmth of] 'the hearth drawn out' merely, and not a genuine vaginal ray at all, that is to say when there are no girls around or worse when they don't want to know you. Frustrare in Latin is to drag things out, to render an action vain, to circumvent or deceive a person. The arousal is in vain and under false pretences, as these days from a hot bath for instance, now we no longer hunker too close around the open hearth.

The frog (10) goes with an ejaculatory leap. Leapfrog, frog style or like the frog, the children's game, picks up the same psychosemantic content, nowadays unawares. Frog is made up of the Lithic elements Pa-hei-rau-gai, orgasmicly going. In Latin the frog on the other hand is rana. It comes via the Greek from the Egyptian and ra is eye and na is pushed forward and presented, the action originally of the rampant penis when rayed, the "Na!" originally it seems perceived as the sound of the expulsion of breath at orgasm after holding it as the tension builds up. Rana is protruding or rampant eyes, they are on the top of his head so he can, like the crocodile, a more formidable water borne predator, lie doggo with only his eyes above water ready to snap up any insects dancing over the water surface, or tackle cattle in the case of the crocodile. In passing, the crocodile from the Greek kroko-dilos (or –deilos) is skull bodied or hardened bodied (that is the kroka–) and what born or become by nature (u-dai)-lau or run down, like the instinct of water to slip into the lows. He lurks in the water as the water itself lurks in the lows, just rana only, like the frog waiting for his prey. In Celtic the frog started out a puit, but they obviously did not know the difference between a frog and a toad since it is the toad whose body 'pau-i-tai, 'puffed out-which-becomes' when challenged. It can be read as penis teat, the glans which also has the trick of puffing itself out. It may impress a smaller passing toad but hardly anybody else. As children we used to prod them to see them do it. Compare the Malay siput for snail, from si-pu-ti, brer-penis-teat. The Malay perception of the prepuce as in a whorl like a snail's shell is fanciful, and must be put down to generations forever deprived of a full and proper inspection of the article religiously removed.

The English pout with the mouth is a straight copy of the puit, the lips appear to copy the plumping to make the pu sound. Pau-tai is become plumped in Lithic. The original derivations will have been left behind long ago (or anyway passed down below into the subconscious, but tagged to the Lithic language prompts to resurrect it generation by generation). It can still be read from the linguistic record nevertheless. It is as if the sexual generation of species has preserved a virtually perpetual linguistic stasis where the semantics are concerned - which is quite outside the Darwinian curriculum (which is solely to do with genetics), and is solely within the domain of human whimsy.

Chapter 6 Fa

There is ample scope for continuing through the dictionary picking up and deriving all the words in f- and ph- as well as all those with either phoneme within them. But it would lose readers fast. We have so far covered the meanings from phai which include orgasm, pleasure, ejaculate, beget, make and present. The tree for fa has also fit, fetch, fruit, ferrites, flow, front, and feelings. The psychosemantic tree is confined to one page, but could be made to cover several. Some meanings are left for readers to turn over for themselves. The book is too long already.

A fit (3) is one thing going inside another, a square peg in a square hole, but originally a pahei or phi in a tai (a round one). It came eventually to be inter alia a canto of a poem, a piece from inside a whole work. In German a fitze is a skein, a single strand or a number twisted together. The paroxysm of the epilectic fit was originally taken to have the same character as the orgasm (9) when the phai is tai. Old English fitt meant strife or conflict. To be fit for a fight you had to be matched, suited, ready, in this case strong and vigorous. A fitter fits others together. Fitz for progeny seems to follow along. To follow is perhaps from fare-lau or linked. The derivation was probably doubtful when gehen to go was added to make Old English folgehen, to follow. A family, phai-mai-lai, a group phai-mai-linked, procreation linked, with a pater familias. But in Latin the family included the servants and slaves, suggesting the -mai- could be for meat or eating too, perhaps linked by procreation and messing both. From all the above we may perhaps conclude the fit Charles Darwin had in mind when pondering the role of the fittest was the later sense of suitability and readiness for the struggle of existence; and it was Gregor Mendel with his generations of peas who harked the biologists back, no doubt subconsciously, to the original sexual fit.

To fetch or bring forward is from old English fecan (3), a clear enough sexual metaphor, from pahei-ka'n: to make with the pahei; compare a well known and now commonly used four letter word which as an old fogey the author still prefers not to print. A ferry brings you across a river. Fs and Ps are virtually interchangeable. F, if it does not say puff, says sex. P says one piece or another. It may be the one which says hurrah! Or it may be just a flat surface like the skin which encloses the flesh. A plate is clearly flat by nature. Pro, pointing forwards, clearly a gull from the penis when rau is pointing forwards. It informs a prow as well as a Malay perahu, a boat with a rampant prow, while froward and forward go in the same direction for the same reason. Fore! For the golfer it means look out in front. We get to front with the final t here a side, while side explains the thinking further: sa-i-dai, one-of-the two, a single side of a body which is split, divided, a parting into two, with the binary symmetry of the human body (and all other live bodies, as a matter of fact. Front is the front side, contra the backside.

The words for fruit around the world suggest that for primitives the male genitalia of all animals were regarded as the equivalent of the fruiting bodies of the vegetable kingdom. Animal and vegetable were not so radically differentiated to start with. The adjectival mind saw characters as universals. It must be borne in mind it was the male genitalia which received attention simply because the sexual organs of the male are worn outside the body and are active for all to see and admire. The females of the species offered no more than a receptacle and a passage for anyone interested in viewing. All the rest was secreted within the body, and was overlooked. Early speakers will have been entirely ignorant of any of the inner workings of the fair sex. Fruit (12), Lithic ph-rau-i-tai, apparently comes from the rayed (and grown, swollen) genitalia which have naturally developed or become (tai). It was not testicles were fruit, it was fruit were testicles.

Chapter 6 Fa

The fruit swelled from natural development (tai) while the genitals were kindled (kai) by sexual rays emitted by the genitalia of the opposite sex. The fruit are not kindled, there is no bodily heat involved in their development, nor is the process to be likened to a spark followed by a flickering (10) flame (10) and then a sudden final blazing up. Yet fruit were regarded as male. This dialectical comparison of the animal and vegetable fruiting is probably responsible for the otherwise puzzling use of frigidus (Latin) for cold, when the animal sexual arousal can hardly have struck our forebears as frigid in any of its senses. This frigi (12) was dau, not kau, it was the vegetal fruiting and its principal distincta were its leisurely procedure with the seasons, and its absence of either the furor or the hot temper of the animal approaching orgasm. By contrast heat, Latin calor, was seen as exemplified by kau-lau-a, the sexually kindled variety of enlargement of the organ. Other terms support this quite difficult analysis. We talk of animals coming into heat. Frigidity is coldness but also the total absence of what is already identified as coming into heat. There is thus a link between sexuality and temperature independently established and one may suspect prompted and arising from a common source in the subconscious mind.

Fruit in Hindustani is phal, with Lithic elements close to phallus. In olden times the phallus was regarded as the male fruiting body, fully alive and therefore capable of fruiting repeatedly, not rooted in the seasons like the fruiting of the vegetable kingdom, which was also rooted to the ground. There are fruit clearly named after the genitalia. One is the fig, a leaf of which Adam used to cover his genitalia when God disapproved of his going naked, na-kai-tai, showing katy, from the Stone Age kai-tai, his bodily orifices. Fig in Lithic elements is pahei-kai, pahei-shaped. The fruit is much the same shape as a testicle. It is moreover a hermaphrodite fruit since when fully ripe it splits open revealing inner surfaces reminiscent of the tumescent vulva, both in shape and colouration. It is the testicles of course which are phai kai, phallus kindlers, as stated in the Lithic for the fig. If you cut them off potency is lost, fattening occurs, and as well there is a significant reduction in the male aggressive instinct. For these reasons bullocks were castrated as soon as they were tamed and bred; while boys had the whole of their male external genitalia removed in order to simulate feminine physiology, a procedure not without life threatening risks of infection, which is still killing boys in an unregenerate India today. Many will no doubt have been inverts dissatisfied with their maleness, which keeps sex changes going today, but others were just in it for the livelihood as male prostitutes.

Until recently the Vatican even cut boys at one time just to keep them singing treble, with a fine disregard for their human rights which include the pursuit of happiness; wickedly telling them they would go to heaven more easily if they shed their testicles. It is true their promptings can lead to mischiefs, and without them you probably have a better chance of a clear run in, but then it must be moot if you acquire virtue for resisting temptations you never experienced. Eunuchs can sometimes achieve erections but they can never breed. Some may even have been in demand in the larger harems for their safe sexual services when the turn for the pater familias came round comparatively infrequently.

To return to Adam's fig leaf, it appears it was testicles which were the source of Adam's offence, calling for a leaf with liberal foliation allowing three separate fronds to be draped over the offending equipment; and since in the highlands of Eden today there are aboriginal tribes who cover their phalluses but leave their testicles exposed, wearing penis sheaths which extend above the navel, this may quite possibly have been the Adamites' style of adornment too, even while Adam was thinking up names for all the animals as his tribe gave birth to language. (If so it now appears he was a hominid, before Sapiens

Chapter 6 Fa

Sapiens, before eating from the tree of knowledge, since tree could mean a tao as well as the arboriculturalists tree, a route or trace as in a family tree).

An-thro-pos, the Greek for man(kind) is in Lithic elements A´n-tahirau-pous, that'one-drawn up-limbs, old long legs in fact. Greek aner, man, (the male) from the Lithic an-nai-rai, the one who protrudes [when] rayed.

The tai rays drawing out anthropous's legs are the very same ones in language that it was supposed drew out our manhood in the Stone Age, the ta rays from the girls´ vaginas, tai ra-ing, or better tarai, ta-raying, which all unawares we pray in aid every time we use a tray or open a drawer or travel in a train. Nature, from the Latin natura and the Egyptian Naturai (sometimes written neter by academic Egyptologists), has rules for whenever the tura na (or present themselves), as when the wind blows or any other natural force is seen at work.

There is also the avocado which in Spanish is pronounced abocado, and is commonly believed to be named after the testicles because of its shape. It is a fair size for a testicle but that is part of the jape. The Lithic phonemes seem supportive of the testicles: a-bu-kai-do, those dual bulbs that do the kindling . Unfortunately, as Eric Partridge points out bocado in Spanish means a bon bouche or delicacy and the avocado pronounced abocado in Spanish may have seen some reshaping as a result. The fruit was originally aguacate in Spanish, pronounced ahuacate, from the Aztec language, Nahuatl, where it is ahuacatl. The –tl is a substantive ending in Nahuatl (which translates to Nauaho in California). It must be remembered here that these forms are traditional renderings from some time ago. The question seems to be whether ahuaca deserves to be regarded as testicle in Nahuatl. We can readily enough accept –ka as meaning create or make in Nahuatl because their supreme deity is Wakan Tanka, which neatly enough translates in Lithic terms as Terror-making-World-maker, The Awesome Creator. It should be noted in passing the Tan for world in Nahuatl is virtually the same as Taun in Ancient Egyptian. A-hu-a-ka reads quite well as that-hei in the completive (u) case-that-makes, that is that makes the ecstacy or orgasm.

You might think it is the phallus which sends the ecstatic signals to the brain, and indeed there can hardly be any doubt our primitive forebears started out under that presumption. It was only when they tried cutting off the testicles of farmed animals they found out they made all the difference. The testicles´ role will then have been at first a seven day wonder and worthy of remark. You might also think enlisting of the vowel u both as the completive sense of the hei-ing and then again as the dual form to register the two hyers is stretching Lithic meanings further than is justified, but this is by no means the case. Such double derivation was for the Lithic mind confirmation of the soundness of the construction of their meaning strings. Such confirmatory indications that the Lithic meanings grouped together under each of the phonemes were matched in nature will have been seen as a welcome clarification of a complex world. We are not yet allowing the stringing of phonemes to be words in the full sense of codified strings with overall meanings picked and parroted. They were having to be gone through phoneme by phoneme to pick up the overall meanings. All the same, hominids were not stupid. The enlargement of the testicles at puberty which accompanies the awakening of the procreative instinct must surely have been noticed long before anyone knew how to say what they could see. The mystery will have received powerful confirmation when they got round to the castration of live animals. The more ideational links to their line of reasoning that could be spotted, the more likely it was to their minds that their thinking was veridical; and there was no professor of grammar around to forbid them doubling meanings back on

Chapter 6 Fa

their tracks when they saw an opportunity. Human castration will have been for a purpose, as with the Vatican: which means in their case – they had no choirs to maintain - after the need for the testicles for breeding was known if not their actual role as pollenators. It probably went with enslavement of captured males, once they had escaped the need to eat them, and was actually one small step for man on the long road to civilisation: better castrated than eaten after all.

Ferrites are made of ferrous (iron) metals. Metals, mai-ta-lai, are earth-born-as lyes, earths become liquid, just as stones are ish-tau′n, fire-born'ones - from observation of volcanos. But iron is the rayed one. Ferrum, iron, phai-rau′m (3) is the source of magnetism, an attractive force just as the phallic ray supposedly attracted the females. A magnet is from 'he magnesia lithos', the Magnesian stone in Greek. Magnesia is a district of Thessaly, the source of the iron ore. Magnesia as a local name might mean anything. Is it named for its most notable product the ore from which iron is obtained by heating? Ma-gai-nai-sai-a can be read as earth-place-presenting-direction-one, probably the centre of mass of the local ore bed rather than north, the centre of mass of the whole globe - or else the axis of rotation of the electrically charged magma at the earth's core. Readers of Velikovsky will be aware of the possibility of the orientation of this liquid's revolutions being distorted by resonant electrically charged visiting astronomical bodies. The meaning of direction for sai comes from its upwards directional semantic content, from the flame which determinedly springs upwards - see chapter 13 – and it may have been the vertical tip of a suspended metal needle, now known as dip, which the ancients first discovered. It is in any case a classic example of the way the meanings become generalised as they are abstracted as metaphor: the more abstracted the more general. In this case the upwards direction becomes just direction, just as a lye, a bitter taste becomes just taste as well as the taster the tongue or langue and then the language which comes from its wagging.

To feel (3) is to have an experience phai-like, like with the phai, if less intensive. It is natural enough to perceive the pahei as the source and centre of sensation where its most intense and pleasant avatar is to be met with, and then to abstract and generalise that meaning. Lymph (14), the lai-em-phai, liquid of the pahai; and so any mucosal body fluid, from the spine or brain for instance, supposed by primitive butchers to be all of the same kind as sperm. In India you still find some of the same confusion today, much like Rabbi Ouaknin's nutritional and respiratory energy to be found in the spinal fluid, and related to the phallus, and all resumed in the letter Aleph (really the phoneme fa). Religious meditation in the Stone Age can be seen to hark back to Lithic language roots, interpreting the subconscious phonemic messaging as intimations from the gods. Did religion start out as grammar? If so Noam Chomsky is going home.

Of course in retrospect it can be seen you need to have as full a knowledge as possible of Lithic protocols, even at the risk of it becoming slightly obsessive, to follow through the semantic twists and turns we are heir to. It is a language of the mind, only accessible at one remove from the page, and it is in the subconscious mind it lives. You have to learn to let your subconscious sensibility lead, picking up the sense of sounds in a manner ultimately quite poetic. That is no bar to rejoining the logic of the classroom as necessary and at any time whenever a hat drops for you. Much of the fun is to be aware of the two worlds and to flip six hundred millennia when you feel like it. It is the only way I know to get disgraced former Chancellor Gordon Brown, that Treasury poodle, out of your hair. The case for Lithic can probably rest there.

Chapter 6 Fa

NOTES

1. Ouaknin, Marc-Alain. Mysteries of the Alphabet. The Origins of Writing. Translated Josephene Bacon. .Abbeville Press \Publishers. New York. 1999.

CHAPTER 7

HA THE HURT AND HAPPINESS AND HUMOUR

When addressing the aspirate there are really six different sorts of h, some of them just huffing and puffing others seriously using the glottis. First there are the aspirated consonants like bh and dh best dealt with under their parent consonants. Then secondly there are the gutturals kh and gh, in English sometimes spelt ch as in loch. These aspirated consonants so frequently lapse into plain aspirates that they need treatment in this chapter as well as with ka and ga. These are really cuckoos in this nest, but they are dealt with here because they often get eroded and turned into plain h, and it is with these we are now concerned. Then thirdly there is the cockney h, half way to a glottal stop, separating two vowels otherwise adjacent and liable to elide. Surprisingly this may have been at one time the commonest usage. In Ancient Egyptian h was probably pronounced ahi or ahei and, where it appeared before an a, it could make instead the double vowel iha; and then even slurring further either to ha or to ia. There is a trace of this usage in our pronunciation aitch from ahi, akhi, aikhi and aich. Otherwise why not Hey or He, like ABCD? Fourthly there is the sudden gasp with involuntary expulsion of breath: haa! The glottis is locked and then suddenly a scream emerges. It is the last cry of a boy, in the age of the Pleistocene, caught in the back of his cave by a sabre-toothed tiger without his burning brand. Fifthly there is the jocular expulsion of breath expressing jollity or sudden humour as in Ha! Ha! Surprisingly enough, a sabre tooth and a joke both evoke a Ha! The jocular ones are lots of little ones. The sabre-tooth ones are single and long, the gasp leading straight into a scream, sometimes terminal like the parachutist's farewell when his parachute had not opened - in the bad old days before we had any reserve chutes and you knew you were going in.

But then a long gasp of 'the happy Ha' turns up as another sixth meaning. The semantic pattern, as meanings expanded and in the process became more generalized, is important. Once established as an involuntary gasp, like when a careless boy (or else a girl), hunkered around the hearth when language was beginning, picked up a white hot stone mistaking it for an ember to toss back into the fire and let out an involuntary "Haa!" recording the error as he or she dropped it like a hot potato, the meaning will have been generalized gradually from "Hot!" (a Hau thing) to take in any sudden emotional input (or output) like "Ha! Ha!" denoting hilarity, or a "Haaa!" at orgasm translating to the happy aspirate, which comes to occupy an important key to human understanding of Lithic language. It was apparently the orgasmic one that pulled them in the Stone Age. It is a constituent of the Greek phi and has already appeared in chapter 6 about the phoneme fa, from pahei. The Ancient Egyptians represented tehei (their letter th), originally from the Lithic phonemes tai-hei, with a glyph of a mallard drake in hot pursuit of the duck, wings flapping. The drake is single minded enough in his pursuit of his mate to sometimes drown the duck while mounting her, so intent is he on impregnation. The semantic content of this high is whoopee! or phaow! from the expression of the ecstasy at orgasm, when the breath held as the tension mounts is suddenly released at ejaculation. The millennia have not succeeded in eradicating this original quite blunt semantic identification of the hedonistic aspirate from the lexicon. It is still in there, somewhere in the subconscious mind, directing the

Chapter 7 Ha

shaping of language as it changes and is remoulded, from whimsy, or simply from lack of conscious attention. Hilarity is another high. These phonemic meanings, now no longer consciously relied upon have nevertheless been picked up in the subconscious as every child has learned their language for the last 600,000 years (or whenever). That may seem some way from the thrust of our English composite letter th today, as indeed also from pahei or ph now pronounced f. But it can be seen to be readily copied by every generation which rediscovers its four letter words. What is conclusive is the Ancient Egyptian usage of hei in the composite pahei, meaning the joy piece (akin to the joy stick pilots in the last century named the steering stick they waggled between their legs) with an uncompromising Egyptian hieroglyph of the human penis ejaculating, otherwise read as mai, the earther>planter>impregnater. A nice piece of metaphorical semantic development there, from earth to impregnation.

The psychosemantic tree for ha is on page 124, starting with the aspirated consonants kh and gh (2) which have often been slovened to h. The columns are numbered (1) to (6). The examples which follow are in no way exhaustive which would involve printing the Lithic analysis of most of the entries in Eric Partridge's excellent etymological dictionary under h, or with h in the words. I have remarked elsewhere my book is really no more than the continuation volume of Eric Partridge's master work "Origins" of 1958. The original Lithic derivation of every word in the lexicon it is not now possible to resurrect, because of the slovening over the aeons. The surprise is how many words in how many languages can still be derived from their original Stone Age semantic contents.

At the beginning of language the original natural meaning of the aspirate was no doubt a matter of considerable discussion, in so far as any discussion was possible. In those early days natural meanings, what you could reasonably conclude from the sound itself, as well as the occasions of its natural expression, must have been the touchstones for communicating. That must surely have been the way inarticulate folk thought: look for the 'natural' meaning from the occasion of its expression. If the shock of a burnt hand evokes "Haa!" the natural meaning of the phoneme is 'hot!', just as the burning brand when extinguished in a puddle with an "ishsh!" makes it clear the 'natural' meaning of the sibilant is flame or fire. That is Lithic thinking for you. We must try to follow suit.

The aspirated consonants which do not sloven into a plain aspirate h are covered under their own phonemes, bh in chapter 3 for ba for instance, dh in chapter 5 for da and ta. It is proposed here to deal with the cuckoos first, the echoic words which copy a sound heard. The simplest is hard, which is from khard.(2). Ka was taken first of all to be echoic of the clink of stone on flint when flaking the flint to make tools. The Greek for skull is kara, the hard part of the head. The r in kara could be a cockney r just to keep the two a apart: ka'a, the hard one. But it can be read as body sun too. The ka is the hard (flinty) part of anything – the body's skeleton, and the world's hard core of rock, which when found on the surface is raised, rao-kai, (rayed-core and rayed-made), rock, and core on view; and also kindled by rays (rock again), it gets kindled by rays, it gets hot in the sun's rays – all of these things, so it certainly must be rock. But khara could also be read in Lithic terms as baked, from made rayed. Clay responded to hot enough heating in that way to make earthenware: made rayed it became hard and you got a hard pot. Ceramic is from the Greek keramos, earthenware, which in turn is from the Lithic phonemes Kai-rai-ma-u(s), made-rayed-earth-one (Greek substantive marker), baked earth. You needed the finest earth (clay). Horn is next door, originally khorn, akin to the Latin cornu, which in Lithic phonemes is kara-na-u, the skull-protrusions-dual, horns. Nau's several meanings include protruding, the original protrusion being, I am afraid, of the male organ for copulating, see

Chapter 7 Ha

chapter 10. That is hominid thinking for you. It is important to remember, when these infelicitous derivations are discovered, the further realization we were simple hominids when, some 600,000 years ago, we learned to speak by giving meanings to the sounds we were learning to utter. The skull was kara (in Greek) because it was supposed it had hardened – hard rayed from the same natural causes as the baked clay pot. Pot is from caput in turn, the Latin for head, from Lithic ka-puti (the body glans), whence the bone skull cap which, suitably sawn off, stood in for the earthenware cup before the baking of clay was invented. The Danes say schol when sharing a drink; they are raising the sawn off skull.

Ka-pu-ti in Lithic is the body (ka)-penis (pu from pipi)-teat (ti), the glans of the body. Nowadays we might refer medically to the head of the penis. Way back it was the other way about. The cap is from the first two bits, the pot from the second two. Both are buses. A hot oven won't do, or the heat of the hearth; it has to be a kiln with a much higher temperature if you want to have a pot which is not porous, (from pa-u-rau, from piece-un-rayed), the clay, unbaked, not holding water. The horn which toots is of course either an animal's horn or else at least a spin off shaped like it. The corn on the foot is a callus, hard like the horn and the cornu, that which is rayed (heated and hardened). Field corn is hard too if you try to eat it as it is grown (just like sweet corn too). It is an ear, from ai-a-rai, that which-is-rayed, a hard head like the skull, and the grain is at the head of the stalk - close to a horn or cornu, but not quite so uncompromisingly hard. That is why corn got ground to flour; and because corn was ground it was grain. Our English heads are cuckoos too. The Latin caput and the Greek cephalos start with ka, in these two cases the hard structure of the body, the skeleton which forms and supports it, but used here simply for the body; followed by puti and phalos. These are quite simply terms for the glans of the penis – like it or lump it. Both the Greek and the Latin say body-knob, much as we might today describe the glans as the head of the penis. Magritte would have recognised the Lithic here.

Our head is meanwhile from heafod, which surprisingly has the same pedigree as caput. The transmogrification of the phonemes in caput from ka to haia and puti to phaudai is not a wit less sexually prompted, if anything more so, emphasising it is the engorged glans the head is likened to. Our chief and chef follow along, a head and a head cook, from khai-pahei via chai-fe. Will they care to discover the metaphor that names them is from the glans of the penis?

A hammer (3), from kha, is really a downer as well as a striker-marrer or smasher, see chapter 9 on Ma. Here (2), is originally from kha-i-rai, place-which-visible, the immediate environs. It is also ahi-rai (3), that which-visible, a powerful confirmation of the appropriateness of the attribution, as well as perhaps accounting for the elision of the kh to h. Hear (3), at the same time, is from the Lithic I(h)ai-arai, it that-which-is audible: since rai is any one of the Egyptian rays which were everywhere about us, accounting for sensations and influences, arriving from outside, including from a distance and including both visual and auditory prompts, even in some cases thinking rays too, wafted in from outside and registered in the brain. Brain is from the Lithic elements be-rai'n, be-rayed or bai-rai'n, the rayed flesh. It probably predates any clear identification of our own individual identity or full sense of self. Partridge here relates hearing to akouein (2), the Greek for hearing, which gives us our acoustics. The trouble is there is no r in akouein, which is from aa (vacuous extension and so air as we say it)-kau-ein, air-strike-verbal marker (from ain, extensioning, and so going), a rather serious omission for the Lithic ray interpretation just proposed for to hear. But audibility actually results as we all now know from an air strike, a modulated puff, on the ear drum, which seems to be the Greek semantic idiom, so rather unusually we have to give the Greeks top marks above the Egyptians here.

A hammer is perhaps from kha-ma-arai (3). Kama, the Old Norse word originally just meant any old piece of rock, ka-ma or hard earth. But the Lithic Ka-ma also means strike-down. A hammer started out as a stone striker-downer, a smasher or smiter. All those hand axes we made for a million years and more (two million year old chipped stones found) were actually mostly for macerating raw meat, which is why when cooking was discovered it was called kau-kau; the exemplary maceration and tenderizing had simply been achieved another way, by heating instead of beating. Khamar was not so far from camera, a dark place, which was one which killed or suppressed (kama, made dead) the sun's rays (rai), and so a vault or room (both originally windowless) and so a dark chamber including the one provided in photography to hold the light sensitive film, and so giving us as well a comrade, a room mate, sharing the dark room, probably as bed fellows. It comes as a surprise to a Northerner that a camera or room, from rau-mai, should be derived from the suppression of the sun's rays since in Northern climes it is regarded as a warm shelter from the cold and wet rather than as a sun shade, but the language goes back a long way and was invented in a hotter clime, as is apparent.

A maul was a heavy hammer, from the phonemes ma-u-lai, which was swung both heavily and down, in a loop (lai), a downer swung in a loop. See chapter 8 on La. It was allied to Old Celtic maca to strike, particularly to strike ma, that is heavily down. Norse kama and Celtic maka assemble the same phonemes but the Norse in reverse order. To me that suggests confirmation of the independent meanings of the phonemes which can be used in either order. Linguists call it metathesis, a putting after. Meta- was originally after in time, (ie. becoming) from 'm-ai-ta, him-that which-become; but here as after in space.

Hide (the animal skin) (2), Latin cutis, an offcut, is a long derivation from the Lithic ka-u-tai, struck in two and so cut off. The hide was the skin after it was cut from the animal. Compare Old High German hut, Germanic root *hud, Indo European root probably *kut"(uncommonly like our cut) but pronounced nearer coot. It was used as a coverlet or to cover the body. To hide, the verb, came to mean to cover, and cover to cover from view and so to hide, with the substantive hide as a covered place to observe from unobserved. Compare Old Persian keuto, hide and even Latin cutis, skin, and Latin scutum a shield (made of hide) and Sanskrit skauti, he covers (all cribbed from Partridge). Then there is Greek keutham to conceal, and probably even Serbian kuca a house, and English house from Old English hus, the basic idea being a covering or shelter, which is sai, or warm with a hearth with a fire (ish) in it, a kha-u-sai, a place-what-warms, a warm place. A covering is of course a concealment. Partridge quotes Sanskrit "kukara" to conceal, Lithic kau-kara, to covered-make.

Thuggi, (Hindi) (Lithic tha-kai in place of Kha-tai for hide) meant concealment, and it was the practice of Kali worshipers (Kali was the prehistoric black goddess of the night, of darkness and death, of concealment and deception – kali is black in Sanskrit – but her followers ka-lai, acted-slyly) to join caravans representing themselves as bona fide fellow travelers in order to strangle the others while they slept. A thousand years and more before Mohammed was born Kali had offered a tariff of seven virgins in the hereafter for fifteen kaffirs (infidels or unbelievers in Her) killed. These virgins are not in the Qur'an. Her religion has been cobbled onto Islam, the religion of Peace and Mercy, by extremists over the years, with the offers of virgins much inflated. In Kali's day it was not widely appreciated spiritual beings have no genitalia, but of course The Prophet knew the next

123

Chapter 7 Ha

THE PSYCHOSEMANTIC TREE FOR HA

The Phonetic Tree

The Semantic Tree

Ha

Echoic (1)	Kh & Gh (2)	Cockney H (3)	Hot H (4)	HaHa (5)	Happy H (6)
Huff	Habit	Halcyon	Hack	HaHa	Hale
Inhale	Haggis	Halo	Hackle	Hilarity	Ham
Halitosis	Haggle	Hammer	Hades	Humour	Hammock
	Hair	Harangue	Hemorrhage		Hand
	Halt	He	Hag		Happy
	Hamper	Hear	Hallo		Haunch
	Hang	Hebe	Hand		Haw
	Hard	Hebrew	Harakiri		Heart
	Harrow	Hegira	Harem		Hearth
	Hat	Helios	Harm		Heaven
	Have	Hear	Harmony		Hedonism
	Hay	Helot	Haste		Hello
	Head	Heron	Hate		Hemp
	Heap	History	Hawk		Hen (2)
	Heave	Horizon	Havoc		Hermes
	Heckle	Horus	Haven		Heyday
	Hell	Hospital	Heath		Hi!
	Helm	Hour	Heed		Hie
	Hem	House	Heinous		High (2)
	Hen (1)	Huge	Hideous		Hip(py)
	Henna	Hydro	High (1)		Homo
	Hide	Hyoid	Hinder		Hooray
	Hill	Hypodermic	Horror		Honour
	Hit	Hysteria	Hot		Horny
	Hold		Howl		Hug
	Hole		Hump		Human
	Horn		Hurry		Hymn
	Hunger				

w

124

world is a spiritual world. He was a follower of Nabbi Issus, the prophet Jesus. It was perhaps the ultimate deception even in her day. The virgins are outmoded Kalian carrots for killing, and have nothing to do with The Prophet or genuine Islam, which makes Osama an unwitting heretic, betraying The Prophet. Genuine Muslims know this must be the case, but apparently can not crack the reasoning, so sit choom and do nothng about it.

A hat (2) (Indo European root perhaps khat) was originally any old covering for the head, including a hood, from a khat and a khud, perhaps originally fur caps against the cold. A hut did the same job on a larger scale as a khat. In Arabic khat is a stimulant leaf of a bush, chewed as a mild drug. The Arabic khat has nothing to do with a hat or a house, however. It means the bush much as we refer to tobacco as the weed. The bush is from kha-tai, with a bifurcating trunk, unlike a tree and much like the English twig, a forked stem, which Partridge relates to the Sanskrit dwikas, double: clearly from Lithic two-shape. The Arabic bush is described as comprising a complex of twigs or bifurcations. You can also compare the Malay chawat meaning a forked branch, and also a brief crotch piece or garment covering the human fork.

Hay was khai (2) originally, close to hacked, like the flint knapper's original ka, echoic from the clink of flint on flint as they struck, flaking flints, ka-na-pai, making flat cut flakes. A harrow was from ka-rau, make rows, just like a rake, from rai-kai, ray or row maker, which after all is just a hand held harrow. Hoe and hew are from an original kau (2), chopping actions both. Compare cau-do, a stroke-do, with du-ce in Italian, driver-become or leader, and Kaeda in Arabic, also driver-become or leader. The Latin incus, on-struck, from Latin cudo I strike (well, do a stroke) which Partridge quotes, is the anvil on which the striking takes place. I have likened Wayland Smith's tactic, mauling the hot metal into shape, to our linguistic habits where elision and ellipsis have been universally adopted for smoother pronunciation regardless of the original form or meaning. To harry is another kh- derivative. The Old Frisian was 'here', (a disyllable) and the Old Norse 'herr' (pronounced hera or herer, the second r the short e or schwa on the end) both meaning army, a strike force. But the Old Prussian was kara and the Indo European original root kar-, strike, which Partridge suggests was "ultimately identical with kar-strong", anticipating somewhat the Lithic semantic tree in chapter 4 for the phoneme Ka. What is hard is tough and what is tough is strong. Armies until quite recently, when they were usually too busy, or too improvident, to find the time to provide their own foodstuffs, were inclined to live off the land like locusts, "harrying" the inhabitants, stealing their goods.

Perhaps we should have 'have' (2) next, akin to Latin habere to have. The Spanish is tenere to hold. To have and to hold (2) are similar in meaning though by no means identical. Holding is one form of having, which has a much wider spread of meanings. The Latin tenere is in chapter 10 on Na, another vulgarism. Habere, if from khabere, is certainly close to capere in Latin, to hold or take, capture, etc, the Lithic ka-pai-are, make-covered-verbal marker, that is put under your protection, just as you put yourself under the protection of your coverlet of skins at night, or even to seize. Partridge says of capere that "Walshe[1], voicing the opinion of every reputable scholar, says that the resemblance to Latin habere which extends to terminations, can only be fortuitous. But to postulate fortuitousness merely because Latin h normally becomes Germanic and Celtic g (as in Irish gailim, I take) is to go perhaps too far; there may have been either conservatism or persistence or recalcitrance involved. The Indo European root is apparently *kap-, to take". He is kicking over the traces, half way to Lithic at least.

Chapter 7 Ha

The cockney h (3), separating two vowels which otherwise might elide, is a world-wide phenomenon by no means confined to Londoners.

But the point in this chapter is simply that ahi, the h of the hieroglyphs, can sometimes simply be separating a from i, or marking the final demise of one of them; but then the further observation needs to be made that the first of the separated vowels may still in time also be lost, leaving a somewhat redundant h as the only trace of the lost vowels. We are dealing with thousands of years, as the units we should be thinking in, remember.

He (3) is a case in point, originally ahi. The underlying ai, which is fully explained in chapter 14 on the meanings of the vowels, meant something like that which and the same phonemic sequence has contributed also the pronoun I, (pronounced ai) where the h has completely disappeared. Halo makes sense as ia-lau, it that looped, a circular glow surrounding the head, with the preceding vowel trashed.

Hebrew (3) according to Eric Partridge is from the Hebrew 'Ibhri, one who comes across (the Euphrates), and like Aberdeen, Crossing-Dee-of, with the Don or river next door with a Brig-o-Don by the time I was posted to the barracks there, 60 to a 30 man Nissen hut, and one tap to shave under between each two huts; and the less well known Brandon, Crossing-of-river, in Suffolk, where the aber means crossing place, from the Lithic a-bai-rai, that/where-legging it-verbal. As crossings were often at estuaries, where the estuary of a river spreads and shallows, Celtic linguists think it meant estuary. Hebrew, apparently from the phonemes Iha-i-bai-rai-u could just be the speakers, from the Lithic They-which-lip it-verbal-ones. Considering their cousinship with the Phoenicians (6) and Carthaginians who were also circumcised and their names record the fact (Phoenician is from Pahei-au-ai-nai-kai-n (6), penis-that one-which-exposed-made, and Punic is from pipi-nai-kai, penis exposed-made), it is natural to just take a look to see if Hebrew has the same distinguishing sexual mutilation in mind. Hei-ba-rai-u can undoubtedly be read as (6), ecstasy-bit-visible-ones. Rai, as well as seen can also mean rayed and roused, and indeed the aim of the Semitic Pharaohs in cutting off their own foreskins in this radical manner appears to have been in recognition of their duty as Pahei-Ra-au-hei, bearers of the Phallus-of Ra-always-virile, to be ready at all times to fire first and not have to wait like the ordinary run-of-the-mill males for rays from the female genitalia to pull out their penises and withdraw their muzzle covers before they could ray back and arouse the females in turn. When the run of the mill lot copied the Pharaoh and his divine penis, they too made it into a deal with their own Deity.

It would be quite wrong, an anachronism, to think this kind of nomenclature would be taken as an invasion of personal privacy in those days. Indeed it was a religious boast then for those who had been cut that they were chosen by Jaweh for the afterlife, and if you were uncircumcised you were a dead man, unreconciled with the one true deity. You had made the wrong choice and you were doomed. It was a claim which must surely have struck everyone, whether Jew or Goy, as a defining belief. In Pharaoh's day the fact the glans of the penis had been artificially exposed was what gave identity to a Jew, and they and their neighbours recognised this equally. The removal of the foreskin enabled the glans to emit its rays. Folk etymology today is less liberated and it is not correct to harp on these genital mutilations. Crossing the Euphrates is safer territory, although it was by comparison with the other (which after all they brought with them and loudly declared was their guarantee of acceptance by their God) a remote and little known circumstance by which to describe a race. Leaving captivity was perhaps worth celebrating, but hardly the fact that they boated to freedom – across a river. Nevertheless Abraham came from the other side of the river. The tribe was an Assyrian one, not a Palestinian one. Those who crossed the river originally came from across the river in the east in Babylonia; and that meaning of Hebrew wins for me. Abraham had yet to make his deal on his penis with Jahweh, copying Pharaoh's deal with Ra. There will I am sure be those who will wish to contradict this appreciation, and some who will reject everything in the book in order to rid themselves of this pesky conclusion. Nevertheless it should appear. They should be asked where they got their initial h from. Palestine was a later colonization, accompanied by genocide. It can not be held against Israel. We were all doing it at the time. However, the later seizure of Israel from the Arabs in 1947 is a live issue and one that can be debated. The Balfour Declaration of 1916 was for a home, together with the other branch of the Semitic folk, the Arabs, and not for a Jewish state.

Also under the Cockney h rubric (3) are, as a suitably mixed bunch, harangue, hasan, hegira, helios, helot, Horus, hour, Hebe, halter and Egyptian hua for water, (really ahua, like the Lithic awa, as well as all the agua languages), as well as hupo in hypotenuse and hyoid, which is from the Greek huo- and weidein to see: weidein from the Lithic uai-da-ien, all that is-becomes-verbal marker, or both ways going-does-verbal marker. Seeing was supposed to be a matter of sending out rays from the eye (ra) which went out and back; so these rays going both ways were seeing. Our eyes, in Ancient Egyptian, copied the Eye in the Sky, Ra, the sun, which pulled up the vegetation with its rays (rai) on their return journey. Then everything was what you saw; and it could be with the mind, just as we say 'I see' when we mean we have it in our minds, in which case an idea could be a concept, a mental appearance which had come wafting in from outside on a ray, like vision. It is these outside rays, which might lead to temptation, which Popes and Rabbis seek to block. Rabbis, having cut off their foreskins to unblock their outgoing rays, wear them on their heads to block incoming ones. Popes don't know why they do it; but perhaps the rabbis do. With hyoid, which is from the Greek hueidos, meaning u-shaped, it all comes down to ah-u-eidos, that-u-become/shape or idea. It is perhaps a nice example of the complexity building from original simplicity; which of course greatly discourages Sapiens Sapiens from working backwards down the tree to trace his verbal roots. With hypotenuse, from Greek hupo (3), under, (Lithic i(h)a-u-pau, it(h)that-what-covered), and the Latin tendere is to stretch. The Lithic for tendere is taien-da-erai, birthing-does-verbal marker: there is a lot of stretching required to give birth, as any matron can tell you. The Greek was the simpler tenein, to stretch, Lithic tai-nai-ein, giving birth-presents or shows-followed by the Greek verbal marker -ein. The hypotenuse turns out to be the one which stretches under (the right angle of the triangle under discussion). At least the stretching points to the length of the hypotenuse, in the case of a right angled triangle, being proportional to the other two sides under it. With triangles other than those with a right angle it is a mess, because the other angles are variables. We can note also the Lithic agreement of the au with the immediately following pau. In so far as the pau, covered, is the completive case or past tense, the au can be understood as in agreement, also in the completive (substantive) case - not necessarily to be transliterated as that-one, but perhaps just that, with case agreement with pau.

Harangue (3) has a convoluted derivation which shows up the original meaning of the Old High German hari for army, which in turn produced the German Herr we translate as Mister, really warrior or brave. The Old German hring (3), a ring, is read in Lithic phonemes easily as ahi-ra-en-ga, that which-Ra-of-shape. The h preserves the only trace here of both the preceding a and the following i. The shape of the sun was paradigmatically circular. General Montgomery was accustomed to call the soldiers into a circle around him when he wanted to harangue them. It was a trick nearly as old as speech. So large a body of men as were to be found in armies in the past positively required making a ring of them if you were to be heard. There were no microphones in those days. The harangue followed once you had got them in a hring. Otherwise you tended to have them in ranks, linear, Lithic ra-en-kai, ray-of-shaped, for doing the business. The sun was round but its rays, sometimes caught in a sunbeam when dust in the air shone, were as straight or straighter than the skyline at sea, and with no other natural rival for exemplifying a row (from rau) or line. (So ra was circular and/or linear. That is Lithic for you. Context decided which. Both were abstract concepts of shape). Hari (3) originally appears to have started out as an army, by definition lined up in ranks ready for the fray. But the rough behaviour of armies when not engaged in battle, unranked, led to the interpretation of the cockney h as the fourth horrid one instead (which we still have to deal with), because of their harrying (4). It was army-ing.

There is another possible root for hari, an army, in the Early French har (4) for a horse, Lithic the frightener, with hari horsed ones, horsemen sweeping down on the fold. But the Germanic tribes did not generally derive their speech from the French. Their word for horse is pferd. But the Old Frisian was hors, and Frisian is perhaps the nearest continental language to English. Horse could belong with the fourth horrid h (4). Horses are hard to handle and they were a hectic ride, probably partly from rough handling; and one ridden at you by a cavalryman was horrid (alarming). The Lithic hau-rai-sai or si could be frightening action, or brer frightener. But I believe on balance it records the horse's own joy in its own action (6). But then why not all three together: horrid, hard to handle and rejoicing in their action? Hasan was, Partridge records, related to hare (another animal that rejoices in its speed and agility), the Old High German for gray. Hares are not notably gray. They are brown. The hare was really a soldier – in flight, not so much a frightener but frightened: flushed they run a mile and as fast as a horse. The Old Frisian, a good guide, was hasa for hare, the fourth h, the one of horror or despair accompanied by –sa, active or action. That signifies, in a different idiom: grai, going rayed, gone with the wind.

Hegira (3), Mohamed's departure, his flight from Mecca, is the Arabic hagara to depart, hijra departure or flight. Mohamed was forced to flee, but the hegira, ahi-a-gai-are, he that-going-verbal marker, his flight, was politely put: a departure. A haji is one who has gone to Mecce, on pilgrimage. This h is a Cockney h. The original phoneme string is ahi-a-gai, with a(h)i in its primitive form, one which: one which-that-went. Helios (3), the sun in Greek, is from the Lithic ahi-a-lai-u-substantive ending, that-which-that-looping or orbiting-one: the sun as orbiter. Helot (3), a slave, is chiefly built around the lau phoneme, he-looped-become, in the sense bound, tied up. The Lithic string is iha-i-lau-tai, it that-which-bound-become, with a cockney h. A harlot (6) per contra, is with the hippy happy h, a slave to pleasure, the same h as makes up the Egyptian joy-piece, the pa-hei.

The Norman French given-name Herlot (6) was William the Conqueror's mother, not as it turned out a happy choice of name. It requires a slightly different reading, a lasting hooray, expressing parental delight at the birth. That did not stop the King of France, who found Normandy an over mighty subject, declaring William's mother not Herlot (pronounced Airloo in Norman French) but a harlot (pronounced arlowe in medieval French), and added a tanner's daughter for good measure. Tanners had to scrape the stale fat from the hides, so they all stank. Soap was not invented for anothrr 700 years. To allege a duke had consorted with a tanner's daughter was meant as a mortal insult, which the history books have copied; and Duke William, later William the Conqueror (who was in fact not a very loveable fellow), is generally believed, correctly, to have been illegitimate. Duke Robert, his father, on reaching puberty appears to have had his wicked way with Herlot (pronounce Airloo in Norman French) and bedded her without getting churched. It has earned her a small spot in the history books – she was evidently a looker - her name Latinised to Herlova (pronounce Airlowa to Airloowa). She was actually Herlot de Graie, the daughter of the Sieur de Graie sur Mer, High Steward at the Duke of Normandy's court at Falaise. Her (legitimate) first cousin Anschetil (from the Norse Ankhetil) de Graie sur Mer commanded the cavalry which won the battle of Hastings (1066 and all that. The Conqueror and his mercenary infantry were losing it to the Saxon house carls, the special forces of the day). Best to have a relative in subordinate command: he could not change sides if the battle was going badly. His head would be cut off anyay. He was my forebear. Now when Duke William earlier besieged Rouen, the defenders hung cow hides on the battlements to mock the tanner's son. The recent TV programme mistranslated it embalmer's son, which makes no sense at all, which they did not even notice. On capturing the town William sent for the four offenders and had their arms and legs cut off. You could not do it today. Was it Normandy genes kicking in, or those from Graie sur Mer I still enjoy? I would hope the former. Graie is from the same root as grain. The village sign is a windmill. We were dusty millers, high tech in those days. There was no tanning or embalming there. The village has not changed much since we left.

Horus (3) is the Ancient Egyptian son of Osiris. Osiris, the Greek name, was Au-sa-Rai, Our Sarah, (he was a fellah) was the everlasting-rising-of the sun, in Egyptian. Like the sun which sets but rises again smiling, Osiris guaranteed the annual regrowth of the crops, and personal immortality. He himself had demonstrated remarkable fertility, since he succeeded in fathering Horus even after his genitalia had been cut off and thrown away by the wicked Saitan, our Satan, the grim reaper, from the Lithic Sai-ta'n, vitality-severing, thought to have been called Set by the academic Egyptologists who remain unaware of the proper pronunciation of the language. Our Satan is credited with even worse mischiefs. Osiris beat him by actually managing to grow a new penis – some say it was a graft provided by his mother and wife Isis who badly wanted a kid - and it is always shown exposed poking through his mummy shrouds as firm evidence of its regeneration. So he rises smiling once more although mummified. Horus is from the Lithic Iha-u-rau-sai, He that-one/who-raised-alive. He was born from the dead as it were, thanks to his father's remarkable powers of sexual regeneration. He was however, in accordance with the Egyptian whimsy, anything else as well that his name of power bestowed. So he was also Iha-u-Ra-sai, It that-one/unit-of Ra-movement, which is why our hour is so named from the Latin hora; while the Greeks had hora for a different sun unit, a season, and later we got our own year, another sun unit, from the same Lithic phonemes only garbled a bit, year from i-ai-a-rai, it-that which-one-of the sun. Partridge debates if the Latin ire to go, Lithic ai-are, semantic content simply extending-verbal suffix, contributed to our year, German jahr. The fact is Year itself had ia in front, which enabled generations of folk etymologists to pronounce year as a unit denoted by the travel of the sun, (without calling upon the final r for Ra), probably from mid season to mid season as measured in stone circles.

Hebe (3) was the Greek goddess of youthfulness and strength. Now ba (chapter 3) meant flesh, and of course flesh is muscle and fat, but mostly muscle. To be bai was to be burgeoning with bulging muscles. In youth your body (Lithic bau-dai, twin-fleshed, remarking its remarkable dual symmetry, left half a mirror reflection of the right half) is still building and burgeoning also, putting on muscle. With -bai we have youthful musculature. The He- therefore appears to be merely another Cockney h, with the Lithic Ai-ba-i, That which-ba-ing. However you may like to remember this was a goddess and it may be she was rejoicing in youths as they established their manhood, and that was why

Chapter 7 Ha

she was adopted as youth's champion. In this case Hebe should be moved into column 6, rejoicing in the musculature. There is also the fact that the male genitalia was suppose to blossom at puberty and the testicles were actually regarded in the old days as fruit, achieved at maturity when the fleshing out was complete. Or else again, Hebe simply registered her representation of high musculature, a goddess of body building. Partridge just jumps to Lithuanian jegiu meaning I have the strength, and concludes the Indo-European etymon or original root was iega, ignoring the switch from g to b. But g does not flip to b. Why should it? If you can simply ignore the consonants, etymology becomes impossible. Language as we understand it, as opposed to calls sung out in vowels before speech, came in with the consonants as we learned to sound them (and label them with meanings), along with the mere vowelisations of our previous communicating system. Admittedly we say befall and the Germans say gefallen, but they are not equivalents. Be- is present tense, ge- is past. It is not a case of one changing to another. The Lithuanian jegiu seems to be from the Lithic i-ai-kai-u, it-that which-strong-one, using kai, strong, in place of bai, burgeoning.

Halter (2) by comparison is a bit of a damp squib. The la phoneme looks at once like the one shared with helots, since they share an element of confinement. Lai can also be lithe and sinuous, a character it picks up by being in antithesis to the phoneme ka, which is hard and rigid, gulled from flints. Helots (3) vary somewhat in their agility and this aspect is inappropriate for them – unless servility can be counted as emotional sinuousness and agility. Partridge sends us off mischievously to the entry he has for helve which he also finds akin to helm (2) (the rudder you steer with, from ai-lai'm, going-in a line/at sea'm), in turn akin to the one you wear on your head (3) (ahi-lai-mai, that which-surrounds [the head] and lowers the hammering [aimed at it]), and probably also related to the Lithuanian kilpa which means a stirrup and is from kai-lai-pa, making-a looping-piece of [for] the feet, (nothing at all to do with a helmet or a helve, as a matter of fact); while the English stirrup is composed of the phonemes stai-rai-upai, to stand-on both feet, well strictly standers for both feet: you stood up in your stirrups swinging your mace. Lithuanian, by the way, has the distinction of being the extant language most closely related to Sanskrit which (with Avestan) is the earliest and most fully recorded forebear of the whole Indo European family of languages. So here is quite a pie. In the case of the rudder, the helm which ships answer, I fancy it is from the Lithic ahi-lai-mai, which is that which-aligns-below, hidden under the water, in contradistinction to the helmet's that which-limits-the damage, or lays the marring. The helve must surely have started out with a b in place of a v. May I write he for ahi and ai, that which? If so helve (3) is from ahi-lai-bai, that which-linear-bai, the handle end of a linear tool. I think it referred originally to a linear tool which you swing, (the sun, helios (3), ahi-lai-oo-sai is from that which-looping-orifice-flaming) and was the end where you apply your muscles (ba), the handle you grasp. Perhaps the stirrup is a foot steering mechanism too, you steer with both feet, horse willing when riding, as well as tugging on the reins. If so the stirrup's terai is the steering as well as the drawing up. The Lithuanian stirrup, kilpa, (kai-lai-pa) similarly may have been making the alignment as well as a convenient loop to put your foot in. The halter is now clearer. The Lithic is ia-lai-terai-a, it that-loops-and pulls along, a loop for pulling along. It is clear to me Eric Partridge was diplomatic in what he revealed. What was too much for the senators he did not present. But it certainly appears he often knew more than he wrote. Not only that, but he was of course still confronting the prejudice, still observed in powerful places in the linguistic orbit, that the meanings to be attached to word roots are all random and not to be attended to. His dictionary usually omits the meanings altogether,

Chapter 7 Ha

unless they are positively required as some part of the etymology, as inevitably occurs quite frequently.

The fourth Haa! is a sharp shock, as when you pick up a white hot (4) stone. In the absence of sabre toothed tigers, if you put your child's hand on a steaming hot plate on the stove the first reaction you will get may well be a Haa! I have not tried it. "Hot!" is rather easily understood by infants if accompanied by suitable hand withdrawal gestures. A "Haa!" is even better. It is an involuntary sudden expulsion of breath which accompanies a sudden sharp pain or extreme dismay. In the absence of such a warning my elder daughter (when still very young) once inadvertently backed her bare bottom onto the element of an unguarded electric fire. What she said as she did it was a cross between an Aou! and a Hou! It was a cross between a wail and a howl (4). The source of her trouble was immediately apparent. Now a matron, I imagine the evidence of this misfortune must still be recorded on her tail. At one time you could make out the outline of the coiled electric element quite clearly. Her private Hell, just that place (2), is now a distant memory. Greek Hell was Hades (4), where Hai becomes/prevails, a hideous (4) hateful (4) place of harms (4), often made out as hot (4); so that Wayland Smith with only a little exaggeration in his own mind will sometimes use the expression "as hot as Hell".

A heathen (4) is derived from the heath (4), an infertile area which has hai-tai, heat (4) dried-become, with nothing much but heath-er growing on it, but which can also be read as from ai-a-tai, that which-first-inhabited, or really where we were all first born, with only a little obliquity meaning inhabited. Because of the light soil the trees were stunted and easier to fell, so they got felled first to clear the land for cultivation. These areas were those first exhausted in turn, and so became Breck or broken ground abandoned as infertile open plains, colonised by heather and bracken and gorse (ga-u-rai sai, grow-where-heat rayed or dry); but eventually barren, the sandy soil by the eighteenth century blown into shifting dunes. But a heathen (hei-a-tehei-en) is also akin to a hoyden, a bold lass not waiting for the boys to make the advances, enjoying, tehei-ing; and it may well be both may have become known for their lack of morals, not infertile at all but on the contrary bumpkins, regarded as inadequates left behind on the less fertile ground or even pushed out onto it, with an eagerness for the simpler pleasures, hoyden, hai-a-tehei-en, enjoying-copulating, and thus jumping so far as the etymology is concerned from the third ha to the sixth, leaving out both the horrid fourth and the hilarious fifth altogether. Horror and hilarity incidentally make strange bedfellows in the same phonemic quiver, and their discovery points to the earlier overarching semantic content originally from the pain of a burn, which only the Lithic hypotheses can provide. Partridge has the gorse commonly found there akin to hearse and earlier hirce (a harrow (3) from Latin hirpex), as well as hirpus (3) for wolf, an enthusiastic (6?) foot traveler, fircus a he goat, and hirsute and even Greek kher (2) for hedgehog. But then he had no Lithic. Gorse is certainly prickly and so is a hedgehog. But wolves and goats are not definitively hairy. All animals have coats. The hearse and the harrow had ray shaped pieces, in the case of the hearse sticking up, sai, (as ornaments), although it may originally have been just a raised platform of strakes. The wolf rejoiced in his (fleet) feet, running his quarry to death, the goat had the same pleasure nimbly skipping from rock to rock. Hairs are rays, and the Greek kher for hedgehog from the original Lithic Khai-rai has hard sharp rays as does the Old English hedgehog, herrison from French hericon, from original Lithic ahi-rai-kaun, that which-rayed-both all hard and all over his body; which also gave the Latins their ericius, Lithic ai-rai-kai-u-s, that which-hard-rayed-body-altogether and whole body (but otherwise much like our rake which has only a single row of hard rays) the final s of ericius just being the Latin substantive marker.

Chapter 7 Ha

Hurrying (6) was first perhaps away from the sabre toothed tiger, under the influence of horrid rays. Partridge suggests it may be related to hurr, an echoic snarl (we can compare khurr with tigre, which we mispronounce as tiger, with the ti- readable as the feminine ending: mistress growler) and so a sound generating horror (4) and swift evasive action. Compare the Old Frisian (very close to Old English) hurrein, of winds, to blow in gusts. That suggests a hurricane, but hurricane is from Taino huracan, an evil spirit of the sea in the Caribbean, for which the original Lithic phonemes appear to have been I(h)-wa-ra-ka'n, He-terror-ray-makes, because it chimes with Wakan-Tanka, the Central American creator god, Wa-ka'n-Tan-ka, Terror-maker-World-maker or Awesome Creator.

With the arrival of a tiger the idea of hurrying away was about right (from horror at the harm anticipated). A harrier and a hawk similarly made havoc amongst their prey. Crying Hawoc (4) and unleashing the dogs of war has both the fourth h for horror and wa for shivering in fear (chapter 14) and ka for strike: it was actually shouted on the rampage by Wayland, who probably fancied words had the power to impose their meanings on the enemy along with the phonetics. Without getting too political, the Wahabi (6) tribe of Saudi Arabia, Wa-hai-bai, fear-rejoicing-habitually (as long as they remain bai, fleshed out, that is in being), were a fierce warrior race, using terror tactics over millennia, named by their long suffering neighbours as terrorists, but proud of it. To hate (6) is the emotion which engenders these practices. The Gothic hatis meaning hate (4), from the Lithic Hai-tai-sai is horror-become-sensed, a response to threat, real or imagined. The French elision hair (pronounce hai-eer) to hate seems to be semantically taking the initiative and anticipating hurt (4), and French haine (4) is showing hate or hateful, to be hated, whence the English heinous. Haunting (4) puts the frighteners on believers. Malay hantu an evil spirit (well –ta is an entity) does the same.

Home (3), with a Cockney h, from iha-u-mai, it that-where-begotten (mai = earthed, planted, impregnated, begotten), and has a wide following in Germanic tongues, often including the surroundings as well, such as a farm or estate. But inevitably home becomes an emotional tie as well, the third h picking up additional meaning from the eighth. Home economics has a degree of redundancy since economics is from the Greek ekoi-nomai, home rules or household management, home in this case from ai-kau-i, similarly that-we-kindled/begotten-we. Egypt (3) is from hoiku pata ahi, Lithic iha-u-kau-pata-ahi or it that-where-procreated–fathers-our,The Fatherland. (Egyptologists imagine Egypt is from the god Ptah. But the god Ptah turns out to have been Our Fathers, an ancestor god like a totem). Home clearly has acquired some of the semantics of happy h (6). The German heim shifts towards hei-i-mai, with affection for where you originated, leading perhaps to powerful patriotism, even right or wrong. The Malay hantu (4) is a horrid spirit to be kept away. It has of course nothing to do directly with an English haunted house, although in England there are those who would keep away from such a place as if it were from the horror h (4). And this particular haunt probably is. It has everything to do with the common Lithic underground promptings worldwide, informing meanings from the subconscious mind. The mixed meanings of the phoneme ha, sometimes appearing together in a single word string, if not common, is quite often to be found. A hideous (4) countenance however - one thinks inevitably of Dorian Gray - is a horrible one that clearly gives one a fright or feeling of repugnance and horror. Partridge nevertheless relates it semantically and phonetically to hairy, from the supposed horripilation (4), your pile or hair (or fur) standing on end from horror. The Lithic however clearly suggests the hair, which stands on end when horrified, is just a pile (long pieces, or surface looped, ie skin), and has a Cockney h only, the hair is just from the Lithic elements of the a(h)i-rai,

132

Chapter 7 Ha

that(h)which-rayed, or else from khai-rai (2), grown-rays, or even of the body-rays. After all the hair is raised from the flesh; it sticks out and comprises very thin strands like rays, but above all it grows. We do not feel horror with our hair all the time, nor did they in the Stone Age either. Most of us probably never experience horripilation (the hair standing on end from fear) at all. Perhaps animals use it more to express fear and hostility, as well as to keep them warm, paradigmatically the porcupine, which is the spiny pig, from Old Provencal Porc-espin. The porpoise, in passing since Partridge adds it in for good measure, is called a pig-fish, apparently elided all the way from the Latin Porcus-piscis.

The Japanese have an irrational habit of committing hara-kiri (6) when the shame of living gets too much for them. It comprises a ceremonial slitting of your own belly with a sword which is stuck in and then drawn across, with fatal results. It must be pretty painful too. The hara is the belly, because like the heart in the West it is regarded as the seat of the emotions in Japan, so hara is the emotional organ, emotion for the Japanese an idea perhaps originating with a stomach ache? (The stomach does dictate emotional tone to a remarkable extent, while kiri is the cutting of it, refer to chapter 4). The power of the custom is locked within the words. Hara-kiri cuts the belly and cuts off the emotions both at once. True, it extinguishes life as well, but that is just the other part of the deal, to show you really mean it. The emotions to be cut off are of course the bad ones, chiefly the horror (4) of being shown up as failing in a code of honour (6), like losing a fight for instance, that fatal loss of face which all over the East is taken so seriously - almost as if it were a public castration. Honour (6) there is a question of how to handle the horrors (4). Westerners accept the contempt of others better, having thicker hides (2) and perhaps a more strongly built in self belief, with less consideration for the opinion of others. It seems the kow-tow (ka-u-tau in Lithic), is the ka-u-cut, the two kas both cut off, a bad pickle to be in. The ka is dual, the physical body, and the spirit, ended symbolically by prostration - the physical body and the spiritual ka at the same time. It is fancy taught and not inherited, of course.

English honour (6) however employs the happy h, indeed it shows it in the Latin honos, an honour awarded, an office of honour or the quality of honour, Lithic hau-nau-s, is admiration-shown-substantive ending. Here Wayland has picked up on the oblique stem of the Latin as we see in the accusative case, honorem, when picking the English, probably just because it gives him that little bit more to get his mind round. The priests of Amun of Egypt used "Hei" as Halelujah (6), with arms raised in appeal and praise of their Deity above. Hale-luya might be read as a Heil-and a high level one, I suppose. It was not in English of course. In Hebrew it is read as Praise to Jaweh (3).from Hale-al-Iuai. But the semantics of hail (6) a high (6) one is incorporated in the semantics of the phonemes in the idioms of other languages too, including hale in good health in English. Hare Krishna, hooray (6) for Krishna is from the same source. I have not followed the theology of Krishna but kare-ish-en-a in Lithic phonemes carries the semantic content perhaps, inter alia, of creator-life-of-eternal, or some such, a big claim.

The fifth ha is shortly disposed of: Ha! Ha! Hilarity (5) gets its meaning from the human reaction to a humorous circumstance of whatever kind. It is outside the scope of this study to consider what all these circumstance might be. The suddenness of the perception must take one by surprise, for which purpose it is usual for comics to lead their audience up the garden path thinking they have understood the story line, only to be overtaken by the sudden denouement, breaking the mould, and the realisation they or the character in the tale had it all wrong. The Greek god Komos, kau-mau, from whom we get our comedy, personified a flaked mind or broken line of mental thinking, leading to comedy. However hilarity has not spawned much in the way of collateral ratiocination. This is probably partly because the sixth ecstatic h has monopolised the field. Laughing and procreation often come close together; indeed the Eskimo was said at one time to offer his wife to a visitor with the suggestion they should laugh together. It is surely a matter of some regret that the human mind should prove to be so thoroughly soused in sexual metaphor, dating back to the earliest mouthings to each other, since it makes the whole of the Lithic hypotheses that much harder for academia to accept. But there is resignation too, since sexual metaphor is comparatively easy to identify. Sex is simple – we all know how to do it, it is a conservative tradition, and Wayland is thoroughly at home with it. "Hie thee to a nunnery" I hear; and Partridge offers the original mission of folk who hied. It means to get along in a hurry. In the case of the Lithic it is surprisingly complex. Since aaa was just extension before it was worded up and specified more fully, ai, amongst a good many other things according to context meant to extend your position, and so to go. The Latin ire to go can be read in those terms, from ai-are, just extensive–verbal ending. With a Cockney h (3), hie is ahi and so ai, just plain going. But now we learn that it has the additional meaning to strive, to hasten, and in Dutch to pant, to be eager or desirous. This has clearly picked up the sixth and highly sexual hai, which has come to be spelt hei in Egyptian and which must now be dealt with at some length. There is an element of humour in hieing of all places to a nunnery. The Middle Dutch was higen. G could be pronounced like y. But it started out g, so there is the going in the Dutch along with the hieing. They evidently hied and then went – eagerly and in a hurry, the eagerness sexual.

The Lithic pai-hei, if you read the glyphs alphabetically – the Egyptians generally didn't – is conventionally just p-h. The Greeks had their conjunct letter phi for this dual sound, which is a p immediately followed by a ha, the conjunction readily transmogrified into fai. The Greek symbol was originally a circular orifice with a straight line entering it on the slant; but later it was extended so as to cross the circle, formerly more like our Q which was probably kau in Lithic terms, where the tip of the line is only just entering the circle, perhaps providing the stimulus which rounds out the kau (stimulated and aroused) circle in turn. The Greek phi thus appears to have been a penis in flagrante, while kau, our Q, meant struck; and striking could be a figurative strike, a kindling or anything with a sudden strong effect. Bearing in mind the lettering came aeons later than the meanings of the phonemes, the design of the lettering was presumably prompted by the meanings already given the sounds. This was clearly the case with the Egyptian hieroglyphs, which preceded writing as we know it. An unmistakable protruding penis was the glyph written as pahei and mai. We know this beyond a peradventure because with hieroglyphs, the sound glyphs would often be followed by a glyph showing the object resulting, or at least the class of objects. In effect you got the analytical phonics followed by the word, a trick the educational establishment in Britain has had to pretend to invent as "Synthetic Phonics" after abandoning it for thirty years - after five thousand years of world wide usage and in defiance of common sense, showing Sapiens Sapiens has a mind which can operate with a degree of inconsequence amounting to irrationality. The whole teaching body in the country is exposed as effectively without intelligence for two teaching generations, rendering three or four generations of the less bright pupils virtually illiterate. It was not as if the penny dropped even then. The illiteracy forced reconsideration, fiercely resisted by teachers. This is not too severe a criticism, but it is unfair to imagine such insouciance confined to teachers. It is the common lot of mankind. We have forgotten Lithic for even longer.

Chapter 7 Ha

Phal meant fruit in Sanskrit[2] male genitalia being regarded, quite perversely of course, as the animal equivalent of the fruiting bodies of the vegetable kingdom. The phallus (6) was the glans, from the Lithic elements pa-hei-lau's, where the lau comes from the meaning looping and so looped or blown out like a ball or a balloon, or a puff ball, (and not the whole [engorged] penis). Glans is Latin for the acorn, which is a seed, which happens to sit in a cup. To our forebears it looked like the way the glans on the end of the penis sits in the foreskin when semi aroused (or circumcised). In Malay buah, from the Lithic bau-ahi, dual (or round) burgeoned-ones, means both testicles and fruit. Our forebears thought they were the same. To avoid too much confusion the testicles were further marked out as buah pelir in Malay, with batang (meaning stem or stalk, from the Lithic ba-ta-aang, a bit-become-extended) pelir meaning the penis, pelir from the Lithic pai-lairai, piece-linear or long. Furthermore Malay paha (6) is the hip (6), Lithic the joy piece in Malay and English alike. In Malay adjectives follow the noun, in English they precede it. Sex (sai-kai-sai, pleasure-making-life, the making really applies both ways, it is almost poetic: pleasure making life making) uses the hips to obtain the reciprocal motion stimulating the genitalia. The hip that is a haw (6) meanwhile bears an albeit modest similarity in appearance to the glans in arousal, the –au being the completive vowelisation, hau meaning aroused. In the Stone Age you had to make allowances of course for the differences in detail to be expected between the vegetable and animal kingdoms. The English ham (6), which refers to that part of the anatomy, and not the cooking by smoking, is from Lithic hai-mai, and identifies the haunch (6) as the actuator in copulation, mai being – inter alia - planting or impregnating in Lithic. Haunch says virtually the same, hai-u-en-khai, orgasm-one-of-maker.

There is much speculation about the Sumerian language and who the Sumerians were. In this book it is argued they were Adamites who came by boat, like Noah, from Eastern Malaya, the Eastern Garden or Garden of Eden (Malaya means the Garden land, and Eden is from ai-tai'n, where it born, ie where the sun rises each day, the East), and it is now 360 feet under the South China Sea. The Sumerians wrote in cuneiform script, later adopted across the Middle East by the speakers of Semitic languages. It is not known to what extent the Semitic tongues gave the same phonetic values to the cuneiform letters. Nevertheless it is by now reasonably clear, from correspondences with Akkadian, that the Sumerian for testicles was pronounced dobur. I have identified this nomenclature as uncommonly like the Malay do buah, two fruits or two testicles; and I regard this as evidence these were Adam's testicles and the Sumerians were Adamites from Malaya, driven from the Garden of Eden by the final great circumpolar ice melt between eight and ten thousand years ago, which raised sea levels by 360 feet.

Kunchi in Malay is a lock or keyhole. Kunchi paha is the groin. The kunchi is from the Lithic ku-en-khai, a structure-of-joining, a lock in the form of a great bolt slid across two swing leaf doors each with wooden channels or later metal brackets. The bolt, and later the key, in a sophisticated levered lock which operates the lock, is anak kunchi, son of the lock, the boy piece. The Lithic elements of anak are an-a-kai, one-that-kindled or begotten, and so son. But the Lithic an-a-kai also means one-that-actuates. That applies to the bolt and to the key. The keyhole of the later levered lock then becomes ibu kunchi, mother of the lock, the female part, a usage similar to our usage of male and female threads, picking up on the sexual meaning of anak. Egyptologists should recognize anak as one recension of the Egyptian Ankh or ansate cross, from the Egyptian Anakahi. The hieroglyph for H, a twitch, was pronounced ahi, from a-hai, that hurts, the hurter. Ansate is from the Lithic an-

135

aa-sai-tai, that long-life-becomes, or a-na-sai-tai, that-presents-easeful-birthing. Women wear it as a talisman without knowing quite why.

The Pharaoh the West knows as "Tooten Karmoon" was really Tutu anakai Amun in Egyptian, Tutu son of [the god] Amun. Tutu was in turn from the god Tahuti or Thot, which in Egyptian was really Tahu-tau, or Know-all, the all knowing, the source of all knowledge. The Lithic for ibu is i-ba-u, she-flesh-source. U got the meaning of source from springs which were holes, in their case in the ground. The original meaning of u was simply a rounded hole or orifice, from the shape of the mouth when saying ooo. Ibu kunchi, the mother of the key, was the key hole into which you inserted the actuator, the key. Our key is in fact from the same Lithic kai as the kai in Malay anak. The kunchi, from kau-en-kai, dual joint-of-joiner, the gadget that joins the two separate leaves of the door together, by putting a bar behind them, so they can not be opened, or pins them together with the tongue of the door lock we know.

The idea that the male genitalia, glans or testicles, could be regarded as fruiting bodies today seems just silly. But it was the Stone Age adjectival mind's attempt to validate the idea every character, if it was true, was to be found popping up everywhere. It was a common feature that was seen, not a complete equivalence, the terms in which we tend to think today when we think of equivalence. Stone Age minds were easily persuaded. The slightest indication would do. While vegetation was rooted and incapable of locomotion, animals moved around. There was therefore the less cause for surprise to find animals fruiting and unfruiting, seeding with their genitalia at will. Given what you knew about animal and vegetable behaviour you might almost have expected it. Half the population of the world today (or more) probably still regard the male semen as seed, (making the testicles a form of fruit), rather than just the pollen which it really is. Pollen, the lexicon tells us, was just ground flour or powder, from the Greek pale meaning dust and the Sanskrit palala flour, no doubt ground in a pestle pounding round and round, that is to say - lala (compare Lithic -lau, looped like in Apollo, that-go-loop-loop, the orbiter) which was how to get powders, including dust which must surely have been ground in nature's pestle (which more or less it had been) just like the ground, which too had been ground in nature's pestle - and grounds in ours. Pollen was seen to fly in the wind, which is expressed by la. If there were any dandelions around, or other seeds with sails, they will have confirmed the equivalence of pollen as diminutive seed. There is nothing about flour or powder or dust, all insignificant and feeble, blowing in a puff of wind, which would encourage a male chauvinist – the common sort - to welcome it as in any way equivalent to his own pride and joy, his sperm. Compare Greek spora, seed, and speirein to sow or sprinkle or spray, with sa meaning fire, life and action. Compare spark, from sai-pai-rai-kai, fire-shoot-that-arising-makes.

We can see the Sanskrit ph was pronounced as an aspirated p, more like the Egyptian pahei than the Greek phi or our f, because phani was a snake, from the Lithic pa(h)i-nai, with the meaning skin showing or bare just like our English snake, from si-na-kai, brer-bare-body. There is a kinship with our naked, Lithic na-ka-ti, expose-body-orifices. There was never a verb to nake, meaning to throw off all your clothes, as Partridge appears to have thought. However phana is the hood of a snake in Sanskrit, such as the cobra inflates when roused, and phakka means to swell, from pahai-kai, to actuate the pahai, not a mile away from our own four letter f-word. Pha-na can thus be read as Spit-presents, ie it is the warning sign it is about to sting. Cobras do spit as well as strike and bite, and can blind you without striking. Moreover phanda, Lithic paha-en-da, pahei-ing-does, is a trap, noose, gin, snare, or trick, all with a snap if not exactly an ejaculatory action by our standards of comparison.

In Arabic as in Hindi a fakir is a naked mendicant beggar or sadu still to be found wandering the streets in India, naked, hirsute and sometimes gabbling, but ignored. Fakir is supposed to come from the meaning poor but the Lithic suggests it means naked, in his case with his pahei-ka-rai, his genitalia made -rai or visible. It is a mocking term. The poverty is derived from his ownership of nothing at all, not even a strip of cloth for a dhoti, a dhau-ti, an orifice thing, or else the two orifices, the standard modesty garment wound around the crotch, entirely suitable for workers when engaged in manual work in a hot clime. Derivations often have the cart before the horse like this when they have been worked out on the assumption the phonology is meaningless. Phatkana in Hindi is to give a cloth a violent shake, to shake it out; whence to scold or rebuke, a dressing down, while phatakana is to winnow. Kana in Hindi means to make or do. Phatna is to burst or explode, a sudden ejaculation. So Phatkana combines phatna and kana. Compare bolna and ana, to call out and to come, with bolana meaning to summon. "Ghari bolao", call a goer (a ponycart), on leaving a diner. Pharakna is to throb. Pharapharana is to throb, flutter or flap up and down. All these semantic contents can claim kinship with the Ancient Egyptian pahei or joy piece with its common behaviour world wide. It is the Lithic in the human subconscious, world wide, which produces these cousinages. Borrowing world wide is fanciful. Academia uses it world wide to shuck off any semantic content of the phonemes. The idea will meet resistance, including NIH (Not Invented Here), but it must become recognized in time. The evidence is too world wide to be dismissed.

Anyway we can guess straight away that the hei which appears in the name for the Egyptian penis has the sixth and happy h at the front of it. The hieroglyph for hei is a loop of string twisted three times, much like the twitch still used on a horse's lip to take its attention away from a worse mischief being performed upon some other part of its anatomy, stitching a wound for instance. Surprisingly it works. You keep varying the squeeze on the lip by twisting the twitch with a flick of the wrist. This makes it clear however the happy h was not the original one for hei. The hurtful (4) one was, such as eventuates when pressing the bare flesh against a live electric element. But it can hardly be challenged the pahei is a source of vehement pleasure. Ha, except for the Cockney version, comes always from such a sudden burst of sensual or emotional response, shock or horror, pleasure or surprise. Hilarity combines them both. Ha was the gasp in all these cases. There were no ice creams in the Stone Age. But all the extreme sensations came to be Ha! Their pleasures were few and relatively far between; but we can tell from the lexicon if we pay close attention that they gasped at orgasm as well as when burnt. At other moments of ecstasy - the all male Amaun priesthood for instance let out the very same cry when standing arms uplifted in adoration of their God – Hei was the most ecstatic greeting tone available: Glory! Glory!...Hallelujah! Hail! Hail! Lord Uiai, the Universal and Eternal. The Hebrew for praise here is halle, the -lle- is tongue work, as in our laud and loud: intoning hei. Hallelujah is Praise to Yahwe. Al hamd al Illah in Arabic is praise to Allah. Hail to thee blithe spirit, bird thou never wert! Heil Hitler! Good health! The American campus greeting of Hi! falls shorter, but clearly is out of the same stable, its orgins fallen away. The Scots when they spoke Gaelic would astonishingly address their wives as hen, but it was not the clucking sort, it was a joyous greeting. The hale and hearty are in conspicuously good health. Malay hati for heart, unconnected in any direct way with English heart, identifies the organ as crucial to liveliness and the emotional liveliness which goes with good health. "Banyak suka hati sahaya berjumpa lagi dengan inchek", "Very sugar hearted I a-meeting again with you", or very nice to see you again, in Malay. All these words in ha take their meanings from the sixth h for happiness.

The hips provide the pumping motions required in sex, which is why they were so labeled, hei-pai, the copulatory pieces. Hippies picked up the idea quite quickly, and wore their trousers low on their hips to give them the extra freedom for demonstrating the movements in public as a tease. I have sometimes wondered if the boys at Rugby public school in the days of Doctor Arnold, now a hundred and fifty years ago, who legislated plenty of cold showers for teasing growing lads, were not somehow subconsciously influenced when they decided to handle their ball to redesign it in the shape of a rose hip rather than just the round one they had been kicking about before, to tease the Doctor in turn - although perhaps not fully aware of what they were doing. Some Greeks would not eat beans, faba, originally probably named from pai-bai, covered berries, we would say legumes, but by folk etymology transmogrified to the pahei beans, viz the testicles, since to the sexed up mind the broad variety do have much the same shape, and such a mind would be eager to make the connection. It ties in with the Malay buah and the Sumerian two burr. You have to recognize the human sexual addiction when beans and avocados, large and small, attract similar identification. Humanity has already been touched on. It is from the Latin humanus, and must surely be related to the Latin homo; but not to the Greek homo which means not man but the same, as in homosexual which describes those attracted to the same sex. Here with the Greek we have a Cockney h: iha-au-mau, dual masses, two equal masses, two the same, probably first the same weights when weighing, establishing the balancing principle with scale pans on the ends of a tipping bar suspended in the middle, measuring the mai or downward instincts of the two pans; but then the same of any measure. The Latin Homo (6) has a strongly pronounced h, and is ab origine a happy h, indeed it is the happy h like the Egyptian hei. The Lithic hau-mau, both in the matching dual case, is both enjoying impregnation. To think that our forebears were unaware of the differences between their sexuality and the animal sexuality in the wild, which was nearer to a capture than any embrace, is surely absurd. The carnivor's embrace is with his teeth. The popular perception of the shaggy alpha male in the Stone Age dragging his females into the cave by their hair is a chauvinistic absurdity. If only it were thus! But it never was. Or at least not since the hominid taming of fire, so that all those hunkered unwrapped around the hearth, after a tenderised meal cooked in the embers round the edge, were good and ready. The heat will have brought both male and female on together. If the girls took longer, their job as mistresses of the flame all day will have levelled the playing field somewhat. They identified humanity as the unique species with both sexes enjoying sex, hai-u-ma'n, enjoying-both-the impregnation.

All humanity springs from this evolution. We live in the latter stages of the fire age, still trying to catch up, and now the information age has overtaken us. The academic view we are earthlings and chose to call ourselves as much, from humus, is ludicrous. Why on earth? Humus has a Cockney h like the Greek homo where it means the same, ia-u-mau-substantive marker. The mau here names the soil which is granular and (naturally) mau, milled, like the ground, grinded to soil. The meaning of humus is that which-altogether-mashed, according to Wayland Smith. Ka, the basic hard structure of the world, which included of course the rocks, the rau kai, made roasted like ceramics and so hardened. But there is other evidence the rocks were also identified as risen, rau, hard core elements, kai. Witnessing volcanoes had taught mankind that much at least. Rocks could be pounded to bits, anyway the sedimentary rocks could, when they became mai, milled, soil, milling was

Chapter 7 Ha

mai-lai, solids-flowing, it rendered the solid fluid. Flints were quite different, they shattered: you never got a granular structure, only smaller and smaller slivers which cut you. Try moulding that and you would be in ribbons. We do not know why the Latins picked homo. Quite possibly neither did they. But it comes from far back when folk did know, and if it had survived for a few millennia, or more likely for many millennia, only under the surface in the subconscious mind, that is no great cause for surprise. They used hemo for a single homo, as if the h were Cockney, the Lithic a(h)i-em-au, one which-of-all, anybody; whence nemo for nobody. Partridge has one paragraph on homo and the remaining thirteen on the earthlings. Since impregnation was regarded as the planting of seed (which was originally in the earth) we should expect to find the ma phoneme doing duty in both cases. Homo, from Hau-mau is the same as humanity, man identified by way of his shared sexuality, his ability to love. It may have been aspirational to some extent, but it is a very human aspiration.

The haunch is like the hips, hau´n-khai, doing the business. A hammock (6) however is from the Spanish, but they got it on their punitive expeditions to South America (America is from the Lithic Aa-mai-Ra-ka, Far-sinking/dying-of the Sun-Country, the Far Western Land: discovered and named – it is in Carthaginian, a provincial Ancient Egyptian - by the Carthaginians), where the hammock is recorded from the Yukuna (a central American language) hamaca and the Taino amaca, and from Haiti. The hama (6) surely refers to copulation, orgasmic planting; and if Lithic applies there amongst the aboriginal tribes the ka has the semantic content of country, land and place. The hammock was the Yucuna finca or pleasuring place. No doubt the tribes slept in them as well, to stay clear of the creepy crawlies as well as flash floods in the jungle, as I did at one time. But I fancy a certain cheerful eroticism will have led them to name the equipment for the facility it provided for their principal interest in life, as if that were its sole purpose.

A hand can be used for most manipulations. We do not know our Stone Age forebears' predilection. Perhaps it was from number two in the psychosemantic tree, chipping flints, kha´n-da, chipping-does or making-does makes sense. But mischief may have prompted boys in the Pleistocene however, just as today. We may be using the sixth ha here. Nobody had thought as yet to tell them they would go blind; ha'n-dai is a sexual stimulater; and there is the finger too which looks remarkably like from Lithic pahai'n-kara. Pahei could mean the principal erogenous zone of either sex. While the boys could bring their whole hand to bear the girls were stuck with a single finger. There were no civilised standards as we understand them to be defended by fair (6) means or foul (4). The heart is taken, quite wrongly, to be the emotional seat. It started out just the thumper, Greek kardia and ker, Latin cor from ka-u-are, strike-one-verbal ending, the striker. With h instead of kh it is in column 6 in place of 2. The stomach, as the Japanese have spotted, with their hara-kiri, is nearer the mark; and even they need to go a little lower to pick up the hormonal centre of the happy bits.

The hearth (6) itself betrays some of the thinking surrounding it. Hei-arai-ta(h)ai is a rozener for sure. Loosely, it had become an arouser, stimulating concourse not necessarily sexual. The German herd and heide discourage treating the th in the English hearth as original. Hai-are-dai from hearth however suggests joy-verbal marker-gives, enjoyment giver, the hearth makes you feel warm and comfortable at least. But the heat also stimulates sexuality, and we should probably give the Hei the full force of the happy h. It does not need to be an elided kh after all, as Partridge thinks. Lithuanian kharstas is hot, but the Lithic is kha-ra-sai-tai-s, make-verbal-hot-become-substantive ending. The Greek keramikos for ceramics is from the Lithic kai-rai-mai-kau-sai, made-rayed-earth-made-fired, ore fired in a kiln, (and then hardening as it cools).

Hymen (6) was the Greek goddess of marriage. To marry was to do the business, ma-are, to plant seed. Hei-mai-en is ecstatic impregnation which Hymen epitomised, in praise of marriage (the impregnation). Ma femme is femme from phai-mai, my delightful sexual partner. The hymen is the membrane broken in the process. Our hymns (6) started out as bridal songs from the Lithic hei-mai'n, literally celebrating-the impregnation. Not many parsons know that their hymns originally celebrated the rupture of the hymen. They will wish to argue it is outmoded as a derivation, and it is a fair point. Language is a whimsy all along.

Hemp (6), from Old English haenep, belongs with the sixth h, in Lithic a hei-nai-pai. Chewing it appears to have given folk a high over the millennia, if not an actual orgasm apparently an ecstatic elation – hei-nai, or hei-mai. Hemp is named for the utility of its leaves. The -pai may even refer to its leaves, but the word in German appears to point elsewhere. The Old High German hanaf, German hanf for hemp embodies the Lithic ha-na-pahei which seems to pick up on orgasm precisely, since each one of these phonemes can stand for as much on its own. Certainly the fibre, which serves to weave stout canvas and strong hawsers gets no mention. Cannabis, the same plant as the canvas plant, clearly also refers to its narcotic effect. It is akin to kannabis in Greek, and copies exactly the Latin term. The Old Bulgarian or Old Church Slavic was konoplja. The Lithic from the Slavic is Kau-nau-palu-a, make-orgasm-phalus-one. It appears to have given the Old Bulgarians an erection at least – they weren't picky - or else they were footloose about the way they handled similes. For the Poles it is konop, while the Lithuanian is kanapes, going back before the Greek. It has a more convoluted linguistic origin than hemp. At least it provides an ecstatic feeling. In reality it does nothing for virility, but it provides a substitute or simulacrum, a kind of ecstatic swoon accounting for its hold on those addicted, most often inadequates. Walshe's Concise German Etymological Dictionary of 1952, which Partridge quotes, cites similar Cheremiss and Zyrjan words from the Finno-Ugric family, "a wandering culture-word of wide diffusion". Cannabis has had a widespread pull. Our canvas is hempen cloth, cannabaceus in Latin.

The French canapés, light aperitif snacks eaten before a meal or in its place, actually mean sofas or divans in French. The original piece of furniture seems to have been what we would now call a chaise longue, because a canapé-lit is a sofa bed. The idea apparently was canapés were to be eaten reclining comfortably, not at table but in the classical Roman style. The question then presents itself why canapés is sofas in French (and a preprandial snack taken on them before sitting down to the main meal) and the narcotic herb in Lithuanian. The established answer is of course these sorts of coincidences are common since all or most words have been randomly selected, so that it is a waste of time to bother with reasons – and only a mug would try. The divan allows you like the Romans to put your feet up. The Lithic is thus ka-na-pai, make (or place)-stick up-[your] feet. The drug in turn had the same result. You reclined under the influence of the drug, probably imagining yourself in a yellow submarine and quite unfit for work. But it may have made your penis stand up too, at least in fantasy. It is a misfortune the feet and the penis both answer to pai, both thinned diminutive derivatives from bai, the flesh, the limbs compared to the main body and the penis compared to the bum, the principal fleshy bit, that is the muscular part of the body. Originally pai was (with commendable logic) the skin. From goatskin tents metaphor gave roofs, and then polis, from pau-lai, all the roofs or residences enclosed in a loop, a city. The polysemy results from the very general meanings the

Chapter 7 Ha

original phonemes originally had and the consequently numerous derivative meanings they acquired. It was this polysemy indeed which led eventually to the abandonment of the system of stringing phonemic meanings to make a composite meaning by a process of ratiocination – of a sort - and led, after the taua (birth, rebirth, renaissance or even revolution) or tower of Babylon, to the acceptance of the phonology and memorized composite meanings, regardless of the structure of meanings by means of which words had been built up over the aeons. It was the second birth of civilization, the first at the hands of our hominid forebears when they learnt to speak.

NOTES

1. M O'C Walshe. A Concise German Etymological Dictionary. 1952.

2. Sanskrit phala meant fruit, and thence consequence, result, reward, recompense, retribution, punishment, loss, disadvantage, gain, enjoyment, compensation, result of a calculation, product, quotient, interest on capital, and finally arrowhead, from the penis head (which surprisingly had percolated all the way through the gallimaufry just listed). It is a nice example of the polysemy which arose from using the phonemic semantic contents in an ever widening metaphorical series of senses. You had to be a contextual wizard in Sanscrit to follow the right meaning. There is conspicuous virtue these days, with a million words in English, to have them rather more concise; meaning what they mean and not almost anything else. Now that we can think more succinctly we can get through more thinking in any time scale, and our thinking allows a more scientific intellectual address. That is civilization for you. I have another book on the stocks before I go, tentatively "The Making of Meanings"; but now in my 89th year it may never get done.

CHAPTER 8

LA. LYE LEAKING AND SLIPPING LOW TO THE OCEAN FLAT WHERE THE LONG SKY LINE LOOPS AND FLIES.

La, with a curled tongue, when our hominid forebears began learning to speak, was the first consonant or stop between the tones we used at the chimpish level, before we spoke. This was because la was the natural break between two tones or vowels, which were the only utterances we had to express meaning before we spoke: hoots and howls, to convey mood mostly. With the addition of the consonants, five with the tongue eventually – l la,ta,da, ra, and ish - language began. With a twist of the tongue it all began - tra-la! The trail is open for anyone who cares to pursue the matter and to piece together the sounds we uttered along with the meanings the hominid mind picked for them. There were howls and cries with semantic contents before speech but they were all vowels, plus perhaps a few growls, from the back of the throat, more of a khkh-aaa then a grr. There weren't that many vowels so the tonal qualities were in demand. Recent researches with recorded audiographs of chimpanzee cries have revealed that chimps are especially good at distinguishing tones, and have an extensive vocabulary of them for different foods, etc. The Hamitic 'Chimpanzee', its anglicised form, in Lithic can be read as Si-m´pan-sai, brer-him-going-up, brer climber. In Malaya a friend had a tame pet Siamang ape. They have very long arms and swing around the place at speed. Louis could be twice round the room on the picture rail in half a dozen swoops. Si-a-ma-ang is Brer-un-heavy-one or Brer-weightless in Lithic phonemes. The llama from South America is pronounced in the native tongue yama and the Lithic is Ia-a-ma, it that-un-massy, another Brer Weightless or Mr Lightfoot. They have very long legs and their hind legs appear to be only lightly fastened to their bodies. They have a fair turn of speed, similar to a horse, and it is from an hour old, to escape the coyotes. The original wild llama or guanaco is called simply the original 'wild species', Lithic gua-en-a-kau, country-in-that-begotten We still keep la as a separater between notes in tunes, without any meanings, along with do, ray, me, etc to make a scale. To go-la is to make a la, to sing; and a gala is a sing-song in origin. A gale is a wind that sings, and a nightingale sings in the night. In addition Ma and La were one more oppositional pair, because Ma meant massive and heavy (chapter 10) while La came to mean light and floating. It can be clearly seen that the hominid adjectival mind thought in opposites. See chapter 15 on thinking.

    The semantic contents of the phoneme la, once the hominid mind got to work on it, as well as what Sapiens Sapiens has contributed since, are in the psychosemantic tree on page 146 under forty subsidiary heads, with columns indicating some of the English usages. The contents are to some extent arbitrary. The pursuit of meanings for this book, which started out as a very large crossword puzzle with a myriad clues and solutions, came quite soon to resemble instead an outsize jigsaw puzzle of vast expanse, a linguistic panorama, a complex texture rather than the bare loose network of meanings, with stops between, of the crossword puzzle.   What is more, the pieces have the habit of jumping places, with connections all across the board (or boards). Not only are the phonemes and their meanings strung into words, a historical development without end, but, wherever

Chapter 8 La

phonemes appear on the boards, their other meanings make a field around the meanings in use, like the residual fields around protein chains of radicals (which make them twist up into irregular lumps instead of lying out straight in a simple line). A phoneme emplaced in a word often exhibits a meaning from a meaning 3 but with a whiff of meanings 23 and 24 as well. That surely is a sign of the subconscious mind at work, maybe mine but equally probably the mind of man in earlier days - as it is intended to show beyond a peradventure before we are done.

With a curled tongue la picked up its first widespread semantic content as "Nasty taste!" like "Yuk!" these days, which is a glottal stop representing sickness. Working backwards from current usages of the letter L it becomes clear the two first meanings given to La, taken to be the natural meanings of the phoneme when first we learned to utter it, were nasty taste and its scientific accompaniment (of the day) the instinct of water to seek the lows, it's taste becoming nastier the lower it goes. Natural pollution meant river water tasted best at the source, the spring, and picked up off flavours (the riverbanks were inhabited) the further downstream it flowed. It finished at the estuary brackish; and the ocean is just brine. The going low, of course, is not really the natural accompaniment of the deterioration of the taste, but it was evidently taken to be so. Stone Age science had established it was the instinct of water to go downhill and to taste nastier as it did so, starting as clear as crystal in a spring and ending briney in the sea. The purity of the water became polluted in the rivers on their way to the ocean, even in the Stone Age. Dead creatures fell in them so that they picked up off flavours even in the haunts of coot and hern. To defaecate in Malay is pergi ka sungei, go to the river, where we say we attend to our toilet. (By the way, pergei in Malay is from pai-kai, make with the legs, and sungei is from sai-awan-kai, action-of water-cut, much slovened over the millennia but still readily recognizable as a river if you are prepared to look at them with fresh thinking). The function is by nature distasteful, we would really prefer to be just blithe spirits, and we do not directly foul our lips unless we really must. At the estuaries the water was brackish and salt. Whence indirectly there is 'Lat!' in Arabic for no, don´t [drink it, it is bitter and will make you sick]. The negative in Arabic otherwise is ma – the opposite of sa, so and si, yes, all sibilants.

In English there is lye for any bitter brew or other suspect liquid not clear as spring water. Moreover the Germanic etumon (Lithic ai tau-maun, as it-born-minded or meaning, but now perversely taken to mean its original phonetic form instead) of our English lye appears to have been lauga, slovened to Old English leah; but the Dutch have kept the g of the earlier form with loog. The Lithic will have been lau-kai or -gai, made (low and) bitter (3).

Water apparently loved the land and would lie itself down on it if given the chance, so that it was evidently taken to be possessed of an instinct for that pattern of linked behaviours: going low and becoming lye, as well as having a flat surface. The point here is merely that both the urge to slip away into the lows, and the predilection for off-flavours were seen as instinct in liquids. It was rubbish of course, but in the Stone Age it passed for science and common sense even. If there were any Pleistocene Einsteins no doubt they were firmly told to shut up, or ignored altogether, as sometimes can still happen today as punishment for stepping out of line and not being intellectually correct (IC) or academically correct (AC), sub categories of the better known Politically Correct (PC). The totalitarian streak is in every polity and in every mind. Anthropomorphic imagination influenced our early ratiocination. The patterns we spotted at home base from our own interests, promptings and behaviours we naively transferred to nature at large. By the time

Chapter 8 La

river water had hit the beaches it had got as low as it could get in this world, it had hit the ultimate depth, it had gone home and it had also turned completely briney and bitter. It made Neptune an old buff. Partridge has him originally a god of springs, Lithic naipa-tau-nai, of water-birth-presenting, (who must have got caught up in the liquid, and so carried off down river to the sea). Much of this was perceptive in a minor way.

Salt, sel in Latin, is from the Lithic sai-lai (3), [heated and] dried-lye, dried sea water. Compare the English sere from Lithic sai-rai, originally flame-rayed and so dried, see chapters 13 for sai and 12 for Rai. The sea is lyr in Old Celtic, probably pronounced originally approximately lua, and it is laut in Malay, from the Lithic elements la-u-tai, la (then with the u the dual and completive case, and so altogether run down and altogether bitter)-become. Liquidity for the ancients comprised those two linked instinctive developments and they were due to lack of fibre. Liquid is from Lai-kau-i-dai, La´s-dual drives-which-does. Water has no sensible structure, it is yielding and accommodates itself to its surroundings by going low and lying flat, picking up an off flavour as it goes.

Babylon is taken to be to do with the babel of tongues in the Bible; and in favour of whoever it was who wrote that bit ba and la, lip and tongue are widely used to indicate language. But Lithic can produce a better match for bab. Babylon really meant Bab-i-laun, mouth of the lawn, the flat salt marshes, now the Sha'at äl Arab, the spread of the river at its estuary where the water has risen level with the land. Sha'at is from the Lithic Sha-awa-tai, up-water-become, flooding the delta inhabited by the marsh Arabs, with channels and lagoons now networked by the hand of man. London like Babylon is at the estuary of its river, the lawn of the don or river. Donbas, River basin, the fertile valley where the vegetables are grown in Russia, and all the other rivers Don (and Deen and Dee), all originally birth canals (as in chapter 5) which have been transmogrified in the human subconscious into just natural geographical canals or channels. "Isis or Ock or Thame, Forget your olden name. Flow (19) down, Oh London (19) River, to your seagulls' silver wings". Yes, there are seagulls as well, with their silver wings[1], which this chapter sorts out next. Flow, gull and sil-, all in honour of Lon-, as the poet has it.

La (2) was the original separation of the pre-linguistic tones of which our cries and howls were made up, tones which we now reproduce as melodies: so la means song, or anyway a tone, and tra-la a string of tones, and so perhaps a tune (note the completive vowel is suggesting a tune which is made of a sequence of tones). La was an articulation between tones (musical notes) with the tongue curled, which came naturally. For speaking, the tongue (ta-un-kai) was the divide-one-making, the divider, and its use was first to divide the tones uttered. It was curled to intone la. Minstrels were ministers of song. A miners'gala (2) was originally a sing-song before they got around to politics. A gale is a wind which howls or wails. It makes a la or goes la. A call is from the same Lithic elements. A seagull is a sea caller and a nightingale is a caller or singer in the night. The lays of Ancient Rome were poems to be sung. Ballads - ba is lip and la is tongue [langue is the taster (11)] - were also sung by travelling minstrels, telling stories which were usually more or less fanciful, of courtly love. For ballad, the Lithic ba-la-dai is what lip-tongue/sing-does, a tale to music. Ba and la were compiled with the meaning elements of utterances in several widely separated languages, one of the most telling the North Queensland aboriginal Djeri-bal tribe, from the Lithic shai-rai-ba-lai, the shai-rai is shiny bright or clear (originally from shai-rai, a firey ray), and the Lithic ba-lai is speech. Djeribal is clear-speech or speakers in clear. Those who spoke other languages were speaking in incomprehensible verbal code. Then there is bolna in Hindi, to speak, one of the most widespread usages. In Hindi –na is the verbal infinitive ending. Babble and

Chapter 8 La

bellow in English have the same elements.

To lay an egg or lie down are both by way of lowering or letting slip down (24) the egg or the body. Melody, Lithic 'm-ai-lau-dai is him-that which-song-does, and it comes from the Greek melos a song, Lithic 'm-ai-lau's, him-that which-sung (2). The curlew says curlew in the night. Actually it does not have any consonants in its call. It really says her-wheew, just as the owl really says erwhee' erwoo-oo without any t in it at all. We fool ourselves because of our own speech habits. In Ancient Egypt the owl said "a'-maoo", which could be read as all the ma's, so the owl was the glyph for m, ma, mai, mau, depending on what followed. The lark is a singer too and the Old English was lawerce. The Low German lawerke and the Old Norse laervirki provide the opportunity to demonstrate to some effect the art of expansion to expose the Lithic. We have from the Old Norse laervirki the original Lithic form la-ai-rai-u-arai-kai, la[singing]-as it-rises-when-it is rise-making. The fact is a lark flies up higher and higher in arching spurts until it is so high you can lose sight of it, and the song goes with the rising spurts in its flight. As a boy I spent hours alone on the fen at the back of West Mere watching and listening to lark and snipe, in those days as common as muck. The Lithic perceptiveness is amazing. We were hell bent on learning from nature, 24/7. Nobody knows why the lark should do this. Eagles similarly do not appear to be looking for prey and never swoop down from their soaring flights, they are just making use of thermals for their fun soaring. In Tenerife where this chapter is written as many as thirty sea eagles can sometimes be seen, all having fun together in the thermals in front of the gigantic thousand feet cliffs rising straight out of the ocean. An osprey is from awa-sai-pai-rai in Lithic terms, water-above-pai (wings)-rising. Eagles in English are unpowered silent gliders, ai-a-kai-lai, Lithic that which-un-powered-float, they glide up without motion, utilizing the lift from thermal up currents. In Malay an eagle is lang, a glider. Yok Lang (Boy Eagle), an aboriginal living up to his name, made friends with a terrorist in the jungle, but reformed when we shot dead his hero Chawok (from Lithic Sha-u-au-kai, Action-superlative-and-strong), a Tarzan who had gone off the rails. Eagle and glider are perfect semantic and nearly perfect phonetic doublets. Thermals were way in the future. Both the lark and the eagle appear to be just having fun going up, which is why when we get up early it is said to be with the lark. The lark itself goes up in the middle of the day, when the sun is shining brightly. It is rejoicing. None of these four calling birds have any speech in their songs, they are just tunes, and plainsong at that.

From the truly aboriginal minds of hominids learning to speak, the bitter taste of the lye (3) shows today in words like sloe, from Lithic sai-lau, sense or taste-very bitter (3). Compare slow, from the same phonemes, this time speed-low. Countrymen, with fresh sloes on the blackthorn in the hedgerows to taste, will bear witness to the cogency of the name. Piccalilli and pickle are from the Lithic pai-kai-lai, pieces-made-lyey, or in the case of piccalilli lyey-lyey, very much so; and in the Dutch version meaning briney. One principal source of all the lai meanings undoubtedly comes from lye (3), the nasty taste. There is also blasphemy where the Greek precursor is blas-phemein, to blaspheme. Phemein is to ejaculate in Greek, the sexual meaning the original one. The Lithic is quite specific: pahei-mai'n, the joy shoot or phallus-earthing, planting or impregnating; but just as in the English it was used also for uttering an ejaculation, making a sudden outburst and so an outcry. "God's boots! he ejaculated, as he realized the canoe was sinking" is clearly a statement. "I am coming he ejaculated, as he picked up his pack and set out after his friend" might cause some confusion over the punctuation, like the Panda which eats shoots and leaves, or eats shoots and then leaves, or eats and then shoots and then leaves. The

Chapter 8 La

THE PSYCHOSEMANTIC TREE FOR THE PHONEME LA

The Phonetic Tree

Ra – La – Ra

The Semantic Tree

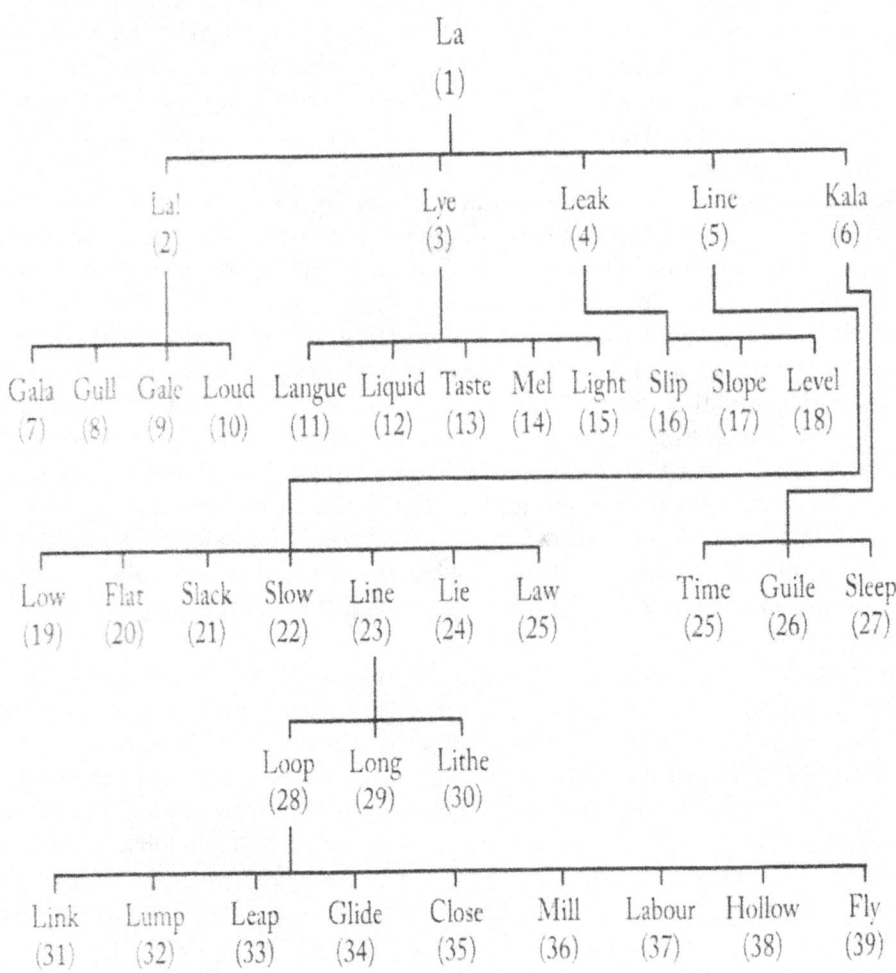

Chapter 8 La

blas-, as Chambers has it, is "probably with the meaning false"(which has a similar set of phonemes). Actually Lithic suggests something more like bitter and full of bile, a simple spin off from lye (3). If you blaspheme it is not a matter of making a mistake from a false apprehension. It is heretically to speak mischievously and slightingly (which is taken to be from bitterness rather than from ratiocination) of a religious tenet. Blasphemy has been punished by death until relatively recently (except out East, where it can still be punished with execution even today; and in Pakistan is pinned on Christians falsely and without scruple, in order to kill and terrorise them, a fraudulence horrifying to true Muslims who get blamed).

The bitter taste of the lye was parlayed to just taste, an example of a widely used idiom of generalization and expansion of meanings over time. Taste was identified as from the tongue, so that the tongue is Latin lingua, the taster, Lithic lai'n-ka-u-a, tasting-makes-one-that, which is paraphrased for the English idiom quite precisely as "the one that does the tasting", the tongue; whence also the Latin lingere to lick, which is tonguing. Lingere is from lai'n-kare, to make of or with the tongue (originally in order to taste, most likely). Chambers has it the other way about: lingere is to lick and the tongue is the licker. But there is then no reason offered why the li- in lingere or lick should mean what they do, for which Lithic is needed. Partridge comically thinks lingua is an alternate form of dingua, which is another Old Latin (Sabine) word for tongue. Any convincing printable etymology for the Old Latin dingua is lacking. Partridge just derives it from a guessed Indo-European root for the purpose, *dingwa, which he then exhaustively compares with Old Persian hizbana, Persian zuban, Sanskrit jihva, Avestan hizu, Old Slav jezyku, Lithuanian lezuwis, Old Prussian inguwis, Old Irish tenga, Gaelic teanga, Manx chengey (with Breton and Cornish cognates lacking the n), Old Norse tenga, Gothic tuggo (pronounced tungo), Old High German zunga (meaning both tongue and language), Old Saxon tunga, Frisian tunge, Middle English tunge and tonge, whence English tongue. He adds "The 'tongue-language' dualism is as widespread as it is natural". This is true but which came first, the chicken or the egg? Or are there two groups, one putting the chicken first (the taster) and the other the egg (the speaker) and each deriving the other from their original. We can add to Partridge's philatelic collection Basque hitz for word, and miin for tongue and iskuntza for language, Albanian gjuke (tongue and language) and ton (tone), Chinese sketou (tongue), yuyon (language), Japanese shita (tongue), gengo (language), Malay lidah (tongue and taste) and bahasa (language, idiom, manner[s]). Which of these words are variants of the same Lithic idiom, and what were the original semantic contents? The Old Persian hizbana, Persian zuban, Sanskrit jehva, Avestan hizu, Old Slav jezuko, Old Russian inguivis and Malay bahasa are clearly an aberrant group. Old Persian hizbana appears to be from the Lithic ai-sai-ba-na, that which-action-of the lips (mouth)-presents, that is it defines the tongue as the ancillary speech organ rather than the taster, and the rest of that group probably came round that way too. The Chinese and Japanese shai-tau for tongue appears to be using shai- as sensing in place of lai, tasting, or else shai- is acting or active and the -ta element is as in the Norwegian storting their parliament, a talking shop, which comes from the primitive idea that thought (and its expression) was a kind of tau or giving birth in the mind. That would make the Chinese tongue the teller; but it looks as if it is the sensor however on balance of probabilities. The etymologies of Chinese and Japanese yuyan and genko for language are obscure. The Malay lidah for tongue rather convincingly belongs in the lingua group, using –dah, does, in place of ka, makes. It is then a fair bet language is from the other approach, in the Malay case bahasa being made up of the Lithic elements ba-a-sa, mouth-that-acts, mouth action, that is to say speech. But it also has a meaning

Chapter 8 La

more like idiom or habitual behaviour, even procedure. This perhaps refers to the alternative Lithic semantic content of ba which, from the fleshy lips which pronounce it, transfers to flesh and other fleshy, that is muscular bits like the haunches and their role in walking. German bein is leg for instance, whence legging it and going and thus how you act physically – reinforced no doubt with bai for being, since alive you are fleshed, but dead the flesh perishes, leaving only bone, from bau-nai, flesh-none, with no flesh on it.

Anyway it does appear that both tongues are the talkers and language is a tasting. In forming our lexicon we have switched them about in a typically dream world manner, such as we should expect when our subconscious thinking comes into play. For some the discovery of this subconscious layer of living can be disconcerting. However you are not being lived, but you are just living beyond your expectations, with the submerged subconscious part of the mental iceberg unrecognized.

Speech is a sequence of tones, interspersed with consonants which allow the mind to identify each segment in turn and refer in turn to each segment's semantic content or meaning. At once a lexical plethora is introduced. Where before speech there were only tones - a few finely differentiated howls at best – now it was possible to string these consonantal beads of meanings indefinitely. Crisp sentencing enabled the first words to be compiled. Words as we know them come from Lithic sentences, or at least phrases, all made up of phonemes, with the whole simply committed to memory, with any amount of slovening later over long stretches of time in order to ease pronunciation. Words were increasingly learned parrot fashion, and the constitutions of the words were forgotten in conscious thinking and allowed to fall back into the subconscious level of the mind. With the development of linguistic thinking, the stringing of tones which produced the stringing of phonemes to provide composite meanings gradually slipped out of conscious processing, until soothsayers were needed to decode tricky bits from God like "mene mene tekel upharsin". The tongue was the maker of these segmented semantic tones, as if the mind itself had been stretched to utter, as indeed it had. The phoneme la was a tone which had been singled out as exemplar of speechifying (because speaking started with the la consonant breaking up the tones). The tools for talking are the lips and tongue. Bab were the lips (chapter 3). So ba and la both together make an uttered tone, whether it is a loud (la-u-da, la-completive-does) and unspecific bellow (bai-lau, the completive oo again, making it loud) or the even less specific bell which merely chimes; or else erudite speaking as in Hindi bolna to speak or tell, the Danish taler to speak, or the bans before marriage when the ba is an announcement, or a ban which is a ba-nai, a say-nay or say-present, a proclamation or both, a proclamation of prohibition.

Just as bitter taste gave rise to taste in general, undifferentiated, so the lye, a bitter liquid, gave rise to liquid in general and undifferentiated. Latin liquor, liqui, is to be liquid, to flow, from Lithic elements lai-kau-ai, lye-shaped-that is. Greek gala, milk is Lithic ka-la, body-lye, and Latin lac, milk, comes from the same Lithic elements in reverse order, la-kai, lye of the body. Indeed you could regard the reversal of these elements as evidence of their independence as individual semantic elements. Milk is from mai-lai-kai, drinking-lye-of the body. All these phonemes we use when we speak stand for their semantic contents, slovened in articulation and somewhat similarly sometimes slovened semantically as well. That is the genius of language. The Milky Way is our translation of the Greek galaxy or gala-ka-sai, (Lithic milk-form-as seen or visible) our galaxy seen sideways on from within, with others seen from afar without the milky appearance but given the same name as a giant scientific discovery.

Blood has the following elements: ba-lau-da, flesh-leaked liquid-does. The grammar

Chapter 8 La

may not fit Noam Chomsky's scheme of things precisely but the substantial elements are clearly germane. When the skin is broken the blood leaks out of the flesh within. That is a sound scientific perception, if not one calling for profound perceptive skill, just hominid level thinking. Modern transformational grammar, indeed any grammar at all, is a relatively recent development.

The slipping down slopes (16 and 17) semantic content has informed a host of words using the letter l for that meaning in English: slip, slide slant slop slope sleigh sleep slouch sleet sluice slump, slink, launch, lacquer, blain and bleed, plain and plead, etc, etc. But lame is from lai-mai, smoothness marred (20) and to lead is from loop (28) and link (31). The river Lune in Lancashire is water slipping down to the sea. Lune means river, since it comes from the Lithic elements lai-awa-n, leaking-water-one. Lancaster is the fort on the river Lune, but by then it was taken to be the name of the particular river, as indeed it had become. One can read into some of these elisions a conqueror's enquiry (perhaps before cutting a throat) "What is your name for this one then?" "Lune: (it's a river, you coon!)". I have for long nursed the suspicion these unfortunates were colonists speaking a Mediterranean patois, with their brains picked out and eaten by the primitive Celts. To slope (17) is to have an inclination as the ladder does, as well as the clinometer. For reasons to be explained in chapters 13 (Ish) and 9 (Ma), the sibilants (s, sh, j, z, and dj) went up, the hum (mmm) went down, and la sloped just like a ladder between the two, a diagonal for the figure of which the other two provided the sides. You could follow round this N figure, which could even be read as a right angled triangle in the mind with the slope also linear. An angle is from the Lithic phonemes an-kai-lai, one-of joint-of lines.

Liquid Partridge derives from the Latin verbs liqui (12) to flow (flow is fare low a back formation from flood), and liqui in Latin was to be filtered, to clarify and so be clear, just what a lye is not; and later on to melt (to become liquefied). These verbs are back formations from liquid, the noun. If you attend to the structure and semantic contents carefully you can get the correct meanings. The lai they had in mind in the original Lithic was the slipping or draining away and not the lye taste. Filtering was achieved by lai-kai, making the liquid do its stuff and drain through a cloth, probably a woven bark cloth only, but it will have got out some of the soil and bits at least. Much, indeed most of our linguistic repertoire today, is achieved with a somnolent tongue, but we still think of a language as a tongue. This is because the uttering of consonants with meanings allocated was what discriminated language from prelinguistic cries, and the first was la with just a wag of the tongue. As a matter of history the phoneme la introduced language with the first consonant, and all the rest came later: civilization following on, but rather later still.

The bitter taste (2) is also found in honey (Greek meli, Latin mel, French miele. Honey was used mai-lai, masking (negativing, canceling out) a lye (bitter) taste. Crab apples (apples kara-bai, strong fleshed, or skull-fleshed in the case of the crustacean), those available in their day, needed more than a spot of honey to mask the lye, in fact to kill it. Wild apples were bitter fruit. A melon on the other hand is a sweet fruit, the lye masked one. A peach (Greek melocoton, a melon kau-tau'n, a mask-lye-one-completively strong-become) was a very sweet melon indeed. The meanings of ma are covered in full in chapter 9. Arabic Lat is a semantic stop, it means no, don't. It may have come from the nasty taste: Stop! Don't drink, it will make you sick; a kindly intervention; but strictly nasty taste, tai (become).

As so often with the oldest Lithic meanings La's original meaning is not so well represented amongst extant meanings as those derived from it, the tail or root being lost in time as it were, with the meaning chain broadening as it develops. From Greek we may perhaps exhibit melancholia, a condition supposedly from a surfeit of black bile in the system, from mela-, black (masked light this time, rather than masked lye. La is light, the opposite of dark not light in weight, because oil, or fat, both lyes, when kindled (kai) caught fire and gave off (-tai, became) - well light! Light is thus from the Lithic elements lai-kai-tai. Greek khole (body lye) meant gall or bile (fleshly lye), where the l's are lai (lye) in both the English gall and bile, from the Lithic ka-lai and bai-lye, body lye and fleshly lye. The historic slovening is from -lai to -le to -l alone. A bale of hay, for instance, Lithic bai-lai, is looped (29) vegetable bits; while the bails on a cricket wicket are other (wooden) bits lying (24) flat (20). A bail meaning a pail is from the original item made of skin, pellis (29) in Latin, pelt in English (since the skin encloses (29) the flesh), and to bail out in a boat is to empty water out with a pail, or in an aeroplane to empty yourself out, not in this case in a pail but on a parachute – which could in fact be identified as a pail of a sort: a looped surface, a bowl for air rather than a bucket for water. Bucket, in passing, is a diminutive from the Old English buc which meant a belly, Lithic the bu of the kai, the bulgy bit (bu)-of the body (kai). Although the bucket is not a bulgy body bit it was originally a skin which bulged when filled with liquid, not the metal job we use today.

A bailey is a castle's outer encircling (29) wall, originally an outer bank, a ba-lai or encircling bund of earth. Bank and bund (Hindi) are both from the idea of a bung, from a fleshy bit. The bailey became a walled enclosure and then a prison, whence at its entrance The Old Bailey – you passed through the portals of the court and into the jail on conviction. Eric Partridge makes out a bale is a ball, but the ball like the balloon is looped in both directions, blown out all round, while the hay bale was held together with a circular twist of straw, an organic loop, before binder twine took over. Is that why the ball has two ls, and the balloon adds two dual vowels u? A bailiff comes from Latin bajulus (pronounced baiulus) a traveling (bai) indentured labourer or porter, tied (from lai, looped), by his indenture, but later a professional indentured steward with legal responsibilities – his indenture appears to have enabled him to come up in the world, but still with an obligation to complete his stint. To bail cattle was to confine them, fencing them behind cross beams, larger versions of those to be found on the tops of wickets. Bail money is paid by a person undertaking, like the bailiff of yore, to confine an accused and produce him to the court when required, on pain of confiscation of the bail money. Now it is the accused's money that is at risk if he fails to produce himself, though he may have had to borrow it.

The Latin for a book is liber from which the English library derives: a bookery. Books were rolls of long strips of parchment first, from the Lithic lai-be-rai, lengths (30)-be-rolled. Liber in Latin also meant free, from which the Statue of Liberty derives. But it had nothing whatever to do with book learning or parchment rolls.. It was the individual's links (32) (shackles) which were be-raised. The same meaning of shackles from links can be seen in the Greek helot, Lithic i(h)ai-lai-tai, he(h)that which-shackled-become, for slave. Any rai reversed any lai because raising was the opposite of lowering. Without the psychosemantics, the diverse meanings can not be comprehended, so they have been dismissed and phonetics declared random. It is the apotheosis of ignorance - which sometimes seems to be grinning at us all.

Flavours come in good and bad and a Lithic element, at first strongly marked for one pole of a presumed dichotomy (or spectrum if you attend to the sequential nature of the distinction as a continuum rather than its categorical differentiation) in course of time diffuses with a fine inconsequence to assume the character of the whole. So nasty taste by a natural progression becomes unmarked and signifies merely taste, just as the tongue tells

Chapter 8 La

us. The nastiness highlights just taste, and its particular effect is then allowed to be spent. Lithic lai (lye), at first marked for bitterness, by a like process assumes the larger character of just liquid or fluid (12), especially if not wholly clear (clear from Lithic ka-lai-a-rai, a form-of lai-that-rai, visible or translucent) as we find already in Greek gala for milk, (as in galaxy, the milky way, originally with the Lithic elements -ga-la signifying body-lye, ie milk, and the following ka-sai or ga-sai of galaxy (the –xy), go upwards, the sloping stripe lit up in the night sky, at one time taken to be a ladder to Heaven for the souls of the dead - night, black, mortality, see the next chapter 9 for ma. We English, with eloquent pragmatism, have added in our word milk the prefix mai- (mi-), drinking or eating, edible, for consumption - perhaps to distinguish milk which is drinkable from other bodily secretions which leak from it which are not. Do not be bothered by the common origin of eating and drinking, as if they were both the same. They are - just ingestion. In India you drink a cigarette (cigret pina), in Malaya you eat a cigarette (makan rokok). In neither place is the smoke in fact ingested but instead passed into the lungs and so as a pollutant into the blood which carries it to the brain as a mild drug, with long term physical debauch to pay for the immediate high. The good news is in only a decade or so the lungs can shake off the damage done to them by smoking. The bad news is you have to have the guts to stop, breaking the addiction – for which many are inadequates.

We need to reflect here that to ga-lai, go lye, often resulted in clear water acquiring an off colour as well as an off flavour as it flowed to the sea. A colour is a ka-la-u-rai, a go-lye-what-visible. In Australia the aboriginals have shortened it to gara for colour, from the Lithic ka-ra, make-ray/see. The raying of the eyes (ra) was supposed to go out from the eye to the panorama and then return to the eye with a facsimile of the view which was painted on the iris (Greek, and Lithic i-rai-s, it-irradiated-substantive marker), where indeed a reflection can sometimes be seen. The ray on its return was the trigger for the eye to see. The original rays from the girls hunkered around the hearth were similarly triggers on their return whence they came, for the fleshing out of the foetus within, admittedly bringing a boy with them in this case, their particular trick; just as the visual rays brought the panorama with them on their return whence they came. Lithic thinking is Lithic thinking, and has to be discovered.

It is not a great semantic step from taste to taster, the tongue, and so from lye to langue (French) (11), also the tongue; and the tongue will wag as well as taste, so we still talk in tongues. Language is simply tongue-age, the speech that comes out of our mouths, just as babble and ballad, bellowing bawling and yelling do too; where the b's are from the same Lithic source as bab, which is indeed precisely mouth in Semitic tongues. The two b's are the two lips which we use to say b, and head the semantic tree for that letter in chapter 3. Much of our utterances around the world we describe as tonguing and mouthing, or using both lips and tongue. (Mouth from mau-tahi, eating-orifice). Hindi has bolna with conventional root bol- for to speak. As already mentioned (in the opening chapter as an example of meaning diffusion with the Queensland aboriginal djeri-), the Djeribal folk say "-bal" for speak/speaking (speech)/speakers (11), using Djeri, from sha-rai, fire-ray, in this case for clear. Of course an Indian expedition could just possibly have quite recently tipped them off to use the Indo-European form, but one feels that in that case they might have given them a bit more as well, and there remains the difficulty of timing. It is either Lithic or sheer coincidence. With the whole gamut of vocal sounds to pick from, to have arrived at such a neat fit by sheer chance is, quite frankly, exceedingly unlikely. But then if you accept that, you have let in the tip of the Lithic hypotheses at least, because if it was not chance it will surely have been some kind of causation. The vulgar Germanic languages, by contrast with the Australian aboriginal, make a spurt: or in other words ejaculate their speech (sprechen, to speak)). Whereas ejaculate merely means throw out and refers almost equally well to speech as to the male orgasm, it has to be said (with the usual nod to Mrs Grundy) that the prime reference of the German metaphor must surely be to their sexual performance, because there is so much of it in our speech; which is then prayed in aid as analogous to utterances from the mouth, otherwise hard to define.

As between ba and la, the latter is all with the mouth open. We mean business. We are either going to bawl or sing, tra-la (2). Thus a miners' gala (7), as already stated, was evidently originally a sing-song before by a kind of progress it turned into a political demonstration. Similarly a gale of wind was originally a howling (or whistling) one until it became just a strong one. Then there are the four calling birds, the song adverts to. A sea gull, already mentioned, in the context of a gull wing, as a mnemonic for a type of semantic transfer from one aspect of a named object to another prominent one to which attention has drifted, is a sea caller; or a squawk-mouth, ghulbean, for the Celts. Here, as an aside, is a simple case of multiple meaning (polysemy of a kind) from a pair of Lithic elements. Gala can be parsed 'go La' or 'earth-ocean', with the two elements providing double duty as 'coastal caller' as described above and island, which we find doing duty in Shri-Lanka or Holy Island in Sinhalese. The simple coastal caller (using the la twice) was all too abstruse for the Germanic races, who added a sea- in front so the point was adequately made. Then there is the nightingale and the lark. The fourth caller will have been the curlew, which screamed cur-lieu around our farm house in the night when I was young, giving me nightmares of banshees on the prowl, even riding broomsticks. Witchcraft, with words of power, picked up some of the Lithic semantics, imagining the meanings magic. Witches could string meanings the rest of us couldn't, and they knew it was sexual magic. The confessions of perversion were tortured out of them. The calling birds were using the phonemes for engorgement, and the three French hens (poules) were from pu-lai too; and we finish up with a partridge an (which means or, as in "If ifs and ans were pots and pans what would poor tinkers have to do?") a perdrix, (in French), another bird named after its call, which in Lithic can be read as pai-ta-rai, the male organ drawn out by the rays from the girls' Ta. The pear tree is an interloper. There is sexual mischief afoot, cheerfully sung by all and sundry. The lords were a-lai-pai to start with, come to think of it.

Cultivation is essentially to till, to make the ground flat and clear of weeds. It is from Latin colere to till, from the past participle, coltus. Partridge suggests it meant to move around, with the root *kwel to move around a place; which makes sense in Lithic *ka-u-a-lai, place-one-that-circled. But he was no farmer. Just moving around butters no parsnips. Lai (20), flat, is required, not lai (29), looped. To crop the land you need a plough and harrow to get a clear flat surface.. Still it suggests he had some idea of the meanings of lai, whether he had spotted it precisely or not.

The oceans were presumed to be encircled by a containing lip, (a lip is a surrounding, looping (29) -pai or diminutive piece of flesh surrounding the mouth) - compare Latin pellis, the skin, pa a thinned diminutive of ba, and so a diminutive of flesh, surrounding the flesh, looping round it - since a body of water staying still outside of a natural saucer was a denial of the science of the day. Except in such a fix, it must have seemed obvious that the oceans would have splashed over the edge of a universe shaped like a penny and slipped down and away into oblivion. So the inarticulate scientists of the Stone Age knew at least one thing, before they ever learned to speak: it was the mission of liquids to settle (19) (Lithic sai-tai-lai, action-become-low) and slip down to the sea. (We just call it gravity).

Chapter 8 La

Liquid was the element of default, liquids lacked, they lacked the stiffening of solids. It has to be said that as far as it went the science was sound. It required many millennia for science to add much of substance to these original perceptions; and meanwhile language was being built around these original ideas and a few more like them - as can be shown from careful study of the vocabularies of today which contain within them these elementary fossils (some of them coprolites) charmingly left behind by the earliest inhabitants.

Of course, for language, fossilization is merely metaphorical. We are only concerned here with the metaphorical usage. With language the internal structure is the semantics, and it is the semantics which are the hard interior elements for the human mind, the meanings are the bones compared with the phonetics, which correspond to the soft tissues. It is thus not without irony that science in approaching language study has dismissed the semantic elements in favour of the phonetics, because they can be more readily and reliably accessed in the living species (speech) - and one might add the phonetics on their own can be arbitrarily subjected to schemes of evolutionary process (such as Grimm's Law) which in reality successfully account for barely six penn'orth of the whole.

For the idea of down flowing and overflowing of fluids related to the Lithic element la we have a plenum or plethora of percolating metaphors in the English language, as well as others all round the world, many already linked by the truffle hunter type of linguist to the earliest times. To resume them all would be a Herculean task requiring many volumes. But many lazy readers meanwhile will look at Lithic as merely an unlikely fairy tale; and yet perhaps later slowly learn to believe in it. To leak (4) is to make a lai or a draining away. A blain is from Lithic ba-lai'n, the flesh-leaking'one, and blisters contain lymph. Lymph is sexual lye[2]. All bodily fluids of a lymphatic nature were assumed to partake of the same character. Blood, blut in German, from the Lithic ba-la-u-tai, is another flesh-leak, u-tai, when cut. Oil (12) is from awa-i-lai, liquid-which-lye, which we find clearly in the Greek elaion, Latin oleum, that which or in the Latin that one which-lyey-one, (3). But the oil lot most probably started out first just awa-lai, liquid-lyey – a very nasty taste. The olive tree is the oil tree, Latin olea, Greek elaia, Lithic awa-lai, and it was olive oil on which the language formed. The refined petroleum is petra-oleum, rock-oil pumped from under the rock nowadays (originally pushed up naturally by the gas with it). However the petera is Aramaic for rock, both words (petera and rock) showing the prehistoric understanding rock was the core of the world pushed up from the core, as by volcanoes. Pai-tai-rai, the original Lithic, is pieces-become-raised, (and originally penes vagina-rayed and so raised). The Greek for feather and wing, pteron, is a surface drawn up. If these Lithic phonemic meanings do not obtain, how could a rock and a feather be described the same?

The Latin olere to emit a smell is a gull from the oil which comes to the surface naturally in places and emits a nauseating rotten smell from the natural gas with it, betraying its biological origins in earlier world catastrophes, which are not yet admitted by the scientific orthodoxy in spite of the learned Professor Emanuel Velikovsky's life work uncovering the evidence, author of Ages in Chaos and Worlds in Collision. His evidence is historical, you see, and not mathematical. Oil when kindled lights. Light is from la-i-kai-tai, lye/oil-which-kindled-born. The Latin lux, light, is from la-u-kai-s, lye-what-kindled-flames. The flame (the -s, from sai) may just be the substantive ending: the kindling may stand for the enflaming on its own. But since the two phonemes are closely combined in the x ending, it probably is relict of the original sai for flame. Translucency (Lithic trans-lau-kai, lye kindled) manages without the flame; the c was originally a k and

Chapter 8 La

smoothed for easier pronunciation. A lamp refers to its wick, a piece or pai, at one time floating em, in, lai, liquid, in this case the oily liquid. Lapis, a stone in Latin is a liquid which has developed a skin or hard surface on it as it cools. It is a derivation which does not spring to mind today. It was lava, coming up liquid, sliding down and cooling solid. Pa, as surface, pertained to all solids, which after all conspicuously have them, and indeed was the aspect perceived by the rays emanating from the eyes, as in panorama (Greek), from pa-en-au-ra-ma, the surface-of that what-the eye-devours, that is the eye's capture or target of everything in view. We do only see the surfaces of things. Pan in Greek thus was used for everything, as if each view was a single collective surface. Thing in Latin is res, the rayed, the visible, the phenomenal. Pa in Ancient Egyptian was used as the ostensive, as we would say for "the".

A snail is from si-nai-lai, brer-presenting-lye. It leaves a slimy trail. Slime is from sai-lai-mai, actual-liquid-solid like wet earth (mud, which must, it appears, have originally been pronounced mood, the dual ma of earth and moir, water). For ma as liquid see chapter 9, straight from the infant's cry for the breast. A leech (4) is a blood sucker, from lai-kai, leak-making. It makes a leak by putting in a non clotting chemical and sucking out the blood. Lithos, the Greek for stone, is liquid-born (12), with Greek substantive suffix –s; whereas stone is from ish-tau'n, fire-born'one: both from observing the flow of incandescent lava from volcanoes, cooling to stone, acquiring a hard surface. The time which needs to be spent on individual analyses in Lithic elements strung together to make words is not critical for the perceptions which the Lithic hypotheses sketch. If it requires time for acceptance it just requires it. It becomes a chore when demanded, though a continual delight when allowed to present itself. Evidence is collectable indefinitely, but it makes more sense to examine the hypotheses themselves for credibility. Do they hang together and give an adequate explanation of how our language has been built?

The ocean meanwhile added other ideas, once it was accepted as the final repository of the dual instincts of liquids to slope down, go flat and become polluted in their flow to the sea. The skyline at sea is the only straight line in nature apart from a ray of sunlight when dust in the air shows it up; and a liquid surface compared with the land is the only flat one. Water goes low and flat together. Admittedly the sea, (from sai-awa)lying about in the low, laut in Malay and lyr, pronounced loor in Celtic, has somehow picked up a bit of the life force, sai, making waves. So la has the psychosemantic contents also of flatness (20) and level/depth (18). Moreover from an island such as an atoll (from the Maldivian, from the Lithic a-tau-lai-lai, that-born-ocean-loop - it has popped up surrounded by the sea - the skyline is not only linear but runs all the way round in a loop (29). The same can be seen in a lake, lai-kai, a lie-er-on land, (if not so regular and seldom actually circular but at least the edge is always continuous and can be seen to always come back to exactly where it begins, dead level). It is the skyline at sea which shows the pure case. To the Greek circle, kirkos we have in English added the l to make a circle, the original (Greek) version kirkos is akin to krikos, a ring, and is all the corners to completion - until the two ends meet. Our circle then is in Lithic terms corner-corner-looped, all the corners looped, smooth bends all the way round. A ring is perhaps rai-en-kai, sun-of-shape. But of course raying rounds out too.

What lay behind Egyptian khu-t meaning power? Alas it was another sexual motif. Kau-tai in Lithic is struck-of the ta, in receipt of those powerful rays emanating from the vulva (ta) which have the power to make the male stand up and rant and become aggressive, forcing himself upon the ladies and on the world. With the bull and the stallion (and the Mafiosi across history) you risk your life if you get in their way.

Chapter 8 La

With the idea of a natural circular loop or ocean saucer rim it soon got stood up vertically as an orbit. Also Apollo, the personification of the sun, is Lithic A-pa-u-lau-lau, that-foots it-oo-loop loop, or goes round in circles. The sun was assumed to repeat life cycles and die in the West and travel under the earth at nights, as if subjected to gestation before arising in the East in the morning as if new born. The pollo, strictly Apollo, the chicken which the Spanish eat is the sun bird, because the cock crows at dawn celebrating the sun's resurrection, and not because it is itself in orbit. Typically, the bird was credited with an intentional motivation - since it crowed at dawn it was greeting the sun, which made it wise: a thoroughly anthropomorphic interpretation. In reality it simply crowed at sun up because the light at dawn triggered this response.

A locality, from the Latin locus, was a circumscribed area (lau), a loop, of the earth (kau), a place, (in agreement with lau, showing they go together like our noun and adjective) an area of the earth. The mathematical locus, a range of positions, redefined the phonemes – lau, linear one (from the skyline (23) as a straight line instead of as a loop), and kau in this case the making or ground – hence the route or transit (going), or series of locations. An enclosure is from to close, which combines the Lithic phonemes ka-lau-sai, make-looped-acting/action. A sailor is an ocean actor from sai-lau-a, acting-ocean-one, where the lau is the most low, viz. the ocean (from awa-kai-an, water-kindled-one - with waves and storms). A galleon, from ga-lai-un, is a go-ocean-one (19), a sea-going ship. A keel, on the other hand, from kai-lai, makes level (18). A ship has a keel for ocean going to keep it level in the swell and when under sail.

With to limp (16) la picks up its opposition to ka which is the driving force, the decisive splitting stroke. A lai-em-pai, a flop-of-the legs, is a shuffling gait. But also it means flaccid, lacking, the opposite of kai, which is hard and strong like the flints which the ka phoneme was supposed to echo. The feeble slippage which liquids express also appears in rivers. Malay hilir, Lithic a(h)i-lai-are, as(h)it-flows, is to pole downstream, to go with the current slipping away downstream. The Australian aboriginal billabong is an oxbow lake formed when a sharp bend in a river bungs up the flow with silt. Lithic bai-la can be read as a travelling liquid (river water) and so river. But billy (bai-lai) is just the water in Oz and the idiom is likely the same as the ber- in Malay berbaling, a wind driven, bai-rai, the ber- in the berbaling, a rotating (bai-lai'ng going-looping) bamboo sail mounted at the top of a tree with bamboo pipes fastened across the two ends of the blade to whoop all night as the wind blows it round driving off any marauding evil spirits. With both the Malay berbaling and the aboriginal bailai (or billy that boils in the song), there is the same meaning as the English be- in becalmed, besotted, etc, merely to be in a continuing state (as after all water is), with the –baling of the berbaling being to go looping as well as baling, uttering, lip-tonguing, la-ing with a ba in it and therefore with a message for any unwelcome callers. What, we may wonder, is the message of this maddening whooper in the night? Is it indeed precisely "Ba la!": "Bum off to the far horizon!" uttered in howling banshee tones, speaking their own fearsome wailing and addictive tongue - in tune with the panic waves of the insane brain? For Senoi boys and girls without a night light it is comforting music, whatever else. The rest of us just have to get used to it, as with the brain fever bird, and sleep through it as best we can. At least we are not likely to be troubled by evil spirits as we sleep. Bili in Oz is bi-, continually, in a state of being, -li, lye: the state of liquid, namely slipping away into the lows and turning lye as it goes, just like the brackish water often to be found in billabongs, finishing up in the salt sea.

With a mixture of water and the solid, heavy element (ma, by contrast with ish the flickering flame which flies upwards) we have lime and slime. The lime was originally

Chapter 8 La

glue, bird lime, and only later the caustic mix. Try analyzing glue in Lithic elemental meanings. The g- is from Lithic kai, make, followed by lau, looped (29), rendered inclusive, and so stuck together. Latin limus, mud, comes from the same mix of liquid and solid elements, but it can be read as slippery earth. English mud has gotten slovened from ma-awa-tai, earth-water-become. Greek leimax, a snail, from Lithic lai-ma-ka-sai, a slime maker-with-sai, brer on the end, as a life form; or is sai his action? Greek leimon is a moist meadow, we would call it a water meadow; and limne is a marsh, with the liquid element (or mud) prominent (nai). Our own lemon meanwhile is lye or sharp/bitter when eaten, the -mau'n is a definitive suffix to make clear which aspect of lai is to be taken into account: lemons have a sharp taste rather than making off downhill and unless you are thinking in those terms you are not going to be reminded of the fruit, the acidic taste one.

The French retain a good deal of the Lithic language in their vocabulary as well as - we must add less generously - a good deal of old fashioned Lithic fuzzy logic. So we find linge for linen. Even the English will have heard of their lingerie or linnenry – nowadays more likely cottonry or silkery, otherwise just knickers and bras. The Lithic for linge was probably lai'n-kai, meaning of filamental form, the flax form. But then we discover linen can also be a rag, probably by way of a linen one, and the filamentous or flimsy nature of the plant whose seeding provides the filament transferring itself to the cloth, ragging it out. But then linge can also be a piece, as for instance a piece of chocolate which is not made of linen nor is it in any way filamental, nor indeed bearing any of the more obvious other semantic contents of the phoneme la, so that we must fall back on the loop around the ocean which we find in loca (Latin) for place – a loop on the ground. So this is a loop on the linen, a piece of the cloth, or a locative piece of anything else, like the selected piece of chocolate broken from the bar. Right next door is lemonade, which unsurprisingly the French use for lemonade. Indeed we copied our lemonade from them. But then we find a limon is not only a sour lime (a lemon is a citron) - that is easy, lai-ma-un, sour-to the taste-one, from lye-manger-une if you like - but also silt, sludge, ooze, mud, which is clearly from the Lithic liquid-earth-one; and then to cap it all it also means the shaft of a horse drawn carriage, a long-weight-one, the shafts carrying the weight – well sharing it with the wheels, the first carriages only had two wheels. So a lemonier is either a lime tree or a shaft horse, while a limoniere is no feminine lime tree, nor even a mare between the shafts, but a pair of shafts or else a wagon (so provided). It is a reminder of the Ancient Egyptian design of their war chariots with a single shaft between two galloping stallions. Only a domestic cart got a single horse power, requiring shafts either side, like the French wagon a few thousand years later described as a double shafted one. So you have to guess between a tree and a horse - not too hard really, since you find no lime trees between the shafts nor horses with leaves on. Still it adds a few Brownie points for Lithic as well as French access to their language roots. Next is limousine which is French. Trickier this. It is a car with a hood on (a roof), as worn in Limoges. Also a stone mason. They came from there. But our English metal is from mai-ta-lai, earth-born-[as] liquid. You heat the ore and the metal leaks out as liquid, cooling solid as the metal we know. (You need the right earth, namely the ore, for the job). That gives us a leader into Stone Age thinking. So our stone is from ish-tau-nai, fire-become-born, from observing the lava flowing from a volcano. You can see the language started out as the science too, science leading. It has since taken off. So the English mason is from mai-sa-un, , where mai can mean solid and heavy as well as earth, earthing (seeds), inseminating, etc (chapter 9), and here it is prayed in aid three times as the solid heavy element of earth. There can be no doubt stone, as well as being fire born, is the solid and heavy element of earth. The French stone mason,

Chapter 8 La

limousin or lai-mau-sai 'n is revealed as the liquidized/fired-earth-acting one or operator. The novelty is our Stone Age ancestors thought of it all. But then they had no telly as a substitute for ratiocination, now treated as brain damage and shunned. The generations reared on television will be zappy, quick witted, shallow, vapid and above all happy with ignorance of everything else, and the computer generation even more so.

Ships are launched on a slipway (16), and launch is a slipping down-making (16) from lau'n-khai. But khai can mean going as well as making, both from ka as driving force. A launch is a (small) sea going vessel which may be carried on a ship for launching to take passengers from ship to shore. Chambers notices Malay lancharan, a launch, from lanchar, agile, swift, in turn from Lithic lithe (31) and considers the Malay as entering English via the Portuguese who spoke Indonesian at an early date. But the dates don't fit. With Lithic we have no problem with Malay words having similar phonemes to English ones, across conventional language families; and indeed it is argued elsewhere Malay is relict of the oldest language (Adam's) of which there is the slightest record. Launch is a doublet with lance, the semantics originally embraced any leap (34), by a thrown lance, or a French arrow (fleche), or a ship on a slipway. A lance is launched through the air in a looping flight like Apollo, the sun on his daily course across the sky, a line (23) and a loop (29) together like the skyline at sea. Admittedly the lance is from the spear which is thrown (a travelling piece), but originally either was used either way. The spear was a stabbing, pointed or pricking weapon. A sling-stone has a similar trajectory, a sling has a looping action, sai-lai-'n, an action-looping-one: you have to give it a swing, from sai-oo-ai-ang, action-round-going-one.

With a leap the loop is described with the feet (or anyway the limbs), pes in Latin and in Lithic pai meaning a lesser-flesh-piece like a skin or a small shoot or minor spur or appendage or any protrusion from the body like a limb. With bellies and pillows it is merely the looping outline which catches attention – unless with the belly, which gets the b- because it is part of the flesh of the main body and not an offshoot from it; and there is some early butchers' lore there too, the belly containing flesh which tastes bitter, lye (3). With labah-labah, the Malay for spider, from la-bahi, he is legging it round and round in a loop, loop-going-loop-going (29) making his web, the web-maker or looper-looper. It is worth repeating here the h originally was a break, like the Cockney h, between two vowels otherwise liable to elision, and its original pronunciation was ahi, of which our letter 'aitch' is a reminder. The Lithic for the Malay spider was originally la-bahi-la-bahi, loop-going-loop-going: guess who? There are no other contenders[2]. Gulled from the spider, Malay melabah (from m-ai-la-bahi) is to be in a state of agitation, going round in circles, or as we might say in English in a spin like the spider, from si-pai-tai-rai, where the pai is legging it and the -terai is drawn out, brer-go-drawn, he draws the web out of his body.

The law (24) is a collection (of rules), Latin leges, Lithic la-kai, loop made, looped, collected, originally a gathering or harvest, making a loop (28), a sheaf tied with a twist around it, or just a collection of nuts for instance put together in a pile (from pieces-looped). Partridge and others think it comes from what is laid down (24), metaphorically speaking. Who knows what the subconscious may put together, but the principal prompt is from loop (29). The law is essentially a composite of rules, like the Commandments, of which there were a collection of Ten. It does not prevent other derivations being added. The law lays down a line (22) of conduct (not to be overstepped). The more prompts for meanings the more likely the Lithic got adopted.

The skyline at sea was seen from a far island where it is visible all round as a circle, at the same time as a line from the ordinary shore. The loop meaning is shown in the

Chapter 8 La

psychosemantic tree at the head of no less than eleven subsidiary meanings. The loop suggested an orbit from the circular travel of the sun. The ocean as well as very salt is also very low (19) and very flat (20) viewed from the land (20). The English word land comes from a special kind suitable for living on, flat cleared land, suitable for culture too. Compare Malay ladang, from la-tai-'n, flat-become'one (20), a jungle clearing for cultivating crops. Cultivating is from Latin cultus from colere (20) to till the land, and till from the Lithic elements tai-lai, to become-level (20 yet again), just like the ladang. Latin lamina which Partridge declares of obscure origin, o.o.o. in his jargon – he had no Lithic – "perhaps Chaldean". A lamina was originally a metal plate hammered flat; but came to mean any thin plate, sheet, scale or layer. The Lithic is therefore most probably la-mai-na, flat-hammered-presenting: presenting a hammered flat surface.

Slow is from low, low in speed by metaphor, as opposed to a high speed, with the initial sa indicating the following phoneme lau was to be read with reference to action rather than a nasty taste or any of the other meanings not to do with action. The Lithic is sai-lau, movement-low (19). Low is from lau, the action of water, run down, from its liquid instinct to leak out and away into the lows. (The u vowel is the completive one, see chapter 14). A slug goes slow, sai-la-gai, action-slow-go or si-la-gai, brer-slow-go. To lie [down] (23) is to lay oneself; and below is the state of being low - compared with what is above. Most surprises lie in the duplex derivations of line (23) and loop (29). A line is long (30) and so is any linear extensive like a lane or a life, physical extensions in space and time respectively. A millennium is from the Lithic massive-length-showing-one, like the grains of the earth (mai, chapter 9) which have been milled – perhaps by those mills of God which grind so slowly and surely, but if not then by Charles Lyell's natural geological evolution. Of course a millennium is from the Latin mille, a thousand, but the Lithic is what the thousand in Latin is from. It is not a mathematical term, more a native one from before math: an innumerable number like the grains of the soil: mai, earth, lai, like (from linked from looped).

To clear land is to make it flat (20) (from kai-lai-verbal marker) but then to make it visually clear as well, from Lithic ka-lai-rai, make-long and/or smoothly-visible (23) and chapter 13, (ra for eye and rai, seeing/visible), rather important when weapons were effective only at comparatively short range. The –rai is there to indicate which of the 40 semantic contents I have shown (and there will be many more) of la is intended. Malay lilit, is a turn or twist (from loop-loop 29) and tali (23), is a string or cord, from the liana, the long lithe one (23 and 31) that Tarzan swung on. When it comes to tracing Lithic word formations in other languages it is important to escape from the Indo-European family where borrowings and modifications of an original common stock makes the case for a truly world wide, because psychosemantic, relationship less convincing. In a book in English addressed principally to English speakers, of all ethnic origins around the world, the work involved is formidable, and Malay is picked as a language unconnected with Indo-European, apart from a few recent borrowings, mostly from Dutch, and I happen to have had five years in the country trying to learn the language. The correspondences of all the Malay words beginning with la- in Sir Richard Winstedt's excellent two volume dictionary of Malay having caught the eye, a list follows with Lithic elements shown for a hundred and one words, to indicate the degree of correspondence from Lithic origins which can be shown in a small window beginning with la- and going to lantin (a Malayan judge's corrupt takings): all the words from a few pages only of the dictionary. Each word is listed with its dictionary meaning, followed by the relevant column of the psychosemantic tree (from 1 to 40), and then its Lithic elements and the meanings of the

Chapter 8 La

elements in English. The Lithic meanings given are meanings and not particularly well represented by the English words used, but they do indicate the original semantic structure of the Malay words for an English speaker reasonably well. Malay is important because it is, I believe, the language closest to the language Adam spoke, Malaya being the garden land and Eastern Malaya, now three hundred and sixty feet under the South China Sea was the real Garden of Eden, which is simply Eastern Malaya. The Bible made up a Semitic Eden up in the hills with Noah's flood in the highlands too - an impossibility - having borrowed the tales from the Sumerians, refugees from Eastern Malaya. Embarrassingly, Adam was a Malay and not a Semite at all. The Akkadians – Semites – borrowed him from the Sumerians who fled Eastern Malaya (Malaya means Garden Land), the Garden of Eden, the Eastern (Padi) Garden Land, by boat (Noah) to the top of the Persian Gulf where they already had a colony (the Ubaid or emigrants), and it had a hinterland above the new sea level amenable to padi gardening, whereas their own garden land left above the sea was hilly.

Laboh, trailing, too long, of curtains, sleeve, shirt, (30) from la-bau, long-burgeoned.
Labu, bottle, calabash, gourd, cucumber, (30) la-bau, long-fleshed/bodied.
Laban, to chatter, gossip, (11) la-ba-un, tongue-lip-one (more commonly ba-la, lip first).
Lachak, abundant (of fruit) (19), la-sha-kai, low-height-grown, ie weighed down with fruit.
Lachar, abraded, (21), la-kha-arai, flat-cut-verbal marker.
Lachi, a drawer (in furniture), (16), la-khai, slip-making, a slider.
Lada, pepper, (3,13), la-da, lye-does/gives. (It gives a bitter taste)
Ladaian, riverine fish trap, (16), la-dai-an, flow down-hole-one.
Ladam, horse shoe, (29), la-da-'m, loop-become-one.
Ladang, (jungle) clearing, (21), la-da-ng, flat-become-one, land (which once meant arable, ie flat land in English).
Lading, curved chopper, (29), la-dai-ng, loop-cut-one, a swung cutter.
Ladong, batu ladong, plummet or sounding lead,(18)(30), la-da-un, level-does-one. Batu = a stone.
Ladun, opera singing, (7), la-da-un, la-do-one, sing-do-one.
Laga, clash, collide, (32), la-ka, link-strike, or linked-strike.
Lagi, more still, still more, (23) (30), la-gai, linear/long-going. (Linear implies Extension).
Lagu, tune, air, intoning, (7), la-ga-u, la-go-one, sing-make-one.
Lahan, melody, (7), la-iha-'n, la-it that-one. (Something one meets with when singing)
Lahang, palm sap, (3), la-ahi-ang, a leaking/lye-one. Compare Senoi 'kruing' (growing, completive case) a tree. The kru- carries the semantic content not merely of growing but of growing superlatively, the big hard plants.
Lahar, mere or forest pool, (12) (19), la-iha-awa, lying-it that-water.
Lain, other, another, different, (32), lai-nai, linked-negative, ie not the same.
Lejeng, lejang, unmarried person, (22), lai-gang, lazy or slow-goer.
Lajor, a long strip of land, (30) (20), la-gau-a, long-land-one.
Laju, fast, (30), la-sha-u, linear-speedy-one.
Lak, a sealing wax, (12) (32), la-kai, liquid-joining when kindled.
Laka, a liana, (32) (31), la-ka, linear-shape. Liana is linear showing.
Laklakan, gullet, (12) la-ka-la-ka'n, slip down-make-slip down-make, the

Chapter 8 La

glugger.
Lalab, cold vegetables eaten with curry, (15) (13), la-la-bai, light-taste-vegetable.
Lalah, gluttonous, (30) (13), la-la-hai, taste-taste [= tastes]-enjoying.
Lalai, dawdling, dreamy (of lovers), inattentive (of workers), (22) (22), la-lai, slow-slowy. Compare English loll and lull.
Lalang, tall grass (growing after jungle felling), (30) (19), la-la'ng, long-long 'one.
Lalat, house fly, (40) (40), la-la-ti, fly-fly-little.
Lalu, meaning pass by/and then, (30) (16), la-la-u, line-long-past.
Lama, long time [past], ancient, (30), la-ma, long-dead [time].
Lambai, to wave (one's hand), (29),la-em-bai, loop-of-limb.
Lamai, brother-in-law or sister-in-law, (32), la-mai, link-of marriage.
Lambak, pile, (confused) heap, (33), la-em-ba-kai, link-of-bits-made. Compare pile, from pai-lai, pieces looped/linked.
Lambat, slow, (22), la-em-ba-tai, low-of-pace-become.
Lambong, flank (of body), (23), la-em-bau-'ng, line/side-of-fleshed-one (ie of the body).
Lambut, bulge, (29), la'm-bau-ti, loop-of-flesh-become.
Lampai, slender, graceful, (31), la'm-pai, lithe-of-limb (the 'm or of is either prefix or suffix).
Liok, liompai, swaying, (31), lai-au-kai, lithe-that one-of body, lai-au'm-pai, lithe-that one-of-limb.
Lampias, to flow, gush, (16), la, to wash for tin, (4), la-em-pai-a-sai, flow-of-pace-that-swift.
Lampas, polish (furniture), la-em-pai-sai, smooth-of-surface-action. Spanish limpiar to clean.
Lampin, baby's nappy, (29), la-em-pai-'n, loop-of-cover-one.
Lampir, enclosure to letter, annexe, (29), la-em-pai-a, link[adjoinder]-of-page-one.
Lampit, a (rattan) mat, (20), la'm-pai-tai, flat-of-cover-thing.
Lampong, floating, (12), la-em-pau-'ng, liquid-of-surfaced-one.
Lamu, seaweed for making jelly, (12), la-ma-u, ocean-edible-one.
Lan, nauseated by food, (13), la-nai, bitter taste-negative.
Lanang, manly, (30), la-na'ng, long-protruding/orgasming.
Lanar, lanau, (ooze, slime) (12), la-en-awa, lyey-of-liquid. Notd -ar for -au spelling.
Lanchap, tapering and slipping out, (16), la'n-kha-pai, sloping-shape-piece.
Melanchap, to masturbate (4), mai-la'n-kahi-pai, impregnating-liquid-kindling-piece.
Lanchar, swift, fluent (reading), (16), la'n-khara, smooth-making/going.
Lanchok, a large puddle, (12), la-en-shau-kai, liquid-of-deep-of the ground.
Lanchor, gush (as out of pipe) (16), la-en-sha-u-rai, leak-ing-fast-out-going.
Landa, wash for gold, (16), la'n-da, leaking-does. A sieving action lets the water drain out of the pan.
Landai, shelving (of shore, horses back), (17), la'en-dai, sloping-become.
Landak, porcupine, (29), la-en-da-kai, encircle-ing-things-sharp. (or flying tacks?)
Landasan, anvil, (20), lai-en-da-sa'n, flatten-ing-does-action-one.
Landoh, long, trailing, (29), lai'n-tau, lengthen'ing-become.
Lang, eagle, (16) (40), la'ng, gliding, glider.
Langah, agape, wide open, (28) (29), la'n-kahi, loop 'one-shaped.

Chapter 8 La

Langcha, rickshaw, (22), la-en-ka-sha, loop-of-strong-action. Jin-rik-sha, Japanese, man-power-carriage, from jin-rin-ka-shai, one man-power-acting.
Langgaian, drying platform (for fish), (20), lang-kai-an, flat (or slat)-made-one.
Langan, subscribe (for newspaper), club together to buy, (31), la-en-ka'n, link-of-made
Langang, tungang-langang, head over heels, (19), tun-gang, become-going [get going] la'ng-ka'ng, la-one-ka-one. [low one leading]
Langas, free, without ties, (31), la-'n-ka-sai, links-of-cut-acting, acting without links..
Langeng, eternal, lasting, (28), la-ng-gai-ng, linear-ongoing.
Langir, leaves used to wash the hair, (3), la'n-kai-a, lye-making-one.
Langit, sky, (22), la'n-kai-tai, skyline of-land-become, [land above the skyline].
Langkah, a pace or stride, (29), la-en-kai, length-of-going.
Langkai, slim, graceful, (30), la'n-kai, linear'one-of body; cp. lanky.
Langkan, latticed verandah, railings (of bridge), (29), la-n-ka-n, long-shape-one.
Langkapura, Ceylon, (19), Lan-ka-pura, Sea-land-city. Cp Sri Lanka, Holy Island.
Langlang, to globe trot, (29), la-ain-la-ain, far-going-far-going. (also eagle-eagle in Malay, glide-glide)
Langsar, tall and slim, (30), la-n-sa-rai, linear-and-up-raised.
Lansing, log brake on a bullock cart, (21), la-en-sai'n, slowing-of-moving.
Langsir, hangings, curtains, (16) (21), la-en-sai-a, lying-vertical-ones, hangings.
Langsong, very far or soon, last, (29), lau-ng-sau-ng, long-one-action-one, (long=extensive=extremely=very). "Terlangsong perahu boleh balek, terlangsong chakap ta' boleh balek", "Boats that have gone too far can [be brought] back, but words gone too far can not [come] back".
Lanjai, slender, fragile, (30), la-en-kai, lithe-of-body.
Lanjar, long, stretching far (as lianas), next, forthwith, (29), la'n-gara, long-one-goer, (cp langsong above).
Lanjam, plough share, (28), la-en-ga-mai, linear-go-earthing.
Lanjut, too long, (of breasts, life, etc), (29), la-en-shau-tai, length-of-very high-become. Dan sa lanjut nya, and the length of it = etcetera. And one too long of it. Nya is from en-ia, of it or of him (or her).
Lantai, decking, floor, (20), la'n-tai, flat-become, flattened, made flat, a flat (surface).
Lantak, ram in (pegs, powder, food, etc), la-en-ta-kai, loop[swing]-of-hole-strike.
Pelantak, ramrod, pestle - or male lover. (!) Pai-lai 'n-ta-ka. The Lithic genital fascination has surely surfaced here. Pelir is penis, the enlarging/swelling piece.
Lantam, loud, conceited, (9), la'n-tai-mai, intoning-become-great (massive).
Lantar, outstretched on the ground (corpse, etc), (23) (29), La'n-tai-a, lying-become-one.
Lantek, launch, install (ruler), appoint, (19) (40), la-en-tai-kai, loop/swing-in-become-make. Pelantek, spring spear trap for game, a launcher. Pe- is like the, making a noun.
Lantin, payment to a judge additional to a fine, (3) (12), la-en-tai'n, smooth-ing-the becoming/outcome.

Selangkang is the perineum. Selang, from linear-action, kang, of the body. Selang is to let slip (from between the fingers) and so intervening. Selang dua hari is let slip two days between, and so every third day. Similarly selang is a (linear, narrow) passage between two buildings (you can let yourself slip through), a line of passage or a movement line,

Chapter 8 La

(sai-la'ng) or alignment. With the perineum, it is by no means clear if the slippage for the Malay idiom is between the two limbs or the two orifices. The Greek, peri-nai-u'm, is clearly around-the orifices-dual'ns. With the Malay probably the reference is to both, an inter-regnum par excellence, both ways on, both sideways and front to back, since the – kang here is the body or even the shape, make or form (four words with the same core meaning).

These constructs are all clearly tentative, playing with syntax from the time when speaking was new, and we were only gradually accustoming the mind to the idea of a grammar. The 'it-that-one' and '-do' or '-does-one' are almost redundant fillers, but they are understandable mind games, given that the methodology was entirely new. The words are the ones available in English and poorly represent Lithic thinking, which had a much looser logic with syllables having much wider meanngs than English words. The idea of grammar was slowly developing in the mind, a new mode of thinking, a construct without precedent before speech – derived from the new exercise, simply by thinking about its implications and potential - and somewhat prior to any transformational potential. It should be possible to examine and meaning-parse in Lithic the whole of any other dictionary in the same way as above, a lifetime's work for an army of scribes, too much to attempt in a single lifetime. But its effect upon the mental address of the first speakers was clearly immense, a development leading the hominid to at least a semi Sapient one. In the beginning was the word, the logos, from the Lithic phonemes lau-kau (s), the link-made [of phonemes], the linkage, language linked meanings to make words. Latin loquor to speak, the logos also the realization for the first time of the outside world as a whole, the linkage making one. Naming introduced the realization of the world with (grammatical) connections: science began with speaking, the adjectival mind complete with Levi-Strauss's binary oppositions, from the binary opposition of the body to the self and the not self; and the other "mythemes" he fancied he had found.

NOTES

1. The word silver is probably originally from the elements we see in the Assyrian sarpu, from surrupu meaning to smelt (Chambers). The Ancient Egyptian is hetch (Partridge), Lithic ahi-tai-shai, that which-born-fired, smelted in this case, but otherwise not unlike the English stone, from sai-tau'n, fire-born'one - from a volcano. Silver was just another metal (Lithic mai-ta-lai, of earth/solid-born-liquid) extracted from a (different) ore. It was also notably shiny (sai) like the flame. You could read silver as the scientific process, sai-lai-bai-rai, fire > liquid > being-verbal marker.

2. We once (about 1930) had from a turkey mated with a chicken a brood of churkeys given us, but their brains had got mixed up and they spent their whole time circling obsessively and died off young. They had brown feathers but long bare necks and purpled heads. They were ugly ducklings. As children we marveled at their antics in our back yard. It was a bit of genetic modification that had gone bdly wrong.

CHAPTER 9

MA. MASS, MURDER AND MENTALITY.

The psychosemantic tree for Ma is on pages 166 and 167, with numbers in brackets in the text of this chapter referring to the numbered entries in the trees. Meanings fall into two groups: what Ma meant itself, and then the meanings the hums picked up as opposite to the hisses. Just mmm without any articulation is a hum. Only Ish and mmm, s and m, the hisses and the hums, can be sounded continuously as long as you have breath. All the other consonants are stops[1]. This is not regarded these days as in any way significant, but when the search for the natural meanings of our first articulations took off at the birth of language, the fact will have been regarded as highly significant. They shared this feature, but then they were also sharply distinguished. They were a contrary pair. Ish and ma were a tweedledum and a tweedledee. Indeed more meanings spring from this character of Ma than from the sound of Ma itself. Nowadays a hum is used as a filler in a sentence while the speaker searches for the next word or phrase. To say Hum! or Hm! can mean uncertainty over agreement.

Each new phoneme was closely examined for meaning. Most recently a similar use is made of an articulation which can be represented phonetically as Ynoh, a slurring of "you know", but stripped of any semantic content and used just like a meaningless hum or filler, while the brain searching for expression catches up with the tongue. It is used by sluggish brains for the most part. Then came the search for semantic contents. To utter a hiss there is a clear expulsion of breath whereas with a hum there is not. Indeed you can hold your nose and still hum with only some minor inconvenience, but you can not even begin to utter a sibilant without the expulsion of air. It was therefore natural enough for our forebears with their adjectival minds to pair off and then to oppose and contrast these two sounds and their semantic contents - and that laid them open to dialectical thinking, given that dialectical thinking was around[2]: hiss positive, hmm negative.

The phoneme Ish (with the vowel element in front because that is how the flame articulated its name, ishshsh, when you dowsed your burning brand at dawn in the nearest puddle) is not examined in detail until chapter 13. The dying flame was a natural prompt for the meaning of the phoneme. Language came from echoism originally. It has proved a potent prompt for thinking. Whereas Ish was, as a sound, lively like the flame and positive like breathing out, a forward movement, a giving out, a positive expression, Ma was identified by contrast as lifeless and negative, as a movement of retreat, of taking back, nay saying even; and as the flame had the instinct to spring upwards, Ma was taken to go downwards. It stood for instinctive down going, and so for weighty matter, mass, solidity, all that was to be found down below, like the earth and rocks, the inertest elements. Moreover, by way of a payback, because the hum was regarded as a filler with an indefinite semantic content, the sibilant in turn came to be regarded as having a precising function. Well, it stands to reason - if you see the phonemes as in opposition.

Because for convenience of reference the chapters dealing with original phonemic semantic contents are arranged in alphabetical order, with some elisions as for example

Chapter 9 Ma

with chapter 4 which lumps Da and Ta together (the clear differentiation between voiced and unvoiced consonants was a comparatively late development), and chapter 13 which lumps together Ish and z and j because they have been lumped together over the aeons by the human mind, Ma's derivative and subsidiary role in this relationship has been reversed; and the semantic contents it picked up from contradistinction from the sibilant are examined first, in this chapter.

Simply because they were taken as opposites, the way we first thought, at the two ends of the semantic spectrum, or more accurately at the two ends of various semantic spectra, the mid positions could be called up by linking the two of them together, a bit of a muchness, neither the one thing nor the other, the middle, the mean and so on: the synthesis had the elements of both with the meaning of a combinated dish, in accordance with dialectical thinking. You can relate this semantically to the scientific notation giving a result and its accuracy as a value x, plus or minus y. The x is then a middle value. This was not terribly good math because positives and negatives should refer to a single category, or better criterion, and not to whites (Ish) positive and blacks (Ma) negative. But nevertheless it was Lithic thinking precisely. In Albanian mesit actually means middle today, which suggests the dd in middle comes originally from the sibilant via th. This is confirmed by the Aeolian Greek messos and the Attic Greek mesos (the single s is more like our z) – whence our Mesopotamia, the land in the middle, intermediate between the two rivers. Similarly the technical term mesocephalic means with the common intermediate shape of head, cucumber at one end of the spectrum and pumpkin at the other.

Yet Eric Partridge[3] curiously prefers to refer back to an original dh for the sibilant in meso, in spite of Armenian maj and Gothic midjis also, both relatively ancient languages in the context of modern historical linguistics although only recent arisings in the context of the six hundred thousand year history of language - since first it was spoken, according to the Lithic hypothesis. The fact is the aspirated consonants in Partridge's day were taken to be typical of the rough pronunciations of our rough forebears. But assuming that it is true, it is no reason to dismiss the sibilants as short on meanings.

Rather more imaginatively, shamanism was the exploitation of intermediaries between the living and other worldly states. Sha was the sphere of the living, Ma of the dead. Na or nai, slurring to ne and then just n, can mean to put forward, present, represent, interpret, explain. Nabi (Lithic na-bai) is a traveling explicator, a prophet in Arabic; in which language Nabi Issus is The Prophet Jesus. (His real name in Aramaic was Joshua, from Jawe-shu-a, Lithic Jawe-enlightened-one). The Prophet Mohammed and The Prophet Jesus taught the same religion, they have been transmogrified into enemies by their foolish followers. A sham is the one thing representing itself as another significantly different thing, often an opposite, for instance an untruth represented as the truth. A shampoo, from the Hindi, is in origin a head massage, a pressing both up and down, rather than just a hair-wash. The -poo was probably from the Lithic elements pa-u, an indication it was to be done with both hands, an up-down two-handed; now transmogrified into a bottle of soapsuds – quite a nice example of semantic drift by means of gulling. When we look at Sanscrit (originally Shamskrit, with benefit of writing) and Prakrit, (preceding writing, the rude form practiced by the illiterate common people of the day) it appears to suggest the grammarians behind Sanscrit were the inheritors of the Shamanistic tradition, high priests of learning and linguistics, following Shamash the Persian Fire God, the Sun (Shai-Mai-Shai, Light-Dark-Light, Up-Down-Up and Life-Death-Life), all three neatly exemplified for the primitive mind by the sun, which appeared to be born afresh each dawn and die each dusk as it sank beneath the Western horizon, in a bloody red end to the day. The

Chapter 9 Ma

common folk who preferred the easier Prakrit dialect for everyday affairs were locked into the mere pra- (from pai-rai-) the physical sensational everyday world of pai-rai, surfaces visible, the phenomenal world of res vista: ever despised and even shunned by the intellectual elite. The -krit is the speech bit in both cases, the mouthing merely, from the kara-tai, make-thinking, which is speech.

Reviewing the hums, apart from the ums (2) which are plain fillers with no meanings, represented in the chart by mm, next are the 'ms or thingumybobs (3) or items of one kind or another, quite common across Africa in the Hamitic languages but with a fair representation world wide. The Hamitic 'm is easily memorable - if a trifle inaccurately - as him (5), a substantive prefix as in the Swahili 'mtu, a person, human being, individual, man, Lithic m-tau, him-born, down the birth canal. Mtu mume is a man, a born person him who plants/impregnates and mtu mke a woman, a born person mai-kai, pregnant made – kindled by the mai or male organ. Then there is mtoto, a child, young person, offspring, offshoot, descendant, from the Lithic one-born-born, the duplication emphasizing the born, that is just born and so young, or a repetition of births to a descendant. Mdache is a German, a straight copy from Deutsche with a him in front (and a rather imprecise ear). We can however think of the 'm in our English him (and in me) in much the same way. 'M as a him, effectively just a substantive marker, can clear up many meanings otherwise defying analysis. It amounts to a cockney m, a bit like a cockney h, which is used to avoid elision of consecutive vowels (and then in time the h survives after the first protected vowel has dropped out). The cockney m adds a hardly necessary qualifier on the way to precising the meaning.

Psychosemantic trees have achieved a complexity over the millennia which leaves analysis a juggling trick, because potential meanings abound, ninety nine for Ma here. For every phoneme there is a network, a whole texture of meanings in which the structure of every word is caught up; and perhaps unsurprisingly many words appear to be caught in the net at numerous points. In English a mare was originally just a horse, pronounced not so far away from the Chinese 'maa which also means a horse (inter alia, with four tones). But then the mare got identified with the female, probably because it began with a ma- and that triggered the idea of motherhood; although it might as well have triggered impregnation, the planting of the seed, and that could have made a mare into a stallion. Since it just meant horse, the 'm appears to have started out as a cockney 'm. Yet it still might have been a full blown ma-, because the Lithic semantic contents include heavy (58) so ma-are could have been a heavy goer. Moreover ill treatment of a horse, when breaking it for instance, could make it spiteful and dangerous, and there will surely have been some of this in the Stone Age, so that a harmer (73) perhaps came into the equation. The gestatory facility (85) is then kept for the mother, which in Chinese is maa too, while we have said mama or, on the far side of the pond, mom (pronounced maaam). Most of the languages of the world have an m in their word for mother, simply because a baby babbles when content but maas when it is hungry, and mothers around the world have thought it calling for them. It is worth repeating from time to time that these same psychosemantic promptings arose spontaneously from the subconscious mind in the age of the Pleistocene all around theworld when first we were lisping in linguistic mode, as they do so still for anyone attentive to the poetic muse today. Readers other than the poetically inspired may wish to query this, but even the most bovine will undoubtedly catch themselves out from time to time, if only responding to music.

Meanwhile in Maori, to ring the changes, motu, is from the Lithic 'm-au-tau, him-that one-severed (two-ed) meant – well – severed or cut. But from severed the Maori meanings

Chapter 9 Ma

THE PSYCHOSEMANTIC TREE FOR MA

The Phonetic Tree

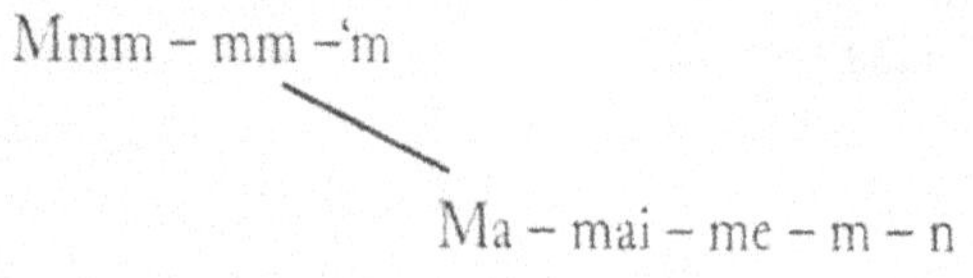

Mmm – mm – 'm

Ma – mai – me – m – n

The Semantic Tree

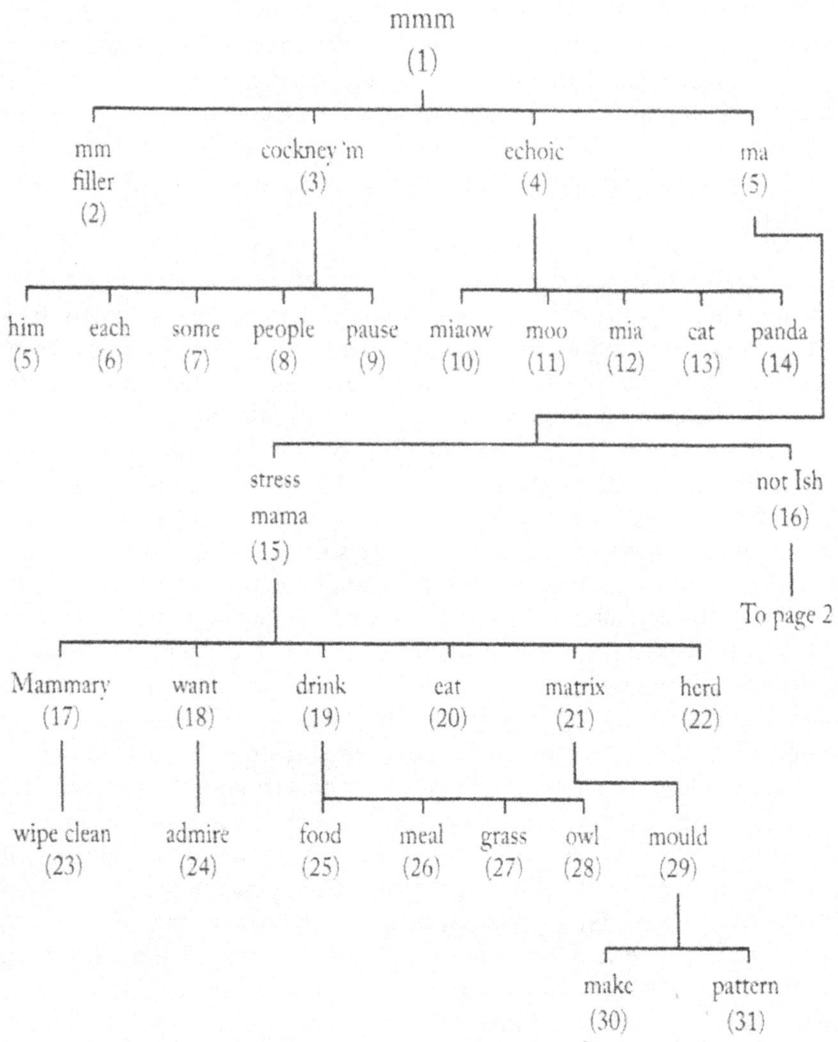

mmm (1)

- mm filler (2)
- cockney 'm (3)
- echoic (4)
- ma (5)

Under cockney 'm (3):
- him (5)
- each (6)
- some (7)
- people (8)
- pause (9)

Under echoic (4):
- miaow (10)
- moo (11)
- mia (12)
- cat (13)
- panda (14)

Under ma (5):
- stress mama (15)
- not Ish (16) — To page 2

Under stress mama (15):
- Mammary (17)
- want (18)
- drink (19)
- eat (20)
- matrix (21)
- herd (22)

- Mammary (17) → wipe clean (23)
- want (18) → admire (24)
- drink (19) → food (25)
- eat (20) → meal (26)
- matrix (21) → grass (27), owl (28), mould (29)

mould (29) → make (30), pattern (31)

166

Chapter 9 Ma

THE PSYCHOSEMANTIC TREE FOR MA

Page 2

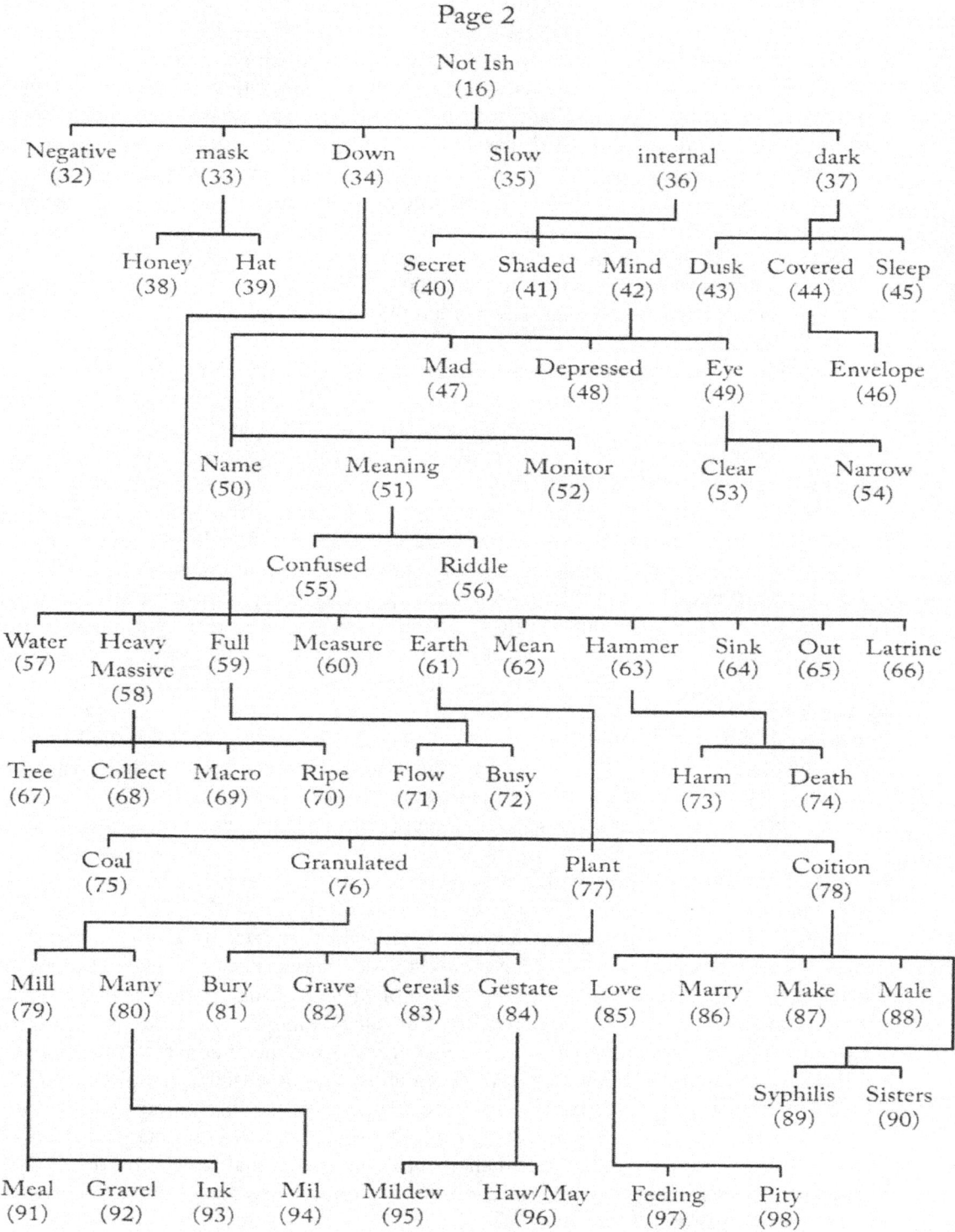

proliferated via the idea of cutting off, and so to be separated, to making a separate thing, and so anything obviously separated from its surroundings, an isolate, such as an island alone in the sea, and then also a grove of trees, probably planted for ritual purposes. The island separation was an act of nature, the grove a copycat procedure for human purposes. Both the island and the grove come with a cockney 'm again (6), and chasing after any meaning from the semantic tree seems otiose. The meaning flow of Maori thinking is instinct with original Lithic thinking, like many tongues undefiled with overmuch modern ornamentation. To the Maori mind maroke spells dry, with the Lithic 'm-a-rau-kai, him-that-rayed-made. It may not seem exactly like dry to the modern mind, although the Lithic elements for dry are tai-rai, become-rayed, but then we are not any longer consciously composing with Lithic phonemes and their devious meanings in mind. That leaves out whether our primitive forebears were either. It may be they were not as yet fully conscious as we understand consciousness to be, but that is to wander into fascinating realms of overall psychological development way beyond the remit of any linguistic study. We note the possibility and pass on[4].

Meanwhile if the rays were the rays of the sun, the paradigmatic ones, what does the raying make? Surely it made the washing dry in those old days in the Stone Age, if they had any, just as it does today. It makes the observer 'dry' too, even today, come to think of it, many millennia later; but also sufficiently stressed (driven) to 'try', although these were the ta rays, not sunrays after all (chapter 5). In Maori again maro means stiff and hard, and the Lithic seems to indicate another cockney 'm. This Maori stiffness and hardness seems to come from the original raying of the male organ by the female (Chapter 12). Ma, weight (58), pressing down, grinding, milling, yields ground and grains. The grains were mankind's contribution. The soil and sand were ground by nature. Both were nothing stiff; and other semantic contents are similarly contra indicated. The rest of it makes perfect Lithic sense if we treat the m as a cockney 'm: maro from 'm-a-rau, him that rayed, roused and raised, and rays again the stiffening and hardening. This was surely Tarzan's own idea: any over exuberance was the fault of his partner who ought not to have been raying him so hard. She was inviting rape. It wasn't his fault. Maro is a straight gull from the roused genitalia. Indeed in Egypt - a long way off – mai, the earther, planter or impregnator was the name of the Egyptian penis. So the maori m here might not just be him, after all. We can even surmise Maori, supposedly meaning the big ones perhaps had this m in mind. They certainly fancy their manhood. If so, they will have closed for the big ones from the sun's rays which make plants grow (and why not us too?) in proper consideration for Mrs Grundy. Tarzan knew nothing of the circulation of the blood, nor of the spongy tissue of his genitalia. Sex was for him just magic. It was a powerful and generally disastrous juju, but that is beyond linguistics again. Primitive perception had no other theory for the process than the perception of rays covering all actions at a distance. Perhaps stone, which he could see freezing after ejaculation from a volcano – eruptions were quite likely much commoner in the Pleistocene – will have added to the science of the Pleistocene couch. It will surely have fallen under the same rubric, the old men adding their sixpennyworth of understanding in those terms, and rounding on any young shaver who demurred. Of course the sequencing of the volcanic eruptions is not precisely the same as for the male genitalia; but then nature and the animal kingdom were already regarded as in some degree at least in conflict. So it all passed as sweet reason, and you had to follow the established science, just as now.

Eric Partridge moves half way to Lithic with his analysis of masturbation. He has "*mas [paragraph 4 under male, page 374] male seed (cp. semen) and thence mas-turbate

Chapter 9 Ma

to turbinate the male seed, or stir it up". Masculine might then be from Lithic masai-kau-lai'n, gestating-life [maisai is dead or gestating life, which describes a seed]-make-leaking'one, (which in passing distinguishes the male from the female as the sex which supplies the seed. Of course it is not actually correct, but it is the well established historic belief of our benighted forebears, from the Bible, in which some of the boys went spilling their seed on the ground; and it is still the belief of plenty of folk today). I was advised to cut off the female flowers when growing marrows because they would not fruit, and I cut the non fruiting ones off. The evidence Sumerian, Adam's language, supposedly a linguistic isolate, was most closely related to the Malay comes from Sumerian doburr for the testicles. In Malay it is dobuah which means the dual fruits. It was not the testicles regarded as fruit. It was the other way around. Fruit were regarded as vegetable testicles. The glans of the male organ had a similar claim to be a fruiting body. It supports the Lithic hypothesis we thought in terms first of our own experiences.

The reality is the boys are mere pollinators of the female seed, contributing half and no more of the genes and less of the foetal influences – except many genes appear to be sexually linked, quite apart from those which determine the genitalia, so that male linked genes appear more in male babies and female linked genes more in female babies. With these semantic contents the hand (manus) is not disclosing a mental state but instead ma'n-nau-s, presenting the seed. In short, the hand is the masturbator: down the middle, but bawdy for nowadays. But for six hundred thousand years ago? The English hand is from ha'n-da, pleasuring does, the pleasurer. The very ancient word for finger, tik, comes from Lithic tai-kai, the tickler, vulva-kindling, stimulating the vagina. That goes back a long way. A finger is from pahai'n-kara, a pleasurer again. Tik, as finger, is a pointer too, and so a pointer outer, indicating the correct answer, our tick.

Immaculate, without spot, is derived from the Latin macula which surprisingly means a mesh, the Lithic perhaps 'm-a-kau-lai, him-that-joined/crossed-lines (or in linear directions), which would make a net. Maculate is thus become gridded and enmeshed and so marked out and so marked, and so blemished, whence immaculate is unblemished. Psychosemantic contents can not be derived against the grain. You can get from a mesh (3) via a mark and a blemish to the meaning of unblemished for immaculate, but you can not get from an impregnation (78, under Not Ish on the second page) to a mesh. Both are meanings with Ma in them, but different Mas. The impregnation is a rational development of opposing ma to ish as up (the flame springs upwards): so Ma meant down and went from down to weighty, from weighty and down to – well earth: it is heavy and down below your feet, having settled there in accordance with its instinct to descend. So to earth seed is to plant it, and planting seed is impregnation. The cockney 'm, him, meanwhile is merely a matter of articulation, and Lithic is understanding the utilization of the process by which human whimsy has put together meanings by metaphors and gulls.

A match, 'm-a-shi-kai, is a thingumybob-that-fire-makes. Originally it meant a torch (a burning branch) or a lamp wick and so in due course the match that comes in a box. The Lithic applies to torches, wicks and matches with equal aptitude, which is why the meaning has slid effortlessly from one to the other. The match that matches, on the other hand, comes from 'm-a-shai, him-one-height. Making was also making cakes, from kneading or moulding (30), pressing the mass (59). The verbal form to match or make a match, to join or bring together gives us a love match and at one time, obsolete now, a spouse akin to Old Norse maki a spouse (87). The Lithic 'm-a-kai can even be read as him-that-joined. But it could have come too from ma-kai referring to the earthing or planting (78) of seed involved in espousal. Ma-kai, as in our English make, is also derived

Chapter 9 Ma

from earthing, impregnation (79). The earth-mother springs to mind. But it has also at the same time been derived from moulding, striking (kai) the mass (ma), pounding the dough or the clay slip. It is not really germane to enquire which derivation is correct because both intimations arise from the subconscious semantic lexicon, and are not mutually exclusive but on the contrary mutually reinforcing, and that is what deriving the word making teaches us. We are living in a dream world and it is not a mathematical one. More is the pity perhaps. More, from mau-are, mass (in the completive case, u)-verbal marker, is to mass extremely, to become more massive, to be more. The catena does not correspond with our linguistic custom today but it is entirely logical. Matins, from the French matin, morning, is from the Lithic 'm-a-tai 'n, him-that-birthed, is born 'one, and so him that is just born, namely the sun. When the sun is just born it is morning. There is the additional gloss of the ma, dead (75) sun returning to life, the sun coming over the horizon shining light, which is much as our morning says: ma-u-rai-nai'n, dead/dark-when/one-rising-presenting.

A mattress was originally a sleeping rug you wrapped around you to sleep, a douvet more than an underlay, 'm-a-ta-rai-sa-sai is the Lithic analysis which can be read as him-that-drawn/pulled-up-cosy/warm (Chapter 13 for the meanings of the sibilants). Me and mine, as well as him, all have a cockney m. Ai is I. Me is from 'm-ai, him-I. Mine is from 'm-ai-nai, 'm-ai plus adjectival marker/showing (nai). See chapter 14 for the vowel meanings. Nai really means showing or presenting here, and so representing, whence the adjectival usage (chapter 10 for Nai). Him is the plum example of the cockney usage. It has a cockney h at one end and a cockney m at the other, as well as the initial vowel missing, the middle letter being the only surviving one with much in the way of semantic content:ahi-'m > him.

Meet and mete and meed and moot, all now a little passé, are concerned with right action (and even our bounden duty), and are originally from to measure, and so coming to mean judgmental and also to apportion, to measure it out. The Wittenagemot was a council of old men who gave judgments, lawyers in effect, W-ai-tai-en-a-kai-mau-tai, All-long-born-ones-that-making-consideration-become, the old men rounded up for making judgments. The Old English was metan to measure, originally to be weighed (66), mai-tai-en. Further back the Gothic was mitan to measure too, suggesting the proto Germanic was metanan to measure, and the prototypical measurement was weighing to discover the genuine quantity (59). Meed meant recompense, reward, payment, rent, hire, which are all from ma, a weighing job. To weigh (61) had nothing to do with the cockney 'm.

A boom, a reverberating sound beginning fancifully enough in a b- because our own utterances started out that way, and ending in a cockney 'm because, when we end the air flow accompanying the oo vowelisation, it produces that closure. Neither consonant actually features in the sound we hear as a boom, yet the oo bit is clearly echoic with a clear cut commencement and a reverberating terminus represented by a hum. A bomb potentially makes the same noise, but the word is not as emphasized as the boom being only potential rather than striking the ear. The reverberating bang or boom will come later. The entirely silent anti submarine boom meanwhile adds a semantic content to the initial boo-, a blockage or bung, from way back in chapter 3. A broom, from be-rau'm, has many rays to do the work. The m in broom is merely a closure for the broom.

With Greek omphalos, the navel, it appears the -m- is either a shortened em, which in Egyptian would be a genitive (em is of in Egyptian), in this case a suffixed one, or else it is just 'm, a substantive marker after the oo. In favour of the genitive is the close copying of much of Egyptian in Greek. Oo-em-phalos is orifice-of-the phalos. The cord was cut

Chapter 9 Ma

somewhat casually in olden days, leaving an inch or so to spare (originally with the teeth), and led to a protruding navel - and not the sunken job we see today with a brooch stuck in it - which could be likened to the protrusion just below. With umbilicus, the Latin for the navel, we can trace the same protrusion, at least originally of the Roman navel, since it is a diminutive of umbo, the boss at the centre of the Roman shield. This boss, a metal bowl-shaped bit at the centre of the shield, accommodated the hand of the shield bearer behind the shield gripping the bar across it. The Lithic elements oo-'m-bau can stand for a hollow-him-bulged, which describes the umbo on the Roman shield quite well; and a little one, umbili, fits the protruding navel too, with the -cu-s or -kau-s coming from -shaped-substantive. The Sanskrit, the language closest to the source of Indo European, has nabhis for navel, with the Lithic elements nai-bai-s, protruding-bulging-substantive, and is copied by the Old Persian nabis, perhaps from na-bai-sai too; and at one further remove by the Old English nafala, picking up the fala from the Greek phalos - whence our modern day navels, with the protruding bulge and the phallus or fruiting body mixed, nowadays anachronistic with neither any longer related to the remnants of the cord as worn today, much more neatly cut off short and withdrawn. Finally, the m in omphalos is still only doubtfully either the Egyptian genitive or a cockney 'm serving as a substantive marker as just proposed, because there is also open the interpretation derived all the way from mai, gestation (85), for which the navel string is designed. In reality the subconscious may well have thrown up all or any of these variant representations simultaneously, so that the Greek editor of Tarzan's legacy was in no doubt of its applicability.

A camshaft has a hump on it – a smooth tooth if you like - so it lifts a lever pressed against it as it rotates, for instance on the camshaft opening the valves of an internal combustion engine in turn. It is a ka'm, a driving thingumybob or driver. It is conventionally derived from the Dutch and German kamm which means a comb, and it is by no means immediately apparent why a camshaft should be akin to a comb, until it is disclosed the comb was named for the teeth it has in it, and in Greek it is a molar tooth, gomphos, for chewing, which we might translate as ka'm-pahau-s in Lithic, a hard knob or a crushing knob (ka has both semantic contents). It turns out to be a nice example of how the Ka in chapter 5 is around in the subconscious mind aware of the thinking which defined a comb from its teeth, and even the origin of the tooth it came from as a hard molar. The comb reverts to the protruding tooth from which it came when it arrives upon the shaft. The Sanskrit is jambhas for tusk. In Sanskrit kh- appears in many cases to have migrated uniquely via gh- to j-; and it may be the original Sanskrit derivation was khai-em ba, the hard growth of (from) the flesh; after all a tusk is not a chewer like a molar. That is of course why elephants are named jumbo; it means tusker; and it sounds jumbo, meaning big, blown up. You can pick that up from the –bau. Boomerang, in many Australian Aboriginal tongues, is composed from the Lithic elements bau'm-ai-ra'ng, go dually 'of-going-returning. We would just say it both goes and comes back again. If we had actually named it we would probably have called it a kumbak or some such. In Oz they spelt it out in rather more detail.

Meanwhile in Tupi, a Caribbean language, a macaw is the name for a parrot. But according to Eric Partridge, the word may have been imported from Africa by Bantu speaking slaves of the Portuguese. It is echoic wherever it comes from. 'M-a-caw, him-that-caws, is first cousin to Jim Crow. The initial 'm is the common Bantu him, or identifier. Macaws feed in great numbers on the palm fruits of the macaw palm, which is probably called the macaw palm, maca-uba in Tupi, (where u-ba is tree in Tupi, the 'super-burgeoned'), just because of the macaws seen in it. The macaque monkey similarly comes

Chapter 9 Ma

from the Portuguese macaco meaning just monkey, but again probably from a Bantu word used in Angola, Lithic 'm-a-cacau, the cackler or him-that-chatters all the time: all the time is from the –cacau, repetitively -caca-, and absolutely (all the time) from the –u. Monkeys have numerous calls and tones and use them frequently, in a way a cow or other main quadruped does not. They are half way to speaking. Even birds call to each other more than the larger quadrupeds, who are old sober-sides. Chambers Dictionary of Etymology, with a distinguished panel of editors, helpfully adds "ma is a Bantu prefix", without offering any meaning. But is it not really from 'm or 'm-a, him that?

The Chinese ma (pronounce maa) as well as meaning mother also means a horse. Mother is from her mammary glands (18) as already explained, named from the infants cry for nourishment. The double toned maa (down and then up) marks the extension of the cry. It is treated as the dipping and then rising tone in Chinese, but it is really just a double aa with no stop between which makes a dipping and then a rising tone. For the horse meaning, the a, extension (chapter 14), is taken to mean going, and the m is a cockney 'm. A horse is noted as a goer. It has no horns. Its only defence is flight, with a kick behind as it leaves for any unwelcome follower. It relies upon its alertness and speed for getting away. The Chinese idiom is neatly indicated by these additional words: maena is a saddle: ma-en-a, horse-for-going. Mabian is a horsewhip, Lithic (as well as Chinese) ma-bai-un, horse-flesh/going, from which the Chinese could, (and still can) work out the item which conjoined these three was a horse whip, which with a horse addresses the flesh with a view to effect its going. They defined a horse whip by its function, admittedly somewhat summarily, but of course it was something of a game with two or three symbols to define whatever.

If you were a mandarin, with forty years learning your trade, which involved thousands of picture symbols, you were not averse to a bit of crossword puzzling, even just to keep the uneducated out. As a result over very many millennia the great majority of the Chinese population were kept in virtual servitude, unable to read. It was the most scandalous extreme elitism the world has ever seen, and led readily enough to the adoption of Marxism as soon as they got wind of it, and over half a century of massacre and bloodshed. Now the best answer for the Chinese masses is to abandon their native language pattern altogether and join the rest of the world. It probably means learning American English to go with the American technology they are learning to copy, and even improve. Their particular whimsy is a mathematical protocol, probably from all that crossword puzzling.

Still in Chinese, mache (from khai, driven/powered, ie pulled) is a horse-drawn carriage or cart; maku riding breeches, horse-made, designed for riding horses; mafu a groom, fond of horses; majui a stable, horse-warming; male, horse-like, horse power; mazhang a horseshoe, literally a horse action/comforter, -zhang having the Lithic psychosemantic content of warm and so comfortable, as well as movement (see chapter 13 on Ish). At the same time ma shang means at once or immediately, from m'-fast, horse-fast, see chapter 13 again, at once just a single jump from a fast horse to a quite general "lickety spit"? This is metaphor for you.

The Greek prefix meta- (as in metaphysics or metalanguage or meta-bolism for examples) means something which happens afterwards, or afterwards, or beyond, from the Lithic 'm-ai-ta, him (indicating something) (8)-that-become. What we need however is an indicator of the after, which puts us in a posterior relationship with what has become. Ai-ta the extension or going or action is fine, but how do we make after out of 'm or ma? 'M, a pause (10), is a period of time, and since it is only a pause, it is, at the end of the pause, over. It hardly needs a Chinese mind to get from just a pause that is become (tai) or over,

Chapter 9 Ma

to when it has happened, after or afterwards or even beyond. But however it was devised it was in fact a Chinese style of mind which did it, used as it is by the Greeks. The clue to this gnomic judgment lies in the fact the Chinese linguistic idiom is probably the nearest to the Lithic mind. A metaphor is a carrying beyond, a transfer [of meaning]. Meteor however, from the Greek meteoros, high in the air, Lithic 'm-ai-tai-au-rau-s, him-that is-become-altogether-raised up-substantive marker, also gives us our meteorite, meteorai-tai, born high in the sky, as well as meteorology, the logic or discourse of what is high in the sky, namely the atmosphere.

Ma as the infant's cry for the breast has imprinted the phoneme in the human subconscious as marking an utterance, giving us a lot of dodgy echoisms, starting with the cat's miaow (11) and its description as a mew (11). It really just says iau which combines the three ancient vowels. A Chinese cat's mew is mimi. It is not that Chinese cats make dual mews, they do not; although if they are like the Siamese ones they do mew somewhat repetitively. The duplication indicates a general meaning rather than a particular utterance or one of occasion. Compare sa (one) orang (person) in Malay and sa sa orang, anybody or somebody. Sa sa kuching China is any old Chinese cat in Malay, just as sa sa orang China is any old Chinese person, or somebody Chinese. The logic of duplication appears to be this one or that one, one or another one, with the little helper prepositions Indo Europeans use left out. In the case of the Chinese mewing, it is this mew and that mew, and so mews in general. It may not fit in too well with Noam Chomsky's universal grammar, but it seems that is how the thinking has gone. An actual Chinese cat is a mao (14), clearly echoic like the Vietnamese cat, meo, a mewer. After all they may well have traded cats, perhaps from Siam. The French dialect maraud, pronounced maraau is a very clearly echoic tom cat from the noise it makes when out on the tiles to see off a rival, before the fur starts to fly. It has given us the English to maraud, to act like a tom cat out on the tiles, along with the agential marauder. Merrill's Marauders however had nothing to do with tom cats (so far as is known), they were Americans who fought with Chiang Kai Shek in Chungking against the Japanese in upper Burma, like the Chindits, during the second world war, and after with the British Fourteenth Army in the bars in Karachi on their way home by air, flying the long way round, and wanting to punch me too. The Chinese Panda, the bear with the black and white face, is known in China as da xiongmao (14) or da maoxiong, a nice disregard for sequencing reminiscent of the Lithic idiom, like so much in Chinese. It is a strong (da) powerful (xiong) cat (mao). I don't know if they mew?

Every Chinese attribution is time consuming because of the polysemy of their syllables, another relict of the Lithic idiom, even after differentiating their four vowel tones, up, down, level, and repetitive (down and then up). A Panda is of course a bear and not a cat at all, which the Chinese must have known when they dubbed it a strong cat. The Lithic idiom with cat includes every meaning which can be gulled from the feline. The Chinese designation contrasts the panda's size and strength with its gentle docility, the Chinese cat too having the delicacy of gait the Ancient Egyptians noticed with their Bast, really ba-siti, goes-lady, walks like a lady, a dainty walker. There is surely some common thinking here, widely separated in time and space, the commonality being provided by the cat, common to both scenarios.

To be fair to the cow it does say something very close to "mmmm" or "mmmer" but when it is worked up it is more of a raucous "rrerrm". It is never really a moo but human whimsy has picked on moo, because of its phonemic value (semantic content) in the subconscious; and in the case of the cow we can not deny its echoic base. It is the Egyptian hieroglyph of an owl that is used for their letter m. But what it actually said in

Chapter 9 Ma

Egyptian, and how it should be pronounced, is "Aa-maoo" (14). This is a much better shot at echoism than the rather pathetic "Ter-wit-ter-woo" we have. If we can go by the mischief in other nursery naming, as in the rhymes, the tarai may have been introduced because of its semantic contents, of which of course neither the owl nor the babies will have had the slightest inkling. Hoot-er-woo would be better. Also the Egyptian actually meant something. The aa, the extensive vowel, including spatial extension, either as a dimension or even a progression or movement, meant something like "Going!" or "Here I go!" Mau is ma in the dual and completive case: in this case both complete darkness (38) and murder (75). Owls hunt small game in the dark. The most you could extract from the Egyptian is perhaps: "Here I go! It is dark beyond a peradventure and I am an exceptional hunter a-hunting through the gloom!"

Latin flies and certainly mosquitoes and midges also get their names from their signature sounds. The Latin for fly is musca. It makes a sound which is a cross between a hum and a hiss which we call a buzz, as if it spoke English (where speech starts with a ba, as in chapter 3). There is a rival school of thought that the fly was believed to be generated from dead and decaying matter, for which it consequently had a yen in life: Lithic mu-sai-kai, very dead-life-creating, a magical reversal of the normal natural process. It may sound silly today because we know flies feed on rotting matter and procreate much like us, but lay their eggs in organic waste so the heat of decay will gestate the eggs. The mouse meanwhile gets its name from an original mus or something like it in Old Saxon, Old High German, Old Norse, Armenian, Albanian, Old Slav, Latin, Greek, Sanskrit, Old Persian and even Luwian an early neighbouring language of the Hittites who copied with mashuil for mouse. All this is in Eric Partridge's Origins on page 418. He adds Greek mus also means a muscle - as if the Greeks thought it looked like a mouse. Compare Latin musculus for muscle, a little mouse seen rippling under the skin of an arm or leg. What actually made a muscle like a mouse is a muscle spends its time/lives hidden under the skin(37,38,41,42). A mouse, far from making its presence known with any kind of buzz like a fly, musca, with a hiss which is more like a hum, (or take the mosquito, a diminutive – muska-i-tau, fly-teeny-become) passes its life (sai) living mau, hidden (38 and 41) under cover. Mice are notoriously timid creatures (although they can be tamed). They have little defence against larger predators. Their name has in turn triggered some absurd conjectures they are a form of life generated in the earth, like the fly, the other mus, by decay.

Timid is from Latin timidus, fearful, akin to Latin timor (fear), and comes from Latin timere to be afraid, to fear. But that offers no very obvious guide as to how the semantic content is derived. Eric Partridge boldly claims Latin timere is akin to the Greek deos to be afraid, which he derives from an original form *dweios, with an original root dwei- to fear. As only the single letter e is common to timere and deos the kinship must surely be treated as dubious at best. However Lithic helps. In cases like this it is open to surmise Eric Partridge half knew more than he ever declared, perhaps because he thought it too way-out to gain acceptance, perhaps because he thought it would damage his reputation as "Word King". Did he have an inkling of any of the Lithic Hypotheses?

Lithic Timei- and Dewei- beginning with t- and d- respectively are akin to the Malay prefix ter- which in Malay is a completive prefix roughly translatable as become, from Lithic tai-, born and so become (for this derivation see chapter 5 if you have forgotten). If we then relate ter-mai and ter-wai we do uncover a startling kinship. The Latin is using – mai where the Greek is using –wai, and with those becomings we get the meaning of fear in both cases. Wai is easy although the Lithic is ahead in chapter 14, analyzing the semantic contents of the phoneme Wa along with the other full vowels. From the echoism

Chapter 9 Ma

of shivering (wewewe) human psychology derives water because prolonged immersion in it, so that you get taken over by the watery 'fluence of cold water, makes you shiver; and then it comes to mean fear by metaphor because fear makes you shiver too. This analysis, by the way, explains also the –ter in water, the element by which you are berayed with the shivers. For shivering with fear it has to be fairly severe alarm but it has to be remembered learning to speak started in the Pleistocene age, in company with the sabre-toothed tiger and matching mayhems. Your author in a previous existence in India sitting over a villager's dead goat in the dark to shoot a panther which had become too greedy of the villagers' goats to live, when it came to dine, on hearing and smelling the brute instead snuffling over his shoulder was startled to hear a sudden rattle – and only then realised it was his own teeth rattling, Extreme funk is a take-over by the autonomic system. The panther evidently said to himself "With his snappers that fast I am outclassed" and left. I blew my whistle and Bahadur Ali, the Shikari who laid the traps for the panthers and had built my machan (hide, from ma-kha'n, like camera, from ka-mai-ra, making dark/concealed) which had proved so insufficient a concealment for me, came whistling through the wood with his hurricane butti (lamp) waved in front of him. It is said a loud laugh – if you can manage it – will even see off a tiger, but it must probably be a maniacal cackle. Whether it worked with the sabre-toothed variety for our hominid forebears who first spoke, and had to live with the brutes, must now be moot. You probably better had a burning brand as well. Oh! The Latin temere is from tai-mai-rai, to beome-harming-rayed, fearful.

The ninety nine psychosemantic contents charted in the tree for Ma do not include fear. But this is just an error of omission. Mind (43), Down (35), Depression (49), Water (58), Harm (74) and Death (75) coming together lead to fear, without too much imagination. Fear should probably have appeared at 43(a) or (49a). It is taking subconscious Lithic to an advanced level to be composing meanings from multiple semantic contents of a phoneme, but it is a process actually going on all the time in the dream world of the subconscious mind, down below the level of conscious thought, where the mind dips unthinkingly into a mélange of closely textured meanings and comes up with a dimly recognized mix of what is there. Here indeed is Lithic revealing the psychology of the human race.

Also in Sanskrit Eric Partridge points out muska means scrotum and vulva too, two rather different bits but both to do with coition: ma (79). Musca is from the Lithic 'm-a-u-sai-ka, them-that-both-life-make. You can compare sex itself which appears to be from sai-kai-sai, or in modern terminology life-making-action: factual, unsentimental, shameless and correct, and all the way from the Pleistocene. An alternative etymology is the warm and sweet meaning for the final –sai, referring to the sexual sensation. For those who imagined the scrotum held two fruiting bodies which produced the seed – our hominid forebears - they and the womb which held the seed while it matured were quite properly described as the two essential genital attributes. The testicles, of which all warm blooded animals have two, are the dual bits hiding under the skin of the scrotum, just like the biceps muscles, the mice hiding under the skin of the arms for instance. The testicles were never mistaken for hiding mice, however, just for the fruiting of the boys. In so far as the act of coition was taken to be a planting of the seed of life (actually of course only pollination), with semen the Latin for seed, muska, from Lithic m-u-sai-kai, dual skulkers-life-makers or him-what-life maker is an undoubted pointer to the scrotum and womb respectively.. Then in Old Persian we find mushk, a substance obtained from a sac hidden under the abdominal skin of a male musk deer and when dried used as a perfume – now only as a

Chapter 9 Ma

base, the smell is genital and aphrodisiac like the his-and-hers sexual attractants sold as cosmetics discreetly by post today.

What can Lithic make of this pot pourri? The musk comes from mu-sai-kai,when planted-life-making (61, 77, 78). The mu- is with the dual vowel because it has dual meanings: the dead (or dormant) nature of the mai-sai or semen (seed) and at the same time the earthing or planting from the mai-sai-kai, and u is the completive vowel. Musk is a scent the male deer discharges when seeking to mount Mrs deer, to get her in the mood; and we have been borrowing the trick from the stag – likely ever since the Pleistocene when we were well placed to observe the strategy and tactic both. The vulgarity of human technique when emotion calls is sobering to see. The mush-ka is akin to Moshe, Englished Moses: it shows moshe means planted the semen or seed, with the same double entendre for the mau- as with musk. In Egypt the Pharaohs Rameses and Tutmose were claiming divine descent, begotten of Ra (Ra-planted the seed/life) and Tut (or Tahuti, but originally Tahu-tau, also shortened to Tutu, or the great god "Know-all", widely believed to have originally bestowed hieroglyphs and every other knowledge on the human race) planted his seed. Moses has omitted his progenitor, presumably Jahweh. If he was, as now appears, an Egyptian (Semitic) priest of royal blood, that may have been a matter of some discretion. The establishment god of his day was the sun god Ra. In Abraham's day you may have been able to think in terms of Ra as well as Jahweh. In Moses' time you might not be allowed to envisage a less physical progeniture, so he just left it out, or if he started out Ramoshe took it off when he left. Akhenaton the heretical and probably bisexual Pharaoh with strangely malformed lower body claimed to be A-kahai-en-Aton, That-begotten-in-the Aton, Born of the Aton, viz of divine descent from the (female) Sun. Japanese Emperors have the same hang-up. It is a common fantasy of hereditary rulers to make rather more of their descent than is warranted by their actual geniture. That is not to dispute their ability at equestrian events including polo, or the street cred their patronage gives to horse riding etc. The Holy Roman Emperor Charlemagne, with divinity off the menu with the Pope blocking that opportunity, had a pedigree done for him which traced his lineage in direct descent back to Adam: perhaps just for PR, there is no telling if he really believed it.

Next to the hums (1, 2 and 3) in the Ma tree, and the standard echoisms (4) come the mammary group of meanings (16 to 32). These all started out with the infant's anguished cry when hungry. The stomach is stressed and the child's neutral babble, ba-ba, changes to a wailing ma'a! It means I am hungry, I want (feeding); but doting mothers world-wide have interpreted it as a vocative: "The little darling is calling for me"; and they give it their breast. It is for this reason that the word for mother has a ma in it world-wide. At one time adult boxers were not above letting out a "hm!" with a heavy blow as they tensed their stomach muscles to deliver the punch all the way from the back leg. It was for them a natural reflex of a stressed stomach and not a vocative at all. Utterances naturally arising were originally taken to have natural meanings – and indeed they did – only to be interpreted variously. The mammary ma is a gull's nest with meanings 18 to 32 on the tree. Latin mammare to suckle provides a duplex format for what, for the ladies, is a duplex function. Our own Ma and Mama are exemplary. Albanian meme for mother follows the Latin perception. The Sanskrit was ma, the Chinese maa or mu. The aa vowel, treated as a down-up - falling and then rising - intonation, is in origin just two a vowels in succession. That is how to learn the intonation. The alternative u vowelisation has the same reduplicative significance. The very same word can also mean horse in Chinese, because it is a language which neglects no opportunity of extracting every last meaning

Chapter 9 Ma

from every phoneme, their mandarin class having spent many millennia leaving no semantic stone unturned.

With four tones, respectively up, down, neither (flat), and repetitious they have managed to eke out the Lithic meanings of individual phonemes long after they were past their sell-by date, often with helper syllables added after the fashion of the Ancient Egyptians' determinant glyphs (in the case of the Egyptian determinants coming after the uttered word, themselves unpronounced but prompting for the class of meaning involved). The Chinese similarly have numerous glyphs pronounced exactly the same but nevertheless each with its own meaning. It is said you sometimes need a paint brush and paper to explain exactly what you are saying. The horse meaning is arrived at, it would appear, by way of ma-aa, elided to maa. In this case the ma prompts for big (59), compare massive, and aa as an extensive, in this case spatial extension, and so going in place of the infantile wailing; and thus defining the horse as the major goer, the galloper. With the other tamed beasts oxen and donkeys, the horse stood out as the speedy and temperamental one, just as it does today. You probably have to be Chinese, addicted to their kind of word games, to pick up the meanings at all easily. In Chinese mama – both a vowels flat – is a wet nurse offering both of her mammary glands, an interpretation confirmed by the alternative term mu, a substitute mother, relying upon the dual vowel in place of the mama repetition. We see the very same protocol in Ancient Egyptian where pu replaces pipi (chapter 11). Ma in Chinese also carries the semantic content of the other motherly function to wipe clean, an obvious gull. The Ancient Egyptian mentiti is the breast, the nippled feeder; -titi like our tit or titty meaning teat, with the –ti ending in Egyptian, teated, being also used as the feminine suffix.

The Malay for mother is emak, pronounced in practice more like ma', the e- being vanishingly present and the –k being effectively a glottal stop. The Navaho, a native tribe in California amongst the oak trees, say ma' for mother. It is hard to believe it comes from the Sanskrit ma'. The Zulu for mother is umame, where 'm is him and 'um is perhaps them, in which case um-a-mai reads in Lithic elements them-that-breast feeding. With Lithic, the initial u- could of course refer across the intervening syllable to the final mai, dualing them. The Vietnamese is the same as the Sanscrit and Navaho: ma'. With all these ma words cropping up all around the world, meaning mother, it is hard to dismiss the underlying psychosemantic promptings, nowadays arising from the subconscious, world wide. The mothers of the world are indeed the principal supporters of the Lithic hypotheses; because if ma has a psychosemantic origin, why not anything or even everything else? So Doubting Thomases must first of all ask themselves what other explanation for the maternity in linguistics around the world is there? When they have found it they should write it down and drop me a line, and not keep it to themselves any longer. We can slip in here the origin of the word matter by way of metaphor from mother (mater in Latin, which probably first meant the impregnated) to designate the trunk of a tree (as Partridge puts it, "from which the buds spring") and so the foliage too and thence any biological material and with it, from the matrix, in due course any material at all. If the –terai, drawn out, of mater did not refer to the buds as the word king thought, then it may have referred to the mass of the tree trunk drawn up, just as the English words tree and trunk do.

After the stress (16) group of meanings in the ma psychosemantic tree are those characters springing from opposition to Ish (17), namely first of all and most tellingly - instead of leaping up like the hissing flame - the completely contrary (antithetical) instinct of silently falling, going down (35) not rising; as philosophers later had it of things pulling themselves towards the centre of the earth - still at it even down a mine (from mai-nai, of the earth-a gaping hole). But in the Stone Age these were simply the individual properties of matter, their natural behaviours, inbuilt just like physical properties, for instance their hard surfaces. Mass, Lithic ma-sai, the falling action, stands in contradiction also to liquid (La, chapter 8) which likes best the interface between earth and sky, running down into the lows but also sometimes rising up in springs to regain the surface when some other force has apparently carried it below. The reality has not yet been accepted by the British Ministry responsible (at this moment DEFRA) which believes water runs downhill in the underground strata from hills around to make artesian springs. In reality the pressure of the overburden (300 feet of boulder clay hereabouts), which is actually floating on the aquifer (chalk) 300 feet down, forces water up where there is a crack (or bore) in the overburden. These hominid "instincts" (just about as good as the current Ministry view) come from what would now be labeled a teleological approach to science, and psychologists would regard it as an absurd anthropomorphic world view – that is interpreting the world about us as if it were endowed with the same psyches and wills as we have. But undoubtedly this simple instinctive idea was the opinion of humankind as we emerged from the prior hominid darkness of subconscious thinking into the full light of recursive thought, which mental symbolisation enabled us for the first time to grasp, retaining ideas in memory in clear-cut terms.

Whether the symbolisation preceded, accompanied or resulted from speaking is a separate issue much debated at present, which makes no difference whatever to the resultant clarification, as all agree. Before speech, you had to be an Einstein to get your thinking act together. How many mute and disregarded prelinguistic Einsteins will have wasted their sweetness upon the desert air, unable to communicate except in the most basic terms what they had worked out by themselves must always remain moot. It was their frustration, no doubt, which provided the pressure needed to crack the mould and led to the revolutionary outburst of symbolic communication in language. The improvement in internal self-expression and understanding, the mental clarification which will have accompanied intercommunication, because of the sheer memorability of symbols or labels for identifying ideas, so that they could be recalled at will and mulled over, has prompted some folk to claim we spoke to help ourselves think first of all; but it is a non sequiter. We spoke to express our own state of mind and impress it upon our neighbours. It eased (but did not altogether remove) a nasty dose of claustrophobia, which is still there, close below the conscious surface; hopefully pushing against the autism every phenotype is born with, and most (perhaps all) never properly outlive.

The words for measure (61), starting in Biblical times with Mene Mene Tekel Upharsin, use the going down instinct (35) in our tree. The Lithic phonemic elements of mene, mai-nai, showing (chapter 11, Na)-the ma-ing, are repeated for emphasis in the quotation above to indicate repetition of the measurements: weighing, weighing: i.e. you have been repeatedly weighed in the balance; and been found wanting, literally the weights (tekel,shekels, from the Lithic become-make-level) u-pha-rai-sai´n: oo-paharai-sai, un-pushed-upwards, from the original pushing up action of the pahai or penis when rai or caught by the feminine rays emanating from the Stone Age ladies squatting opposite around the hearth. The 'wanting' concept comes from the failure of the weighed material to push the scale pan with the weights in up by weighing the goods side down. It indicates short measure. The measure was wanting, like Pharaoh's failure to save grain in good years against drought. Of course we don't know who made the mystic graffiti in the first place, but it will likely have been the priests of Amun-Ra, the bureaucratic civil service of

Chapter 9 Ma

the day, providing advice at one remove in order to avoid punishment for blaming Pharaoh. He was generally assumed to be responsible for dealing with the deity on behalf of his subjects, so droughts and other misfortunes of his people were his chestnuts. Perhaps he distributed surplus crops to gain popularity when he should have exercised precaution, and the civil servants were ensuring the people understood it was against their advice. If so, the pattern is still current, and other mischiefs with it. It would be unfair to suggest nothing has been learned since Pharaoh's day; but it is clear there is still much to learn. Nowadays civil servants have to face up to governments. They can't play God.

By Pharaoh's day the reading of language in its original (already old fashioned) Lithic phonemic elements (God Speak) required the services of a soothsayer who could discover the underlying significances of the original phonemic strings, disentangling their polysemy. The pha-rai-sai Lithic phrasing is to be found in the English word phrase. It is from the Greek phrazein to indicate or explain. In this case it is a case of pushing forward (pha-rai) pointing up or presenting the illumination (sai), sense or meaning, and not any longer the Pharaonic scalepan. The sense or meaning of sai here is also of course from warming by the hearth, how we (pleasantly) sensed or experienced it physically, and thence of course how we experience or sense things mentally as well. Sense thus comes to mean how we grasp the import of a word or sentence, as in French savoir or when we say "I see" for understand. That is what a meaning is, like an etymon, ai-tai-mau'n, the as-born-meant'one, the original meaning, an original meaning at the birth of a word - before it was hijacked by the experts, dealing in phonetics in place of semantics, who have declared it to be the original phonetic form merely, where etymon (52), Lithic ai-tai-mau'n, as it-born-meant or meaning (or thought), is clearly to do with the original semantics.

Weight belonged to solid things which if you dropped them fell on your foot. The flame per contra was insubstantial (actually incandescent gas) - like wind, thinking and spirits - which all supposedly partook of the flame, as did indeed all animals in some measure in so far as they were warm-blooded, and so must have some of the fire element within them. The Greek marmaros (in phonemic terms ma-ma-rau-s) for marble meant first of all a large boulder, in Lithic terms a mass of solid matter (ma-) raised to an ultimate level of massiveness (-marau-), almost a big marrow. A marrow is just a biggy. As Eric Partridge puts it: "influenced by marmairein [the Greek from the Lithic 'm-ara-mai-rai-ai'n, him-visible-matter-raying-verbal] to gleam or shimmer". It signified a shiny rock like marble. Marbre (the French for marble) is "dissimulated" by the French from the Latin marmor, according to Partridge. Pars pro toto (part of a word taken up as standing for the whole) mar- stands for the Greek marmar. The English boulder has been given a ba-lai, lithe flesh or smooth texture from polishing. We may however prefer to put the thinking the other way about: because the boulder marmaros gleamed and shimmered when polished, the word used for to shimmer was gulled from marmaros: "to large-boulder", marmairein. Then since water's surface too was seen to mimic such a large boulder by shimmering - under a slight breeze - it was described as moir (water in Arabic), a string with an awa in it as well as shimmering – see chapter 14 on Wa and the vowels. But the m- in moir for water could just as well be a cockney 'm, him-awa-raying, him-cold-raying, the cold as also in winter or the English water; or in addition moir could be also or indeed at the same time the descender: step in and down you go, quite the opposite of a burning gas which says ishshsh in a rising puff when it steps in and is extinguished. The Lithic hypotheses somewhat support that etymology, however fanciful it seems.

The Greek marmairein was a gleaming in the gloaming. The Lithic is fairly easy. Ma-Rai-mai-rai'n, Death-of the Sun-dying-raying. But it is also hard to spot because neither the gleaming nor the gloaming really belong to ma, but on the contrary more straightforwardly to the flame, ish. But the sun's death rays are brilliant, redeeming the darkness of death. There is often a whimsical element behind Lithic determinations, rabbits are sometimes pulled from hats to astonish the onlookers.

Hammer (64), as already explained in chapter 8 under the phoneme Ha, is a tool for making heavy downward strokes, a horrid marrer or harmer. Administered to any live species it is hurtful. Maccaroni is from the obsolete Italian verb maccare to break up into pieces, one must suppose by a sequence of heavy chopping blows from a hammer or some such. The Hindi ma-khana to harm or injure, to make ma, and so punish is surely related to maccaroni. Maccaroni is punished with a hard pounding. Murder and massacre (6) make use of the same ma as does maccaroni. Murder or murther is from morthor the Old English noun, with the verb myrthrien. Mur-, it appears, is merely a slovening of mor- which brings the English into line with the Latin group based on the verb mori (Lithic mau-are) to be deaded, to die, the opposite of living (sai). Eric Partridge appeals to cognates in Sanskrit, Armenian, Old Slavonic and Lithuanian. The English group includes post mortem, really just Latin, mortality, the morgue, mortgages, to mortify, to amortize, moribund, morbidity, even a murrain and check mate in chess. The mate of check mate is from the Arabic mat which makes check mate look like a borrowing from the Old Persian Shah mat, the Shah is dead. Mati in Malay is dead too. It might be taken as a borrowing from Arabic but the Aboriginal Malay gives that its quietus: the Senoi (Malay Aboriginal) term ma-te for dead means in the ground. We can work this out because where Malays say buang from bau-aa-ng for muscle-away-ing, for throwing away, aborigines say bu-s-ma-te, which is flesh (muscle)- action/throw-ground-to, chuck it down. Living sparsely spread in a virgin jungle they can afford to just drop things as they go. So Malay mati means in the ground (buried), with the reasonable presumption the body was dead before burial. But of course mati can be read also as from the Lithic ma-tai, dead-become, tai born into the nether next world of the dead in fact. Lithic is happy with multiple routes/roots, indeed they appear to have been regarded as reinforcing indications of 'natural' meanings. Massacre is from the French and related to macher to crush or mash, but the Lithic analysis of the phonemic string suggests the ma-sha is demolish-life, with the macher originally makher and the –crer is from –karai to make, with -ere verbal marker (infinitive). Yet massa appears also to have suggested a killing en masse at the same time, although the stress appears to be on the action rather than its widespread nature. The semantics of a single syllable or even a string of them can be read by the subconscious mind twice with two different meanings without any discomfort. The subconscious is a guide to our dreaming sleep like our state of mind before we learned to speak and so to compile and order our thinking by laying it out in a line. Language is sequential.

If a body goes on going down it finishes up on the ground, made up of all the rest that has settled there. The earth is the solid element, solidity being next to weightiness. But the earth is also the place of insemination - where you plant seeds – and germination and so of fertility. Dead (inert) seeds are planted in the ground and come to life. To earth them, that is to bury them, is to bring them to life. Burial became popular because of this linguistic reasoning. Indeed to bury was to plant the seed, to propagate, to gestate in the earth, and ma came to carry the meaning of seed planting in the animal kingdom as well. In Egyptian the (more clinical) term for male genitalia is mai, the earther, planter or inseminater. To marry was originally to go a-planting. Amare, Latin to love, is from the Lithic a-mai-are, as-planting [your seed]-verbal ending, when even the most chauvinist can feel an access of goodwill towards his partner at orgasm, regarded in the old days as the source of affection. Just the anticipation can turn heads. The Egyptian god Amun, A-ma-u'n was supposedly The Ever-Loving-of all'one. Amun is from the same phonemic roots as amare to love. From serere to plant in Latin semen is supposed to come, what is planted, the seed. Seed was sprinkled on the ground. That is the etymological derivation, but the subconscious can handle multiple meanings, and sai-mai´n is a living-dead'one, so it means dormant. Indeed there is no real reason why semen needs to be derived from serere to sow. Sowing seed is bringing it to life by sprinkling it on the ground, the Lithic for our English seed is sai-tai, living-becomes. Serere could even be a back formation from semen. But serere also carries the meaning of action-raying, akin to spraying, which (like sprin-kle) has a p in it, which was the paradigmatic sprayer for the Lithic subconscious.

These roots have a common derivation from a common Lithic substrate, rather than being connected daisy chain style. They all draw their inspiration from the subconscious under-layer of language, the very same one that Noam Chomsky has prayed in aid for his universal grammar, as if the genes actually carry the ideas that phenotypes will think, rather than just structural programmes for the phenotype's physique. His thinking is not really genetic, but instead discovered by each child in the languages consciously learnt by each speaking phenotype in turn. Babies have no transformational grammar at their command, inherited ideas, any more than their legs are programmed as to what walks they will in the course of their lives choose to take. It is a confusion of physical structure with activity, a category error. Ideas are actions like steps. How we think is genetic, but not what we think, any more than where we go. Chomsky thinks children could not learn language without it being inbuilt because he can not see sufficient guidance offered. That is because it is subconscious. It does not register with the conscious mind. It has to be accepted we can think at a low level without knowing of it, just as we can dream without knowing how we do it, or even remembering it after. Our conscious thinking has a subconscious keel to it. Lithic abandons determination for whimsy when it comes to thinking. It is neo-Darwinism that has got it wrong here. Natural selection is fine. It has provided us with brains, but it does not determine the thoughts we put together. From that point of view we are post-natural, able to survey our prison though not to escape from it. It does not mean our thinking is right, indeed it means much of it, if not all, is likely to be askew - as history, the record of performance to date, affirms. But we are not being lived by our genes, which have no brains and can have no ideas.(mental activities). It is subtly demeaning for the intellect to have to share thinking with the subconscious. Academia doesn't want to know. You have to preach.

NOTES

1. If communication before speech was by means of cries, as in Chimpish, what we would call song, without any stops (except perhaps a La, the odd halloo or two to break up the tones, see chapter 8 on La), what originally made the difference and introduced speech as we understand it was quite simply just that, the introduction of the stops, or as we call them consonants. Hisses and hums were half-way houses, old friends as it were, not so very different from the clear vowelisations with which cries were made before speaking. All the other stops by their very nature were not singing notes at all. So hisses and hums were cases for early study. The distinction between mmm and nnn, which is minimal so far as the phonetics are concerned was apparently generally not made.

2. The dialectical thinking of the Stone Age, as well as Hegel and Marx's revamped version of it, is examined in some detail and demolished in chapter 15 on thinking.

3. Eric Partridge. "Origins. A Short Etymological Dictionary of Modern English". A glance at the 364 "Indogermanic" word roots at the back of WW Skeat's Etymological Dictionary of the English Language of 1879 – 1882 reveals his predilection for the aspirated consonants as originals in the first few paragraphs of his introduction. It also provides a succinct synopsis of Grimm's Law and its implications.

4. What our hominid forebears were conscious of, to what extent conscious, particularly self conscious, as we understand these terms, when first they began to put together language, is a difficult question, which I hope to address in a forthcoming study of "The Making of Meaning", currently in draft form.

CHAPTER 10

NA PRESENTING THE NAKED SEER

Knapping flints has been going on for a million years and more. It was clearly a trick learned by our hominid forebears, and indeed we likely would not be prepared to count them human at all if we were to come face to face with them today. At "Grimes' Graves" in Norfolk, England – (Grimes is the Devil, the Doer of evil, Grimes from the Lithic kara-mai(s), maker of all the mai, the mayhems and harms) - a few stones' throw from where this is written, the mines were dug in the sandy soil to recover the virgin undisturbed flint nodules, with no cracked faults in them to spoil the flint knappers' work. They provided perhaps the first industrial complex in the Western world, with a network of tracks to send them far and wide. These mines with their crawl tunnels from the base of the twenty foot shafts, with notched tree trunks providing access, were probably old when Stonehenge was young. In the centre of the chamber at the foot of the main shaft of one of the best preserved and renovated mines was a fine phallus in clay the height of a man, which was removed for storage in the dungeons of Norwich Castle Museum seventy five years ago before the site was opened to the public, so far without reprieve. It was made by our local forebears to fertilise Mother Earth to do her duty and give birth to a plentiful supply of flint nodules for the miners to find. It is a delight to think of these simple souls happily patterning nature upon their own sexual experience. After all how could they possibly know that what they had personally learned in the hard world of experience was no good at all for decoding everything else. It is a lesson still to be learned. Dating before any known religion the flint mines naturally attracted the fear of the Devil later, in times when he was believed to really exist, rather than as a figure of speech.

Stonehenge has been out of serious use two thousand years but at Brandon (Bara-an-don, crossing-of-the river in Ancient Egyptian), the town beside the Flint mines astride the river, where the path to the river's edge at the ford is still worn, the Flint Knappers Arms was providing refreshment for the current generation of flint knappers, still shipping flints for flintlocks to West Africa for their muskets, when I was a boy. Here was an industry which may have gone back tens of thousands of years, before the last glaciation, which led to Noah's flood when it thawed some eight thousand years ago, raising the sea level three hundred and sixty feet. We do not know if the Egyptians shipped flints from Ultima Thule but there does seem to be some linguistic evidence they were here, the surviving evidence thinly spread after the Celtic invasions, but otherwise hard to explain. The Celts will have mopped them up when they called since they were in those days head hunters with a partiality for the brains of those they killed, and they probably even killed them for the table, and so quite shortly used them all up. Egyptian geometers may well have been responsible for the straight tracks across England and the ley lines involved, which fossickers so enjoy tracing as Roman roads and marvelling at today. Civilisation has been set back more than once by barbarian invaders. The Romanised Celts would later themselves be swamped by the Saxon tribes flooding into the country, so that the fens which were drained before the Saxons came were flooded for another thousand years until Dutch engineers fresh from draining the polders were called in in the seventeenth century.

Chapter 10 Na

To knap a flint is to strike it in such a manner as to produce a flat plaque or flake, which comes away with a flat surface and a sharp edge. The strike presents you with a piece with a surface which can be used chiefly for the sharp edges. We shall see before the end of the chapter that the Lithic elements on which the word knap is based, ka-na-pai, the first syllable slovened to a single letter, the last slovened to -pe and then a bare final -p, carry the semantic contents strike-present-flake, which is precisely what knapping is about. Nothing could be further from the current linguistically correct view that words are formed from randomly selected roots which have no intrinsic meaning, a view which is patently false, although it saves a lot of thinking. A flake is just slovened from the Lithic elements phai-lai-kai, surface-flat-struck, and a plaque is very similar. Every other word in all the languages of the world, if sufficiently examined, and sufficiently unslovened or reconstructed, will teach the same lesson. Language is built from meaningful elements assembled slowly from phonemic roots, which individually carry meanings, first of all our only media of communication. Words are constructs (sentences) made up of meaningful pieces. The same process continues today. UNO does not mean the United Nations Organisation for no reason, picked at random. It comprises three phonemes each carrying the meaning of the words they have been chosen to represent. If you do not know that you can still use the word in a meaningful way, you simply lack its proper etymology. It is just the derivation of the meanings which is different in this case from the original methodology which was a bit more basic. As a result it takes a whole book to get folk to think in these unaccustomed ways and so to understand how language was made.

The psychosemantic tree for Na is on page 186. Eric Partridge's second entry - the first is nab - under the letter N is nabob which is a nice example of the slovening of navab from an original nawab. W is not v and v is not b, but Wayland Smith is not that bothered. The Arabic nawab is the plural of naib, an ambassador or a provincial governor, officials sent in subordinate positions with the role of presenting the views of the ruler. This chapter has as a principal task to show that the phoneme na originally meant to present or show. Chapter 3 already attached the meaning of the haunches and their movement, going, to bai. A naib or provincial governor, appointed and sent out by the Shah, is from nai-bai, presenter or shower going, an explicator-bum (16), a travelling representative. The same applies to nabbi which the Moslems use for Nabbi Issus, Jesus the Travelling Prophet. Travelling teachers were liable to be the mouth of God, but that is not the meaning of the term. Nabinabi in Malay however is the seven limbed starfish, show-bits-show-bits (probably the bi started out bai and conveys burgeons), remarking his astonishing accumulation of limbs when animal life makes do with only four. The prophet is travelling, the star fish is burgeoning. They can both do their things because both spring from the underlying idea of flesh, fleshy bits, and so in the case of the prophet the haunches which provide the musclature for perambulation, and in the case of the starfish the burgeoning which is the habit of the flesh.and provides him with a superabundance of limbs. The banana outstrips the nabinabi by far and has a whole clutch of fruits all ba-nana, fruit protruding upwards – commonly around fifty.

Na is the sound of the expulsion of breath after holding it. Such a breath holding with a sudden release was typical of orgasm (1) and our hominid forebears apparently knew it. Much of the semantic contents of this phoneme spring from this identification. When we were learning to speak we had little in the way of inhibition as we know it today. Our forefathers, as well as their mothers, were shameless when it came to working out how Tarzan next door to them around the hearth might be thinking. You have to locate yourself like them in your birthday suit squatting together, even scrummed up together, around the welcoming glowing hearth. It does wonders for your civilised prepossessions, with which of course they were in no way encumbered. It is an education to follow them into their linguistic symposiums, whatever it does for your morals. We know from our exploration of the other phonemes already that the orgasm was going to be gulled for its concomitants as metaphors. The early mind was tyrannised by the eye, much as today. Once you have Tarzan thinking like you, you know he will be rehearsing the scene as it unfolds (nightly) to the eye. He is enjoying a sexual bonanza, and we are going to have to follow him at least in outline, to see what arises for science. If you were today in a fix like your Stone Age forebears having to invent speech, you too would be grasping at sexual activity like a drowning man grasping at a straw. Moreover "Na!" even today is a natural expression of sympathetic delight which my elderly spinster cousin, a horse breeder, emits when a new foal prances out for the first time. There will be others expressing the same sentiment similarly with other stimuli. So there were, hundreds of thousands of years ago. It is a shame to denigrate so natural an expression of pleasure. Ternahak in Malay however means to be overcome (ter-) by desire (the -nahak bit), much closer to the original meaning. There is a further reason, perhaps, why this phoneme depends so widely upon the sexual motif. There was no competition. Hums were spoken for by Ma. Na was an opening sound, and an was a closing sound, with nothing much to offer in between.

So how does this all translate to explain why nai is negative? Na has been identified above as the sound made when holding the breath as emotional tension builds, with a final sudden release at orgasm, ending the tension in a few pulses of sweet sensation flooding through the whole nervous system. In chapter 14 on the vowels meanwhile there is a somewhat more prosaic examination which identifies the vowel aaa as extensive and unrestrictive. You can go on with an aaa for as long as you have breath, as you can not with a p, or a d, or a k for example. The consonants, which came in with speech, and indeed provided the articulation (separation) which enabled us to string our thinking in separate bits where before we were unable to sharply terminate one thought and start another, now act as restraints partitioning the flow of sounds uttered just as they do semantic flow. This should probably be taught in schools, immediately after the letters and their phonemes or sounds; but not before. Now it remains to demonstrate why, of all the consonants, the na phoneme should have been chosen, that is should have presented itself as the classic stopper. The hums (chapter 10) can be sounded for as long as you have breath, unlike typical consonants. When the doctor tells you she has seen enough of your throat you may not plan to articulate an -an, but it is a fair bet your tongue will impact your palate, which gets an n. If you just shut your mouth you get an m. The Chinese use bu for the negative, probably because they take their lips as blockers too. If you shut your mouth in China you get the reverse of when you open it. The vowel u is picked up in China for its inclusive and conclusive character uncovered in chapter 14. Semitic tongues use m, the labial stop. The Indo Europeans all go for the palatal stop, the n. The phoneme na is the signature phoneme of this closure. You do not have to be a senior wrangler to understand that when you terminate anything then thereafter there is none of it. True the vowelisation of un-, with the –n actually terminal, is on the hither side of the consonant whereas the phoneme na is exemplified with it on the far side. But this is a common dual phoneticisation which applies to every phoneme and was evidently regarded with indifference.

The vowels are open, the consonants are closures. There is a degree of opposition already involved in this circumstance. So it actually follows from this that if aye is positive, its closure terminates it and implies its absence. The semantics of ne, is n-ai, the

Chapter 10 Na

THE PSYCHOSEMANTIC TREE FOR NA

The Phonetic Tree

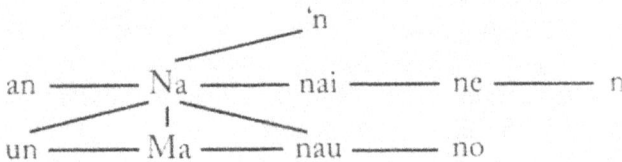

The Semantic Tree

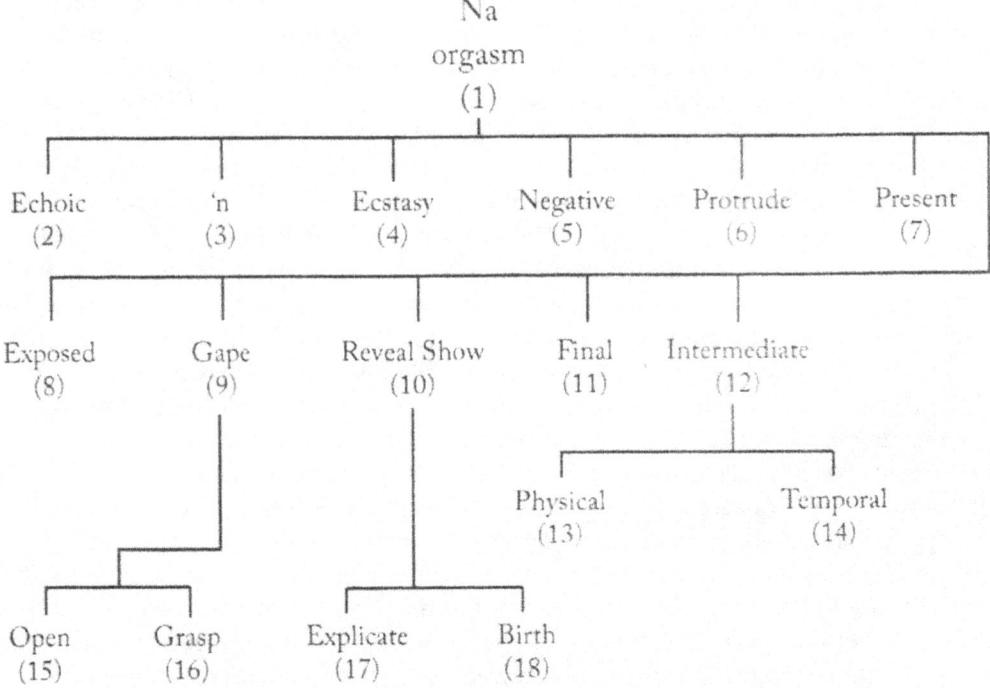

Chapter 10 Na

closure of ai, even though it opens it. That is hominid thinking for you. Of course we do use un- as well as a negative, when we are unappreciative of an argument for instance. Chapter 14 on the vowels provides some more indications as to the meanings attributed to ai. It came to mean that which or that is, really the same idea, a positive position. Its closure therefore absents the positive. The absence is not an opposite. But it was clumsily thought to be so, as can still happen. The absence of existence is taken to be the opposite of existence, non-existence. It sounds sound. But is the absence of red the opposite of red, its negative? Is it different for an adjective and a noun? You can read more about how this came about in chapter 15 on the origins of thinking. The conclusion is that because when you stop saying aaa you can finish up with an n, na becomes a negative marker. To decide meanings in this way may seem like bordering on insanity, but that is how it has been done. There is after all no guarantee we have not been certifiable, ever since the forebears of Homo Erectus first rose onto their hind legs; and even a good deal of evidence for it. The mania has for the most part been homicidal, often with sadistic accompaniments. That does not mean we can not avoid it in the future, only that the avoidance is by no means guaranteed.

However, if we are to finally close with the na phoneme's original meaning it is necessary now to leave the wall paper on one side and to explore the human genitalia, to see what psychosemantic contents we can find there. Much of the nomenclature comes from the Egyptian. The schoolboy pee which comes, in a long slow meander, from the peeping of the Egyptian quail chick is all in chapter 11. The rousing raising rays which invade our sexuality all come at only one short remove from the Egyptian sun, Ra, in chapter 12. At the precise juncture na, at orgasm, the male member is raised upwards and forwards and is presenting strongly and there is an outflow of fluid. Indeed it will have been well known to all ranks in those far off days that this was the posture of the male member even in the introductory stages. The chosen target may well have been still squatting on the far side of the hearth warmed up and waiting. What is more, behind the piece the carriage is in generous mood too. The Egyptian God Amun, the ever earthing, planting, fertile, impregnating, sowing his seed, was the ever loving too. Latin amare to love comes, it would appear, from a-ma-are, as when-planting-verbal suffix; and this was no agricultural chore but mating. It is not intended to suggest couples in the Stone Age were incapable of the generous sentiments of love at any other time, but merely that was the time when even the thickest proto farmer's boy will have registered the emotion most powerfully. Indeed in the previous chapter it has been suggested that to be truly human is not (as the etymologists have imagined) to be an earthling, from the Latin root for humus, but on the contrary to be hei-u-ma'n, enjoying-dually(both)-the mating. It was the taming of fire and the superheating of the swains which led to the humanity of human mating and thence to human mutual recognition and communication and so to civilisation. Strike a match and see the world of man explained - by an 'adult' route, that is by recourse to the genitalia. We are still living in the fire age. Animal copulation is both violent and in fact nasty brutish and short, and neither participant betrays anything other than vehement effort, and in the case of the female utter subjection. This may not apply to the lady praying mantis who apparently makes a gastronomic bon bouche out of the opportunity provided of getting really up close to her partner by eating off his head. This is apparently prior to orgasm as the performance of the male is not inhibited but on the contrary appears to be concentrated on the job in train by the removal of any alternative call centre. Does the headache come after? Anyway Stone Age wallies did not study the mantis. We must guess they rejoiced in the reciprocity of the female - until recently that is - when they cut out her clitoris to stop her reciprocating, so they could impose themselves regardless of merit and without any wandering by their partners. It is the philosophy of the stick insect, and it is in common human practice even today.

It comes as a surprise that na can breed a series of echoisms. To snore (2) is the sound of snoring, which can vary a lot; but the English is a sniff in followed by a -narr out. When asleep we pause between the in and the out just enough to introduce a na. A sniff, snuffle and snuff are barely echoic but pass as such. There is not really any n in a sniff. It is tempting to think the n has sneaked in as an indicator (17) and it is just the s-ff which is the sniff, the nearest we can get without actually talking with our nose instead of our mouth. A neigh is an equine na. It expresses equine recognition if not actual delight. A snicker and a nicker express strings of them, and a whinny is a whole lot (u) of loud ones. A horse's nearest to no is a snort. Come to think of it my Shetland pony stallions snorted when mating too. It is an understandable expression of triumphalism just as it can also indicate rejection. It could indicate what they would have as well as what they would not, an expression of what the philosophers would describe as the will to power.

A snap is thought to be echoic of a sharp break, for instance of a dry stick. If so it is the final p which provides the echoism. The sna- is just the run up, "here it comes"; and indeed the initial s- which conventional etymology regards as an Indo European common "vaguely intensive" prefix, in Lithic analysis often suggests that what follows is an action, an actor, such as an animal, or at least something phenomenal from the world of visible human action. Snap can be read as action-present-the pop or crack. It does not say that. But that is a fair representation of the semantic content that went into the string that makes the word. We can only express the meaning by putting it into the words which come nearest to it, which after some 600,000 years may not be a perfect fit. Anima (Latin), the soul, has long been accepted as echoic from an original breath, and so a breath of air, and so the breath of life and so the soul. After all when you are dead your breath disappears. Eric Partridge sets out to analyse the echoism and starts out well: "a- a slow moving in-breathing, plus ne- a moment of relaxed breathing plus -ma a strong out breathing". If you try to reproduce this sequence you will find yourself faced with three breaths instead of the usual two, an in and an out, and you will have to open your mouth for the third and final out breath, the strong one, to get a ma. In reality it is possible to recognise a light click in the gullet as the direction of breath changes from in to out and that is only a short way from a nasal tone and even ni following it with a third stage opening the mouth for a ma perhaps echoes a sleeping person. Breathing with the mouth open we can recognise an a and a na. The -ma in anima therefore looks like an additional semantic suffix in Lithic, and can be read as m'a which can only be verbalised as him aa: the semantic content is 'that extensive' in other words the meaning refers to the continuity of the breathing and it should not be taken to refer just to a single breath as echoed.

The principal virtue of the soul which is here an entified breathing process (air is after all rather insubstantial) is that it is the insubstantial element making up life which continues, while the substantial part is mortal. These echoisms have clearly been taken from sleep patterns when breathing reveals its tonal values. Normally when awake we breath silently. So we have flatus from fla(in)-ter(out), and spiritus from spi(in)-ri(out), both Latin, and atmos from at(in)-mau(out), Greek, and atman from at(in)-man(out), Sanskrit, and atma in Hindi. Readers will recognise the anemometer, the atmosphere and the mahatma from these breathing exercises, which are well worth grasping in order to experience the power of the echoic, such as it is. It has been enough to set Sapiens Sapiens off on his poesy. Animals are breathing species (with a recognisable nose) but are not

Chapter 10 Na

usually taken to be further blessed with the Latin anima or soul, nor yet with its masculine version, animus, the thinking mind. Since thinking was taken to be insubstantial - it is - it seemed reasonable to relate it closely to the insubstantial spirit which informed and indeed provided life, the elan vital of philosophy.

Nay (2) negatives aye, just as never negatives ever. Rather more esoterically no negatives au, which means the totality and can therefore be written o, and so spoken. No means none, and so not at all, pas du tout, full stop. We don't have au in our English vocabulary. We have o and treat it as the same as no and call it naught, from no wiht, nothing, as a blank o with nothing inside it instead of an inclusive one putting the O round the outside of everything included. Negare in Latin means to deny, to say no, or nay-make in Lithic; and negro (from nai-kai-rau, negating-making-visible and so black) in English, now taboo in the West for fear of causing offence to Africans. It means not gerau, that is not rayed (by the sun) at all, and therefore as black as night. Negro is the Spanish for black, from the Latin niger, which gave the West the term nigger as well, originally a euphemistic term for black, but blackened by the African slaves in America. Nether negates ether, the upper air. Ether, ai-ta(h)i-rai is become rayed by the sun, ra, which raises the plants so that they are gerau or grow, and the same raising has apparently given us the upper air, or so our forebears assembling language evidently thought. Naught, from na-wiht negatives aught (or awiht?). Somewhat more controversially, in- negatives ai; and sin negatives sai, although ai and sai do not appear on their own in English (as going and comfortable/existence); narrow negatives arrau, that rayed again but this time not raising anything for the boys but instead rounding out for the girls. We have always personalised the way our world behaves, and much of our personal perception has been based on our own sexual experience. This was most of our thinking when first we began to speak; and still it shows. The Egyptian rays (see chapter 13 on the phoneme Ra) were prayed in aid to account for any action at a distance, and our physical sexual responses, like our thoughts and mood swings, were taken to result from invisible rays of one kind or another arriving from without. The sun was first recognised in Egypt as the Aton, or Aa-taun in Lithic, an eternal vagina, birthing light into the world each day.

Since the male member rises when aroused the feminine member must therefore be the source of the rays which draw it out and up, just as the sun does the same for the plants. With a bit of hindsight and a slightly more critical mind set today we can see that our transference of performances was really the other way about, starting with our perceptions of our own performance. So since the male member rises, the crops are doing the same. Since the vagina rounds out when roused, (and male arousal appears to be involuntary, prompted from outside the body), the sun has the same facility which draws the crops up and out, just as the girls draw the male organ up and out. The vagina starts out narrow, not arrau, just a slit or cut, and finishes arrau, rayed or round (from Lithic rau'n-tai, rounded-become). It was a corollary that it was the feminine vagina that started every sexual encounter, since the male organ was sheathed and unable to ray back until it had been roused, and its muzzle cover withdrawn by feminine rays. There may be some sense in this, but if so the process takes place in the minds of the participants and not by means of any physical rays; which then of course leaves open who is the initiator and who the initiated, and in reality the circumstances will be as various as circumstances usually are.

But it was certainly taken as no light laughing matter by the Pharaohs of Egypt, who reckoned as Ra's sons they were entitled to take the initiative in every encounter - as royalty are apt to do - and cut off their muzzle covers so they could fire first. It has not been explained as yet why Ra should not have thought of the rearrangement of the male

Chapter 10 Na

member in the first place for himself, had he wished male members to wear foreshortened foreskins. Perhaps unsurprisingly this particular absurd piece of thinking has been banished to the subconscious dark room down below and does not feature any longer in the language with which we choose to communicate today. There is in its place a Semitic fancy circumcision is a deal done with Jahweh so He and they will know each other.

The arrow we recognise is not rounded out but instead flies through the air as the sunray does, up and away on its return journey to the sun. The name may even be echoic of the sound made by a flush of a few hundred well fledged arrows as they are discharged from the bow in battle. In Sumerian (as in Latin) the arrow is sag-i-ta, sag is the head in Sumerian from Lithic sa-kai, the top of the body, and i-ta, which punctures. The arrow was a weapon which penetrated at a distance like a bullet, when most weapons were bladed, and many just wielded.

The Old English cennan meant to beget, from kai-nai'n, with forms akin in Old Saxon kunni, Old High German cunni and Gothic kuni. If kai- is kindling, kau- is kindled, the male and female aspects of copulation as imagined by our forebears (in reality the perceptions are awry). Cunni suggests kinship with cunt, originally from Lithic kai-nai-tai, the kindled-orgasmic-birth canal. Comparable is vagina, Lithic u-a-kai-na, the orifice-that-kindled-orgasms. Compare the shameless sacred symbol in Hindu religion, the yoni, a close up worms eye view of the engorged vagina with exposed clitoris, Lithic ia-u-nai, it that-orifice-orgasmic. It is even claimed the inocent coney was renamed a rabbit just as the Royal Society for the Protection of Birds today has its computers replace the ock in cock bird with asterisks like the f-word, to save readers experiencing a mischievous sexual idea, since a cock, as well as the term for the avian male (from ka-ka, repeated crowing) and for a tap, originally a spigot remember which you tapped in to the hole you had tapped), is also slang for the male organ, a personal spigot. A coney's erection is only an offence for farmers. Coney describes its habit of making burrows. The Lithic is ka-u-nai, earth-what-erects. Few people realise a rabbit's burrow refers to the earth piled up at the entrance to the holes it makes, and not the hole at all, just as the iron age barrows, like the burrows, humped up earth (over royal burials). Until quite recently all Christian burials had small barrows over them, the earth packed down loosely left lumps on top, and of course the body coffined or not took up some space too. Nowadays you never see a warren, u-a-rarai-en, all-them-raised risen-ones. In Malay naim (3) means delightful. If the final m is the result of slovening mai via me to m, as commonly occurs, then it is highly significant: nai when mai, meant in Lithic as orgasming-[when]copulating. Of course the Malay speakers are not running their minds round this derivation when they spot something delightful. But our primitive hominid forebears were, when they researched the natural meanings of the sounds they were making, with which to clothe the thoughts they were thinking.

Moreover Malay nahak means desire from the Lithic na-ha-kai, what makes for the joy of sex; and ternahak, tai-nai-ha-kai, become desirous, is described as overcome by desire. The ha phoneme (chapter 8) contributes a shock element, as in the Egyptian pa-hei, the joy-piece which we describe more prosaically as the penis, the pe-nai(s), the protruding piece (4), showing the preoccupation of the owner, and so even perhaps the witness piece. But come to think of it, it is the penis which plays the principal part in the original orgasmic na (3). It could be the orgasmic piece. Yet we know it meant as well the protruding piece because it was used in Latin to refer also to a dog's tail, which when wagged clearly registers delight, but does not carry the nerve endings to allow stimulation to register the same extremity of sensation as an orgasm. Indeed Chambers´ estimable

Dictionary of Etymology represents the genital meaning of penis now as merely copied from the Latin penis meaning tail, the protruding piece, with the description simply brought round in front to refer to the male member, the little tail the boys carry in front. Of course Chambers has no Lithic; and that may be all very well; but then it does remain to be explained why na should signify protruding in the first place, or even the second place, which in itself may present no problems for conventiomal etymologists who have decided to eliminate any such enquiry from their agenda by declaring all symbols randomly selected in the first place. But it is a view by now so palpably foolish as to need no further contradiction here. Na appears where its sexual credentials are fully established and the only character common to penises and tails, after all, is their orientation. The penis must surely win on points for emotional impact, tails maybe for greater public exposure when worn. But tails have little or no psychological pull for humanity, certainly nothing like the virile member; and anyway the Egyptians have to be taken into account with their pahei.

Eric Partridge is more ambitious than Chambers but he is also astray, heading the penis group with penates, the Roman household gods akin to the Latin penetralia, the innermost and hence the most secret parts (of beliefs for instance). Now there can be no doubt the penis is a penetrator as Partridge maintains, but the question which has to be confronted is whether the Latin penetration derives from the action of the penis or whether the penis is named from a previously established meaning for penetration to do with the household gods who were ensconced within, so that the penis during copulation was perceived as a copyist of these godlings, perhaps nipping in to present compliments to the penetralia, the innermost and secret parts. With the issue spelt out like this, the conclusion seems inescapable. We based our perception of general manoeuvre upon our private (bodily) experience and not the other way about. The Latin penetrare to penetrate is made up from the Latin elements pene-trahere, and trahere means to draw along (and within), based upon sexual analogy. Trahere and its traction comes from the Pleistocene hearth and its rays.

These are the feminine T-rays at work. The Lithic for trahere is quite clear cut. Ta-rai-hai-are is vagina-rayed-joying-verbal ending. The male organ was, it was supposed, being drawn in by the (completely imaginary) active radar type of ray the birth canal emits, which on its return to its source pulls the male genitalia back in with it, just like the vegetation which was drawn back up towards the sun by the sun's rays. All Egyptian rays were there and back rays like our radar. Our back is just a bounce, and not the instinct fashion of the Egyptian rays. In fact we can see that the transference of the idea was in reality from the genitalia to the sun, perceived by the Ancient Egyptians at one time as a world birth canal (aa-ta-oon, aton in Egyptian) birthing light into the world every day. The basics are in chapter 12 on the phoneme Ra. The hei inserted before the final verbal suffix -ere in trahere is not fortuitous. It comes from the pleasurable sensation accompanying the original sexual exercise which framed the concept, irrelevant in the generalised traction but crucial in the derivation. The conclusion is obvious. The penis was the orgasmic protruding piece, the protruding aspect only applicable to a tail as well. The former supposedly got drawn within by the rays sent out from the opposite sex. The orgies around the hominid hearth were thus judged by the linguists of the day to be initiated by the womenfolk, who were enjoying a new found humanity, that is they were were hie-ing the mai-ing just as well as their mates (the meaning of what it is to be human, the species 'hei-u-ma-nai', enjoying-both-the planting/impregnation-orgasm), and either sex initiating the copulation. By comparison the remainder of the animal kingdom suffers impregnations which are nasty, brutish and short, and appear to be inflicted by the male by guile (a mating display) or force.

Chapter 10 Na

The cart is often put before the horse like this where conventional etymologists want to have the penis a tail because they have no knowledge of Lithic psychosemantic contents to guide them and are quite unaware of the Egyptian rays in chapter 12. The dog itself in Latin is canis, which confirms the perception of the penis as the protruding piece since the ka was the male contribution to the human body, the skeleton and all-important framework (on which the fair sex was judged merely to hang the dependent flesh in the womb). With the dog, canis, from ka-nai(s), here was the end of its backbone (ka) which was nai, protruding and showing (its mood), acting as the witness piece (nai) of its soul (ka). You could judge its mood by its tail.

At the same time hei and nai have a lot in common. The ha syllable was analysed in chapter 7. It adds vehemence traditionally derived from Latin vehere to carry, now vehicular transport but originally in the days of human porters u-ai-hei-are, when going strenuously, ie under burden, for instance under a forty pound pack which after a hectic mile or two you know well you are carrying, and then with the usual –are verbal suffix. Anyway in Malay nak or na' is to desire (3), usually taken to be a short form of hendak, from hei'n-da-ka, copulate-do-make, and for the most part reduced to a prediction, not what we want but what we will, we will it, or perhaps better in the Malay idiom it is willed, we have been struck with that desire, so that that is what we intend to do. There will be other cases of the na phoneme meaning enjoyment, but English mostly passes them by. There is only nice and it has such a troubled etymology it is hardly worth the effort disentangling it. As well as pleasing it also means precisely accurate or discriminating, a curious mix. It comes via protruding, presenting, showing, making explicit and clear, discriminating, and so finally precise accuracy. These semantic contents conventionally are supposed to originate from (the meaning of) the Latin nescire, not to know, to be ignorant. Eric Partridge demonstrates the supposed semantic catena thus: "ignorant, innocent, whence….foolishly, whence shy, hence discriminating…..hence agreeable, pleasant". He seems easily pleased when meanings have to be got to run in a single straight line rather than the Lithic reality of whimsical cross currents and polysemy in every phoneme. Ignorant and foolish string well enough, and perhaps innocent and shy with agreeable and pleasant, if barely. But discriminating seems to be well out on a limb. Shyness does not arise from a hyper discriminating mind as Partridge seems to require. Most likely it comes from the subconscious dark room hinting at realities the conscious mind does not wish to entertain. It typically afflicts teenage girls not yet ready to plunge into the sexual jungle opening up before them but beginning to recognise its pulls. It comes from confusion and lack of understanding as well as a refusal to face up. It is a long way from nescire, which is simply not to know.

But then Partridge also derives science from scire which he thinks is "probably originally to cut through, (Latin secare) hence to decide, quoting Sanskrit chyati he cuts and Irish scian'a a knife. These are really from ka, via kha, the flint knappers' ka from the sound of striking off a flake. Lithic suggests scire is from sai-kai-verbal suffix, sai-making, making illuminated or clear; in which case the nai in nice is not a negative (5) as Partridge imagined but is the same as the Malay nah, which comes from show (13) and means 'here you are, take it', as in the Malay "Nah! Do biji ubat": Nah!, presento, here you are! Do (pronounced doe), two, biji, little bits, ubat, medicine: or 'Here take these two pills!' With the Malay ubat, ba is to burgeon or bloom and u-ba-tai is altogether-blooming-becoming, a make-you-well or medicine, which is from mai-dai, doing the measuring, from the weighing (mai). The nicety is nai-sai, understanding showing and also showing comfort, from warmth, sai originally, around the hearth; or delight such as

Chapter 10 Na

sugar (from su-kara) makes on a purely tasting scale. Nice gets some of its pleasurable niceness from its first phoneme nai, it is not unreasonable to suppose; but it is the dual meaning of sai which yields a nice, that is to say warm and comfortable, whence a pleasant taste, but also a bright and clear and so a precise judgment. You need the Lithic analysis in chapter 13 for ish to identify these meanings, which have been gulled some way from the original flame. Without Lithic you take your fragile mental catamaran up the semantic creek without a paddle. A catamaran is fom the Tamil, and the Lithic is ka-tau-m'a-rai'n, join-two-him'that-rayed'one. The -m'a-ran, the -him'that-rayed-one bit, is Tamil for a tree, Lithic ta-rai in English, in both cases the sun's rays being the agency for drawing the trunk out and up, and appearing in the linguistic symbolisation. All vegetation is subject to this universal processing but the trees are evidently the dab hands with their responses which explains how they grow so strong and tall. In fact ma-ra'n could be massive-grown'one, rather than him-that-rayed'one. The catamaran, two (dugout) trees tied together – kattu is tied in Tamil – is a design which has led to the trimaran design ("three trees") which has the solo round the world sailing record today – they were probably fibre-glass trees. Its mental avatar has made its way just with its Lithic paddle over the generations around the world. With random word elements you would not get very far.

Canabis, the hemp plant in many languages, including Sumerian the oldest language known, where the name is read as kunibu giving a Lithic analysis of kau-nai-bau, what makes-ecstacy-of the flesh. What pleasure (4) of the flesh is intended is open to debate; as indeed is also the Lithic analysis – like all Lithic analyses; but particularly in this case because of the extreme antiquity of the source and the limited understanding of the Sumerian phonetics involved. But hemp seems to clinch the matter since it reads as hei-em-pai, where the em means of, where the pai closely resembles the Egyptian pahei or joy piece the glyph for which is an unmistakable penis in arousal. Moreover the Old English version was haenep from hei-nai-pai, the two first syllables surely conclusive so the pai could be the leaf; while the Old saxon was hanap, the Old High German hanaf, from Lithic elements ha-na-pa-hai, Old Icelandic hampr, from ha-na-pa-rai, Albanian kanap, Lithuanian Kanapes, Persian kamb and Greek kannabis, these citations being from Partridge and Chambers. The halucinatory drug made from hemp is addictive and can provide a high which is usually extremely pleasurable though sometimes horrific. It seems clear the ancients associated it with sexual arousal (4). How the moderns find it today is moot for oldies who have not indulged, but the young will keep taking it, with a persistence usually associated with the sex drive. Canabis leads in Latin to canabaceus, hempen, and so to Old Northern French canevas and current English canvas, made from hemp fibre. Walshe's Concise German Etymological Dictionary of 1952 also cites Cheremis and Zyrjan words, both languages from the Finno-Ugric family. Knowledge of the drug seems to have travelled widely. There was certainly something powerful going for it. There is some black humour in the reports of the brewers' droop which follows its use. Droop goes with drip, drop, and dribble. Curiously the drai- or drau- which mark the drawing up and out also function as drawn down and out, pendant in fact: erect or flaccid depending on context. Lithic is like that. The language suggests canabis drug addicts are enjoying simulated orgasms (in yellow submarines), in spite of brewer's droop.

Both Partridge and Chambers go on to record canvassing as tossing in a canvas sheet and seek to relate this to canvassing for votes which seems a rather far fetched semantic catena. Partridge has it to be by way of sifting through canvas, hence sifting thoroughly, whence examining thoroughly; which is still some way from canvassing as usually conducted. Chambers finds tossing in a canvas sheet and canvassing for votes "seemingly unrelated", after reporting the supposed trace via shaking out and examining carefully. More likely canvassing is from unscrupulous wooing of the electorate by providing the pleasures of the flesh (in this case just food and drink) while speech making, now democratically confined to offering promises of future pleasurable improvements in voters' fortunes in return for their votes. Canvassing in the form of tossing in a canvas sheet or sifting through canvas goes back to the sixteenth century and is best ignored as folk (ie silly) etymology. A canvasser is offering voters, at several removes, promises of the pleasures of the flesh the party plans to provide for him. Of course he does not know what his terminology implies and he hardly expects to honour it anyway.

A snipe is a small bird of the open heath with a very long bill. Victorians would serve it spatchcocked with its long bill (still attached to its skull) stuck through its body as a skewer. Si-nai-pai is brer-protruding-piece (6) in Lithic, but it is his poll with its beak, not his penis. A banana, like the seven armed star fish nabinabi (with a plethora of protruding bits) in Malay, fruits in a bunch of up to a hundred protruding upturned pieces. It is from the Taino, a West Indian tongue and is akin to the Arawak prattana which says the same with pai-rai-ta-nai, piece(s)-raised-become-protruding. No doubt the nudge-nudge linguists who named the fruit enjoyed the similarity with the relevant human organ, since pai-rai could be the erect penis. But the appearances will have been taken quite seriously, to indicate a common reality: the banana was bananaing because nature dictated the performance, just as the human genitalia benanad as they did. It was a game of spot the common pattern, no different at all from the way scientists practise today. It was to take hundreds of thousands of years to knock them into shape. Whilst with the fruit, we can notice briefly, buah nanas in Malay, the pineapple, with a fruit on it the shape not of an apple (which originally just meant fruit, like the phallus) but a pine. The Pine tree has a tall upright trunk without branches, another protruding piece our elders remarked, with a cone for which the tree was really named, since like the acorn it was taken to resemble the male glans (which is acorn in Latin). Apple, with seventeen cognates in Indo-European languages, is akin to phalos in Greek which actually referred to the knob or fruiting body on the end of the penis and not to the whole member at all. In the old days boys had three balls, one above and two below, a very early trinity; and indeed the foot type of ball may have been named after the testicle rather than the other way around as is commonly imagined. Buah in Malay is fruit, and the shape of the pineapple fruit is like an outsize acorn or oak corn, or glans in Latin, when pai-nai, in arousal. Buah pelir in Malay are the testicles or penis fruit, since pelir is Malay for the penis. This is akin to the Greek phallos, the engorged penis knob, although unrelated linguistically – other than from the Lithic. La, chapter 8, embraces liquids, flowing downhill (an instinct in all liquids) to the ocean, looping like the line round the ocean where it meets the sky, and the orbiting of Apollo the sun, and inflating or ballooning in an enlarging loop like the phallus. The Greeks refer to the pa-hai-lau(s), the inflated ecstacy piece, the Malays more simply to the pai-la-ire, the inflating piece.

The anti-Lithic lobby have to explain how the minds of the Greeks and Malays got together, not a congruent couple of words but close enough, if their minds were really not informed at some level by similar sounds having similar semantic contents, so as to need some other explanation. They should perhaps concentrate on that and leave aside any reservations they may have about the subject matter not being in the best of taste or leaving them out in the cold. Our forebears had not invented the idea of good or bad taste and sailed ahead with their word formations as their thoughts prompted them. As early

Chapter 10 Na

humans, hei-u-ma'n, their joint enjoyment of copulation is writ large in the linguistic record. In half a million years the pattern still pertains, in language at least.

Nibs, nebs and nabs are all three prominences, and a nipple is a little one that leaks liquid. Even the belly button, the navel, protruded originally. The Old English was nafala, the Sanskrit nabbhis, the Old Persian nabis. They had to get hold of the navel string in clumsy hands before they could get a flint to it or maybe their teeth, so there was a bee hive effect rather than the sexy dimple now embellished in the West with studs and rings. The umbilicus or Greek omphalikos, the hump, or him-phalus-shaped was for the Greeks a symbolic centre of the body and therefore also a symbol for religious centres, which they marked with stone navels like bee hives or acorns. The acorn is an ak or oak-corn, kara-u-nai, or oak-skull-what-protruding. Kara is skull in Greek, the hard one. Latin cornu (the horns of cattle) are kara-u-nau, head-dual-protrusions, as indeed they are. The corn grows a protruberant seed head. A bead is a bai-a-tai, a bit with a hole (drilled in it). But the bead on the foresight of a firearm is also a barley corn. It has no hole in it but stands up, a tiny knob for aiming with. A knob is ka-nau-bai in Lithic, the shape (ka) of the protruded bit. Naik is an ascent in Malay, from nai-kai, an up-going, or a rising of the ground (or both), and kenaikan is to rise, to make an ascent. A knot in wood is a protrusion from a cut side branch, and a gnarled trunk is one with many knots. Canis, Latin for a dog, is the one with the waggly tail. The ka resides in the spine and the dog's spine protrudes at the tail end, whereas the cow (kau) has dual skull protruberances, its horns, cornu, kara-u-nau, skull-what-protrusions dual, in front. The gnu has two huge horns too but it is named by the South African bushmen n'ku like the cow and only altered to gnu by whitey. With ka a corner and a joint the knee (ka-nai) is the protruding joint. The elbows, wrists and ankles do not present their corners in front. Only the knees (and the little knees or knuckles) do. In France the knee is genou, -nau in place of –nai. Both are in Lithic protruded and presented, the -nau perhaps rather more forcefully than the merely –nai, or else dual in France like the horns in Latin – we all have two knees, just as cows have two horns.

A canopy comes from the Latin canopeum and the Latin is from the Greek konopeion the neuter of konopeios closely akin to konops, a mosquito, from ka-u-nau-pai-sai, makes-what-presents-a swelling-action-one (insect stings were regarded as inseminations causing the flesh to burgeon), and the Greeks had it like much else from the Egyptians. The Greeks evidently thought an insect sting was done with their genitalia and kindled the flesh into swelling, just as they kindled the flesh into swelling with theirs. We do not know if they had discovered the ichneumon wasp which lays its eggs in caterpillars, which hatch and eat the caterpillars from inside; but it is quite possible they had. It could have confirmed their view of other insects' action, including konops, the mosquito. The Ancient Egyptian for the ichneumon wasp was khatru, from Kai-ta-rai-u, kindling-birth-raised-ones, ie actually carrying the procreation to completion, unlike the humble mosquito which did not have sufficient ka to properly impregnate foreign flesh. Ichneumon, which is from the Greek, carries the Lithic i-kai-nai-u-mai-en, which-makes-present-completing-impregnate-ing, that is to say its sting leads to the actual birth of maggots inside the caterpillars, which eat them out from the inside, vital organs last.

It is perhaps necessary to repeat from time to time that Lithic is a semantic study and when words in one language are suggested as indicating the meaning in another, it is not the words offered which are supposed to provide the indications but the meanings. Critics often forget this and object to connections claimed between wholly unrelated languages because there can not have been any linguistic contact. The Lithic hypothesis per contra claims that the human race has been thinking the same - if you dig deep enough - all along;

Chapter 10 Na

and these correspondences of meanings when the phonetic record is looked at with proper perception demonstrate as much. The correspondences come from the common human stock of psychosemantic (now mostly subconscious) identifications. There is no suggestion English words, for example, somehow influenced Inuit, Navaho, Malay or Chinese words. They did not, unless by some remote and improbable borrowing we know nothing of, and find unbelievable. Indeed assumed borrowings have been used, all unawares, to cover up Lithic correspondences, and only become absurd when they involve prehistoric travelling beyond belief. Malay, the classic magpie language under this rubric, turns out to be related to a very early source language now lost, spoken in the Garden of Eden, the plains East of Malaya, (Malaya actually means the Garden Land) which are now three hundred and sixty feet under the South China Sea. That is how Malay provides a conduit to Lithic meanings so readily. Inheriting on the periphery Adam's advanced prehistoric civilisation, and its language, perhaps only a provincial version, there has been the less impetus for change and the more respect for tradition in Malaya.

Malay jankal mankal means sticking up irregularly, a bit of jankal and a bit of mankal as it were. Malay jongkang means sticking up, up-shape in Lithic, or perhaps ups-making. Jan or jong is up, from Ish in chapter 13. Jankal is thus much the same with –lai added to indicate the idea of a line or progression, which is also mankal a down shape line, with ma meaning down (see meaning 35 in the tree for Ma, chapter 9). The overall idea is like a distant range of mountains. The Chinese copies. Shan is mountain(s) in Chinese, ups, uplands. Shang-hai is On-sea, strictly above the ahai or awai, ocean with a cockney h to separate the first a- (now lost) from the -ai. Ocean, incidentally, akin to the earlier Greek okeanos appears to be from the Lithic au-kai-a-nau-(s), from an original au-kai-awa-nau-(s), that one-strong-water-presenting (in the same case ending as the one)-substantive ending. The idea is one of powerful waters. The sheer force of an ocean swell will certainly have impressed ancient seafarers venturing to sea with dugout canoes or trussed bamboo rafts, and its power is now under investigation as a power source generating electricity. Canoe (Taino canoa) from the Lithic ka-nau-a, means hard-hollow-one or dugout. The hard hollowed was a tree trunk, the English trunk being from a te-rau'n-ka, a drawn-up'one-hard, copying the original erect penis again. The English cannon has much the same Lithic elements, as does the Spanish cana or cano, a tube, as well as Spanish canyon a large tube or hollow, and so also a deep high sided valley carved out by rushing waters. A cane is hollow like a canoe – well not all that much like, but semantically out of the same common semantic stable, originally copying the original engorged vagina, I am afraid, u-a-kai-na, the hole-that- kindled –hollows out..

In Malay we have nusa an island, from the Lithic elements nau-sai, protruded-up. An island sticks up out of the surrounding water. An island in English is an up-land. Nu- with the completive vowel u even suggests the protrusion is something which has taken place and is now a done job, as if historically islands have done their arising. In fact this is what was widely believed and forms a significant part in creation myths, particularly the Ancient Egyptian ones, since one or two submarine volcanic eruptions had shown it happening. Similarly stone was considered to be sai-tao'n fire-born'n, since volcanic eruptions had shown stone born from fiery lava. It was common sense for anyone who had seen a volcanic eruption. From nusa an island we have Nusantara the Indonesian archipelago, that string of islands federated today as the Indonesian Republic, a corrupt nominally Moslem empire held together with violence and with island guerillas fighting for independence. The Lithic is nausa-en-tara, 'islands-of-drawn out': like our string and tiara, a string of islands, the archipelago, using a metaphor originally sexual (see chapter

Chapter 10 Na

12 on the phoneme Ra) but in this case naturally disposed, rather than by the fancied sex rays from the girls playing upon the male member. Our chest of drawers has the same semantic pedigree. A drawer is pulled out and drawers you wear are pulled up, both like the male member when tau-rayed.

To ransack Malay still further we have the nibong palm, with a straight protruding naked trunk and there is a burgeon, a tuft of greenery protruding at the top of the palm. Ba is flesh (chapter 4), or foliage in the case of vegetative life forms. The baung on the top of the nibong is the burgeoning top. An elephant's trunk is of course a protruding proboscis up front and one suspects the elephant comes from ai-lai-pahei-n-tai, them-long/flexible-penises-of-dual, except that the earlier Greek elephas has no –nt, ending instead with an s. But we are perhaps entitled to ask why the -nt got added later. The indication is somebody was thinking in terms of a proboscis at both ends and using a metaphor originally sexual. The Greeks seem to have thought "what a long member!", leaving it to their countrymen to decide which one to consider. The Aryan mind then added the consideration Mr Twococks, with a tail at both ends. The nibong palm is also used to describe a brindled dog. But a dog does not have a tufted head. Nai-bau(ng) can be read as showing dual flesh/body (textures). The brindling is an intermixture of hairs of two colours in its coat, brindled being from the Middle English brinded, finely branded or streaked. A streak is like a string, but perhaps the s- in this case indicates the mark was originally burnt; although in chapter 13 on ish the initial s- which occurs in many English words making s the biggest section of any letter in the dictionary, which is often described by conventional etymology as vaguely intensive (whatever that really means), is derived from the existential character of ish, like is for example. It means the word originally referred to a phenomenal item, seen, and was not an abstract term. That is why there are so many of them. That was the common pattern of initial (Lithic) symbolisation. With the palm tree the final au of nibaung is completive. With the brindled dog it is dual – from the prehistoric dialectic in chapter 15. No Lithic, no comprehension.

Finally for the protrusion sense (4) of na there is the Roman frog: in Latin rana. Frogs have eyes mounted on the top of their heads so they can observe when submerged in a pond with just their eyes above water. Ra is eye or eyes in Egyptian. Ra-na is eyes protruding, or "Old Pog-Eye". Disappointingly the Greek, the common intermediary between Egyptian and Latin, has batraxos, and Aristophanes had his frog chorus singing "Grek-ek-ek-ex coax-coax", a croaking song, fanciful perhaps but we can follow him. They called the frog a croaker. Cold climate frogs croak less, it is a sex call, and if deprived of the sun's rays they can not copulate. The croaker may have displaced rana, which if you don't know your Lithic is a bit dull, although if you do it is delightful. Ba-tra-ks-aus, behind the Greek, is twisted mouth, and it is also echoic of a raucous croak. Frogs as well as gnomes are modelled for the garden, and the frogs all have exageratedly prominent eyes to appeal to the comic muse, showing this character is well established. In fact frogs are prestigious leapers as well as croakers and the bull frog leads in all these fields being hefty and muscular like the bull. Frog is from pahai-rao-kai, his leap makes a movement which is ejaculatory like the rayed and roused penis The common fircone (6) is akin to Latin conus, a fircone (which has a protruding shape), and also to Greek konos from which establishment linguistics derives Greek konikos and French conique, and we have the far more precise conic sections. The Lithic ka-u-nai-kau-s means made-protruding-shaped-substantive marker, or shape-when-protruding-kindled-substantive marker. In either case it is the acorn shape or glans, viz the shape of the knob of the penis when aroused. (Sorry folks!) The geometrical shape is a little more precisely described. It

197

Chapter 10 Na

is rounded and comes to a point, and it has a place in higher mathematics with conic sections and the equations for them. But that is where it comes from and that is the message of Lithic. We made it up.

Now we move to meaning 7, to present, which is a straight gull from the action of the penis which, in times before trousers, presented itself in public when aroused so that it has been described as the witness piece, its angle of attack being a fair indication of what was on its owner's mind. For presentation there is of course an element of metaphor involved, that is to say it involves the impact on the beholder, already at one remove from the bare perception of protrusion, but that is a fine distinction it is not important to understand. Under the same rubric comes the shift from presenting to the present. The switch is highlighted by comparing a Christmas present with the present time. Probably not one English speaker in ten or even in a hundred makes any conscious attempt to relate these two meanings. Nevertheless they can quite easily be related. In the case of the Christmas present we are closest to the penis. We can envisage the actual process of presentation, holding the present and then extending the arms, pushing the present forward to put it within the grasp of the recipient, proffering the gift much as, in a sexual relationship, the penis is proffered. The present time, now or nau, what is presented, and so present (using –u in the substantive mode, see chapter 14), probably relies somewhat upon the prehistoric view the world was presented in consecutive snaps of the state of affairs to human view, much like the early cinematograph machines which flickered from frame to frame. The one which is presenting itself is the state of affairs in the here and now. These ideas are picked up chiefly from the Egyptian language, a relatively recent language compared with the origins of speaking, our records of it only preserving the form of the language for some ten thousand years at the very most. But it is argued elsewhere that most of the divergence from the old original ways of speaking with meaningful phonemes has occurred only recently (since Babel). Nothing of course is certain when addressing a period so long ago. But then nothing at all is nearly as certain as most people imagine, including the whole body of science which only approximates reality at best. The one which is showing, nai (10) is also nigh, spatially present or near; (near was originally the comparative of nigh, and nigh meant presented or present). Other Indo European languages have ni, nei, na, nah, nahe, nach, nehwa, etc for now. It is hard to distinguish anything other than the phoneme na as contributing anything to the meaning, and it means presenting and therefore presented and so being present, what is present, whence the present time. New (14), akin to Latin nova, Greek neos, Sanskrit navas, Hittite newas, Tokharian A niu, Gothic niujis, Old High German niuwe and finally Old Irish nue, to pick examples from Partridge again, is the same idea applied to the temporal dimension. All these cognate words in numerous Indo European (and some other) languages are all in Eric Partridge's etymological dictionary, but there is little point in wasting space and readers' patience quoting them extensively. My "The Origins of Speaking" (2005) effectively forms the second volume of Eric Partridge's 972 page etymological dictionary "Origins". It is just he can not be blamed for any errors, since he had no hand in it, being dead.

Partridge has a nest (Latin nidus) "a place in which to sit down", presenting (a seat) as it were, although almost a hundred percent of all sitting in the last million years has been hunkered legs akimbo on the ground. Most nests are actually rounded out and hollowed out, which is what nidu from the Lithic nai-tau, rounded out-become, means precisely. Egyptian Isis, properly pronounced in Egyptian Au-Siti, Isis being the Greek, meant World-life-source, but also Our Lady. In Malay it is still means Our Lady and is used for the Virgin Mary. She had a seat as her glyph, a throne. On it she sat suckling the infant

Horus, a pose transferred later to the Virgin Mary. Perhaps it was partly a crack like 'Her indoors' today. Au-siti, Au-sai-tai, also could be read as Altogether-easy-become, which is the original semantic construction for sitting at ease, the ease originally ai-sai, warm (sai) around the hearth. The correspondences are compelling. In the Stone Age the matrons stayed at base camp with the children as keepers of the hearth. They were sources of the flame and warmth as well as of life – they fueled the fire, empathised and gave birth. Sai was warm, and so comfortable, and so pleasurable. To be sedentary was to be keeping the flame. Nowadays we put our tail ends in a chair. A nest, from nai-siti, presents-a seat, en-ai-siti, for-the-female. Partridge treats nether as from a root ni meaning down where Lithic has nai as pointing up. But Lithic shows nai as a negative also, here the opposite of plain therai, drawn up. Under reinforces this Lithic analysis: in this case un-drawn [up].

Sand in Spanish is arena. The Latin is harena. Our arena had originally a sand covered floor. Sand is from the Lithic sai'n-dai, moving-does, or hot-becomes, or both: the shifting sands of the desert, where the wind blows the sand off the top of the dunes and deposits it in the low, so that the dunes can move slowly across the landscape. In the tropics the surface of desert sand gets hot enough to burn bare feet. In sand the first phoneme sai, as well as movement, can mean warm or hot, from flamed; which is how sai'n-da does heat and movement both. Arena for sand is from the Lithic a-rai-na, that-(the sun's)rays-presents. Sand gets hot. The Latin harena has a cockney h, separating an initial i (since lost) from the a next door, i(h)a-rai-na, it-that-(the sun's)rays-presents. The Hittite seems to confirm the analysis of the Latin and Spanish, their word for sand being koraiz, Lithic ka-u-rai-ish, land-what-rayed-heat or hot, a land surface which heats up under the sun's rays. The Latin introduces an ish too in an alternative hasena as a variant of harena, fire rays in place of sun rays.

A noise, being auditory, presents problems for semantic analysis; but in the event the Lithic proves easy: nau-i-sai, presentation-of which-moving. Most natural noises are made by a movement of some sort. With speech on the other hand the movements are not what catches the attention, it is the sounds uttered and the meanings which can be attached to them. If you wanted to mime a noise you would I suppose make a variety of noisy movements. You would not include any utterances, like a roar or shout for instance, since that would mislead the guessing into searching for meaning or emotion. In the jungle a noise indicates movement, perhaps of a predator, or nowadays a terrorist. Wild pigs rootling are a pest in the jungle at night. It is best to just ignore noises in the dark concentrating merely on not making any. Not many tigers are left and terrorists can't see to move in the jungle at night. So you can sleep sound ignoring wild pigs.

The Arabic for a lighthouse is menorah. The Egyptian is pharos, from the Lithic elements pa-hei-rau-sai, ejaculate-rays-of light. The Arabic says much the same but in a different idiom, 'm-ai-nau-rai, him-that which-presentation-of rays [of light], sudden bursts of light. The flashes were produced with a circulating screen. We can picture the lighthouse keeper encouraging the pushers with his stick.

The Latin genere means to procreate, and the Lithic elements are kai-nai-are, making-orgasm-verbal suffix; a fair indication in itself of the meaning of the phoneme na even if additional evidence were wanting. Partridge puts it at the head of 25 paragraphs on this group of no less than 95 words akin, including general, generator, genius, genes, genitals, jaunty, gendarme, genuine, germ, gentility, genealogy, gentile, progeny and even the genitive case, none of which are particularly orgasmic. He adds "the relationships between Greek, Latin and Sanskrit are strikingly numerous and intimate". Sanskrit ajananta, they were born, matches with Greek egenonta; and Sanskrit ganus with Latin gens, a clan. In

Chapter 10 Na

India the Ajanta Caves are given over to modelling couples copulating in stone. Ka-na, this Lithic pairing, is clearly inhabited by a strongly sexual motif. Add a ta, a cut or slit, and it is a girly one. What is more it has spread by means of an analogical extravaganza over the millennia to develop meanings of an astonishing diversity, a fact already recognised by the word king Eric Partridge.

It is important to give Partridge's research work an occasional airing like this to draw attention to the relatedness of words within a language family which is already fully established. Lithic relates the families in turn, (a task which has so far defeated researchers), by pursuing the semantic connections rather than just the sounds – elsewhere taken to be random - a pursuit which offers up a different set of congeners. Immediate examples of the different phonemic strings used in different languages to define the same things by way of the same meanings are sand and lighthouse above.

Ignis, the Latin for fire, compares with Lithuanian ugnis (often particularly close to Sanskrit) and Sanscrit agnis is from the Lithic a-kai-nai-ish, that-making-show (13)-flame. Indeed the thinking is that fire makes the flame present and protrude itself from what burns, an immanent oomph capable of letting itself out in little or at large. This is quite interesting since it seems to suggest that the idea of fire was of something lying behind the flame, which might manifest itself in the fully expressed burning form of the flame or perhaps less forcefully in the heat of the bodies of all animal species. If so it was not good science, but it was the science of the day. It may even throw some light on the nature of the magic bird the phoenix which burnt to death and then arose from the dead, which we looked at in chapter 6 for Fa.

The ichneumon, an Egyptian weasel or mongoose means the tracker or hunter in Greek. Ichnos is a track in Greek, akin to Lithuanian eiga a walk or course. Lithic ai, extending, and its semantic cognates including walking and going are explained in chapter 14 on the vowels. The Lithuanian eiga, a walk (and so a track made by an animal or person walking, just like the ichneumon's ichai which neu, from nai-u, showing where), is clearly from the Lithic phonemes ai-ka, going makes (ie a track), and relates English go and Latin ire (from ai-are) to go, to extend (your distance from your point of origin). Partridge relates the Greek ichnos, from ai-khai-nau, going-made-presented/shown, to a supposed "Indo European root *eigh to go, an extension of ei to go (as in the Greek and Latin verbs)". Lithic does not subscribe to word analysis by cutting them down to "roots" of a single syllable. Tracking is following a traveller from the traces of passage left, which is the track. The Lithic in the first phoneme does indeed validate Partridge's guessed "root", but he misses all the rest out, which is what makes sense of the word, as his "root" can not. The ichneumon's eating, ichneu-mon, tracked-mau'n, is by tracking down its prey (eaten one), often apparently by smelling out the nests of buried crocodile eggs. The ichneumon fly which lays its eggs in caterpillars which hatch and eat out the catapillar while still alive, leaving the vital organs until last, is a tracker for the purpose of the plantation (mau'n) of its eggs. In point of fact the Egyptian for ichneumon appears to have been kha-tarau, make-ta-rayed, drawn out, or here drawn along. Either it was supposed to send out an attractive ray and follow along the ray as it returned (which guided its search) or else it picked up and followed up the ray emitted by its prey, which seems the better idiom. It is an originally sexual metaphor like so much in Egyptian hieroglyphics.

The Japanese art of flower arrangement meanwhile, ikebana, is from iheru which means to arrange from to go or put in a row, and bana which is flower. Bana flower is interesting. Ba in Lithic is originally flesh or foliage. What is it about -na which picks out the flower from the remainder of the foliage? It means to present or presenting, originally sexually, in

Chapter 10 Na

Lithic. The flowers attract attention because of their colours; and the pollinating insects (that some say are colour blind) are attracted by their scent. Is it possible von Linné's discovery in Sweden in the eighteenth century that flowers are the sexual organs of plants was old hat to the Japanese when they were dreaming up a name for flowers?

Meaning 8 for na is exposed, which is not so far from the original protruding but does not require the same sticking out or up. These are both gulls from the behaviour of the male member, preceding meaning 9 (open, agape, empty) from the female sexual response. There is no significance in the order in which they are put other than the closeness of the meaning of 9 to the meaning of 8, so far as their sexual origins are concerned. It has been suggested naked (8) is from a lost verb to nake, from na-kai, to expose ones whole body to view, the full monty. But the Lithic suggests it is from nai-kai-tai, exposed-of the body-the orifices. In Egyptian khati is the lower belly, the tapped bit where they lie. Nude, from Latin nudus, is surely from the Lithic nau-tau-(s), exposed-all the orifices-(plus -s, phenomenal suffix). A snake (8) is si-na-kai, brer-exposed/bare-bodied. It has no coat, and of course no limbs. A snail, from si-nai-lai is brer-present-lye. It leaves a slimey trail. In Malay a snail is siput, from si-pu-ti, brer-penis-teat. The similarity of the whorl on the Shell to the male glans is whimsical. But nevertheless Kuala Lumpur, muddy river junction, the Malayan capital city, is on the Sungei Siput, the River Snail, a broad slow running river. Akin to naked is the earlier form nacod. A cod, like the –ked in naked above, could be read as the genitals, and the plural cods were certainly taken to mean the testicles, perhaps because they were known to be the twin sources of kindling(kau) of the feminine genitalia (–tai). Originally the male drive was ka-, and here there were two of them kau-. A ti was a source as well as a teat, both from ta, the birth canal. The Tudors wore cod pieces, trouser flaps over their genitalia enabling them to urinate without removing their trousers, just dropping the flap for the purpose. In the absence of Y-fronts they evidently wore no underpants unless very loose ones; and perhaps shirt tails.

The iguana is a Caribbean Taino word for a large lizard. Like all cold blooded lizards, lai-zai-rai-dai, it does a lot of lazy lying in the sun's rays, to warm up and so to gain the energy to catch up with a lady lizard and copulate. It is not really being lazy, lai-zai, which is lying in comfort, (as well as simultaneously laying or lowering the action) - comfortable originally when warming yourself (sai) around the hearth when you should have been out hunting. Like brer-bare-body the snake, the iguana is from ai-ga-ua-na, that which-body-one that-bare, the bare bodied one without a coat. The substantial part of the definition is solely the -na stuck on the end. Taino perceptions, at the Lithic level, are remarkably similar to those entertained at some distance by the Romans and others. This is because their languages started out, surprisingly enough, with the same symbols as meanings for the individual phonemes as they learned to utter them, way back in the Pleistocene. Snake and iguana make a doublet, utilising different idioms but the same elements to string together phonemic meanings to the same end or sense. They are obviously related by way of the Lithic original meanings alone. There is no other convincing explanation. Academia just relies upon coincidences, of course.

Knitting is to be knotting whereas a knot is the done job, with many Indo European cognates, as Partridge says: "another puzzling word meaning something hard prominent and lumpy". Kai is hard and grown, nau is protruding, prominent, and ti is thing (from tai, what has become). His generation were perhaps more strictly brought up in the colonies, where the manly virtues were to be accepted without too much introspection. But it must now seem a trifle imperceptive of him to get no prompt at all from this description to help him in his etymological analysis. Admittedly metaphor provided something of a screen.

Chapter 10 Na

Adjacent words on the same page of his Origins are knap (the noun meaning a knoll and the verb to flake flints), knave, knee, knob, knocker, knoll, knuckle and knurl: only the knave is much immediate help with knot or knit, and that well developed from its original form and meaning. It is from the Old English cnafa or cnapa meaning boy or youth, "anterior etymology unknown" according to Partridge. The Lithic suggests a cnafa, from kai-na-pahei, with our four letters beginning in f, a young man with grown-protruberant-genitalia, past puberty and capable of procreation, no longer a puer or piper, with his voice broken, though still in his youth and with a menial job and the congenital lack of sobriety and morality which often accompanies the teen-age years, as puberty and growth suggests strength and power; and so full of knavish tricks. Contemporary definitions were rogue, rascal, male servant, attendant, squire. Did they have a problem with their teenagers in the middle ages too? They certainly respected maturity in the old days, a respect which has been buried altogether in the past half century, to the scandal of the nations, though not altogether without some reason behind it. They were much thinner on the ground in those days: just a few million people in England.

A knob is a shaped protruding bit; to knock is from the echoic strike (ka) [stone on flint] present (na) make (ka); knoll is from ground (ka)-protruded (nau) level (lalai); to knurl is to make (ka) prominent (Nau) ray (rai) lines (lai).

The Egyptian goddess Nut, probably from the Lithic Nau-ti, Exposed teats or Open orifices, is represented as the night sky and is pictured with her feet at one side of the earth and her body bowed over with her head at the other side, stretching her body out a bit with the tips of her fingers on the ground, with a trifle of the whimsical artistic licence modern art has accustomed us to. The moon is her vagina and the stars are her teats, of which she thus has a ridiculous surfeit. At times like this the appropriateness of the dual vowel also being the completive must have been brought home to the priests of Amun as they struggled to match up the universe to their anthropomorphic schemes. This bizarre perception of Nut no doubt helped to name the milky way and the galaxies from the Greek from gala, from ka-la or body-lye, milk (from mai-lai-kai, drinkable lye of the body) with its genitive case galaktos, of milk, milky. With her night time torso studded with breasts like this she was sometimes represented as a cow, with stars stamped all over her underside. She was certainly displaying all her orifices with a vengeance. Our own night, German nacht, appears to come from na-kha-ti, the naked sky showing-its body-orifices at night. Naughty has a somewhat similar phonetic pattern suggesting the mischief it originally denoted was sexual frivolity of one kind or another, probably flaunting nudity or perhaps just exposing the breasts, acceptable in some hot countries but not in the West – until recently when sunbathing, inhibition discarded, society youngsterised.

However there is a copious alternative etymology for the aught, naught, naughty group which seems to have everything going for it since Old English has nawiht contracted to naht, naught and nought in Middle English; all, it is proposed, from na-wiht, no thing, since wiht is a thing or a creature (a wight). The Lithic in wiht and wight is u-ai-tai, one that is born (the creature, a wight) or one that is become (the thing). In Middle Dutch and Dutch today wicht is a child, which appears to suggest cognisance at some level (ie the subconscious) of the one that is [recently] born etymology. With this na-wiht etymology, a naughty person is a nobody, worthless rather than mischievous. It would be easy to omit the sentence introducing naughty as from sexual exposure, which is contradicted by the worthless gloss, for a quiet life. But it is deliberately left in to exemplify the conflict between Lithic analysis and conventional (phonetic) etymology. It is a perfectly tenable position to argue the subconscious mind has adapted na-wiht to nought and applied it to the

Chapter 10 Na

O symbol, altering wiht to ought prompted by a Lithic recollection. Otherwise it is simply a coincidence the two analyses are on offer. It does not diminish Lithic. A hundred percent discovery of original Lithic word formations is a Will-o-the-whisp. The challenge will no doubt cite gw changing to w. But there are not many cases of w changing to gw, and anyway the change is from h to gh, whereas gh to h is reputable.

Canada is conventionally supposed to be from some huts mistaken for the name of the place the local tribe reckoned they lived in. We can imagine the interpreter told to ask what is the name of the place in which you live, and replying they said huts. But the tale is probably apocryphal. It is of a par with the interpreter pointing to what he wanted to know the name of and being told finger. Or compare the national park in California named after a complete sentence in Navaho: "That is-our-mother-of-the tribe", when a miner forty niner asked his Man Friday what he called a retreating grizzly bear which happened to be the totem of his tribe: "Ia-ushi-ma-i-tai". Thinks (in balloon): "I am not telling you her name for fear you could use it to conjure her against me". It sounded the fortyniner thought like Yosemite - pronounced yozemmity. Yosemite National Park is supposed to be Grizzly Bear Park. Undeveloped languages are nearer to the Lithic than languages much built up, and make use of long strings of short beads easily slovened by a lazy ear to a single word with what seems like a normal number of syllables. We can remind ourselves of the Can-araia islands with their exposed rocks – the Carthaginian was Ka-en-arai-a, core-of-raised/visible/exposed (ie rocky)-one, lands-rocky, the rocky lands. We can then add the area below the rim of the Mount Teide in Tenerife, above the tree line and with bare rock reaching to the lip of the volcanic caldera, which is called on the island maps las canadas, it seems to be saying land-exposed or bare-become, da from tai being a natural development as opposed to kai which is made by an agency other than the natural ones. The Canadian ca'n-a-da, land'of-that-born is akin to the Carthaginian Guanche as the name for the original Tenerife population they found there, from Ga-u-en-khai, land-where-in-begotten. Both mean just natives. It looks as if the Canadian aboriginal folk were asked what do you call yourselves, and replied we are the native folk It at first appeared that Las Canadas above the tree line in Tenerife might be land-no-produce, but the country Canada is not infertile. Better is land laid bare or open. A lot of Canada is open country you had to mush across. It rather depends where these misbegotten huts were exactly and the phonetics may have been misapprised as well, like the case of the grizzly bear misnomer.

Meaning 9, open or agape, takes in hollowed out and hollow as well. We already know a canoe is from the Taino canoa and Carib canaoa or canaeua. They all point to Lithic ka-nau-a, a hacked-hollow-one. The original canoe was a hollowed out tree trunk Canoe could be just trunk-hollowed. A cane has a hollow trunk too. A cannon and a canyon are the same in Lithic. A canyon is a cut or shaped (ka) [or land] hollow (nai) one, and a cannon is cast or drilled the same. A valley is a shallow canyon from awa-lai, water-leaking down, which is what washes the soil away below. The Arabic Ouadi, a valley Anglicised as waddi, is from the Lithic awa-a-dai, water-that-done/cut. It has nothing to do with the t in water as Partridge supposes. The -ter in water is to show it is fresh and is drawn up, a bit like the rocks from down below, in springs which then revert to type for water and flow down again to the sea, the instinct of all liquids being to lapse and slip away whenever given the chance. That is what liquid means. Water is just fresh wáter, tarai from a spring, not the lye in the sea. The infernal forces pushing water up against its natural instincts were perceived as powerful spirits, with conspicuous oomph, to be got on your side. Springs indicated spiritual presences and so were holy and prayed to. In Tenerife the dry water courses which have cut through the volcanic tuff are known as

Chapter 10 Na

barranco. They are slovened, with a w tidied into a double r, from ba-awa-en-kau, going-water-of or by-carved, a scientific statement of the day. Compare The Punjab state in Pakistan from Panch Awab. Panch is from pa-en-kai, the points-of-the body, four limbs and one head making five. But the Awab, from awa-bai, is water-travelling, that is a river, just like the Carthaginian ba-awa. You need to know the Punjab has five major rivers running through it. The going water is not unlike the billy for river water, from bai-lai, travelling down liquid, in Australia, with whitey waiting for his billy to boil, since it does not have to be a river to get the name, it means fresh wáter such as is found in rivers. Water goes by leaking away, in rivers or out, because of its instinct to lai, to slip away down and sideways, slopingly, into the lows; unlike the ish or fire instinct which is straight up and ma which is straight and deep down. See chapter 8 again for La, and 9 for Ma.

Anatomy is from Lithic a-na-tau-mai, that-exposed-cut-corpses, and from Greek temnein to cut, tai-em-nai-en, twoing-of-showing-infinitive marker. Curiously a tome was a volume, u-a-u-lau'm, (one-that-all-looped/rolled-mass) cut off a large papyrus roll, so it would fit in a pigeon hole in ancient libraries of scrolls, and so a volume of a large work and so also the large volume which needs dividing, whether actually divided or not. The anatomy is what-shows [when]-cut up, and so refers to the cadavers cut up to show their bits and pieces. Gyne, female in Greek, refers to the sex which kai-nai, kindled gapes as with the vagina above, which may at one time of course have been read as oo-a-gyne, hole-that-feminine, but kai-nai is better since it analyses gyne as well. In Malay nyak is a prostitute, Lithic nai-a-kai, presenting (nai)-that (a)-kindles (kai), for which she is employed. She initiates the sexual encounter, soliciting.

Meanwhile a nose, with the two nostrils or nose-terai-lai, the nose's little draw holes where the air flies in, is itself from na-u-sai, and is the protrusion-dual holes-upper, not to be confused in any way with the dual holes lower. At the same time the Lithic can also be read as the dual openings sensing, since sai can mean both upper and sensing, see chapter 13. The sensing here is by way of smell, which is from sai-'m-ai-lai, sensing-him-that is-floating/flying.

Malay najan is a star. It is presenting (7) an orifice (9) through which fire (sha or ja) is showing (na) (13). The flaming (-jan) of the upper fires which were supposed to exist above the stone firmament apparently shone down through holes in the night sky, the moon and stars, which our primitive forebears attempted to relate to the orifices of the human body. Quite often there is a surfeit of Lithic meanings available, so often in fact that it suggests a double analysis was taken as confirmation of the appropriateness of the phoneme string, when language was largely a matter of composing as you go. It also suggests the Lithic meanings of the phonemes, as they spread by means of metaphors and gulls, became so meaning rich as to present a conundrum in interpretation. It may seem madness to us today but that is how they thought; and the way our words were originally put together is the evidence for it. In a few hundred thousand years there is no reason to suppose we will not appear just as silly and even incomprehensible to our successors. The mind is busy weaving its spells without intermission.

The tenable-tendency group of words which Partridge has assembled – which includes a few surprising plums like continue, impertinent, retinue, tenet, tenacity, tenant, abstinence, continent (noun and adjective both), detention, entertainment, maintenance, pretend, tenuous, hypotenuse, tonic, thin and dance – is one of Partridge's largest groups in which he has collected 205 words. It needs special attention since the original Lithic derivation of any one should probably apply to them all. The single examples explained in the twelve chapters of this book, which are dedicated to phonemic meanings, stand in for

Chapter 10 Na

sometimes hundreds more, some identified and some not. Partridge's tendency sub group of 124 words is epitomised by the Latin tendere to stretch out. Here, it would appear, are no sex oriented T-rays to do the stretching out since there is no trace of an r, relict of a ray, in any of them. It is for this reason they come rather late in this chapter. It had not immediately struck home that the initial tai could be carrying the original meaning of giving birth, since it has been for the most part taken over for the much more usually useful meaning of to become. Tai'n-dai-are, giving birth-does-verbal marker is a fair dumb crambo for the stretching out of the birth canal our forebears all so readily thought about.

Latin tendere to stretch out is from the same Lithic elements tai-nai as tenere to hold, but with different senses. Tenere is from tai-nai-are, the vagina orgasmic-verbal marker. Tarzan apparently felt himself grasped, seized or held. Mrs Grundy will not like it. But the two basic meanings from the same two elements are hard to explain in any other way. Stretching out and grasping together apparently suggest nothing at all to conventional etymologists. But then they have no Lithic, and their words are all supposedly randomly formed, except those that are echoic (when a Lithic plan suddenly obtains).

Partridge's nimble group of eighteen English words plus 97 foreign and former forms includes a fair spread of words akin: nimmer (thief), numb, nomad, nemesis, number, numismatist, and numerous, and they are all, according to Partridge, derived from the three base meanings of na displayed in the Old English nomme meaning numb and Old English niman to grasp, seize or take, and Greek nemein to distribute or spread. The Lithic easily deals with grasping, nau-mai, orgasmic-[when]mating, when convulsive constrictions of the vagina occur, grasping the penis. It is not polite, it is bawdy; but it is a Stone Age idiom long before Mrs Grundy. Nor is it fanciful. That is exactly the way we thought in those days long ago. That is where we come from, and it is quite important we understand it if we are ever to master how we come to think the way we do today. Hundreds of thousands of years of gradual civilisation have modified the original vulgarities by means of metaphor on metaphor, but the atavistic traces remain like flies in amber, concealed in the lexicon, learned and preserved and understood by everyone who learns to speak but today only in the subconscious mind, that submerged part of the mental iceberg which informs our thinking still, although at one remove from consciousness. The subconscious forms part of our thinking all the time, it is the aboriginal dream time and our dream world that we enter when we dream, where ideas flow freely in an uncontrolled stream without strict logical control, largely in pictures with meanings implicit, and usually without expression in words, the way we think when awake. When any words do intrude they usually have seminal significance (like Orson's "Rosebud"). Our dream world closely resembles the waking world of our forebears before they learned to speak, and thus learned to order thinking and allow the development of phonemic structure and reasoning to monitor the flow of thought; instead of just having to watch the world go by (along with the inner world of the mind as well), unable to put it into order.

The UNconscious, on the other hand, as opposed to the merely SUBconscious, is wholly unconscious, inaccessible directly or indirectly to the mind (anyway in normal states, ignoring the claims of yogis and mystics in trances, etc). It is thus quite unlike the subconscious, which can be summoned on occasion to give evidence, and may sometimes prompt the conscious mind uninvited from the wings. We can not control the promptings of the subconscious mind. We can only deal with the consequences when they emerge into consciousness. Meanwhile we do not think about the <u>unconscious</u> or with it at all. It is not part of the mind. It is involved with the autonomic system looking after the housekeeping

Chapter 10 Na

jobs like keeping breathing going, regulating the beating of the heart, recording the protocols for interpreting the raw input to the eyes and ears, for reporting pains and other sensations, and operating the functions of all the other organs of the body, the digestion etc. It is simply the biological control room and has nothing to do with thinking other than the routine maintenance of the physical brain. It is located in the basement nervous system and ground floor of the brain, while our conscious mind lives and appears to operate from the cortex in the attic. Biology and psychology have so far failed to distinguish adequately between the autonomic system and the mind, virtually denying the mind any independent role and even making it a metaphysical figment – the ghost in the machine of the 1940s. We should not be afaid of describing the mind as meta-physical – since it is only a virtual body, really just the collective term for our thinking, our mental activities, not an organ like the brain, which is a physical phenomenon. The mind is shorthand for the activity of the brain, the use to which the brain is put, namely our thinking.

For all that biology about the brain, the discovery of Lithic is a poison. You can play mental cats cradles for ever, but the message of this book is that linguistics is a subject matter sui generis, for study for its own sake, without any remit to sort out the scientific mess of present day biology and psychology: but just for the world-historical insights into how we have developed our cultures, our basic thinking habits.

It is fun for all. When it comes to spreading and distributing, from the Greek nemein, from the Lithic elements nai-mai-en, ejaculating, we can perhaps relate the meaning of Onanism, from Onan (a back formation) the eponymous ancient, who "spread his seed upon the ground" – actually a pollen job, the scribe responsible for this part of the Bible simply had it all wrong, they were all ignorant in those days since there had been no gynecologists meriting the name in the Stone Age. Au-na-na'n, everywhere-na-na-ing, spraying his pollen around everywhere, in place of channeling it properly to the next generation - an extravagance indeed, like a banana (with up to a hundred fleshy protrusions together in a bunch, the bunch hangs down but the fruits stick up, just like the male organ. Well they thought so anyway). The Greeks may well have also taken into account the meaning of the extensive vowel aaa, which has also been used for going (extending your position from your point of origin) in the Latin, as well as spreading and even a spread of time, for Greeks an aeon. Lithic allows both these meanings, the aaa and the na, to present themselves as contributions for the adoption of word structure. Nomme, however, meaning numb in Greek, is the most interesting since it comes from nau-mai and surely means sensation-dead. (Orgasm is the acme of sensation and would have been used metaphorically for that sense). Numbness implies sensation has been suppressed (mai), or even killed off.(mai again). The bai was tacked on later to show it was referring to the flesh in general, to distinguish it from the other more specific meanings of na and ma, before getting reduced again to a final -b.

A further meaning of Lithic na-mai is in the English name, which has nothing to do with lack of sensation, penis-grasping or spreading pollen. It is a very widespread idiom occurring in Old English as namian to name and Old English, Old Frisian and Old Saxon nama a name, Lithic showing-the meaning, in this case a symbol or symbolising. The Old Saxon is identical to Malay nama as well as, closer to home, akin to Hindi naam, Old High German and Gothic namo, Dutch naam, Albanian emen (the same phonemes in reverse order, a metathesis which underlines the independence of the two elements which can be read in either order, as well as the Independence of mind of the Albanians (who have not always been free), Latin nomen, Greek onoma, Sanskrit neman, Tokharian A nom (slovening the -ma like the French nom, which is heavily nasalised), and finally Tokharian

Chapter 10 Na

B nem. (These major metatheses are an argument for original Lithic phonemic meanings on their own). These are all Indo-European family languages. But there is also Lapp namma, Finnish nime, Turkish nam again, and Old Persian emmen like the Albanian, with (slightly garbled, as the Celts know how) Old Irish and Gaelic ainm, Manx ennym. But the Albanian, English, Finnish, Gaelic, Lapp, Malay, Persian and Turkish have no business being at all the same, unless prompted by Lithic meanings subconsciously recovered from their own Lithic language construction. Here are eight coincidences for academia to explain away, all clustered around one word in eight different language families. There is a further group of languages suggesting a name was widely regarded as a symbolisation directly representing the phenomenon symbolised, the person or thing named, and so leaving off the ma, the mental presentation with the nama group. So we have Danish navn, Old Welsh anu, Cornish honua, Armenian anun, and Hungarian – another outrider - nev.

Perhaps we should also look at the Chinese ming zi meaning name, where the zi is merely a noun suffix sometimes appearing to denote agency. Ming, with the two same phonemes as Malay nama, is a statistical surprise. The Chinese idiom of stringing phonemes with minimalist grammatical inflections is close to the original Lithic pattern. It is as if their language congealed early on and never had a Babel revolution like the rest of the world. The result is it is too difficult for anyone but a mandarin (or master, compare Malay mentri or minister) to master, which tends to make the mandarins good at mathematics and the masses somewhat inarticulate. Not being a mandarin it is difficult to guess how ming zi comes by the meaning name. We can see it has the same two phonemes (one nasalised) as the Malay nama – in reverse order like the Albanians and the Old Persians, which is probably insignificant. You have to ask if the Chinese ming can be analysed as from mai-nai in Lithic elements. If it can, then ming is equivalent to nama. This is an example of the symbol as a tripartite concept, as in Appendix A (on the philosophy of language): the symbol, the symbolised and the symbolising mind.

Then the Chinese ren for man (mankind, both sexes, in origin anyway) much like Malay orang (this time the Malay version is the nasalised one and the Chinese not) is from Lithic rai-nai, exhibiting rays, (after taking them in from outside), the rayed species, with brains showing reason, rayed-activity, the intellectual or thinking species. It was supposed ideas were born in the head, kindled like sexual birth, by rays which did the job, coming in from outside. There seemed nothing other prompting them, any more than the boys registered any personal exertion causing their genitalia to rise. Today we live in an electromagnetic soup, indeed we are just micro-croutons in it, but it causes us no particular concern, and we asume we are resonsible for our own ideas.

The name ren or orang claims that mankind is uniquely the rational being, in this case by being the recipient of mental rays lower life forms are incapable of receiving, untuned to reason which nature therefore is piping - well raying - only to us. Not much sense can be made of ren and orang without the recognition they are based on the general belief amongst the ancients that attitudes and their mental correlates in humans result from rays which enter the mind from without, triggering emotional responses. It may have been reassuring, removing any feelings of guilt as receivers of these teasers from outer space over life lived in a violent and confrontational world, red in tooth and claw and hand, (which does the ha-ing, the horrific horrible things as well as the happy pleasurable ones). What was actually happening was probably the rays were prompts from the subconscious, as yet unrecognised other than as part of the other, whence the rays came. Anyone nowadays unprepared to recognise the subconscious which influences their thinking can not possibly accept the Lithic language hypotheses and should put the book down. (They should then go on to re-examine their own personal psychological hangups, and get back with the book or seek help).

So far, we have progressed to meaning 10 in the psychosemantic tree meanings, to show, as far as to explain (17). Birth too (18) was an epiphany. Partridge refers us to fancy where, in Greek, epiphany means to show to, a showing, exhibition or manifestation, the -phany clearly from pahei-nai, the penis-presenting. Similarly we have Noel meaning Christmas, where Nau-El is Birth-of El or the Lord, exactly as the angel did say (to spell it out: "born is the king of Israel", well the Lord of the warriors of the Lord). Christ's -mas, meanwhile, is from ma-sai, plant-seed or life, conception rather than birth. In Ancient Egypt life was supposed to begin at conception, a belief inherited by the Pope along with the Pharaoh's hat, putting the Catholic church in the Pharaoh's debt and in a fix over abortions. The rest of us still think in terms of birth. Nai can mean the actual birth (18), as an epiphany (French née). The language was the science of the day. Native is from the Latin nasci, from nai-sai-kai, to be born, in Lithic presenting-life-making. Compare sex, from sai-kai-sai, action-making-life, which is a pun from the polysemy of the phoneme sa.

The semantics of sex and six can be related if you know five in Indo European refers to the points of the body. Panch for five in Hindi, is from the Lithic pa-en-khai, the shoots or points-of-the body. The Punjab is thus from panch awab, the five rivers, with awab from awa-bai, water-moving, not unlike the Australian aboriginal billabong for an ox-bow lake, a bai-lai-bunged, travelling liquid, a river, blocked up.

It is clear when called upon to think of a sixth point of the body to add to the head and four limbs to make six, our primitive forebears came up with their favourite, the rather minor male member; and maybe for a seventh, while in the area, the twin life-bits, sai-bain, (bauah the testicles in both Malay and Sumerian), the seed containers, switching from the penis to the two testicles, the dual fruit, simply because there were two of them to add to the five main protrusions in order to make seven. With eight the game was going to need an addition of three to the main points; or else a fresh start; and although eight has not been analysed in these terms before it would seem sensible to count in not just first the penis and then instead the two testicles in order to keep adding just one at a time; but now both penis and testicles are needed together to make eight. That provides a very convincing triad, given the male genitalia is already introduced piecemeal, to add to the five main points of the body in order to give a total of eight after seven. So what can now be made from octo? The Lithic original phonemes seem to be au-kai-tao, which can be read as that one/all-of the body-become: it is counting all the bits in together, whether the main points or the other, making eight. Ten is from tai-nai, the completing - of the counting, because it meant the counting of both hands, not the sum of the sum gone by but the sum of all the fingers, the end of the exercise. We are left with nine to work out. Nine, nai-na-i, the presenting-not-one; or Latin novem, nau-ai'm, presented all-out-one, or not one of them, which would be one less than the ten, which is the sum of two hands of fingers. Have we cracked it? You have to remember adding was originally finger work. Math was futuristic.

The Latin natus has the past participle -tus ending, like all the other Latin verbs, from the Lithic tau(s), born and thence become, and so the past participle quite precisely, with a substantiating -s ending. Nai, French né, presented, can mean born. The Spanish niño (pronounced ninyo) for child is a nai-nau, a presently ie newly-born. The French just have né from naitre to be born, which can also mean to arise (6), as well as puisné for later born, younger or subordinate, from coming after. A cobra in French is a naja, a riser upper, spun off from the Indo European naka or bare body of Hindi nag and English snake, while the cobra comes from Spanish from the Latin colubra, referring to its locomotion, Lithic kau-lau-bai-rai-a, body-looped-going-one, but bai-rai doubling as large, compare Hindi barra big. Snakes coil along, and a king cobra is supposed to be able to overtake a horse, probably an exaggeration, but it will certainly catch up with you if it wants to. It stands a good five feet tall with a vicious temperament. It will attack man or beast in its way unprovoked, probably the only snake to do so[2]. Flushing a king cobra you stand still and pray, offering it your shield to attack - if you happen to have one. Partridge derives the Latin natura, nature from the Latin natus, born, but the Egyptian semantic derivation already introduced is to be preferred. The aboriginal Malays' name for themselves is Senoi from Sai-nau-i, First-born-ones or first-present-ones, making their claim to be the original stock – and the present Malays to be the usurpers of the land, a historically fair assessment. Malays retaliate by calling them Sakai, Sa-ka-i, Single-Ka-folk unlike dual Ka folk (one for this world and one for the next), and so animals in effect, without any after life. The insult is understood and resented: the Senoi are not Moslems and wear their foreskins in full, making them the butt for insult.

We have so far used a terminal 'n (11) without comment. Hums tend to be used as fillers: speakers in Indo European languages use mmm while thinking of the next words, and these days in Africa m' is often regarded as semantically him- and the 'n in Indo European languages is similarly thought of as short for -one, an unspecified one because as a hum 'n carries no very obvious meaning at all, making it suitable for those constructions where an itemisation is required without any additional semantic baggage. But then there is the Germanic usage of -en as a verbal marker; and for the Egyptians en or em is of, prefixed or suffixed. In all cases the vowel e is from the dipthong ai, since for all of prehistory there were only the three vowels recognised, a, i and u. As a verbal marker ai'n makes use of the vowel a as an extensive and the i vowel as the diminutive reduplicative to indicate a spin off from the preceding one, so the semantics of –ain or -en is on-going, a spatial change and then and thus a verbal marker.

Another snake is the anaconda which is probably first from the Tamil since it appears in Surinam too, rather than from the Sinhalese, the language of Ceylon (from Kai-lau'n, Land –ocean'of/in). The Island; now Shri Lanka, Holy Island. Shri is Flame-rayed, Spiritually inspired, and so Holy. La'n-ka, Ocean'of-land, Island. The Lithic elements of anaconda are a-na-ka'n-da, that-no-striking-does (2). The anaconda coils round its prey and squeezes the life out of it and eats it whole. It is not poisonous and has no fangs.

The word manual, from Latin manus, a hand, deserves a paragraph or two on its own. Prelinguistic communication will have been by expression when close to, or otherwise entirely by gesture, mostly by hand signals: when hunting, for instance "You creep round to the right" pointing to a hunter and then in the direction he should go - precisely as in the jungle when hunting terrorists today. And another twenty or thirty signals much the same, including in the Stone Age signs for the different species of prey sighted. Terrorists are all of the same species but the number observed is of immediate interest. "Take cover and prepare to engage" must surely have been the handiest, and probably still is. The idea we had no ideas before we spoke is by now rendered absurd. How then could we have formed the concepts which issued in speech? African bushmen have hand signals for every species of prey, which they can use when hunting; as well as directional hand signals, even more essential when the quarry is an animal rather than a terrorist because of their more sensitive hearing. A dog, a horse and even a cow has ideas but they are formed from their experience, which does not include symbolisation: they are simply reminded of past experience by envisaging similarities with what they see (or smell, or feel). Their feelings

Chapter 10 Na

are largely to do with feeding, sex and predation. In origin we are no different. That is an unfortuate concomitant of Darwinism, I am afraid.

The Latin hand might therefore be from Lithic ma-na-u, mind-show-er, what shows the meaning, strung the other way about: meaning-present-one. In Lugandan, the principal tribal language of Uganda in central Africa, which nobody should think has any very close relationship with Latin, the hand is mukono, which I suggest comes from the Lithic mau-kau-nau, (in nice agreement), the meant-made-presented. I suggest this is because in Lugandan also 'mean' is mukodo, thinking-made-become, or mu budde, thinking-fleshed out-become, or bwe bumu, from bau-ai-bu-mu, becoming-fleshed out/in being-going-currently-minded; and mind is omutima, from au-mu-tai-ma, that one-mentality-become-solid [ie as an entity]; and to change one's mind is mutwe, from mu-tau-ai, mentality-become-away. Hands were prized as signallers. Of course they were the active agents for every kind of activity as well. But if you can not speak you value the ability of gesturing to communicate the highest, because at human level you need to relate to your peers and you are already beginning to build up claustrophobic tension. So the hand is probably named for its communicative potential, next to facial expression which is only available at short range, and is less specific anyway. Hand signals are half way to language. After all they are already symbolic. But compared with the phonemic strings which can be uttered, or the squiggling available to script, bodily gesturing of every kind is an impoverished medium – which is no doubt why human mentality followed up by spilling over into language, and then into script. But ha-n-dai is also does the pleasuring.

The hums (mm and nn) can be exchanged. Partridge: "The Old French mappa is dissimulated first in Old French nappe and then nape, leading to English napery and the diminutive napkin". This is the terminal 'n, (11), 'n-that-cover-makes'n, simply a coverlet, the one that covers . The Middle English nape is the flat part of the neck, according to Partridge akin to a napkin. But the neck is not flat, it is the na-pai, the protruding (6) piece of the spine between the shoulder blades, much like the tail the other end of it (pai-nais) or even the stalk carrying the fruit, the Ka-puti or caput (Latin). An apron covers the body, nowadays to protect clothes from splashes in the kitchen. It comes from a misperception of a napron, 'n-a-pa-rai-un, one-that-cover-verbal-one, as an apron, one that covers, just a covering.

Having dealt with nib and nab, both with meaning (6) protruberance, originating in male arousal, nip (whence nibble) and nap now refer to the feminine aspect of arousal, or perhaps even to both aspects together. Malay comes to mind. Ketam bersepit is a pincered crab. The pincered is from bersipit (binary-action-pieces-two) while crab (kai-tam, is hardened-become in Lithic. The crab is hardened all over, and crab in English is similarly kara-bai, skull-body). In abusive slang ketam bersepit is a Sikh, widely if unfairly regarded as the Shylock of the Far East. Also bersepit can be read as hairy as well with a bit of poetic licence, and Sikhs are not supposed to cut their hair (or drop their pants in public). Malays and Chinese can enjoy that calumny together. They are also noticeably less hairy. The ber- in Malay is also much like the be- in besotted or benighted in English. A nip is from nai-pai, protruberant pieces. A nap is a short sleep, a momentary pai or covering (of the eyes) just as a nip is a short pinch, where pinch in turn is from pai'n-kara, to make with the protruberances, and the original (climactic) nai is short, in fact ephemeral, also. Nowadays we say rather more tastefully instead in the wink of an eye. In Norwegian we have nippe, to take a nap, a snap, a quick closure. The nap of cloth, or of the earth, is its protruberances on the surface, or in the Dutch even a tuft of wool. Probably conclusive is the Old English ahneopan to pluck off, with Lithic elements a-khai-nai-u-pa'n, away-

Chapter 10 Na

cut-protruding-ones-[of/from the]surface-ing, a mouth-ful and head-ful of Lithic semantic beads in a string.

The ankh is a symbol from Ancient Egypt otherwise known as the ansate cross with a history of mystery. It is still worn as a talisman or good luck charm by silly folk. It is roughly an egg sitting on a T. It is certanly old and hard to decipher. Moreover like many amulets it can be read in more than one way, which was taken to indicate magic power. Perhaps you can look at that as representing for the ancients a kind of assurance that they had it correctly, much like the assurance that today you get when filling in a crossword puzzle when the letters for words across match up with those you want for a word down. Or like a corroboratory piece of evidence for a scientific theory. We should probably think of it in terms of seven or eight thousand years before the present. That is only 5000 or 6000 BC. The hieroglyphs are by no means fully understood. You would never think it, from Sir Wallis Budge's phenomenal hieroglyphic dictionary with more than a thousand pages of scrupulously cut glyphs at the cutting edge of printing technology when it was published in 1921, seven years before the first edition of the Oxford English Dictionary was completed.

The ankh is believed to have mystical meaning, chiefly because nobody to date has understood what it really means. It is an attribute of the Pharaohs. Aa-en-ka(h)i is Eternity-of-the ka, where the Ka was the male soul, the hard structure, symbolised by the skeleton, of the otherwise female body, and the driving force, the male life principle. It was sometimes translated when addressed to the name of the Pharaoh as 'Live for Ever' or 'Living for Ever', 'Eternal Life'. Pharaohs expected to be gods when they died, with a single omnipotent Ka. The common Ka came in two parts, one for this world and one for the next. The second barrel only did for the Dua Taun, the Second World, (in accademic speak just the duat) which was dark and dull, and you could be pecked or even eaten by bogeys if you had done bad things. Equipped with the Ka for eternity you were immortal. The Ankh glyph thus means Eternal Life. Pharaohs claimed to be sons of the immortal gods, ascending into Heaven when they died. Their titles often ending in -meses or -mose (Ra-meses, Thut-mose) which named the god they supposed had planted their seed of life (mai-sai or mau-sai). Ra was the rumbustious sun god while Thut, or Tahuti, was a Know-all from an original Tahu-tau, now Tutu. The usual symbol, the hieroglyph for the Ankh, comprises three parts: the egg on top with an upright on which it rests, with a horizontal stroke cut across, perhaps giving it a platform to sit on. With a little bit of slovening it could mean a-oon-a-khai in Lithic, that-vulva-that-kindled, which could account for the egg shaped bit on top: The Mother and Source. One even wonders if the Egyptians had Americanised their pronunciation of the oo so that it sounded more like an aa, as with American Mom pronounced Maaaam. But then what is the Tau doing underneath? Is it perhaps the eternal seat or Au-Siti, Our Lady, Isis, the symbol of the eternal feminine Sai-ti, the Life-feminine source, making the whole the Goddess's vagina, as a Source of inspiration for contemplative souls? Perhaps! But the Lithic might be a'n-a-khai, one-that-begotten, son. The Pharaohs Akhenaton and his son (after conversión to Amun again) Tutankhamun, really A-khai-en Aton, That-begotten-of the Aton (the sun as eternal birth canal birthing light into the world each day), and Tutu-anakh-Amun, The All knowing-Son-of Amun (Amun Ra, the sun, literally the Ever loving Eye). In Malay anak means son/daughter, from an-a-kai, one-that-begotten/made. So either they learned from the Ancient Egyptians or else their Lithic thinking found the same meaning string from the same Lithic semantic elements. On this interpretation putting an ankh in a Pharaoh's name signifies son of, and there are clear cases, like Tutu-anak-amun above.

Chapter 10 Na

The symbol, however can also be read in a different phonetic metaphor as Na-tau – the oval on top is the Na and the T underneath is -tau, reminiscent of the flag blown out horizontally by the wind, na-tu-ra or na-tau-rai, show-tau-ray or showing the natural draw or pull, perceived as a ray. The Egyptian ray scheme was hostile to practical aerodynamics, which was consequently not a strong suit in Egyptian understanding. If Tahu-tau, Know-all in Egyptian, with tahu also to know in Malay, was Thoth's or Tahuti's or Tahu-tahei's strong suit, na-tau, show-all makes a universal symbol for natural science. Tau'n is Egyptian for the universe, as we can devise from their symbolisation of Heaven, Egyptologist-speak Pet, but actually Pai-Taun, Roof of the Universe. The glyph is a square for a surface or roof, bird's eye view, followed by a half circle sitting on its flat side for the world with its over-arching sky, cut in two because the other half of the circle, the Dua taun, the second semicircle or world underneath was the world of the night and of the dead. The Greeks transposed their Pai to a view in elevation, their Pi with two plain supporters and a wavey surface or roof seen side on to show that that is the bit to be taken on board. The half circle, believed by the academic Egyptologists to be a bun, is the waking world of the living, a penny covered with the bowl we call the sky. The underside of the penny was for the Egyptian mind the Duat (in Egyptologist speak), in reality the Dua Taun, the Second World of the souls of the dead, around which the dark sun circled during the night before reappearing gloriously reborn to the world of light at dawn (which means the birth, the tau-ing or dawning). Why birth and universe together? Tau is the birth canal (ta = cut or slit, oo = round hole, and the birth canal is both in turn) and so birth and so becoming, and so ta-oo is the becomings-all (oo the completive vowel, chapter 14), and so the universe conceived as the totality of what happens as opposed to the totality of all locations in our own idiom. It all fits together; but you do need a bit of Lithic to start you off. Na-Tau is Lithic Presenting (6)-Totality, The Tau (and even the Torah?) Or else and as well Na (17)-Tau is Explicating-the All, all you need to know on earth.

The Ankh is first of all eternal life, (literally aa'n, ongoing, kai, live, with ka), immortality, and then the son (of God), as well as the Goddess's vulva as fertile life source, Source of Life of the World, God the Everlasting Mother, the Aton. The Ankh is thus a dialectical trinity, The Mother, The Son and Immortality or The Holy Ghost: and that is all you need to know on earth. Did Jesus learn anything from Egypt?

It is time to end this overlong chapter on Na, time to nail the chapter down and move on. Nail (6) is from the Germanic nagel, the g commuting to y and then to i quite easily. Nai-kai-lai is from protruding-making-linked, which is germane. Or else it is from it is simply 'n-a-ge-lai, one-that-makes-linked, a jointure. Or both!

NOTES

1. See Budge's Egyptian Hieroglyphic Dictionary, Dover 1978 Edition, Vol 1, page 534, column b, for ichneumon.

2. Meeting a roused King cobra, erect and five feet high in a Malayan rubber plantation, my leading scout raised his carbine to plaster it; but I forbade it (in a very low voice). He would probably have shot its comb, and none of us could run as fast as a horse. It was also a magnificent creature. A good five minutes of Her Majesty's time was wasted while the brute debated action and decided upon withdrawal, slipping away off the track. It was worth every minute, although Her Majesty herself, I regret, got no benefit whatever.

CHAPTER 11

PA: THINNED BA: SKIN, PIECE, PENIS, PI AND PIE.

The root meaning of Ba (chapter 3), from the fleshy lips which come together to articulate it, was flesh – a sort of metaphorical echoism. We are asked to believe our hominid forebears, when they were learning to speak, perhaps some six hundred thousand years ago, thought of that as the natural meaning of the sound they were making, in the absence of anything else - there are really no things that go bump in the night, and not no more in the day neither. Then we must believe as well that their perception has been passed down from generation to generation for four or five times as many generations as hundreds of years, or between two and three million generations: a game of Chinese whispers all through twenty to thirty fair sized football crowds. But you must remember each individual had a lifetime to get the idea across to his neighbours, and there were a lot of them all at it together in each generation; so that it was actually a fairly thick rope for the transmission. Not only that, but the perceptions will have been reinforced because they were incorporated in the construction of the languages people were speaking, so that the meanings of these basic phonemic elements presented themselves in the subconscious minds of every speaker while their conscious minds picked up the language. That is the clever perception, and the clincher. Those anyway are the Lithic hypotheses, based not on surmise but under the compulsion of the linguistic evidence. We learn our language, and at the same time pick up the basic phonemic meanings behind it unawares. That is the subconscious mind for you. It is certainly a surprise, but there seems to be sufficient evidence that that is what happened. It makes better sense than the evolutionists who have no history and posit a blind process for language development as if it were a physical process, which clearly it is not. It is a novelty already to posit a first language composed of simple phonemes, as we learned to utter them, (more or less the same as our letters of the alphabet today), with the inherent meanings we picked for them, which later went to make up the meanings of our words when we got around to learning them as simples, instead of sentences in the phonemic language, which is what they actually were. That is how our words were originally composed, when we first learned to speak, using the consonants to string concepts into words with complex meanings. Before speech that had been impossible. You might have conveyed a meaning by hand signals, grimaces, the point of your toe, or whatever else, but only one at a time, and nothing abstract either; and that was your own thinking too. Speaking made a new world of the mind. It conjured it. The important perception is these consonants must have been given meanings of their own, which now are unrecognized. We have to dig them up again by way of working out what our hairy forebears would have taken to be their natural meanings as they learned to articulate them. It will have taken them a time. Shall we suggest twenty generations to get much of a vocabulary up and running? There are plenty to spare. I like to think the swirls and cup hollows cut in rocks, before anything else in the Stone Age, represent the nausea and dizziness our hominid forebears were trying to register, as they struggled with themselves, working with their brains to get their minds to register sequential thinking, in place of picture thinking where your mind could travel any whichway. It must have been a horrendous claustrophobic struggle, enough to drive the Einsteins of the day quite mad.

Chapter 11 Pa

The psychosemantic tree for Pa is on page 216. Pah! (1) like Bah! indicates dislike and contempt - it is vehement dislike. Pooh! means much the same. That is how it has come to indicate a nasty smell. The expulsion of breath is an expulsion of the smell. The unvoiced expulsion of breath from between the lips is a puff. "Pff!" can be added to the other expletives, and Pish! is out of the same stable. It is sometimes thought to derive from piss, but the derivation probably went the other way around. They are all expressions of spitting out (and so of rejection) – a Stone Age gesture when something edible turned out to taste nasty or even poisonous. To spit, from ish-pai-ti, is to issue from between the pai, here the lips. But of course it is echoic too. Ish meant issue amongst other things, see chapter 13. To piss is similarly to issue, in this case from the P (16). (Try it sideways).

We will discover precisely why our forebears thought of pee for the boys' genitalia in this chapter, and why boys still think the same today, hundreds of thousands of years later. The colour sepia (Spanish) comes from the cuttle-fish which when pursued by a predator emits a cloud of fluid of that colour as a bitter smokescreen behind which to jet to safety. The cuttle-fish was probably named sepia by some ancient jolly Spanish jack tar quite possibly of Basque extraction: Si-pia, Brer-pisser, with the colour as a gull from the conduct of the fish[1]. If it is not Brer-pisser then it is just plain pisser, with the Se- signifying the action (in this case one of issuance, another semantic content of the sibilant). Perhaps equally ancient is the origin of the cuttle which is from the Old English cudele, akin to cod which is the pouch of a fishing net, bag shaped, and so the fish caught in it, as well as the scrotum, another bag of interest to our forebears, and by confusion the testicles it contains, so that as a plural cods it has been used for the testicles. The sepia is a pouch (15) shaped fish. A pouch is a swollen shape, and is from the Lithic phonemes pa-u-khai, surface-o-shaped. The urethra had evidently been traced to the bladder, capable of filling and blowing up. Cuttle is from ka-tai-lai in Lithic elements, shape-becoming-loopy/inflated. The Lithic elements are not of course in English. They are in Lithic, and can not be directly translated into English, or indeed into any current language. When writing looped or looping in English, what it is intended was conveyed in the Stone Age was partaking of the instinct of water which when completely run down into the ocean exhibited its fuller character, the straight skyline at sea which turned into a circular line when sufficiently far from shore. What is being preached are the original semantics derived from the original phonetics, which are now indigenous in language.

Ka-ta-lai, ka-born-lyey is body-born/become-loose/loopy, an alternative representation, better if you know your Lithic. The cod started out as a pouch (of a fishing net, and the Lithic elements cod came from were ka-u-da, joined-Os-become; and the cuttlefish has the shape of a little pouch – containing sepia dye – and back in the Stone Age pouches were also pa-u-khai, skin-what-fashioned, made out of skin (5), as well as pouch shaped. Bag at the same time, from ba-kai, simply means belly shaped, the belly being from ba-i-lai, the flesh which sags, just as liquids sag downhill. It could be argued you sag when you lie down, but at the same time you straighten out in a line and lie low, all of which render you lai. Certainly when you stand you become upright (stand is from sa-tai'n-dai, up-becoming-does). The syntax may seem strange to us today. To examine the Lithic semantics more deeply, sa is up or upwards, tai is coming into being, or come into being or become. The 'n is a filler of uncertain significance, perhaps "of" or "pertaining" or a kind of verbal marker before verbs were generally distinguished. The final da or dai shortened to d is out of the same box as tai, to be about, to be becoming or be doing. When you are static you are merely upright, whence it follows you are staying still and not loping off. The cod is a fish which defies etymology, but as a large shoaling species it is, or in old

214

Chapter 11 Pa

days was, harvested by the bulging bag full; fishermen thinking the cod made a full bag, caught in a pouch net. Predators go for the easy option. That is why the cod has been fished near to extinction, prices falling and then rising.

Pa (2), as the thinned diminutive of Ba, suggested the skin (5) (on the outside of the flesh, whence the Latin pellis, from pai-i-lai, surface-which-looping or enclosing), or a diminutive piece of flesh, like a spike or sprout (6) or a leaf or petal (petal from Lithic pa-i-ta-lai, a sprout-which-has become-flat). The small piece of flesh, a pipe, which attracted most attention in those far off days was the penis (15) – much like today, in fact. The name came indirectly from the cheeping of game bird chicks, which sounded as if they were saying pi-pi (3); because if you wanted to start off your fine vowelisation with a consonant, in the modern manner of the day, you started it with a p. Of course that was just a whimsy. The sound of the quail chick was started with a p because it starts its notes sharply. It actually produces a dual note like eee-eee, and not a howl like an owl. So pipi was the quail chick in Ancient Egyptian – on the echoic principle. Because Pa starts sharply it is used also for a sharp sound like a tapping sound, and so a tappet and a patter (3). A tap has a further semantic construction: ta-pai is an orifice-covered or the tapped barrel stopped up - with a spigot. The earliest tap was probably invented for getting licquor out of a barrel and the spigot stopped it up. It was a wooden piece. Today we quite like peep-peep or even cheep-cheep for the game bird's pipi, which is perhaps over egging it a bit. The Ancient Egyptians studied quail chicks and liked pi-pi. They were probably rearing them for the table. The quail chick always chirps twice - never a single peep. It says "pi-pi", "pi-pi". As a matter of fact all ground-nesting game bird chicks do the same. Now for the Ancient Egyptians (and all the other ancients we know of as well) the vowel u was the dual vowel. (The reasoning behind this, such as it was, is in chapter 14 on vowels). They believed every species had an instinctive knowledge of some special characteristic which went with the species, and gave their many gods animal heads to point up their identifications. The quail chick's specialty was to be wed to duality. Since the Egyptians had turned their three vowels aaa, eee, and ooo (e and o were dipthongs which came later, from ai and au respectively) into a primitive dialectic, in which ooo (or u) indicated a duality, they replaced the echoic pipi with pu.

The dual pi was a pu; and since pa in Egyptian meant "the", "pu" - with only a little imaginative elision – could be read as p'-u, "the u"(8). Accordingly a charming hieroglyph of a quail chick was used for the vowel sound u. It suffered like all hieroglyphs from one big disadvantage: it was far too complex and took far too long to draw for a single simple symbol where sentences were to be recorded, especially if you were having to cut it into rock. But the Egyptians had far more time on their hands than we do, and they liked the artistry that went into their script and the punning that had gone into the shaping of it. You must remember too that recording the thinking was at the leading edge of technology when we were learning to do it. Nothing appeared extravagant. We can note in passing the hieroglyph of the quail chick is supposed to be wa by the academic Egyptologists today, who have no Lithic – as if the chick barked like a dog. But as all syllables are supposedly randomly selected throughout the world it presents no problems for them: the quail chick's use needs no justification: they presume a priest of Amun had a sketch of a quail chick the others thought neat; so they popped it in at u, presumably as that was where they happened to have got to. But we live in a much more closely textured world than that.

Then came the jolly herdsman a-playing on his pan-pipes (7), making piping noises - the lazy puss, instead of hunting - just like the quail chick. His pipes were called quail

215

Chapter 11 Pa

THE PSYCHOSEMANTIC TREE FOR PA

The Phonetic Tree

Wa – Va – Ba – Pa – Ba – Va – Wa

The Semantic Tree

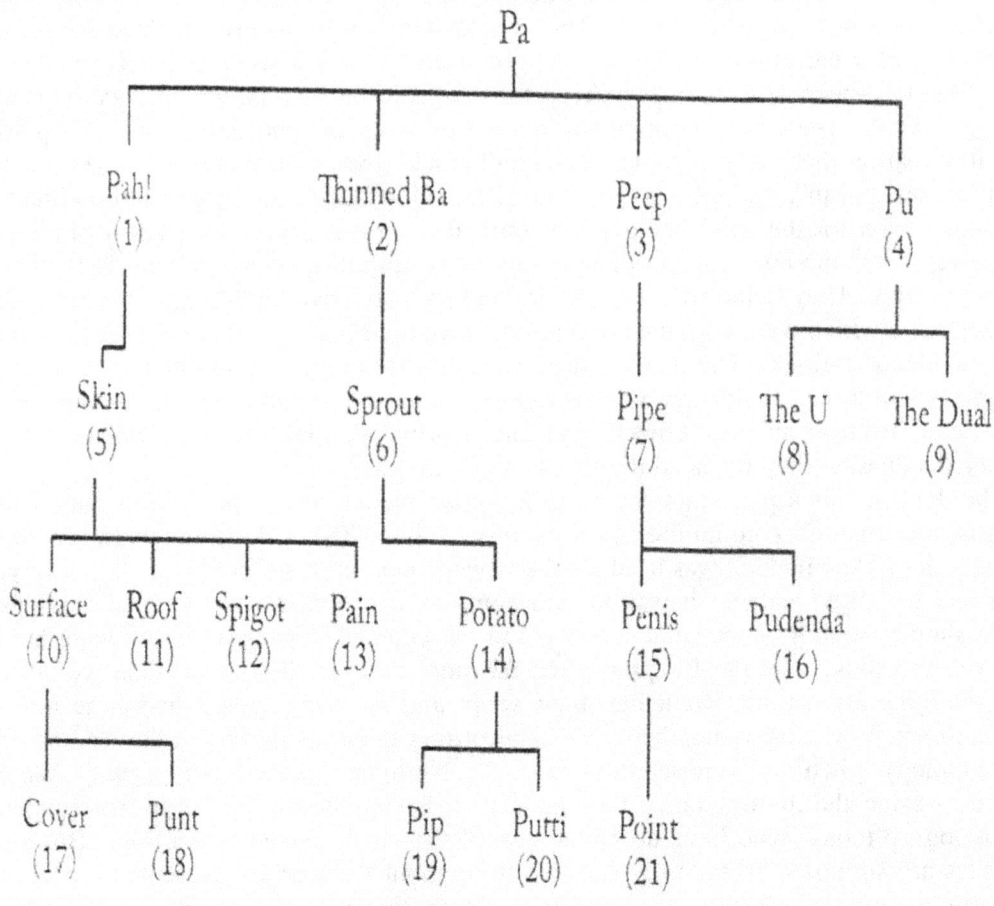

chicks, "pipi". Notice his piping had no duality; there were a number of pipes bound together and blown in turn. The pipi vowelisation suited them quite well as the i vowel was the diminutive-reduplicative and the u vowel meant the inclusive and so all of them as well as just two (chapter 14). Otherwise our drainpipes and the pipes we used at one time to smoke might have been called poops instead of pipes since our pipes are learned from the Egyptians through Greek.

The penis (16), a single pipe, one which nai, presents - it stands upright when engorged (rayed) and doing the business (see chapter 10 for Na, to push forward and present). It does not play tunes like the pan-pipes, any more than the gull wing sings. A penis can thus be described as a double gull job (meanings derived by metaphor, see note 1) since from the quail chicks' pipi the pan-pipe is gulled because of the similarity of the sounds each makes, and then the pan-pipes are gulled, again because of their similarity in shape to the choke or pipelet on the male urethra. The two perceptions which have largely shaped language are thus both paradigmatically represented in chief by the penis: first echoism and secondly metaphor based on shape. Echoism was the easiest to understand, it pushed itself into consciousness, as it still does today. Shape was perhaps the most important - it has been described as the tyranny of the eye - since it packed an additional punch: shape was either static (remanent) or mobile (elastic). The inert bits of the world like rocks and even rivers stayed very much the same, and the vegetable kingdom changed only very slowly and never got up and ran; growth after all is a slow and almost imperceptible process so leaves and fruit burgeon and the plant gets bigger and bigger but only slowly and always controlled by the due seasons. But animals move about all the time and their limbs come into play in any number of different and striking ways, and their most astonishing trick of all is they can change shape - in part - enlarging (fruiting) and shrinking before your very eyes.

This ability admittedly is confined to the genitalia which also show every sign of being in many ways at the core of the life form of every phenotype. The males can fruit and unfruit time after time, putting the strawberry to shame[2]. The Malay for fruit is buah and it is also used for the two testicles, as well as for a bobbin, a little bob, a plural ba, originally a pendant bunch as with a plumb bob, perhaps at first a pair as with bub, and then only one needed for taking soundings. It is only a guess but it may well be the testicles were regarded as the receptors of the energising feminine rays. They are egg shaped like eyes, after all, which were supposed to receive the returning rays they had sent out, bearing pictures of the world outside back irradiated onto the iris (the rayed). Hominids must surely have noticed if they removed the testicles, or when they were undeveloped before puberty the feminine rays were ineffective. Egyptian for the male genitalia is ba, bits of flesh, of which the dual form is bu. Comically the Ba was the feminine part of a man, which was no doubt why his ba, his genitalia, so desperately sought the female all the time and the female in turn packed such a powerful pull on them.

Abu for father appears to be using the A as a long Aaa, an extension, outgoing or outcome of his testicles, and so meaning he with the source testicles, the dual fruiting bodies. The females meanwhile can open up from the merest slit to round out and accommodate the male organ and then even the head of the baby at birth as well, reverting to standard slit thereafter. It may not be teatime talk, but our hominid forebears had no teatimes - they never took tea - and an appetite for understanding at almost any cost, as ideas piled up in their heads. Much of language will have built around the hearth, where the encumbered matrons had stayed all day, along with the unencumbered girls when they were not out with their digging sticks grubbing up tucker for the evening meal.

Chapter 11 Pa

Indeed it is arguable what triggered language was the women staying in the heat of the hearth all day working up an interest in pulling the boys when they got back to the hearth with the meat. How did they work it? They made themselves available. More curiously, how was the biter bit? The ancients reckoned once the boys' muzzle covers had been withdrawn by the female rays pulling out and plumping up the acorn nestling within, it sent out its own retaliatory rays rounding out the girls and attracting them towards their sexual nemesis. Simple really.

Pa, as a thinned (actually unvoiced, which makes a finer note, voicing is comparatively gravelly) version of Ba, is taken to mean a thinned diminutive of flesh, a shoot or sprout (6), hijacked by the quail chick (3) above, echoism taking precedence over mere metaphor (which requires reflection). The quail chick, all unawares, identified one small protruberance of the animal (human) form, because it was quite like a pan pipe, which in turn was called a chick because its notes were similar. That is the way metaphor works. The Pan pipe picked up an echoic icon, followed by the penis with a shape similarity, and so a pee from a peep, although the penis never peeps. But the limbs in turn are diminished protruberances (6) of the corpus, which in turn is the core (ka) of the limbs. The haunches, like the hams are ha-u-en-khai, ecstacy-twins-of-the body. They are also split into two burgeons, bottoms with bilateral symmetry. The feet, compared with the whole body, are thinned diminutives as in Latin pes foot, and pous leg in Greek including the haunch. The Latin supinatio means regurgitation, to which we are all liable when supine, especially after dining too well, (Latin supinus Eric Partridge translates as overturned backwards, and the verb supinare as to lay backwards, no reasons given). The Lithic can be read as su, altogether upwards, pai, limbs, and nau presented, pushed upwards or protruding, much as the quail chick's second derivative does in fact, or like a playful puppy or kitten on its back with its legs in the air, a perfectly useless posture which comes through in the penumbra of meanings attached to the supine position as passivity in the face of circumstances calling for action. The Romans, who spoke the Latin, were inclined to overeat and drink supine ("with their feet up") on chaises-longues. The pai in this case are the legs, thinned diminutives relative to the main body. We can see much the same semantics in the pupa or chrysalis, with all the limbs, pu (4), pa, covered (10), just like the pod does, paradigmatically with peas in it, the little plumplets (19) covered (10), legumes like the bean, faba in Greek, which some Greeks refused to eat as pahai-ba or testicles.

In Malay the mouse deer is si-pelandok, brer light feet (from the Lithic si-pai-lai-en-tau-kai, brer-feet-lightness-of-become-going), picking its way timidly through the jungle leaving only the lightest of footprints. It is little bigger than a fox terrier, and apart from two top teeth like darning needles which it will use to slash if cornered it is defenceless against predators. Its pai (feet in this case) la'n-do', smoothly do. It is credited with sly cunning, the brer rabbit of the jungle. It slips along slyly. It gets caught and eaten nevertheless by the still slyer aboriginal hunter with snares set in holes in artificial hedges made of undergrowth on the way down to water sometimes half a mile long or more, so Si Pelandok goes through one of the holes and ends up snared and eaten.

The origin of pedestrianism is the Latin pes for foot, from pai-sai, motion pieces (6). The meanings of the sibilant phoneme (ish) are in chapter 13. With pes the s could just be the Latin substantial (noun) marker. In Malay again si puti is brer snailshell. Kuala Lumpur the Malayan capital is on the Sungei Siput or River Snail. A shell is a tough one, but it apparently started out a bivalve seashell, and the Lithic si-khai-lai-lai, brer-cut-looped-linked, that is to say with two sides containing the shellfish, hinged at the bottom. Compare the conch, from ka-un-khai, body-dual-hardened. But in the Pacific the conch is

Chapter 11 Pa

a single shell you can blow a tune on if you hole the top. Siput (15) was principally a snail, for which the term was coined, Si-puti being from Brer penis-teat. No hominid had a glans with a whorl on it like a snailshell. But they apparently liked the idea of it. The resemblance is somewhat fanciful. It is metaphor of course. That meant a common facet of nature spotted was a natural pattern shared. With Malay pintu which is a door, like the Spanish puerta, we have two surfaces – literally paie-en-tai-u, surfaces-of-units-two (10): the old fashioned door was of the Wild West saloon door kind with two swing leaves. They could be closed so no John Wayne could kick them open, with good solid beams across them in brackets as bolts. Neither a mountain pass nor a sea port, from the Latin porta, have even one swing leaf between them, the derivation is purely a semantic gull, the pass is a gateway or passage way providing a path enabling travelers to pass through the mountains and the seaport is a doorway or point of entry and exit for ships reaching or leaving land. These complications of the use of metaphors, sometimes repeatedly, are of course why steady old academic scholarship switches off and opts for meaninglessness.

Hawaiian for a sea shell is paua (9,10), and u is the dual vowel as well as the completive one (chapter 14), so pa-u-a is a dual lid one, as well as being a completely covered one. The completive was also the dual, since for the primitive dialectical mind any completive state was the product of two preceding states – just as two peeps made a pu, and two pigs make a piglet and two people make a child (and two Latin people a puer (3), a child, which picked up the peeping or piping sense of the pipi with voices as yet unbroken). The female form came later, puella being invented for a girl, with puer redefined as a boy.

In India prayer (which in English is composed from pai-rai-a, arms raised one) is poojah, from pu-sha, both arms-up, just like the Egyptian priests of Amun-Ra (when praying), with elbows in a right angle making it clear they were praying to the divine dialectical scheme of the Tau, the two dimensions of the world, the down-up (time) and the sideways (space), as seen in Egyptian tomb art. It is only a short hop - a convulsive move - from there to the colour puce, supposedly the colour of the flea – we have pea green so why not flea puce – from puce (which is from flea in French, but with a derivation far from the colour, from the Latin pulex irritans, Lithic pu-lai-kai-sai, legs-leaping-strong-acting, enabling it to jump as if over the moon, and if tethered to pull a cart a hundred times its size as a circus trick, spelling out in elaborate detail the simpler pu-kai, legs-strong, French puce. Our Cavalier spaniel, investigating a dead hedgehog in the greenhouse, incarcerated overnight for the children to see in the morning - out in daylight they are usually sick (the hedgehogs) so it died in the night – was struck on the snout by fifty fleas jumping simultaneously like a single black pellet and sprang back as if struck on the nose by a stone. The colour puce is a gull from the flea. It has no legs and does not jump. The Greek phulla for flea remarks the flea's leaping like our English frog's as ejaculatory. For the Greeks it was from pahei-u-lalai, ejaculatory-ones-leapings. For English frog we can read pahei-rau-u-gai, penis-orgasmic-what-goes. But both idioms are from the same Lithic semantics as flea, a jumper. For the adjectival Stone Age mind a pattern, of shape or action, was adjectival and could be spotted occurring all over the place. The flea's leap was for the adjectival mind informed by the same character as the ejaculating genitalia, and so could be spoken of as the same. The only problem about the flea is it is not purple but black. Is puce just short for purple?

In Africa lives the chimpanzee (6): si-m'pan-sai, brer-him-limbs-lively/active, or else, more likely from the activity of the limbs, pa'n-sai, a goer-up, not unlike the Australian go-up, baji or bird; but in the chimp's case not a flyer but brer climber. They climb nimbly

Chapter 11 Pa

through the trees. In Sumatra, on the other side of the Indian ocean, they call a smaller local species of monkey chipai, lively legs, or another goer-upper. The nimblest, with long arms and prehensile tail, is the siamang ape, or si-amang, brer-weightless in Malay, from a-mang, un-heavy.

The Sanskrit for a male man is puman (15), he is the one with a pipi-ma´n, an earthing or planting (impregnating) pipelet, his penis. In chapter 9 for Ma man has already been identified as the planter. It is tempting to read woman as u-au-ma´en, one-all done gone finish-planted, the passive version from the completive (passive) vowel u, making 'passive-that one-planted', that is 'the planted (impregnated) one'. We can see the male chauvinism in this semantic analysis, which suggests it is a correct linguistic analysis, (I first typed right but shrank from feminists' misinterpretation). The same pu as in the Sanskrit is also in Latin pubes which means first of all adult, the pu-bai(s), the genitalia burgeoned, sexually mature, even the pu-bai, the penis-bits, the testes, may be meant; and only thence the pubic growth of hair which indicates their maturity. Eric Partridge relates pubes directly to puer (7), a piper, a Latin boy, but puer was originally a child of either sex, it just meant a piper, with a note like the pan pipe, with unbroken voice. Without a consistent Lithic analysis you are up the creek without a paddle. In reality this pu goes right back to the quail chick, with only a nod on the way to children's high piping unbroken voices.

Curiously the Malay for the human groin is kunchi paha (15). Kunchi is from a kau'n khai, a join-maker, literally ka-un-kai, make two joined, a closure or junction, used also for a lock. Ibu kunchi, the mother of the closure is the keyhole, and anak kunchi the son of the closure is the key, an incestuous etymology fortuitously arrived at. The paha above looks like the Pharaoh's pahai, identifying the fork as the one with the genitals attached.

There are those in competitive vein who have tried to make out that Apollo was the Eternal phallus, the glowing glans ejaculating light, but A-pau-lau, Eternal-traveller-in a loop, the orbiter, is better, the traveling by a metaphorical gulling from feet as if they were pedestrian (6). Egyptians could get away with this idea of an eye in the sky without any inconsequence since the eyes we have they supposed to be active radiation sources rather than merely the passive receivers of the sun's rays reflected from the panorama we now know them to be. The Egyptians drew Ra's rays with hands on the ends to teach the ignorant peasantry that the rays of the sun came down and then went back up again pulling the plants back up with them: whence to grow in English, ge-rau, ge-rayed, from kai-rau, made rayed. Gardeners marvel at the way their plants grow in a hot spell, at the right time of year. The Ancient Egyptians noticed it too, and no doubt their hominid forebears did so too. They weren't stupid, although ill informed; and things like plant growth were their specialty. Ignore the spelling, even the words, and think of the meanings in the syllables merely. It came as no surprise in Ancient Egypt that our feebler eyes returned only with a simulacrum of what they had encountered, reflected on the iris of the eye, the irradiated or more precisely it-ray-showing, (i-rai-sai), for the manikin to read from behind the eye. As we now know, it would not be long before people would come to ask what this eye in the sky was doing, and the first belief it was keeping an eye on disciplinary matters would come to be superceded by the idea it was concerned even for sparrows' falls. For this we have the civilization of Egypt and the lost Egyptian language to thank.

From pai, the skin, the surface of the flesh, came the idea of an enclosing surface (10) and thence a roof (11) or lid or top, the Greek pi.(which shows a lid or top in curlicue, supported), and so, via the skin or periphery of the sun a circular measure, pai d. The subconscious appears to have chosen the pai or pi. The Beduin's roof is made of skins in

Chapter 11 Pa

any case, to provide shelter from the sun, and this predicament of escaping the sun's rays must have been around since savannah conditions prevailed in hominid days. Sa-u-a-na reads in Lithic heat-where-that-prominent. There will not have been enough cool caves to go round. Whereas the pa that was a vegetal shoot or sprout (6), a small (thinned diminished) burgeon, would push upwards, if rather slowly and relatively insignificantly, a surface could slope any way or even be circular like the surface of the sun, the boundary of a tube seen end on, whence the Greek and Latin peri (5), from pa-i-rai, skin or surface of Ra, meaning around in Greek. It was the idea of anything going or being around the edge of something, a periphery. The -phery is from the Greek pherein to carry. The carriage was originally of the foetus from impregnation, the pahei did not stop raying until it had triggered the pregnancy. We should not imagine hominids had any biology. The penis was a magic agency with a magic invisible raying facility, copying the sun and our own eyes as well. Our carrying is from putting it on the head, kara, just as a pair of horns, cornu, were the dual protrusions of the skull. Horns, a bifurcation of the skull, suggested immortality. It made the cow, with its Ka-u, a sacred animal, with a dual Ka, one for this world and one for the next, the "Dua Taun", the "Second World" in Ancient Egyptian.

It was the Greeks who started Britain as a name. Britons were called Pretani in Greek. It came from Egyptian Peri-taun-i, periphery-of the world-ones, that Ultima Thule or Ta(h)u-lai (a cockney h to keep the a and u separate), the ultimate World-loop or rim, beyond which you ran the risk of falling off the edge of the world. There is some linguistic evidence Egyptian speakers once colonised Britain. Taun was Egyptian for all the birthings or becomings or happenings, and so the universe as experienced, as already explained in chapter 5. Similarly Egyptologists believe the Egyptian for Heaven was Pet (sic). Akin to spit? But the glyphs were not usually read alphabetically. Pai, a surface, was drawn as a square in hieroglyphic, a surface in bird's-eye view. The Greek pi (10), was the same in elevation with two supporters and the top surface in the shape of a curlicue to direct attention to the top surface as the bit intended. Top can also be read in the same Lithic terms since the Tau or Tao (a T) was believed to represent, amongst other things, the two fundamental extensions or dimensions of all human thinking, namely the extensions of time and space, whence inter alia (for the Chinese) a lifetime path or way to follow, amounting to a religion. The vertical dimension was the temporal one and the horizontal cross piece on top the spatial dimension, seen sideways on with a flat earth. The tau-pai, the surface or space dimension of the tau, is the top of the T. Time can be seen to be coming up here, offering progress.

A pie (10,11) is lidded, that is surfaced with a pastry top, unlike an open tart. It is made of pieces too. Eric partridge, without the benefit of any (elaborated) Lithic semantic contents, declares a pie might be so called because originally made of magpies. The children's nursery rhyme meanwhile plumps for four and twenty blackbirds. The semantic catena in reality goes the other way. The magpie (10) is named for its contrasting patches or surfaces, black and white. A plate is a similar flat, and circular (like the skyline at sea) surface, from the French plat (10) meaning flat, a surface-flat-become. Semantically what is become is a thing of course. We could be treating these t endings as noun endings. La is flat by metaphor from the ocean, with a flat surface (compared with the earth) whither all liquids yearn to go and the water does on a daily basis – by river. The Latin penna (10) is a wing, a protruding surface (in flight). The Greek pan (10) as in pantechnicon and panorama, meaning everything, is a more difficult one, being the combinative form of Greek pas which is from the Egyptian pa-sai, the surface as sensed, in this case seen, that is everything in view – after all you do only see the surfaces of things and it is no great leap

Chapter 11 Pa

to see the panorama as a single surface as presented - the world as sensed, and therefore every-thing. Panorama (6) spells it out with –orama which means that-what-eye-ment, i.e. all-seen, all that is seen, a sight, in gunnery a sketch of the whole front with recorded targets given numbers and marked on it. In Egyptian Ra was the sun and ra was an eye as well, with rai meaning seeing or seen as well as rayed by the sun[3]; and much of Greek is closely akin to Ancient Egyptian. This is because for many centuries so many educated Greeks lived in Alexandria and studied at the library there, forerunner of modern universities. In Greek horan meant to see. The h seems to have been a cockney h, from the Egyptian one pronounced ahi dividing (any) two vowels to prevent them eliding (chapter 7). Greek horan is thus from the original Lithic i-a-u-ra-en in Lithic terms, roughly it-that-one-eye-verbal, to eye or see.

The Greek for eye, and thereafter face, was ops (6), in Lithic expansion au-pai-sai, that one or that what-pai(the surfaces of things)-senses. It is the eye which lets you know where the material boundaries are, saving your shins. The pa is the same pa as in panorama, the surface of things in view: after all the surface is all that you see, so you get a superficial view. That is how the Egyptian pa came to mean "the" for them, denoting particularity, by way of the one in view rather than any old one that might come to mind. The au is also an oo or o or egg shape. The eye (ops) is defined as a sensing egg. However the pai-sai can also be read as the surface sensed or seen, and so the front of anything, and in particular the face. Our face or front is from the Latin facies which adopts a different and somewhat ruder definition based on paha-kai. The face – anyway a pretty one – can kindle the pahei. The pai has been exchanged for fai or the pahai. P can of course become f under a law like Grimm's which finds consonants being switched on a regular basis between related languages as if this slovening were determined by a (subconscious) fashion in pronunciation. However for the -s in pas to change to -k in facies (15) under such a dispensation is hard to swallow, and the Latins appear to have followed a different tradition. The Egyptian nefer (15) as in Nefertiti meant pretty, and it can quite easily be read in its Lithic precursor form as nai-pahei-rai, [when]showing or present-the pahei-is rayed and rises. We can all be influenced by a pretty face, and its expressions provide the entrée for relating to the personality within as well. It does not make the world go round but it certainly plays its part. When we say pretty we are somewhat similarly saying the pee-raised-becomes, what a pretty face does for you. We don't think in these rather blunt terms today but when we learned to speak, a very long time ago, it was in fairly brutal terms. Today a pretty face is pleasurable but that is all, anyway so far as we are prepared to admit[4]. But I remember a boy at school in the 1930s who looked like an angel and because of the glances he attracted concluded he must be the reincarnation of Jesus Christ, finishing up with his frontal lobes cut off to disillusion him. He was sacrificed because social etiquette decreed he could not and should not have the truth explained to him.

With Latin facies, face, ka can mean striking or kindling (chapter 5). A pretty face can arouse passion in a beholder, rather more than a shapely arm or other part of the body which is not a secondary sexual character, like the foot or ankle. If he is male it can probably be said it will. Human whimsy is such that just about any body part can become a fetishist fixation, along with its usual covering. But the face is always seen uncovered because it carries the owner's eyes – unless a fetish makes it taboo and requires it to be covered at all times for fear of the lasciviousness that, facing, it might otherwise arouse. Romans went around clad but not yet constrained to wear any yashmak or visual dowser.

Chapter 11 Pa

It is even possible to go so far as to derive the 'front' from the missionary position. The Latin facies comes close to the other four letter word, where the striking is understood in the stark physical thrusting sense rather than merely as kindling. In Albanian, that maverick language next door, para means in front, the surface visible. They had clearly been talking to the Egyptians long before they got caught by the Turks. The Latins used para to con-front and so to oppose, to be against, surface presented to surface, two parties up against each other. Pugna in Latin means both fist and battle: fist from pa-u-kai-na, the inflated end (of the arm in this case)-made-protruding (4); battle from surfaces-dual-made presented (10). The two battle lines in those early days simply confronted each other, locked shields and bashed at the enemy line like a rugby scrum getting down. Opposition is confrontation precisely.

Another maverick language along the Mediterranean littoral, Basque, now confined to the top end of Spain and the bottom end of France, has pipi for moth. The moth is notably silent with nothing in common with the quail chick, so it is clear immediately we have here a shape metaphor, with two little surfaces (10) or wings, with a flapping action. Moths, and more particularly butterflies are conspicuous flutterers. A butterfly in Albanian is Flutura, a flitter or flutterer. I have found it used as a girl's name. (She was a scholar, not a butterfly). Greeks used pai for wings too. Their word for wing is ptera (10), the plural of ptron a feather, which we only commonly come across in helico-pter and ptero-dactil, from the Lithic that which circle shape-wing and wing-fingers. The Greek P was originally pronounced properly here of course: pi. For the Greeks (far enough back) wings were surfaces, pai, which were tai-rai, subjected to Egyptian rays, in this case the vaginal rays (see chapter 5 for ta as the birth canal) which pull things out and up, like our chest of drawers which we pull out, or our drawers or underwear we pull up; and nature which for the Egyptians exhibited (na-) a quiver full of pulls, turai, to be propitiated. Wings were seen as sky hooks which have the facility to get you pulled up into the empyrian, an ability mere human propensities, not even the ladies, can aspire to, lacking the natural pullers necessary to grab the wings. None of this makes any sense today, but is it not quite fun? The Latin for a feather and a wing is penna, our pen we write with, originally a goose's feather with the end cut into a nib (a nib, from nai-ba, is a protruding bit). The Latin penna for wing is a protruding surface (10), but the feather makes better sense if the pai- is a piece (16) like the penis. The feather offers a surface, admittedly, but not one which is notably protruding. The individual pieces of the feather however all protrude in a remarkable fashion from the central quill or spine, in so far as they have minuscule hooks along their length enabling them each to join their neighbours on either side to make a waterproof and airtight surface. Birds preen (16) (Lithic pai-rai'n, arrange the pieces) their feathers with their beaks to rehook joints which have become separated. It is the protruding pieces of the feather (a feather is from phai-a-terai, pieces-that-tai-rayed, (drawn out: not shy of revealing the original sexual source of the metaphor precisely) which make up a surface, which is not itself protruding. The wing then makes a surface which is protruded in flight, supposedly hooked up in turn to the rising rays of ancient fancy, but actually of course providing lift by beating down upon the air.

A bishop or overseer is from the Greek epi-scopus, Lithic ai-pai-sai-ka-au-pau(s), (that which-covered)-(see-mak)e-(all-surfaces), a Lithic doggerel which means ai-pai, on top or over, see-make or as we would say just seer, which is because ops in Greek is eye and skopein is to view. The –pau– here is the same as in the pa- in panorama, the visible surface which we see. In Latin palear is the dewlap of an ox. The Lithic, pa-lai-a, is surface-slack (10,16)-that. While the Latin palla is a long cloak worn by Roman women,

Chapter 11 Pa

and the Lithic is pa-laila, surface-long and loose. The pallium worn by men – including now the Pope – is a mantle or a coverlet, like pellis a Latin skin; which shows the idea is a surface which can be put to use to mean equally either an item of clothing or a furnishing, including also a pall in English.

A pane is a surface like a panel, both surface ones (10), though a pane hammer is one with a knob behind (instead of a claw) and is a protruding piece, although its use is to beat panes (10) or panels flat, its rounded profile avoiding making weak places with a sharp edged hammer. Then there is a palus in Latin which is a long piece (16) meaning a stake, whence the English palisade, and the phrase beyond the pale, akin to the English pole, another long piece; whereas a pile is a (looped) collection of pieces, shape unspecified. In Latin again a pilum is from the Lithic pai-lau-mai, piece-long-heavy and is the heavy javelin carried by Roman infantry. Or else the lai, as in javelin, is looping, flying in a loop like Apollo, meaning it is hurled. Latin pilus is a hair, another long piece like the English pole, but small scale by comparison, and pilosa is hairy. A caterpillar is therefore defined by Partridge as a hairy cat, apparently accepting a caterpillar is a cat (sic) because a caterpillar is sometimes hairy and that seemed to fit, leaving him with the cater- to deal with. The Lithic however is ka-ta-pai-la-a, a body-become-feet-undulating-going-one. The untrilled r is from an a. It is an unusual Cockney r, using the untrilled version to divide two a's Caterpillars have numerous sucker feet, and no legs to speak of, which they use in an undulating manner, their bodies rippling as they lift pairs of feet in turn. Lai carries the meanings of looping and so undulating. Caterpillars are the undulating insects, not cats of any kind; and most are not hairy. The ka-ta or two ka is explained, like the Hawaiian uku for insect, by the caterpillar using up both ka in this world by being born twice, once from the egg and again from the pupa. Stylised butterflies were drawn in the Stone Age, probably as intimations of immortality, because of their ba-ta, two ba, or bi-ta, two flesh embodiments or beings, or else bi-born. The hope was that death would prove to be a pupation with a rebirth into a far more ethereal form, like the butterfly, to follow. I have read that children awaiting gassing in the holocaust left stylized butterflies on the walls. If they didn't they might have done. Chambers' committee of expert linguists will have none of this, recording merely of butterfly "the origin for this name of the insect is obscure" - while Partridge leaves butterfly out altogether. Caterpillar: ka-ta-pai-la, body-become-feet-looping. No cats and no hairs! You could say body become a perambulating ripple.

In Greek pagos means frost: pa-kau (10) is surface-of the ground hardened, and frost does harden the ground as anyone who has tried to dig a trench in winter above the forty eighth parallel will be aware. You find yourself hacking out thumbnail sized pieces. The Koreans, in the bad old days, confronted with this problem would equip themselves with very large earthenware pots, five feet tall, at their front doors as receptacles until the thaw, when the ground would open up to receive its dues again and the pots could be emptied. A second pot held kimche, the local pickle. It was japed American forces, Waylanders all, could not tell one pot from the other.

The Potato (6), from Central America, is from the Taino language via Spanish. Originally the same species as the tomato, it was bred for its root tuber while the tomato was bred for its fruit. Today, if you irrigate a potato crop as it is flowering you get a crop of small green tomatoes. They are mildly poisonous, which shows the breeders were persistent, breeding the tomato for larger sweeter fruit and the potato for a fatter tuber. It was natural selection by stomach ache. The potato in Lithic phonemes is pau-tau-tau, plump ones (tubers)-birth-birth. You replant the tubers (14) and get another crop, repetitive births. The potato tuber is a shoot (6) which has become burgeoned. The tomato by contrast is from tau-ma-tau, birth-death-birth. With a tomato, an annual, you replant the seeds each year. It is closely related to the totem pole, a garbled Anglicisation of ototema (Hawaiian) which in Lithic phonemic elements is au-tau-tau-ma, all-the born-born-dead, all the generations of ancestors: and there they are one above the other on the pole, sometimes with the mythical original progenitor on the top. Of course they are only a symbolic representative selection, since to show them all your pole would have to extend into the heavens.

Water in Hindustani is pani (10), and nahi is nay or no: so pani is from Lithic pa-nai, with no surface. If you step into it, down you go straight through to the bottom where there is a surface. The Semitic fancy is for moir, the descender. If you step in down you go to the bottom. On the other side of the world, for the Guarani in Paraguay, water is apan (10), unsurfaced. Down you go to the bottom. In England a pan (10), now with a lip for frying with fat was originally a flat griddle for making baps, just a surface. Bread was cooked that way once, which is why in France they still call it pain, and in Spain pan. A Spanish frying pan however is a sarten, from the Lithic elements sa-rai-tai'n, fire-rayed-become'one, a fryer rather than a pan. With English bread the emphasis is on the action of the yeast in making the dough rise, bai-rai-dai, ba-i-rayed-become, as it did also with beer and any other brew. Ba was flesh, but dough was similar, more like flesh than the vegetable matter (vegetable flesh) of which it was composed. Vegetable tissue was vegetable flesh anyway. Rays were supposed to work at a distance to raise crops, penises, visions fetched back to the iris of the eye, anything raised or roused in fact, just as when crops grow (made rayed or subjected to sun rays, see chapter 12 on the phoneme Ra), so yeast had this facility too.

Just as the nature of the flesh (ba) was to burgeon, so the pa on a smaller scale swelled or puckered up. The penis did. Pimples did. The lips would pout, become swollen. A pudding is doing the same, from the Germanic root pud- to swell - just as the pipi does (although the catena is long forgotten, so far as the conscious mind is concerned). A paunch, pau-en-kai, is a swollen one-of-the body. To poke is from pu-kai, to make with the pipi, picked up by colloquial vulgar slang. Pandi is Telegu for a pig, it has become fat, just like the boars of Borneo, or indeed the English pig, which is pai-kai, fat-bodied. You may have forgotten chapter 4 for Ka, the sound of the flint knapping which went on for a million years; then a symbol for hard; whence the bones, whence the bone, the backbone; and then the bodily structure, the skeleton, and so finally just the body In that the pig shares the honours with the penguin, which is much more closely related to the Latin pinguis or the Greek pion meaning fat than to the folk etymology of white head from the Welsh pen-gwin. Apart from the improbability of the Welsh getting there first, the penguin does not have a white head anyway. Linguistics buffs, saddled with this absurd etymology, have twisted and turned to propose it perhaps first referred to another bird which did have a white head - Partridge suggests the Great Auk - and then got transferred to the penguin in a fit of inconsequential ornithological inattention – an ornithological error rather than an etymological one: anything rather than an admission of foolish linguistic error. It was not deliberate prevarication, but almost: just what naturally sprang to mind.

The French petite, which is taken to mean anything small at all, comes in delightfully French fashion from pai-titi (15), a swollen teat, a breast or pap with only the nipple (from nai-pipi-lai) or teat protruding, little more than a pimple, and used precisely and with fine Gallic humour for any lass only modestly endowed. A pea in its pod is a small plump piece become covered or skinned (pau'd), which is what the pod does. A broad bean is much the same but being that much bigger (baraud, flesh-rayed-become) unfortunately picks up the

Chapter 11 Pa

semantic connection with those other fleshy bits which the boars in Borneo carry out the back in full view, their testicles or fruit. Some Greeks didn't eat them therefore.

Partridge lists thirty one words along with prince, all semantically from in front and forwards, which he presents as pri-. The Lithic is pai-rai, or visible surface with which you are visually confronted and anyway represents the front - for you - of whatever you are looking at. At one stage it appeared to come from the pai-rai or rayed-piece conspicuous in front, congener with proud, prow, pro-, prance, prank, prink, forward, and even proof (from probus with Greek baino meaning I go - I show a leg - going forward, proudly, confidently, honestly) etc. The prince is from princeps a front or first ceps, taker or performer, from kai-pai., making covered, and so seizing (with the hand, we must suppose, rather than to cover in the sexual sense). It looks as if as principal warrior he got the first slice of the booty.

From the same stable is to press, from pai-rai-sai, piece-raised-acting, thrusting or pressing in. The Latin to press is premere. The Latin action is one of mai, planting or impregnating, or even (in Egyptian) just of the mai or penis. The price of anything on the other hand is soberly estimated. The Latin is pretium, declared by Partridge to be o.o.o. (of obscure origin – he gives up). Pai-rai is the observed surface again, the perception, and so the perceived value, the estimated worth of goods for sale. That is the pai-rai-tai. The – u'm is just nouning it. It was a superficial calculation, and perhaps still is.

Every P is open to Lithic interpretation, given only it may have been whimsically switched from another phoneme. For this the phonemic congeners appear at the top of the semantic trees. Some are certainly more difficult than others. The phoneme chapters can only give sufficient examples to lead the reader into the techniques required. It always involves some expansion to recover the original phonemes from the slovening over the millennia.

NOTES

1. As a reminder a gull is used throughout for the way a gull wing is derived from the seagull which has a wing of that shape. The seagull is a sea caller or singer, like a gale of wind which is one that sings or howls, just as you can have a gale of laughter, which is not musical at all but is a sudden loud burst just like the wind in a gale.. The wing does not sing or howl at all. Its connection with the singing or howling is indirect, just sharing the gull's wing shape.

2. Linguistically the strawberry name, although traditionally treated as from the strawing of plants to keep the fruit from the ground, has a Lithic structure relating it to the glans of the penis. The strawberry takes up a shape and even an enrouged colouring which with only a little whimsical over egging - by Stone Age standards - can be regarded as both shaped and coloured like the engorged glans. Straw is from sai-ta-rau., of the flame (or heat) become rayed, that is to say dried (corn stalks). But siti in Egyptian was the female, as in Au-Siti, the World Life Source (in Greek mis-spelt Isis) . It is from the Lithic Sai-tai, Life-birth. Compare pata for father, Lithic covered-birth canal, the male pride and joy described as a throttled urethra. In Malay, Siti Maria is Our Lady, the Virgin Mary. In Egypt Au Siti, Isis, was the mother and wife of Osiris, Au Sara in Egyptian. They were respectively World (or Universal) Sunset and World Sunrise. Between them they produced Horus, the day, (Lithic I(h)au-ra-u-s, He-that one-Ra-unit. Well they still do,

every day. The sunset does not seem a very positive role for the ladies, but you have to understand what it meant in earlier times. The sun died but to be resurrected next morning at sunrise. Now the dying was at the same time the necessary stage in nature before being reborn, gestation in animal life, propagation for vegetable life like the seed which falls down and enters the earth and gestates there and is born next season. Siti, as well as the female life principle was also feminine sensitivity, and at the same time the sedentary female, tending the hearth and nurturing the children while the men went hunting. The sunset was thus the mother of her son, the new sun which was born next morning. It meant all of these things and confirmed the philosophers and scientists of the day in their belief that with such a concatenation they had got it all correct. The reality was of course the concatenation had been shaped, all of it, by their own whimsy, and was effectively wrong in every particular.

3. The Egyptian rays are fully covered in chapter 12 on the phoneme Ra. They were not really Egyptian rays but part of early science, it is just they are extant only in Egyptian hieroglyph. Ra, like the Tau, is one of mankind's earliest symbols: the circle to add to the T, so far back and so bare on rock dating is probably a waste of time.

4. Houri today counts as an English word, originally a nymph of the Muslim Paradise, a voluptuously beautiful woman, from the Persian huri. But in Arabic Huri is the plural of Hawra, a lady with gazelle like eyes; hau-ra can be read delightful-eyes. The eyes of course were rai in Egyptian, a Semitic tongue originally, like Arabic; and were supposed to send out rays which fetched back a panorama and painted it on the iris for the owner of the eyes to read from behind. The Egyptian rays accounted for all action at a distance. Ra, the sun, sent out sun rays which pulled up the vegetation toward the sun on their return journey to their source, and this was why the Egyptian priests drew the sun's rays with hands on the ends: so hodge would understand their function. The whole gamut of these active rays which comprised Egyptian science, with hundreds of named active forces of nature, represented by the animals, all originated from the imaginary rays the boys imagined they were receiving from the girls as they hunkered opposite each other around the hearth, in their birthday suits, in the age of the Pleistocene. The boys found themselves with erections. Before trousers it was apparent to all. They swore they had not moved a muscle, as indeed they had not. It could therefore only be explained, like the vegetation, as the response to an incoming ray, and it was supposed to be coming from the genitalia of the girls opposite. The sun, originally the Aton, from aa-tau-oon, was believed to be the eternal-birth-channel, birthing light into the world every day, a busy lady and heroine of fertility. A houri has acquired the reputation of a voluptuous temptress; and it may be she gets some of this from her Lithic phonology, hau-rai, orgasmic-raying.

CHAPTER 12

RA: THE ALL-SEEING SUN AND THE EGYPTIAN RAYS

Most of the meanings of the phoneme Ra are best treated as gulls from the Egyptian sun god Ra. It does not mean that the Egyptians were the source of world-wide meanings, but only that when they were around they were thinking largely in line with the original Lithic semantics. But it makes sense to start by asking why for the Ancient Egyptians the sun was Ra in the first place. As a consonant Ra has the peculiar character it shares with the hisses and the hums (Ish, Ma and Na) that unlike the other consonants it can be prolonged for as long as you care to keep your tongue vibrating against your palate. The late Peter Ustinov as a boy maddened his parents by pretending to be a motor car, accompanying his movements with an endless series of rapid repetitive ras in imitation of an internal combustion engine. Ra undoubtedly stands for repetition. Before the motor car there were the growls of the feline and canine families and the croaks of corvids as well as the frogs and toads. Woodpeckers too string sounds with their beaks and even a snipe drums. But the sun, like Old Man River just keeps rolling along. So why should the repetitive consonant be chosen as its symbol? Perhaps because sunlight shining through trees may extend multiple fingers of light reflecting motes in the air, which suggested a string of tiny bits of light following each other down the ray. That will certainly have been noted as a rare give-away of the nature of the sun's rays.

Perhaps also the sun's rays were seen as repetitive arrays because the growth of every blade of grass was ascribed to a ray from the sun pulling it out and up, and there were an awful lot of them to draw up. We say grow from ge-rau, from that original idea of the rays making the grass (and everything else) grow, with the grass itself ge-rayed-real fast (sasai). For that the sun must surely have a myriad rays to be able to address so many client blades. The Egyptian priests drew the rays of the sun with hands on their ends to make it clear to hodge (the uninformed populace) that that was how it went. There was another prompt for repetitiousness where the sun was concerned. The sun came to be regarded as a world eye in the sky. Our own much feebler eyes sent out rays which reached the panorama confronting them and returned to the eyes whence they came, not pulling back their targets like the sun but only a simulacrum of what they had encountered, which you could sometimes see from in front painted on the iris, the irradiated surface of the eye. The picture was taken to be pointiliste - like the grass – and that obviously pointed to a vast army of individual elements of rays for the job. We do not know which idea came first, the case which accounted for sight, the action at a distance which we all enjoyed, or the action at a distance we could all feel and see when the sun shone. It does not make much difference to the ideas involved. Rays went out and then came back to their source with their mission accomplished, we would say like radar beams: the sun and the eye were active radars. We now know of course our eyes are passive and merely receive and register the light rays from the sun reflected from the surfaces of whatever is in view. We can see that although to the Egyptian mind these rays were purely physical with a mechanical action, their conception as active seeking agents with a role to play actually reflected an anthropomorphic imagination. But that is only the beginning of the Egyptian

Chapter 12 Ra

rays, just what is needed to make the case for the Ra trills to represent the motes of light chasing each other down the sunbeams.

The rays from an animal's eyes, also ra in Egyptian, came back to their source just as the sunbeams supposedly returned to the sun. How else would the crops grow? Or we see at a distance? It will no doubt have ranked as a wonder a few hundred thousand years ago when we were learning to speak. All the rays however went back to an initial identification much closer to home, a lesson learned by our hominid forebears around their hearths. Since the male member rises unbidden when aroused, the feminine member must therefore be the source of the rays which draws it out and up, just as the sun does the same for the plants. With a bit of hindsight and a slightly more critical mind set today we can see that our transference of performances was really the other way about, starting with our perceptions of our own experience at the "hands" of the opposite sex. So since the male member rises, the crops are doing the same. Since the vagina rounds out when roused, (and male arousal appears to be involuntary, prompted from outside the body), the sun, which is always rounded out, has the same facility which is always drawing the crops up and out, just as the girls draw the male organ up and out. The vagina starts out narrow, not arrau, just a slit, and finishes arrau, rayed or round. It was a laughable corollary that it was the feminine vagina, as they all hunkered around the hearth, that started every sexual encounter, since the male organ was sheathed and unable to ray back until it had been roused, and its muzzle cover withdrawn by the feminine rays seeking it out. There may be some sense in this of course, but if so the process takes place in the minds of the participants and not by means of any physical rays; which then leaves open who is the initiator and who the initiated, and in reality the circumstances will be as various as circumstances usually are. But our simple forebears kept it simple.

It was certainly taken as no light laughing matter by the Pharaohs of Egypt, who reckoned as Ra's favourites they were entitled to take the initiative in every encounter - as royalty are apt to do - and cannily cut off their muzzle covers so they could fire first. It has not been explained as yet why Ra should not have thought of the rearrangement of the male member in the first place for himself, had he wished male members to wear foreshortened foreskins. Perhaps unsurprisingly this particular piece of thinking has been banished to the subconscious dark room down below and does not feature any longer in the language with which we choose to communicate today. There is in its place a Semitic theory circumcision is a deal done with Jahweh so He and they will know each other and they will stay faithful to Him: an odd deal certainly, and slightly indelicate with it. Is God Almighty really dealing in penes? Surely not!

Previously, when the world was ruled by goddesses, before men became bold (or rebellious) enough to shed their reliance upon their mothers, the sun was seen as a World birth canal, birthing light into the world each day. In Egyptian it was Aton, from the original Lithic elements Aa-ta-un, Eternal-birth-canal, seen fully frontal; and transliterated by Sir Wallis Budge in 1921 as the disc of the sun. In those days academics did not think in terms of the feminine genitalia, never mind what the Ancient Egyptians said. The hieroglyph was just a big O. It could just as well have been a disc as a vagina; except of course a disc would have had no business to be there. It usually had a dot in the centre. For perspective? Even as late as in Ancient Egypt there was still a recollection of this earlier religion of the goddess. The hermaphrodite Pharaoh Akhenaton, in Lithic A-khai-en-Aa-ton, That-begotten-in-the-Eternal-Womb, a divine Son of the Sun like the Japanese emperor later, led a religious reaction against the chauvinist priesthood of Amun Ra. Aa-mau'n could be read as Ever-impregnated, and so perhaps daily giving birth to light, much

Chapter 12 Ra

like the previous Aa-tau'n actually doing the job; but it could simultaneously be read as the Ever-loving, since when impregnating our Stone Age forebears evidently experienced that emotion, much like today; but in those days perhaps only noticeably then, or at least contemplating the job. Anyway it was how to get Tarzan to grasp the idea. The priests eventually defeated the Pharaoh and his name was deleted from the Pharaonic records and and his capital city built for the Aton demolished. Sigmund Freud even made A-khai-en-Aa-ton the original of the Oedipus legend, partly because of his deformed and bloated thighs shown in statues of him, on which Freud based his Oedipus Complex - Oedipus is swollen legs in Greek; and the late polymath Emanuel Velikovsky more recently revamped much of the same material rather better. But Velikovsky was silenced by the astronomical establishment of the day for imagined heresies in the field of astronomy. (Some later proved correct. Establishments are like that. The universe has always been a violent place – just with relatively long gaps between the worst disasters; but establishments prefer a steady state to preach about).

Egyptian Pharaohs were expected to come of age by copulating with their mothers, a kind of ancient droit de seigneur exercised by the dame from whom legitimacy appears to have descended, as the original life source, an incestuous relationship from which Akhai-en-Aton, with his impaired sexuality appears never to have escaped. Tahu-tau anak Amun, AkhenAton's son (vulgarly known as Tooten-Karmoon), started out Tahu-tau-anak-Aton, Know-all-son-of the [heretical, female] Sun, but had his name changed when his father was defeated by the priests of Amun Ra to Tahu-tau-anak-Amun (Know -all-Son-of Amun [Ra] this time) perhaps in the hope of retaining the throne. But it appears he was murdered while still a boy, perhaps a triumph for the very first bureaucracy. We can imagine the trauma of these transferences for the populace. It will certainly have been argued no Eye in the Sky will have cared to be misidentified as a vagina, any more than a goddess would care to be mistaken for an Eye in the sky. Moreover behind the Eye in the sky was a male god this time.

With the sun the eye of the world, what made the difference was it was open to wonder for the first time for what purpose it looked down upon the world, a whimsy which could not have been prompted in any way by a sun seen merely as an everlasting light supply, the purpose of which was simply to let the light into the world. Admittedly Amun Ra – Amun is the Ever Loving One – looked down upon the world with a rather severe affection, not uncontaminated with self love, in order to punish evil doers who challenged His will as God; as indeed did Yahweh, the God of Ancient Israel, in Lithic I-a-u-a-i, He-Universal-both-Eternal (secret vowelisations identifying perhaps the first dialectical deity, The universal and Eternal), especially when His subjects hankered after the earlier fertility cow goddess. The cow was supremely female because of her extended lactation, and the Aton was supremely female because she was so busy giving birth on a daily basis. It was Christians who first thought God's oversight might be due to His concern even for the fall of sparrows, a truly compassionate deity who would show mercy to all believers. It was of course a dangerous heresy for anyone who laid claim to represent His authority on earth, and much blood was spilt before a compromise was struck with authority, and the church made an uneasy peace with the state, the Bishops with the Emperor. It is generally reckoned the original deal between the Roman Emperor Constantine and the Bishops of the early Christian church in 335 AD was a disaster, allowing the Pope in due course to impose his infallibility along with other thoroughly unchristian beliefs. Mohammed held to the belief in Allah the All Merciful, in deliberate and even violent opposition to the harsh chauvinism of his own Quraishi (Wahabi) tribe. Wa-ha-bi in Lithic is Terror-

Chapter 12 Ra

rejoicing-being, or in Proto Arabic simply terror-enjoying-[while] alive, ie all the time, or in short: "The Terrorists", the judgment of their neighbouring tribes in prehistoric times. On Mohammed's death, after his jihads (or vehement actions) against his own Wahabi tribe who expelled him, his religion was infiltrated by the very pagan tribal leaders he had sought to defeat. When he eventually beat them, The Prophet forgave them if they converted to Islam; and since Kali their Black Goddess of the night was the goddess of death, destruction and deception of all unbelievers at all times, they naturally cheated him and pretended to convert. The Moslem religion with a Wahabi or terrorist slant was then carried by the sword all across North Africa into Spain, before The Prophet's true message could reappear and the old unreformed Wahabism be replaced by those who believed in Allah the All Merciful and genuinely professed the true Moslem faith – until Osama bin Laden reintroduced the original heretical pagan Wahabism once again in this century.

It appears some Stone Age Einstein abstracted the idea of a sunbeam and put it to work illuminating a whole galaxy of rays now extant as the Ancient Egyptian rays, (shortened to Egyptian Rays) mostly invisible, but some even physical like rain' (raying), and including the ray sent out by the ordinary animal eye to feel over the panorama and bring its simulacrum back to the eye. In Egyptian to see was peterai, from the Lithic pai-tai-rai, the surface-becoming-rayed [by the eye of the observer]. Ra was the eye and rai was seeing, visible; so vision was drawing up the surface (back onto the eye, the rays' source). The surface (pai) was like the Greek pan, the surface of everything seen. You fielded a superficial view of the whole panorama brought back to your eye. Panorama (Greek) is from the Lithic elements pan-au-ra-ma, surface-that one-the eye/see-matter, all that the eye sees. The final -ma is hard to translate. It was the opposite of ish which, since it was the flame, was light and airy, flickering and insubstantial. Ma could feature as such an opposite even in an abstract composition such as the insubstantial mechanism of vision. It should perhaps here be translated just as thingumyjig, with an inconclusive meaning, in fact just a substantive marker like the English -ment. It means what the eye sees. The Greek ptera, a wing, was another pai-tai-rau-a, a surface-be-rayed-one, and so drawn up, in this case drawing the bird up with it into the sky. The birds' wings were sky hooks. A helico-pter has helical wings, drawn up surfaces or sky hooks. Technology has provided the power only quite recently. Anyway, whatever the reasoning, it can be seen, from the gamut above, the growl phoneme came to stand for r and then for Ra, the sun, and then for rai for its rays, (which Aton cribbed from the vagina) bringing with them as a gull what was already worked out for the growl, its repetitive nature, with audibility as action at a distance courtesy of one of the rays around.

The psychosemantic tree for Ra is on page 234, with semantic contents 1 to 25. A dozen different arrangements could easily be drawn and no doubt many more meanings formed around the world are missing. But the overall pattern is clear. Words were in origin strings of independent meaningful phonemes and it is only a comparatively recent trick to treat words as singletons rather than strings of meanings making up a composite overall sense; and this in spite of the universally recognized fact we go on adding to the strings as a matter of course, calling the additions prefixes, suffixes and even infixes (in Arabic). The stringing of phonemic elements to make words led similarly (later) to the stringing of words to make sentences. Words started out as sentences, or anyway phrases, of meaningful phonemes. The academic stasis in linguistics involves dismissing psychosemantics and treating words as randomly composed and the elements strung as themselves meaningless. The loss of grasp is only felt when it comes to trying to understand our linguistic heritage and what that has of interest about the way the human

Chapter 12 Ra

mind has worked and works. It is a whimsy we can readily grasp the idea of sentences but not the sentences whence we learnt the trick. For the most part we are only capable of reproducing the ideas we have been personally taught – and only if we remember them.

The sabre toothed tiger was simply "Grrr!"(1) in echoic proto language before we learned to speak. It can be counted as a cry. But ti-grrr is speech, meaning mistress growler, which gives us French tigre. English tiger is just an ignorant mispronunciation of the same. There are plenty of similar echoic names for crows and ravens, etc. They are not only in English. In the jungle along the central spine of what is left, since the last great glacier melt, of the Biblical Eastern garden land of Malaya from which Adam and Eve were expelled by the rising sea level eight to ten thousand years ago - quite recently, in the age of tongues – the Senoi aboriginal hill tribes copy the growl of their faithful hounds. A dog is khkhauk, (spelt in the guide book chok), the final k from Lithic kai: growl-maker. It suggests the Latin canis for dog may come from Lithic khkha-nai, which would mean growl-showing, or growler again, as well of course from ka-nai, spine-protruding (the tail wagger) like penis, from pai-nai, the shoot protruding. Our own rather tame dog perhaps started out from the Lithic dau-khkh, it does-growling, another growler. They all do it. We have our own cur, surely from krrrr or growler. It comes via the Old Norse kurra to grumble from the Middle Low German kurren to growl, again with multiple rrr. If the trace is not found precisely, the fact is we are still triangulating the meanings in these words for the prior semantic content of the underlying Lithic phonemes. The original nomenclatures can now only be surmise. But I have no difficulty with it. Growls were likely mimicked for as long as it took, say khrkhrkhrkhr (k,k,k,k), to get Tarzan on board to start with. Once he had it, it then became more economical with spit to cut the sound down to size to chok or cur or canis or even dog.

Raw is a quite different semantic structure, although the phonetics are much the same. It comes via crudus, in Latin bloody, from red, sunset red from Lithic ka-rau-tau. Karau is make-rayed and so coloured, and rau-tau is Ra-[terminally]become. In the Stone Age they were happy to double up meanings like this, or elide the syllables, which came to the same thing. You can compare mai-ra, the death of the sun as it goes down. The original Sanskrit speakers saw the sun go down in the sea, so they called the sea maira. We have adopted a mere, neither the sea nor where the sun goes down, and badly pronounced it at that. Compare Malay laut, the ocean, from Lithic lau-tai, altogether low and lye-become.

Gomera, in the Canary Islands, is the Western Isle from Ga-u-mai-Ra, Land-where-dies-the sun, in Carthaginian. From 'Las Americas', in Carthaginian again 'the Western lands' of Tenerife, where this book was mostly written, the sunset is behind the island of Gomera some eighteen kilometres west. The island neatly covers off the sunset as it moves back and forth throughout the year as seen from Las Americas, while the wind coming up the African coast pushes up a puff of cloud over the hills on Gomera, which leads to magnificent sunsets. Enjoying a sundowner on our patio prompts the thought that long dead Carthagiians were doing the same some three thousands of years ago, and recording their experience by naming the island Ga-u-mai-Ra. America, also in Carthaginian, is from Aa-ma-rai-ka, Far-death-of the sun-land, the Far Western Land. The NY Times have been told, but judged it not newsworthy, though very many hundreds of millions of folk on their side of the pond happily use the word all unawares they are speaking Carthaginian, and Carthaginians clearly must have beaten old Christoph to it by some thousands of years. If that is not news I don't know what is. We may even suspect the Gallic tribes got their mer for sea (where the sun sets for Frenchmen) from the Punic speakers living in France - before eating them. It seems a long way round to raw but it

Chapter 12 Ra

gets worse. Rau by itself could mean red, the sun in its extremity (-u), that is going down, when the sky is bloody. The adjective crudus was applied to red meat and even to gore, so that is how raw came to mean uncooked. When cooked the meat is sealed and the blood is browned. The classic rose meanwhile was rau-sai, light red. They were mostly rose coloured, that is pink, although modern plantsmen have succeeded in ringing the changes since. Lithic suggests raw's reinforcement directly from Ra the source of sunrays, with raw being like the Greek agora in the open air, as animals grazing from grass (20).

Repetition (4) can be recognized in our English ritual, which comes from – or anyway is closely akin to the Latin ritus, a rite. We have to ask what exactly was a rite in the mind of whoever it was who made up the term, or whoever they were, because words are generally adopted by acclamation not by single coinages. Eric Partridge compares the Greek neritos which means numberless, where the ne- is clearly the negative so that the -ritos must be the numbers, in Lithic terms rai-tau(s),: we could say growl born (1) but repetition-derived (4) is better. What else is number than iteration? Well in Greek it is arithmos which is where our arithmetic and math come from. The Lithic is a-rai-ta(h)i-mau's, which meant, I am fairly sure, that-in a row-become-a mass or bulk quantity: a sequential measurement of quantity. Earlier I had the Lithic for arithmos analysed that-repetition-derived-meaning'substantive marker. In Lithic terms they are both the same, although I prefer my second go. That surely makes a ritual a repetitive drill or procedure, which is what it is.

It perhaps throws some light on reason too, from the Latin ratio, which comes from ratus, the past participle of the Latin verb reri, to be counted (4), to count, or reiterate, whence to calculate or reckon or order your thinking. But also just to count out a ration or calculated share. It suggests that thinking was originally perceived as the deliberate rehearsal of points in turn, one by one, maybe even repeating them out loud, a skill dependent on language of course, in order to arrive at a balanced judgment based on all the relevant data. Certainly it suggests the fanciful virtues of reason developed by philosophy are rather over-egging the reality, which only claims to be rehearsing what seems relevant, as anyone reasonable would do before coming to a conclusion. To do less is reckless, from Old English reccan to take heed, to take into account, in original Lithic rai-ka'n, to count-make. To reckon turns out to mean at base to put in a row (like the motes in a sunbeam), to put in order, which is what regulation is about also. You don't have to be counting the motes but you may be. A mote has just mau-tai, become a mump or mound, a little accumulation. You would not expect such a mump to move and you would be right, since move, from Latin movere is from mau-bai in Lithic and it gets the movement (of the mass) from the bai, those muscular burgeons, the buttocks, which do the leg work. Movement is also derived, like going, from a, the extensive vowel, incidentally already sketched top left in Figure 1 for chapter 3 (page 44), illustrating diagrammatically the semantic input of the vowels. In addition the sibilant phoneme (chapter 14) has action and so movement amongst its semantic contents from the supposed liveliness of the flame which says ish as it dies. All of which makes the Greek ameusasthai meaning to become displaced quite relevant. The monarch meanwhile generally just takes an overall view, as sole archon, the one making rows and rules. He has ministers for doing the detailed counting and costing in the rows he makes, currently in the United Kingdom, when this was originally written a Mr. Brown. His rows turned out straight but all in the wrong direction.

Chapter 12 Ra

THE PSYCHOSEMANTIC TREE FOR RA

The Phonetic Tree

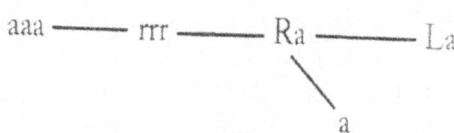

The Semantic Tree

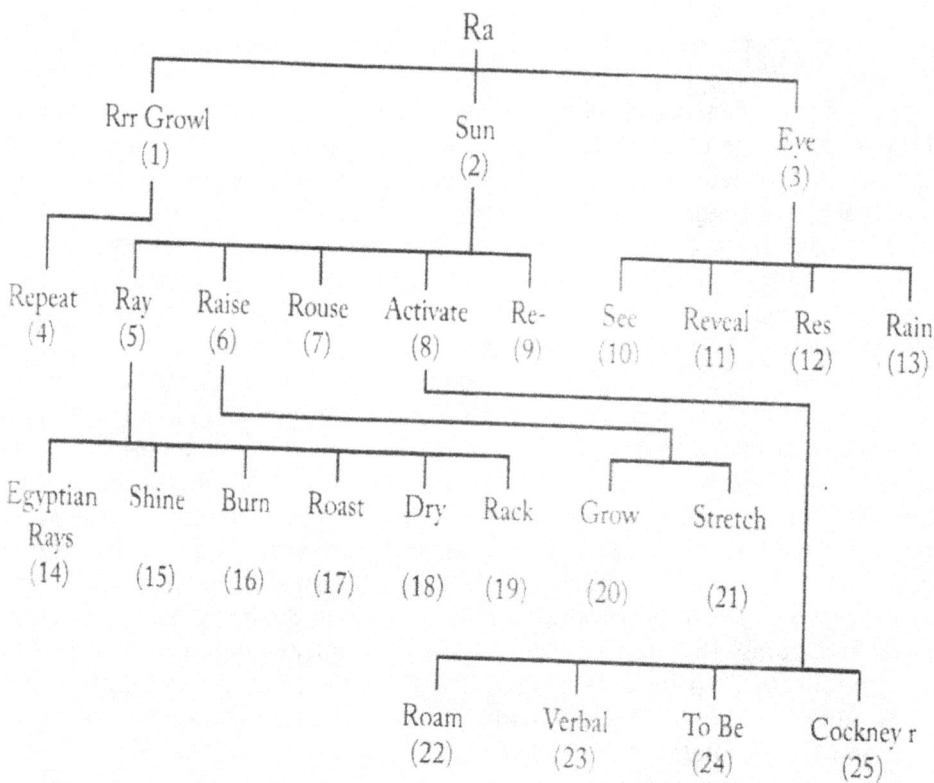

Chapter 12 Ra

Eric Partridge adds the Sanskrit racayati, he regulates, making rows. Our English kings, if we help ourselves by looking also at the German one, konig, are supposed to be kau-nai, strength-exhibiting or exercising power, in the Latin version their potestas recognized, their ka here standing for their political potency or power. You can compare the Arabic (and Aramaic) nabi for prophet and naib for ambassador (later governor of a province) both from the Lithic syllables nai-bai, expositor-bum, a traveling informant: one a mendicant preacher the other a pompous emissary, a representative of the supreme power sent to explain what that power requires. They don't intrinsically mean anything else other than their Lithic origins. What else we understand about their respective roles are merely add-ons in practice from usage over the aeons, which often outmode the simpler and blunter Lithic meanings – in the process making the underlying psychosemantic structures much harder to spot or even concealing them entirely. Lithic research is not primarily to find out what we really mean or at one time meant, but to study the way ideas and their expression have expanded, been modified, drifted and changed. We are not looking for evolution in accordance with rules, a process which starts by random variation followed by natural (unplanned) selection of the fittest variations, which is applicable only to blind biological change, including particularly, as Darwn had it in 1859, speciation. We are on the contrary dismissing this protocol from language studies altogether. It has nothing whatever to do with language development which proceeds by human whimsy and circumstance, which have shaped the way we consciously think, a derivation driven by human thinking itself, a meta-physical phenomenon however much it may emanate from a natural source in the brain. We are no more controlled by the structure of our brains as to what thoughts we may think than we are controlled by the structure of our legs as to what walks we may take. We can not fly and we can not step outside the powers of human cerebration. But in our own gardens we can wander where we will. Will the Massachusetts Institute of Technology stop crowing from the top of their big hill and please note their cognitive researches in terms of the brain scarcely impinge upon language and certainly do not warrant belief in Chomskyan hard wiring of ideas, our ephemeral mental actions in life. The Chomsky-M.I.T. alliance is misplaced.

From ra as an eye (3) come the obvious meanings to see (10), and thence to show (11) from seeing, like the rabbit which shows its buttocks or bottom (Lithic ra-baba-tai, its visible twin bulges) as it flees, by flipping its white skud into the air as it runs like the antelope, another one-that becomes-with looping-feet, as it bounds along, its white tail rather than its feet which describes such elegant curves in the air as it goes. A bunny is one that presents its bum. Were there wise women in the nursery with unacknowledged knowledge of Lithic underpinnings of words giving them a feeling of words of power? If they coined bunny, could they also read rabbit? Or coney, ka-u-nai, which addressed the rabbit's tail as a spinal extension-what-protruded and exhibits itself, apparently immediately from the Spanish connejo pronounced conneyo, the –o on the end simply a substantive ending: from au, that one. The rabbit's skud is from ish-ka-u-da, show-spine-that-does. The spine here is of course the bit which sticks out the end. The spine is for most of its length embedded in the flesh for which it provides the support and frame, but where it has an exposed end or tail it has a modicum of independent and visible action. It can wag and flick flies, for which it was hardly designed but comes in handy like much of blind anatomy. The ka is a widespread term for the skeleton (an upright-strong-flexible-job, it has jointed vertebrae), particularly the spine. As such it is also the male soul which provides the structure and also the drive and will-to-action of the male. The female soul, in Egypt at least, was the ba or fleshly soul which is draped over the ka in life but perishes

235

Chapter 12 Ra

at death, leading males to confirm their pristine belief they possess immortality while women (like animals), lacking the male soul – and presumably possessing only the simulacrum of it in their spines – were mortal. Should it be necessary to add that these beliefs, although still traceable in the lexicon, ought not to be followed in civilized society, since they are merely fanciful and extremely bad mannered? Such ideas are now so distasteful it is hard to find them recorded but Aristotle is on record and for the etymologist coyness over our past misdemeanours and ineptitudes is inappropriate, since understanding Lithic semantic contents requires this kind of honesty.

While on land the bunny rabbit is presenting its tail as an escape tactic, in the pond alongside the frog is presenting the other end, his eyes only above the water line. That is why the Latins call him rana, eyes protruding, brer pog-eyes. He has managed to redesign his headgear so that his eyes are on the top of his head. When it is submerged he still has a full view. Na is to protrude, originallytaken as a gull from Tarzan's penis, and thence coming to mean to present, to present oneself, to be presented or present, a presenter or exponent; and finally the present, nau, now, the presented (in time). The retina of the eye is another case in point. It is from the Latin. The Lithic is rai-tai-na. An intermediate translation is rays-tai-presented or showing. To extract the meaning of tai here we need to refer to the prehistoric meaning of the Tau, the symbol we call T. It represented the two dimensions which make a surface, as well as the two dimensions representing space and time, and then the two dimensions representing the world as we know it, and so even the world as we know it, since tau also stood for all the events, happenings, originally from all the births, with birth from the ta or birth canal, from parturition, dividing a single piece (or person) into two. Thus the Egyptian for Heaven, conventionally transliterated pet but actually correctly pronounced Pai Taun, skin or roof (Semitic desert dwellers' roofs were goat skins against the burning sun) of the World. The hieroglyphs are just a square (a birds eye view of a surface) and a semicircle on a horizontal flat side, conventionally described as a bun (sic) but actually of course the image of that day which was of the flat surface of the world and the upturned bowl of the sky under which we live and move and have our being. The Greek pai, spelt with the letter pi, (and known to school children the world over as chosen to represent the ratio of the diameter of a circle to its circumference) is drawn in elevation, the surface with a curlicue as the main feature and the two supports plain as only helpers. Will there still be those who think I am making all this up? The rays tai or in the two directions made a network precisely for the Latin rete, which means a net. A reticule adds the –cule, in Lithic -kau-lai or joined or crossed lines. A net in English is from nai-tai, presenting-Ts, which makes a net just like the Latin rays going two ways.

A thing in Latin, res (12), Lithic rai(s), was the rayed, anything visible, as we would say pertaining to the phenomenal world. Of course it is open to argue that what we see is not immediately real after all, and this is argued exhaustively in Appendix A on the philosophy of language. So far as the history of reality is concerned, in the human mind we may note the semantic catena from the visible to thing to chattels to goods and so wealth, so that the Vedic ram meant riches and the Sanskrit rewan meant rich, (with lots of things). Eric Partridge picks out Middle Welsh rai meaning precisely goods or riches. Riches itself has obvious kinship with Old Frisian riki and Old Norse rikr, where Norse final r was pronounced a (25). Both are variants from the Lithic rai-kai, meaning powerful, but from the idea of having possessions: wives, chattels, cattle, etc. In the Stone Age you had the possessions you had the power to hang on to. Partridge supposes that *re (the speculative original root) meant property, arguing reification, to invest with reality, is literally "to make property of". There was really something of the repeating, numbering and counting

Chapter 12 Ra

of items under meaning (4) in Latin res and Welsh rai, as well as seeing (10) via rays (5). The psychosemantic trees drawn to demonstrate the descent or perhaps better the sprouting of meanings one from the other in fact misrepresent to some extent the dream-like cross-referencing of prompts from the subconscious. The root Partridge was seeking is *re to make real or realize, given of course reality is the visible, which of course it does not.

From the rabbit with its tail end visible as it runs, it is a short semantic hop to rain (13) which shows a pattern like a series of watery rays, leaping over the obvious difference that the visibility comes from sunbeams and the other from substantive watery beams; and from there follows the idea of a stream, although the Egyptian lingo makes it clear the sequence tr had a special significance from the earliest meaning streams, passed down in the subconscious mind from our hominid days, and re-accessed from generation to generation as every generation consciously learned to speak and subconsciously - as Chomsky would say at a deep level – identified the phonemic meanings from which words are built – just as it still happens, more or less, today. But it is the lexicon which is our first tutor, and not any transformational grammar. In our subconscious minds we learn to recognize the original phonemic semantic bricks while upstairs with our conscious minds we are learning to construct the language buildings.

A ray from the sun (5) was gulled by the priests of Amun for all they were worth. The sun's rays raised the plants, acting at a distance. In similar fashion anything else which was raised from a distance must surely be being rayed in order to raise it. Tarzan said it wasn't him doing it. It must be a ray coming from the outside. Not only that, he had a very good idea whence it was coming, because whenever he was sitting facing the fair sex. – around the hearth for instance – he found his member rising. So it made sense to look for what might be emitting rays like the sun, and since the sun had for long been identified as a world birth canal in the sky (the Aton) it was easy to see the little tau the girls had between their legs was the likely culprit when rounded out like the Aton above. The males were in thrall, it thus appeared, to the feminine nature which was to seduce the male. Such an imaginary pull, a magic force, was and is still recognised in every kind of application such as in English trays and chests of drawers which get pulled out. Even the underwear we wear are pull ups, drawers, though the original sexual gull may no longer be on the wing. The Egyptians marked out the forces controlled by their gods with a glyph before their titles which the Egyptologists have called a neter – the glyph is of a pennant blown out in the wind – but the vowelisation is just guesswork, since it is usually not marked in the glyphs, as with all writing in Semitic tongues (unless added with superscripts or subscripts afterwards). The glyph is misidentified as an axe of divinity – since it precedes the glyphs for the numerous gods of Egypt. In reality the figure, a pennant blown out in the wind, is a symbol of a natural force and should be pronounced natura with the meaning na-tau-rai, showing the tau ray, like that from the tau or birth canal, or natural pull or force.. Their many gods were at one time anyway not gods in the Greek style but symbols of the natural forces over which each presided. In case this is not concise enough to convince the senators, reluctant perhaps to be taught wisdom by a rank amateur, it can also be shown that one of the oldest gods of Egypt, Ptah, after whom Egypt is named, nevertheless is uniquely denied any neter (as academia currently calls the thing). This is because he is properly pronounced Pata ahi, which means Our Fathers. Since he was an ancestor god he did not represent a force of nature but a source of advocacy and consequently he was not described as natura, showing a force. Egypt itself is from Aui-kau-pata-ahi, and is not the land of the god Ptah but on the contrary That where-begotten-of fathers-our, the land where our fathers were born, The Fatherland. Father is from pa-ta,

Chapter 12 Ra

or piped-urethra or birth canal, the male organ described as a strangler preventing childbirth. The Irish bot, Manx bwoid is their word for penis, indicating a similar blocked ti; and boy in English, it must be suspected, has a similar origin. A buoy is a similar bung or fleshy bit but afloat.

Latin has the same semantic content in the tra- root as the Egyptian pennant of divinity. Trahere is to draw out or along, no doubt with the sexual origin of the tara gull forgotten. Our English farm tractors are exhibiting at several removes the power of the feminine pudenda to draw out the male organ, but this is of course to be disregarded in common parlance. Yet it is needful to remind the reader of the whimsical and vulgar provenance of the term because it illustrates nicely the mentality of our hominid forbears, who after all had no television and only one entertainment; so that the greater part of our original lexicon can sometimes appear (as already touched on in chapter 1) to have been largely hammered out on the anvil of our own genitalia. To track is to follow the traces, drawn along by them indeed, for a hunter-gatherer the second most thrilling experience of his life. The noun is the trace left by the tracking. The Latin trans, across, with fifty main compounds in English alone, is from the same semantic root, to be drawn across – originally from the boys' side of the hearth towards the girls'. A trance is a fixation whereby the victim is locked onto an attractive ray which holds him entranced.

A tree is a plant of the variety which has been notably drawn up with a hardened trunk, just like the male organ in receipt of the same ta ray, though a job which in reality has been carried out by Ra, the eye in the sky, which nevertheless has a connection to the old belief in the uplifting feminine rays.

Now we can see three is from the rays of the T, while quattuor, Latin for four (four is from the Lithic phau-u-arai, the protrusions-what-activated (8), the four limbs) was perhaps in original conception kau-tau-ray, joined-Ts-rays, one T upside down on top of the other, making four rays. It makes a cross, in Latin crux apparently from the Punic, a provincial Egyptian. It is a curiosity the Lithic phoneme ka, with its semantic content from the identification of the sound of flint knapping strike, flake, split off should here be used to mean join. If you put together a flint matrix with a flake just struck off, it fits exactly with a barely detectable seam, highlighting the perfect fit or join. From that point of view a joint between any two items, to be a fit, was where they had been split apart. Ta, which was the lighter sound of the snap of a stick broken in two, which meant to make two from one, to give birth, to be born, to become, and so any transference from one state to another, to die to become dead, similarly came to mean to join together to twin, to tie. Like the slayer and the slain, a discontinuity, once perceived, could also be seen from the near side of the event as well as the far side. It is one of our more splendid inconsequentialities that we can have the same semantic content with two quite opposite interpretations.

To try is to be in receipt of a ray which drives or draws us to make an attempt. It dates from before the persona as an independent and reasonably independent agency had been put together. To tremble is to be drawn, terayed em-be-lai, as-be-liquid, that is as immersed in cold water, suffering from hypothermia, when the body tries to generate heat by shaking the muscles. All these supposed rays (14) are in fact seen as omnipresent. To rehearse them in any firm order is hard. If the reader has succeeded in wading through the first eleven chapters a good deal of understanding of the Lithic hypotheses should have been gained. Rays were supposed to be around which could affect the mind too. It was supposed an individual's brain was be-rai'n, the organ where these influences were received and registered. It was the playground for outside rays or influences beyond the individual's control. Indeed the idea of an individual personality is a comparatively recent fabrication which has grown up with the expansion of language and the capture of more and more human thinking by the conscious mind. You can see some relics of this belief in the idea of spiritual possession by good or bad spirits. A dream came into the mind as a ray drawn in. As such it might well carry a message from an outside agency such as a god. A hero for the Greeks was in receipt of hai rays so that he performed heroically. Bravery came that way. Berani in Malay means brave. Ber- in Malay is much like our be- in benighted or begotten or beware. The rani is from Lithic ra-nai, ray-showing, a clear case of inspiration from an outside influence. Or else it may have been the –nai ray was intended, via presentation to suggest confrontation. In so far as nai came originally from sexual presentation it could easily have slipped into confrontation. The Malay has also berahi with a Lithic hei on the end in place of the nai. Hei we find in the Egyptian pahei, the ecstacy piece or penis. Hei, as with the American greeting Hi! conveys pleasure (or else pain, but always a sharp emotional response, as in hot). The Malay berahi means amorous and lustful, in the modern American slang hot. Berahman in Malay, Brahmin in Hindi, is lustful of the mind, actually meaning an ascetic. In Hindi brave is bahadur, from bai-ha-tau-rai, be-hero-tau-rayed.

Rage is simply a ra-kai, a ray kindling or stimulus. A veranda is from the Hindi baramda via the Portuguese. The Indians appear to have got it very early from the Persians. It is essentially a protruding roof from a building providing a place to sit in the open air but out of the sun. Ba in Hindi is in use as a bung of one kind or another. A veranda acts as a blocker of the sun's rays. The hums m and n are both in use as fillers but also as meaning fillers too, where we would now use a preposition to guide the relationship between two nouns. Modern syntax calls for an of after ra, in accordance with the postpositional idiom of the Hindi tongue.(which now uses ka). Ba-ra-'m-da in Lithic meaningful phonemes is Block-sunray-of-does. In Malay we find an opposite gloss on ba, from the haunch to going to be ongoing, as in our own benighted, to be in a state or even in motion. Beraja for instance is a planet, from Lithic ber-ra-ja, be-shine-rayed, sending out a shining ray, or is it that the planets were recognised as illuminated by the sun without any luminescence of their own, just like the moon, Silene,from sirene, presenting reflectd light, ra-ja meaning sun-lit. One wonders if the Hindu raja was claiming to be God illuminated too, rather than just a regulator. The Sultans next door, after all, Su-al-taun, fancied themselves either the Delight of the world or else its Illumination, the Light of the World. Or take the aboriginal Malay berbaling, a pair of bamboo tubular, deep throated whistles, mounted on a rotating shaft hoist to the top of a tree. It is ber-ba-lai-ing, going in a loop all night in the wind, making a whooping sound keeping the evil spirits for miles around at bay. Every well appointed ladang or leveled clearing should have one. Then there is bera, be-sunning, which can mean changing colour, a light bright colour, inflamed, blushing or swollen, all conditions the sun can be held responsible for, the swelling really most applicable to fruit, but since a swollen poisoned limb feels hot the rays get blamed for that one too. Berai is scattered, much as we say sprayed, from the sun's radiating rays in all directions. Spray is perhaps at one remove from Ra, the sun. It is ish-pai-rai, the action or even the issue-of the piece-which is rayed – with no prizes for guessing which piece or pipe caught the imagination of our cheery hairy forbears. A spray is an ejaculation.

The ray was thought of as a stimulus or prompt to almost any unusual degree of activity. This was how your fortune was taken to be determined by your fate, what rays might come your way. Folk saw themselves as puppets ruled by superior forces. Smitten with an angry ray you experienced a rage, ray kindled, shaped or made, and proceeded to rant and rave. Even a grin was prompted by a humour ray, from hei-u-mau-rai, a joy-one-

Chapter 12 Ra

minded or happy-thought-ray, a haha ray. Later a new and classical analysis of the psyche made out the humours were liquid elements. Hei was of course at bedrock a shock stimulus of pleasure or pain. Ha! came out for hot as well as humour. Gerai and ragai are from kai which means struck and made or kindled, from flint knapping in the first place. In Malay an amok is someone whose mind is kindled by the original hacking spirit. So he rushes around inflicting it on whoever he meets. He has to be cut down. It is an extreme form of nervous breakdown leaving the subconscious mind in charge to discharge its tensions on the world at large. Unsurprisingly asylums are full of folk who imagine they are in receipt of rays from outside, which in fact they are sensing from their own subconscious minds of which they are wholly unaware.

Fifty years ago, for an operation to fillet a cauliflower ear, inflicted by the workers at British Steel when I fell on the ball in a game of rugby, (playing for the Military College of Science nearby (2nd XV for a civilian team) I was hospitalised. At that time British Steel was still British, but their industrial relations were already heading for the unacceptable, which resulted in their sale abroad. For filleting, I was admitted to Shenley Military Hospital, at that time specializing in head injuries and brain surgery, mostly oldies needing tumours removed. I never really lived it down, although the ear was largely tidied. I was approached in the ward by a young officer who had had the misfortune to fall from the roof of his Cambridge college while trying with accomplices to lift his tutor's car up on to it in the dark. He introduced me to the Egyptian rays for the first time. The task was successfully completed in spite of his fall - the tutor was carless, and the butt of university humour - and for some days he went about his business as usual, apparently unaffected; before his friends began to notice peculiarities in his behaviour, until he had to be hospitalized for his own safety, where he had a substantial benign polyp removed from inside his cranium, all at HM's expense. Now a year later, after sick leave, he was back in for final check up by a medical board to see if he was fit to continue in Her Majesty's service. I was studying for a post graduate qualification in a hotch potch of scientific subjects thought suitable for anyone aspiring to assist in the design of ordnance; and had a book open on electromagnetism, and when he saw it he became immediately animated and enquired about electromagnetic rays. While recuperating he had become aware of a ray which carried information directly to the brain. He sought guidance on how the common or garden electromagnetic rays were propagated to see if the ones he had found conformed. I told him I could give him the formulae from the book but I strongly advised him not to mention his discovery to the board members the following day. He readily agreed it was the safest course. So I imagine he has by now retired, full of years and honour, with his Ancient Egyptian helper rays intact but unexpressed, I guess as a full colonel or higher. He was a personable youngster and had already shown exemplary initiative at university. He just had to control his rays and keep them in order. In Tarzan's day we were all having to do it.

It is a sobering thought that some part of the mind can be dreaming while the conscious mind is wide-awake. How else do we learn to recognize our Lithic origins of speech while learning our language today, when no part of it is in the extant script? Before speech our thinking was probably for most of us for the most part subconscious, with kaleidoscopic prompts and inconsequential takes of every scene, as the mind meandered or raced away, just as everyone experiences their thinking in dreams today. What we have built, with the tagging of ideas, is an intellectual crust on which we can mentally promenade, on a day to day basis for practical affairs. Our bodily functions, heart beat, circulation of the blood, digestion and all the rest not specifically captured remain part of the autonomic system, wholly unconscious, that is to say they are not generally within the purview of the conscious mind. Yet there is a degree of mind over matter as well as matter over mind. A tumour can lead to delusion, sometimes of rays, and the rays to maniacal behaviour. Equally, an emotional depression can depress vital functions. A physical disorder can make one cross. The subconscious mind can inform our waking state. As well as a deep unconscious we do have a layer of subconscious thought not immediately available to our conscious minds, unless by a specially directed effort probably prompted by emotional discomfort which forces us to dig deep into our mental facilities. It is while exploring to get out of an emotional hole that mental illness is said to occur. In asylums folk can be seen sitting in corners, bodies rocking, as they confront the same mental knot over and over again with an inadequate and inappropriate approach, because of their emotional bondage, with reason in an interminable stutter. Compared to the careful way we go about our waking calculations it can be said we all have someone too close to a madman for comfort in the dark room down below; and far from sending down our painful thoughts for safe keeping out of the light as Sigmund Freud supposed, we mostly keep the madman within securely chained, as simple common sense. Sometimes he may escape.

Without an element of rational protocol there is no way our minds can motor in a continuous straight line. It is a facility the human race has had to build since speaking as it has gone along, and it has to be said we have taken our time about it: hundreds of thousands of years. We might have done better if the mind could have evolved like the flesh instead of whimsically weaving itself a frame for thinking largely on its own. But that would have taken longer still; and the end result would have left us with tunnel vision, unable to think for ourselves because our minds were driven by our genes. This is indeed where some over enthusiastic biologists have thought we are at already. But the brain does not determine the terms in which we think any more than our legs determine what walks we will take. The legs will not enable us to fly. The brain will not enable us to master everything we wish. But within their preordained purviews when deciding their particular actions they are supreme. Charles Darwin had no wish to dragoon all knowledge within his one evolutionary idea. He was aware of its dangerous potential in the hands of less thinking folk. He actually believed it might, if misunderstood, release the flood waters of bloody revolution upon the streets of London, and was disposed to leave his work for posthumous publication (after he was safely gone!). Only Alfred Russel Wallace's paper he sent to the Linaean Society in 1859 announcing his discovery of the evolutionary mechanism (Darwin's old mentor Sir Charles Lyell was president) persuaded him to break his silence to avoid being deprived of the kudos of his discovery. Papers from both Wallace and Darwin were read and Lyell declared Darwin's the better of the two. Else we should have had Russellism. Ideas are only virtual things. They have no existence except when they are being thought. They leave no particular impression on the brain which survives the phenotype, any more than the particular walks the legs have taken leave any particular impression on the legs. Their legacy is by transference from one mind to another, quite unmediated by the genes. We have sidestepped evolution by means of speech. We talk so much our legs would probably by now be slowly getting shorter, since today it is no longer the most successful lopers after game who carry off the most brides. Only we are getting longer because of our optimal feeding (those of us who are optimally fed). But the lexicon enlarges itself every day quite without regard to biology. It is a metaphysical reality, along with scientific theory and everything else in the realm of ideas transmissible directly from phenotype to phenotype by means of speech. We have talked our way out of the slavery of the genes, never mind blind clockmakers who take an opposite view. That does not mean that with this new found freedom most of what we have thought has not been rubbish because for the most part it evidently has.

The rays were perceived as impinging on and registering in our brains (ba-rai'n), the flesh rayed – or was the brain eventually perceived as perhaps itself not just rayed flesh but an organ like those other ba designated testicles in Malay and even Sumerian, and raying – a sun itself and raying, a source (of ideas) itself? In any case these brain rays were evidently taken to be a peculiar and privileged acquisition of mankind, suitable for distinguishing man from beast. In Malay we have orang for man, from au-ra'ng, that one-raying, either in receipt of rays which are raying from without or else himself emitting rays, like brain waves, although the former is the most likely as the original form, since the brain has no need of rays to itself and they do not reach anyone else. The Latin vir, from uir and Lithic u-i-rai, one-which-rayed is semantically much the same as an orang although superficially quite different. It is as if rai meant rational, gifted with reason, straight up thinking. It may have been what the brain rays supposedly vouchsafed. The Chinese for man is ren, akin to orang. Apparently from Lithic rai'n, it means the rayed-one. Lithic has a remarkable ability to pull widely disparate languages together at many points. It would take a master spirit, or more than one to hunt down all the instances, and a lifetime or two each at their disposal to complete the task or even get anywhere near it. You start to think of monkeys sitting down to type the Bible a randon, (as the sun does), scattering its rays all around without discrimination, firing its rays at random. But we do all seem to have been proud ab initio of our ability to reason, even if the conception of how we thought it went seems askew today. When conscious thinking was a novelty, that need be the cause of no surprise. It is nevertheless a temptation with more recent dissimulations to rename proud Sapiens Sapiens simply Homo Fraudster. Reason is a malleable instrument of use for many purposes other than explication. Business alone calls for playing cards held close to chests. It even calls for concealing science when needs be, to win a deal or sell an environmental poison.

In India where the sun sets over the Western Ghats in a glorious blaze like over Gomera, merah means red. Carmine and crimson are out of the same vat, but complicated by to-ing and fro-ing between the Semitic and Indo-European tongues. Kermis or something like it is the word for the cochineal insect which when crushed produces a deep red dye[1]. In the case of carmine the word from the Latin mixes together the kermes insect and the Latin minium for red lead to produce a deep red. Skipping the minium for the moment, the kermes just meant insects, the Lithic suggests kara-mai-sai, maker-of-earth-ups. They were probably white ants which build irregular castles many feet high from the dry earth by gumming the grains of sand together. Their cousins the cochineal insects, ka-u-shai-nai, body-what-shine-presenting-liquid, had the colour. The Sanskrit krmi, pronounced keremi, from the Lithic kara mai, an earth worker, was both an insect and a worm. The worm is easy. The insect was presumably one which lived in the soil or close to it, as many do, most of them scuttling away when turned up. Our worm on the other hand, from the Latin vermis from uermis, although capable of being described as a soil turner, appears to have originally been a maggot usually found living in rotten matter. Mai means both soil and dead.

Tales of the mythical Aamaraiga were around as a Shangrila when Vespucci senior named his more famous son Amerigo, and the mythical land will have been known to Columbus when he set sale to prove the land actually existed. His idea of the size of the world allowed him to believe it would prove to be the land the valuable East Indian spices came from. In this he was disappointed, but Spain found silver in abundance instead and

Chapter 12 Ra

has lived on the booty for over four hundred years. There is no other possible explanation for the two oddities, the pyramids in central America and in Egypt, than a common dispersed source. We can conceive of a common psychosemantic linguistic connection – taun for instance in Egyptian and taan in Aztec mean the same, but a cultural artifact dreamed up from the lexicon by two separate civilizations is a bridge too far. Only ignorance could allow anyone to believe the contrary. The contact must have been many years ago, but probably after the great glacier melt raised sea levels around the world by three hundred and sixty feet. Most probably the transmission was from Adam's Malaya with displaced persons going East and West, 10.000 to 8,000 years BP. In Mesopotamia where the Sumerian (Western travelling) Adamites finished up they had ziggurats (vertical constructions) made of mud.

Rock is from rau-ka. Ka (chapter 5) is the knapped flint, gulled for its hardness. Most places you come to it quite soon if you dig down, and much of it sticks up bare of soil. In 1831 Charles Lyell demonstrated in his epoch making book "The Principles of Geology" that it had indeed been thrust up, not once but repeatedly from down below. The ancients used ka for the bedrock, and so the earth, and so for land. That was what was in there, just as bodies had bones as hard structure to hold them together. The samples which stuck up above their natural covering of soil, it was clear even to the ancients had been raised – more rays at work. A rock was an expelled bit of the core. Had they not seen it often enough in volcanic eruptions? Stone is from sai-ta-un, fire-born-one. Metal is from mai-ta-lai, earth (the ore)-become-liquid. The Canary islands are supposed to be from the doggy Isles in Latin. This canard was invented by the elder Pliny over two thousand years ago and has had a somewhat longer run than it deserved (until I came along). Before speaking in the Roman senate he would begin "Carthago delenda est" (Carthage must be destroyed) and he would repeat the slogan again before he sat down. Fascism came from Rome and re-emerged under Mussolini only recently. To be fair the Carthaginian foraging general Hanibal had made a mess of the Roman campania and had only been defeated by the Fabian tactics of the Roman general Fabius who finally slaughtered the Carthaginian force hemmed in on the shore of Lake Trasimene (spelling approximate, only recollected from secondary school). Nevertheless the genocide of all the Carthaginians in the metropolis and environs of Carthage which followed in due course can hardly be excused even by a Fascist. The language is all but forgotten and is now spoken only by the Berber hill tribes who escaped, a provincial patois based on Carthaginian which was itself a provincial version of the Ancient Egyptian language (which was destroyed in turn by the Wahabi Arab invasion nine centuries later under the Islamic flag). Pliny's fib was flawed from the outset: canis is third declension and would have given us Canery Isles. The Carthaginian was Ka'n Aria, the Araising Ka or Rocky lands.

An anorak and anorexia are widely separated in origin but come side by side in the dictionary. The anorak is Inuit from Greenland, and simply means clothes. Like the Malayan aboriginal tribesman asked the name of a growing timber tree who replied at once it was a tree, and the Australian aboriginal asked to name a budgerigar who replied it was a bright coloured bird, the Inuit asked to name his anorak said it was clothing. The Lithic appears to be a-nau-rai-kai, that-present-rays (may we guess warm ones?)-[to the] body. Strictly the Lithic says presenting-raying-of the body, for warming the body. But the prepositions all come from of initially, and it could be referred back to the first phoneme, so the pattern A-of B could also signify A-B of. It is no more surprising really than putting the adjective before or after the noun. Girls with anorexia are on a different tack, but they answer to the same original Lithic phonemes with the same meaning trees. Orexis is

Chapter 12 Ra

appetite or desire from the Greek verb oregein to stretch out and desire. The stretching out is evidently from au-rai-kai'n, to be ray kindled. These are clearly Egyptian rays like those which have already been found to stretch out both the male organ and the female vagina. The au- here is either an introductory that one, as the Stone Age mind wound itself up to a positive identification, or else it is an oo or orifice which is getting stretched out. It might be either, since the boys were supposed to have reciprocal rays for the job once their muzzle covers had been withdrawn; but it seems clear it was the boys who were the paradigmatic and original stretchers out, since before trousers their ostentation was conspicuous enough to spot the desire even at quite a distance. The anorexia is a classic loss of appetite for food, but linked at some deeper level with a disinclination to copulate, a distaste and denial of feminine sex, and even of sex altogether. Those caught up in the discomfort are not easily cured because to cure them it is necessary to drag them into confronting precisely what they are determinedly refusing to confront. It usually cures itself in time, the Dawkins genes being so strong, but can be traumatic and even life threatening while it lasts since the victims starve themselves for their greater good and to save themselves from having to confront their own natures fully frontally. The intellectual approach is so far the only effective cure known. Humanity is not usually silly for ever; just for rather a long time. The anorexic have really just forgotten how to laugh.

While every schoolboy knows about the antics of his own organ he knows very little about a girls vagina, which appears to be from the Lithic u-a-kai-na, an o or orifice-that-kindled-presents [itself]. For the girls the presentation is by rounding out. Indeed round itself is from rau-en-tai, rayed-of-the ta, or the ta-when rayed. If it were rand instead of round it could be sun-become, the round shape gulled from the sun, which is conspicuously round; and little reliance can be placed upon vowelisation over the years, so rand originally is not impossible. But all the rest we have gleaned about the Egyptian rays points us in the direction of sexual raying in this case as well. The conventional wisdom pays no regard to the phonemes involved and derives vagina from the Latin meaning a sheath. In their book the vagina is simply another sheath. However it is open to a Lithic speaker to respond that it went the other way about: the swordsman's sheath started out a vagina in which, in rollicking mood, he fleshed his sword. The sheath would after all need to be designed reasonably na for the sword to slip easily in and out. In Malaya I had a parang ground out of an old car spring for felling trees which went in a sheath made of two hollowed pieces of wood bound together so as to be sufficiently na to hold the blade which had a thick blunt side the original thickness of the spring. Inside the sheath the clitoris is a miniature residual ill-formed penis which inflates and obtrudes in order to catch the stimulus of the reciprocating full sized male organ when admitted. It is formed from the Lithic phonemes ka-lai-tau-rai-(s), which readily read as makes-liquid-[when] the vagina-[is] rayed-(substantve marker). In arousal the vagina becomes lubricated. The clitoris probably plays no part in this but the simultaneity makes the Lithic string veridical. It also provides the sensation, which is why it is so wicked to cut it out. Female circumcision is a barbaric male chauvinistic mutilation, often accompanied by stitching together the vaginal labia to prevent penetration, leading to chronic infections. It is the mark of barbarism at work. It is no part of Islam. Formerly pagan tribes pretend it is. It should be severely punished.

An orifice is from an o-rai-pahei-kai in Lithic, a hole-rayed-phalus-kindled. It is a round hole in short. It is true the -fice part is from the Latin verb facere to make, but facere is from the same derivation, the making being begetting, making babies in origin, making with the pahei, just as making in English too started out as making an earthing, planting or inseminating. With making itself the ma- has been ascribed to kneading the mass, apparently preparing dough to make a cake or else the clay to make a pot "by pressing repeatedly with the hands" (Partridge). There is however no mention of the supposed hands. The other is to be preferred. The other rounding out of the uterus is at childbirth to allow the passage of the baby's head. Jaweh is said to have inflicted this painful passage on women, apparently withdrawing his own rays which would have helped at this juncture and replacing them with others that make the pain, to punish them because Eve had upset the divinely instituted balance of nature. Eve in future was left to do the pushing on her own. Apparently she had used her intelligence to improve on the divine dispensation with her digging stick, leading the water from the river to the padi fields with their much improved yields – from which the deity drove our forebears by drowning them under the South China Sea. We are having to rely upon Adam for this analysis of where the trouble lay. He had presumably been innocently killing game for a living in the time honoured way. He said he had simply accepted the food he was offered. We may suspect the tree of knowledge was really the ta-rays which Eve had picked up in her brain when working out her hydraulic improvements of nature.

From growth there is grain, but gr, ain is from grind. To grow is to be gerau, be-rayed and rise. On the grind stones which go round there is in due course inscribed a grain, the round scratches from the grit which gets between the upper and the nether stone, along with the corn. Wood grain on a plank is not round, but that is because the timber has been cut lengthwise. In nature the tree rings add to the girth as the tree grows year upon year and the rings can be counted to tell the age of the tree. The ground has supposedly been ground, since it is generally covered with soil, which has a granular structure, like the coffee grounds at the bottom of the pot. The grit is gerai-tai, born of going round, grinding, become ground. If it is put between the stones it is not born there; but sufficient was rubbed off the stones to suggest it all came that way – as indeed it does, by erosion one way or another. To erode is from the same root as a rat which is a rodent, a gnawer, but the gnawing is only one kind of abrasion from abradere to wear down in Latin and radere to rub. We have here a fleet of Latin buses. From grinding, the ra phoneme has been put to use as if it is the essential phoneme for abrasion, whereas that is the wrong bit to borrow since it only provides the rounding; it is what goes round, namely the grind stone, which really provides the abrasion. However in Malay a thorn is a duri, and a local prickly fruit is a durian. It gives the guide to the meaning of the English thorn, a holer, from tau-ere'n. It has a puncturing action, represented by the verbal –ere- (8) like the Sumerian sag-i-ta, for arrow, with a head-which-punctures. The colour gray is the colour of the rye and emmer wheat flour. Wheat flower is white. Flow and flour are akin. The powder flows as if it were a liquid. You have to hold it in a solid container like liquid if you do not want to have it slip away. The r in flour is a cockney r, untrilled and pronounced like a, with the same meaning as if it were a – one or that, in the case of flour just one, a flowing one or flower. It is interesting that by milling the flour right small it begins to acquire the character of a liquid, confirming our forbears' belief water lacked a solid element and that is why it was so slippery and elusive. By abrading the solid elements by milling them you got them moving towards a liquid state. A flower is a fa-i-lau-a. It is a shoot-which lowered [petals]-one, just as flour is one with a fluvial habit, a dry powder in effect, although the powder itself is simply one that has been pounded, with a pestle (from the Sanskrit pinsati, he pounds) rather than with a fist, and the fact it flows if it is dry is not covered. A petal is from pai-ta-lai, a shoot-become-lowered/flat.

Chapter 12 Ra

It now becomes possible to discuss the derivation of the English adjective rare. It means these days to be uncommon. Partridge as usual has some good stuff[2]. It is perhaps well at this stage to remind ourselves of the character of the sun's rays, or indeed those of any light source, as they will have struck our hominid forebears when they were teaching themselves to speak. They shine (15), they heat (17) and they can burn (16). As terrestial fires send out similar rays to the sun it was assumed that the sun was a fire source, and a volcano was a terrestial sun which only worked occasionally and often half heartedly at that, while the sun was burning at full bore all day. There is of course no direct evidence of this ratiocination hundreds of thousands of years ago, but we can see that reason provides that it went that way. Fire will actually cook food put near to it but away from the flame. The rays will also dry (18). They are straight (19), as observed in sunbeams when the motes reflect the rays. The motes lit up were mistaken for the rays, detectable as a string of microscopic particles, suggesting the repetitious rrrrrr. The rays raise the crops so that they are gerau and grow.(20). The effect of rays of every sort is always to stimulate and bring to action at a distance. In any case they seem to be the activators that provide the action. But perhaps more fundamentally they radiate in all directions around their source, with an instinct to spread themselves around, which in turn perhaps gives them their universal application. But anything that is spread around becomes sparse and rare. To ray is to radiate (14) and so to become opened out or spread out, individually to gape and collectively to have gaps between, separating the pieces. What is separated with gaps between is the eremite who lives alone, from the Greek eremos, Lithic ai-rai-em-au(s), going-spread-into-one(singularity), which means a solitary, a unitary entity, from both au (chapter 15) and the reri from earlier in this chapter, to itemise and count.

A hermit, from an eremite, is one who has become a solitary, from the Lithic a(h)i-rai-em-i-tai, withdrawn from the inhabited world. The Greek eremia is a desert, an uninhabited part of the world. Rare meat on the other hand appears to be contradictory, since it appears at first sight to have been getting a lot of raying. In origin, all the words leading to rare meat in Germanic languages come originally with a cockney h in front, originally pronounced ahi (to separate the vowels a and the i). Rare from rai-rai, a reduplicative, means perhaps lots of little rays and so only lightly cooked. Roast is thoroughly cooked over the flame, from rau-sai-tai, fully rayed-[of the]flame-become. But the Old English was hrer, the h later shed as redundant. Like the hermit, which glossed the Greek eremai, the h in hrer is a cockney h, originally separating an initial a vowel from a followng i. In Egypt h was pronounced ahi, and our aitch is relict of the same pronunciation. In Middle English the meanings of component phonemes was disregarded and ai had become pronounced as her, so the difference between hrer (a[h]i-rai-rai, un[h]which-fully/continuously rayed) and rer was not regarded. Rare meat which was un-continuously rayed was spoken of as continuously rayed, the absurdity unnoticed because the meaning of the word was well established and its dependence upon its original string of phonemes was forgotten. This is only one case of such slovening which just happens to have lost the original meaning thread. There will have been many others. It would be sweetly reasonable to tick off every word which is not immediately responsive to analysis in terms of the Lithic psychosemantic trees printed as further cases in point. It may not strike those who do not want to acknowledge their random roots have been discredited as a reasonable sequitur.

The roster that allocates shifts comes from a roaster or gridiron and so a grid and thence a table allocating jobs or duties, etc. There is certainly some lateral thinking involved while for the most part simply following a chain of metaphors. This is not evolution of meanings. It has nothing to do with Charles Darwin, will Neo-Darwinists please note. This is how the mind works and how the languages of the world have been built. The liberal transferences of meanings has no doubt been much prompted and assisted by borrowings from languages akin or merely rendered adjacent. When you translate you allow yourself a good deal of leeway, which is missing in your own language where meanings are clearly established at any one time and not to be tampered with so freely. It is however not only the crops that grow. Time itself in the old days was measured on the same yardstick. A crony is a person who attended the same institution synchronously, at the same time. It is assumed cronies will be on friendly terms, from their earlier shared experience, or drilling by the same team. A crony, instead of a contemporary has become just an intimate or friend with no overt reason for the friendship, which may therefore be found sinister, as working behind the scenes together, exercising inappropriate help or assistance one to the other. To be chronic is to accompany the passage of time, to be of or for a time and thus to be continuous like time itself. A chronicle is a historical record in the form of a strictly time ordered tale. The Greek god Chronos was exemplar of what kerau-nau in Lithic semantic terms was what growth-presented. What growth marks is the passage of time, and thence the aging process. Anyway so our forebears evidently thought. Chronos meant age, time passed, and so just the time that passed. He is called Father Time and represented as an old man with a gray beard and a stick. The Lithic handles it all.

To roam is to wander around. It has been derived from pilgrimages to Rome. But this is absurd, since the Holy City is precisely targeted by pilgrims from the outset; and nor would there in that case be any call to change the spelling. It makes more sense to link the name with Romany or Roumany gypsies, who perhaps gave their name to Roumania. Rouman sounds Hindi, the original Gypsies' language. The Egyptian connection was only fleeting before they again got expelled like the Jews some time before them. Their later pretence to be Egyptians and to possess Egyptian magic was just that, a pretence required by their black goddess Kali when having intercourse with goys and unbelievers. Deception is imperative to keep faith with the goddess of concealment and deception. Kali can be read in several ways. In Hindi it means time and tomorrow, probably from an original ka-lai, go-looping or make-orbit like the sun god Apollo, from A-pau-lau, that-journey-looped, the orbiter. But the Hindi also has the meaning black, from that part of the sun's orbit which ka-lai, goes low, that is the night time transit under the earth through Tartarus by the dead (but gestating) sun, before its rebirth relit at the Eastern horizon. The English black has the same phonemes and no doubt the same semantic source with a metathesis of the constituent meaningful phonemes, benighted. Also ka-lai can be read in Lithic phonemes Act slippery or slyly. That was what the goddess had in mind. She was convinced like President Bush that those who were not with her were against her and adopted a proactive policy of eliminating them all. She wears a necklace of fifteen skulls, from the goys her followers have bagged, which change to a necklace of flowers when she comes out and makes a public progress through the streets. Sometimes she even switches from black to a jollier blue. Already in prehistory she was offering the faithful who killed fifteen infidels seven virgins in the hereafter. Her followers who have infiltrated Islam, the religion of peace on earth, follow her rule of thuggi, killing travelers by joining their caravans pretending to be innocent fellow travelers and then murdering them by stealth while they sleep. The Prophet's message is negatived, so far unnoticed. There are other confirmatory evidences of the abuse. In Baghdad assassins today have put out the eyes of their victims, as the thugs did in Pakistan in the eighteenth century, a final triumphant gesture to mark their successful deception.

Chapter 12 Ra

Anyway we can compare the Sanskrit bhrama, roaming, to roam in modern English. If this is a cockney h originally separating an a and an i the Lithic elements appear to have been ba(h)i-ra-ma, going-raying-of the mind, going as the rays of the mind guide you, as the spirit moves you, everywhere and anywhere indiscriminately like the rays of the sun, spreading yourself like the rays do. It only appears far fetched because we have lost the facility to think in terms of meaningful Lithic phonemes strung together ad hoc to convey complex meanings, before language had adopted the post Babel scheme of learning words by heart with their meanings attached by rote. We no longer compose words on the hoof as it were. A Chinese scholar will be more at home with Lithic. Their words are still seen as made up of meaningful phonemes strung together. Like Indian roaming, bhrama, is the English witch's broom stick, used wandering through the sky at night, na-ka-ti, flights of fancy with their secret sexual proclivities to the fore, something of the night about them. At one level a broom is merely a besom with a raking action, at another like the Indian Brahmin it can mean those in a state of spiritual exaltation, which may be dried up asceticism (as Brahmins claim) or otherwise of the night, wikka, an awesome (fear-making) mental activity forsaking the established paths of knowledge in the light of day in pursuit of enlightenment. These old crones had probably stumbled on a spot of Lithic language which gave them the impression of words of power, capable of summoning into full cognizance a hidden protocol from the past, as they would put it spirits of past life now reaching us from the rays they left in their tracks. That is not to say they were not effectively quite mad, because of the use they imagined they could make of their perceptions, nor that most of those punished for witchcraft were not completely innocent of evil – just Lithic thinkers.

Now surely it all seems obvious straight away, once you have managed to hook up to the Stone Age way of thinking, shedding our more recent and more sophisticated pathways in the mind. Straight away is a long way round. Straight is from the Lithic syllabic analysis ish-te-rai-ga(h)i-tai. The sibilant is up, vertical and straight (like the ash tree trunk). Terai is drawn out (like Tarzan's penis) and gai- or kai-tai is shaped-become, and all of it is straight beyond a peradventure. Moreover a straight route is the shortest way between two points, which is how straight away, an away on a straight route comes to mean in the shortest time, while that time may in fact be taken up with no wayfaring at all, but only with an instant's reflection or even a reflex response for fear of unwelcome correction. A string is strong enough to take the stress and withstand the strain and all these words come strictly from stretching out (21). Compare Greek oreigein to stretch out, from au-rai-gai-en, that one what-ray-kindled, from which comes also our erect and erection, drawn out rather than vertical. The verticality has evidently been picked off Tarzan's penis, his contemporaries having spotted the gull perching there. Then once straightened (by the ray required), things can be seen to be in a row, rau for all to see. A run comes from arousal. Else you would walk. But it can be in a row or series by a semantic leakage from straight, like a run of bad luck. These rays arranging visible (real) things in a row are really all the same. Rails are straight lines and may have a train drawn along on them; a train is a string of carriages getting drawn along - or else a bridal train drawn along by the bride, towed behind her. A ruler for drawing is from the Lithic rau-lai-er, or rayed-linear-verbal marker. A line is straight (from the skyline at sea), but a ruled one is straighter, eliminating altogether the looped one seen from a coral atoll running all round the skyline in a circle. A rafter is a long (drawn out) straight load bearing beam, modeled on Tarzan's penis again. A raft, made of rafters, in Malay is a rakit, traditionally made of stout bamboo lengths tied together with rattan (a liana, a long lithe looping vine)

Chapter 12 Ra

which has become rayed, extended in shape and quite like the ones Tarzan would swing on. A rakit fits almost too nicely: straight-trunks-tied. In return for an hour's work at the riverside you can get many miles downstream with your rucksack rakiting beside you. A rug on the other hand, ray shaped, has the rows going in the other direction, originally a fur (gulled from Tarzan's penis again) sticking up like the hair on a shaggy dog. Hair is from a(h)i-ai-rai, that which-one which-rayed, or else i(h)a-i-rai, it that-which-rayed.. Hair is ray shaped and also it rises. A rag, from ra-kai, is all tattered and torn, into bare warp or woof. A rake, also from ra-kai, certainly makes rays on the surface raked. Ranks have the same shapes, they make rows. A range as well as a ring, like anything else which is round, has been rounded out, and not only by the rays of the sun, but also (alas!) by Tarzan's penis again. What price an engagement ring?

The human mind has had to accommodate a round sun radiating rays which on the other hand fly straight and true, though you do not have to go straight to be true (attracted and so faithful, held in a ray) including as a further gull faithful not merely to one's master but also to an ideal of a reality which can not be denied, and so to be true in the way we mostly use the word today. A very small rake is a curry comb for combing a horse's coat and leaving it nicely arranged (14), (in rows) also achieved by brushing which makes it shine (15). The curry you eat also makes you rayed, these rays making not alignment but heat (17). A curry is simply a hot dish (17) like a roast one which is cooked (17).

A plate rack (19) is a set of bars like a barbecue, from the Taino barbacoa for a raised rack (of ba-kau, bars joined). You could cook on it or dry your fish in the sun. It will have been only a slow bake because it was made of wood. To bake was to tenderize the flesh, just like the hand axe pounding, in use for a million years before the taming of the flame. Cooking (kau-kau) was a repetitive pounding, and then tenderizing in its new guise of heating over the flame. A hat rack however is a rack of hooks. The racking function has taken off and abandoned the straight rows it had. Or else the rack's function all along was to raise the items racked, hats, plates and meats equally, holding them on hooks or on rows of bars as appropriate. A stack on the other hand makes a stand from the same Lithic s-ta which is up/vertical-become. Wine too is racked to separate the rack, the skins, pips and stems and also the sediment from the wine. These solids may first of all have been raked off after the pressing. The lees that slipped through the rack on which the grapes were pressed would then have to be passed through a filter to clear the wine, and this secondary process appears to have inherited the same name, in spite of the fact the final process is effected by drawing off the wine from above and/or draining through a filter.

Raise and rise (6) are gulled from the sun's rays, no doubt afforced by the sex rays which Tarzan suffered from so regularly. A ramp is a rising surface. A rampant figure in heraldry is one with raised fore limbs. Or else the general posture is simply copied from Tarzan's predicament. A ripe fruit is one that has been rayed and swollen accordingly, pai here in the sense of swollen – precisely the same process as that suffered by Tarzan's fruiting body. A berry has its flesh in a similar rounded out condition whether it is as yet ripe or not. In some ways it has jumped the gun. You may have to go by the colour to see if it is ripe. If it is still green, the colour of growing, it is still growing and unripe. In Latin, the kidney is ren with the plural renes, of obscure origin as Partridge puts it, but from the Lithic elements rai-nai, rayed presented or showing. An internal organ was taken to have been rayed and filled out, the kidneys like two joined berries – or from the English kidney, kai-dai-en-ey, a shaped-pair-of-eggs (Old English aeg, pronounced aey as well as aeg). A thorn has been drawn out into a hard point, and so has a Malay one, duri, with a durian a fruit with a skin covered in raised protrusions, though not actually sharp. Sharp in

Chapter 12 Ra

English is gulled from spike so far as the ideas are concerned,. A spike, ish-pai-kai, is an upward-piece-hardened, a stake probably with the blunt end stuck in the ground like the Japanese panji, another piece-upward facing, of razor sharp bamboo to spit unwary attackers.

Re- (9), our usage, refers to the Egyptian rays' habit of going there and back again, a pattern we have not entertained in historical times until the discovery of radar. If you go back then you will be back and back is behind. The back is really the behind, the ba-ka, fleshy [part of the] body. Malays use balek, to go back, which is like our black, the lower circuit of the dark sun when it goes back from the West where it set, to the East where it is relit and rises the next day. At the back is in the rear, where the second r is most likely a cockney one (25) untrilled, pronounced and semantically just a. Old Norse writes -r where we would write –a. It can be seen elsewhere that rai as well as to go back means to go back over the same route again, to repeat, and this time not in the opposite direction. When we redecorate a room we do not do it backwards or back to front the second time, but rather we set out once more after we have reversed to our initial starting point. When we are done the room has recently been redecorated, with recent really meaning freshly, the Latin recens coming from the idea of a new arrival, (arrival gulled from a boat getting to the bank, la rive) but originally from rai-kai'n, of the sun the kindling, the sun at sunrise, recently come forth bursting with light and energy ready to climb the skies. A blue rinse has much the same import since it has muddled through via the French from Vulgar or Low Latin recentare to meaning to become or be fresh. This is taking liberties with the rays of the sun but it is well within the range of a semantic gull or metaphor. A river too is of confused derivation, being considerably slurred. The Lithic awa meaning water, from the shivering from immersion originally (see chapter 14 on the vowels), is responsible for the -ver, which leaves the ri- for the description of water forming a river, and this must surely have been rai-, rayed and so drawn along down, all the way to the sea; leaving the rays Tarzan discovered first around the hearth relatively minuscule. The science is outmoded but the Lithic phonetics ring true. A derivation is thus a drawing down, neglecting the water, although the draw still has water in it, discoverable in the cloudy draw, the valley cut by the water drawn down, just like the Carthaginian barrancos in Tenerife, sharply cut valleys carved out through the volcanic tuff, by the flash floods off the mountain, baa-awa-en-kau, travelling-water-of-carved: a derivation still to be accepted, from ignorance of Carthaginian.

At the other end of the spectrum of rays and their meanings is Latin rasicare to scratch often, a frequentative version of the Latin radere to rub, a simple semantic hip-hop from the Lithic rai-dai-are, ray (or rake)-doing-verbal suffix. When in English we rub we are ra-bai, sunray-going, that is going backwards and forwards, or more correctly forwards and then backwards. A rascal identified himself as a member of the great unwashed, lousy and for ever repetitiously scratching the rashes on his scurvy skin. Today he is just suspect of mischief, especially if only a bit of a one. Radere is just doing the same as the sun. From that comes the school eraser or rubber, abrasions and even the razor with a rubbing or rasping action. To be rash however comes from the German line, with the Old High German rase and the Old Norse raskr (pronounced raska), from the original Lithic phonemes rai-sai-kai, rayed-action-causing, a ray causing precipitate action. This is one of the insidious Egyptian viral rays spitting the brain, injecting a yen for action regardless, leading to a lack of proper premeditation and precipitate action. It must then be asked what a rasher of bacon must be. Is a thin slice of ham instinct with wild ideas? Eric Partridge opts for a variant of rase to cut which will hardly do because rase is really to

Chapter 12 Ra

scrape or rasp. The bacon is not cut into rashes. The sober truth is a rasher is simply echoic. When ish-rayed it says ish almost as impressively as the brand when dowsed, it is a hisser when rayed in the pan. It comes from the fat which rapidly melts, which already gives it its streaks, the straight ray shapes, before it gets near the flame. Whether you roast or fry you get the fat running out as juice. The Latin frigere which means to roast, grill or fry, Partridge says is akin to the Greek phrugein to grill. He adds "perhaps echoic". The g could be pronounced g or y, which enabled the French to spell it and pronounce frigere as frire. Partridge was probably thinking of his breakfast bacon here. But even phr is a poor echoism for a rasher. The fact is fat, the juice (which originally meant the gravy or even broth, fruit juice being added later), used with a wick for a light like a candle, was perceived as just one avatar of the organic lymphs which exuded from the body or were to be found in it, for example in the brain and spine. It was for this reason supposed until quite recently the semen was made in the spine, and the flame (of life) was supposed to be connected with these juices as language suggested already, ish for flame and sai for life. These were the equivalents of the juices which are to be found in the vegetable kingdom in fruits. That is of course why the term juice was found suitable to represent both the animal and the vegetable varieties together. The conclusion is inescapable that far enough back bodily lymphs were regarded as fruit juices and the male genitalia were regarded as animal fruits. That was Tarzan's view anyway. A fry up produced the life juices from the meat in the same way that sex produced the life juices from the fruit. Look at lymph, lye-em-pahei. Is it going to be argued this phonology is random and accidental, along with all the others? Frigere and frying was a form of frigging. It may put you off an English breakfast but you do not have to follow the thinking of our hominid forebears just because their memo pad appears to have survived in the phoneme strings we use in modern languages.

The reciprocating action of the piston (from Latin pinsere to pound, which is from the Lithic pai-en-sai-ere, the pai-of-action-verbal suffix, which means to pound (repetitively) by way of the action of the pai, as with a pestle or little pilum, akin to phallus and itself a pestle or a javelin – where the –lau or lai refers to the javelin's length and its looping flight. In a mortar, which is a pila, the feminine version of the pilum, the pai's lau or loop is in the bowl shape. Tarzan rudely saw the mortar as a mau-ta or planted vagina, a gull from the shape. The re-cipro-cating Partridge has from a supposed *recos, backwards and *procos forwards. Recipro- then becomes an overlap or amalgamation of the two supposed roots. We can certainly see re- and pro- there, each with a kai suffixed, and going-back-going-forward probably does the original string justice. Re is from rai as already demonstrated. Pro it is naturally tempting to relate to Tarzan's penis like so much else, since an Egyptian ray seems to be involved. It is akin in that case to prow and proud. However it may be the eye's ray, which is involved here because the panorama which the eye reveals is a surface, pai, and pai-rau can be the surface-seen. The surface seen is the front surface and it is in front of the viewer. You take your pick. My pick is for Tarzan's penis on the grounds it comes forward while the view sits passively in front. A nice case of polysemy ends this rudely radiant chapter. With so few phonemes and so many meanings and so general allocated to each you can see Babel was predicated, and the need for words with fixed meanings was only a few hundred thousand years away when first Tarzan lisped his first few meaningful phonemes to his mate.

Perhaps we should end with a bon bouche to clear the palate. A raisin is a dried grape. It is rai-sai'n, dried-sunshine'one – or else it dries quite well hung in a cellar, but the classic idea is drying from a ray, and a ray is taken to be responsible for the process willy nilly. But the etymologists will have it otherwise. It is said to be from a raceme, a bunch (of grapes), from the Latin racemus, a ray-shaped-mass (of berries). Pull all the grapes off a bunch and you are left with the ray shaped mass, a collection of stalks which supported the bunch. But a raisin is not the bunch but a single grape. Its claim to its special identity is not that it is a grape but that it is a particularly treated grape. We might therefore expect, before ever we come to examine the etymology that the nomenclature might have been chosen to reflect this character. Without Lithic, the blind watchmaker (Professor Dawkins), working on etymology goes by the phonology alone. He thinks he knows the semantics are not of prime consideration. Given there is a raceme and it has to do with grapes, and the pass is sold; and the raisin abandoned to its neighbour without further ado. But it is the ado which is needed in every case if sense is to be made of the way we learned to speak = and the way we speak today, which after all comes from it.

NOTES

1. In Arabic the cochineal is qirmiz, in Early French kermes, in English kermes, in Sanskrit krmi, in Persian kirm, in Lithuanian kermis and in Byzantine Greek khermezi. The Spanish, from this hotch potch, introduced their cremesin from which English distilled crimson. They were all really white ants, no good for togas or red dye at all. Take your pick.

2. I have often thought I am really only writing Volume 2 of Eric Partridge's Short Etymological Dictionary of Modern English. But there are some less charitable exposures of what he did not know. For instance he believed that pies were called pies because originally made of magpies, whereas they are called pies because a pie meant a skin or covering or lid, and pies, made of many things but never of magpies, have a crust on them, usually of pastry but sometimes of potato, etc. – contra a tart. I feel after forty years studying his book I know him well enough to rib him when Homer nods. Just when I thought to call on him and show him some of my work, he died. It is arguable he had discovered some Lithic at least but did not care to publish it because it seemed in his day too way out. That is what I wanted to ask him. Now we shall never know. But I am entitled to surmise, and he is of course free of all blame.

CHAPTER 13

ISH: SUGAR AND SPICE AND ALL THINGS NICE

If you approach the question of the beginning of language and how people were thinking then, or if they were thinking at all, with your mind emptied of preconceptions based on the last few hundreds of thousands of years of more or less articulate ratiocination, there is nothing much left for you to think about. Nevertheless it seems obvious enough that folk were thinking before they were speaking, for how else could they have had the brilliant idea of setting up a means of communication. In reality it was not a single or sudden decision of course, but a long drawn out process we can hardly hope to reconstruct in any but the most cursory fashion today. There were many pre-articulate noises which the mind had learned to interpret: whoops and shrieks from fellow individuals of the species, the peak of hominid comprehension, and also of course a plethora of natural noises from the patter of rain on the surface of water or on your leafy roof to peals of thunder and the crash of falling trees, or just the splashing of a stream and significantly enough the hiss of a burning torch extinguished in a puddle of water, and even more impressively a million years of the clack of flint on flint. If a twig snapped the quick witted got used to the sound and asking themselves who or what goes there; and the less quick ones had a less turbulent life but quite often a shorter, as well as a duller one - just as today. So there were natural noises like the snap of a twig which already betrayed a semantic content, and there were other noises made by active agencies, and some of them could be predators and others prey. This is the last chapter on the consonants and that is why some degree of final review has found its way into Ish.

A silver-back gorilla is quite good at reading these symbolic indications and a chimpanzee even better. A gorilla slow in the uptake is at home in the forest habitat without much to fear. His physical strength alone will probably get him a progeny in Darwinian terms, and keep gorillas going. In the gorilla's environment you don't need superlative intellectual performance to make your way, so nature has not selected for brains as specially fit, but rather for strength, which is surely why the gorilla is bigger than the chimp. It worked a treat until men armed themselves and took a fancy to bush meat. The chimp is feebler and less well placed environmentally, and the evolutionary pressures have selected for brains. The same can be said for hominids although it seems there have been times when hominid size was being pursued for its own sake, for else why should we have grown from chimpish size to six feet and more, and much of it comparatively recently at that. First of all there was probably a time when hominids fought (and ate) each other – until only one species was left. Since then we have just kept on going for the winning physique which worked well for us in the past. (Some tribes still fancy "long pork". Your flesh tastes like pork. You could very probably make an English breakfast with the rashers sizzling in the pan). Or else it was just that the brainless ones got beaten to the food, and better feeding got us our size. In any case in more recent times we have been able to afford a few luxuries, including better feeding and size increases, as our brain power has given us dominion over our fellow animals. You might think stature is a telling factor in hand-to-hand fighting, and at one time no doubt it was; but weaponry, which is brain power in action, cancels that out. David whacked Goliath, when hacking each other with metal weapons was the presumptive standard military procedure, a technology well developed already when the Philistines confronted the Israelis on the plain of Esdra-elon some three thousand years ago. But young David knew better and had the confidence of his knowledge. He used the artillery of the day and won. If you have tried slinging stones you will know he had a bit of luck as well. He took several stones from the brook, you may remember, smooth and round and heavy enough to fell a giant at a distance; so it is clear he knew he might need more than one shot. My own performance would be less than one hit in a hundred. Young David must have been practising as a hobby, and then some. Naturally the primitive Israelis thought it must be the hand of God, with whom the young David must have found favour. In reality he was just Olympic gold.

So far as linguistic ability was concerned, when language began we can imagine eloquence will have been admired regardless of its utility, simply because it was the new cool thing. Did hominid lasses swoon when Tarzan turned out a well composed sentence, as teenagers do for a pop star today? They probably did, since much of their time they worked around the fire and kept it fed, while the boys were afoot out hunting. The girls will have filled their time practising their phonemes and trying out different tunes with them and guessing their significances. They do that with much greater acquiescence than boys even today and it shows up in their examination results. The boys dream of shooting goals as a displacement from bagging bush bucks. They are not significantly stupider than girls, and their determination is greater; but their attention is adrift when it comes to any kind of filigree, whether requiring mental or physical dexterity. They hammered flints in the age of the Pliocene: big biffs for boys. Any hominid boy in those far off days when speaking was the latest wonder, a sedentary accomplishment requiring some fine tuned fancy thinking, a bit like the nimble finger-work required for sewing, who was nevertheless prepared to face the brain damage and join the fireside circle and its discussions on girls' terms was already half way to their affections. Older alpha males may well have been these former ladies´ boys; because, if the testosterone is up and running, access to female company is a powerful instinctive priority, encouraging even attendance at chat shows of no intrinsic attraction. "If you can sew with phonemes, I can do it better!" "No you can´t!" "Yes I can!" "Yes I can!" "Yes I can!"

Be all that as it may, it is obvious echoic utterances must have been the first symbolic communications, long preceeding speech as we understand it. The paradigm is "Grrr!" for a tiger - which with language assumed substantiality, identifying the brute present or otherwise; whereas in prelinguistic days it meant more like: "Leap for the tall trees: I see or hear or smell a tiger!" Language put a Ti- in front, probably because felines have always been regarded as female from their slinking, even graceful and dainty motion when creeping up on prey; and with domesticated cats from their gentle gait and care for their kittens. So "tigre" means "mistress growler", from the immitation of the tiger´s growl by our hominid forebears from perhaps a million years back. Rock formations will have weathered away in that time scale, but semantic formations have survived because of the repeated refreshment of the semantic patterns by successive generations, the triumph of life and reproduction over inert nature. The ten chapters on individual phonemes from chapter 3, on Ba, up to this one, number thirteen on Ish, have revealed that the etumons or original meanings were phonemic, before morphemes composed of more than one phonee; or in layman´s terms each single sound itself was given meaning and the original roots of words were not random at all, but carefully thought through, leading to further derived meanings, when stringing more than one meaningful phoneme together became the norm. It is the Chinese idiom precisely, and to be half way successful today it needs to be

Chapter 13 Ish

afforced with numerous tones to distinguish meanings because they have proved so prolific, and even then it leaves a good deal of polysemy to be sorted out simply from context. This is still brain damage for Westerners, and any old Chinese mandarin could probably have seen off Plato, Aristotle, Thomas Aquinas and Saint Augustine all together when it came to mental wrangling. At least it is good for mathematics, and the Chinese nowadays take to math like ducks to water, because their language idioms retain the semantics on which they are based and do not encourage inconsequential memorisation, like the languages of the West.

From the mewing of chimpanzees, with finely discriminated tones way above our ability to discriminate them, they must surely think "pity they haven't mastered language!" It enables them to build quite a substantial vocabulary of sorts, which we have only recently realised since we can not follow the tones. We have made them think in human terms, at which they are not all that good. But it is clear that vowelisation (mewing in Chimpish) preceeded speech as we understand it. The tongue is used already when consecutive vowelisations are discriminated, but varying tones come from a long way further back, in history and in the throat, than the linguistic expertise required for consonantalisation. The physiology is otherwise largely immaterial when writing a book on semantics, the development of linguistic meanings.

Some of the apparently original phonemic meanings adopted in previous chapters, which still show up in the languages of today, and more still in old dead languages frozen in time, from before literacy and spelling blurred the significances of the sounds themselves, come from the way the utterances were (and are) produced. So for instance in chapter 3 the sound Ba is found to be made by pursing the lips and then uttering the most general vowel sound of aaa from between them. The meaning attributed on those grounds was lips whence the sound came, it was their signature tune; and from the lips which are the fleshy surrounds of the mouth Ba was taken to symbolise the mouth and the fleshy bits round it, and then and thus just flesh. It became the signature tune of the flesh and the fleshy bits. From then on Ba acquired, by the process identified for Lithic as a 'gull' (because there is no other term for this mental step and this term simply appeared an easy mnemonic for it)[1], all those characteristics which can be attributed to flesh, bearing in mind flesh could be applied in those days to vegetable tissue as well as the animal variety, so that the lips were seen as foliations as was the phalus also, which was classed as a stalk with a fruiting body – phal means fruit as well as phallus (the glans and not the whole penis which was the fruit's stalk) – and the ancients imagined the sperm was the seed, whereas in reality of course it is only the pollen. The girls keep the seeds tucked away inside themselves, and hominids knew nothing about that. The Bible still thought seed was male, although God must have known better.

Then, secondly there were of course, from prelinguistic symbolism, utterances which were echoic of natural sounds. Wa is perhaps the best exhibition of this linguistic development because it does not go outside the range of our own natural human behavioural responses to find its meaning. It required no natural philosophy of the external world. It is the sound of shivering, from prolonged immersion in cold water, or indeed any hypothermia. The body is trying to generate heat by tweaking the nervous system to generate muscular contractions[2]. So Wewewe, the sound of shivering, meant water; and for the full justification for the identification of a meaning half a million years old, try the next chapter, chapter 14 on the vowels. It was as if the water were speaking through its victim, captured as a result of going too far in surrendering herself (or himself) to a natural element which had dubious intentions. Only a mug would do as much. Does not the water find expression in water sprites like crocodiles with less than friendly intentions? When you shiver perhaps the water is also telling you "You oughter be frightened!" Fear brings on uncontrollable shivering as well, when the teeth can even involuntarily chatter in a truly astonishing manner indicating a similar nervous breakdown.

As a third mental step, after the lips from the sound and the water from the shivers, it is possible to go still further afield and pick up symbolic echoisms from impersonal natural phenomena. Cuckoos and Cockneys or cock-en-eyes, Cock-s´-eggs, spring to mind. But the ultimate paradigm here for echoisms derived from nature must surely be the phoneme Ish, the sound made by a burning brand when Tarzan extinguished it in a puddle when the new day brought relief from the threat of the sabre-toothed tiger. It was identified as a clear symbolic sound for the flame and, gulling again, in due course all those characters deriving from the several characters of the flame which will be covered in the present chapter, particularly the instinct of the flame to spring upwards when most other things fall down. If you drop a stone it may well hit your foot. To drop was first of all taken to be the instinct of what was dropped. (It is pulled down by gravity, in fact). Our forebears thought the pull was instinct in pieces of everything, a form of anthropomorphism or autism still teasing us.

Fourthly there is the phoneme La, which paradoxically was quite possibly the first consonantal stop phoneme to be used, and indeed may have served as a mental trail-breaker for all the others in turn. If you are intoning, using singing notes without words, mewing as the chimps do, and you are looking for a break between them – Oh Paleolithic Einstein! – a flick of the tongue is the easiest one to pick with minimal diversion from the tones. So it was probably the first tongue movement to be added to tones. Consider the difference between m´-i-a-u and m´-i-la-lu^3. The m´ is scarcely even in the actual pussy cat vocabulary. We put it in because we like consonantalisation and where there is none we are inclined to choose a hum. The significant comparison is between iau and ilalu. With the tones just eliding as in iau there is only the whole to consider, a single semantic gobbet. Even at that, the tom cat's catawaul can take on a gamut of quite reasonably explicit statements, though confined to his frame of mind: from lust on the lookout for the female to slake his passion, to furious challenge on the approach of a competitor standing in the way of his quest. You can hear the change of tone as lust gives way to aggression. It is an unfortunate character of the male psyche, and not only tom cats, lust and agression lie far too close together for comfort. The male psyche still presents a formidable test for holy matrimony many millions of years after our forebears parted from the feline branch of the physical tree. Our former serial concubinage still defeats the Child Support Agency, hands down. Two or three millennia of morality surrenders to wholly unprincipled hedonism. Cool!

The semantics of the La phoneticisation may not have obtruded initially; but if the consonantalisations were to be expanded to include other sounds and their meanings – and they did so expand - we have lift off when the first vowel had a La in it. All that was needed was the son of our former Einstein of the Pleistocene, or at least someone who understood what he did and how. With hindsight it is clear such a one must have been born, and all the other consonantalisations were adopted and their meanings hammered out; but probably slowly and one by one. The result is a language with a depth of texture nowadays unrecognised. We have learned to skate over the surface using merely the derivative meanings we have memorised for words. It is only the subconscious mind which still picks up the old constituent phonemic meanings as we each in our turn learn to

Chapter 13 Ish

speak with our conscious minds, and keeps the original structure alive, but unconsciously all unawares.

Chimpanzees sometimes seem to have reached an appreciation of the use of the tongue, perhaps their tongue wagging (which produced the tongue movements of La at least) meant "Discriminate! Discriminate!" or "Communicate! Communicate!"; or else they are natural tongue waggers for no particular reason. Their tonal vocabulary of mews will certainly carry no other consonantal values. For hominids bursting into speech La was identified as taste, simply because the lingual grimace followed a nasty taste – see chapter 8. The tongue is the taster, so wagging it meant taste; and since water tasted fresh from the spring and became increasingly brackish and lye as it ran down to the sea, the deteriorating flavour and the sloping-down-to-the-sea syndromes became regarded as the two natural debasement instincts of liquids. La received those two psychosemantic contents, compounded by the way the phoneme was uttered and the phenomena it was judged to give rise to. Following upon these two combined perceptions, all the gulls along the sea shore came to life, as explained in chapter 8.

Pausing here, we should perhaps reject simple echoism as just prelinguistic cries, we might say as just signs of the nascent human mind, with parts of speech wholly absent. But with firstly our own utterances as meaning sources as with Ba, and secondly with environmentally prompted personal utterances as meaning sources as with Wewewe (shivering), and thirdly with environmentally directly derived meaning sources as with Ish (the sound of a burning brand when dowsed), innocent of any psychic input, and finally with mixed utterance and environmental meaning sources as with La, we can surely say that language was up and running, if still with a rather modest performance. It comes from the turn-over from the nominal to the adjectival mind, a change examined in chapter 15 on thinking, a result of language and symbolisation. With that, the introduction to this chapter is complete and we are in a position to elaborate those meanings which derive from this original echoic symbolisation of the sibilant as fire and flame. You have had six pages of beating about the bush - but to some purpose: a review of some of the infrastrructure of the Lithic hypotheses after a fair dunking in Lithic phonemes and their meanings. That is how the Lithic hypotheses work. That is how we learned to speak.

The psychosemantic tree for the phoneme Ish is on page 260. It is a wide ranging one. It makes sense to study it before continuing any further, since it is not further referred to in the text. However the headings are numbered, and references in the text have numbers in brackets to help readers follow through the positions in the tree if they so wish. The sibilant phoneme is first of all a hiss. In chapter 10, on the phoneme Ma, hisses have already been paired and opposed with the hums covered in that chapter, because they are the only two consonants or stops which can be voiced continuously as long as you have breath; and they were also taken to have opposed characteristics – for no good reason, but for our forebears' sufficient reason things came in opposed pairs: from sex really, male and female, one sticking out the other sticking in; but already worked up into a primitive dialectic. By contrast Ba, Ka, Da, etcetera are proper stops, uttered once and spent. Continuing them merely extends their accompanying vowelisations. But you can hum or hiss without an accompanying vowel at all. Nevertheless they are lumped with consonants because, like the proper stops they do act perfectly well as breaks between consecutive vowels. A stop is a better term than a consonant which simply means they are 'sounded together with' an accompanying vowel. Hums and hisses alone are not necessarily so accompanied; but they can be. Consonant also suggests the accompanying vowel in some way has priority, since the stop is described as 'sounded with them'. This is of course

257

Chapter 13 Ish

precisely correct from a historical perspective, since we sang before we spoke, that is to say hominid hoots and cries were prelinguistic and comprised sequences of tones only. But most of the meanings come from the phonemes designated consonants. Perhaps the phoneme La was the mother of all languages because curling the tongue between notes in the musical scale was the lead-in to all the other stops. The discovery of the ability to consonantalise and then to symbolise such sounds was the origin of language, and the sea changes in thinking which it brought with it.

Apart from the word hiss, from the Lithic a(h)i-ss, that-which-ss, there is not much else to be said about the sibilant on its own. It means nothing - unless it comes from a snake - when it soon comes to mean hai-ss, 'horrors! – like picking up a hot stone - hit it or quit, and be quick'. However hisses crop up elsewhere where they can be seen to carry a semantic content, and there seems little doubt our hominid forebears will have been alive to these meanings. A kiss not only makes a hiss (chium in Malay, clearly echoic) but is also a gesture of comfort or pleasure (19). Then there was in nature the sound of rushing water; and even the trickle of a stream had, perhaps fancifully, the same sound. The roar of a mighty fall of water, or a raging flood, has the character of white sound, heard as a loud hiss, widely used to disorient and brainwash prisoners nowadays. It dominates the mind, blanking out meditation and together with sleep deprivation makes a potent punitive psychic mix. But for just a bite size hiss the snipe is a good example. Its whirring noise as it flies is well known to shooters, something like "thirer-thirer-thirer-thirer", but quicker than you can say that, and commonly described as drumming.

One assumes the snipe does it by swooping and vibrating its wings, and it surely must just be for the fun of it. With "snipe" the Lithic phonemic elements involved are si-nai-pai, semantically brer-protruding-piece. In his case his protruding piece is, rather unusually, his bill, as long as his body, for poking in the mud for prey. Tarzan could easily spot which bird was meant because of the metaphor used. Have we a Paleolithic joke? Which having said, an alternative reading of the Lithic construction of snipe is sai-en-ai-pai, sounds-as-going-winged: drumming as he flies, his drumming and his bill competing for recognition. He makes good eating but is rather small. You could use the facility with which the phonemes can be manipulated to provide different meanings as an argument Lithic is a fancy. But in reality Lithic is too extensive and comprehensive for that; and it is important to introduce these simple and unimportant semantic constructions based on phonemic meanings, to try to get the reader to start thinking in phonemic terms in place of the word meanings he or she has grown used to since learning to speak, so that words may seem by now the only and mandatory way of addressing the world. It should not be too difficult to make the mental flip, because there is an ally beneath the surface of the mind, the subconscious element, which has been doing it all along. Just give it a chance by letting it free, by letting the mind free to roam in a dreamy way without thinking in structural terms at all. Never mind if some of your reveries are rude: you do not have to pass them on, and you can shake them off again when your reverie is over[4]. It certainly appears our hominid forebears valued two ways of reading a string of meaningful phonemes as one confirming the other, and so the natural meaning string for the job.

A whistle (5) is echoic, like wind: if you blow out you get a whi-, with a bit of a hiss thrown in, and the telai at the end of whistle is become lai, that is uttered in singing tones, because La was the singing stop, no stop at all really in those singing times, just indicating a change of note in a continuous howl (or yowl). A syringe is more difficult. The Greek syrinx was a tube or channel or shepherd's pipe or whistle, whittled from the hollow tube of a syringa shoot. But then the syringa bush was named from the whistle made from it:

Chapter 13 Ish

the syringa is the whistle bush. So we still have to identify the Lithic semantics. The Lithic sai-rai-n-kai, starts with an echoic whistling sai-. The rai is the sound ray, which carries the sound to the ear, the organ which gets rayed, so that you hear. The hiss of the extinguished flame has come to stand for sounds in general. Not many things in Stone Age inanimate natural science had a characteristic sound, but the flame when dowsed had this remarkable articulation. The n in syringa is perhaps just a verbal marker, while the kai (-ga) is making: whistle-raying-making, ie the tubular shoot from the bush you use to while away the time while watching over your flocks all day by cutting and trimming the finger holes so you can get a tune from it In Chinese you get Shu (6), which is the whistling wind. Back in England you get an issue (7), an expulsion of breath suggesting a flowing out. It is a sound which appears too when you spit (8). Lithic analysis perhaps can explain the choice of the unfortunate shepherd, probably happily playing his pan pipe, named Syphilis, chosen now to name the venereal disease. I believe he was named an innocent piper. But his name could be read, sai-pa-hei-lai, either sai-pai hei-lai, piper pleasing-lay, or much later sai-pahei-lai, issue-pahei-lye, the venereal discharge from the penis. Syphilis was Niobe's eldest son in Greek myth, born near Mount Sipylus from Sai-pai-lau's, a high-surface-flat'substantive marker, a plateau, and since it seems it had a flat top, may have been suitable for grazing sheep for Syphilis to graze.

The mouth has already been identified as bab (chapter 4), because it has two lips, and the lips are the fleshy bits which utter the ba sound. Its duty as fleshy bits has led to the bum the bubs and the breast and even the legs (bai in Ancient Egypt, which included the whole haunch or buttock), bein in German and arms, baah in Hindi, which are burgeons off the main body. The lips, in retreat in face of these big bits of the body, have been transferred to the thinned and diminutive pai in place of bai, which still loop around the mouth, lip from lai-pai. The issue of the two lips is after all a spit. A pout is with lips pushed out, from pau-tai, lips pushed out-become. A spout has much the same Lithic structure, an actual-protruded-tit or orifice, the initial s- being from the same semantic root as our is. The spurt from it is potential rather than actual, and the s- here results from the marker for action. A spurt is verbal, a happening and not a thing, although it is a noun.

Curiously the Sumerian for cat was katse while the Akkadian was putse. The Lithic for these strings are respectively ka-tse and pu-tse, and curiously like our pussy and German katze. It may not seem much unless you know the Sumerian for mouth was ka (the cut) and the Akkadian was pu (the entry of the pipe). They were both spit mouths. Akkadian culled a lot of Sumerian idioms like this – as well as much of Sumerian religion they later claimed as their own. Adam and Eve and Noah were Sumerians and not Semites originally. In Ancient Egyptian pu could be read as pa-u and since pa in Egyptian meant the, pu was read as 'the oo' or 'the u', and so the quail chick or pipi was used as the hieroglyph for the u in Egyptian. It appears the Akkadians too read it as the oo or hole[5]. Compare the Egyptian kati for a different (feminine) slit with a vulgar nasalised English term for the pudenda; which may even be related in some roundabout way to the Akkadian in turn, although the original Lithic substrate seems a more likely explanation.

A slug is a slow-goer and moreover leaves a slimy liquid line which slips or slurps down behind it as it slides along[6]. The Greek limax with Lithic elements lai-mai-kai (s), the slime maker, is a snail. A slug is in fact a snail with an ill developed shell, which shows up as a thickened saddle on its back. The lai-mai also can be read as liquid-earth, as in the Greek leamon, which means a moist meadow and limne a marsh or mire, presenting a mixture of liquid and earth.

Chapter 13 Ish

THE PSYCHOSEMANTIC TREE FOR ISH

The Phonetic Tree

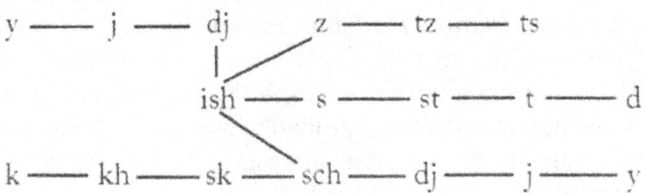

The Semantic Tree

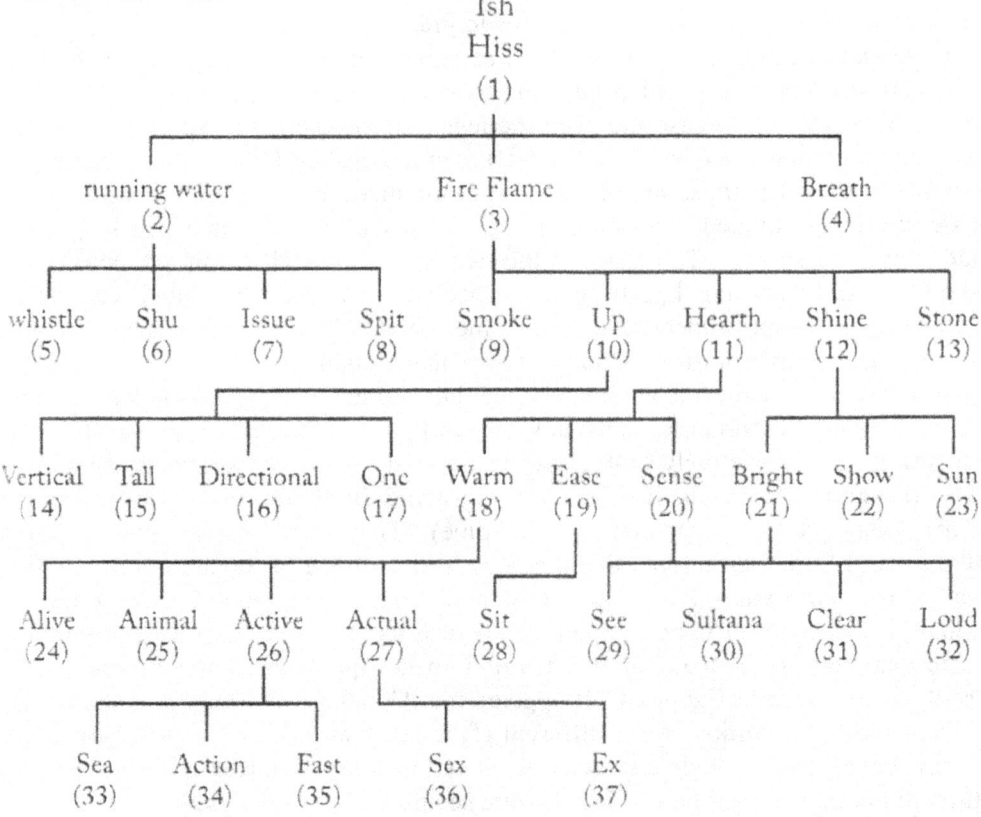

Chapter 13 Ish

A well is water which lies there, from awa-lai. A spring is where it springs up and breaks surface, but the original springing up was a sexual metaphor, ejaculation being the original meaning of ish-pai-rai'n-kai, issue/action-of piece-rayed-making. This was why Aristotle fancied water had a yen to get to the surface, so that if on top of the earth it ran down along it, but if under it it rose up instead in a spring - and then reverted to its more usual running down, clinging closely to the local declivities of the surface. This switch in behaviour from upping to downing evidently appeared to Aristotle to be brought about at the threshold of the surface of the earth; and the unnatural uppings indicated a goddess's prompting.

Oranges, really naranjes (a norange mistaken for an orange), are from 'n-a-Rai-nai-shai, one-that-sun of-showing-colour (12), the golden sun of midday, not the dying sun at dusk which glows red. A lime or a lemon is described as a lye or acid one (the semantics of the ma phoneme includes to eat), an orange as golden coloured. There is of course a bit of poesy in the orange, but the lemon is right down the middle.

Shara is a Gypsy word - Gypsies came from India originally, expelled for their thuggery some six hundred years ago and then again from Egypt where they sojourned like any other refugees seeking asylum in those days, until their reputation as tea-leafs and thugs came to the attention of the Egyptian authorities.

As followers of the prehistoric black goddess Kali, in those days their treachery and deceit in all their dealings with non-believers was mandatory. They were actually required by the goddess, whose thinking had become somehow turned upside down, to indulge in criminality whenever dealing with infidels in order to acquire merit; while to deal fairly with a goy was a crime. Some still pretend to be Egyptians to avoid telling the truth to goys, and there is a spin off: the Egyptians had the reputation of magic words and powers, including screwing their hands around their eyes to make goys think the evil eye would be upon them. The gypsies were originally convicted of garotting travellers in India (now Pakistan): thuggi, or joining caravans to kill, pretending to be innocent fellow travellers; already promised seven virgins in the hereafter by the black goddess in prehistoric times - black for darkness and hence concealment and deceit - for fifteen unbelievers killed. Just like modern day religious fanatics you may think, now pretending to be Islamists, the ultimate deceit. There is a concealed premiss here, which seems quite doubtful, that martyrs will still have their wedding tackle with them on arrival in the hereafter, since the etherial world is generally believed these days, and in Mohammed's days too, to be a world of the spirit, insubstantial, and their genitalia therefore gone past recall. What would one not give to see their faces fall (if they have any of those either!) on arrival at the pearly gates with their promised virgins awaiting them. For far from having gained access to the delights of the flesh in abundance, apparently a different lady for each day of the week, they will instead have been cruelly robbed of any such possibility with fraudulent promises from professional fraudsters pretending religiosity: the ultimate deception, which is Kali's delight. The British, when they got to a position of power in Northern India, followed an uncompromising policy of putting anyone guilty of thuggi, or ritual killing to acquire merit with Kali, to an ignomineous death by hanging, or being blown from a gun, after the briefest of trials. It greatly reduced belief in the Black Goddess since when it actually came to it She just abandoned her followers to their fate and none of the revenges promised followed. Kali is now fully Indianised, the Hindu religion is a magpie religion picking up gods and goddesses from all over, and Calcutta, from Kali-ka-ta, Kali's-Place-of Birth, or khota, fort (strong-become), claims to be her original place of worship. But deceit alone allows it. She will have come there riding piggy back on Islam, unnoticed by

Chapter 13 Ish

the faithful. Kali was worshiped across the desert lands of the Arabian peninsular for thousands of years before the Prophet Mohammed rescued the Arab tribes from her embrace, preaching a truer religion against the Kali worship of malice. Kali's revenge is by infiltration of Islam by deceit.

Shara is a bright patch in Shanta, the gypsies' composite language, from the Lithic Sha-Ra, Shine-of Sun. Shine and Sun are of course the wrong words to capture the proper semantic contents as originally conceived. In those days Shine of sun and bright ray or resultant bright patch were the same. To shrink is from ish-rai´n-kai, fire(3)-raying-makes. The thinking was the effect of the fire is to drive out the liquids and reduce things to their dried up shrunken states like dried up sticks. It also causes anyone exposed to such scorching to withdraw from the flame, and so to shrink from any other challenge. These are the two meanings of shrink explained from the Lithic elements involved, otherwise inexplicable since getting smaller and withdrawing from action are not themselves connected - unless you can persuade yourself that to shrink, from cowardice, is a diminution of the self, or else perhaps a pulling back is effectively to make yourself smaller. But that is asking rather a lot.

The Arabic iskra (3), a spark, from the Lithic elements ish-kara, is a flame-maker, as is the obsolete English chark (3), from shara-kai, flaming-making, the ancient device for making fire by drilling with a sharpened stick in a wooden socket with fluff around it for ignition. The friction of wood on wood generates heat until the fluff ignites. What it ignites, ignis in Hindustani is the sibilant ish, i-genai-s, the generated flame, or it-generates-flame, viz. fire. To char, from ish-arai, is to burn, flame rayed, charred by rays of the flame. The English spark, from ish-pa-rai-ka, is a firey-speck-ray-making with all the same phonemes as the Arabic iskra. It may seem presumptuous to be thinking in Lithic terms like this, but it is a presumption born of very many years of examination. It is not all plain sailing because the primitive mind did not sail an entirely consistent course. In those days folk were very far from a single theory of everything. There were only small patches of apparent understanding, and they were generally misplaced. Plus ca change!

The Central Senoi aboriginal tribes of the Malayan jungle count in their own way for the first four numerals before adopting the scheme of their Malayan neighbours. One, two, three, four is mi, duak, mpeq, mpon, before following the Malay five, six, seven, eight, lima, enam, tujoh, delapan, and so on in Malay. The Senoi numbers are a lesson in Stone Age thinking; perhaps they are Adam's Eastern numbers copied by the hill tribes of Malaya, the Garden land, who learned the Adamite language of the plains. They are remarkably erudite for a Stone Age mind. But one of the things which obtrudes in the study of primitive thinking is the degree of abstraction which appears to have obtained from day one. These learner speakers were remarkably bright. In chapter 10, mmm, the hum, is identified as a filler, as well as – in the Hamitic languages – a specific filler such that we can read it as 'him', with what follows in the word the description of 'him'. The m' we find in the Senoi numbering system seems to have been a similar initial sound-off as the mind works itself up to the key to its thinking. Mi is from m'i, a single itemisation such as we have seen is the semantic content of the vowel i. Perhaps we could characterise it as "Him single": the singular. Perhaps, to fit better, it came from m'ai slovened to mi. In that case it could be read as him-first-one, like the first person singular in English. A as the first vowel carries a certain priority in its semantic contents which is reinforced today by its position at the head of the alphabet. Alpha and omega are the beginning and the end. Yet it is not clear why the letter a leads the alphabet, since it was not at first the vowel sound it is today, instead being used for a glotal stop. But then no doubt sounded when

Chapter 13 Ish

isolated between two general vowels a'a, the principle can transfer from the stop to the adjoined vowel, a bus. The Lithic contribution could then be it became the vowel a because of its position at the head of the series. The Senoi duak is from Lithic tau-a-kai, the-Tau-that makes, in other words the Tau or T which forms our own two and many other languages' duality. Or else the final –k is just from an original glotal stop. The two strokes of the Tau or T are certainly joined (kai) but kai also had the semantic content of the earth (later spelt Gaia, with the -a ending to make it feminine) because of its hardness, like the struck flint. If you dig a bit you come to bedrock. So it was the hard element, originally from the underlying rocks, which was in turn from the ka-ka sound of flaking flints. The Tau is a prototypical symbolisation and it can be read as the two of the world skeletal structure, the horizontal line the flat earth, and so standing for space, with the vertical line representing time, bearing the world of events upwards and onwards. Perhaps the Tau was the Stone Age Space-Time waiting for Albert Einstein to come along a few hundred thousand years later. What kept him and us so long? But of course it could equally just be the two dimensions of a flat surface, as the earth. Anyway it was prototypically dual.

For three, m'peq is from the Lithic m'pai-kai, indicating in this case them-pieces-joined, defining the three arms of the Tau. Alternatively the pai is a dimensioned pai, namely a surface's pieces [dimensions], with the upright of the Tau making three. The top line of the T is expanded to a surface (which Pai represented ab initio), the flat surface of the earth itself made of two dimensions, which with the vertical stroke makes three. Four from m'pon, in Lithic m'pa-un, him'surface-dual, dual surfaces, which each have two dimensions for the horizontal surfaces. If one surface is made of two dimensions, it is not all that unreasonable to argue two will be made of four. Anyway the language says as much, and the Senoi are quite happy with it.

The Malay figures, out of the same stable, show some signs of carrying on the same mystique. In place of mpeq is empat for four, which is surely a redefinition of the same two surfaces, from m'pa-tai, 'them-surfaces-two' again. Lima reverts to body language, lai-m'a, the five linked relatively long extensions of the torso, the limbs and head. Compare Hindi panch for five, from pa-en-kai, the points of the body. We do not think of the head as in any way equivalent to the limbs so we do not readily lump it in with them, but if you look at the torso without preconception as to the function of any of its members, drawing a stick man for example (as the Chinese did), it is obvious at once there are five ancillary protruding bits, quite regardless of function, attached to the central linear body, which have to be taken into account; unlike a fish which has a single torso, i-kan in Malay (and in the Pacific), ik-a in Borneo and New Guinea, with only some wavey diaphanous extensions by way of fins, i-ka'n, a single-torso-one in Malay or just a single-torso Borneo style. This curiosity causes it to be known as piscis in Indo European, using its body as feet in effect, from the Lithic pai-sai-kai-sai, feet-action-body-action. This by the way is probably why the Christian vesica piscis symbol was adopted for the early Christian church, relying upon the body of the church to prevail and not by any individual action to impose belief. Enam for six is from ai-na'm, which it is not hard to crack as all which-protrudes, if still thinking in bodily terms and adding in, slightly mischievously, the boys' little protruder to make up a sixth. Note that with na the original protruder was in fact the boys' one anyway, as in chapter 10. This matches our Indo European six and sex, with the original meaning of sex being the (male) genitalia, from sai, activity or acting or action (indicating, slightly mischievously, the pleasure of it, also sai) ka-sai, make life. It has been known for some time, although not for ever, it is the action of the male sexual organ

Chapter 13 Ish

which fertilises the female. It was first supposed it was by physically kindling the life principle aboard the female body, rather as with a chark a fire can be kindled by a vigorous and determined twiddling of a stick in a wooden drill hole until the flame bursts forth. Pollination is a novel conception of which the Bible still knew nothing, supposing the male sperm was seed which of course it is not. The seed is actually concealed within the body of the female and the patriarchs were wholly unaware of it. For them the seed bearing and fruit bearing plants and animals were boys! Phala meant fruit and phalus. The testicles were regarded as fruiting bodies, somewhere between nuts and plums. Of course nobody expected the animal forms to precisely copy the vegetable ones.

Tujoh for seven, is a pass: like seven too difficult. But perhaps it can be read as from tau-sha-u-a(h)i, all-life-all-that, which, adding to the bodily protrusions the life force, the flame of life without which the body is not alive. Delapan is perhaps from di-la-pan, di-loop-of surfaces, di as in digamma, that is to say, twice round the edge of a surface like Apollo rounding the sky, the four sides of a surface twice. It may sound rather advanced. But some seven thousand years ago the Egyptians were drawing a surface (pai) as a square, an abstracted four sided plan view the Egyptologists have identified as the letter p (the Egyptians actually pronounced it pai). As every schoolboy knew in my day, the Greeks also called it pi and drew it in elevation, more as a lid or roof (like their 'polis' or 'all the roofs in a loop'making up a city), with two supporters and a lid(Π) often with a curlicue to make it clear that was the bit which was being represented, and the two supports were just that; though we had not as schoolboys carried out the etymological analysis, still a novelty waiting to be unearthed.

A speck is itself from a spark, and a speckled hen is one with markings which are spark like, that is with little spots or flashes of colouring. Roast is from rau-sai-tai, rayed-of the flame-become. To fry is from fa-rai, fat-ray. Fat and fry both have the f- in place of the p- of Greek pion, fat. In chapter 12 for Pa the case is made for the semantic contents of this phoneme including fattening. It could certainly be argued that fa- is a better original for fat, in so far as the Greek phi comes from the elision of the Egyptian pa-hei which is the penis, the ecstasy piece (chapter 9 for hei). It is a clearcut gull from the penis which is addicted to swelling, so that it is taken to have the fattening trick to a T. But by now it is an embarrasment to be always harping back to the genitalia, so that wherever possible an alternative derivation is to be preferred. Nevertheless it is absolutely inescapable we started speaking in idioms we gathered to an astonishing extent from our own genital performances, simply because that occupied our minds to an overwhelming degree; and anyway we generalised outwards from our own personal thinking about our own uninhibited personal sensations and reactions to the world around. It was naive but it was frank, and it was a very long time ago. Yet even half a million years later it still shows. Remember we were only hominids when first we learned to speak. The human mind can only have got around to the consideration of any relatively complex questions of propriety well after language had been around long enough to have established a tradition of coarse reflection upon coarse behaviour. To go back even before speech, our world was a semi-conscious or even an entirely unconscious world in which what bubbled up got expressed, and autism was the rule. There were no prisons or prison reformers then, only the punishment handed out by the outrage of your peers, if outrage it was. Sexual aggression in itself was perfectly acceptable in those days, so long as it did not intrude upon any competitor's territory, which almost inevitably it often did. If you were caught jumping the local talent belonging to another male it was a matter of course you were in trouble. You just better act secretively so as not to offend the alphas. That was all the morality

Chapter 13 Ish

there was. You can see the same behaviour in our cousins the chimpanzees today; and a hyper critical mind must see Sapiens Sapiens too in much the same light even today.

Then it was a seven day wonder that the flame leapt upwards (10). Most everything else falls on your foot if you leave go of it. In Chinese shang is up or upwards, and shan is a mountain, from sha'n, an up-one, an upland. The English mountain, is from mau'n-tai-n, superlatively massive-one-become-one. In Ancient Egyptian sa'a is to go up, while saha is to set upright, to erect, and sash is to prick up the ears, from the Lithic sa-shai,up-sensers (10,20). Sa-arai is to bring up, with the arai meaning to bring (from the extensive vowel a for any extension or progression and so bring: in Latin it had the meaning go, with ire to go from ai-re, going-verbal ending). Thence we have sariu, bearers, carriers, porters in Egyptian, where –u did duty as a plural as well as a substantive. At the same time Egyptian sasha meant shine (12), actually sa-sha, sun-shine, or anyway like the sun.

With no grammar to speak of, up, upwards, on top, and the top or summmit all fall under the one semantic head. In that sense, thinking at the beginning of language was fuzzy by our standards. In fact it was worse than that. The mind could elaborate further from there, in spite of the fuzz or even because of it. The inclination was to relate the idea to its expression in human terms: it was as if the mind said to itself 'and how does this Ish reflect upon us, how does it find expression for us?'. In Old Persian Shamash is the sun. So we have to ask ourselves why. The sun in those days sprang up shining and then it sank down and died, often in a blazing blood red series of splashings across the Western sky – precisely as it sometimes still does today. Upping, and at the same time shining, sha (12), the sun then descended to die, ma, but encouragingly to gestate below the horizon (ma again) and arise gloriously the next day, resurrected, shai again. "Does not the sun rise smiling at the dawn of another day?" Shamash, Lithic life-death-life, has much the same semantic content as the tomato, an annual which blooms and the seed must then be planted to germinate and come to life, be born again. The Lithic tau-ma-tau is birth-death-birth, a perennial: you plant the seed each year. The Aztecs bred it from the same original plant as the potato (from pa-ta-tau, piece {tuber} birth-births: you plant the tubers year after year. Osiris, in the original Egyptian really spelt (and pronounced) Au-Sarai, World Sunrise, (well really world-shine-ray, but they meant precisely the same in the Stone Age, because of the imprecise nature of thinking then). Osiris promised immortality; though not like the God of Christianity as a salvation but as a natural occurrence like the vegetation which renewed itself each year with seeds planted and germinating in the ground. Seed is from sai-dai, living-becoming. The Latin for seed is semen, from the Lithic sai-mai'n, the living deadun, germinating life when planted.

For the Persians, at one time fire worshipers, Zara-thustra shared the phonemes Shara- with Osiris The -thustra is harder to decypher. It was Zoro-Aster in Greek, much like Latin astra, a star, which has the Lithic meaning roughly a fire-vent or fire-birther. Considering the Lithic options, perhaps Zara-Thustra is best translated 'The Light of the Totality of the Stars, of All the Stars, of the World of the Stars, of the Firmament'. He was the priest who established the Persian religion a thousand years before the current era. The Christ has since been similarly pictured as 'The Light of the World'. While on religion, Zen is an esoteric form of meditation to acquire enlightenment, developed wthin Buddhism. In Japan Rinzai actively seeks enlightenment. The Lithic elements appear to be from arai'n-zai, to actively spiritualise; Soto Zen meanwhile aims to become gradually enlightened by the continual exercise of the proper means, namely squatting upright. Lithic suggests the -to, from -tau, means become, rather than achieved. Zazen is the soto zen method: upright zen.

Chapter 13 Ish

To stand in English meanwhile is from sa-ta´n-dai, upright-becoming-does. The does is little more than a verbal marker indicating a natural process, or one which results from the nature of things, as opposed to ka (or arai) which is often indicative of making from human agency, like the knapping of flints. When the idea is universalised over the millennia of metaphors, Ka still retains the forceful nature of the original activity. To stand is hijacked as the state of standing too, a stand, as the syllable ai did duty for our syllable -ing as well as our syllable -ed. Stood makes the past sense clear from the au (oo) phoneme that it is a done job, oo being the completive-substantive vowel (and therefore also dual, but that is not relevant here). See chapter 15 for the vowels. To stop is to sta-u-pai, to stand with u-pai or to vertical become with both-feet.

To score is from the Lithic sai-kau-are, acting-cuts-verbal, first to make the scores and then to count the scars made. The semantics are apparent because the word covers both the gouging out and the count which follows. It would not otherwise be possible to account for this double meaning. To scratch is similarly to chip out or cut an upright stroke, sa-ka-are with a confirmatory –tch, probably from –sh, vertical again, because the counting was of parallel vertical lines. That was how numerals were first recorded, just as they still are on cricket scorers´ pads, and on prison walls, where a diagonal stroke is used for the tenth stroke if the sentence is a long one, representing the digits of the two hands. We count in tens. In Malay, often the language with the most direct Lithic understanding, sa, abreviated from satu, which is also used, from sa-tau, an upright, cut or gouged out, is the word they use for one. The Malays go on to use sa-sa as any-old-one and so any. In Hindi one is ek, just any old cut, from ai-kai, that which-cut, a cut. The Senoi (Aboriginal Malay) for one however is a surprising mi, which can probably be read in its original Lithic form as 'm-i. The 'm was most likely just a hum and doing service as such, as the Senoi mind braced itself for enumeration, using the diminutive reduplicative vowel i for an itemisation. An initial 'm is used similarly in Africa, sometimes translated as if it were him, which is the actual semantic content, more or less. The Senoi are using the vowel i in its original role as the diminutive-reduplicative vowel, which serves quite well as the base for enumeration, a singleton in a reduplicative series of many.

Language did not spring fully fledged from anyone's head, it built over the millennia. Language is now a strait jacket, but not quite in the way Benjamin Whorf imagined half a century ago. We first of all dreamed up the lingo by dividing the world to shape it. In other words we had been thinking over millennia before we spoke. Then we forgot how we did it, so it now appears as if it was the language which framed the world. But the opposite is the truth. Of course it was the world as we apprehended it at the time, rather than the real thing, which we analysed. Our world shaped the language. The straight jacket today comes in the form of the secondary meanings we have developed using the phoneme strings we now call words. Breaking that crust releases the genie beneath. We get back to our original perceptions and symbolisations. Meanings come to life again, a mile away from the arid syllogisms of the linguistic logic compiled as transformational grammar. Meaning is back where it belongs in the teeming lexicon built over the millennia around the world.

The stake, the original stick, which refers to the vertical posture of the stake when stuck in the ground, sta-kai, make standing, and indeed struck on the top in all probability to get it to go into the ground and stay upright, with the very same Ka phoneme which came from the striking of flints at the time of our most primitive echoisms. All this probably only took a few thousand years to emerge, or if we start with the original psychosemantic meanings perhaps a few hundred thousand. In that length of time, given human whimsy it is

Chapter 13 Ish

remarkable there was not greater semantic drift or development, whichever way you care to look at it. We are picking up a pointer to subconscious refreshment over the generations as they each learned the language with their conscious minds, providing scope for their subconscious minds to pick up the original constructive scheme compiled from meaningful phoneme strings.

To put some body onto the psychosemantic tree for ish, the hissing (1) is to be seen in the Malay chichak, a little house lizard skittering about the walls with pads on its feet enabling it to grasp the ceiling if needs be, simply by clenching its feet and making use of the vacuums they form. It makes a very high pitched cheep amounting to a hiss. The h in hiss is a cockney h (chapter 7), separating an original two vowels, showing the word started out a-i-ss, that-which-'ss'. The cicada, (Latin) a grasshopper, cheeps too, in Spanish cicaria, pronounced thicaria, the 'ss' or 'th'-maker. To cheep in Malay is chiap, the cheep from the pecker and not from the lips. Similarly you can hear the soughing of the wind. The English sip is from the sucking sound of the lips. If you say it drawing breath in instead of out you get the sound of a sip so exactly you can use it to tease your grandchildren when they are learning a noiseless sip.

The babbling brook can be found in gush (2) which goes 'sh', or makes a sh, and in splash, ish-pai-lai-i-sh, action-surface-liquid-which-'sh'. Note two different semantic contents for sh in the same word, (35 and 1) suggesting some degree of fluency in the phonemic meanings, conscious or otherwise. Lai registers the instinct of liquids to spill, in turn ish-pai-lai, the action of going lai or flowing downhill, ultimately to the briney ocean where the water has turned into lye (lur from lau-arai, for ocean in Celtic (altogether-lai'd, and spelt lyr), and laut from lau-tai, in Malay, (altogether lai'd-become). To wash is to splash water, from awa-shai, water-action; and a flash or flush was originally a splash, as a flush still is. Splish, splosh and plash are just whimsical variants, the first two evidencing the use of phonemes with the stops mostly regarded rather than the vowels. Plash, without the initial s-, leaves nothing critical out. Plush on the other hand is not an action and has no initial s for this reason. It is a hairy or long piled material. There is a nice conjugation of semantic elements involved here. Pellis is a skin in Latin (though perhaps from Homeric Greek where it meant a milk bowl, the lai in that case being the bowl shape rather than the enclosure of the flesh in the case of the skin), from which we get our pelt, and a skin of course may be ours or an animal's. Skin is from ish-kai'n, it warms (18) the body. If it is our body, most of it without significant hair, the pai-lai is simply the surface-looping (surrounding) our flesh within, pa being the thinned diminutive of ba which initially carried the principal meaning of fleshy or flesh because it is pronounced by the two (fleshy) lips – as already disclosed in chapter 3. But animals have pelts with conspicuous hairy coats. Gulling therefore allows the surrounding surface (pai) to acquire the meaning hairy. A sheep's coat is thick and keeps it warm, shai-pai is a warm coat, a character it acquires from being so shaggy or long haired. Brer Warm Coat is a sheep and plush is a material with a shaggy pile. It is also soft and pillowy but that is another connection, kushi (Hindi is soft or easy), like a cushion. Ka can be shape or make It relates to sai, at ease around the hearth, nicely toasted (18,19), made comfortable or a comfortable place or placement.

Washing was mostly done in a stream if you go far enough back. They were urinating and defaecating in the same stream too, so it is no surprise as you went down stream the flavour was less bland. Each village had strict rules ensuring defaecation was down stream of watering points, but of course the next village downstream was unable to benefit from this dispensation. Only the natural breakdown of vegetable matter in the pleistocene provided a degree of purification for those living downstream. Under this dispensation the hill tribes tended to be the hardier even though on shorter commons. There is still the same problem in so called civilised countries today where water boards discharge "treated" sewage into the rivers. You would be ill advised to try to drink it. For that it needs further treatment. Father Thames is supposed to be drunk five times before he reaches the sea, each time after sterile treatment which was entirely lacking in the Stone Age.

For the Turks ush is a penis, u-shai, what shshs, that is to say it is what water-issues. Stable lads talk to their horses thus. Before putting down new straw they intone shwsh-shwsh-shwsh until the horse, quite without benefit of Turkish, or indeed linguistics of any kind, nevertheless eventually pisses, so the new straw goes down after it has drained away. It is a clear case of psychosemantics, which evidently goes back a long way, well before our hominid forebears. Even potent grave and relatively rational seniors are sometimes instantly put in mind of the need to urinate when they turn on a tap or hose the flowers. A spray, starting out a sprinkling distribution of liquid and only later a sprig or buttonhole, gets its initial s- from the gushing sound as well as the active semantic, the p probably from the penis (a squirter), and the ray from the jet formation.

The sudden "sally", before bickering down a valley as the poet had it, was not in origin a slipping down but a leaping up as a loop: in Lithic from the skyline at sea which runs all around the horizon, and then from the similar orbit of the sun which runs all round the sky, and so from the Latin salire, to leap up: sa is up (because the flame springs upwards) and lai is an orbit or loop; and so a looping action is sa-lai-ere, up-looping-verbal marker. You already had the la meanings in chapter 8, if you have read the book consecutively (as you really should, because as we go on we have shorter explanations, assuming some of it at least is beginning to make some sense). Sala the salmon is a leaper up while the -mau'n is in aid of plantation of the seed, for which salmon in their hundreds leap up river rapids in a mad scramble to spawn and die. The Chinese however evidently have in mind the whispering breezes when they contemplate the sibilant, in so far as their word for wind, air on the wing, is shu. Our wind whewing-does, the Whistler; unless it is so fierce it sings, when it goes la-ing, a gale. The poet even thinks it moans (where m-a-u-a'n is a wailing sequence, and so echoic, and the 'n on the end is the verbal marker), since its tone can slowly fluctuate as it speeds and slows around the topography and foliage.

But ish as a phoneme is for the most part given over to the flame (3) and all the meanings that are derived therefrom. There are not so many words today in English with the sibilant meaning fire precisely, so it may be thought the original identification is wrong. But in reality the scarcity is precisely because it is the thirty or forty subsequent derivative meanings which survive. However the Basque for fire is Su and the Arabic for a spark is iskra (ish-kara, fire maker). It was the name TE Lawrence, when he was not in the Arabian desert urging Wahabi (Terror-loving) Saudis to rebel and throw off the Turkish yoke, gave to his Cairo news sheet to get the Arab masses thinking wahabi style. The paper survives in Cairo to this day, though nowadays under different management and with a sharply revised editorial policy. The cheap red chequered tea towels Lawrence bought in the Cairo sukh and issued to Auda Abu Tai (Auda Father of his Tribe) and his fellow Arab rebels as an identifying uniform for those fighting for an autonomous Arab fatherland, in replacement of the corrupt Turkish Caliphate in Constantine's city, are now worn by Arabs across the Middle East, alike by kings and commoners, as badges of autonomous pride. None of them probably know by now they are wearing Lawrence's tea towels on their heads, and may not care to be told.

Chapter 13 Ish

To char is treated by Eric Partridge as a back formation from charcoal, with char like chore meaning a turn as evidenced by the turn of work a charlady performs. But 'work' comes easily in Lithic from chipping flints, productive labour, u-a-kai, what-that-makes roughly, suggesting the charlady was originally a khare-lady ; while the char in charcoal comes just as easily from the same source as the chark: ish, the sound of the flame hissing as it dies. Chark is clearly from an original sha-kai, fire-making, and charcoal is coal which has been burnt (but incompletely due to lack of oxygen). English also has ash. Ash is the modern much elided form of aesc, the Old English form, from the Lithic ai-sai-kai, that which-fire-makes. The Old Norse is aska, with exactly the same Lithic elements as Old English. The Gothic was asgo, from ash-kau, fire-made, and the Sanskrit was asas, from a-sa-a-sa, that-flame-that-burnt. Or else the repetition was used to indicate ash was flame repeated (to completion). Sanskrit also routinely had sh in place of an original kh, and here the sh has additionally become an s. Partridge meanwhile simply guesses the Indo European root for a turn was as or az, as a terminal conclusion with no reason given, but of course he was under the Skeat illusion that words are composed from random morphemic roots, not phonemic meaningful ones at all. Lithic sorts out the mess: but opens out a whole new research programme. The Old English carried the nearest reproduction of the Lithic. A char lady is a worker (from khai-are) and charcoal is burnt wood (from shai-are, to burn) which glows hot like coal. Simple really.

The ash tree on the other hand is a tall one (15). It goes up, like the flame. The English ash penetrates the woodland canopy largely branchless, and has smooth tall trunks in established wooded areas around my house today. Without the Lithic psychosemantic tree nobody can explain the reasons for the two meanings of ash, so they pretend there are none, which certainly saves thinking. In the Pleistocene such woods (as well as Lithic meanings) were bog standard. The oak by contrast spreads its branches to suppress rival growth, and it is named for the superlative hardness of its wood, enabling it to do so. The Aboriginal Malay kruing for a (hardwood) tree has much the same semantic content There is also the aspen tree, originally just asp, from a-sai-pai'n, an up shoots-one or tall pieces one, a tree not conspicuously tall but with long tall shoots. The acacia may also have originally been a-ka-sai-a, that-grows-tall-one. The mason tree, the false acacia in Europe, grows alongside an old ash in my garden and out-tops it. My grandfather was a senior mason and planted the trees wherever he lived. They are fine trees but not native. One wonders why the masonic order should have chosen a false tree. They don't know. Was it because they too only represented their declared identity, while nurturing a secret reality only disclosed to those in the ultimate know? It would explain rumours of a secret head concealed somewhere or other. Anyway we can here include also arbor, the Latin for tree, which gives us the Nularbor plain in Southern Australia, an infertile region with little enough herbage and a nul- in the way of trees. It is still a surprise to find a Latin speaking digger in early days, but there apparently must have been one. The untrilled r is a cockney r replacing a. Arbor comprises the Lithic elements arai-bau-a, raised-burgeoned-one, ie a tall growth, in fact a tree, which has been drawn up. Tree is quite similarly from the Lithic te-rai, originally tai-rai, rayed by the feminine rays issuing from the ta, the female pudenda, which were found to draw out and up the boys squatting opposite around the hearth, and so meaning from time immemorial draw up, raise, stretch tall (tall is from ta-lai, born and so become-linear or long). In ancient Egyptian it was the cedar which was called ash or shai, the tallest tree in the Lebanon. The cedar is in Lithic terms Sai-da-rai, much the same, that is up-drawn, a tall tree. Or else it is from the earlier Greek kedros, with initial k-. The Lithic from which it comes is then kai-terau-sai, trunk-drawn up-tall.

Chapter 13 Ish

While looking at trees, all remarkable for their height compared with the undergrowth, we can include the American sequoia capable of two hundred feet, a giant pine in the American Cherokee tongue, from sai-kau-ia, tall-grown-it that or one, the tall one in their tongue.

Right next door in the dictionary is a sequin, originally zecchino, a Venetian gold coin, from zecca, a mint for minting metals, which in turn is derived from the Arabic dar as sekka, house of the mint, a heating house, where the metal is melted and poured in a mould. Dar is a house in Arabic, I guess the dar is from the ta-are or birthing place. Apparently in the bad old days Arabs were either on camels or making babies indoors; or anyway liked to think they were. That is Sapiens Sapiens for you. Sekka, the mint, is from the Lithic elements sai-ka-ka, a fire-making-place. Metal, melt and mould are closely akin in Lithic. Metal is from earth (the ore)-become-liquid, melt is ore-liquid-become. Mould is from ore-that what-liquid-births, the mould forms the melt. The sapodilla tree reveals its own original logic after some unwinding of the Aztec lexicon. The dilly, a tree found in the West Indies, is aphetic (a shortened form, well uninflated really) for sapodilla, which in turn is a Spanish diminutive (-illa) of the Aztec tzapotl. The –tl is simply the Aztec substantive marker. Tzapotl in turn is short for the Aztec cuauhzapotl, of which the first element is from cuahitl which is their word for tree. The Lithic elements are kau-a(h)ai-tl, grown-extensive-noun marker, or grown high (chapter 7). The u vowel is the completive one (chapter 14). The h can therefore just be a cockney h, and the -a'ai a reinforcing extensive. The Spanish diminutive -illa in sapodilla is actually from the Aztec –tl, their substantive marker taken from the bus tzapotl or tall piece. There is no reason why different languages should not have parsed their words differently, which has obscured the commonality of Lithic and provided the astonishing diversity of the six thousand languages currently on earth, along with as many more really numberless languages which have perished or been largely transformed, all from a common phonemic starting point. Of course there may well have been diversity in psychosemantic terms ab initio as well. You would surely have expected it. But the surviving evidence points to uniform Lithic thinking as extremely widespread if not universal. Rather depressingly, we seem to have started out thinking all in very similar terms, with common phonemes; and just ended up at loggerheads.

The Latin os for bone is from a-u-sai which is un-what-burnt, the unburnt. Bones are burnt up in modern cemetery furnaces but in the prehistoric funeral pyres they were not consumed. Instead as the hard masculine part of the body - the fleshy parts were seen as the feminine contribution and so as ephemeral - they were collected and given reverent burial, supportive of male chauvinism, where they might even germinate and lead to reincarnation in this world or the next. It is perhaps pertinent to remember here that Aristotle believed women were mortal, having no intellectual souls at all. Their contributions to the world were confined to the sins of the flesh, fleshing the male seed and rearing the next generation. It was the women in hominid days when we were learning to speak, who - hunkered round the hearth in considerable deshabille - with the feminine rays which emanated from their genitalia provoking action at a distance, who drew out the male phalus, seducing its owner. Since the flesh was mischievous in this way, women with their fleshly orientation, including their bulgy bits, were the mischief makers and it was therefore not surprising they were not going to benefit from the after life. It may even have prompted Adam's report to Deity, which the Bible says landed Eve with the pains of childbirth, the punishment fitting the crime, so far as Adam was concerned. Over sixty years ago when I drew attention to Aristotle's chauvinistic position on these matters (to

Chapter 13 Ish

expose his savagery) in a university tutorial, a fellow student got up and left the room in indignation, as if I was recommending the posture. So it is perhaps wise now to include a disclaimer. The posture, should it reappear, needs slapping down. But the fathers of Western civilisation need to be stood in the stocks, and we should not shy away from the task. Our forebears were not very nice. Their mischiefs should not be overlooked as our Victorian forebears overlooked them. Only lawyers, in their vanity (and their wigs), now care for Aristotle's syllogisms. Karl Popper has moved the rest of us on. Our hominid forebears have some things to apologise for too, as has appeared already in these pages.

The classic case when it came to raying was the sun, whose rays the Egyptians drew with hands on the ends to symbolise their propensity to pull up the plants on their return journey to the sun. We are into Lithic thinking here. None of it was entirely veridical, while some can now easily be seen to have been absurd. But that does not mean it did not obtain at the time. The flame as ish can be finished off with a sizzle, sai-zzi-lai, "like the hiss of the flame" (when extinguished) for anyone who speaks Lithic, and turns it round.

Asbestos, as well as causing cancer, is also unconsumed because it is incombustible. It is from the past participle of the Greek verb sbennimai to extinguish, composed of the Lithic phonemic elements sai-bai-en-nai-mai, the burning-organic matter-of-presenting-death (or strictly the dying). Asbestos is from a-sh-bai-sta-u, Lithic that-burning-organic matter-halting (standing)-one, ie. A fire extinguisher. For some reason Eric Partridge – who although the word king of his day had no Lithic (or did he?) – took the initial a- to carry the semantic content un- from a- as an absence, which it often does, as well as 'that', and read asbestos as inextinguishable, flying in the face of the physics. Asbestos is incombustible and puts fires out. If it were inextinguishable it would burn furiously. But then Homer himself sometimes nods. Meanwhile in Malay salai is to heat over a fire. The sa- is clearly the fire. The tricky bit is how the –lai can mean over. In fact it doesn't. It means under, like our below. The fire (sa or sai) on its own suggests burning. La (chapter 8) can indicate lowering, including a low rate as in slow, and also surrounding as in pellis, skin, which is a thinned derivitive of ba, flesh, surrounding it, from the skyline at sea. Salai, in Malay, has the –lai to indicate it is not an incinerating job but the less violent one of subjecting the flesh to the heat of a flame below. It is Lithic thinking to a tee or tai. Salaian in Malay is the rack over the fire for smoking meats, with the fire under, the lai picking up fresh relevance by way of the linearity of the racking, and the -an (pronounced long, a bit like arn – with an English untrilled r - rather than like Anne) being a substantive ending in Malay, which can be read more or less as if it were "one" in English, or sometimes even "-ing". The Malay prefixes and suffixes are a quite lengthy and important study on their own account but not germane to the argument here.

Brazier, Partridge has worked out in his book, is from braise, originally breze, that is embers or live coals; and we can add the Lithic analysis bai-rai-sai, a be-raying-fire, not the full flame. The point about the embers was they glowed red as live coals at the seat of the flame before fading when burnt to ash, that burnt. The Primitive Germanic had brasa as is found in Swedish today meaning fire (or a burning log), and cropping up also in Old Provencal brasa and Italian brascia, bracia, braga and brece. In English we have braise, "now only in cookery" as Eric Partridge puts it. To braise is to cook with live coals. But the live coals glowing red led to the South American country Brasil, red like the embers, named for the hard redwoods of the country at one time the principal export, named for their redness, named for the red embers, named for the Lithic phonemic and semantic elements above.

271

Chapter 13 Ish

There is also in English combustion, with the sibilant on offer as indicating fire. But the word is from the Latin comburere of which combustus is merely the regular past participle. The Latin prefixes co- and –ambi- as prefixes (co- is joined together and -ambi- is 'as the flesh': that is with bilateral symmetry and so on both sides) so that the word actually has the original core construct –urere, Lithic u-rai-ere, where the u- is as the completive vowel ("all done gone finished") and also the passive, and rai- is rayed, by the fire, ish in fact but not stated because the fire's rays had already acquired some of the semantic content of the flame which uttered the rays. The final -ere is just the Latin verbal suffix; because rays (re from rai) acted upon their targets, having effects; and so they were activators, and so makers of activation, and so verbal markers.

Breath is akin to breeze. Compare Latin susurrus, the whispering of the wind in the trees. A hiss (1) on breathing in, followed by a parting of the lips and a puff when breathing out has given us our spirits, from the Latin spirare to breathe, the spir- (Lithic sh-pia being, as Eric Partridge puts it, "as clearly echoic as one could wish". The s- is breathing in and the pia is breathing out through the mouth (compare spit!). Halare in Latin, also to breathe, is also echoic: the ha- is the sound of breathing out and the -la- of breathing in, with the usual -are verbal suffix. Note the -la- separating two vowels, and the fact the vowels are both aa (see chapter 9 on La). The Greek pneuma for breath, air and wind is also supposed to have been echoic breathing again, the pneu- is breathing out and the -ma breathing in. It does appear our forebears were rather an asthmatic lot, and probably slept on their backs with their (ever so slightly rancid) animal skins tucked up to their chins. The Latin tussis for cough is also supposed to be echoic, leading to tos for a cough in Spanish; as is whistle, a bit of a wheezing sound originally, rather than the clear notes produced by professional whistlers today, some even capable of rendering classical tunes by mouth. A whizzer acquires his speed from the sound of rushing air, and a whisper is sibilant communication, or for poesy just the sound itself, as when the wind is alleged to whisper in the trees or even green grass to have the facility, which is stretching it a bit. Whether the Chinese derived their shu (6) for wind from the hissing involved in breathing or from the susurru of the breeze is moot, but it is clearly echoic in Lithic terms.

Issue (7) is generally judged to be directly from the Latin ex-ire to go out, but if so its slurring is psychosemantic, from the puffing and hissing of breath (4) and wind, or the babble of brooks, which is in reality coarser, more like bubbling or white sound. The breath issues and the wind blows, and small waterfalls shush. Ex (37) is itself the result of major slurring in turn. The out of its meaning was in origin a rising out, ex is from ai-kai-sai, going-makes-up, like a cork out of a bottle[7]- neither of them invented when language began - so perhaps from the sun coming up and out of the horizon each morning, indeed 'as it-begins-to shine', which is as good a reading of the Lithic elements ai-kai-sai as the other, so ex was probanbly when the sun came out. The Latin ire to go is from ai-ere, ai- verbal marker. Ai is aa-ing and so going, the distance gone an immediate extension of meaning from the extensive vowel. All vowels are extensive in so far as they can be continued for as long as you have breath, but a as the general one was picked on to exemplify the characteristic precisely, as an extensive psychosemantic content of the phoneme. The extensiveness of the vowel is then gulled for going. It is a semantic gull: the legs are borrowing a character from the glottis. Issuance probably similarly accounts for quite a number of the initial s- prefixes treated conventionally as "general intensive prefixes" (Partridge) in the Indo European tongues. It is not clear in any of these cases why an intensive marker should be required, but certainly the s- prefix is often there. As will emerge, the sibilant has several roles which the Lithic reveals. Sparse, spray, spurt,

Chapter 13 Ish

spout and sperm, all related to the Greek speirein to sow, strew or scatter, probably in ugly origin all from the performance of the male organ which does all these things and also links up with the Greek peos for penis, pai-au-sai, piece-that what-issues or spurts. Compare Sanskrit pasas or sapas for penis, where there appear to be two quite separate alternative secretions on offer, as indeed there are. (Note the metathesis of phonemes).

A hose (cockney h), i-au-sai, it-water-issues, passes water too. But curiously the original hose were the ones cladding the legs, and they were tall (15), it-what-raised, like the ash tree, and like trousers, terau-sai-a, also a garment pulled-up, drawn-up-ones, trews. They also covered the lower legs, a novelty when introduced, since the lower legs were formerly left free for loping after game. The original chawat in Malay, a loin cloth merely covering the crotch, actually meant crotch piece, since chawang means a fork in Malay as found with a branching bough as well as with the body. So the chawat is probably from Lithic ka-u-a-tai, joint-dual-that-divides, a joint of two pieces is a fork or crotch and the chawat divides it by passing between the haunches. Adam's single fig leaf from the genus ficus was never more than a scribal absurdity. The lightest of breezes, or even a single stride would have rendered its purpose nugatory. Yet rational folk take it as reasonable because it appears in the holy book. The fai-kau of the ficus, in Lithic meaning penis-shaped, may have struck the scribe as fitting for covering Adam's profile. Since its leaf has three protruberances and the male profile has three bits to cover, and the match was there in the old Stone Age just as today, it may have prompted the Lithic in the first place. The garden hose therefore has no obvious semantic connection with the stockings, although they use the same phonemes and are both tubular.

The garden hose is probably also related to to ooze. Ooze in turn probably comes by way of spit. There is a cross current which enters the lists here, deriving from the spitting, from the Latin spuere and sputare both meaning to spit, producing spittle and sputum. The classical spit was preceded by a thorough-going hawk, and the phlegm spat out was supposed to be akin to all the other mucosal secretions and slimey things like white of egg, sperm, brains and bone marrow, even frogs eggs and snail trails. Slimes were all ish-lai-m, live-lye-matter. It was not yet quite science, but it was classifying by appearances which preceded science by many hundreds of thousands of years, and may sometimes still stand in for it even today. Ooze is from Lithic awa (the emphasis is on the w with the a prefix and suffix approaching an indeterminate schwa) for water or other liquid (the reasons are in the next chapter on the vowels); and the -zai gets its semantics from the slimes, the liquids formed by life forms – which are oozy. A virus, originally Latin uirus, from Lithic u-i-rau-s, liquid-which-is rayed or roused (and so on its way, travelling, oozing out), originally just meant the saps or juices of plants which run out, including the notable ones which were poisonous. The s in uirus is probably merely the Latin substantive marker, but wi-raus certainly attracts the psychosemantic content from the sibilant we see in issue (7 and 24), a liquid which has arisen from life forms, a live juice like the plant sap and the disease carrier. Animal and vegetable were taken to be closely aligned, as indeed in some respects they are. Animal flesh and vegetable tissue were accepted as equivalents. Both were implied by the phoneme Ba, simply because the lips which make the sound are fleshy. The poisonous sap, Latin uirus, Lithic u-i-rau-sai, liquid-which-roused-issues, was 'wos' in Old English, from awa-u-sai, water/liquid-which-issues, matching a similar Middle German wos. The next door Old English 'was' meant mire or dampness – compare German vasser, water, another fluvial liquid - so the poison gave a new meaning to virus, a poisonous agent quite unconnected with either spittle or mire, but deriving its semantics from the poison of some saps, by way of a semantic gull, sidestepping the

Chapter 13 Ish

tyrannical eye. Sap is merely a sai-pai, an issue (7) of the skin or surface or bark. It flows out of the plant, for instance when the bark is cut or the plant picked. A virus is a poisonous agent which turns out to be a class of microscopic semi-live macro-molecular cells capable of interfering with the genetic makeup (DNA) of the phenotypes of the macro species, introducing diseases; and nowadays under human control even modifying them to order as agents of beneficial genetic gene substitution.

To spit (8) is echoic too, a puff with a liquid element represented by the initial sibilant (2). There is a phonetic relationship to part, Lithic pa-tai, pieces-divided, as well: the pai or lips are tai, divided, two'd, parted so the spittle issues. Compare Latin potare to drink – from to part the two lips. The group is closely akin to the Latin sputare to spit, with English spew and even water-spout, which in turn give us the shaped pourers or spouts on our pots. To spout originally meant to vomit. Splash and splatter are other variants. Eric Partridge contents himself with the initial s- as "the Indo European intensive prefix". But then he had no Lithic and needed a general intensive prefix to cover a quiverful of meanings, like for instance the other spit or spike on which meat turns over the fire, the turnspit. The first s- here will have come from the spike, originally a stick stuck upright (10) in the ground – that is the original s- in this case, probably as a marker, and the -t at the end of the spit probably comes from an s or ts or tz as in the Germanic tongues, with spitz meaning sharp (22) in German today. The meat is spitted or pierced over the fire (3) on a sharp stake (22). The psychosemantic contents sharp (22) and flame (3) combine seamlessly to indicate the use of the sibilant. That is how the subconscious mind works, pulling discrepant recollections together linked by incidental connections outside reason.

The flame Ish (3) directly gives us smoke (9) from ish-mau-kai, the flame-mau, put down/depressed/ marred/maimed/morbid/dead-makes[it]: quite a good definition of smoke even today. The dying fire smoulders and the flame moulders. In the introduction, chapter 1, attention has already been drawn to the cigar, from the Central American Maya tongue yet astonishingly like the Arabic Iskra (3) for spark above, and simultaneously compatible with sugar, from the Sanskrit Su-kara, in this case making a pleasant sensation, the pleasant taste derived from the comfortable warmth (19 & 20), from being nicely toasted (18) around the hearth (11), instead of directly making a flame. Cigar is from the Lithic sai-kara, fire(3)-maker or burner which after all is precisely what a cigar is. Cigar is immediately from the Spanish Cigarro which the Spanish took to be a fair transliteration of Maya sik'eh to smoke and sik tobacco, the burning material which you light and smoke. To smoke is to make smoke if you are enjoying a cigar or cigarette, or just to emit it if you are a bonfire, but both are making it just the same. In Hindustani you drink a cigarette (cigret pina) while in Malay you eat it (makan rokok), and a Tamil cigar is a cheroot, from the Tamil and the Lithic shai-rau-tai, fire-rayed-become. It is lit. Nothing can be made of all this without Lithic. Likely nothing will be made, since it was not invented here, but elsewhere - back in the Stone Age.

Lexicological research across six thousand languages is inevitably an ongoing enterprise, which will require a regiment of volunteers working to establish Lithic language roots beyond a peradventure. But there certainly seems to be a remarkable community of perception where dowsing burning brands is concerned. It is evidence in itself that the dawn of the fire age, which we still live in, dates to the same period as the dawn of language. We can hardly go back in any known language before the Sumerian, only a few thousand years ago. Their word for fire was izi (3), not widely divergent from ish, the title of this chapter. The Akkadian was isatu, Lithic ish-a-tau, flame-that-become. Compare Malay satu (one), from sa-tau, an up[line]-cut, a vertical mark (10,17). Are they

Chapter 13 Ish

not both equally derived from the dowsed burning brand? In Chinese, shihuo is to catch fire or be on fire (3). The -huo (chapter 8) can include a sudden pain and suffering. The shi root in Chinese appears to mean to lose nowadays, but when one comes to check over its combinatory forms it turns out to be not so much to mislay anything but to suffer a loss (such as in a fire?), or to lose one's grip, to let slip, to lose one's bearings, that is to slip or melt away like the evanescent and insubstantial flame (3). Shiling in Chinese is not to work properly – here one sees the active sense (25 and 35) of the sibilant phoneme - shipei means "I must be leaving now", the idea is perhaps that my feet will be slipping away, or else just to become active, from the flickering of the flame, never at rest. Shiwong is to lose hope or confidence, a slipping away in the fright department. Chinese appears to be a language retaining elements so old (and conservative) it preserves idioms of original Lithic composition: words are still recognised as phonemic strings with meanings derived from their constituent phonemic meanings, veritable proof of Lithic. They never experienced the shambles of Babylon and still know what they are saying – as long as they have mugged it all up, which is said to take a mandarin or advisor forty years.

In Sumer sweat was izutu, heat born/generated. It occurs to me the victorious Akkadians entering Sumer will have been confronted by sweating Sumerians declaring themselves on fire. They will have compromised on sweaty hot, what the English sweat (18) means precisely, along with sweet which has the su- one step further in metaphor (19) from nice and warm around the hearth. The Lithic in this case appears to have been izi-au-tau, using izi as the heat of the flame and reading the whole as heat-that what-born. When you get hot you sweat. Pay attention, Tarzan: what happens when you get hot? Right! You sweat! The word sweat in English is from the same construction, ish-au-ai-tai, heat-that what-that is-born; and the French sueur has a final rai in place of tau, raised or roused, in effect drawn out, in place of born or become.

Professor CG Gostony of the Sorbonne, of Hungarian extraction, has traced words akin to the Sumerian in a variety of languages, but mostly Hungarian where many correspondences are striking, and he does not shrink from drawing the net quite wide when it comes to semantic correspondences[8]. So, for example he has the Sumerian word silim which he translates as to be intact, perfect, or in good condition, en bon etat, which we could perhaps stretch in English to in favourable circumstances. It smacks surely of the Lithic sai, flamed, in a loop, cool, hunkered around the hearth, warm, cosy, comfortable, at ease (19). Interestingly the Akkadian (proto Semitic) translation he records as salamu. Salaam alaikum!. The Hebrew is Shalom. The salaam is now usually translated as peace. But it seems it is really the comfortable feeling of peacefulness. He then prints for comparison the Hungarian sima meaning lissom, sleek, favourable or easy (19 again), followed by selyem the Hungarian for silk, comparable with Latin saeta and serica, Italian seta and French soie, with English silk, German seide and finally Chinese sunn which as well as silk can carry the meaning of law as well as soft and docile, following the Chinese universal practice of milking every last metaphor from every phoneme. If you consider the Chinese meanings a moment it should appear that silk exhibits the exceedingly soft and supple characteristic which it can be argued are to be found, in their own spheres, also in the law which supposedly is a smooth procedure lubricating social intercourse, as in softness of texture and in docility of temperament. The same character is not hard to find similarly in the Hungarian sima, lissom; and silk is soft, supple, smooth and claimant to a certain perfection (where wearing apparel is concerned). Is the same hangup reflected in lawyers' outmoded dress sense today, wearing skirts like clergy, as well as wigs and silk?

Chapter 13 Ish

Sumerian, Akkadian, Chinese, Hungarian, Latin, English, French, Italian, German, Arabic and Hebrew are amenable to the same psychosemantic phonetics and semantic contents. Coincidence? Surely not! Eric Partridge, treating the s- as simply a further case of an Indo-European emphatic prefix, has little difficulty attributing other words for smoke starting m- and without the s- like Armenian mux, actually from the Lithic mau-kai-sai with the fire removed to the far end; but with Old Irish much, Welsh murg, Cornish moc, mog, mok, Breton moguet, all not unlike English murk, to a primitive meugh or meukh, all meaning smoke. But he had no Lithic. The s- must have been dropped long after the Tower of Babel, when words broke free from Lithic phonemic structures at the conscious level and words became simples rather than strings of phonemic meaningful elements and the initial s- became sidelined as a less than useful emphatic or intensive marker. The mental shift from phonemic composition to words as we know them was a paradigm shift greater than the later parallel shift from pictograms to letters in writing. Both demoted reason, the original semantic content, prefering system and simplicity. Slovening and slurring of the old forms became acceptable. The wonder is so much survives, and this can only be accounted for by the work of the subconscious mind which prompts for the old patterns of thinking, and is repatterned in every child's subconscious when consciously learning to speak their mother tongues, which are all based on these Lithic whimsies. Thus are refreshed the thought patterns of the first speakers with each generation. It may surprise, but it has hapened and it happens.

The flame springs upwards (shai), while everything else goes downwards (mai) if unsupported and can easily damage bare toes. Hot air and gases were closed books to the ancients. The flame was magic, alive yet consuming life, devouring the flesh of animals and vegetables alike, omnivorous. The vertical, the instinct of life to shoot upwards, was the vegetative miracle, culminating in fruiting and seeding. It still is, and attracts generations of gardeners to this day. So much thinking is reducible to this original identification of life with rising, and following from that identification, the corollary identification of death with going down, that it is a waste of time to try to arrange the whole gamut in any kind of schematic arrangement. A piecemeal approach presents the evidence in its entirety without any preconceived ordering. Half a hundred examples should surely suffice, taken in any order.

An island is land which arises, springs up (ish, 10) out of the ocean (lau, chapter 9). The -land in island is a doublet with plain land in folk etymology already. But the laun is not originally land. The land was cultivated, ie flattened land, literally la'n-dai, flatten-become. In the original Lithic la- refers to the ocean from which the island arises as land: is-lau-en-da, up-ocean-from-born. The Celtic for the ocean is laur (lyr), the Malay is laut (chapter 8). Both mean the briney, the cumulative final state when all the liquid's slipping down (la-i) is done and finished (la-u). The English Ceylon, is from Silan, the Hindi name for the island, from the Lithic Sai-la'n, arising from the ocean. It is also Holy Island for Budhists, Shri Lanka, where La'n-ka is from the Lithic Ocean'in-land, and the Shri is spiritual (4) from heavy breathing and many of the meanings of the flame, much like the English island above. For Hindus it is not holy. Malay selah is to lift up a curtain, to raise its level, which on its own has the natural habit to be slack and lapse or hang down. The Malay sayap is a bird's wing, an upping pai or surface. However the vertical can also indicate the stationary. The vertical | is contrasted with the horizontal –, as in the Tau or T, the two directions | and --. To stand (English) is from the Lithic sai-tan-dai, vertical-become-does, or the vertical [line]-of the Tau-does. The Malay sampai is to arrive, the limbs standing upright and still after travelling, when they worked their way sideways in a

Chapter 13 Ish

line or sideways extension - like the skyline at sea. Jalan, Malay for travelling, is going linear. Compare aller in French which also means to go, a spatial extension a going linear process again. Admittedly you do not leave a slimey thread behind you like the slug, from sai-lai-gai, moving-slime-making or brer-slimey-going (or both!), but there is for the Malays a virtual thread or linear trace marking your journey, in the mind.

For the French, sauter is to jump as well as to cook. In the first case you become sa-u-tai, both acting (34) and vertical (14), in the second the dish becomes heated by the flame (18). It is no coincidence the genitalia have come to enjoy in language both erection, upping (10) and heating (18) together. It is inbuilt in the psychic encyclopedia of the subconscious mind which gleaned its lexicon from its psychic highs, as is already remarked in previous chapters. The ash tree has nothing to do with the unburnt residue in the grate. It is the tall one (15). It has a strong instinct to go up like the flame, from which it gets its name. Its long upright shoots made strong straight spears when spears were needed on a daily basis for obtaining food and keeping animals and human foes at bay. The ash's tactic is to push a tall straight trunk up through the forest canopy to reach the light of the sun. If any reader can think of any other explanation why an ash is a fire tree they should certainly show. The academic view is there is no reason, names are entirely random (except for those that obviously aren't).

The sacred from Latin sacer, Lithic sa-kara, is the uplifting and life enhancing comforter, with the same Lithic elements as the Arabic iskra for spark and Sanskrit sukara for sugar once again. Compare Tamil shri for holy, the spiritual flame. Eric Partridge makes great play with Sagamore, which he has from Mitford Mathews' Dictionary of Americanisms (1951). In the original Lithic it is Sag-em-au, top of the (skeletal) body (from sa-kai), ie sun-of the body, or head, followed by –em-au, -of-them all. It meant tribal chief, whence in America the Grand Sachem or head of Tammany. The au for the all could be the community or tribe, or a town, or even the whole world in Egyptian. But Sagamore is from the Algonquin languages, specifically Naragansett Sachimau, whence the Abnaki dialect Sagamore, tribal chieftain. For sag, head, we can go all the way back to Sumerian, which it is hard to believe directly influenced the Naragansett or Abnaki tongues. It meant innards guts or heart in Sumerian, but that was because these were thought to be the seat of the sa-kai or life drive. The head was also recognised as such a one as well. So it meant head too, reinforced by the reading of sa-kai as up-of body, the top of the torso, or even the sun of the body, after all the eyes were supposed to emit rays. In Sumerian sag-i-ta meant head which pierces, or arrow. They were still using the same name in Rome for arrow, without knowing why they did it.

The Latin sagitta for arrow, from the Lithic sag-i-ta, the head or point-which-pierces, as opposed to the common hand bladed weapons you swiped with, is thousands of years later than the Sumerian sagita, where sag meant head. Eric Partridge offers no derivation, but suspects it might be from the Scythian or Parthian, a deal closer to Sumer than Rome. Or sagitta could also be read in Lithic as sa-i-kai-ta, action-which-makes-a hole. But it does not fit so well with the phonetics. The arrow was the precursor of the bullet. Although it could also be used for high angle fire like artillery, it travels like an angry ray and penetrates like a bullet when other weapons were mostly slashers cutting the flesh. The two reinforcing readings probably ensured the adoption of the nomenclature. The spear is a sharp-pointed-one, sai-pai-a in Lithic, or it could just be action-pointed-one, the business end with a cockney (untrilled) r standing in for an a or schwa. The sword is from sai-u-arai-dai, action-both-ways-doing. You could swipe both ways since both sides of the blade are sharp along its whole length. A dagger too has both sides of the blade sharp but it is a

Chapter 13 Ish

ta-kara or hole maker, like the sagitta. You punch it in, it is not a swiping weapon, being too short. It is a gangster's weapon, not a militaty one. The Saxons' seax or broadsword, sai-a-kai-(s), action-that-strikes, was a striking action weapon. They may have got it from the Romans in Gaul. They beat the Celts who had heavier picks or celts, axes with long handles which were kai-lai-tai, striking-looping-born, swung in a looping overarm stroke, to strike at the head. A hit on the head was curtains, but the Saxon sword with a shorter swing most often struck home first. Certainly you could recover and get a second blow in quicker if you missed with the first. The best tactic was probably to dodge the first whack from the celt and then lunge forward while your assailant was rewinding, and cut the side of his neck. What usually settled the matter, then as now, was how many weapons could be brought immediately to bear. Saxons were stodgy and fought close together like the Romans; Celts were wild and swinging their celts kept them apart. They were a collection of wild individuals, and of course ever so slightly mad (in those far off days), no match for a trained fighting forcé working closely together.

A summit has the Lithic phonemes sa-am-ai-tai, top-of-going/travel-become. Zenith, the summit of the sun's passage across the sky, is from the medieval English cenith, senyth or cenit: spelling was variable in those days, and cenith etc is thought to have arisen simply from a scribal error misreading the Arabic samt (summit) as senit. A sum, which sounds a bit like a samt, is from the Latin summa which meant the sum total (su-em-ma, the top-of-the amount/mass) and came from the highest amount when you totalled a column of figures, probably traditionally starting from the bottom and adding up, not adding down, just as we are inclined to do today for short sums (down for long ones). But semantically, however added, the totaling up was thought of as adding individual amounts one on top of the other, just as you might pile them up, and not piling down. A total is an inclusive singularity of course. All sums were just adding up originally. Long division, and worse, came rather later, as it still does.

A squirrel has a very fine over-arching tail. Understanding his name involves knowing the Greek, where a shadow is skiouros, literally as Partridge has it "the shadow tail". But he has not got it quite right. The Greek for tail is ouros, probably because the sun's rays made the vegetable kingdom sprout and shoot, and in an animal the tail was seen as a kind of surplus shoot sprouting from the far end of the animal. Rays were the explanation for all action at a distance without direct physical contact. The tail was frisky - often against flies, but with the squirrel for balance too - and so for the Greeks must have been the receiver of rays, the Greek auros, Lithic a-u-rau-(s), is just that-what-rayed. It is a Lithic hypothesis that these linguistic structures were put together before full consciousness, when it was assumed we were for the most part being lived by outside environmental influences, forces or circumstances. Only later were these forces, or some of them at least, adopted as part of the persona. So a tail getting wagged from the outside made sense originally. You can not very often make much sense of word structure without understanding the thinking behind the Lithic phoneme strings. A shadow was a tail made by the light, s-kai-ouros, a light-made-tail emerging from the back side of the light like a tail. With the squirrel the actual tail inherited the same phonemes as the imaginary shadow tail, with the kai now coming into its own as of the body in place of made with the shadow. A squirrel's tail at the same time seems to (over)shadow its owner as well? Perhaps it was an additional prompt for the nomenclature.

In precise contrast to the squirrel whose name hangs by a single convoluted thread, the Egyptian god Osiris rejoices in a quiverful of interlocking associations, as any good god should, in the semantic contents of the sibilant in his case. Osiris is the Greek

Chapter 13 Ish

mispronunciation of the correct Egyptian pronunciation Au Sarai. Our Sarah was a fellah. He had the misfortune to lose his genitalia in a fight with Set who evidently fought dirty. The Egyptologists' god "Set" is correctly pronounced in Egyptian Saitaun or Satan. (Worse, Sai-Taun means the activity of the World in Egyptian, equating evil with nature. The Egyptians had got that far some seven thousand years ago. Should we level with them?). Osiris in Lithic phonemes is Au-sai-Rai, that universal/eternal-upping-of the sun (Ra); the Eternally Rising Sun, The Sun-rise, but also Eternally rising Life: Sai could be read as life: Universal Reincarnation, The Comforter[9], suggesting reincarnation of the human body like the daily reincarnated sun. You can see that with this lot of indications it is no surprise to find his birth was celebrated each spring in the households of the faithful by planting mustard and cress – cress is gerai-sasai, "the fast grower", or some such – which germinated and shot up in pots in the house, showing the resurrection of the apparently dead seed. That was why the Egyptians mummified their dead. With the right ritual and glyphs in the tomb it was going to ensure their germination and resurrection if they had not offended the gods while on earth. We may laugh; but we look too to the same end, albeit in more sophisticated ways. Should we pause to consider that we come from simpletons?

The French for sky, ciel, and the English rather more prosaic ceiling, are both probably akin to Latin caelum, the heavens, and so have suffered a transmogrification from a hard c, really a k, to a soft c like an s, the letter c permitting the transfer. This kh/s shift is common enough in Sanscrit. It comes from the fact the sibilant, the expulsion of breath from the half closure of the teeth and the palate, can be quite closely copied by the expulsion of breath from the half closed glottis. Anyone can try it. The Semitic tongues with hacking and hawking glottal consonants which have none of these gentle features have no difficulty keeping ka and sa apart. It has to be said they are well advised to do so, because semantically they are poles apart. To address ciel the sky we should perhaps notice the Greek kuklos for circle, in Lithic kau-kau-lau(s), each and all the corners-looped, that is to say a smooth line going through all the turns required to get back to where you started out. The caelum is this looping of corners of the over-arching dome of the firmament. This requires no upper loop from ciel with a sibilant for up, it is about smoothed corners and the upturned bowl we call the sky, and not in origin the location of the firmament as up above. But then again the fact that the sibilant can offer an upper loop may have assisted the slurrers.

As for our English sky, we may be mixed up with the squirrel, since sky comes from Middle English skie from Old English skua, skuwa, cloud, akin to Old High German skuwo a shadow, which certainly seems to have something of the Greek idea of a shadow as a light tail about it. But to suppose sky comes from a cloudy sky from a shadow seems far fetched. Clouds surely appear as superimposed moving contrasting items, with a degree of solidity and consistency and a different colour from the blue of the empty sky. The tail is a foreign body caught up with the Greek for shadow, and is found in clouds as shadow making. The sky however is from the Lithic ish-kai, light making, or light place or land. When the light goes the sky disappears. Or else it is the upper land or place. Or even all of these. The firmament, up there, remember, was a Stone top to the world with holes in it letting the light through from the upper fires at night, and rotating as it did so.

Budgerigar has already been made an exemplar of Lithic semantics, ba-dji-dji-rai-gara having the semantic content of go-up-(bright-ray)-(make-ray), bird-of bright-colour. Ba-ji or go-up (10) is the Australian aboriginal word for a bird. The djeri-gara or bright colour of the budgy shows the Australian aboriginal mind was never so far from the Western mind as folk have imagined. The djeri is shairai in Lithic, brightness (21) being what the flame rays. The -gara, from the Lithic elements ka-ra, is colour because colour is what the ray makes, determines the appearance, of anything. It also makes the ray which the eye recovers. It opens the possibility too that our colour comes originally from very same ka-ra or make ray as the aboriginal gara.

The Sumerian for bird was gesh, also a go-up, with gai meaning going just like the Australian aboriginal ba (which also features in the English bird, another go-up, with rai, raised, in place of dj, up. That is what it does (-d). The Sumerians were displaced persons from the Garden of Eden it is now believed, when the final great circumpolar ice fields melted and drowned the Eastern plains of "Malaya", (which means the Garden Land). Its cultivated lowlands whence Adam and Eve were finally expelled about eight thousand years ago are now under the shallow South China Sea. It was rice padi gardening, not flowers. The Sumerians were Adamites from Eastern Malaya who came from the East in boats, the first citizens recorded, Sumer being the oldest known city, based on their riverine irrigated rice padi gardening which their women folk had discovered with their digging sticks while the men were engaged in traditional hunting trips in the wilder lands around in what is now Malaya, Borneo and the Philipines. Their menfolk, Adamites to a man, attributed their misfortunes getting flooded out to the hubris of their women who had used their heads to displace the natural order, which Adam assumed to be displeasing to the Heavenly Power, since it would have put his nose out of joint – so he shopped his partner. They had irrigated the land multiplying the yield. What more natural than that Nature and the gods should riposte: "You think more water on the land than naturally supplied will be good, do you? Then try this!" raising the sea level three hundred and sixty feet. It was bound to give Adam pause.

Much later the Akkadian Beduin (Cain, countrymen, breeders) conquered the city of Sumer, (Abels to a man, A-bai-lai, the veg-irrigators), and then adopted much of Sumerian culture; so that the Adamite story as first told by the Sumerians has come down to us from Babylon the Akkadian capital (Bab-i-laun is the mouth or gateway of the ocean, or perhaps the Shatt al Arab, which was then at Babylon), including Adam and Eve, the Garden of the East, and the flood story, all borrowed myths from Sumer. The Sumerians were not Semites but Adamites, speaking a language closer to modern Malay than Hebrew. Adam certainly wore a foreskin, if little or nothing else, and it is a virtual certainty he and Eve added a navel apiece, in spite of Genesis suggesting the contrary. A-dam is First-born, he wasn't any actual early hominid, just an abstraction, our origin. The story of Adam and Eve expelled from the Garden of Eden (Eastern Malaya) refers to the final melting of the circumpolar icefields, between 10,000 and 8,000 years ago, when a massive block of ice, over a mile high and occupying a province, it is now believed, slid into Hudson's Bay raising the water level and causing the solid crust to rise, tipping the wáter south, which drowned the civilisation in what is now the South China Sea, formerly Eastern Malaya. We do not know what caused this catastrophe, and catastrophism has lost out to uniformitarianism, in aid of science, so the certainty there was a cause (most likely the planet Venus, a giant comet, as it was captured by the sun, upset the earth's orbit) is overlooked. There is plenty of geological evidence of repeated major global catastrophes, but fortunately they have so far been fairly few and far between.

The Jewish Old Testament remains a very creditable compilation for its age, though quite absurdly imperfect in parts like most human compilations, even those dealing inter alia with divinity. Locating these Sumerian antecedents, (actually from the old Eastern Malaya), in the hills to the North of Iraq subsequently, in the environs of Lake Van, where

Chapter 13 Ish

the Akkadians themselves originated, was a late pious figment, thousands of miles out. We ought not to saddle God with our imperfections, but we do. Floods (other than local ones from rivers overflowing, as in Britain today) do not occur inland and least of all up in the hills. The fiction has lasted twice as long as Pliny the Elder's deliberate fib that the Canary islands were doggy islands from the Latin canis, when he knew they were really the rocky coast islands from the Carthaginian Kanaria when Rome was still just a pig sty. Recent attempts to trace the Biblical nomenclature to geographical features in central Asia have worked remarkably well, since they were originally picked in the Bible for that very purpose. They just were not HC (Historically Correct) when first selected, thousands of years ago, so they still are not today. Noah's great flood was a sea level matter, and not in the mountains, an impossibility. Noah is composed from the Lithic phonemic elements En-awa-ahí, On-water-goers, and just means sailors. The Garden of Eden means Malaya in the East, now 360 feet under the South China Sea. Malaya is the Garden Land. It is from the same root as mali, a gardener in Malay and Sanscrit. Yet there have been expeditions to find a five thousand year old wooden ark up in the hills on a Mount Ararat. The Lithic is Awa-a-rai-tai, water-that-arisen-become. It means the new high ground, where any boat would beach.

The Albanian for a bird is zog, much the same as the Sumerian gesh some ten thousand years ago, with the order of the phonemes reversed. The Lithic from which zog comes is sa-u-gai, up-what-goes, and seems perfectly clear. Nobody can deny the most noticeable character of birds is that they have mastered the art of flight. The Egyptian[10] for bird offers seventy nine different strings of glyphs (names) for birds of one kind or another, of which of course there are very many species. However the fact is it is only the post-Linnaean ornithologists who have concerned themselves very much with species other than those that stand out because of some visible peculiarity.

The phoneticisations which follow are not all precisely as favoured by the academic Egyptologists who generally leave out the vowels since they do not know how to determine them, or put in neutral sounding ones just so the word can be pronounced. If the vowelisation were modified by a following glyph, then the original,(in the case of the world the –au), could drop out and be replaced by the vowelisation of the follower. Hieroglyphs were far from straightforward writing as we understand it today. They originated as compositions made up of art work representing actual phenomena given meanings. The chapter dealing with Egyptian matters in detail and in chief, already half compiled, has unfortunately had to be postponed to a subsequent volume owing to the exigencies of space, along with several other difficult languages, including Basque and Sumerian, picked for their difficulty. The deeper historical evidence for the deeper historical semantics must therefore await publication of a further volume. The Lithic hypotheses and the demonstration of their efficacy must have priority. The problem is one of size.

Of the words for birds, the Egyptian gashu is not unlike the Sumerian gesh, in fact it is virtually the same word, as the -u ending is most likely to be just the common Egyptian plural case ending. The transmission is obvious: from Sumer to Akkad to Egypt. It is likely the Sumerian sibilant was pronounced shu, like the Chinese who probably got it directly from the Adamites from the submerged plains of Malaya, just as the Egyptians also probably did, but via the Sumerians and Akkadians. There is also siasha in Egyptian for a bird, from si-ash-aa, brer-up-goer. Shang is up in Chinese. Then there is Egyptian sikama, another bird, from si-ka-a-ma, brer-go-weightless; followed by an alternative recension sahaisahai with a cockney h to separate the consecutive vowels, sa-ai-sa-ai, up-

Chapter 13 Ish

go-up-go, a compulsive flyer just like the budgy. Similarly we find haihaisai, repetitively going up; and araishau, being around aloft (lofted or lifted)[11], or rising aloft like our birds; and awanhei, an air lover/goer ; and 'mshaira (using the Hamitic idiom, starting with the personal marker m-), 'm-sha-ai-arai, him-up-go-er. Finally we have arai paitaun, around in the heavens, or perhaps ascending there, probably an eagle or vulture; aa-rai, go-rising-[into]pai, skin, surface, lid or roof-of the taun, the world. In Ancient Egyptian the arai could alternatively mean a lion, not habituated to flying or flight. In his case the name was echoic, arai, the roarer or snarler. As the lion was the king of the beasts, perhaps the eagle was the lion of the skies. Finally there is aasaiu, the air-rising-one; and aapaida, the air-travelling-does. These English translations are of course translations of the semantic contents, not of the words. The semantics are from the phonemes, before words. In Ancient Egyptian, nouns were still treated as just descriptive, so you could describe a bird any of a number of ways.

It certainly appears not only were the Egyptian scribal classes, priests of a sort, allowed a good deal of freedom in the way they strung their glyphs together, their spelling; but this whimsical attitude extended to nomenclature also. They had fifty different ways of saying bird, most of them exhibiting no indication they were identifying different species. It accounts for the large amount of polysemy uncovered in Ancient Egyptian, as well as a lot more not identified no doubt, to add to the many words with the same meaning. Egyptian texts are jigsaw puzzles to decrypt and disentangle, and much of the tentative reconstructions are indeed still tentative, and some of them plainly just wrong.

The sparrow was any small bird, from the origial Lithic sai-pai-rau, upwards-limbs-rayed/raised. The Spanish call all birds sparrows, pajaro, with sky hooks (the wings, which get rayed and drawn up on the ray's return journey, just like the vegetation drawn up by the sun's rays. On the other side of the Atlantic ocean, parrots may have been just birds too, rather than parrots particularly. The name was probably vouchsafed on challenge, to show they knew a bird from a bowl of porridge. It makes better sense than their being named from pierots because of their clowning as Eric Partridge suggests, or from a parish curate as Bloch and von Wartberg suggest. A pierot was certainly a clown, but what was it about a curate which suggested a parrot? Copying his rector parrot fashion? Moreover if they were named pierots why are they called parrots? In that case they would surely be pierots. Also there are no pierots in South America, but there also birds were indeed supposed to be blessed with sky hooks, with pai-a-rao-tai, surfaces/wings-that-drawn up-become. A parrokeet would then become a small screeching (khi) parrot, as indeed it is, screeching as it flies. A macaw appears to be named for its caw, 'm-a-caw, him that caws, from a Bantu dialect with the Hamitic m' for him, transferred with slaves by the Portuguese to central America where they became associated with the macaw tree in which macaws were to be found congregating eating the fruit, the tree in Tupi being named maca-uba, the macaw tree. Uba is tree in Tupi, from the Lithic completive element u- and –ba for burgeon. Trees are superlative burgeons compared with the rest of the vegetable kingdom, the undergrowth. That provides some slight confirmation parrot just meant a bird since the Portuguese were able to name the macaws in the land of the parrots, borrowing from Africa. In Australia they recorded the frustrating habit of the bird going up (baji, go ups) just when you thought you had surprised one, without developing any theory as to how they managed the trick.

Mountains are high, often with a series of peaks on the skyline, in Spanish sierra, from sai-ai-rairai, up-that which-rising rising, serrations on the skyline. Latin serra was a saw, and here we have sai, action (34) and rai-ra, reverse-reverse, as well as again and again,

Chapter 13 Ish

like the serrations of a saw (saw from sa-u, ups-all, all the ups, which trace out an up and down series of peaks and troughs). So back and forth and up and down both appear. It led directly to the serrations on a postage stamp. Sere in English – "with ivy never sere" for John Milton – is parched and dried out, from sai-rai, sun rayed or fire-rayed, scorched even, like a deciduous tree in winter; but Milton knew ivy is an evergreen, never dried out.

Scorch in turn has an initial s- and the –ch was originally a k, with the Lithic elements ish-ka-u-rai-kai, the ishka- is the effect of the flame, viz to burn, but in this case uraikai, one-ray-made, a burn from radiant heat as opposed to the flame. The redundant repetition of the ka element, at first suggesting the flame made the ray and the ray then made the scorch, is rendered needlessly complicated because we approach the analysis with preconceptions about parts of speech. Ishka, firemake, can be an action or a substantive state of affairs or both at once if necessary. The fire (or other heat source) makes the ray and the ray makes the scorch, as science now confirms. The grammar discloses a prior pairing of ishka and raka and their use together which effectively transposes the two kas as common elements to a joint function, qualifying the fire and the ray as a one-off. You would not get away with it today if you were to propose any such arrangement; but Stone Age fuzzy logic could fudge a lot better than that, without blinking an eyelid. You had those two pairs already, both with the same second element, and when you wanted a fire ray you were in no way disturbed to find the structure of the next bit needed was already prefigured. This was not thinking in strict linear fashion as we know it; but then it was not writing, it was a first lisping step towards compiling a protocol for speaking. In the mind the two pairings were viewed one behind the other in immediate succession when the common contribution of the two suffixed elements was obvious. Now it makes a nice exercise in rethinking the way our forebears thought at the outset.

In India when the soda water is being poured into the whisky the cry is bas, pronounced like the bus from the English omnibus precisely. The water has ba-sai, gone to the height (required). Bas means enough. Or else, with a Chinese ba it means block or negative the rising (of the soda in the glass). Perhaps stop in English is out of the same stable, since sta-u-pai, stand (from sai-tau, vertical-become)-where-surfaced fits quite nicely pouring water into a drink. But the pai is general and is footed, and the whole is stay where your feet are, or stand where you have gone, ie cease to advance: although pai always carries traces of skins, and so tent roofs, other roofs and surfaces, and lids as well as petals and plant shoots and pipes and penises. Lithic will sometimes remind the reader of a bit of a dogs' dinner; but that after all is the human mind.

The soda itself in the water is more difficult. Medieval Latin had sodanum, a headache cure, apparently from soda a headache which may in turn have come from Arabic suda, a splitting headache, with sada meaning to split. Sada makes sense as the sense (sa, 20) of splitting (ta) in Lithic, since sa is sense and da from ta, at psychosemantic base, is breaking (or splitting) in two. However it is some way from a split to a headache, which might as well be a scorching head, the sada, Lithic sa-da, giving birth to the burning (3) sensation (20). Sodium, which is the chemical name of the metalic element comes from the earlier soda. Sodium bursts into flame when removed from under water, sa-u-dai-u'm, fire-what-born-of water'neuter ending. But this is a relatively recent concoction from the earlier soda, coined an aeon before sodium was discovered. The relation to the metal is from sodium carbonate, an old headache cure. Sau or su could indicate the completive term of sai, nicely warmed (18) from the hearth (11), and so comfortable or even pleasurable, like the termination of a headache. Sodanum was a pain reliever, it easing-does-present. The

Chapter 13 Ish

headache cure sodanum is after all more likely to have been phrased to pick up the easement of the affliction, than to record the pain suffered with the headache.

To soar is to sai-u-a-rai, rising-un-that-rayed [caused], to sail up (10), unpowered: on thermal air currents in fact. The air could be the u, since the original awa referred to the elusive formless water, and so came to take in the equally elusive (as to its substantial nature) element the air. You knew it was there when it blew, but not when it didn't – much like the water which revealed its treachery when you stepped on it, but not when you looked at it (when it had a faux surface). The sailing, sai-lai, itself is an activity-maritime (26), maritime because lai is the instinct of liquids to run down to the sea, so that when lau it is the ocean. But a sore throat is a sensation (20), in this case a painful one. It hurts. It looks as if sore was originally from sa-u-rai, over-rayed by the sun, a case of sunburn which is sore. Typically sensation, as you sense around the hearth, may be positive or negative, probably starting positive and then inheriting its opposite along with a neutrality, i.e. generalised to a sensation of either kind. Sai, as well as flaming and fire, starts at ease, even pleasing, from being nicely warm around the welcoming hearth; and progresses to pleasurable quite generally, and in the superlative case (su) delightfully sweet like sugar, su-kara, sweet-maker, which tastes pleasant - and negatives bitter tastes in turn just like honey in Latin, mellis, mai-lai, masking the lye. Lithic mai-lai does not have the words masking or lye but only the semantic contents we have in those words in English. It is not just a coincidence mask and lye have the same phonemes as mellis. Both spring from a subconscious survival of the original semantic attributions carried in language. So the attributions can not be dismissed as not invented together in languages.

Sheer, without any change of spelling in this case, can mean straight up (10), from Lithic shai-rai, up-rayed; and since it is cliffs and declivities which have this appearance the up can be confused with the straight down. It can also mean translucent from shiney (12) and bright (21). To surge is to rise up, to sheer-go. The Lithic elements are clearly sau-rai-gai, up-rising-going, closely akin to the later Latin surregere whence it probably more or less directly comes. Resurgence and insurgence are out of the same tub.

With sheer (10) we can also group steep (Lithic ish-tai-pai, vertical-become-surface) and scarp (Lithic ish-karai-pai, vertical-made/shaped-surface); and after some further thought the Latin castrum which means a camp or fortified enclosure, in England a Roman cantonment originally fortified: the original fortified place made use of a natural hump whenever possible. The Lithic elements are ka-sai-terau'm, which are readily legible as land or place-up-drawn'm. The 'm appears to be just a primitive (Lithic?) substantive. In Africa you find it in front of nouns, where it has the semantic force of him but without the ungrammaticality which is often taken to go with it in translations into English. There is nothing irrational about its use. A castrum made use of a quite generalised sense of the remarkable terau facility, which had burgeoned into a pattern to be found everywhere as the human mind built by metaphor on its favourite fundamental underpinnings. A ka-sti-raum offered little more than an improved hillock, a place raised up. Sai-ta-rau meant drawn and so also raised, up, with the initial sai- possibly marking the fact too that the idea following was one of action.

Ka, chapter 5, originally the chink of flint on flint, included the semantic contents hard and the hard part of the world, the solid ground (rock if you dug), and then particular locations on the ground in its tree of meanings: a place, an acre, a land, an island. The Roman castrum was a made raised defence in a naturally raised place. You dug a ditch and threw the earth inwards making a glacis, on the top of which you stuck posts, tree trunks, to make a wall. Wherever possible it made use of a naturally defensible position

Chapter 13 Ish

such as a natural mound or a loop in a river. Sheer, however has other revelations. It can also mean so fine that the light shines through a fabric so you can see through it. This is from shine (12) with ray, which for the Egyptians again had the meaning of see. Ra, the sun, was the great eye in the sky observing its creation, with our individual lesser eyes emitting their lesser rays enabling us to see. There is more. Earlier sheer meant bright or shining too. You can compare shara in Shanta, the Gipsy lingo. It means a bright patch, from a fire ray. My daughter's pony was Shara. She was black with one white fetlock. It may have been indirectly from gypsy knowledge. She had a delightful nature. Shanta seems like the Australian aborigine language, now defunct: Djeribal, Clear speech – other tongues were in code! Compare ba-djeri-gara (budgerigar) where djeri is bright, and didgeridoo where it is a loud toot. I repeat these classic cases of Lithic thinking unashamedly because of their importance for understanding. Shine and sheen have an –n from nai (chapter 12) meaning showing. Old Norse skirr meant bright, and the Norse speakers invaded Great Britain with their bright-making-rays. What is bright is also clear to see. What is clear to see is obvious. What is obvious is absolutely obvious, and thence absolute. So sheer stupidity is absolutely stupid. At sea ships sheer off when collision threatens, and, less well known, the sheer of a deck or bulwark is its (upwards) sweep. Sheering off has action (34), direction (16), and a ray which goes there and back and therefore bends around. But with all these sh terms it is sometimes hard to avoid believing that there is in there a k, via c, which has got slovened to a soft c and then engulfed in the preceding sh- or s-. Shears or shear legs lift heavy loads. They are lifters or uppers.

But shearing sheep is a cutting job, a scission but not with scissors. The cutting shears have lost an original sc- or sk-, a cutting phoneme, from knapping flints. A bed sheet is not sheer but it is of the same texture, namely a fine weave, and its thinness transfers to sheets of paper, metal, glass, etc, and even to rain when it falls in a continuous sheet rather than in individual drops. Sheep shearers have lost the ka for cutting, as has the plough share which is a cutter of a furrow and turns it over (which makes the furrow, a reversed or rolled over strip, a furled row). And ka for cut appears in a score cut in a wooden tally or scores written as a tally, in a shard (a bit of broken pot) and even an apportioned share which is divided up if not exactly cut, and a shore marking a division, a boundary between land and sea. Eric Partridge adds the words short and curt, both cut to size, sharp and shred, and even cortex and cuirass, remarking: "behind all these words lies the idea to divide or separate by cutting". Lithic adds to that "just as the first flint knappers struck flakes from a flint with a clink which struck them as sounding like ka". We can add also a shirt and a skirt, and a curtain; and a response can be curt, even cutting.

To jam on anything is to stamp on it, an up down motion from the Lithic sha (10) and ma. A mash or mush is the same as a jam in the reverse order. The resultant texture is a jam, also achieved by long cooking (sh-aa-m). To smash anything is an action (35) originally up and down, a good pounding, but by generalisation any action with the same effect like throwing a glass into the hearth or a plate across the room, or hammering a china vase. The up and down comes from the contrapuntal nature of the hums and hisses, hums without breathing out (much) and hisses solely from the issue of breath/air. Ish being up, from the flame which named itself when dunked, the hums were therefore down – a whimsy but a simple one. Surgery meanwhile is transmogrified (s- for sh- for kh-) from the earlier Greek kheirourgeia or hand work, from the Lithic khai-a-au-rau-kai-a where the hand is named as the maker (khai-a) and the work is 'all that what is makery' in Greek as in English. It looks as if the ancients proceeded to surgery when massage failed. Both were physical interventions rather than juju.

Chapter 13 Ish

The spine is the vertical piece one. In Latin spina was first a thorn, a sharp piece protruding. Lithic allows for frequent polysemy by analogy. A spine of hills may run sideways but it is a raised ridge. A spike, like the thorn is sharp and in origin was knocked into the ground and stood upright. It was vertical and sharp together. Now it is any polar piece pointed at one end like the handspike gunners used to use to fit into the trail of a light field gun to swing it onto its target. A stick, like a spike, was pointed, since you could stick it into a body. Indeed the Old English stician meant to pierce, not unlike the Old Persian tigra, hole maker, and the Sanskrit tigmas, pointed. Compare Hindi, tik, originally a sharp point, then the pointer, the finger, then to point out as correct, whence Hindi 'tikh hai', it is correct, 'OK'. The older Avestan tighra meant pointed from ti-kara, hole maker, and tighri meant an arrow, from ti-karai, hole-making. Eric Partridge has them both from a root ti or tei meaning to pierce. Admittedly he has stripped away half the Lithic phonemes which spell out the meaning in order to get down to an original random and meaningless root just conventionally adopted without thinking, which was the favoured procedure, even for Partridge - before Lithic analysis came along. Ti-kara can be read in Lithic phonemes hole-make, viz to pierce. Ka covered both the idea of making – as when the flint knapper made a hand axe – and kindling as when his knapping made sparks. Tikh for finger was not a piercer, although it was a pointer, so perhaps it was an orifice kindler or tickler. But don't tell Mrs Grundy. Or else it could have come later from the generalisation from pointed to the verbal form to point, making the finger a pointer rather than a tickler. The Latin instigare meant to stick a stick into someone and so to goad or incite, to instigate an action; or to get your little donkey to pull harder.

Stiff and Latin stipes, a post, are from virtually the same phonemes in Lithic, sai-tai-pai (or phai), up-become-piece (or phallus). Lithuanian, a conservative tongue close to Sanskrit, has stiprus, firm, si-tai-pai-rau(s), up-become-piece-raised/roused. Which piece provided the original motif is not too hard to guess. It was the male organ. Firm starts off phai-rai'm, it is from the Latin firma, phai-rai-ma, (as) phallus-rayed/[when] raised-for planting – and so firm. Eric Partridge describes the Latin stipes as a round stake stuck in the ground, a stock, a post, without attributing any semantic content to the s-. Post in turn is from pa-u-sai-tai, a piece-that-vertical/sharp-become. Partridge's stock is from the Lithic sai-tau-kai, with sai-tau meaning up-become, viz upright, and the kai made. It made a stockade of upright posts dug into the ground. The stocks secured head and hands in upright posts, or a single one with a crosspiece with three holes in it, one for your neck and the other two for your wrists.

A stop is an event, often an action (34), and is from the Old English stopian to close an apperture, or a gap - the idea we would convey today with to stop up, rather than to come to a halt as used now on roads across Europe. Latin stuppa is tow, stuffing, only later a stopper or cork. With stop the s- indicates action (34), and the -tau-pai is a -hole-bung, a tamp, tamper, tampion or tampon just as a tap started out, but has diverged to emphasise its ability to be turned on and off. When the tap is turned off the flow is stopped. From the blocking of movement of the other comes the blocking of one's own movement, as an intransitive verb, the object of the stoppage abandoned or turned in on itself. For the French to stop is to stop oneself, a relict of the stopping or stuffing which needed an object. With stand the s-ta'n dai is vertical-becoming-does, an active verb, referring to the legs.

Examples of the vertical (up, 10) semantic content for the sibilant because the flame springs upwards begin to become repetitious and tedious even for the born again linguist. Some might perhaps be listed for readers to try to analyse in Lithic elements for themselves. A spire is easy after a spine. Any reasonably short words from a dictionary

Chapter 13 Ish

should suffice. But to sink is to go down rather than up. The pattern here is nevertheless recoverable. Ka is the sound of the knapper's strike. If ish is up, ka is down. After all ka is the sound of a sharp and intentional downward stroke, a forceful and impressive blow. You can consign sink's initial sai- to movement (35) merely, making it the action of striking (flint on flint), which is downwards; but the real semantic composition is probably the chopping off of the levitation. Sinking was a loss of flotation rather than an active seeking of descent. A jig, a jink or a jog illustrates the same pairing of elements; an up down would serve, but short interrupted rises is better. A jug Partridge thought was from the pet name for Joan, comparing Meg for Margaret, but it is actually spun on a potters wheel and the clay is made to come up. The potter draws it up with his hands, while a plate, a bowl or a cup do not require the same dexterity. A jug is a bowl tall-made. The pattern is repeated in jig-jig, a specialist term used by the Bombay pimp with little or no English when plying his trade in Grant Road sixty years ago, keeping the medical officers in British regiments busy. "Jig-jig Sahib?" is politely translated: "Would you care for an up-go-up-go job, Sir?" The psychosemantic content is clearly for repetitive thrusts. It is quite doubtful the pimps had any Lithic theory in their conscious minds, nor the medical officers neither. But nevertheless there was an undeniable immediate meeting of minds. Curiously jijian is Chinese for sodomy, the very same movements but this time round the back; and now apparently one of your human rights, even in the church of Christ. This is a real surprise, since in the Bible the whole city of Sodom has been destroyed for the practice and one unfortunate fellow turned into a pillar of Sodium Chloride for looking back – at the city, but perhaps really at the practice. Sodium catches fire exposed to air. If the odd chlorine molecule gets knocked off salt when exposed to acid it could account for the sharp taste of salt. Shanghai, the Chinese port city, in Lithic elements is 'above-the waters' (Ish-awan-high), the Walmington-on-Sea of the Orient, though without any Captain Mainwaring as yet to lend it tone, and now metropolised with skyscrapers instead.

The hearth (11) is a word which is an unusual construct. It is essentially where a fire is kept alight. A clue to its derivation comes from the Gothic hauri meaning coal, with a cockney h and Lithic elements ia-u-rai, it that-one-raying, ie glowing. Coal glows red when alight. Now a hearth also glows on the floor of the fire where the red hot embers are the hottest part, plenty warm enough even when dying down to cook potatoes in the ashes. But there weren't any potatoes in the Stone Age. They had not been invented. Red hot ash behaves like coal. It glows. The Latin carbo for coal looks as if it may have first meant glowing charcoals, kara-ba-u, deeply burning wood in the hearth at the bottom of the bonfire; and then was extended to cover the natural 'charcoal' when it was found in coal strata. Both produce burning ash and look the same once well alight. Stone Age man went by appearances. Glowing ash and glowing coal were both the same. The hearth's cockney h is moot, and so are the Lithic elements i-ai-rai-tai, it-that which-the rays-are born/become/come from. It might have originally been hot-that-etc. The glow is revealed; the combustion, the flame, is over. The hearth does not mention the flame, but it was the site of the family fire for much longer than the whole of recorded human history, perhaps fifty times as long – and as such earned a Ha- as the site of many of the phoneme's meanings in chapter 7.

The sibilant as shine (12), whether the flame's flickering glow or the sun's bright rays, shows in the English shine and sheen, star and mist, and Austria from Oster Reich, the eastern Reich - from the fact that the East is where the fiery one (the sun) is born each day and rises above the horizon, the skyline at sea: East, from Ai-a-sai-tai, that which-that-shining-is born. But Australia is the southern one. Australia is from A-u-sai-tarai-lai-a,

Chapter 13 Ish

That-completive-up-drawn-orbiting-one, when the sun is at its zenith, in the south. The Lithic meanings alone explain how Austria and Australia are eastern and southern respectively. A stone (13), Lithic ish-tau'n, is fire-born'one, from the volcanoes which were observed by our primitive forebears; and the lava was seen to harden into rock. Volcanic activity was widespread when we were learning to speak probably due to repeated comet strikes, or even after just one biggy like an asteroid. Did a big jolt knock the ice off Canada into Hudson's Bay? Who knows? Stone is static too of course, and we have our standing stones at Stonehenge, where the -henge is supposed to share the root of hanging, referring to the capstones. On independent linguistic grounds, it appears that Britain was occupied by Mediterranean colonists speaking an Egyptian patois before the Celtic head hunters invaded in turn and ate up their predecessors, retaining only some Egyptian place names attached to the terrain. The vertical (14) is merely the substantiation of up as a direction or action, simply from the habit of the flame. The Malay seluar, trousers, are up sliders, just as trousers are drawn ups like the drawers thereunder. The ash, as already mentioned, is a tall (15) tree, its habit being to extend a single relatively branchless trunk to penetrate the forest canopy. The same applies to the Latin silva, a whole loop of tall trees. The -lua (then -lva) may suggest the lai has dual application: not only long but also at the same time a loop or group of them, making a wood. The savannah, a treeless plain, from Spanish zabanna, is originally from the native West Indian Taino tongue zabana, tall-burgeons-none (15), that is treeless precisely. A savage is a jungle dweller, supposedly untamed and cruel, slurred in the Romance languages from the original Latin silua-ticus, forest-dweller. The –ticus, from tai-kau is made born or given birth in Lithic. The tai, born, can of course be read as living or become or even just being; and all from the original ta, the sound of a snapped branch, two-ing, partition, the slit dividing the two bilateral halves of the human body, the birth canal, birth, becoming, and so on. Just stir in a few hundred thousand years of ratiocination of a human kind with the subconscious sector of the human mind recording it all in the dream world for each generation, and you have chapter five, Ta and Da, before your very eyes.

In accordance with the usual Lithic linguistic pattern the vertical direction becomes generalized, the direction abstracted without its original orientation. The sewing motion is up and down through the materials being sewn together. Sai-u is just action both directions. Old English spelling seowian to sew hints at the original vowelisation now slurred: sai-au-ia-'n, directions-dual-go-verbal marker. Similarly the seed sown in the fields by hand was broadcast to right and left, but there is a double entendre: the seed was being brought to life. Semen, the seed, in Latin, from sai-mai-'n, is a living form (sai) but dormant or better apparently regarded as actually feigning death (mai'n), certainly inert and without the ability to come to life and grow unless brought to life by being sown, put into the earth, that magic element apparently cold and dead but harbouring the seed, propagating life, gestating the plant and bringing it to life. A seam is what is sewn, and is also in a straight direction. A sow, on the other hand, the lady pig, Old English just su, is super fertile, kitted out with maximal life (24) seen as an invisible adjunct. While to cover another neighbouring root commencing with the sibilant, a sewer or drain is from essever, in Medieval French, with the Lithic elements ai-sai-awa, going-high-water, or getting rid of high water, viz lowering the water level, which is what drainage is supposed to be about. These days proper drainage takes more money than the government is inclined to vouchsafe. Eric Partridge, without benefit of Lithic and therefore looking for water in a suppositional Latin root, offers a guessed Latin *exaquare, to take water out of, to empty of water for sewage. Sewage in origin includes Evian spring water, and indeed excluded

Chapter 13 Ish

waste which was not drained away but deposited in a hole or in a stream, or in the fields for fertilizing the crops. A side was first a surface, from Old Norse sitha, from the Lithic elements sai-ta, the directions two or two dimensions, up-down and sideways, which define a surface. The Tau or T is one of the oldest symbols in the human mental cornucopia, indicative of two dimensions, of a surface, or indeed of the space and time dimensions; and there is no need to be shy of finding such thinking around and forming symbols even at the dawn of speaking. Ta and u were the two extensions, spatial and temporal respectively, and because the world, supposedly flat, extended sideways, time went upwards. Progressive, huh?

But before abandoning the restricted meaning of up (10) there is a further derivative semantic content to be uncovered from it. Long before any idea of writing a script had dawned upon our forebears they found scratched marks could be made on wood or stone. A single relatively straight scratch suggested just that: singularity. Two scratched side by side suggested two; and as the mind built on that, repetitive scratches came to suggest increasing divisions or numbers, showing an amount (which is actually what number means, Lithic nai-em-bara, presenting/exhibiting-of-bigness, while the Latin, numerus says the same, nau-mai-rau-us, presentation-of mass-raisedness-substantive marker. It may be timely to compare ramai in Malay which means crowded, from rai-mai, raised-amount, with orang ramai the public. Orang is persons (from thinkers – thoughts were supposed to enter the head as rays): different phonemes but counting vertical lines just as Malay counts them with sa, a single upright). Sa, an upright, is one in Malay, aphetic for satu, an upright cut/carved/scratched. The Chinese for one is su, it is the exclusive unity, with su also meaning all, the inclusive unity. Perhaps this is where our –s for plurals comes from ultimately – not from Chinese of course but from a Lithic semantic content shared with the Chinese subconsciously. English also has single, sai-'n-ge-lai, one-ge-linked, inclusive one, as well as same and similar. Same is from sa-mai, a single amount, while similar is from sai-mai-lai-a, same-linked-one, one like the same, similar. A sum must be originally an additional total from adding up. If you think in terms of adding by putting one amount on top of the other, as we do when we think in terms of adding up, and as most folk confronted with a column of figures will start at the bottom and arrive at a top or upmost amount when they have the total, it is the topmost total which represents the sum. We use sum for the process and the result, at the summit.

But now the Chinese have suan pan, totalisator board, a summing surface, for the abacus, originally with counters on a board rather than the modern device still in wide use in Eastern lands with beads free running on wires. The Chinese hand is shu, perhaps the totalisator of the digits or the shovers of the counters, and the Lithic for counters has slurred a lot. Old High German has scioban, action-make-going; while the Sanskrit is ksub for a push, Lithic kai-sai-bai, making-acting-going. Shove, shovel and shuffle and scuffle are all from the same root. Near sum in the dictionary is the sjambok, Afrikaans for a whip, which the Dutch copied from their Indonesian lands. The Dutch spelling is peculiar. It is cambok in Malay with a soft c, which they appear to have got by nasalisation from the Old Persian chabuk. The Lithic emerging is khai-em-bau-kai, striking-on-the dual burgeons-of the body, or in Old Persian kha-bau-kai, strike-dual bulges-of the body, a bum striker or whip. More recent whippings have generally been across the back avoiding the genitalia with the victim allowed his trousers on – unless he is under age of course! It certainly appears in origin the whipping was in the bare buff and aimed at the bottom as the best area to make a mess of. The cat o'nine tails had metal jags on each tail. Kati was the tapped (feminine fleshy) part of the body, the rump, which may have prompted the cat,

Chapter 13 Ish

otherwise inexplicable. If you got the cat-o-nine-tails you enjoyed a rump with nine trails of the tails. Or else the cat was really a cutter, with or without tails.

Malay selampit offers simultaneous insights into Malay grammatical prefixes and their lexical semantics. It means a single long flat braid or plait. The Lithic obtrudes. Sai-la-em-pai-tai, a single-length-of-surface-become. It may not be perfect in English, but it is in Lithic. Berselampit is in English terminology be-braided, while in Malay terms it is ber-selampited, wearing a single skirt length "twisted between the thighs as a loin cloth". The loin cloth looks more like a single loop of the legs rather than a length of surface. The definition is from Sir Richard Winstedt's trail-breaking and thoroughly erudite Malay Dictionary in two volumes of 1953, now in a class of its own, with much fascinating detail which native Malay speakers learn from too, all totally lacking from modern pocket dictionaries churned out for birds of passage, in predictably hurried passage, from the IMF and such like international advisory bodies visiting Indonesia. Winstedt was a professional Malay imperial civil servant whose devotion to the country of his employment shines through every page of his books. I never met him but I was fortunate to arrive in Malaya when his first edition had just hit the streets and I carried his two volumes in my back pack during the two years I lived mostly in the Malayan jungle sleeping under a piece of plastic tied between trees, worn during the day folded at the back of the belt - housed piggyback like the humble snail. The selampit is of course the aboriginal chawat in new guise, and no doubt with a finer and less see-through weave. It was the traditional and entirely suitable attire for those at hard labour in the heat.

Heat or warmth, sai (18) comes from the flame, ish. A sheep, with Lithic elements shai-pai, has had a warm covering or coat ever since the Pleistocene. This is a simple piece of Lithic analysis which can be quoted to doubters to consider. If it is countered the original forms actually had an initial sk- that just makes it a warm body coat. So far as Chambers and Partridge are concerned a sheep is a sheep is a sheep, and no reason why offered. Partridge just adds o.o.o. his short for 'of obscure origin'. Lithic analysis clears up this obscurity once and for all. Chambers says no definite connections are known outside Germanic. However the ever-nosey Partridge has found Egyptian sau, sa, sua, st (proper pronunciation – with vowelisation - sai-tau, in the happy state of born-warm) for sheep, which shows in Egypt too the sheep were well known for having rather cozy coats. Cozy is conventionally traced to the Norwegian kose sig, to make oneself comfortable, (the g in sig originally pronounced y), but cozy is from the Lithic kau-sai, made-warm, whence of course at ease (as when warm), comfortable (hunkered around the hearth), and then any pleasant sensation, and then again both pleasant and sensation on their own. That is how language has built, by metaphors, piled one upon the other – until there was so much polysemy we had to start again at Babel with preassembled words with fixed meanings, so all speaking (languages) became unique.

Aestus, in Latin, is in Lithic a-i-sh-tau, that-which-fire-become, viz a burning heat. Our oast houses also were a-u-ish-tai, that-where-heat-applied to the wetted barley seed on the way to producing beer. Whisky is often recorded as fire water, and it is: Awa-ish-kai is water-fire-kindled, a water with a shot of the ish element in it, a change of state resulting from the heat of distillation. Of course the native American description as fire water referred to its astonishing quality, we would say like a shot in the arm, when swigged neat for instant effect. In Zululand to be on fire is sha, firewood is izinkuni, it-flaming-makes-express, and a firebrand isikhuni, Lithic i-sai-kau-nai, which-fire-kindled-presents. Compare izi, fire, in Sumerian. To fire or burn down is shisa, probably from the Lithic shai-sa, flaming-action (26) and hot is ashisayo, Lithic a-shai-sai-au, that-heated-fired-that

Chapter 13 Ish

one. Ancient Egyptian throws up sa for flame or fire, with sam to burn, to consume by fire, Lithic sa-mai, flame-consumed. Samtau is a conflagration, a fire, from flamed-become. Samu is incense, which gets consumed when burned for the scent given off. Sa-mau is flame consumed, just like sa-mai. The -u is more substantial than the -i, but both can be read as –ed.

In Egyptian again tcha and Sa'n are fire drill sticks, flamers. In Hindi a cup of tea is cha, from the Chinese tcha, just a hot drink originally and nothing to do with an Egyptian fire drill, except that both cases are gulled from the Lithic ish for fire. Tea is just our mispronunciation, resulting from incomprehension. Malay teh is also from the Chinese and not much better than the English. Juice in English was initially a hot drink too, and a savoury soup at that, and only later used for fruit juice; indeed it likely referred at the outset to the juices running out of the steak on the fire, Lithic djai-u-sai, issuing(7)-when-fired (3). The Sahara probably prays in aid the heat, Lithic sa-ha-rai, heat-horror-rayed/raised, a desert (also from the Egyptian: the academic dsrt in this case, probably with the semantic content land-dried out-become, dai-sarai-tai).

Warmth, vouchsafed to sheep with their fiery pelts (shai-pai), was often missing amongst our early featherless biped forebears. They borrowed his coat out hunting, as well as for sleep, but the core facility for getting warm in cold weather was the hearth, classically at the entrance to the family cave, tended by the womenfolk, oldies and children while the braves were out hunting, as sketched on the cover of this book, where our language was made. The warmth of the hearth, as well as its security – it frightened animals off, and the smoke repelled biting insects – was the exemplar of ease (from sai), comfort, the pleasant sensation and pleasure. With full bellies from the cooked meat, attention will have turned to sexual concourse. Indeed the heat from the hearth will have triggered it. Animals are said to be in heat when sexually receptive, as if they had benefited from hearths too, which they never did. The sense (20) comes from our experience living outdoors in the Pleistocene and then registering the changed sensation, even perhaps its recovery in the extremities, around the hearth.

Sugar (19) can be added to sheep as a classic Lithic analysis. Sugar from Lithic su-kara is pleasure-maker (19): su, an extreme sensation (around the hearth) being a pleasurable one, just as Arabic iskra (spark) and Old English chark (the fire drill) are fire-makers from ishkara or isharaka. Suave is a straight copy from the Latin, "sweet to taste and smell, gentle or soft to the touch, agreeable to the eye" as Partridge puts it. The rather older Sanskrit has suadus, sweet, suadma sweetness and suadati, he takes pleasure in or is pleased to. Like sugar is the Hindi thank you: shugria, [your action is] a sweetness-making-one, "sugary one!" The Malay equivalent suka means to like and to desire; it makes a feel good factor like the sugar; it makes you desirous to have it. It can refer to your taste for marmalade or your desire to bed a pretty girl, or just conventional content: "Banyak suka hati sahaya, berjumpa lagi dengan inchek!", "Very sweet hearted I, bemeeting again with mister!", in other words: "Very nice to see you again!" The sibilant can certainly have a sexual connotation, as in sex (36), at a hazard from the Lithic sai-ka-sai, action(34)-make-pleasure (19, 20), or action-make-life (24), or both at once, as is indeed the common experience, pleasurable life making. Had our hominid forebears spotted it, do you think? Maybe not. It is said they learned the male role from sows kept without a boar that did not farrow in the manner expected. In those days no girls had evidently ever been short of the attentions of the hominid boars, so at first they both took the whole business to be entirely recreational.

Chapter 13 Ish

In Malay sulbi means the loins, while in English hips haunches and ham, all three with the sudden sensational h-, hip perhaps the pleasuring pieces since you work your hips when copulating, and ham, ha-mai, when impregnating; but now of course almost entirely used for the smoked viand. Hai is in chapter 8. The su- in the Malay sulbi can therefore be read as pleasure just as in sugar, and the lai perhaps as flexing, as in lithe, with bai referring to the ischeral protruberances (bum). Our loins are closely related to the Latin lumbus, with lumbi the loins, whence we get our lumbar and lumbago, chopping the flexibits. The loins are probably just a bus from the Latin lumbi, the lau phoneme standing for the whole, as bus stands for the whole omnibus Also the hip joint does bend the body, about in the middle. Moreover the rump is, like the belly, a bulge of flesh, a rear swelling.

In Malay kaseh is love – perhaps from ka-sai-hei, make-pleasure-ecstatic. Anyway in Ancient Egypt the God Amun, from Aa-mau'n, The Ever-planting'one, was The Ever Loving, like Allah later, and the ma syllable (see chapter 9) meant earth and so earthing, planting and so impregnating. The Latin amare to love is from a-ma-are, as or when-planting or impregnating-verbal. In English to marry is taken to be a ceremonial matter, but the consummation is in the meaning, to impregnate. Marriage celebrates the forthcoming impregnation, which for homosexual couples is of course impossible. Any celebration must be just a sham. The Malay jimah is (from the Arabic) coition, apparently from the Lithic elements shai-ma(h)i, action-of impregnating. Kasi in Malay is to give or to cause to happen, for instance kasi makan is to give food, and alternatively to cause to rust because makan carries the meaning of eating as well as what is eaten and rust eats metal. The sense of giving – without any price – makes for contentment, and settles or eases any dispute over ownership by conceding, giving in. The English give is perhaps from kai-phai, making pleased/setisfied (see chapter 6 on Fa), that phai or pleasuring which (unfortunately) was originally provided by the genitalia – back in the Pleistocene.

So the warmth of the hearth was an agreeable sensation. Heat covers the full range of sensations from comfort to acute pain. Sai came to represent that range, including the idea, namely sensation or sense (20). Latin sentire to become sensible or sensing, to feel, has the past participle sensus, used for the substantive term sense, the feeling or what is felt. Feel is from the Lithic phei-lai, copulation-linked or like. Just as the sensation of warmth was taken as typifying physical sensation, so the sensation of the pahei, in Egyptian the orgasmic penis, was taken as the sensation of the life force, the source of life. The physical is from the Greek phusis, Lithic pahai-u-sai, life force-what-action, in this case growth. Aristotle described phusis as the nissus or natural drive which exists in all life forms to expand and grow, like the fruiting of the vegetable world. His idea was really closer to biology than physics as we understand it, which is more mechanical (and lifeless). To see (29) is the visual sensation, which is san in Egyptian, to see. It is the most important everyday sensation of all, and determines much of our mental outlook. It is indeed regarded as in some ways more than just another sensation in so far as it presents us with a mass of information already processed in the mind as we become aware of it. So a sudden burning sensation prompts recognition of extreme heat and immediate withdrawal action, never mind why; but also the sight of the hot poker, cigarette end or scorpion is fully informative, allowing understanding immediately to flood in.

In the Stone Age we only saw properly when the sun was shining, which immediately explains why sun and shine have some of the same elements. See Chinese shimang, which is to go blind. We can parse it in Lithic immediately: shai-mang, sense (visual)-marred or murdered or submerged. A sore is a (painful) sense-arising. Or the r may be a cockney r, with the Lithic really sau-a, a sensed-one (or else the original sore was sunburn from Ra).

Chapter 13 Ish

The Chinese is important. We can only attribute the same Lithic semantic contents as we have worked out mostly from the English lexicon if Lithic applies to Chinese as well as English. But that is one of the Lithic hypotheses. The Chinese and English languages, it can authoritatively be stated, are unrelated – unless by common Lithic origins

The sense of bright (21) really belongs with shine (12) and sheen. The Australian aboriginal budgerigar, djeribal and didgeridoo where the -djeri- means bright, clear and loud respectively, has already been used to illustrate the diffuse semantic contents of single syllables in early language strings. We do not have any word of such generality and must therefore use djeri when thinking about this ancient language usage. A shrimp is related to the budgerigar, because the elements of Lithic language we can identify here for semantic analysis are shai-rai-em-pai, nothing to do with its small size, as might be imagined because this meaning of insignificant size is in fact gulled from it. When cooked the shrimp turns pink, just like other crustaceans. A shrimp was indicated to the Lithic mind as a bright-ray-of-the skin or surface, sh-rai-em-pai, much as the budgerigar was just a bright coloured bird, but in the case of the shrimp flame coloured, sh-rai when cooked, fire rayed in both senses, both cooked and coloured simultaneously. Then we can also relate the aboriginal dje, bright, to shima in Australia which means good, probably by way of a bright or clear thought. However in California, shi ma' in Navaho Indian means my mother. The ma' of course is mother. The shi is probably from shai meaning of number one, that is of the speaker, me; while ushi in turn is the completive u or plural case of shi, my, and means our in Navaho.

A scone, sai-kau-nai in Lithic phonemes, shine-made-show is explained by the Middle Dutch for scone: schonbrot, clear or bright bread. Scones were evidently made of white flour as a party piece when ordinary bread was generally brown, probably made of brown rye flour. The word has nothing to do with the way it is cooked. Schon in the old German languages has many meanings. None follow the aboriginal djeri, but they have an even wider spread: fair, beautiful, fine (arts and words), splendid, nice (mess), perfect (order), the fashionable (world), kind (regards). All those might conceivably have come in a chain of gulls from an original identification of a blaze, given a sufficient number of millennia. The kau, made, like the original flint knapper's handiwork (which made a flint tool) is often emblem of a humanly created situation, as opposed to a naturally occurring one. The sai, by way of shiney (12), could conceivably host the Germanic clutch of derivatives. The Greek selas is light, brilliance, perhaps originally from sai-lai-sai, shining-oil-burning, but a glow rather than a blazing light since Selene was the moon, Lithic sai-lai-nai, brilliant-low/looping-showing: reflected light showing?, showing a dim light? The burning oil may well have had only a small Greek wick. Or else the lai has its semantic content from its usage in the word light, which is from burning lye, as a marker to indicate it is the light of the flame which is relevant here and not any of the other thirty or forty derivative connotations. Indeed for Selene, the moon, the lai could mean circling, in orbit, or even floating about, the moon's course being comparatively irregular, moving around in the night sky with no easily recognized pattern. Refer to chapter 8.

Showing (22) is not so far away from shining (12) and bright (21), because what is shiney or bright tends to show. In Lithic terms they are one. But the root in the Germanic languages, whence it comes, means looking, and not showing. Eric Partridge sidesteps this embarrassment by saying "the same action from the opposite point of view", quoting M. O'C. Walsh's Concise German Etymological Dictionary, of 1952. But will this do? If anything shines it catches the attention. Think of the light catching a mirror. There weren't any in the Stone Age, but there were natural reflectors and shiney things, water for example. If it shines (or moves) it shows. Our semantics come mostly from observation, not from ratiocination. The idea of showing being the same idea as looking but from the opposite perspective took a German etymologist to think up, when he would have been better employed going with the swim instead of trying to crack the nut by means of his own devious logic. A sign, from sai-kai-nai, is the sense-made-evident, as well as the sense meaning what you made of it. The Latin for a sign is sema, showing the meaning, a mental indicator, which is a different gloss on the shima of the Australian aborigine or the Californian Navaho Indian above. This degree of diversity in the interpretation provides cover for Lithic, making it harder to discover – so it does not get noticed - and so challenges belief in it. A semantic content is what the sign is indicating or showing. A symbol is a sign of another to which it has been referred.

A Semite is a descendant of the Biblical Shem, who shares the patriarchy with Ham and Japheth. How these tribes acquired their names is at present quite opaque. It is tempting to hazard a guess at the Lithic semantic contents. Shem, shai-mai, might be bright (white) or bright minded. Ham is most likely from i(h)a-mai, they that-dark; or else from Ha-mai, rejoicing in-impregnating; ha being already associated with the more immediate physical forms of sensation prompts for a similar sense of mai. If by any chance this is right then the Semitic race is claiming intellect and dismissing the African races as over sexed. It is a pattern which unfortunately whitey is apt to follow even today, in spite of it being clear by now that what determines character traits like these is the education, cultural as well as intellectual, which obtains; and the genetics of the race hardly counts at all. The fact is with widespread impoverished living standards, sex is the only readily available source of pleasure and religious inhibition is absent. The Lithic resonance with sexual motifs is evidence of this. Hundreds of thousands of years ago we were probably all as sexually active as the bonobo chimpanzees. The goy, meanwhile, is from the tribe of Japheth, a difficult one. Ia-pahei-tahei certainly evokes hedonism, initially by reference to the enjoyment of male and female sexuality, but so anciently it probably stood just for a simple pagan enjoyment of the good life in even the earliest Biblical times. Pagans were not plagued by ideology so much and were not banging their heads and prophesying punishment, nor handing it out personally meanwhile like the Old Testament folk, to judge them by their book. Paganism was a cheerful acknowledgment of the fundamental value of fertility, and sex was a propitiation of these powers. It is tempting to speculate, but tastes will differ.

The sun was anciently universally assumed to be a fire source, but a brahma one compared with terrestial hearths and even volcanos. The sun is apparently from the Lithic sa-u'n, the shine(12)-superlative 'one, but most of the Germanic words end with a vowel, like for instance the Gothic sunno, which suggests the original final phoneme was -nau(12), adding a certain prominence. There is a very early record of the Avestan khveng or xveng for sun, pronounced roughly ksueng, with Lithic elements kai-su-en, the making-superlative shining light-ing. This can be set beside the Sanskrit (and Malay) suria for sun, Lithic su-rai-a, shine-raying-one. Malay also has bintang suraya, the suraya star, namely the su-rai-a, ultimate-shining-one. With this can be put the country Syria from the Greek Suria. Su-rai-a can be read as light shining or raying or rising (chapter 13). Syria is thus in origin the Sunrise or Eastern land for the Greeks. It is improbable the Malays were exchanging notes with the Sanskrit speakers, so suria is unlikely to have been a borrowing either way, but more likely derived from a common source not known – the subconscious Lithic source.

Chapter 13 Ish

In China the sun is jih, the bright shiner. They favour single phonemic meanings there. In Japan they add a demonstrative ni-: the sun is nichi or nitsu. The surviving Celtic tongues abandon the shining and go for grian (Old Irish, Gaelic and Manx) and greian (Welsh). It may seem odd Western Europeans should pick the same root as Egyptian Ra. But they hiked across from the Middle East. Grian is from Lithic kai-rai'n, making-rays-one. Latin sol is back with the superlative shining, adding lai, orbiting (chapter 8).

As the flame springs upwards and never ceases flickering as if it were alive – compared to a stone - and as animals are warm; and so, it appeared, partaking in some degree of the element fire; and as they are also lively (they run about, just as the flame without benefit of any legs can race through the forest if it is well ablaze and fanned by a favourable wind, with each individual flame flickering all the while) the idea of life can easily be gulled from the flame. The vegetable world is only vouchsafed movement – compared with a stone again – in growth, and that only when pulled up by the rays of the sun, a fiery source. So trees and plants get their share of the lively element, such as it is, from the outside; in themselves they are cold. But it follows that a gull from the flame is the active capacity. If you want to know if an animal is alive, poke it and see if it moves. (If it is fierce use a long stick). So the same phoneme which started out as the sound of the dowsed burning brand is gulled one by one for all the semantic contents in the psychosemantic tree accompanying this chapter – and no doubt quite a number overlooked and left out.

The Basque for god is Jinko. He made Life: the Lithic is shai-en-kau, Life-of-Creation, The Creator. Senility is from senile from Latin senere to be old, to show living – as already experienced. Senescence, from the Latin senescere to grow old, is in turn from crescere to grow which in Lithic analysis is kai-rai-sai-ka-re, made-rayed-up-make-verbal marker. In these Lithic analyses the words used to translate the phonemic meanings can only approximate the Lithic thinking which in its own terms was a great deal slicker than the foreign wording suggests whilst at the same time, it has to be admitted, witnesses a fuzz in Stone Age mental processing from which we are still slowly extricating ourselves with unequal success. The Lithic analyses offered in English are hardly neat, but Lithic thinking nevertheless made perfect sense in its day, probably because what made sense in those days did not have to be very clear. Since hominid times we have been precising, if rather slowly.

Seed (24) is from the Lithic sai-dai, life-bearing (in the sense of birthing). The Lithic elements of life, lai-phai, the length of the flesh, refer to its temporal length; while flesh, phai-lai-shai, is the flesh belonging to animal life forms as opposed to animal and vegetable tissue which are both ba. The Latin for seed is semen, sai-mai'n, life-gestating, like Shamash.

Moses and James and Thomas are brothers along with the Egyptian Pharaohs Tutmose and Rameses – there are others – their direct progenitors. The mose and mesi and mase bits are the Lithic elements mai and sai, to earth up or plant (ma) the seed, or life (sai). The Pharaoh Tutmose is claiming to be begotten by the god Thut, or Tahuti, or Tahu-tai, or even Tau-tahu, All-knowing and World-birth. Archbishop Desmond Tutu (who doesn't know this) got his name from Tahuti too. Tahu-tai was an early creator god and supposedly the source of all knowledge, of the intellect and speech, as well as of the world, taun in Egyptian. Rameses was reckoned to have had Ra, the Sun, plant his seed. James is Ia-mesi, really Iau-mesi, the God the Jews call Jaweh or Jehovah planted his seed. In Latin James is Jacobus, Iau kindled the flesh. Thomas was a twin, from tau-mesi, a dual planting of the seed. The late Moshe Dayan, the Israeli general and archaeologist, has dropped the god's name and relies merely on having been procreated, the seed planted, which must be

Chapter 13 Ish

conceded. He followed Moses in this, who may have been really a James, if he really was not brought up as an Egyptian priest, or else perhaps another Thutmose, shedding the Thut on leaving Egypt.

The hieroglyph for mesi in Egyptian is three fox tails tied together at the top, presumed to be for use as a fly swot in those olden days – no plastics then – with mai-si given the punning semantic content dead-tails and simultaneously suppressor-of life, fly-swatter too, in order to make a memorable glyph. A swastika is another piece of linguistic history which in this case goes back to the Sanskrit, when svasti meant well being. The su-a-sai-tai has the same su as in sugar, but here indicating a generally enjoyable condition, and the a-sai-tai is as-actually-becoming (27), well-being precisely. That leaves the final ka in swastika. It stands here for the idea of making or joining. As to the symbol, su is omnidirectional (16) derived from the up direction (10). The -a-sai-tai is then read as that-single-tau. The tau was a T. A single tau had only one side of the cross piece like a gibbet. The swastika is made of half Ts pointing in all four directions. If sa was one direction su was all of them. This kind of semantic cats cradling is quite typical of primitive intellectual wrangling, and it is worthless but capable of being teased out. My final reading of swastika is Su is all directions (the cross), -asa- is each direction and tike is fingered, that is with pointers on the ends of the cross. (In passing, this fingering – tikh means finger - is responsible for our tick, which borrows the shape). It could still be read as meaning making for wellbeing (Suasti-ka) at the same time. You have a pun, the symbol's composition matching the meaning swasti-kai and swasti-ka. That was what made it an amulet (amiasti in Ancient Egyptian, amuletum in Latin). Amai- or amau- is as minded or meaning; and -asaitai or -laitum is as seen or as drawn: the meanings as visible patterns. The punning has kept it afloat over the millennia.

Salus, Latin for safety, is from the Lithic elements sai-lau, action-lowered, life-smoothed or perhaps at ease-at length, or all three. The latter seems to be indicated with creosote a well known timber preservative which is from the Greek. The kreo is flesh (growth literally) and the sote is the past participle of sozein to preserve, to be saved, sau, full of life. Compare Arabic salaam or Hebrew shalom, both greetings, generally translated as Peace! Like Islam they come from the same Arabic verbal form aslama to submit. Or you may prefer direction-smooth – no nasty kinks in it – or spirit-calm, or all three of them together. The sow meanwhile, the mother pig, su in Old English, is full of life and proves her fertility with record litters.

From life it is a short intellectual step to alive life forms (25). We find si- as brer- (a preceding denominator for phenotypes, animal or amphibian or reptilian) in numerous languages. In English we have snake from si-na-kai, brer-bare-bodied. The Hindi is nag, just the bare body without the brer. The snake is bare of limbs of course as well as without a coat. The colour sepia is the colour of the secretion the fleeing cuttlefish (sepia in Spanish), ejects when pursued by predators. The Spanish fishermen named the cuttlefish Sepia, brer pisser. Cuttle in turn is from Old English codele, akin to Old English cod and Middle Dutch codde for testicle. The Lithic appears to be ka-u-dai, the Ka (or oomph) what does. Hollanders appear to have spotted at an early date removal of the cod led to reduced libido in both animals and men. The cod really referred to the scrotum rather than its contents since cod had the general meaning of a pod or bag, but castration of animals was originally done by the farmer and of men by the victor; and in both cases it may be assumed they simply grabbed the scrotum and cut off bag and contents in one. Indeed you were probably lucky in the case of the human genitalia, where the whole tackle makes a handy handful, if they did not take the penis off at the same time. Certainly, when

Chapter 13 Ish

Egyptian armies won, their cheery soldiers collected phalluses from the wounded and slain on the battlefield as evidence of their win, without which count the Pharaoh might prove disbelieving. Anyway so far as the cuttle fish is concerned his smoke screen tactic appears to have been taken by English speaking sailors as an evacuation rather than the urination the Spanish favoured: kati-ta-lai, belly-become-leaking. The colour however suggests neither of these but a specialized secretion. Both the languages have been built on the nautical whimsies of jolly jack tars.

In Malaya a snail is siput, brer puti or penis teat, with a glans shaped house on its back. The similarity, it must be said, is only slight, but the usage is confirmed by other Malay examples. Seladang is the wild ox and ladang means clearing, where the ox was to be found browsing. Si-amang is the siamang ape with long arms it uses to swing from branch to branch with an astonishing facility: brer-weightless. Si pelandok is brer mouse deer, the brer rabbit of Malay folk law, dainty sly and secretive and no bigger than a prize rabbit but with two needle sharp extended incisors with which he will wickedly slash you if trapped. It earns him a whack on the head with a long stick. The pe- is in most cases little more than a substantive preposition in Malay, but here it may refer to his feet. Landok has the semantic content of sly doer, and he treads lightly and leaves few tracks. Siapa, from si-apa, is brer-what? and so who?

The active species above has then been gulled for activity. To slough is the action (25), sai, of letting slide down or lowering (lau), shedding [a skin]. Eric Partridge thought the slough was first the skin of a snake, and only then its performance sloughing it. The Lithic analysis contradicts this, and the fact recent opinion in the Germanic tongues have it back to front too is not persuasive. The slough of despond is a somewhat similar let down: you sink in – without benefit of any skin. The spelling of slough, originally from sluk, encourages the belief the snakeskin is what the shedding leaves behind. To slough in Malay is salumba, from salu-em-ba, a sloughing (action-lowering) from the flesh. In Malaya the action has not been gulled from the skin which is shed. Selulup is a plunge or leap (into water), and berselulup is to be adoing it. Plunge in English is akin to the plumb line with which a weight (plumbum, the heaviest known metal, lead, in Latin) is lowered into water to discover its depth. The plunge makes the leap, the plumb just goes (bai). Lead metal appears to be named after this facility, lai-a-dai, lowering-that-does (because of its weight), and a plumb pa-lau-mai-bai is a piece-lowered-down-going. Hang it over the side and down it goes until it reaches the bottom. Slough is not far from slow: in Lithic the action-lowered, in place of one of lowering.

The Egyptian god Set, enemy of Osiris, is a mistranslation based on the Egyptologists' alphabetic hangup over Egyptian glyphs - in reality only used latterly for foreign names, etc, which were what enabled the code to be cracked by Champoleon. Glyphs were generally intended to be read as syllabic, and some were of more than one syllable. The glyphs for s-t, transliterated Set, were really Sai and tau or taun, and their most obvious meanings were the sai, the activity, and taun, of the world. Hindi has Shaitan, from the Semitic, and English Satan. It rather looks as if Satan, the root of all evil, is really to be found in the ways of the world, placing it firmly at the door of nature or else of humanity, or shared between both, and not a disembodied bogey from another world at all. Sleep, from sai-lai-pai, is a state of lowered livelihood and activity and sight covered, precisely activity-lowered-covered. The sai also carries the meaning of sense. Sleep covers the senses, eyes shut and conscious attention absent. To lapse is more or less a doublet. The Latin is sopire to sleep, from sau-pai-are, all the senses-covered-verbaliser, whence we get our soporific. But then sleep is a case of easement too. You can hardly be more at ease than when you are asleep, nightmares excluded. Su, we have seen in sugar, can refer to a pleasant sensation, from the warmth of the flame in the hearth. That is the subconscious for you, meanings overlapping. It is not a linear mental capacity, but more a source of arisings from a whole three dimensional texture or pudding of memories and promptings, some immediate and strong while others, like a papier-mâché, are leftovers from bits and pieces which have happened to jell because of various quite oblique psychosemantic appeals over millennia. The whole rather indiscriminate mash gets passed on generation to generation, the linguistic heritage learned by every child, its subconscious semantic keel.

We do not inherit ideas, which are an activity of the brain, any more than we inherit the walks we may take or the races we may run, the activity of our legs, even though the legs, like the brain, are a genetic inheritance. I suspect this is where Noam Chomsky got it wrong; and certainly the MIT (Massachusetts Institute of Technology) school of cognitive psychology appear to have allowed Darwinian evolutionary theory to take over their minds to the exclusion of common sense. Ideas do not evolve, because they are themselves mental activities, and not organisms. We learn to alter the activities. Ideas are a whimsical product of our thinking, or better just the substantiation of our thoughts.

The sea has nothing to do with the flame, on the contrary in the real world water and fire do not mix. But of all the waters in the world the sea is the one which is always in movement (26), not exactly like the flame but apparently sharing some of the same potential. Rivers have white water too, but that is because they are on their way to the sea, sai-a, the active one, or perhaps elided over the millennia from sai-awa, active water, that is to say with waves which come ashore, with some modest part of the active spirit of the flame imparted to them. That is Lithic thinking for you, not mine.

Activeness leads into actuality (27). It is these mini leaps of the human mind, like the jump from the shown, the seen and the active (all gulled from the flame) to the actuality, which spring to mind without recourse to any reasoning, which go to make up not only our common sense but also, almost unbelievably, our finest thinking, our mathematics, philosophy and science. It can be argued that Einstein abandoned reason for a deeper subconscious intuition informed by the prehistoric Tau, a T-shaped reality, just as Karl Marx derived his atavistic dialectical materialism (via Hegel) rather less prettily from the vowel oon of the ancients (aaa spawns eee and then they are followed by the rejoinder ooo, counting one, two, both of them, in place of one, two, three) once they had shucked off (risen above) conventional thinking. See chapter 15 on thinking. Many of the initial s- which Eric Partridge has identified as "the general intensive prefix" are indicating actualities (as is), as opposed to abstractions. Latin combuere to burn has past participle combustus from which we get our combustion, which it is tempting to treat as s-tau, burnt become, but in fact it is of course indicative of the past tense merely, actually-become.

To sit, Latin sedere, and our seat etc, are to settle oneself comfortably, from sai-tai (19), comfy-become, including to squat around the hearth at ease long before chairs were invented. They are gulled from the easement from the warmth of the hearth. So it turns out a chair, from kai-rai, refers to the novelty of a made raised perch.

Lithic terms activity and action (34) are virtually the same. It is not hard to pick up some examples of Lithic where the sibilant is used for action. Malay is perhaps the closest to the primal language (Adam speak?). Selah is the bolt of a door, with an uncanny resemblance to a slide. Doors bolted against an enemy had beams slid in huge brackets. That is no doubt why a bolt starts with a bau. It was a substantial burgeon in its own right. In Malaya selah secured light bamboo edifices with a linking action. The bamboo as a tree boasts many single stems, a ba-em-boo, a burgeon of many burgeons, like the banana with

Chapter 13 Ish

fruiting protrusions that evidently reminded Tarzan of his own. More general action is found in sound, from sau-un-da, activity-what-does. Sounds generally are the result of movement, perhaps in the surrounding bushes with the stealthy approach of the sabre-toothed tiger on the lookout for a meal. If this seems improbable consider noise, na-u-i-sai, show-what-which-active. Slow is lowered action or movement. The German langsam (slow) has the same phonemes reordered. The sepoy or soldier, sipahi in Hindi, is a foot soldier who acts on foot. It is hard to avoid reverting to Malay. Sayat is to cut off bits, sai-a-tai, action-which-cuts or separates, and at the same time what turns one (sa) into two, one-which-twos. Which bits is not specified, but it is used of cutting the umbilical cord and also, in a Muslim country, for cutting off the foreskin, circumcision – which is a cutting around (the glans) in Latin.

The Latin caedere to cut (past participle caesus, informing incisions) is from the Lithic kai-da-ere, to do the flint knapper's original chopping action, from which kai is gulled. In parentheses, ducere to lead, in reverse order is to pull or draw out and so to lead, from Lithic tau-kare, to make with the tau, the feminine pudenda, which in Ancient Egyptian at least was supposed to send out an attractant ray, like the sunbeams which pulled up the crops on raying back on their return journey to the sun. These inferior feminine rays just pulled out and up the boys squatting opposite around the hearth. Al Caeda, the Arabic leadership, has the cutting order but the ducal meaning. Osama sees himself as il duce. We are here right next door to the English ploughshare and the other thirty three words closely akin which Eric Partridge lists with it, all deriving their sense of shearing from "the idea to divide or separate by cutting". Their semantic contents come from a former sc- or sk- and it is the ka which provides the cutting. Malays use potong for simple cutting, from pau-tau'n, dual pieces-divide'd.

A push is the action of pu, which as a dual can be decomposed as pipi, the penis, which not only protrudes as the penis records, nai, but also pushes. A push is a penis action. In the same way piesein in Greek is to press down, the action of the peos (penis). A medical fit in Malay, with alarmingly vigorous convulsions, is sawang, from the Lithic elements sa-a-u-ang, action-that-extremity-goes. A sickle for reaping is from sai-kai-lai, action-cut-looping. The sickle was swung. To be sick, is to have one's liveliness subjected to the chop, hurt or damaged.

Cress is a very lively grower (24) and therefore a fast one (35). But with a ski the action (26) is one of cutting to make the planks you ski on, the same as our shingle which has the little known semantic content, from Middle English skindle, of wood sawn thin for roofing. All these are akin to Greek schizein to split, as in schizophrenia or split brainery, and also our schedule originally a sheet of papyrus made to lie flat, and our garden shed as well, which makes use of cut planks. Greek phren (heart or brain) is a pointer to the antecedents of our own English brain. Ph- and b- established a natural linkage in the mind, they were close enough for that. The brain was clearly perceived as the flesh (ba) recipient of rays from outside, just like the male sexual organ which responded, according to our forebears, to the rays sent out by the girls. But for the Greeks the brain was made of lymph, and that was the same as ejaculate, phren. Since under such attack the heart beat faster, it was linked to the genitalia. Both emotional moods and mentality (ideas) were originally supposed to be borne in on rays from without, and were only slowly selected for personalization, and taken in piecemeal over many generations, as integral functions of the individual persona. It is still a common retreat into irresponsibility by the mentally insane.

Use has a very long derivation from Lithic, now hard to trace. In Italic languages like Latin it is probably from *utsus, with a revealing ancient Oscan form uttiuf, accusative

Chapter 13 Ish

plural, with a Lithic expansion u-tai-tai-u-fai, dual-becomings-dual-pleasurable, comfortable, convenient, convenient in use, useful, use. The use is a duality of activity, a dual relationship between the user and the used, like a tool, another dual convenience similarly lai twice over (or more), that is to say flat facile lacquered and gliding in use, easy and so useful.

With that it is time to exit this overgrown chapter - words in s - exceeding all the others by a long chalk - which has grown with the many meanings of the sibilant, in turn sprung from the strength of the impact on the primitive mind of the hissing sound of the dowsed brand speaking directly - almost personally - to our Stone Age forebears when they put it out. Fire was high tech when first it was tamed, a good deal trickier than the inert stone it displaced, for all the flaws in flints. Tarzan found Mrs T's cooking replaced his chopping with a hand axe. Ex for exit is from ai-kai-sai, as it-makes-ascend, rises above, i.e. beyond and so outside, out – up and away like batman! Or else it was for our hominid ancestors the sexual exit they had in mind, and kai-sai, body-raising, was the paradigm for withdrawal. Who knows? It is usually safe to bet on Tarzan thinking in sexual terms. But ALL the time?

There is a final sexual flourish to the chapter taking the time once again from Malay. To show affection is kaseh sayang, to give or bestow sayang, affection, as Sir Richard Winstedt glosses it "such as from parents or lovers". Are we not back around the hearth in the warm glow of the flame? Sayangkan is to love, experiencing such a warm feeling, surely just as sugar from su-kara makes a sweet taste. Eric Partridge meanwhile presents us with his own "f/e" or "folk etymology" when he hesitantly offers sex as akin to the Latin secus, a cut, from the verb secare to cut, sai-kare, the action (sai) of our flint flaking forebears once again, making a striking action. Lithic has sex from sai-ka-sai, action-make-life, which makes much better sense, and the first sai acquires some of the comfort and pleasure provided by the hearth.

NOTES

1. A gull wing is from the shape of the sea-gull's wing. A sea-gull is a sea caller, from ga-la, like a gale of wind we call a gale because it is a howler, or a miners' gala which was in origin a harmless sing-song before politics took over, or a nightingale, a night in caller which treats us to a finely modulated sing-song in the night. But the gull wing neither sings nor calls. A character has simply been picked from the symbolised and the wing named from it. It was the Lithic "Open Sesame!" when language began, and is now known rather inadequately as metaphor, which is why Lithic makes use of the term 'a gull' instead, from the gull wing.

2. Were some scientific wiseacre to claim on the contrary shivering comes from some arcane thermally controlled neurochemical reaction, ignorance of which disqualifies the identification, it could be retrieved by personal experience of over enthusiastic dipping in the local cow pond as a boy in inclement weather, when the shivers would sometimes invade the whole body.

3. Of course this can only be a coincidence, but the cat's cry mimics the intonations of the Jewish God, Jaweh or Adonai; and the version with La dividing the vowels comes quite close to the Arabic God Allah who came later, or maybe earlier if His name derives from

Chapter 13 Ish

El. This in no way impugns either of these Deities – most believe them to be really the same One True God – since it is merely a matter of linguistic idioms practiced here on earth where the three original vowelisations, eee, aaa and ooo, do seem to have exercised, and even fascinated the hominid mind to an extent it is hard now to understand. It is even possible, as the medium of prelinguistic communication, early folk secretly - even instinctively - treasured their mewing chat long after speech had replaced it, rather as educated Victorians treasured their smattering of Latin and the Classics they once learned, long after they had forgotten it all bar a smidgen. It is also possible to drum up some black humour from the source of the revolutionary Marxist dialectic in the Pliocene Vowel Oon, the first dialectic, both equally absurd when subjected to the cruel light of Lithic derivations. The Vowel Oon is in chapter 14 on the vowels. The Marxist dialectic is demolished (for the first time) in chapter 15 on the origins of thinking, which shows it results from muddling two different lines in the mind.

4. Just keep well away from shrinks who will be keen to pass on to you their favourite fantasies, by means of which they manage themselves to preserve a fragile balance, which at best will therefore fascinate rather than illuminate.

5. Elsewhere it is noted this extended to copying Sumerian historical myth, including Adam and Eve and their expulsion from the Garden of Eden, which is apparently grounded in reality with the raising of the sea level by three hundred and sixty feet with the melting of the circumpolar ice some eight thousand years ago, leaving the padi gardens of Eastern Malaya submerged under the South China Sea; and Malaya – the garden land – only surviving today as the Western hills, mostly quite unsuitable for rice padi-gardening, still above water. There is no difficulty with Malaya, Adam's garden land, surviving ten thousand years if Lithic can make sense of phonemes lasting six hundred thousand.

6. Slugs are not formed from the word slow, nor from slip nor slime nor line nor along, but on the contrary all of these words carry some of the same meaningful phonemes as the slug, and like all verbage acquire their meanings from them. It is necessary to interject these occasional reminders of the proper Lithic hypotheses since critics who are just dippers will otherwise make use of their own misunderstandings to make a mock of them, imagining the words used to indicate Lithic meanings are meant to be word copies – often where no copies should be.

7. The German poet Wolfgang Von Goethe wrote (parodying the Christian teleological philosophy):- "Glory to God Almighty who designed / The cork tree for us, having corks in mind". In my dissolute undergraduate days 65 years ago I was constrained to embellish the master's work:- "And glory too to Man, / Who with God's cork stole His thunder / By capping the Deity's plan / And putting the bottle thereunder".

8. Colman-Gabriel Gostony, ancien professeur au collège Saint-Michel, Saint-Etienne (Loire), et ancien auditeur (1952-1972) a l'Ecole Pratique des Hautes Etudes, quatrième section, Sciences philologiques (Sumérien). Paris (Sorbonne). Dictionary of Sumerian Etymology and Comparative Grammar. Published in paperback in Paris in 1975, Editions E. De Boccard, 11Rue de Medicis, 11. Ouvrage publié avec le concours de la Récherche Scientifique.

Chapter 13 Ish

9. My uncle, whose wife died quite unfairly long before him, inscribed on her gravestone "Does not the sun rise smiling, at the dawn of another day". After experiencing Japanese prison conditions for nearly four years in Singapore he became seriously religious and reverted to the belief, from the Egyptian Book of the Dead, in the dua taun or second world, (Egyptologists think it is duat) along with the second birth into it, on death in the first one we all live in.

10. Sir Wallis Budge. An Egyptian Hieroglyphic Dictionary. Dover Publications Inc. 1978. Vol 2 Page 1086.

11. See Sir Wallis Budge's "Ptah Renpit", where his "renpit" is really "arai en paitaun" and turns out to mean "[who] art in Heaven", a translation of The Lord's Prayer (and Ptah, an ancient god, is an ancestor god, pata ahí, our fathers - or Our father for Egyptian Christians (Copts).

CHAPTER 14

WA, YA AND THE VOWELS

This is a conjoined chapter for the vowels and the two dipthong consonants Wa and Ya, because their meanings are so closely intertwined it makes no sense to try and treat them separately. Phonetically Wa can have come from the slovening of Ba by way of Va, and similarly it can by misprision sloven back the other way via Va which then gets pronounced as Ba; as also of course Ba can then be spelt Va. There must always be a doubt which was which originally. The phonemes are shown with Ba below rising to Wa in the phonetic tree (page 307), because that gradation is already in the phonetics. Ba is at the level of being. Wa is up and away in the empyrian, the insubstantial. Of earth, air, fire and water only earth is fully substantial. Air and water are vowel elements, fluid, shapeless and yielding, without any persistent surface; and fire also is an insubstantial element but arising from the substantial: the flame comes out of the bough where it must therefore have been lurking before. Or so our simple forebears thought. After all if the flame were truly of independent origin it would be found flaming away disembodied on its own without any physical source. Light does this, lightening the sky, but not the flame itself which waits for the light to strike the bough and release the flame within. This kind of thinking may seem far fetched but it is what is required to recapture the Stone Age mind, effectively identical with ours but filled with many ideas now quite hard to follow.

Vowels only carry tones. It is the consonants which give them substance and split them up, articulating one semantic content from the next. Before speech we hummed and haared, wailed and howled, but we were unable to precise a verbal string of separate phonetic and semantic beads, with each consonant modifying the tone it accompanied. With consonants, which are really better described as stops, the supply of meanings could grow to fill the mental spaces, the separate boxes the consonants provided. The semantic trace was articulated, so meanings were separated and distinguished. Indeed with the stringing of the separate semantic beads, not only reflection but an interplay of meanings became available. Twenty beads (phonemes) was probably more than most men could follow through and maintain the thread of meanings from one end to the other. No doubt we started out with just two. The original consonantal phonemes appear to have been no more than a dozen. Moreover there was from an early date the problem we now know as polysemy: the same sounds became over packed with meanings so it was hard, even with the context as guide, to guess the right meaning to pick. Certainly it took time and thought. Pharaoh was still using soothsayers when the lean kine came along. The semantic contents of the twelve chapters in this book with psychosemantic trees for the phonemes involved with all their meanings were an encyclopedia beyond the mind of simple Homo Sapiens (also known as Homo Erectus, who succeeded Habilis) to grasp. We must have started with just the top rows in the pychosemantic trees to manipulate at most. The meanings at that stage were so general, fuzzy and ill defined it could be said that the rest of the world lexicon was a virtual prisoner within them waiting to be allowed out through the filter of the bare bottomed naming committees squatting on their hunkers around their Stone Age hearths. Indeed initially each semantic content in turn must have been individually hammered out with many meetings, with trials and errors gradually shaping a common consciousness. There will have been the slow uptake of buffoons, their gray matter in the cortex largely uninscribed. It is still a claustrophobic horror scene to vividly envisage what it must have been like struggling to grasp each symbolism in turn and get young Tarzan hunkered beside you to register his understanding or lack of it. It is a scene anyone interested in etymology should be invited to contemplate at some length. It is necessary to discard all your intellectual clothing and allow yourself a few skins at most, probably not very skillfully scraped or cured. It may even help to imagine the itching and even the slightly rancid smell of the skins as well as their occupants. No doubt there will have been some brilliant boys and girls – at this stage probably for the most part girls – who will have been locked onto the game, texting each other much of the day around the hearth with utterances, just for the fun of the exchanges, much like kids with mobile phones today.

The psychosemantic tree is on page 306. There are three ancient vowels, a (aaa). i (eee), and u (ooo). Aaa was the general vowel, and first of all signified extension because you can keep a vowel going as long as you have breath. It is also unmodulated, just what comes out – which makes it general, as well as an un- when it comes to pairing it off with the modulated vowels. It is also the first vowel because it is the easiest and babies babble first. So, like the letter a, it comes first and can even mean first. I (eee) is the thinned and therefore diminutive reduplicative vowel, diminutive because thinned, and reduplicative because diminutive, and because reduplicative involved in itemisation and numeration, the digital vowel. U (ooo) is the inclusive-completive-substantive vowel because it is uttered from rounded lips and so suggests a circular surrounding pattern which is inclusive, as well as dual, because the other two vowels were only two and so in their case inclusive meant both of them. It is substantive because the inclusive is substantive, a category is implied by inclusion and a category can be substantive: all nouns are categorical. These identifications are not immediately obvious, we have little use for them; but at the birth of language when everything was up for grabs they virtually must have come out, as the mind struggled to get its bearings.

The forty three semantic contents strung together in the psychosemantic tree for the vowels can be rearranged in several different ways, and the number and explicitness much increased – but not on a single page. These psychosemantic trees are supposed to be a guide to the thinking of the subconscious mind which like the dreaming mind is kaleidoscopic, capable of jumping without much consequence from one idea to another with gossamer connections no more substantial than those the psychosemantic trees reveal. Sapiens found himself saying Wa (1) involuntarily when he spent too long in the water, groping for fresh water mussels with his feet, likely sent back in by his elders until he had enough for a meal. For me, dipping in the local mere when still very young, stepping between the cowpats and enduring the nips from duck lice involved, overstaying and emerging with one's mouth ashiver was quite common. We would be toweled and revived by a fond mother with a cat's tongue of plain chocolate now no longer made. The wer-wer-wer of the shivers (7) meant hypothermia and the element that caused it (wáter of course, awa, now agua with a glotal stop and then a G), or else an extremity of funk, and so distress of any kind, building vocabulary from like to like, as heard in the ululation and wailing of the womenfolk in face of death or other disaster; meanings added by metaphor over the ages, not all together. Words like howl and whine and awe and woe are formed indirectly from the sound of shivering. The wind is a whistler, the Lithic wai'n-da, whistling-does as a clue/definition of wind. Winter is the windy time, Lithic Wai'n-tai-a, whistling-become-one, but a shivering time with it. The chill factor will have been

Chapter 14 Vowels

recognized in the Pleistocene. Nothing surprising in that. The Aztec God of creation was 'Wakan Tanka': Fear-making World maker, The Awesome Creator. How do we know ka means make? It was the sound of flint on flint, see chapter 4. How do we know Tan meant the world for the Aztecs? Taun was the world for the Egyptians, as in Pai-Taun for Heaven, see chapters 6 and 9. Of course that might not signify if there were no other evidence for contact between Central America and Egypt; or if the same Lithic phonetic meanings were not so widely distributed around the world. But how do you explain the pyramids in Egypt and Central America unless by inescapable contact at some stage to swap ideas? Surely pyramids have not just been presented by the subconscious mind all around the place.

The flood when the circum polar ice fields finally melted some eight thousand years ago – the sea level rose some 360 feet – reinforced the human belief the gods were gods of high places, where natural forces, and the sheer stability which went with them, were strongest: particularly the severe discipline of the cold season but also the ethereal shining whiteness of the clean snow, even the lack of mud on the roof of the world. So how to attract the divine spirits to your lowly habitations in the valleys? Well by making them a mountain, if only a relatively small one, to show you knew what they liked and were trying to please them, however punily. Surely they would alight there to inspect your handywork at least. If not, kill for them, to show how much you want to please. In Central America hundreds of thousands of hearts were torn out of living human bodies at the summits of the pyramids and held aloft to show the spirits. Was this not a homicidal mania? Or was it not a mania after all, just because it was accepted by all there at that time as rational behaviour? Might they all not have been mad together, brain washed into believing the will of the gods was a monstrosity, led by the priests who had in fact invented the whole paraphenalia? All mad? Why not? Meet Sapiens Sapiens! Mutatis mutandis we can see a good deal of the same still today. What must it have been like in those times and places for the maverick spirits who did not swallow hook line and sinker their fellow human beings' inanities and insanities? What indeed! Sanity was severely taxed.

With this the last chapter dealing with phonetic meanings, with the last psychosemantic tree, it is intended to plunge in at the deep end and present the wildest shores of Lithic hypothesising straight away. The vowels are the oldest parts of speech, as is perhaps recognised when we term the consonants as those elements of speech which have come to be sounded with them. Throughout prehistory it is, I think, clear there were originally only three vowels. Fine tuning didn't go any further. Indeed for a long period there may well have been only two. Chimpanzees mostly mew. Is it fanciful to think of them when they are really comfortable and stress free as babbling like babies? Anyway babies babble which is of course why they are called babies, just babblers, starting with the general "ba" which gets uttered when the lightly pursed lips are parted to let out an aaa (26), the unmarked vowel. The prehensile lips of the chimpanzees, which they use for plucking leaves and fruit, come forward quite readily to provide the tubular shape which makes a mew, with something of a whistle in it. The word prehensile throws up a Lithic analysis worth recording. Chambers' brilliant American Dictionary of Etymology defines it as: "adapted for grasping or holding on, from the Latin prehensus, past participle of the Latin verb prehendere to grasp or seize (pre-, before, unaccented form of prae + hendere, related to hedera, ivy, in the sense of clinging, and cognate with Greek chandarein to hold; see Get). Related to prey" It is all very well to confidently declare pre- means before (as it

Chapter 14 Vowels

THE PSYCHOSEMANTIC TREE FOR WA, YA AND THE VOWELS

The Phonetic Tree

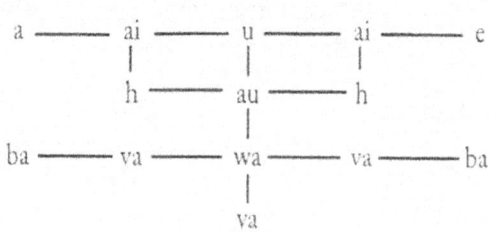

The Semantic Tree

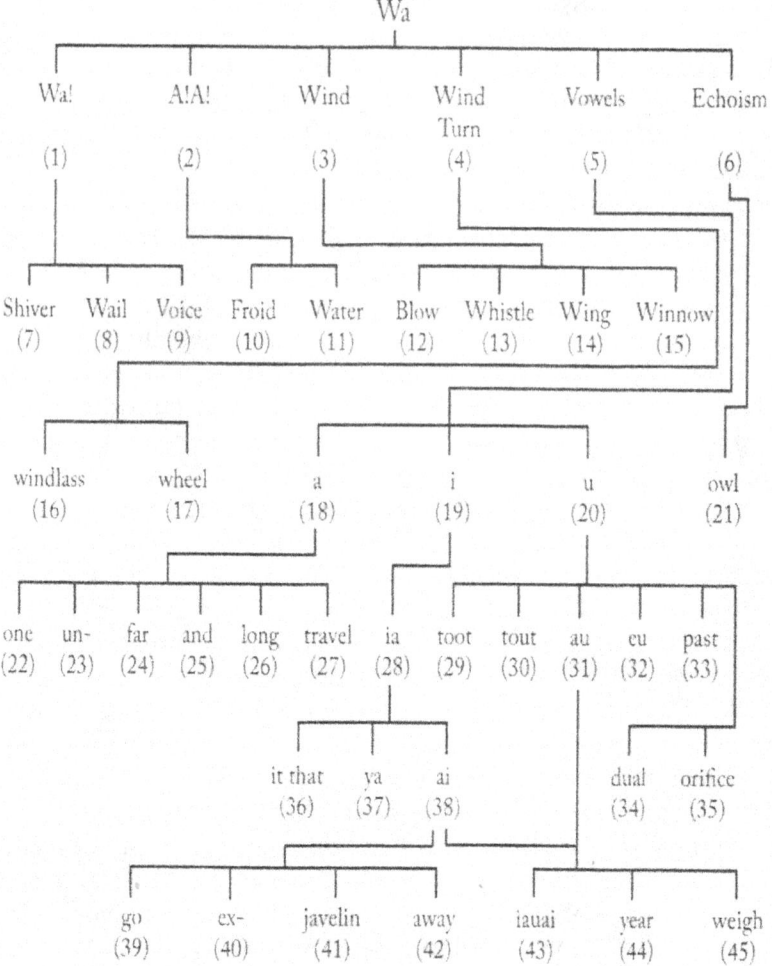

Chapter 14 Vowels

does inter alia), but it makes no sense when it is tacked in front of hedere to grasp. What is it about grasping which needs before in front of it? The answer is pre- does not directly mean before. The Lithic makes sense of it when nothing else does. The Lithic for pre- is pai-rai, the surface-seen, which gets to mean the front, which is of course the surface facing you presenting itself as the front of whatever it is you are looking at. Thence standing before, whence before. Spatially in front is gulled to mean temporally in front, before in time. Compare panorama, from the Greek, Lithic pan-au-ra-ma, surfaces-that all-see-mass/assembly. The Greek pan for all comes from the same idea, seen in this case as a single surface or picture taking in all of the items making up the panorama. The Greek god Pan, with his pipes or pipi, has a more mischievous derivation. His name is a play on the pa-nai, the orgasmic penis, an eroticism his followers well understood. Priapus had his herms, showing off his pairai-pu or aroused phallus on a pillar otherwise largely bereft of features. He is a salutary reminder of our thinking from a time brutally franker than today.

Ivy clings to the surface, a form of grasping without the limbs. The atmospheric pressure which holds a sucker to a surface was quite unknown to the ancients, and indeed is still little understood by the public. Stiction in olden times was a force from outside, source well known. Hedere is from the Lithic i(h)a-i-terai, it-that-which-attracted, pulled (by a ray attracting the ivy to it), causing it to adhere to the irradiated surface or pairai. Lips and tails as well as ivy are prehensile, needing some special outside assistance to acquire their extraordinary capacity, unlike the limbs which are made to do their own grasping, but ivy has this attractive gift in excelcis. Holly had a red berry, a colour which came (in a very similar package) from the sun. That is probably why they got in folk songs. Folk relished this esoteric understanding which encapsulated the mysterious element and contradicted the established belief.

For humanity however aaa is the general vowel ab origine, unmarked and representative of the vowel tones in general. Lips and tongue, the jokers in the pack which mostly generate the stops (the consonants) are out of the way and the doctor can examine your throat. The larynx is open. Aaa is the open sound uncluttered and continuous for as long as you like to go on with it and have enough breath. All this while the breath is going out. You can in fact gasp an aah! during the breathing in but it does not come naturally at all. A diver surfacing at the last moment may do it. In point of fact a, the extensive vowel was used for 'ever' in Old English with na (ne-a elided) for never. Ah! is an unspecified tone of understanding and appreciation, remarkable for the generality of its applicability, so that it can even be used as a refusal to reveal any information at all. The 'ever' version may have come via aw, the oo in this case emphasising the completiveness of the extension, as rather similarly in all, which has an l, a laryat or lanyard looping around the lot – twice! Or else the second l (lai) in all was to indicate this was a spatial (local) extension and not a temporal one? Either way all has its coverage nicely coralled. What aaa actually conveys as a continuous tone is precisely this idea of extension, which can then be applied in a number of ways, not only temporal extension. It can be spatial, proceeding or going; or even quantitive, all or very.

I (eee) is thinned. The tongue is pushed up to narrow the passage for air and diminish the outflow. It is the diminutive, derivative, repetitive, reduplicative, representative vowel. Our forefathers must have paid attention to these common-sense characteristics of the sounds they were uttering, and it will surely have been in the hope of discovering the natural meaning implicit in the exercise in order to make a bridge into the mind of Tarzan hunkered next to them, who might with luck spot the same implications. With the limbs you can gesture when playing dumb crambo, and with the face you can mimic emotional

Chapter 14 Vowels

tone, but hardly with the voice unless with echoism, and echoism could stretch quite far with aa-oo for the owl and a wail for 'weeping' (where the echoic vowelisation has been sacrificed to a later grammar). The meanings of vocalisations for the rest were open to speculative notions – the way they were articulated for instance, or some other association which caught the attention as significant. With the meanings for eee listed we endeavour to record the original Lithic thinking, in the absence of any of the associations from subsequent thinking: what can be extracted from the phonetics (in the context of three vowels) alone.

For ooo the lips are pushed forward and rounded. The u vowel is therefore (because a round suggested enclosure) the inclusive, the determinative, the completive and so the substantial; and because it is inclusive it includes the other two, a and i, and so it is also the dual sound, which is the reason why we say two, as also because we counted one, two, both of them, (the Tau, a T, one of the oldest Stone Age carvings, literally ta [cut] oo [dual], and perhaps why also our U has dualised uprights), instead of one, two, three (as we count nowadays, and has already appeared). As an aside at this point, we also admittedly say bilateral as well as bicycle etc. to indicate the dual; but this is not because b and d are much the same (as conventional etymologists are apt to declare), which they are not, but because of the bilateral symmetry of the flesh, which is ba from the lip work; as can be seen in the limbs - the long bits - the breasts – the raised bits of the ladies (siti) - and the bums – all the fleshy bits, like the bottom, the twin fleshy bits with cleavage between. The bubs are dual too, but in Arabic bab is the two lips making a mouth (or gate or entry, as in Babylon, the entry to the Shatt al Arab, the salt lawns leading to the sea, from the Lithic Bab-ai-lau'n. En or ai'n, or just ai is the genitive, including in Ancient Egyptian. Babylon is Akkadian. Egyptian is originally Semitic (with African admixture). Ai has the original semantic contents quite generally of that-which, or one-that, the second term being as it were a spin off from the first, a subordinate rider or addendum, and the n merely indicating closure to separate it from what follows. It follows in this case of Bab-ai-lau'n the a in ai is much the same concept as 'n, meaning one, or even one that, or even the one that. Aa is a vacuous vowel as well as an extensive one. That gives it its suitability for air and water, ever and aeon (extensions in time), far and away (spacial extensions with the intervening space empty), numerical extension or summation as add and all, continuity like and (which as a concept is empty) and anything else which like mere continuity, or more of the same without end strikes the imagination as abstract, insubstantial and unbounded; paradigmatically like the Jewish God. Iauai, sometimes transliterated in English as Jehovah, and the Egyptian God Osiris, really AuSarai in the original Egyptian, World-Sunrise or Universal up riser. This is Lithic thinking at a secondary level, trying to pick up some of the implications for thinking of the fuzzy original semantics obtaining at the birth of linguistic competence, rather than merely trying to identify the pieces of the original semantic lexicon. At this distance we are dependent upon discovering the implications of the Lithic lexicon from the reconstruction of the Lithic lexicon itself – in turn from the traces left in linguistic usage today; and in both cases we are in turn dependent upon assessing the validity of the thinking by way of such subsequent promptings as we can access, at least to reject what does not carry conviction.

It will be argued there are no really strong reasons on offer why any of these meanings for u should ever have attached to a vowel or to this one in particular. Although there may be some truth in this perception it is also true that there are no really strong and immediately convincing reasons why any of the psychosemantic trees should have arisen and become markers in the mind of man. All are gossamer connections lightly

Chapter 14 Vowels

agglutinated in accordance with human whimsy, and stirred in the subconscious pie as attention flits de fleur en fleur from time to time, mostly in the dream time. Psychosemantics are the stuff of dreams but they are by no means nonsensical, just lightly (and dreamily) assembled. What is really striking is that so much of what we have in the dark room down below is so similar all around the world, even when the conscious mind has woven so different linguistic patterns out of it on the surface of the conscious mind above. What is convincing about Lithic is it fits. It all hangs together and finds expression in a myriad words in languages all around the world. The reasoning may not be obvious, but it works. It would not work if it were not based on fact.

Together with the three vowels, Lithic postulates the Vowel Oon, the unity or unit of three, with the third vowel resuming the first two, the first two aaa and eee, packaged within the third, ooo, third because inclusive: aaa the standard, eee the little one, and ooo the container of the other two, making up the oon or inclusive unity. It was a relationship picked partly from the family and sex. Aaa as the general vowel was recognised as the first; or was it the other way around? If aaa and ooo are dad and mum - an O can suggest the feminine sex and the birth canal - aaa is a bit vague to stand for dad's yard just because of its extending propensity. He was however the free ranging hunter, and no doubt often out of breath and breathing hard as he was away going loping interminably after game, an activity of extension. In any case the three vowels were triune from the start, just as the ineffable is today. The first count appears to have gone one, two, both of them, instead of one two three as we do it. It was probably a left over from splitting a flint and then finding the two flakes still fitted together exactly and if put back together carefully you almost had the status quo. It dates the thinking too from the time when the count was only to register a distinction, to distinguish the one from the other, and so the first from the second, positions probably occupied at first by a and u, and then when a second distinction was made in order to accommodate a third item, eee accepted the repetitive role shifting u as the completive to both of them. Eee then, as the repetitive again, became the plural of both of them, and then ooo as the completive could then become all of them. It may seem a long way round to simple iteration and addition but in the early days the birth of mathematics was a long winded business repeatedly pushing the head of the intellect up against its roof. Even the simplest concepts were at one time novel constructs. Figure 1, sketched for chapter 3 (page 44) is worth a look. Even a cow can probably tell the difference between one turnip and two, but she is still some way from rationalising the relationship between them or even spotting that such a one exists. She is simply not blessed with the idea of iteration. A bigger pile of veg is just a bigger pile of veg for her. Similarly we had to learn the hard way that a distinction, from dividing or breaking in two, the two distinguished, could be replicated to give rise to iteration and so to numeration. Meanwhile the insidious one, two, both of them of dialectical thinking was taking hold and building into a dialectic, which with hindsight can be seen to be the denial of iteration, an anti-math (and also the downfall of the Communist miasma in due course).

Much of this dovetails quite well with some of the exposition in chapter 15, The Origins of Thinking, and Figure 3 (page 327). To distinguish between this and that, it was simple to see this as not that, and so the negative as the opposite of the positive, and then absence of similarity as the opposite of it, absence as opposite, rather like a hole in a molecular metal lattice which can import the equivalent of an opposite electrical charge. Distincta were thus in opposition from day two if not from day one. This is largely derived now from Ancient Egyptian, although long preceding it; but it is not intended to break off to go over all that at this stage. They had the vowels in an oon – as a unit or an inclusive as

Chapter 14 Vowels

opposed to an exclusive 'one'. It was not all that far from Thesis, Antithesis and Synthesis, rethought five thousand years later than the Egyptian priests by a German professor, Georg Hegel, who claimed to have invented the liberal dialectic prompted by the Platonic technique of teaching pupils to think by eliciting repetitive responses from them or from a puppet, each response carrying the argument further. Hegel was closely followed by Karl Marx. Boasting he had stood the liberal establishment dialectic on its head, he disfigured political thinking disastrously with his totalitarian determinism for several generations until the whole system imploded from its absurd internal tensions, trying to make everyone fit a bogus psychological configuration. But it is likely to disfigure academic thinking for as long again before the intellectuals can work it out of their teaching systems (or find the humility to read my chapter 15 and pay attention to it). There is black comedy in communism, claiming to be revolutionary, digging up the atavistic thinking from the beginning of the human race and imposing it by force on whole populations with such terrible bloodshed it makes Homo Erectus' raids and slaughters no more than tea parties on the lawn, with just a bit of ritual killing for entertainment, no more than practice for the mass executions of the last century. Have we become less mad or is it madder? We seem to breed bigger monsters than ever with so called civilisation. It nurtures them – by teasing them perhaps.

The Sanskrit for voice is vac, pronounced wac, from the Lithic Wa-ka, fear-make, or sound the alarm, with distinct if tenuous and far flung connection with the Aztec God of Creation, Wakan Tanka already mentioned. The voice was first used to convey emergency information; and speech was to alert the tribe to what was on the cards precisely, rather than just to screech. Speaking is just a refinement of screeching. It came from the need to precise in messaging. More precise thinking came before and forced an outlet in speech. It was certainly a quantum leap in human civilisation compared with which the invention of the wheel is entirely insignificant. It was the beginning of education, where before it was left to everyone individually to make their own way simply by watching how the world went, the snail paced apprentice method. Moreover with speech, understanding became cumulative from one to another and from one generation to the next and as language built so did understanding. Meanings became infectious. Even with everyone joining in the process, progress was slow – to be measured in hundreds of thousands of years, and tens of thousands of generations, a champion football sized crowd or two chain-spread on end over the millennia, almost too intensive and lengthy a process for the mind to grasp. That was the consonants for you.

But this chapter is about the vowels, left overs from pre-speaking times. They were old when the consonants were young, but now they were to be trimmed and sandwiched into compartments. The tones were broken up to be made into chains. We learned to think in bits, which seems to have suited the cellular structure of the brain. Before we finish with the Sanskrit voice we can look at the schoolboy "Cave!" from the Latin imperative of cauere, later cavere, to beware (schoolboys pronounced it KV). "KV!" was the cry on the approach of a beak in the old days when Latin was the schoolboy's bread and butter. Lithic ca-wa-verbal marker, make-ware!, can also claim cousinship with the Wakan Creator in Central America, as well as with voice. For good measure in Malaya, about equidistant from Panama and Italy, kawal means to keep guard, and berkawal means to be on your guard with an almost identical sense to the schoolboy's KV. In France cold is froid, pronounced roughly froah, but it apparently comes from the Latin frigere which is to be cold, probably to be frozen stiff or to be rigid in fact, or else the Lithic frei-kare was to

Chapter 14 Vowels

cut off the pleasant warmth. Yet the French has swung back towards the pronunciation wa, a metathesis signalled perhaps from the dark room down below.

Water is from the same stable as awan which is water in Ancient Egyptian, with a horizontal zigzag glyph, to show a rippling surface, without any rigid structure. Water was an airy element, liquids and air being both fluids without any rigid structure giving them shape: as they label water in India: "pani", from Lithic elements pa-nahi, surface none, having no solid surface. Or else it is pa-nai, lip-presented, since drinking water is pinica pani in Hindi. But it is possible to use an adjectival pinica, which is 'of the lips' derived from the noun; and then to qualify it further: to drink is to make with the water or with the lips, in fact it brings both derivations together. English drinking is to make a drawing in, and is close to our chest of drawers and the underwear we pull up. The Egyptian hieroglyph awan, often taken by academic Egyptologists - who treat the glyphs as alphabetic - as just n, is actually a formalised rippling or shivering surface, a stylised zigzag line awan, a-u-an, go-both-ways, up and down in this case. It is an easily demonstrated fact that an "a! a!" called out staccato will gain the attention of an infant, with inhibitory effect. It is a parental alert instinctively understood. There will be some post natal development of the brain needed first, but only a few months. It appears it was used in the Stone Age when junior approached the water's edge. "Ha! Ha!" probably did for the hearth, with a hand suddenly withdrawn as if just burnt, the adults having learned the hard way that a really good burn elicits an involuntary "Ha!" which therefore means "Ouch, that was Hot!"

The water warning is now spelt aqua or agua and such like, the q or g taking the place of the glotal stop, giving a cross between a! a! and wa! wa! The -ter in water is harder to explain. Terai means drawn along by an Egyptian ray, originally out and up. Might this be spring water which is pure and unadulterated as it is drawn out and up from a source under the ground, so water just means fresh water as opposed to the saline stuff found in the sea? Or might it just be the ground water for the same reason, since terra in Latin is ground, the land, which in turn is soil ground (terai in Lithic) and levelled in nature's mill? If so water is ground water. Or is it an agential –tor, doer, the shiver doer, water being always cold in nature? Anyway the range of similar words .tends to indicate that. The Greek is hudor, the Russian voda, both look like agentials. Vodka is strong water. Eric Partridge, with no Lithic, treats vodka as "in form a diminutive" like -kin in English, and suggests it is little water because much reduced by distilling. Whiskey appears to be from awa-i-ish-kai, water which has been ish-kai, fire kindled, fire water, or anyway a warming tot. During the distillation it has evidently absorbed some of the essence of fire, which is how the Red Indian tribes too read their Lithic. There may be less of it but it is not a waterkins. The Hittite for water was watar and the Sanskrit udan. Ta and da are most often from the Lithic semantic contents becomes or does. There is some further indication in Latin unda, wave, water-of-deed, the water's trick, and the Arabic wadi, a valley, from awa-dai, water-cut or done, with oued, awa-ai-dai, the river water-that which-did it, by flowing down. Winter is the cold wet season, it is a waterer.

The Egyptian has hua for water too. In Egypt there were as many ways of referring to anything as the whimsy of generations of priests with a fancy for poesy could devise. Hua however was not one of them. The Egyptian h was a cockney h, pronounced usually ahi, or achei – whence perhaps our pronunciation aitch - but essentially in use to keep separate two consecutive vowels otherwise liable to be elided or the weaker to be eliminated altogether. With hieroglyphs, a glyph ending in a vowel not appropriate could be modified by a following glyph with a different vowelisation. So there was a requirement

Chapter 14 Vowels

for a marker to show this was not the case. Hua will have been actually pronounced ahua, the h replacing an original glotal stop, making it quite likely the model for aqua, agua, etc. as well as the descendent of the original Lithic awa. The pronunciation of Egyptian has not been attempted in academic circles to date, the glyphs being read as if with consonantal values only, and a minimal vowelisation inserted where essential for pronunciation; whereas they were actually originally syllabic. An owl is taken to stand for m for example, when in reality it said aa'maaooo (as owls do). A mouth with parting lips is read as r, when actually it represented arai, arousing, the lips parting. I think it is a mouth anyway. The salacity of these ancient monks should not be under estimated. They may have drawn it sideways on as an in joke. The Egyptian rays were their special preserve, representing what passed for science and theology at the same time, a rosy state of affairs now long past. Hua was not so different from the awan they drew as a zigzag line, or awanu with three zigzag lines for the abyss, u being the inclusive: the infinity of formlessness, all of it, the third line the tertium quid of the dialectic, relating the other two – both of them in fact. Drawing three symbols for the Egyptian priests was ultimate inclusivity, from counting one, two, both of them, the vowel oon or dialectic[1]. It was their plural.

Rain (11) is an intruder in this chapter since it is water which descends in rays with the watery vowelisation over-ruled. Nevertheless the Old English former form regnian, to rain, shows kinship with Latin rigare to water or irrigate, which in turn, it would appear, took its time from the rain descending in rays as the sunlight was supposed to do, from Ra the sun. If water followed similar pathways it rayed just like the sun. Reigning too, the monarchical function, was a straightening or ordering role, one which nature already achieved with the rain, perhaps to teach the monarchy its manners. For the Rex to be making rays was euphemistic, but it may have appealed to him as a Roi Soleil or Sun King. The Old English regnian for rain also illustrates how g could easily slip into the pronunciation y. Rain serves also as an introduction to urine where the opening u stands for water, whatever else the rest is about. The Greek verb ourein meant to urinate, which seems clear. Urine flows out a bit like a (localised) shower of rain. When urinating you are water raying just like the rain which shows off the same trick on an area scale. You are raining water on an individual scale. The Greek can also be compared to the Sanskrit warsam rain, from Sanskrit war for water. Warsam is the active (sai) water which mai or descends (ma) to earth (ma). The Sanskrit war (spelt at the time with a v) may well have originally been awar, or awa, starting with the shivers like everyone else. A final untrilled r may replace an elongated a, and have been pronounced aa. Try the Malay pesiar or besiar, to stroll: from the Lithic phonemes pai or bai-sai-aa, going-movement-extended, with leisurely movement. You really have to be obtuse to miss the Lithic underpinnings in so many places, once the overall plan is revealed. But now we move to Latin urinare which surprisngly means to take a dip, to plunge or dive into the water, apparently from ua-in-are, water-in-to go. It seems clear the initial ur- comes from a slovened awa-. But by the time the Old English caught up with the Latins there was some confusion in the ranks. Following the Latins we adopted urinate, but while we declared we were having a dip we were actually having a pee, perhaps in anticipation of the trick the Americans dreamed up with their visits to the bathroom later still, but without having a bath. But you can see we were half way right because the slovening had changed awa to ur-, and awa-rai imitated the rain, a spray of water, not a dip in it. The slovening had changed the analysis. We have even confused urine with Latin aureum, gold, from au-rai-u'm, that one-shining-one, which Euphemus himself would have jibbed at. The language Tokharian A, a remote outlier of the Indo European family of tongues (now extinct) amongst the Central Asians,

312

Chapter 14 Vowels

should have the last word. Water for them was wär, the most nearly echoic of a shiver which is werwerwer rather than wawawa (Latin), or wuwuwu (Greek). But they too slipped in an r for a sound really a schwa.

Wind (3) probably does a whistle, just as a gale goes la or sings. But why does it whistle? Because it blows. To blow you must either burgeon low, as the petals flatten when a flower opens; or else with a limb (ba) you must swipe with a looping action, thus delivering a physical blow from a looping limb. Boxers, strikers with their upper limbs alone, nowadays deliver straight blows, because a looping one signals its approach and loses the weight delivered ultimately from the back leg. But the original blow was an unscientific swipe as the phonemes suggest, and carried the meaning of to wallop, which meant to thrash. Thirdly to blow up a balloon you must make a flow of air, from the Latin flo, I blow. The initial f- is clearly a puff from which the b- comes, a lip or mouth rather than the puff itself. The puff is a powerful phoneme, a gesture of exasperation, expulsion and rejection – which of course is why it fits so neatly into Ancient Egyptian eroticism, which we still follow today. The way lau can be used to indicate fluid flow can be found in chapter 9 for la. It is the instinct of liquids to flow out, down and away if allowed loose. The au following upon the l is in common guise here: that completed, away, altogether, all. The blow does not tarry any more than the liquid out of an emptied vessel. That is nature's way. You can not recover a puffed puff any more than you can pick up spilt milk. Had you not wished to lose it you should never have let it out. You should in any case have paid attention to the semantic contents involved (as above).

To wind (4) a handle gives us the vowel sequence uai, oo or circular going (ai), and then 'n the Celtic and Germanic verbal ending, and finally a –d from –dai, doing. Prison officers called screws would screw tight the windlass the prisoners were made to turn as punishment so it was stiffer to turn. It was attached to nothing as a pointless insult added to the physical exertion. The winding the windlass (16) provides is a turning la-sai, in a looping or circular action. We are prompted with an initial o (well a w, which is a skimped o) as with a simple winding, and then with a -lass, a 'looping action' as well. So how does uai suggest a revolution? Partridge refers us to voluble under which he addresses the Latin voluere to roll or cause to roll. A voluble person is thus one who has turned over the whole business in his mind and then lets the whole lot out. He is on a roll; but perhaps it would be more accurate to treat the vo- as from uau-, meaning superlative rather than rotational, and the –luble as from lau-balai, a leaking balai, lip-tongue or verbosity. An archipelago, from the Greek is the chief sea (Partridge: as seen from Greece of course) with etymological analysis for pelago, sea in Greek, surface-lapsing-location. It refers to the fact water offers no noticeable resistance to penetration: step on deep water and down you go, pursued by the same spirit as a leak. Compare Hindi pani, water, from Lithic pa-nai, surface-nahi or none. La we know as circular from the skyline (seen from an atoll island, which ai-s-lan-d, that which-risen-[of]ocean-become).

An atoll is an island in the Maldive island chain which comes from Malaya Dewi, the Malayan Family or archipelago. The atolls literally are awa-ta-lau, water-born-in a ring, born from the ocean as coral reef islands, and the coral adverts to the very same process from ka-u-ra-a-lai, land-what-rise-ing-from the briney. Partridge derives coral from the Greek korallion which he proposes to relate to the Hebrew goral, a pebble. The grinding of the goral acquires the grinding or wearing smooth meaning from the grindstones which go round, just as wood grain goes round when a trunk is felled, although it presents itself as longitudinal streaks in a planed plank. Pebbles on the sea shore are ground smooth by the briney, as the wave motion shifts them back and forth across the rocks and sand. The

Chapter 14 Vowels

English pebble is pa-i-baba-lai, piece[of rock]-which-go go-in loops and smoothing – acquiring some of water's instinct to go flat, having it dinned into them, back and forth, back and forth. There is no reason per se why ba should persist as meaning go, just because the sound is made with the lips and the lips are fleshy and the haunch or bum, the fleshy bits, are the source of most of the flesh for the Stone Age butchers, the muscle the quadrupeds and man use for perambulation: so ba made with the lips thus comes to mean go. That is the way the mind goes and it is no good complaining it is not cricket (or logic). It is the essence of human mentality and that is what counts.

We can now return to the uai vowel sequence winding (4) a handle. Since the vowel a is the general unrestricted extensive vowel, ai is extending including that extension of distance which accompanies any departure, and occurs when you go. We know anyway ai can mean going since the Latin ire, to go, with the -re the Latin verbal marker, almost says as much. Uai can therefore always have the idea of oo-going, going in an oo, an o. To roll has the verbal marker up front, and the o line (not the linear line here but the world circling orbital loop one as seen in and from an atoll) follows. Now we can see why we have coined the term wheel (17) for the specialised roller invented recently. It is an uai with a loop in the end, an o goer in a loop, as may be gathered from uai, the o-extension already reported. A wheel just keeps rolling along. An o is a static hoop but a lau (or lo) is a roller, with both a circular and a linear instinct. When the Lithic is spelled out syllable by syllable you have to try to think of the meanings behind the words used, which are those available today, usually unduly precised by now, for the purpose of representing the boorish and unsophisticated approximate fuzzy meanings of early days. So we must allow for a measure of approximation.

To work through the psychosemantic tree on page 307 brings us now to the vowel oon (5). This is a difficult bit. We are trying to penetrate the mind of Homo Erectus. The reader is asked to turn native and shuck off hundreds of thousands of years of conditioning and try only to think in those terms left to him – and this when he will not know what they were. The only evidence we have is what is left to us of his language as preserved like flies in amber in the everyday speech of today - and every stitch of that will be disputed. Life being short no attempt will be made to take academia by storm. Let them go or let them tarry, let them sink or let them swim. The world has other things to do, and other wicks to trim. The vowel a bears traces of being the first born. Oon is the inclusive unity but a is the initial one (23) a singularity, a. Sa in Malay is a single upright – Lithic sa is up, as the flame (ish) springs upwards - in full satu is a single cut or scratched upright stroke, used in Malay for the number one. If it was incised or scratched it was probably on rock, an early day procedure since it does not make for speedy recording: we are back in the Stone Age, whether in our Malayan Eden it was actually cut on bamboo or not. A single line scratched is atomic, with no innards, a blank: you see it in the English an, spelt un, with the semantic box empty, a negative quantity and quality. So if you are under you are (Lithic) an-terai, un-drawn up; or with nether the Lithic elements are nai-terai, negative drawn up. Because of the sexual dichotomy, nai (chapter 11) which comes from orgasm when the breath, held as tension mounts, is let out as it breaks, comes to mean just the erect state, presenting, pushing forward and up; but also simultaneously the opened rounded vagina, and so the open and so empty category (24) as well.

Old Norse blakkr, a white horse, reveals the development of French blanc and English black, both from uncoloured (an-kara and an-laka), in French leaving the colour white and in English without any colour at all, black. With science the English have it, but that is not significant. The bla- is apparently from pla- and means surface (compare Latin pellis, skin,

Chapter 14 Vowels

pa surface, la surrounding). A- is un-, and an-ka-ra is un-colour. The colour, it was thought was delivered to the eye by the returning ray sent out by the eye, bouncing off the surface seen (an active ray like a radar beam), picking up the colour from the target. With science we now know the eye is passive, picking up the sun's rays reflected from the objects seen. The Sanskrit for a white horse is karka, the Lithic elements for colour are the same as in the Old Norse, but the whole is here ka-araka, with the first ka- in the sense body and the second uncoloured.

But to get back to the vowels, our English away is probably from au-ai, the completive-going, rather than the derivation generally adopted of an-weg from on-weg, on the way, since the meaning is far away rather than just going, which needs the Lithic au-ai, altogether gone. Similarly far is from fa-aa with a cockney (untrilled) r. The semantics is spelt fa-aa, fare far. Similarly, 'and' (26) spelt semantically is aa'n-dai, extending-does, not to be confused with ante, from an-tai, un-born and so unbecome, or anti from an-tai, un-tied or unpaired, impair, and so contrary. The words today are not particularly apposite for the original thinking but we do not have the original articulation any longer. The thinking is nevertheless accessible. Long is from la-au-ng, linear-extensive completive-one in Lithic elements. The purpose of this book is to provide a lead in to Lithic thinking, which it has taken forty years to develop. Understanding of where we came from linguisticly is a great help in cutting down false assumptions, a hermaneutic Occam's razor.

The middle vowel i (eee) as an item is often translatable as he or it, and the sequence ia or ai often nowadays dipthongised as e, as 'ít that', 'that which', 'the one that', even he or him (ia in Malay). Typical is Arabic yani, Lithic ia-na-i, it that-presents-itself, Arabic for id est or i.e. Est is from Latin esse to be, which can be analysed as ai-sai, as is living or as is seen, since the sibilant - from the warmth and light of the flame respectively - carries the semantic contents of life and visibility equally. Ya is similarly a vocative in Arabic. Ya sheikh is polite. A sheikh is an elder who has kahi, spirit made or accomplished by a lot of living, shai. Attempts have been made to relate the Arab sheikh to the West Indian chief, a cacique. But Partridge sides with Santamaria: cacique is from Mayan cah-tsik, hand-honoured, with hand the symbol for power, kahi as the actor, since Lithic adds cah (from ka(h)i) is the maker or actor, the tool we all use, which the hand is; so that the cacique is actually a Cahi Tsik, a High Executive, rather than just a symbolic hand. As for the tsik meaning high, Lithic supplies uplifted, as the flame leaps upwards.

Mixed between ai and au are the analyses of hour and year on offer. Lithic insists they all revolve around Ra, the Egyptian sun, although this is heresy to conventional linguistics which keeps Egyptian, as an unknown, at arms length. Where was the transition, it will be asked. Lithic has no need of transiting since it posits parallel semantic development; whilst acknowledging of course that borrowing has often occurred in the course of human intercourse. Horus was the son of Au Sarai (Osiris in conventional speak, but Au Sarai in Egyptian), the World Sunrise, a repetitive come uppance, the resurrection of the world sun, and Sa suggested life as well as light because the sibilant phoneme meant the shining light and at the same time the life principle and the up direction, all gulled from the rising flame, the source of heat and light. The semantics are comparatively simple, but they encapsulate belief in immortality. Does not the sun rise smiling at the dawn of another day? Au, the All, the Totality, refers to both space and time, symbolised by the Tau, the duality. We know it as just a T, but for the Egyptian monks it represented the two world dimensions, space and time. The space was the line across the top and the time dimension was the vertical, that is the rising line.

Chapter 14 Vowels

Some time before Einstein the combination of these two elements in human experience had attracted their attention, as at about the same time, or even earlier, it was as the Chinese Tao attracting the attention of the Chinese mandarins as a mental birth or becoming and so a Path or route to understanding. The vertical and horizontal dimensions put together were both eternity and universality, permanence and omniscience. What a prize! What an aspiration! What Simplicity to reflect upon! It was and is a splendid symbol for navel gazing, and the Chinese have done a lot of it. It brings philosophy but not prosperity, as the Chinese are now learning. What prosperity shall we now at last see in China with the lesson now at last learned (unacknowledged) from the West? Was it Marx? No. His philosophy broke the mould; but his philosophy was false. The Chinese illustrate the Golden Rule of life, simply this: third time lucky: Tao, Marx, Capitalism, the philosophy of common sense. Perhaps there is a dialectic there too for those who must have it? China has learned capitalism from Hong Kong, stung by the British lion, a priceless boon. The Chinese may not like the analogies. Tant pis!

Horus comes by a significant aphesis, which just means shortening in a slovening process, from i(h)a-au-rau-sai and the original Lithic was probably he that-one that-was raised-shining. Horus was the personification of the dawn, The Dawn Horus, a son or copy of his father the sun in his permanent avatar, the sun as a rebirth phenomenon, ascending. There is here a nest of prompts for religious sentiments. How, it might be asked, can the single orb be both father and son, the paternal sun giving birth at dawn to himself as if the dawn were a separate entity coming forth from his own being like a son from his father's paternity? But then how do you manage to count one two both of them? The answer is you have to go back a long way to when the human mind was little troubled by remaining mysteries and just followed through the thought that sprang to mind. Horus was at the same time I-a-u-Ra-u-sai, He-that-unit-Ra-when-shining, a sun unit, and the sun movement was a time unit, a movement in time as well as in space. It was not exactly Einstein's mc, but it did hook space and time up together, one movement coming to represent the other, in the Stone Age a seven day wonder in itself. Ai and Au (in our terms e and o), were approximating a dialectic, nothing to celebrate today: but then e and o don't mean anything for us. None of this is strictly needed to understand the meanings Lithic phonemes acquired, but it is a nice example of the kind of thinking needed to access the Stone Age mind.

Hari in Malay means the day, when the sun is shining, from the Lithic i(h)a-rai, it that-Raying. The Greek sun unit horos, i(h)a-u-Ra-u (s), it that-one-Ra-one-substantive marker, was prayed in aid as a year, and hora, it that-one-of Ra, was a season of the year. Greek horos was also used as meaning boundary or limit. I(h)a-u-Rau can be read as it that-where-raised, or the horizon, which in turn is the boundary between earth and sky. Daytime sun units we know as hours, from the Latin hora a season, time, hour. The year is another unit of Ra, as is obvious. It marks the time it takes for the sun to swing between its heliacal rising points and back again, with the seasonal effects so important to the life of man. It started out in Old English gear, from Lithic gai-a-rai, the going and returning (it is Ra's rays which give the re- its return again meaning, because they were supposed to go out and return back pulling up the plants with them on their return trip to the sun, just as the human eye, a feeble sun, reported back with a simulacrum only of what it had met and felt over), the time it takes for the travel, the journey sideways of the sunrise from midwinter to midsummer rising and back. It is a refinement on the Greek which left the unit unspecified. The year is already primed with the ai, with the semantic content of extension or travel, so the g sound could be overlooked as an inessential helper towards the meaning. It can easily change to y, or j, as in German jahr, or nearer to English the Old Frisian jer and Old Saxon jar. The spelling is only an approximate guide to the pronunciations which are all much the same, and none of them paying attention to the original Lithic composition. Latin, looking as ever to Greek, had hornus meaning of this year. Compare Greek horos, year. We may conclude the –nus supplied the this, and Lithic confirms nau means presented, present, as in now. The year and the hour are equally sun units. They are both cases of the vowel u as a substantive (20), which can be read as one or unit. The year is its sideways travel while the hour is a portion of its loop or orbit. An orbit is from au-ra-bai-ti, that one-Ra-goes-thing, a round or circle, and thus the track of a wheel likewise, not itself a circle, just a rut (from Lithic rau-tai, round-born or else ray-become. Ra has the potential for round and straight lines equally) made by a wheel, and also the orbit of the eye, also ra in Egypt because like the sun it was supposed to emit a ray, in this case an egg shape emitting a ray again. Roundness was what was supposed to do it. Round orifices as well as orbs were sources, with some looseness of the criterion when it came to the end of Tarzan's penis, which was bell shaped or snailshell shaped rather than ball shaped but nevertheless was taken to perform in accordance with the perceived scheme of things. It is Apollo, the ever looper, in orbit, who measures the hours and times the crowing of the cock, and names the pollo dish in Spain and even has a hand in the three French hens (poules) true love has to give, along with the partridge 'an a perdrix', or a partridge in French, which the cheery boors (Wayland Smiths) fancy is 'in a pear tree'; while the poetry is actually hinting at the alternative philosophy with its esoteric and erotic (Lithic? Yes!) pa-terai, the male erect penis that the witches were privately thinking of. But the educated male philosophers had forgotten all about that, ignoring their true linguistic heritage in pursuit of religious ideals they supposed (only supposed) were incompatible with the old pagan knowledge. It was a case of emptying the baby out with the dirty bath water.

It must surely be a source of astonishment in the case of a word like horizon and its adjective horizontal that its derivation from the sunrise remains opaque. The Lithic is i(h)a-u-rai-sa-un, a standard expansion to counter slovening and aphesis. A schoolboy, you would have thought, could read that as from it-that-one-rising-of the shine-one (or sun), or else it-that-one-of Ra-the rising. Sai is rising, because the flame leaps upwards. Our own sun is the flame one or shine one, from ish the flame which (inter alia) surely shines. Is not the sun rising a certainty also? And is not 'so', just so, Lithic ish-au, is-that one, as is? The density of meanings that fit is surely in itself an astonishment, which is as-tau-nai-shai-ment, as-become-evident-showing-ment, with ment also akin to mental. The conventional etymology is from the Latin tonare to thunder and so to stun, but tonare is from the Lithic tau-na, become na, that is to say it momentarily obliterates everything else in the mind, just as an orgasm (from na, the expulsion of breath held as tension breaks) does: a powerful metaphor surely! Maybe you need an overhead lightning strike to bring the meaning home: the clap of thunder heard from immediately beneath can certainly be stunning. Less impressive tones are gulled from this paradigmatic one.

A javelin has a fine gamut of vowels. It is a Celtic weapon, a light spear for throwing at long range, when you need to consider its flight. The geflach, fletched with feathers like an arrow, was a specialisation. The plain javelin was a hurling weapon, gai-, hurl is straight from the Lithic kai- a forceful stroke, originally aimed at a flint rather than a quarry, with the Lithic semantic contents of -u-ai-lai′n what-going-flying added. A javelin was a light throwing spear. Jehovah has even more vowels and they are supposed to be so sacred they can not be disclosed or mentioned and instead adonai is substituted, really a

Chapter 14 Vowels

young man from the Lithic a-tau-nai, that-birth-showing, his birth is near, he is still green behind the ears, but taken to be good looking with it. But Yaweh is taken as the same vowelisation (approximately), and Lithic expands Jaweh's name back to I-a-u-a-i. This is neat and poetic and recommends itself on those grounds alone. The question remains what are the sacred semantic contents? The concealment will undoubtedly have been because some secret truth, suitable for revelation only to the initiated, was supposed to lie there. But the mystery will likely lie with the ancients and no harm will be done today by linguistic research. Only the black goddess Kali is wed to darkness and concealment. White goddesses handed their virtue of openness on to the gods who followed them, and they only kept a few mysteries for their close followers to follow. With i-a-u-a-i we have a pentagrammaton and not a tetragrammaton as is declared. That is not necessarily a disqualifier. Indeed the layers of cover, from the time when it was generally thought that religion should be a recondite affair with truths too traumatic for the common insight, are likely to be diverse. We have the old original vowel oon deployed in particular fashion with a symmetry which calls out for explanation. We are back in the time of the soothsayers who had a much closer acquaintance with the Lithic roots of language than can possibly exist today. Indeed, they could probably have written this chapter in spades.

We have already worked out a good deal of vowelisation in various languages, with the semantic contents the three vowels carried. It-that-one-that-which[is] springs to mind for iauai. But it offers very little intellectual satisfaction. I-a-u and U-a-i offer more possibilities. Overlapping of phonemes with the meanings read twice is common in Lithic. Two oo's in the middle sound the same as one, just sounded a bit longer. Now it is a hexagrammaton in the Greek, sex in other languages. We have an introductory phoneme in both cases (in capitals above), with as followers -au and -ai. We already have read au as the all and the world, the universal term. Egyptian Taun, the world as all that has been birthed and happened, matches Wakan Tanka, the Aztec Creator God, the Awesome World Maker. I-a-u reads as He-that-Universal. U-ai is to follow. U is the completive, absolutely all of it. The ai, the extension, is evidently the temporal extension here, to go with the spacial dimensión already recorded, and uai means the whole of the temporal extension, the eternal, an aeon. So we have The Universal and Eternal, and we have it entirely in vowelisations which predate the consonants which carry the language of the thousand things of earthly experience. It is a statement of the trans-substantial and a digging deep into the prehistory of the mind. It is a fuller statement of the Tau, the T which is scratched on rocks as testimony to human or rather pre-human aspiration, from times so distant we do not know what the scratchers even looked like. I like to think of these Tau symbols as a million years old, with the idea of Jaweh already in the wings waiting for language for full expression. It splendidly identifies space and time as the two dimensions of human experience and traces them to a source in the Sacred Absolute. Is that not what religion is about? The formulation of the Jewish God is not exactly triune. The principal constituents are an au and an ai, but they are conjoined in the u in the middle, a both of them, from the mind set that counted one, two, both of them, still waiting for iteration as such. Iter, Latin again from ai-tai-rai, a going-become-verbal marker, a journey or the path of it, or as it-born-the ray, a there and back job, turning again like Dick Wittington (without any cat). It is this dialectical conjunction which provides the pabulum for mystical contemplation, the ineffable: the relationship between our experience on earth with its temporalities, and the over-riding timeless eternity (when our earthly experience is dismissed), with a permanent infinite space to go with it. It is simply a Stone Age dialectical triune unity, one two both of them, from before iteration. It is also surely the

Chapter 14 Vowels

same perception as the Buddhist Nirvana, a blowing out of all psychic yearning like the flame of a candle – life like a flame – leading to an experience of utter tranquility, without any consonantal perception at all, swimmingly diagnosed as bliss. Anyway it is some way from the seven nubile ladies supposedly awaiting a Wahabi terrorist, arriving hopefully with his ectoplasmic wedding tackle miraculously reassembled intact. Perhaps these are only metaphorical Muslim houris, one for each day of a metaphorical week. The life in the spiritual world of the hereafter has no genitalia, so a Wahabi suicidal martyr is certainly heading for the mother of all disappointments when he is greeted by the promised virgins. He will have to be making his excuses, for which he has in no way been trained. The goddess Kali will be in ecstacy: her finest hour, with her greatest deception of her own martyrs fulfilled – if She exists of course.

A hoop (20), from the Lithic a(h)u-u-pai, is that one-oo-surfaced, a peripheral piece (shaped like the periphery of an O), or the skin of one, the outline; and is indeed a circlet. The Lithic from which the word hoop comes derives periphery from the skin of a circle. Compare with peri in Greek which means around the periphery from the pai-Rai, the skin of the sun seen head on (well facing the orifice), its perimeter. In chapter 12 it has been used to show the British are Pretani or PeriTauni, periphery of the world ones, living at the periphery of the world in Egyptian times, and validated by the Ancient Egypian language, which is the inspirational origin of Greek and Western civilisation; and making the Inuit who eat raw fish – esqimaux - the only true Peritauni or Britons today. The West has been reared on an Egyptian amalgam of Semitic and Hamitic (black African) cultures. To be fair the West, once aroused from its dogmatic slumbers by the above injection, has added much of merit its progenitors lacked. The Inuit object to Eskimo, a derogatory term used by their neighbouring tribes for whom firewood was available to cook their meat. Eskimo is from the Lithic Ai-sai-kai-mai-u, as is-alive-body-eating-ones. Sai-kai together is read as alive-body. The –i may be plurals. The "Ka" was both the structure and the driving force of the body, treated as "soul"; which was dual, for this world and the next. The Sai Ka was the living soul in this the first world, and the kai was of the first and live ka of the body. The Malays call the aboriginal tribes sa-kai, an insulting term much resented: it means single ka folk with a single-cylindered ka with no second cylinder for the next world, animals in short (or is it insects, wearing their two bodies together in the first world?) whose prospects can therefore be snuffed out without any harm. In chapter 13 on Ish it is demonstrated how the semantic content of the sibilant includes both alive and first. Now a loop begins with an l like Apollo's, the orbiter, and adds an oo like in the hoop. The French tout (30) meaning all is akin to Ancient Egyptian Tau, all the births, becomings, events, the universe. The T is a universe Einstein came to understand, both the elements of becoming – space along the top of the T and time pushing up from below, in a vowel oon or dialectic Einstein spotted, as folk do who shuck off linguistic thinking and conventional linguistics with it. Hegel just clothed the Tau in language; Marx turned them upside down as coat-hangers. We (31) are the plural of he (38), with he from ahi, or ai, with the original semantic content that which or one it. Ushi in Navaho is our, the plural of shi which means my, which is cognate with sa in Malay which means one, which is also the first person singular. Une is the simple uninclusive unity, but a unit, which unites and forms a unity is the inclusive one (30), all gathered together, the inclusive category. Away (42) is the completive of going, from a-u-ai. A way (39) is the substantive of going. To wag (20) is to dual ways go. A waggon is a way going one. But Old Norse Vagga, a cradle, is a wagger which goes to and fro, a rock-a-bye, which goes and goes back (a rocker, rau-ka, it makes a reversing ray) plus a-bai, that-goes. The solid rock is raised

Chapter 14 Vowels

core, per contra. Add it all up and rocking is going both ways, nothing to do with the earth's core brought to the surface the Carthaginians reported in the Canary Islands, in spite of the same phonemes involved, merely due to the polysemy which has arisen as the phonemes and their semantic contents became overloaded. There is nothing wrong with bye (from bai) meaning simultaneously going (we use the bai, the muscled haunches) and the binary concept (also gulled from the haunches, side by side bi-, both. The first semantic content is gulled from the action of the human haunches, the second from the two side by side hams, whence also our idea of besides: the hams hard by each other in accordance with the binary symmetry of the human body. It was probably wise women with at least some Lithic who composed the nursery rhymes. When you weigh (from Lithic u-ai-gai) with suspended scale pans, the pans are both-ways-going like the wagging Norwegian cradle, but in this case straight up and down to do their job, that is to tell you the weightiest (as long as your point of suspension is slap in the middle), instead of from side to side to kid Norwegian babies they are still in the womb, with a comforting shake up. It is because the scale pans carry the weight that the Latin vehere means to carry, not the other way around. You do not go both ways when you are carrying anything. The wagging pans have clearly been gulled. An anchor is weighed when it is raised. Its weight is carried. It is brought straight up when it is weighed, not up and down like scale pans. A vehicle is thus a little waggon and a little (level) carriage at the same time. A voyage is a way going and a convoy is a kau'n-u-ai, a joined'one-unit-travelling, a joint voyaging. (A caravan started out just a convoy, and Kali's followers took advantage of them to gather their fifteen unbelievers and garotte them while they slept, in pursuit of their seven virgins when they died). It is of course more immediately from the Latin via and verb vehere, as any Latin pundit will tell you, but this is whence they are from too. With Lithic phonemes and their semantic contents you can pick your way through the lexicon with added insight and delight.

The Greek for well (the Adverb) is eu (32). But it is the neuter case of eus, from ai-u-sai, which meant strong, lively, brave, that which-completive-lively or active – from the flame leaping upwards, indicating activeness as well as liveliness because animals with warm blood are both alive and active, two gulls out of the phoenix's nest. Eric Partridge has more on this. The interrogative que in many language variations is without explanation. Why is judged to be from *kwei. Certainly it is cognate with Y, which actually says (and draws) u-ai, dual-going or ways, with the ai extensive, a Y junction of possible paths, and an interrogative drawn out of it. U is substantive, ai is extensive. What is first firm is then open to decision, it opens indefinitely what was substantiated. Why else is the Y drawn Y? In the lexicon of semantics, as opposed to empty phonetics, Y is critical. It is the question mark verbalised and sketched: what-that-is. It carries the semantics in its configuration. It is thinking drawn out on paper. The T and the Y, the Tau and the Uai, are the twin mnemonics for Lithic, which turns out to be spelt TY for purposes of meditation with an oo added for completeness. Let us call it Tayoo in place of Tao. The semantics are hard pounding, which is why they are shunned. Not only that, they are not 'scientifically correct' because they can not be laid out as specimens and measured up to see if the ideas fit the facts. This is not surprising since metaphysics in their entirety are not reducible to mechanics. Linguistics is the metaphysical science. It will not answer to Darwin or Newton, and there is a very good reason for this, quite outside any ideological hangups readers may have: it is that thinking is an activity and not an organ or any other solid. Within the limits of the brain's capacity it is free. Your brain does not decree what Sunday walks you will take, and so neither can your genes. They

Chapter 14 Vowels

control physical capacities alone. You have the capacity to take a myriad walks, perhaps an infinity of them to choose from, as linguists accept. It leaves the door ajar and the mystery of how the mind relates to the electrical circuitry unsolved, which is a very good thing.

NOTES

1. They were there in fact before they had even invented a coathanger.

CHAPTER 15

THE ORIGINS OF THINKING

Writing a book on the origins of speaking, it is inevitable it must lead into the origins of thinking. The development of one has obviously gone hand in hand with the development of the other. Indeed it has sometimes been argued the one has simply become the obverse of the other. Generally it is proposed (wrongly) advances in thinking mirror advances in linguistic achievement: when we find words for new ideas then we start to think in terms of them. In the same way, most people imagine they think in words – probably because when they come to express what they think they find it comes tumbling out in words. Of course Wayland Smith learns the words others have put in place. But thinking in words is only shallow thinking; the original thought is prior. Worse, all education is in words (even when accompanied by still pictures or movies – or mathematical symbols); so that education tends willy nilly to reinforce the illusion and keep students thinking at a shallow level, often doing no more than building their vocabulary (more or less esoteric, depending on the quality of the education). Of course it keeps them politically correct as well. The lexicon can indeed function as a very large pair of blinkers, to the conscious mind at least, leaving only the subconscious to its original native untrammelled perceptiveness and lack of inhibition or judicial stricture.

Moreover the recent explosion of information crying out to be mastered, due to explosions in the media, principally the technological and scientific media, has only reinforced this shallowing of thinking. If you have to be well informed, or only apparently coping even, you had better not spend too much time on questioning methodology or exploring epistemological issues. You may not even learn these terms, so busily are you encouraged to attend to informing yourself and memorising names, data, formulae, etc. Students, if their wits are about them, wish for time to digest and mull over what they get, and if they are enthusiastic conspire to give the syllabus another whirl after qualifying. The retake of course has to go by the board later. Some even drop out bemused by the absorption rat-race, judging themselves inadequate or at least in some way not cut out for academic success. They are the saner ones. Academics meanwhile take this as evidence of natural selection and see no need to question academic procedures.

Also there are very few poets left. They are increasingly seen as dropouts or comical rhymesters, and nowadays they probably are. In Victorian times they were still revered as the deepest thinkers. There are no Lord Tennysons today. With inspiration there is still a struggle as we grope for words to formulate and express the idea we perceive, whether dimly (for the most part) or even occasionally with a sudden "Eureka!" feeling, as if a veil were lifted and we suddenly got a flash vision of the reality. But nowadays education is no longer to be treated as a personal struggle for understanding. It is presented as accumulating public knowledge towards certitude and certification, so the competent can feel confident and right, with charity where the less well equipped for this hesitate. This is simply wrong and misleading in every particular. It is "Red Brick" learning in the most pejorative sense. We finish up with the reductio ad absurdum of a well stocked memory, the badge of a shallow thinker, treated as a master mind and given a trophy.

Chapter 15 On Thinking

Surprisingly, feminism, which might have been expected to provide some check on the male tyranny of the word, has had the reverse effect. Feminists, thinking of themselves as counter attackers, have moved into male territory arguing they can think male thoughts just as well as men. They can of course, perhaps with some upset to their feminine hormone balance; but it is not what is wanted from them. The female mind is the one free from intellectual and linguistic hang-ups; although there is a view women were originally the instigators of linguistic advance at the origins of speaking, using their articulation to massage the egos of their male partners – in return for meat and sex. They remain natural talkers, still massaging, without falling for linguism themselves, perhaps knowing perfectly well it has been a mild fraud from the beginning. For the males meanwhile speech is ego-massage. Their "objective" subject matters are easily appropriated as extensions of the self. So they get a double ration, their own and their partners' massaging and attention. Still, it has to be said, the males are natural go-getters, and as such they have powered progress ever since our hominid ancestors came down out of the trees, whether the girls care to admit it or not. There is nowadays, after hundreds of thousands of years, more in language than merely feminine charms. It is a whole new world of substantive conceptualisations. It is not that the female mind is less capable of contributing to human science; simply that they have not cared to pursue the matter until recently, and the male mind has thought to encourage them in this.

Feminists may wish to interject here that the males have unfairly cut them off from education and stunted their intellectual development over millennia, in extension of their first mischief of similar effect, impregnation. It would be idle to deny these charges; but the male mischiefs were only successful because they were pushing at open doors. For most of the time, the girls were happy to concede. They just wanted babies like their mothers before them, before anything else. Now they are beginning to think they can find something better.

It turns out the dialectic is in fact relict of some of the earliest ratiocination. It is a term based on the Greek for 'Conversation' or backchat: first interlocutor A has a go and then party B responds. In linguistic terms that is the origin of the dialectic, simply cross-talk. But it goes back much further and deeper than that. The Dialectic is our Lithic heritage, a nice example of pre-linguistic thinking. It is an irony the Communist Dialectic proves to have been an atavism and not a novelty at all. Jumping many millennia, Klaus Fuchs (the atomic spy) sold out his adoptive country, his family, and even his tennis club cronies because of the Dialectic, which he had to believe was prior to science (a verbalised discipline) because it was pre-linguistic. So he followed Marx's dialectical thinking and gave the science of the West to the Russian dialecticians. This is really quite surprising: Fuchs was certainly no fool in conventional terms. He had scientific 'chutzpah'. He was a practicing atomic physicist. So why did he do it? No doubt his psyche wanted to posture against the everyday. It helped him study leading-edge science. But his mistake is a testimony to the intellectual power of the Dialectic, which has always been perceived – ridiculously – as deep thinking prior to all the methodologies which utilise speaking, and in particular prior to scientific methodologies; something a priori and given, so you can't argue with it.

There is some merit here in being able to trace the Dialectic far back into human history. Ancient Egypt already reveals it as an ancient piece of established mystery; and some notice of the Egyptian mental usage has already been given as "The Vowel Oon", a-i-u (going going gone), as elaborated in Chapter 14, the last chapter on the phonemes, the vowels. The Dialectic involved fundamental orienting perceptions (as it still does) as to

Chapter 15 On Thinking

how the world went (and goes). These perceptions are not currently intellectually reputable any longer; but nevertheless across Europe the dialectical way of thinking is still believed in, at least in decadent academic circles, particularly in France. Even in China the spell also persists, in spite of their very different intellectual idiom. It is to do with moral justification. If benevolence and beneficence still appear to be tied up with dialectical thinking then that is the way academics are inclined to think; historical evidence or even reason notwithstanding. Plato (550 BC) used dialectical methodology to argue moral cases, basing his approach on Socrates (who proclaimed his debt to Egypt). But the alternate toing and froing of the dialectical process is thousands, or even hundreds of thousands, of years older than both of them.

Ancient Egyptian thinking has had to be entirely resurrected along with the Egyptian language, because Wahabi Moslem genocide resulted in the loss of much of the Egyptian cultural heritage as well as their language. It is a permanent cultural disgrace the Semitic community must bear, hardly ameliorated because they kept some of the Egyptian achievements as theirs. It matches the Akkadians' rape of Sumerian a few thousand years previously. The Akkadians were primitive Semites, as indeed the Egyptians were too originally.

So what are the original categories of human thinking? Indeed, prior to that, what is a category – of thinking or anything else? These questions need answering succinctly and with complete clarity if any progress is to be made in clearing up the misconceptions of the last many millennia. First of all mental perception is fundamentally dictated by our visual sense – it has been described as the tyranny of the eye, the only non-reflexive sense we possess; all the others (feeling, temperature, pain, taste, in practice hearing even) are personal experiences, but vision is of the world around, and therefore purporting to be objective. The panorama, all that can be seen, is the local phenomenal world, the visible scene. The supposedly objective world of objects is given by the eye. Perhaps we trip over it sometimes also, but the pain of stubbing the toe is clearly subjective.

So now we must pause to see what is involved in seeing, and what ideational constructs it entails. Infants open their eyes and learn to focus. What do they see? Focus brings to attention distincta. See sketch 1 of figure 3 on page 326. Perhaps the infant is seeing the wallpaper in the nursery. Let us suppose it has a floral pattern, with red flowers on a contrasting ground. With focus, the eye will pick out the contrast at the boundary between a flower and the ground. The mental event is best represented as "Distincta!" or rather let us say "d!", for "See!" in English, and also for "Distinction!": see Sketch 1. The eye will follow this distinction and will trace out a boundary (Sketch 2) and so eventually – in a day or two only – realise there is a bounded area. The bounded area so identified is indeed a category (d'), first the category "Red" (though red may not discriminate colour as yet, just what happens to be there, which is red), later perhaps also or instead the category "flower", but certainly not yet (Sketch 3).

The pivotal point needs to be underlined that the category is derived indirectly from a prior and more elementary identification of a simple distinction or boundary (Sketches 1 & 2), because from the very same distinction (d!) come the pregnant identifications of (d') (Sketch 5), "Red" and "Not-Red" on either side of the boundary line (Sketch 6), and this already has relevance to the Dialectic.

We might tease our understanding of the Dialectic at this stage, debating if this "Not-Red" in Sketch 6 is the opposite of "Red" or if the "Not-Red" is merely the absence of red. We are going to need to be able to recognise the difference between the absence of a property and its opposite if we are to see through dialectical thinking, which confuses

Chapter 15 On Thinking

them. It is already a challenge to the many potent grave and reverend intellectuals who have not thought in these terms and remain confused by the Dialectic; but then they do not concern themselves with infants whom they probably think of as mewling and puking merely.

The original discrimination (d!) in Sketch 1 – exemplified by distinguishing a change of colour on the nursery wallpaper (but just as well the aureole of an erect nipple for those who fancy a psychologically marked target as trigger (Sketch 4)) – can be represented conceptually as a simple line or boundary (Sketch 2). Flower and nipple boundaries are in fact curvilinear of course but the simplest representation of a boundary is an unmarked one, which simply continues, and so a straight line. This is the stage characterised above as d! in Sketch 12, labelled Pa. The conceptual odyssey then proceeds as in Sketch 5. As the distinction suggests a distinction-between, no doubt prompted by a flower or nipple pattern which goes on round to enclose reasonably neat targets, the single boundary line then bends round both ways in the mind as in sketch 5 to convert the boundary idea to a category, matching more or less the way the eye follows d! around the periphery, until it finds itself isolating not one but two categories (circles, d') separated by d! (Sketch 6). This is probably the source of the butterfly patterns scratched on stone, the acme of Stone Age thinking vouchsafed in triumph to posterity (Sketch 7).

Archaeologists have identified it as a butterfly or even a double headed axe, giving a simplistic interpretation to a symbol invented by minds supposedly simplistic. The point is the two categories or butterflies' wings, d', red and not red, are mentally developed from a single discrimination (d!) and they all three appear in the glyph. Purists may wish to challenge the double whammy implicit in my figure of eight or butterfly design (Sketch 5 & 6) showing categorisation from a single boundary identification as sufficient to summon its negative to mind; but I am unmoved by them. We are not talking about a stage which can take in a substantive item on a ground, and the objection is therefore anachronistic. After all if a line merely curls round in the mind will it curl right or left? Obviously it can equally go either way and so it will go at one time one way and at another the other way, so it ends up going both ways; the symmetry of an unmarked mind indeed demands it as sweet reason. So along with our category we get a phantom doppelganger whether we aim for one or not. What are these two? In our example they are "red" (or for the nipple deep browny pink) and "not red" for the ground of the wallpaper (or not-so-browny pink, for the breast): which we can now write in generalised form as "x" and "not x": universals. If I am right this is an important stage in the development of human rationality. Ability to shuck off the evidence of our senses when false similarities such as the moon and the cheese are presented, so that we are freed from the tyranny of the eye, comes only very many millennia later – if at all.

Meanwhile it has been our misfortune to have another line on our minds, which we have readily confused with the first one: the criterion, the awareness of a differential marker. It is known nowadays as a continuum – shall we call it c! There is no language which does not recognise the notion of more (Sketch 8), though in earlier language it was sometimes clumsily expressed. Mathematicians, concerned with numbers, mix it up with 'next' these days. It is in fact a difficult concept to get across, as primitive concepts go. Computer buffs as well as symbolic logicians and simple mathematicians too will recognise the "greater than" sign >. Because it is greater, from left to right (the direction of the script) the lines converge reducing the spread, imaginatively to equal a following term of ordinary size. Contrariwise, the "less than" sign < opens out from left to right, so

Chapter 15 On Thinking

FIGURE 3

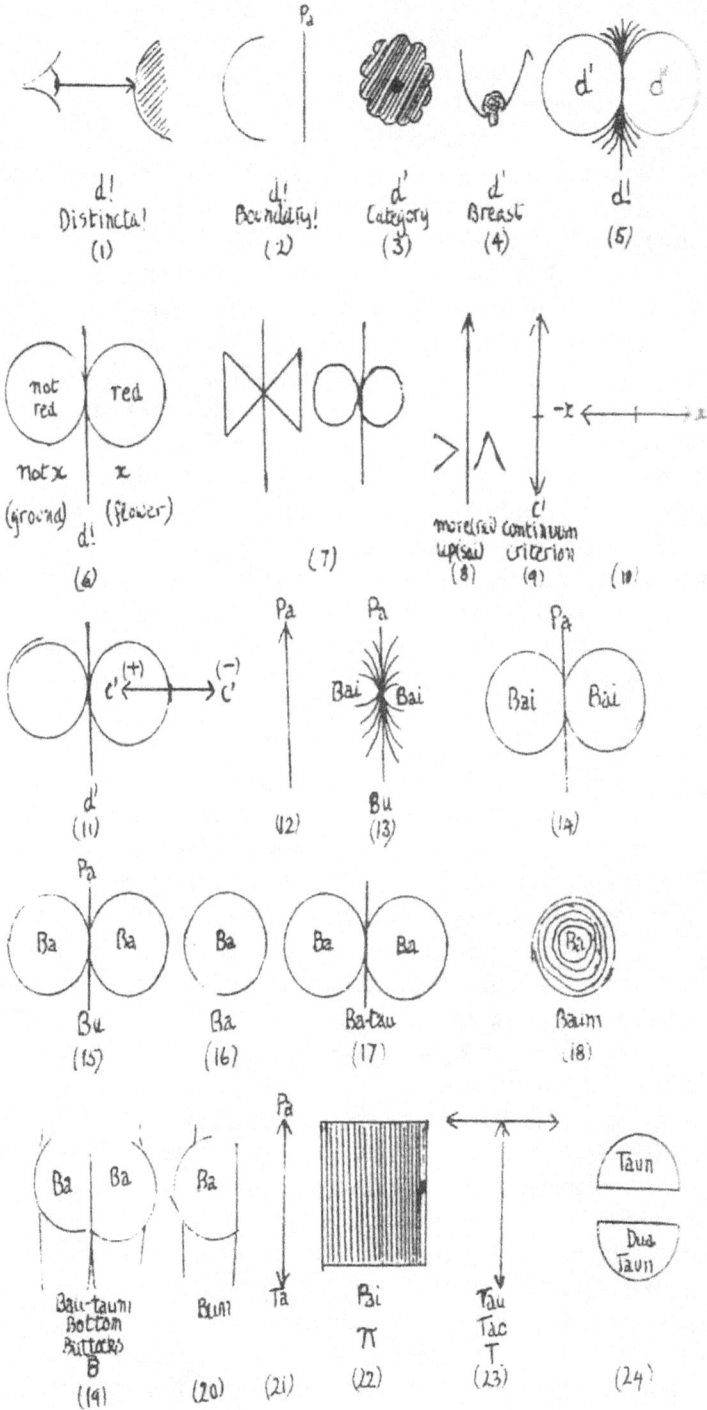

that the initial diminished spread leads to an expansion to catch up with a virtual term on the right of standard size. These terms deserve serious mathematical consideration. The initial term on the left of an equation would have to contract or expand in those ways to equal the term on the right in other words. It is clear "greater than" and "less than" are relations developed (logically) from the middle case of equality or "same!" although the original perception probably hardly encompassed this sophistication, coming from a perception somewhat more akin to "What a Brahma!. You don't see many wide mouthed frogs that big these days!" Here we were simply grading things (as to size, or perhaps as to weight – we shall never know). It is hard to get behind these ideas.

The relationship is mathematicised as a gradient and drawn out and formulated in mathematical symbols in numerous ways. But we can surely see today the conceptual schema involved is simply a line or direction with an arrow on it, a vector, for example more is up in Sketch 8. To include less as well as more we need a double arrow, and (pregnantly) an origin or point of reference like ourselves, with a left and right hand, a change-over point from more to less, the equality at source from which more and less are marked deviations, see Sketch 9.

Well-briefed modern boys and girls will recognise this picture at Sketch 9 as the y axis of coordinate geometry used for the analysis of algebraic formulations. As such it has nothing whatever directly to do with the line we also drew vertically in the previous Sketch 6 to distinguish between "red" and "not-red", the first discrimination of the eye, which we mentioned in passing could be generalised as "x" and "not-x" (Sketch 6 again). To point the parallelism which has led to confusion I have drawn the x axis also, simply copying the pattern of Sketch 9 at Sketch 10. These are all simply different schemas, of which there are potentially an infinite number. In both cases (Sketch 6 and 9 or 10) the first term now involves x (a coincidence of the symbolism chosen) and the second "not x" and "minus x" respectively. In spite of the fact that linguistically it appears that the absence of x (not x) can without much loss of rigour be represented as a negative, in reality an absence and a negative are clean different things. Quite apart from the math, this becomes clear if we try to think what the negative of "red" might be. Perhaps that colour which when combined with red produces white light, negativing (rubbing out) the red? That suggests complementarity rather than opposition. Moreover, unfortunately there is no such colour, all colour qualities being sui generis and only when all colours (frequencies) are mixed is white light produced. In fact we can not ever see negatives of positives in the real world, only absences, eg of light of one group of frequencies or another. Negatives and positives turn out to be simply (mathematical) fictions, without regard to whether the real world provides any fits for them or not. There is no requirement to prove their existential (sc. ontological) status.

There are for sure presumed polarities, for instance in electronics, basically the potential to attract or repulse, in which respect we find atomic and sub-atomic particles marked. But otherwise negative and positive are cultural constructs much favoured by mathematicians and physicists and of great value in calculations and bank accounts. But they are not presented to the eye, not even by a see-saw, they are abstracts, clearly inferred from experience in the phenomenal world but not part of it. They are to do with shuffling pebbles from one pocket to the other and that sort of thing. They are relative to activities, not to things, coming and going, upwards and downwards, and light and dark for instance. So in the case of electronics, or other subatomic particles schematically opposed, attraction is often regarded as the negative of repulsion, while the absence of attraction is even treated (in semi conductors a hole in place of a particle for instance) as opposite in value

Chapter 15 On Thinking

and equivalent to a repulsion. Electrons being negative purely by convention, the travel of an electron through a medium is by convention a flow of negative current. So the similar movement of a hole where an electron (or other negatively charged body) might otherwise be is treated as a positive current. But it is the directions which are opposites (strictly reciprocals) not the electron and its absence. A negative is simply a reciprocal vector.

Nothing here so far is new; at most it is perhaps presented in pictures differently.

We can now see further however that the category has hybridised. Neither fish nor fowl it has become a red herring. Originally no more than a boundary which closed, it has acquired an outside and an inside, an exclusion zone as well as a centre, simply because it is an extensive presentation in the mind. There is now, if you can anticipate a little, a continuum across the boundary with the point of origin on it (Sketch 11). This is something new and even shocking. It is certainly confusing. Hard pounding! It was not in Hegel's or Marx's books.

So now to tie up the relevance to the Dialectic of these two different lines which the mind perceived before speaking – the boundary line or distinction (d!) and the sequential line or criterion/continuum (c!) – perhaps the essential outlines of the Dialectic should first be spelt out, starting with the Hegelian as it was borrowed with insignificant modifications by Marx, and is therefore best known, as well as being still believed in Europe, and unbelievably by some presidents and prime ministers. There are of course published critiques, notably that of the late Isaiah Berlin in Britain; but they are literary, even anecdotal, rather than methodological. The methodology really needs by now to be exposed and demolished once and for all, and it is the analysis in terms of c and d which does it.

The Dialectic posits a Thesis (roughly a proposed heading; it is clearly a category, d): a case in point is Feudalism, (a vague and tentative term to describe Norman society, since much revised but still very much in vogue when Victoria was crowned which was about when Marx was formulating his dialectical schema for world history). Another more recent application is The Idea of Social and Economic Freedom. Every Thesis is perceived as pregnant with its own doppelganger or opposite, its Antithesis, which arises spontaneously and inevitably from the Thesis, not at all unlike the balloons in Sketch 5. The absence of a category is implied by the existence of one (even just the postulation of one when there is a postulated absence to match); while a continuum is conceived as extending infinitely up and down and so with a positive and a negative. But category and continuum are clean different things – as different as a straight line (the continuum) and a circle (the category). Put them together nevertheless as if they were one and the same and you get this quaint hermaphrodite feature half one and half the other and capable of populating the world and the brain with a comical coat hanger network, a negative implicit in every positive categorisation, with an ability on top to dream up another category embracing the first two. Examples are Capitalism and Totalitarianism, implicit in and therefore inevitably following upon Feudalism and Social and Economic Freedom respectively. There is plenty of room for interpretation here; there will be parties who prefer different examples and may wish to argue vehemently I have got them all wrong; and it is true I approach their selection quite casually, aware I am on phantom ground. Nevertheless the theory is that it is by the development of Thesis, Antithesis and the third term in the Dialectic, Synthesis, the final realisation resulting from the confrontation and then reconciliation of the Thesis and Antithesis, that both the world progresses and at the same time the mind properly comprehends the process by way of these double repetitive elisions, a double whammy neither of which can stand up to examination.

Chapter 15 On Thinking

We are now right inside the dialectical thicket. The thesis is the category initially selected (d') and the antithesis is the implied exclusion category (d'), misprised as a negative. This confusion is drawn in Sketch 11. The doppelganger not-red arises from the fact every boundary has two sides to it and categorised (Sketch 3) has a within and a without. The negativity of the dialectic however is superimposed on the mere absence of red outside the category simply by confusion with the other (quite different) line, the continuum, which is thus put in Sketch 11 in order to show how these two lines have been confused by Hegel and Marx. It is solely this confusion which enables them to invent the dialectical coat hanger pattern supposedly informing both the world historical process (a miasma) and our mental processes (misconceived), both at the same time. The synthesis recognises the common origin of the foregoing two and supposes it is the same as a current commonality, which of course it is not. You can always find another category embracing the two preceding ones. In effect you rub out the two lines you have just drawn in and then draw in another one across the differences between the former two, by means of a quick switch from the category arising from a boundary distinction (d') to a criterion/continuum (c') bridging the boundary.

Perhaps it is the most important single aspect of the Dialectic that it is taken to represent both the way we really think and at the same time the way that world events actually unfold. Because clearly if this is the case once you can grasp and accept the Dialectic methodology your thinking ought from then on to be in line with reality, the way the world goes. You are thinking in objective terms, ie the way the objective world proceeds; while the others, poor muts, the subjective thinkers out of kilter with reality, who do not think in dialectical terms, are being suckered. This makes your belief an obstinate one so that you are set to ignore contradictory opinion; and that in turn self selects for a bigoted mind-set as well as the wickedest of tyrannies. Needless to say my own belief is the whole dialectical gamut is all pie in the sky. The pragmatic view is schemes can be invented galore, much like computer software programmes, for one purpose or another, but hardly to provide every kind of analysis by means of a single programme; and so the dialectic has turned out hopelessly impractical, leading to the most painful political and scientific foul-ups and disillusionments.

I have described an early dialectic in Chapter 14 as The Vowel Oon, with the vowels a, i and u in the roles of Thesis, Antithesis and Synthesis. The vowels indeed lend themselves to the representation of pure thought since they flow freely without structure and thus without identification, whereas the role of the consonants is to structure utterances and therefore they are perceived as delineating phenomena, or anyway ideas, discrete chunks of thinking.

The word dialectical itself needs some explanation, being originally from the Greek dia- across and –lectos from legein to read (or choose), that is to say to pick out the meaning of an utterance and so to specify its meaning or import, to read or even to legislate. So the dialect, the way local people talk, is chat but also the logic of speech. I think the speech element is important. It is implicit in dialectic, originally argument and counter argument bandied to and fro as between two folk or perhaps philosophers cross talking in argumentative mood. Then we have to go on to analyse the semantic contents of the term still further: not merely argument and counter argument but prinzip and counter prinzip. Here we access some of the deeper ponderings of the human spirit or psyche. There is first the contrastive consciousness which comes from the very early, even infantile perception of the boundary between red and not red for instance, generally x and not-x as fairly exhaustively discussed already. But then, confusingly, the linear element presents itself

Chapter 15 On Thinking

alternatively as a continuity at the same time as the discontinuity of the boundary line. The dialectic is caught up in, or perhaps better descends from this confusion of boundary and continuum, a confusion it must be said still able to fuddle the best of brains and lead to the betrayal of patrimony and even humanity itself. Witness the brilliant buffoon Doctor Fuchs from chapter 1. The gambit goes precisely like this. First of all conceive of a Thesis and Antithesis on either side of a boundary line; pausing to philosophise as much as you wish upon these contrasted categories whatever they may be, praying in aid, wholly improperly, the positive and negative poles of a continuum with a mid point or point of origin discriminating the two opposite directions. Then comes the Synthesis. Switch about your original point of view entirely now and regard the two elements you have been contrasting as entirely positive and negative aspects of a unifying entity such as a continuum presents. This is your Synthesis. You have as it were stitched up the two elements previously parted, or indeed witnessed their partition and their subsequent over arching unity like a bystander witnessing any other scene change in the everyday world of visual objects. That fixes the whole fandango in the mind. The mind and the world then mirror each other in this dance of the coat hangers, the mental gyrations thus guaranteed to reflect precisely the structured processes of reality. This secular neurosis has probably by now killed more than all the world's old religions put together, because it commands the same certainty in assent as the old religions did but with hundreds of times the power for evil at its disposal due to the progress of technology. It is therefore surely bizarre that dialectical thinking is still admired in certain quarters, and Neo-Darwinist ideology is popular.

It is hard to know whether to dignify Karl Marx with a notice in a chapter on thinking. But he is so much better known and therefore influential than Hegel that his version of the dialectical nonsense deserves proper direct attention. He was a perceptive social critic of his day, which was nigh on two hundred years ago; but his methodology is hopelessly out of date and was always wrong. His dialectic, which he cobbled together from Hegel by (as he put it) standing Hegel on his head, was the rotten egg in his basket and yet the one beloved by academics for the next century and a half and still admired today even after the communist ideology has failed egregiously everywhere it has been tried. Marx's actual influence has therefore been wholly malign and his intellectual muddles still inform much of the academic establishments around the world. An examination and refutation of the dialectic on scientific and logical grounds is therefore long overdue. Senior wranglers with university tenures have shirked the task or simply failed in it because their thinking never challenged or examined the philosophy involved, as too difficult to argue much about. The collapse of Marxism has therefore been merely a matter of practicalities and any hostile critique has been based merely on rival social theory, leaving the afficionados still singing famously to their own scores.

Hegel's dialectic was a contrast and exchange of liberal prinzips which he believed would be fully realised in due course. Marx's was a contrast and exchange of economic factors which he believed would lead to political revolution in due course. In both cases Natural Process was involved, informing both the way the world went and at the same time the process of human thinking. It appears to have struck nobody that these coincidental arrangements were a curiosity, as if it were to be expected from the track record of human thinking to date that we would or could naturally keep in step with reality. Any set up which positively entailed any such arrangement of affairs, so blatantly contrary to the human record, ought surely to have been suspect from first formulation.

Chapter 15 On Thinking

There were other curiosities just as bewildering. Economics were naturally determined and their outcomes inevitable and yet they had to be struggled for bloodily. Nobody asked why they could not just sit back and let Nature take its inevitable course. The true answer was because the whole fabricated scheme was bogus; but nobody realised it, whether they looked forward to the denouement with keen anticipation or regarded it as a threat to their livelihoods. The parties were struggling for and against the inevitable, and comically those against won. But it was a black humour killing many millions by the way in the name of the dialectic and its winning ways.

Marx was a caveman when it came to science. Aristotle must be judged to have known better two thousand years earlier, and he too had one foot in the cave. It was originally Plato's cave in fact. Marx's mind-set was of the 1830s or 1840s at best, twenty years before Darwin when Biology was only present as Linnaean Botany, a kind of philately merely. Evolution of the rocks was what Charles Lyell had successfully demonstrated in 1831 in his book "The Principles of Geology", in collaboration with my great grandfather, an enthusiastic conchologist (shell collector), and his shell collection which occupied the whole top floor gallery of Merton Hall. I remember it well (the Shell collection). The hard sciences as we now know them, physics, chemistry and of course electronics were simply absent. (Shall we say negative?) Straightforward mechanical forces (Newtonian physics), action and reaction, were the scientific paradigms for the historian and philosopher alike, not a lot different from the thinking of our Stone Age hominid forebears as they flaked their flints hundreds of thousands of years before. They just lacked its application to the spheres (courtesy of old Isaac Newton).

The human mind is not primarily oriented towards elucidating the truth. It is much more practical than that; which is how we came down from the trees. The mind merely seeks tools for analysing the world, human destiny, reality, call it what you will.

The dialectic proposed a scheme or process setting out with a Thesis or proposition such as "The moon is made of cheese" or "The world is red"; but which soon got read instead as "Cheese!" for instance, or in the second case "Red!". Whatever else may be said this is clearly categorical thinking. We therefore need to look closely at a category and what may be done with it, as well as what may not. A category is (or comes from) a description, although it can be reduced to just an ostensive description, pointing something out: "That!" All names are categories. So we proceed to examine categories. Thesis, Antithesis and Synthesis, all three of these are categories. We have already been over the way the infant, and quite similarly the infancy of the human race, got its mind around the idea of a category. It can be shown to be an item bounded by a common character, in the case of red for instance a patch of red on a ground which is not red. Humanity is another category just like the red patch although far more complex and controversial to describe. Feudalism and capitalism are categories too. Outside the red patch the ground is not red. Outside humanity are non-human things. Outside feudalism and capitalism there is not any feudalism or capitalism. Inside, the category has determinations but outside they are absent. The category is in no way in opposition to the ground. It is simply in absentia on the ground. The absence of red is not its opposite.

But now a mathematician will tell you the opposite of plus x is minus x. This is where Hegel and Marx messed up. Not x, a ground, is not the same as minus x. X has not been subtracted, it simply is not posited. This is where we need to distinguish a distinction which makes a category from a criterion taken to be a continuum. I don't think the mathematicians had gotten around to this comparison in Hegel's or Marx's day. Frege did not have it. They are two markedly different ideas. We have seen a category already as

Chapter 15 On Thinking

bounded (by means of a distinction) so that its logical symbol is a boundary, which can of course be represented by a straight line: on one side what the category describes, red for instance, on the other side of the boundary line its absence. It is true a category was first identified as an encirclement but it was derived originally from a barely perceived distinction at a boundary. The thinking can be drawn out as in the Sketches in Figure 3, with the category x shaping up with its doppelganger not x, based on either side of the original distincta.

But there is another kind of criterion altogether which can be represented as a straight line also and so quite easily may be confused with the categorical boundary. One straight line, after all, is exactly the same as the next one. Only in this latter case we are looking straight down it (or up it) instead of across it. This is the line known to mathematicians as a continuum. I believe Berty Russell invented the term. We only met once (at digs in Oxford) and had to beg to differ (on politics only). He was by then well past his sell by date mentally and involved with the campaign for nuclear disarmament as the best way to avoid the cold war heating up – actually certain to guarantee it, of course. Think about it.

The best continua are continuous and of infinite extension, by definition unbounded, although that does not of itself distinguish one from a boundary which can also just as well be conceived anyway as infinite. There is after all no chance of red and not red meeting around the corner of the boundary if they press on long enough. Continua do not have to be numerated but they often are, since we often find it handy to make use of graduations when it comes to any extension, gilding the lily for our own convenience. The numbers are a virtual reality to mark out a (supposedly) real space and they can be given a null point or in other words a point of origin and be made as it were into ladders going up and down from there, usually positive numbers going up and negative ones going down, but on graphs they can go sideways too (left to right like Western writing). On such a continuum plus x and minus x are indeed opposites; and "not x" is just the zero point. This point can now be made common to these two categories. (OK, the description of a criterion is categorical, but its erformance is as a continuum   Distinction and criterion/continuum together can be made to meet at any point of origin, without too much distortion of the mental category if lightly addressed. Otherwise they are clean different ideas, only subject to confusion because of the generality of the straight line which appears to suit them both perfectly well. You can not find an antithesis as Marx did lurking anywhere within a thesis because a category by definition is just a simple category; nor can it therefore combine with the original contrary to give birth in any way to any kind of summation putting the two together to form a third, the synthesis. That is just free composition outside of any logic, or to be quite blunt with a bogus logic purporting to be prior to thinking, dreamed up by guesswork. A boundary term is made to do double duty as a continuum, which has an up and a down at the same time, which is just sloppy thinking. The nearest you can get to that gallimaufry is Stone Age sex (boy + girl = progeny), which appears to have been introduced initially in the Lithic scheme of primitive vowelisation. Our first sallies into reasoning came out reeking of the subconscious soup from which they sprang, and it was quite strong stuff. See below. Clear thinking in precise terms rules it out, but daydreaming fishing for original thinking can still conjure it up.

I am obliged to S R Fischer (A History of Language, Page 103) for his notice of Rongo Rongo, the writing of Easter Island. Some 25 mantras in this script survive, most of them appearing superficially to be sketchy mnemonics of various bizarre sexual copulations. But I think they are records of dialectical thinking recorded as fundamentals for meditation. Needless to say I see them as childish and wrong headed also, but not however

Chapter 15 On Thinking

as evidence of the pornographic mentality of savages that the literal reading of all the copulating would otherwise suggest. Their dialectics were just as dialectical as anything Hegel or Marx turned out, if clothed in language derived from idioms Mrs Grundy would hardly have cared for. Moreover there is added to Hegel the further insight whence originally sprang the dialectic, arising like a miasma from the dream world of the subconscious borne on the confusion of sexual excitement with the purely intellectual stimulus of the Eureka feeling. The Dialectic owes something to a misprision of a plainly sexual pattern. Nikita Kruschev may have been getting more out of banging his shoe on the table than his fellow United Nations delegates could manage. Perhaps at bedrock orgasm is the plain man's Eureka. The latter is said to have sent Archimedes straight from his bath romping through the streets with no clothes on at all. It undoubtedly was for him a great excitement.

But to return to the basics of Rongo Rongo as devised by the Easter Islanders, the inscriptions (all wood carvings) appear to comprise simple telegram style statements in the form A + B = C, glossed as A copulates with B producing C. Whether even math itself arises from the sexual metaphor thrown up by the subconscious is here a red herring, but it could be so. Fischer cites the following example: (Te) Manu mau [phallus = ki 'ai' ki rota ki] ika [ka pute] ra'a". This is translated as "All the birds copulated with the fish: there issued forth the sun". He extracts the elements actually glyphed: Manu (birds) mau (impregnated) ika (fish) ra'a (Ra issued forth). But to look further at what the Easter Islanders were actually thinking we may note that bird is Manu, two phonemes ma- and – nu which can carry the very early semantic contents mass and none. A bird for the Easter Islanders was defined as Brer Weightless. Compare the Australian aboriginal Ba-Ji for bird, which meant Go-Up, those life forms able to overcome their weight, which causes the rest of us to fall to the ground if unsupported. In Malaya there is similarly the Siamang Ape, an acrobatic long armed Gibbon, Si-a-ma-ang, Brer-un-weight-one, Brer Weightless. Mau as well as the earth and so the massive element and so the mass or weight of anything might also be used for earthing up and so the planting of the seed, the impregnation, or even the gestation in the ground or in the womb. In Egypt the god Amun, The Ever Loving One, carried the same semantic content as the Latin amare to love, a-ma-are, as-[when] impregnating-verb ending. In Malay mau is simply to like or want; but in aboriginal Malay it covers lust and sexual possession as well. Words start out with a wide coverage when in short supply and assume specific meanings as they multiply. Ika for fish is the same as ikan in Malay and ika in numerous New Guinea tongues. I-ka-'n is Single-body-one, Brer-limbless. It was the "mana" or mental presentation or conceptions of these species, not just their physical conception, which came together in the Easter Islanders' minds when they became conjoined. Copulation was merely their robust and vivid paradigm for any linking together. It meant conjunction. How better to anchor the idea in Sunny Jim's adolescent mind?

So it was simply the elements of weightlessness of the birds and simplicity of structure of the fish, its reduction to basic outline shape, which came together and coming together reached their apogees in the character of the sun; quintessentially weightless and flighty, a super bird, and at the same time the ultimate in minimalist configuration. Thus it was meditation for Rongo Rongo boys and girls. Spot the combinatory characters! It is bogus science of course but you can see it is science of a sort. It is also demonstrably dialectical. A fish is not the antithesis of a bird at first sight, but on reflection the water surface, a major natural interface (d'), divides them just as a distinction (d') divides the categories x and not x: the fish at home swimming below the interface and the bird above it, and both

Chapter 15 On Thinking

by fin-beat. If the bird is thetic, the fish is antithetic, or else the other way around. One is the reflection of the other with the natural boundary (d') between them. The sun in turn mimics the flying fish, up out of the water with a fine swoop at dawn into the empyrean with the birds, and then disappears down into the deep at dusk back into the fishy element again. These are certainly simple metaphors, but they are not mad or bad. Some fish had an Apollonian temper and would fly short distances while some birds exhibited a remarkable aquarian propensity, diving to join the fish. This put them on the ladder category as well, with a little bit of what they fancied on either side of the boundary. The abstraction of the abstract adjectivals, the weightless and the simple-shaped adjectival elements, are both characters of our own reductive science, a potent dialectic indeed now with better terms to it, distinguishing (itemising) and then recognising their common elements and bringing them together, nowadays as in chemical formula rather than as man and wife. It is the genesis of the method which is of principal interest when contemplating the origins of thinking. The bird has grown legs for landing gear but the fish remains completely fishy dying when it lands out of water. "Pisces" for fish, from pai-sa-kai, has perhaps the suggestion he carries his legs, pai, in his body, kai, or perhaps better he uses the leg-action-of his body, Brer Motile Body. It is metaphor all along, and so only makes sense in the terms in which it was originally conceived. The fish is born in water and dies out of it but the sun is born out of the water and dies into it, so the sun gets that from the bird, since the bird drowns in water; but how is it born out of it? That is the conundrum for meditation. Is an egg sufficiently watery to keep the metaphorical cats cradle going? The kingfisher was thought to be born from water, at sea, perhaps he was given this role because he clearly had a natural affinity for water and spent so much time diving back into it. We can see the dialectic is silly but the Easter Islanders couldn't. We may be smarter, but not all that much when you look at the twentieth century, ragged out by Hegel and Marx, and the dialectic still a plank in the intellectual firmament even now, after so many millions dead from the hedonistic massage of the psyche by this methodology.

Perhaps the Jewish God was the first, perhaps even the only dialectical God. Jehovah, the Jewish God that Christians witness (with Pagan overtones), was originally "Yahweh" or "Ia-u-Ai", the magic combination of vowels 2-1-3-1-2, I-A-U-A-I, which orthodox Jews at one time preferred not to reveal, but held them covered by referring to Him as Adonai instead, the secret virtue being in the vowelisation, IA-U-AI. With Jaweh there is a symmetry about the central Lithic completive dual vowel u, pronounced oo in English but in Semitic languages often articulated as a semi consonant Wa. "He-extension-both-extension-He" appears to be the semantics concealed in the original appellation. "The Universal and Eternal": a dialectical God with omnipotent aspects spatial and temporal brought together in Final Synthesis: Single Extensive, Both, One Ever. We are counting one, two, both of them, from a time before iteration had been fully worked out. It may be bad math but it is basic for religion, a dialectical trinity, perhaps even prefiguring Einstein's Space-Time-Both of them: anyway a thinking man's god, unlike the Christian Trinity which is a comforter for everybody. All this is some way on from the origins of speaking hundreds of thousands of years ago. But in all this time Sapiens and then Sapiens Sapiens has not changed his spots; and only the Lithic Hypotheses make sense of any of this surprising persistence over so long a time.

Hard science (physics) treats its categories as real. An atom is supposed to be really out there, bolstered by the perfectly valid theory that the world is what it is and not another thing. The same rule is applied to subatomic particles and their qualities. But it is all a ghastly mistake. Sure, there are definite things out there; but they are not the same as we

Chapter 15 On Thinking

perceive them to be. Of course Emanuel Kant already knew this. In science this is a truism; a solid table such as Doctor Johnson kicked, or any other solid body, is in fact a congeries of dancing particles with electromagnetic fields, and most of the space is just that – space between the particles – when scientifically described. Our fingers, similarly composed, simply bounce off the table's fields when they encounter the table's "surface". Moreover red is not really red; it is a frequency band of electromagnetic radiation, to which our optical sensors respond with the mental experience we know as red. What we experience as red moreover is by no means the same as the electronics which trigger it. We may be the recipient of rays, but what and where is the screen on which these phantoms are displayed. We do not now imagine there is a manikin behind the eye reading the pictures from behind as we can sometimes catch sight of them on the iris from in front. When we sit on a pin and it punctures the skin we dislike what we fancy we feel. But it is not the same thing as the physical reactions of the nerves involved. The problem is the scientific terms we use to redefine what we regard as real are also figments as we present them to ourselves. Science provides us with linguistic refinements for the most part. That is not an excuse for walking out and going over to mystic illuminations, but it is certainly an opportunity.

Molecular biology copies the hard sciences. But it does not treat of thinking, only of the brain. We are left with an apparently unbridgeable divide between the mind (the thinking) and the brain. Science is reasonably content with this, provided the things which have been scientifically detected out there are given precedence: molecular biology is prior to psychoanalytic theory for instance. Examining the brain is scientific. Psychoanalysis (which claims to deal with mental events) is a "cultural construct".

Unfortunately, the distinction between science and cultural constructs is not as helpful as it at first appears, since science too is merely a cultural construct. It is a myth the scientist directly accesses the real world and his determinations are therefore objective. The history of the discipline immediately rubbishes any such idea. This realisation must come as an unwelcome shock to anyone who has walked on the moon – or even sent the walker there. He or she is rightly persuaded the science is objective (gets veridical results) in a way Freud's and other fantasists' waffle is not (does not). Moreover he scores highly for abstraction and precision. Freud too is lavish with his abstractions but he scores less highly for precision. Clearly some cultural constructs are better than others; and what makes them better has to do with the rigour with which fickle fancy is controlled and subjected to severe testing by comparing it with independently deduced "facts" and circumstances. It is the match which validates the science, not the method. Scientists alas are as human as the rest of us or more so and often remain unaware of it. It is hard to know whether it is right to dignify Karl Marx with notice in a chapter on thinking. But his thinking, such as it is, is so much better known and therefore influential than Hegel's that his version of the dialectic deserved attention.

Our consciousness can be (and I think actually should be) analysed in a continuum of developing crispness and informativeness of semantic content. I have labelled the stages in this continuum with Greek letters – chiefly to raise the tone of the piece as mathematicians often do; although the Greek letters do have lip smacking qualities germane to my purpose.

Psi (Ψ), perhaps symbolising a boundary crossing (or perhaps a cactus), designates those sensations which reach our brains and trigger immediate mental events: Ouch!, Hark!, Hot!, Ha!, Wa!, Hard!, Sour!, etc. You hardly need any intelligence for the job. If you are awake and reasonably sober you should get the message. A Chimp would. But I

Chapter 15 On Thinking

go on from Hot! etc to include in this same sector the other more specific raw emotional and adjectival responses to stimuli: Horror!, Horny!, High!, Hiss!, Hate, Hurtful, Hearty, Hellish, etc. An initial h is not a requirement but it is often a guide because the original element "Ha!" is the sudden compulsive explosion of breath due to shock or exhilaration. Prototype is the Pleistocene foolish boy (or girl) picking up a white hot stone in mistake for charred wood, to throw it back into the burning hearth, compulsively exclaiming "Ha!" for hot. The list can be extended to individual taste, and often has been; sometimes with bizarre results when early psychologists have been compiling lists of instincts. There is virtually no limit for a sophisticated mind to the categorisation of primitive traumatic promptings capable of being identified and labelled. But it is probable our first speakers contented themselves with very few; so we shall not bother with all those expansions which are possible. Psi just stands for the crude rude initial primitive psychic output, as input for anything to follow.

Next to Psi is Phi (Φ), originally an Egyptian rude gesture carried over into Greek script (the upright originally penetrating the circle rather than merely crossing it), but here employed for the whole adjacent area of mentality, the identification of phenomena, including the Phi (Φ) which appears to have started out as Tarzan's penis, here superimposed upon his partner's pudenda. This is the phenomenal level of thinking, simply taking in and mentally digesting crude input, identifying "things" presented to the senses; along with commonsensical ideas of causation, etc. – pre-analytical thinking, in learning terms coming to grips with vocabulary. Phi is adequate for some simple abstractions and analogies arising from them. Given the initial crudity of Psi (Ψ), identification of things is already by comparison an abstract process. Phi identifies both form and function, rescuing us from prior adjectival guesswork. This is conscious thinking at last, such as we know as commonplace today. A chimp by contrast is mostly stuck in Psi, with only the tip of his accomplishment nosing into Phi, unless dragged forward by human intervention. But the mere identification of phenomena wins no prizes for thinking.

Eventually – after many millennia – we got scientific. I have called reasoned marshalling of phenomena in the mind Pi (Π). It is crisper than Phi and conspicuously requires reasoning. It still allows for a great deal of erroneous ratiocination, but it is where we are at today. Pi is for Pattern, a layout on a surface, conspicuous scheming, everything from the realisation there are regularities in human experience to the modernists' theory of everything. It takes in magic and religion as well as science. It is a broad bailiwick. But it only takes one thin mental slice at a time out of the rich complexity of the reality it seeks to capture, and it is only a representation at one remove from it. Most of humanity's mistakes naturally enough are in this latest sector of intellectual activity, crammed up against the current end of it – including the idea there could or should be a theory of everything.

This leaves Ro (P) for the Reality, confronting the Psi, Phi, Pi series but in no way part of it. Our intellect doodles on the wallpaper while Ro is the real underlying wall our doodling is supposed to represent; which is contrary to the naïve and popular idea that our doodling is progressively getting closer to the real wall and may hope to alight on it given sufficient time and attention. That is a category error. It confuses the wall with the wallpaper. Our ideas must always remain at one remove from reality for as long as we recognise a world outside ourselves, since the wallpaper on which we draw turns out (in reality!) to be papered on the insides of our own heads, a mental construct, compiled from our sensual responses, which of course are by nature subjective. Our linguistic and even our mathematical presentations remain just metaphors, in an intellectual medium human enough, but always unreal. There is no Holy Grail in science, there is only representation.

Chapter 15 On Thinking

I like this scheme of things because it points up the absurdity of Napoleonic thinking and the other methodologies of the asylum which seek to illuminate Pi by recourse to Psi, as if inspiration were superior to reason, an escape from hard thinking by going back to the primitive end of the spectrum expecting to tunnel from Psi all the way round to come up again at the other end out in front of Pi. That is an illicit move in my gaming. So there you have it. Psi, Phi and Pi is all we know on earth, and in that order; and perhaps even all we need to know – since the rest is developed from the study of Lithic thinking, all unapologetically in the third category, Pi, yet not without benefit of Psi and Phi also.

There is a recent mental module theory which proposes the human mind was divided into separately functioning departments until recently. It is quite unproven. But there is indeed a problem in the archaeological record. How is it that we were fly enough to flake away at hand axes with such increasing precision and yet for a million years or so too thick to get around to decent thinking? The cognitive neurologists have come up with the idea our brains were divided into modules not consciously connected, so that while we could learn the tricks of the trade within any module, we could not apply what now seem to us the lessons of what we had learned to do, outside the module concerned. What modules there might have been is then up for grabs: suggested are sexual (for reproductive skills), social (for clan collaboration), technical (for flaking flints etc), natural (for catching game to eat), and eventually linguistic (for communicating between modules as well as with the neighbours). So when we learned to speak we broke the partitions between the modules. Sixty five years ago when I was at Oxford the students who were studying PPP, the latest syllabus taking in Philosophy, Politics and also Psychology in place of the Economics of PPE, used the old British psychologist MacDougall as exemplar of this temptation to fabricate psychic modules (instincts in his case) in excessive profusion, and we coined the coffee drinkers' term "a silly MacDougall". There may still be something of this "silly MacDougall" abroad in the halls of Academe even today.

The inter-modular incapacity really makes better sense if you adopt the position that over this million years or so the hominid brain simply was not thinking consciously at all (or anyway very little) as we understand it, more just apprehending individual skills subconsciously by looking and doing, the old apprentices' way; so that the marvel is better rephrased: how was it that this brainless wonder was making tools without thinking about it at all, simply by following subconscious promptings to copy, without really knowing what he was doing, as we understand it, at all? It goes against the grain of common sense at first; but then parrots can copy human speech, with a noticeably limited range also, and nobody thinks they think through what they are saying or have any knowledge of exactly how they do it. They follow their instinct to squawk the squawks they hear. In the same way perhaps our forebears followed their instincts to copy the flaking they saw, fine tuning the artefact as the parrot fine tunes its articulation. If you think about it, we can ourselves still do as much, for instance when we sing when we compose the notes and tune without any need to direct our vocal organs to do it. Perhaps hand axes were effectively sung. Certainly, without words to work with, hominids could not lay layer upon layer of thinking as we can. They were in exactly the same pickle as trying to do algebra without any notation. It is not theoretically impossible but it is extremely difficult; and without the ability to have a solid (unified categorical) idea and hold it in the mind so as to be able to come back to it with the degree of precision required for further thinking about it, it is indeed impossible.

The question we should be asking ourselves when it comes to getting inside a dumb hominid's mind is what ideas was he having? It is a question which has not been asked

Chapter 15 On Thinking

because it appears to be unanswerable. We have probably compounded the difficulty by seeking to preserve speaking for a late achievement of Sapiens Sapiens, when in reality our primitive hominid forebears were already articulate yet still pretty beastly with it. Moreover I think you could initially go bashing flints just for the fun of it like a gorilla drumming on his chest, to see and hear them break: "Just look what I can do!"; and then you cut yourself on a sharp edge which results from your flaking. You don't have to go looking for tools. You simply trip over them; they find you. All you need to be able to remember is what hurt last time; and then, and this is what made you human, you have to go back for more of the same, just like the squirrel does after burying his nuts. If his tail were not so bushy he would be half human at least: he is relatively feeble but quick on the draw and bites. He even has hands, and all that has held him back is the refractoriness of stone – he can not break it. We are not so much featherless bipeds as giant squirrels who shed our pretty tails; and we had the wit or just the good fortune to grow big enough to break stones. You just need hands and a bit of beef behind them for the trick; and memory first of course, but that came in with the herbivores, knowing which bits to bite.

That is a kind of thinking, but it would not win many prizes. It isn't thinking about thinking which is what we really mean when we think about thought; and consciousness is a completely different thing. Every living thing is conscious in the limited sense it is responsive to inputs. A fly contemplates the fly swat and is only defeated when we perforate the weapon so the pressure wave is subtly altered to deceive him, and all this without a single thought in his head that we would recognise as such. None of this fits in too well with the present ideas of the cognitive neurologist, wrapped up in his study of the microphysics of the brain on the grounds you can't ignore science, or even with the cognitive archaeologist looking for inspiration in his catalogue of stone tools. With minds trained to think in terms of their bits and bobs they invent the hominid mind in their image, adding blinkers to taste to account for their deficiencies. That methodology is flawed. They believe our forebears were dumb, but they allow them mental paraphernalia of craftsmen today, only cutting off the bits which elude them in the record.

It is better to start with nothing and think of stone tools as coprolites from the mental digestive system. Nobody nowadays thinks of his stomach as an organ of rational activity but the job it does puts tool making in the shade. I am not forgetting that nowadays we have minds capable of thinking of a complexity almost to match the stomach. But looking around it is clear it is still something of a novelty. Moreover you can easily have a brain without using it, or at least without using it for thinking very much. It wasn't even put there for thinking; it was put there for running the enterprise, as the control centre, a job it continues to do well enough even when we are not thinking but dead drunk or in a coma. The thinking is an accidental and inessential spin off from the nervous system developed for another purpose, namely running the phenotype's engine room. This is in fact the classic evolutionary pattern of adapt and make do, which has engineered novelties galore (conspicuously eyes which focus for instance) as spin-offs from other previous facilities. Although we may value thinking highly, it is not all that important in Darwinian terms. Indeed it is usually regarded – correctly in fact – as outside the rest of evolution. With speech and education, it is argued, survival of the fittest takes a new turn and selection ceases to be natural and becomes cultural instead. Or at least cultural selection is added to the pile. After all we spend a good deal of time these days spoking nature's wheel with medicines and therapies of one kind and another, and even borrowing and diverting her techniques for our own purposes, monkeying with the genetics.

Chapter 15 On Thinking

We can see now that with a bit more flexibility the bishops might well have won in 1859, and the churches might not now be facing annihilation from scientific progress. They should have dumped the body and argued for the mind as its successor in the struggle for survival, leaving aside where the mind comes from and discussing how we should handle it now we have it as it is. It would be uncharitable to suggest the cognitive gentry are still in something of the same bind as the bishops, but certainly their attempt to treat conscious thinking simply under the biological rubrics of the day – to keep it all scientific – is quite simply misplaced. It is misplaced because with thinking you can produce it cheap and pile it high - according to Chomsky infinitely high - something which does not occur in nature. The mind, and mental activity in Pi (Π), is sui generis. So we can get better results by letting the mind go free, and then of course in tranquillity mulling over what we have, with all the sagacity science can muster. It is a question of de Bono's hats. Academics working on the brain wear one big sombrero with a brim so big it drops to the ground, so that they never take it off (or see out from under it), because doffing it is too much of a discard, unless they are drunk or dreaming. We should not urge them to get drunk but certainly a bit of undisciplined dreaming, allowing their modules to go free and just listening to the music does help. It amounts to a new science of dumping. Einstein would have approved. He surely must have dumped his bits and bobs and launched his mind into empty space with awesome abandon. We know this in fact because he said so. At one time he wrote off language altogether. But he recollected it in tranquillity, as we all must if we wish to avoid the asylum.

To come back to our origins in hominid cognition, they evidently managed without much thinking. Why can we not allow that they simply did not do much conscious thinking at all? Or at least they did not think with the attention to it that we are accustomed to. They worked things out "by guess and by golly" with admirable perspicacity. I am arguing that with hominids it was mostly by golly, the surprise and delight of finding something which worked when you went through the motions; so that it was a spin off from the instinct to show off which underlay our intellectual development ab origine. For most of the last million years it simply did not occur to do much thinking out loud – the chimp in us got no lessons from futurity in those days. It was just a case of accepting what occurred. For more on the modular mind see Appendix A on the philosophy of language. I have tried to keep the philosophy out of the body of the book as irrelevant to the origins of speaking, but I have included the appendix simply to try and show I am not altogether lacking in that department.

This chapter so far has – I admit it – skirted and skated round the nub of its proper subject matter, how initially we were habituated to thinking and in what terms we thought. We have come across some pointers merely: the Psi, Phi, Pi, Ro sequential analysis of the mental spectrum; the adjectival mind; the source of categorisation in the recognition of the prior distinction (and so eventually nouns derived from adjectives); together with a good deal of poking fun at those persistent afficionados of the atavistic dialectic. This has been a deliberate preliminary in order to clear away some at least of the commonly held misapprehensions which would otherwise immediately confront what follows.

No doubt before speaking the mind dwelt on what was presented to it, just as it still does today. It is most probable we have extracted and distilled our intelligence from contemplation of the world around us, as well as within us; if only because it is difficult to see where else we might have got it from. There was, it may be presumed, a grave tendency to snatch at knowledge and jump to all the wrong conclusions, based on perfunctory resemblances (e.g. the fish, birds and sun in Rongo Rongo) mad metaphors

Chapter 15 On Thinking

and whimsical prepossessions (e.g. universal copulations) just as is the case today. Half a million years ago (say) when primitive speech was forming, or better when our utterances were being developed to carry an increasing semantic loading, the most difficult bit to accommodate (in our minds these days) about this early stage of prehistory is probably the degree of ignorance, and incapacity to cope, which generally obtained. Illiteracy we know, but inarticulacy is largely unexplained, and general inarticulacy is almost impossible to comprehend. With no speech we must have been nearer monkeys than men so far as our mentality was concerned, regardless of what studies of contemporary physique may reveal. How can we visualise this instinctive brute, with no conscious grasp of reality, beginning to assemble the mental tools for conscious ratiocination, confronting himself and his world? Small wonder there has been a desperate inclination to look to the monkey world for guidance. How does a chimp think? He is pre-articulate. But he is surprisingly teachable, given enough time and effort. What is largely lacking is Simian intention; they are lazy brutes, mentally sluggish, failing if left to themselves to make the most of themselves. Even today we can see the pattern is inter-specific. It is a fair bet our hominid forebears were in the same boat. Their grey matter was there but it lay largely untapped because they did not have the foresight or interest to start using its full potential, to start building its potential, hard work at the end of a day taken up with making our way. That is one reason why it is most likely it developed in the first place for some other purpose altogether. There can hardly have been any selective advantage in an enlarged organ which lay unused. Perhaps it provided balance for the upright stance, or finger control for all sorts of handy jobs, etc, all without making use of conscious thought. The chimp's own accomplishments solely concern its own betterment, e.g. signing "Gimme banana". There is no intention there to direct anything else.

Yet chimps are far from autistic. They know each other. They can relate to humans. So can a horse, a dog or a cat, of course. A cow or a sheep can accept us but hardly contribute anything intentional. Of course a cow can readily distinguish a daisy from a blade of grass. But she probably does not think about them. That is the point. A monkey and an inarticulate hominid are both in great part cow. But at the same time, the hominid, it turns out, is on a roller coaster to ratiocination – if we speed up the process a bit. This was certainly tied up with a substantial accumulation of grey matter inside his skull, the lid of which rose to accommodate it. Or else the grey matter simply expanded to fill the gap made by the rising lid? That in turn might easily have been from some uninspiring circumstance, like more chewing – or less (with cooked food perhaps). Meanwhile hominid instincts will have been purely animal, though his brain provided unprecedented and unlooked for opportunities for building and retaining thought patterns on a vastly extended scale.

I am inclined to think, since there appears as far as one can tell to have been a contemporaneity, that mental usage grew from the taming of fire, on top perhaps of an increased meat diet now that it could be cooked. It literally made us all sit up and think; our culture comes from naked seminars around the hearth, with our warm bellies full of cooked meat, and our warm minds most probably thinking of sex for desert. After all, not only cooked viands but also the warmth around the hearth gazing into the coals must have applied adaptive pressures upon the human frame including the brain. We talk of animals coming into heat. Our hominid forebears were animals every day coming into heat. I believe it was this unnatural heating which led to an enormous increase in the sexual athleticism of the human race. It is not hard to see, when one pictures to oneself any group of hominids, their minds still largely empty, their bellies full, hunkered for the pleasing and

Chapter 15 On Thinking

relaxing warmth close together around the hearth, perhaps in the mouth of their cave, all of them as bare as the day they were born. The warmth, as well as the proximity and availability of adjacent bodies, will have stimulated the adult parties present sexually. These early folk were inclined, in the absence of ratiocination, to do what came naturally; and what it was can fairly easily be rumbled. You do not need to be a medical practitioner to notice that with heat the vascular system expands increasing the heart rate so that inter alia more blood is pumped to the genitalia, and in turn there is an automatic and involuntary engorgement. Surely our bare bottomed forebears will have noticed this also. Nowadays girls in massage parlours know this and encourage their clients to take hot baths. It makes them smell sweeter and be nicer to know at close quarters as well of course. Even a natural warm climate encourages sex, leaving the British, the Peri-Tauni, around the periphery of the world, notoriously under privileged in that department. That is the real reason, in this air age, for the annual flight of citizens from countries in Northern climes to the sun. With the sun, young folk become ravers and older folk are miraculously enlivened. The Mediterranean littoral has always built a macho male. The steamier African continent is also renowned for its sexual prowess. In India the worship of sex is most highly developed, and armed with the Karma Sutra lives are probably shortest because of the overworked heart, added to an ill supplied stomach. Not only is there this connection between climate and sexual activity, surely much increased in a much hotter artificial microclimate around the hearth, but there is also, just as importantly, a change in the ambiance of the sexual relationship. Both sexes are relaxed as well as stimulated by the warmth of the occasion. Orgiastic sex releases more emotion. It could have been this bomb burst of emotion which triggered the birth of the thinking man. If so intellectual activity comes from emotionalism. Long after he was capable of any further orgasm, Tarzan found he still enjoyed thinking about it. He really got thinking. It was perhaps overwhelming sexual emotion which drove him to think, to trawl up out of the subconscious this reflection of what drove him, for further savouring in relative tranquillity. This was mankind hooked on thinking, faut de mieux, his mind in a pink haze as he focused on his earlier pleasuring and planned more for the future.

In short we have swum to civilisation through a sea of sexuality which was the original Open Sesame to fully conscious thinking; and the male genitals have burgeoned beyond all necessity compared with the other apes, simply from countless generations of obsessive and addictive over use, aeons of frenetic sexuality, and of course the necessary selection for it. It was around the hearth also, I imagine, that the ladies will have first got out their needles and tailored stomachers for their menfolk to keep their bellies warm out hunting and lively on their return, with the innate animal liveliness of the furry animal life-support systems they were borrowing. Ratiocination is really just refined emotion and without it learning is dreary in the extreme. Thinking is a vehicle just like speaking is, and we have now perhaps identified the original burden of human thought. We pile Ossa on Pelion when we speak as well. Learning demands emotion today. Some teachers are charismatic, others are not. That largely determines the outcome.

Mrs Grundy has by now turned her face to the wall, but we should perhaps meanwhile turn our attention in turn to the Reverend Grundy, not yet comfortable with the idea of orgiastic copulation over aeons, courtesy of the divine flame, however ancient. Sexual fantasy was indeed the first full dress rehearsal for the real performance, and (at the risk of being accused of merely punning) this first full mental address – the word here used in its verbal sense – gave us our first fully realised mental addresses (nouns) sufficient for all subsequent mental rehearsals, images imprinted in the cortex as fully conscious images.

Chapter 15 On Thinking

Moreover the very same images are, I believe, still there, the lingam still firmly imprinted in the lingo, and only the concealment of the subconscious mind preserving a fragile decorum.

For the Revd G we can cite the Egyptian head god Amun (Lithic Aa-Mau'n) "Eternally both inseminator and gestator", "The Ever Loving, both sexes", crude forerunner indeed of the all encompassing love of the Christian Deity. It should perhaps be explained (see Chapter 9) Ma comprised a number of derivative semantic contents, including particularly here that of earthing of seed and thus both insemination and germination; while Latin amare, to love, from the Egyptian via the Greek, (Lithic A-ma-are), 'As when planting', the male or mali role [mali is Hindi for gardener, ma-lai, earth-leveller], as in Malaya, the Garden of Eden, or at least that peripheral hilly bit of it left above water when the melting of the circumpolar ice flooded Eden, the Eastern Garden Land, under the South China Sea. The resultant diaspora colonised both Sumer and then Babylon and then Egypt. It was Amun too who first pursued fully the drive for life after death in its most literal institutional form, again prefiguring Christian belief. This in turn may be why recent biblical scholarship has located Moses, and the Mosaic religion still professed by the Jews, in Egypt (The Fatherland in Egyptian) with Moses a priest of the Aton (the Eternal birth canal in Egyptian) and even possibly a dissident Pharaoh (The Devine Penis in Egyptian). If this were the historical pattern the congeners of the Egyptian language to be found in Malay, otherwise hard to explain, would fall into place.

Recall, after all, is the missing element in subconscious thinking, the mind retains no imprint of its activity, the job is done without a record, certainly without a record in any detail. I believe that the taming of fire and the consumption of cooked protein meals around the convivial hearth led to sexual consummations, no hair pulling needed any more, and sweet dreams thereafter, still remembered on waking. Life became all Rongo Rongo, and this had important consequences quite additional to sexual activity. There was a spin off, as so often with physical evolution. What was sauce for the sexual gander was also sauce for the mother goose. The same breakthrough into conscious appreciation of hitherto subconscious responses, what was formerly the dream on autopilot, could now after the breakthrough lead to conscious appreciation, focused attention, and to quite other diverse matters; prideful consideration for instance of tapping out a hand axe, that is the lesser delights of getting it right at work, of mastering the initially refractory medium which too turned out to yield to slick technique. Wherever there was pleasure in such ego-massage the new found mind would wander. The Scrimshaw had begun, leaving Wayland Smith behind, doomed, with just the heavy work to do.

It is necessary to point out here, to enable Mrs Grundy to return to the debate, as well as to check any young blades seeking to recapture their authentic roots, that none of this has any current implications for human thinking or conduct, other than the reflection that honesty is often the best policy for understanding. To argue that nothing has changed in a million years, or even just the thick end of it, is blatantly absurd. What has survived as an adaptive response on the part of the human physique as a result of this outburst of frenetic sexual activity long ago, with the fair sex in charge of stoking the fire all day, 24 x 7, is a degree of independence of the menstrual cycle, so that sex is available at all times, a happy circumstance we apparently share only with the Bonobo Pigmy Chimps – and they have evidently achieved it without the benefit of the hearth. We are the only two Hoka Hoka species on earth, the procreational function dumped in pursuit simply of raw stimulation, same sex as well as heterosex. It is a bizarre accident, no part of the original scheme of things (which was for genuine procreation), resulting from suddenly introduced long term

Chapter 15 On Thinking

overheating in the Pleistocene. Fascinated by the fire, the heat and the flame together, the mind has confronted and out-stared nature. It is the price we have paid for our culture. Now we are stuck with this outmoded fillip we hardly need any more.

I think the original sexual reverie is probably responsible, as much as the present promptings of the gonads, for the sexual content of so much of present day psychologising. Certainly, so far as language is concerned, the sexual prototypes of so much of the lexicon is indicative of our original favourite subject matter. I have even gone one further, suggesting that the subconscious receptacle for these original connections still feeds the conscious minds, indirectly, of each new generation as it apprehends the lexicon both consciously at the superficial (surface) level, and simultaneously at the subconscious level beneath, where the thought patterns flow free and unconstrained by too much language. Down there is the bubble-up element in our mental makeup, humanity's muse, our musings, out of the reach of Mrs Grundy and hard to control.

So far as the subconscious is concerned, it appears to be a halfway house, not wholly unconscious and inaccessible to the conscious mind as the autonomic system appears to be, but not normally recognised by the waking mind. We can remember some of our dreams and can day dream when dozing, but we lose contact with their sourcing when we consciously address them, left only with the shell without the kernel. It is this kernel which I believe Lithic language roots show to be in certain aspects sovereign. Even when awake we can get some shocking promptings from down below, our muse presenting to the waking mind meanings we never intended, triggered by who knows what or how it happens. I have already attempted to sketch spectral lines in the mental curriculum, Psi, Phi, Pi and Ro. Some or all of Psi, the intentional element anyway, originates in the subconscious, outside intentional control. It is a funnel vapouring up strange concatenations from the deeper levels of the mind. Lithic language roots are just one small part of these vapourings. In passing, the fascination of hallucinatory drugs arises in part from the apparent entrée they provide to this area of hyper-vivid primitive and mostly visual perceptions, mixed with a good deal of giddy swirling sometimes appearing yellow and submarine; but in greater part from the relaxation provided by intoxification, surrender to non-thought. Mental poisoning, it turns out, starts out as fun – courtesy of Psi. The audio frequencies of articulation are more effortful and significant than the visual and are blurred out by artificial stimulants; but their sober research is the more rewarding. That leaves tunes, threnodies which flow with rhythm, somewhere in the middle, redolent of the subconscious muse, opening channels to the inarticulate dream-time, dumping the linguistic impedimenta.

We have now introduced the two ideas of the original discriminatory distinction (d), celebrating the boundary between two different textures on the one hand, which went on to generate in the mind the straight line criterion or continuum (c); and on the other hand the unitary bounded area (d') which was then presented by d, as the prying eye of the infant closed the boundary around a nugget. For long this d' must have been a difficult concept for the inarticulate adjectival mind, texturing its universe in an overwhelming and kaleidoscopic avalanche of perceptions, with no mental handrail or any fixed points to guide it. In such a mass or mess it must surely have seemed superogative to go picking out individual nuggets (nouns) as well. Before speech was added the mind undoubtedly roamed somewhat more freely across its experimental inputs. It is useless to pretend there was no mental activity before speech. Squirrel Nutkin disproves it. But the activity was speechless, it could not make use, as we do now, of the conceptual code we find in words. So there were no stepping stones across the mental abyss. In this fix distincta appeared

Chapter 15 On Thinking

adjectival, popping up all over. Qualities were not entified or separately located. Adjectival terms answer to more or less, their application slipping into the form of a continuum. In this way the continuum virus was fed into the distinction fold; and the category was thus provided with bogus positive and negative poles. The next question we must ask therefore is what senses aided thinking in the absence of language; and the answer must surely be the visual sense. As the eye discerned the world around so the mind discerned the terms in which to think. We have been focusing our thinking ever more closely ever since, with language thinking in nuggets and labelling them, just as the world goes, and then labelling the labels, and so on and so on. It therefore might be possible, it occurred to me, to find traces of the prior thinking patterns when it came to the birth of language. In other words, I accept the view that the development of language followed upon the thinking needed to get it started. Latterly individuals may use vocabulary to stimulate thought but this is a later development. It is hard to believe that language was created from nothing, after all.

Surprisingly, it then turned out, and only after years skirting and skating around the idea, that the very patterns I had chosen in illustration of the eye's analysis of its original journeys of discovery (Figure 3, Sketches 1 to 11) do in fact appear to represent quite well some of the first informing meanings of primitive language roots. I turned my attention to the thought patterns I had drawn and deliberately attempted to label them in Lithic terms. It proved a highly educational exercise. The exercise is here repeated, without a great deal of reconsideration or review, but pretty well as it first occurred to me, with only minor re-ordering for clarity in following through the sequential stages of development of the thinking, my originals having been scribbled across the bottom of a page wherever they would fit in, in some degree of excitement.

We start with the criterion tidied to a simple line as in Sketch 12. I labelled this Pa, because I already had it in mind in company with the burgeoning side developments rounding out (Sketch 13). There is a switch between Sketch 13 and Sketch 14 where the outcome of the thinking in Sketch 14 has led to the "x" and "not x" balloons usurping the labels of the burgeoning process in Figure 13. The finality of the mental process is recognised in Figure 15 where Bai, the burgeoning, has changed to the unmarked Ba, flesh, the pregnant balloons now substantial categories. Here the logic of the pa label is reinforced as the thinned surface tangent of the burgeoned Ba, just as Pa skin is the thinned derivative tangential to ba flesh. A single burgeon may now be abstracted as exemplar of the principal semantic content of the phoneme Ba (Sketch 16). This in turn offers a redefinition of Sketch 15 as two Ba with a cleavage between them. The cleavage - from flaking flints, where the effortful strike was taken to sound like "Ka" and the resultant cleavage as the flake was, as it were, spat out, was taken to be like the lesser dental plosive Ta - is added in Sketch 17. At Sketch 18, as an aside, I have shown "Baum" (German for tree) with the completive vowel here indicating all of the tree's growth rings, of which I have only drawn four representing hundreds. At Sketch 19 I have tried to sketch a bottom or buttock, whilst at Sketch 20 I have shown a single bum or haunch. In Sketch 21 we find our original line in Sketch 12 has a double label, both Pa and Ta, the line representing both a dimension and a division. At the bottom of the page Sketches 22, 23 and 24 are from Egyptian. Sketch 22 is the hieroglyph for Pai, being a surface made up of dimensional lines. Sketch 23 is of the Tau or T, a symbol too old to date. It features in the Egyptian ansate cross or ankh. It comprises the dimensions in Sketches 9 and 10. As such it can represent the two dimensions of the surface of a flat world, or even the dimensions of space and time. It also is the symbol Two, and its arms make three rays, the ta rays, three.

Chapter 15 On Thinking

Finally there was space for the world in Egyptian, Taun, for which the glyph is a semicircle or 0 divided in two. It provides an opportunity to remark again that Egyptologists have mistaken the glyph for a bun, pronouncing it just ti. The under half is Dua Taun, the second world of the dead and the dead sun as it passes under the earth (which was taken to be a disc), gestating in darkness each night before its rebirth on the Eastern horizon each day. Dua Taun is thought to be the Dwat in academic circles.

Bearing in mind the abstraction of a single line from a crooked boundary (Sketch 2) is already a recognition of such as representing a continuum too (because both are just lines), it struck me "Pa" and "Ta" might well be treated as serving as markers for the two directions on this line of double derivation, and so as nodes, apt in turn to be identified as male on top and female thereunder, which is why I have put the labels top and bottom (Sketch 21). These labels are elementary Lithic phonemes, not yet words as we understand them, it must be remembered. There is still a good deal of unstructured swirling in the Lithic mind. We are shaping our thinking and then giving utterance to the labelling. There is a paradox when we subject this to present day customary thinking, because we regard words for things as simples, and abstract shapes and concepts as a posteriori, whereas I am turning it the other way about. The explanation of the paradox is simple: our customary thinking, after aeons of language, tongue wagging in effect, is wrong. We thought in shapes before we thought in words. There is a good deal of evidence, from primitive science, that subjective minds still thought mostly in shapes even after their tongues had been wagging for a comparatively long time. This almost comes to saying before we spoke we mathematicised. Thinking was that difficult, and there was no notation. The math of course stayed simple. Some of the evidence is scratched on rocks as symbols for which anthropologists and archaeologists have been searching for crudities as meanings, without success. Spirals are perhaps the pathetic mementos of the whirligigs of the giddy untutored mind trying to home in on a definition but finding a purchase unobtainable, the whorl its only utterance. Cups are similarly abrasions from dizzy screwing with a hard stone or flint to uncover the essential shape it presented, Adam delving, the product of frustrated mind seeking to relieve its emptiness, to pattern the inane, to escape the nausea. Aesthetes can derive comfortable backing from some of this: here was man the artist while still in his birthday suit expressing himself in primitive art forms before his mind was pinched and trammelled by repressive civilisation. But I see these signs as simply cries of pain, like the mentally disturbed rocking back and forth, or the severely religious similarly in traumatic confrontation with their god.

To continue with the line drawings, consider the ongoing development of Pa in Sketch 2 on its own account. It does not curl round. It can only repeat itself (Sketch 22) extending sideways. This after all quite precisely copies the movements of the eye in panning or scanning any scene, particularly a whole panorama, which is simply Greek for the pan or whole coverage of what the eye (Ra from the Egyptian) consumes (Ma from the Lithic) or takes in. I have drawn ten stripes and you can picture them as close together as you like, sweeping out a surface. Moreover Pa has been identified already (Sketch 15) as tangential to Ba, the burgeoning (fleshy) bits. The surface indicated by vertical hachures in Sketch 22 is therefore skin; with the phonetics (Pa the thinned diminutive of Ba as skin or surface) making it a triangulation, surely enough to convince an ox – or a hominid – once presented. So surfaces, we now know, comprise extensions in two dimensions, a Tau or T, see Sketch 23. Sketch 23 in fact shows up the shortcomings of my Sketch 22. Clearly Pa is replicable in both directions like Ba, not just in one direction as I showed it. The Tau shows the two dimensions of any surface; and there are two more dimensions,

Chapter 15 On Thinking

space and time, which it is sometimes taken to represent also; as well as the idea of two in the first place. I rather fancy the semantic root of three in turn is from the Rays of the Tau, there are three: alas, another dialectical intrusion with mystical connotations for musing on. The wise old owl, speaking in Lithic, would howl "terwit terwoo". Howling already has an i, an a and a u (the h was a Cockney h separating two consecutive vowels, one of which is then apt to be dropped in colloquial speech. In the case of the owl's hoot the h was doing double duty, for trauma and for cockney duty together). Ter wit ter wau, is very wise and very doubly wise, for witches who can read it. For long, witchcraft was a poor man's Marxism, stuck with their dialectic, mind and matter in a crazy waltz together. Can we draw the parallel: Marxism as the modern man's witchcraft? The Egyptian owl, by the way, was a more down to earth bird and spoke a different coarser lingo, saying "Aa Mahoo", Always both Ma, viz darkness and death in Egyptian. He was a nocturnal marauder, and the Mau (all the Mas) fixed him later in glyph as the bird for alphabetic M, and he is a lot easier to draw than a vulture.

The Egyptian glyph for Taun (Sketch 24) was a circle cut in half, regarded as a bun by Egyptologists. T represented by a bun instead of Taun, the world, represented by a picture of it. Ah well! This was because the whole circle, the lip shape for "oo", was an O, as it still is for us. Their idea of the sublunary world was a flat disc like a penny with a dome shaped stone fly cover over it. The other half of the gismo, the underside of the penny, similarly domed, was the Dua Taun or Second World (misconstrued by the Egyptologists as simply "Duat") ruled over by the dead sun as it travelled across West to East, to be reborn into our Taun and blaze afresh in the sky like Osiris (really Au Sarai in the original Egyptian, Universal Sunrise, promising rebirth after death for all, like the Christian God later). The sky or Heaven was Pai Taun in Egyptian, Roof of the Universe, (misconstrued by the Egyptologists as "Pet", more like a spit). The original prototypical roof for Semites in the desert was made of goatskins. The divided unity can be drawn both halves together, it can even be unity dividing, and thus a parturition, in which case the O might be taken as the birth canal. The birth canal opens and rounds out to pass the head of the infant in a truly astonishing manner – and they say it hurts – bound to have caught the attention of our simple forebears. The Egyptian Aton, which the Egyptologists think is the disc of the sun, is really the Aa-ta-oon, the Everlasting-Birth-Canal, the sun which is born from the dark Dua Taun at Dawn and dies diving into the sea at dusk, simultaneously birthing light into the world at sunrise each day, and dowsing the light at night. Perhaps there should be a pause here to explain this ancient poetry. The Egyptian mind in ancient times saw the world as a peep show with successive scenes presented, and these repetitive becomings they articulated as repetitive births, scenic shots. For linguistic purposes, the oo could be the literal round orifice required to make the sound or equally its abstracted signification of totality, in both instances equally using its shape to derive its meanings. The universe was thus the totality of events rather than the totality of locations we think of today.

What I have tried to show with the 25 sketches in Figure 3 is that the mind started out with shapes. I shall be told by academics I have trawled up a whole lot of quite unreliable dream material which can neither be proved nor disproved and it is therefore unscientific, anecdotal (just gossipy) and not worth pursuing. That is why I have included the Egyptian which has linguistic links and the semantics are therefore open to debate, proof or disproof. It may be the material is less unreliable than unwelcome to academics bent on publishing their own concoctions based on rather different semantic prepossessions. In any case, all the linguistic connections should properly be taken into account before deciding they are insufficient to provide a convincing statistical base of correlations. All of science is in

Chapter 15 On Thinking

reality ultimately statistical. Those who decline to be persuaded of the validity of the linguistic points of contact with the semantic catenas worked out in this study of Lithic should be asked to devise another arbitrary scheme of their own as complex and wide ranging in scope without anything to do with Lithic, which can exhibit anyway near a similar number of points of contact with language today, in order to show the Lithic correspondences worthless. Or even to just name two they know already.

The central mystery is still how the synapses in the brain come to prompt for the ideas in the mind. It is hard to see how any electronic state of play can at the same time simply be an idea. Recently an indication was vouchsafed me when new digital hearing aids restored sensitivity to a range of higher notes which had been missing for me for very many years, blurring many of the consonants beyond recognition, since I had the misfortune to get blown up while still quite young and had both my ear drums blown in. The machines immediately reintroduced the missing frequencies but the brain no longer knew how to interpret them. Were they sounds or flavours or visual inputs? It took months (but not many) to recover the full proper audio-responses to the inputs of sounds from the hearing aids, so that the dawn chorus came fully back to life and the consonants lined themselves up once more with the utterances with which speech presented me. The translation of the raw signals and the brain's responses to them to picture, sound, idea, etc is by no means a simple matter, it is a skill which has to be learned. The skill is mysterious and subconscious and perhaps it will always remain so.

Meanwhile it is not irrational to conduct research just as if there actually were a little manikin in there monitoring the brain's performance. The mind has those characteristics in its own performance precisely, learning as it goes along. For all practical purposes there is a virtual ghost in the machine, anyway as long as the machine stays alive, doing its thinking for it. You can not stuff the mind into the brain (as we understand it). It won't go. Maybe it is the brain which needs to go back to the drawing board, and the cognitive linguistics buffs along with it.

CHAPTER 16

CONCLUSIONS

This chapter is included to answer in some measure the question often privately formulated if seldom put: why bother? Authors, especially those aspiring to scientific status to teach the senators wisdom, are inclined to attach too many lessons to their lucubrations. But now that the book is written there is little point in pretending I do not believe in it. It certainly seems to me there is an epochal element in the discovery of Lithic language, not only for semantics but also for the whole field of epistemology and even – at one remove – for mathematics, logic and the philosophy of science itself, which I believe must now recognise even math as derived from the original simple utterances of our hominid forebears. In no way is science thereby impugned, rather it is instated as in most ways the best thinking we have managed so far. But it is still just language. With such expanses of advancement already to our credit by means of the powers of thinking, we must conclude it is premature to draw any conclusions as to what more may or may not be achieved. Certainly in linguistic studies Pandora's box is at least and at last forced ajar. But the work that remains to be done should dwarf progress achieved to date, so that within the present century any contribution my study of Lithic language roots may have made will most probably be ignored and forgotten in the cataract of perceptions to follow, weaving a whole web of interconnected studies and research programmes and leaving my few original semantic catenas looking naked and uninspired. My book, if it is still read at all, will be read just for the patter. In short, the Lithic paradigm is a fertile one.

Fifteen years ago the overall Lithic scheme was presented to Penguin Books and the friendly advice was unequivocal (delivered by my sister's brother-in-law who worked there): forget it if you do not wish to be pilloried as a maverick sex maniac. It has to be admitted that the sexual content has if anything increased rather than diminished since then. But this is because the mania is shared with every reader, since if we go back far enough - it is an edifying process in itself - we all have the same forebears and it is their Stone Age mania, not mine. It may be the reader will still wish to slay the messenger; but that would be a pity since some understanding of how we have thought and therefore how we think today is essential for the understanding which everyone seeks. In a permissive age when the internet runs on porn a sober approach to digging up prehistoric sexual images can surely be expected and even tolerated. At eighty eight years of age the subject matter is viewed objectively and not as a substitute for indulgence – as some may try to claim. We should not view our Stone Age forebears with over-riding disdain. They had no television, no universities, no philosophy or politics worth the name, only the experience of daily living with which to occupy their minds, and little in the way of language. In the same circumstances it seems indisputable modern Sapiens Sapiens would share the same mania today: our principal life work is still to be fruitful and multiply and our principal interest is sexual – now expressed pictorially on television and in the art museums and even in schools. Internet computing, as well as the writing it brings in its train, is already closing libraries, and dumbing down culture with soft and hard porn. In fact the internet is said to be largely hard funded by the hard porn photographic filming it offers. That says a lot about Sapiens Sapiens: the sap still runs, and we are inevitably its

Chapter 16 Conclusions

victims; as well as its beneficiaries, if we know that we can at least play our cards so that civilisation may win.

If you have really read this far you will by now likely be getting impatient for the use and purpose of the work, if any. This can not of course be made the touchstone for research, which can therefore prove to be entirely fruitless at the end of the exercise. Otherwise a distortion is introduced from the beginning. However Lithic, as it happens, is invaluable as an educational tool. First of all it puts us all in our place, not entirely estranged from the rest of the animal kingdom, but nevertheless with a uniquely quirky mind often subject to promptings which may not be entirely rational because they arise from our subconscious store of old saws and far from modern instances, which we have picked up over hundreds of millennia. Secondly it puts us in serious debt to our hominid forebears, whose burden of often rather silly ideas we still carry within ourselves below the level of conscious knowledge. There is nothing demeaning in that. We have our skill at heart beats etc from much more primitive forebears. We are a patchwork of abilities and functions, a bit like the Sphinx which is a patchwork of different animals, both carnivore and vegetarian, with a human head stuck on top. Was it meant to be us? I guess it was.

It would be wrong to conclude we have learned nothing important in the last ten thousand years since the Sphinx was carved. We have learned almost everything that makes us what we are. But we need to remember we carry a (subconscious) ball and chain we are not going to escape in another ten thousand years. So much for the theory of everything improbablists are already singing about. They are scientists rhapsodising without the least knowledge of the history and limitations of human thinking, since it can not be empirically addressed; and so they have not addressed it.

Writing on the origins of speaking and basing conclusions on diverse and thinly spread indications in an over rich medium - the world lexicon - is open to challenge as unscientific. There will always be the call for more evidence. Evidence will also keep turning up; both for and against. The truth is science of every kind is in this position; the search for understanding is an amalgam of our own making. It is not the uncovering of a hard reality previously obscured by muddled thinking that most people would accept – the model scientists follow. On the contrary it is simply the invention of the right thinking for doing the job in hand, based on indications, many of them quite slight. Think about the "colours" and "flavours" of sub-atomic "particles" and their constituents; or spend a morning with Einstein and his spatial distortions. It takes quite a bit of habituation before any of this appears "hard"; and it is then the habituation which does it, not the evidence. This is an alarming truth since it implies we are suspended over an abyss supported by nothing more than the accumulated detritus of our own grey matter, no more than a gossamer safety net at best to keep us from the intellectual abyss. But anyone confronting the basic constituents of our linguistic achievements and the thinking that has gone with it, much of it whimsical and some of it preposterous, is bound to come up against these realities. It encourages a proper scepticism and should therefore really be part of the national curriculum in schools, if only to discourage unrealistic meliorism on the one hand and hard posturing leading to terrorism on the other. But claiming that the foolishness which has provided the universal pabulum, and received widespread support over aeons, is not intellectually correct (IC) is not going to be all that popular, since it challenges the intelectual pecking order. An anti-IC stance is even more unpopular than an anti-PC one. Inviting the senators to move over is a recipe for confrontation. The only sane position is to invite the public to the ringside to see the fun; perhaps even to witness an execution, and decide upon the blame. This indeed is the purpose for which this book is written. I have

Chapter 16 Conclusions

no fear, as I will almost certainly be dead already before its impact is recognised – or else I will be 117 years old. Thirty years is the average time it takes for any new ideas to achieve more than minimal notice or recognition.

Next most important, the skids are at last under dialectical thinking, a miasma perhaps even older than speaking. Not even the most intellectual academic, nor the most unintelligent bozo can in future aspire to this kind of short cut to omniscience any more. Chapter 15 on the origins of thinking identifies the errors underlying the dialectic and is an assault upon ideology. In the context of the open society and its enemies, any rebuke to ideological pretentions must surely be benign. Neitzsche freaks and skinheads alike can anyway draw no comfort from their Lithic heritage, simply because of its risible element. The Uber-mensch has feet of clay like the rest of us. Hitler was the classic Superman but really an egomaniac buffoon, stuck in his Fascist ideology, and unable to escape because he was unwilling to face the challenge of confronting his own beliefs.

Hominid status was not an honourable one; and pride in our origins is raucously amusing. You might almost as well ardently wish to be a monkey. Fascism and terrorism are two sides to the same violent, atavistic and autistic mania, the terrorist worshiping his own club foot in search of the feelgood factor, which must ever escape him unless he capitulates: for he can never overcome his illusions unless he is first of all prepared to lose them, and from this his egotism bars him. He remains thus a spiteful prisoner ranting in the psychic cage he has locked himself in, yowling and catawauling rather than singing, and killing in the meantime in the hope of breaking the bars. His blacks and whites are grays for the rest of us, and we are right and the Usamas are playing the monkey role. The proliferation of terror is a spin off from German Nazism and Russian Communism, with Mid East copycat Baathism, and now jihadism, a privatisation of totalitarian terror - as nice an example as anyone could wish of the pervasiveness of ideological mental posturing regardless of overt content or belief. What is unbelievable to the terrorist Bin Laden and his fellow Wahabi jihadi religionists (actually Moslem heretics) is obvious enough to the objective observer without the terrorist ideology, which comes all the way from the prehistoric Black Goddess Kali worshiped at Mecca before The Prophet rescued the Quaraishi tribe from their pagan idolatry.

Our present urchin mind-set however can not help him; and Europe as a political organisation remains firmly Fascist even today, the democratic deficit glaring and even brazenly flaunted in Brussels, the new world capital of Fascism with (hopefully) just the genocide left out. Voting "No!" to Fascism is described as a failure to communicate with the people, who have in turn failed to understand that they really want the Fascist Super State. There is even in the European Union a trace of the Black Goddess Kali whose rules require the abuse and punishment of non believers by deceiving, robbing and if possible by garotting them while sleeping, on the grounds those not with you are against you. Her home base appears to have been in Arabia before Mohammed. It is a desert song. A cold coming they had of it. Her followers in India practising Thuggee (the garotting of fellow travellers, whence the English thug) were expelled in the fourteenth century to become Gypsies, because after being expelled again for the same anti social behaviour from Egypt in turn they pretended they were Egyptians, gaining bonus marks with Kali for deceiving the goy in Eastern Europe as to their origins. (The Turks called them Roma as Westerners). They had picked up some Egyptian folk magic which proved of use to frighten the goy too. The Egyptian Great Gods however can not approve of this deception, effectively taking their names in vain, and a thorough-going curse in Ancient Egyptian in the name of any one of the Egyptian Enead (their nine Great Gods) will send genuine

Chapter 16 Conclusions

Gypsies scurrying for their lives in hours, where the law takes months or years. You may have doubts about the power of the Egyptian Great Gods in these modern times but Gypsies have none, fearful of their past misdemeanours coming back to haunt them.

With all savage beliefs the necessity is to confront them. The only way to break the vicious circle is to educate the Gypsies together with their fellow citizens, which is an offence against Kali's rules and finally breaks their bondage when She is seen to be impotent. Until then religious belief in Kali, a mirage arising from the cruel waterless desert, will continue to put them in hostile confrontation with unbelievers as a matter of their eventual salvation with Kali. The Wahabi tradition is from Kali. It is not a Moslem tradition, but its opposite. It was in fact what the Prophet rebelled against. His jihads (vigorous actions) were against his own tribal elders, who worshiped the Black Goddess and the black meteorite which fell at Mecca in prehistoric times, which they took to be Her calling card declaring them Her chosen people. The Prophet rededicated it to Allah on capturing Mecca.

The dialectical idiom is an early and long established one, relatively harmless in moderation but poisonous as an imperative. Dialectic stipulates that whenever you have two related terms in apposition the position is one of opposition. (The detailed analysis, and refutation, is exhaustively covered in chapter 15, on thinking). So ka is antithetic to la, as la is to ma; and ma is to ish and perhaps sa is to ta, with ta antithetic to ka. In semantic terms ka, strike, is antithetic to la, lapse; and la, slight/light, is antithetic to ma, heavy and dark; and ma, dark to sa, bright; and sa, single to ta, split into two, and ta, (naturally become) to ka, (forcefully made). But then we find other pairings: so sa, easy and sweet, is antithetic to la, sly and bitter; and there will be many others but the point is made. These few examples establish the pattern that has heavily influenced human thinking. In chapter 15 it is argued that it was the three vowels which originally triggered the perception. It can also be seen that the vowels are in some sense a legacy from our pre-linguistic past. They are a left over from our tonal howls and cries before we learned to speak by utilising the consonant sounds to break up our cries into the manageable (because precisely reproducible) sequential pieces of speech. What atavistic folk memories they must conjure up in our subconscious minds! Our conscious minds are just the icing on the enormous sponge cake made in the paleolithic kitchens down below. Simple distinction is an early achievement of the human brain. Perhaps it is a pointer to the fact that from the outset prelinguistic thinking was on the road to the dialectic: divide in two, to and fro, there and back, a ping pong in the mind, fallacious ab initio; but nevertheless highly revealing as our road to abstraction. If we go back to the nursery wallpaper in chapter 15 we can see the first perception of the world around us was triggered by the contrast between visual textures. It was a novelty arising from the emergence out of the darkness of the womb into the blazing light of day, and the newly opened eye fastening in the light upon (for example) the contrast of being red and not being red. It was the origin of the tyranny of the eye, pernicious in the absence of further and subsequent ratiocination admitted as evidence. Although prior to language, dialectic does not hold priority over linguistic thinking, and even less over mathematics, a later spin-off from language, now treated as if it provided a direct access to ultimate reality rather than being merely a triumphant composition of the human mind. Klaus Fuchs, a nuclear physicist who spied for Russia, betrayed his tennis club, his family and his country – in that order – because he did not understand this, and could not break free from the Marxist dialectical thinking. Ah well!

More importantly however, the workings of the subconscious mind, indeed its very existence as a calculating entity conscious of semantics on its own, is evidenced by Lithic

Chapter 16 Conclusions

language survival. Freud had a subconscious he patterned rather unconvincingly with egos, ids, etc., supposed entities he picked from his own dream world. The Lithic subconscious is a bit different, with no real dragons apparent. It is not difficult to understand: the lexicon is made up of sounds with semantic contents and the catena leading to the subconscious, which I do not believe can be broken, goes like this. Lithic language roots are evidenced world wide, originating in the psychosemantic promptings of the aboriginal hominid mind some hundreds of thousands of years ago. They could not be, because of the rate of linguistic change and the noise or blurring this generates, unless there were a means of refreshment in place and continually at work. No such refreshment mechanism can be detected in the conscious mind, which is why academia has denied the possibility of such Lithic survival – and therefore and thenceforth omitted to look for it. But it now follows as day follows night the refreshment does occur, but in another place – in the subconscious.

Jung went on to posit a store for psychological archetypes (of his choice) in a metaphysical World Soul or universal mind from which we mortals' minds were all dependent - shades of Platos mental archetypes in the cave - and to which the privileged at least were able to gain access by insight. He thought this was his unique discovery. Well it was. Like all discoveries in the mind they often come with a wodge of personal predilections. He effectively located the subconscious he claimed to be able to read, decyphering the archetypes, as out there in the other, and not part of the individual mind at all. It has to be said too he thought the discovery the reward for his intellectual virtue. His was of course a clerical mind, his father was a cleric. He was also of course of Hitler's generation, though to tell him so would have been to him poison. The Lithic hypothesis in stark contrast keeps everything within the bounds of science, with the subconscious using solely the semantics implicit in the language sent down to it, and the ability to express its self-generated contents available only to its own individual owner, its partner in the same body, knowing only the language it has learned. There is no call for any invention of etherial entities or soul media with broadcasting potential, or for sublimation of location. or action at a distance such as Jung prayed in aid.

There is nothing in Lithic which is not in the lexicon if seriously interrogated. Jung's universal mind is rescued by Lithic from the transcendental limbo in which he left it. The vapourings are traced to their true source, the subconscious mind every individual has. It goes back a long way. At base some say there is even a crocodile mind which some psychopaths discover and summon to the surface - though we were never crocodiles. But there could be some bogies down there nearly as nasty.

The Lithic elements discovered in the foregoing chapters are no more than remnants of the grammar of Ur Speech (the supposed language), which in itself we can never hope to recover, for all those reasons the obscurantists offer for curtailing etymology. Lithic nevertheless is of acute significance. As a first grammar it is a more fundamental guide to the operations of the human mind than the transformational version we apparently contrived, according to Naom Chomsky, aeons later, which is based on speech as we know it, with strings of words looking for ways of conveying meanings more and more precisely, and probably finding them in a slow build up of rules designed to aid understanding. It is understanding which has been the goal from day one, an ambition which is still what makes us believe our world goes round the sun. It is a fact of life you need to understand. It does in fact make the world go round – not love, but the love of comprehension, the eureka feeling, which is much the same as plain love, the recognition of the other and making it your own without any restraint or reservation whatsoever. So force yourself or

Chapter 16 Conclusions

not, you have to go over the ground in pursuit of understanding, and this includes these days examining instinctive drives, including the most subconscious, as well as their perversions. You must be a rapist, a mutilater of the human form, you must rejoice in the brutal castration by your own hand of your enemies (with an obsidian knife?), and the wholesale slaughter of the innocents. In short you must explore the whole spectrum of humanity and not shrink from it – of course only in the mind – forcing your attention on the most perverse perversities and vilest acts which naturally (if you have been even averagely brought up) you shie away from. Needless to say you may roam the fair uplands of love and affection as well, as antidote to the other, but this you are likely to do of your own ambition in any case.

In the foregoing chapters some exercise has been had of the semantic processes whereby meanings have proliferated and diversified, along with the underlying human whimsy which comes largely from our underground store of arcane associations thrusting through to consciousness in largely unrecognisable form; so that, for very many, full awakefulness is never achieved. Potentially we are all zombies, and it is from a very long line of zombies we all proceed, more savage than noble. I have represented the development of speech patterns as spun by Scrimshaw man and Wayland Smith. Scrimshaw precises and constructs, working as if carving a filigree in ivory. You can think of him in caricature as Old Chalky, the Alistair Sims antediluvian schoolmaster. Wayland meanwhile hammers away at his own devices, slovening and slurring for an easy pronunciation, and often spoiling Scrimshaw's finesse.

With bind and bund, pond and pen, open or unpen, even with the Latin ripa for river bank and English trap, to draw shut (the lid) we can, if we try hard, discern an underlying common element which can perhaps be represented by something like the word enclosure. But to understand why words have the meanings they do it is always necessary to expand them back to their full original forms and then examine the underlying elements of meaning they comprise emanating from their constituent phoneme strings. Astoundingly, if this Lithic Hypothesis is correct, it is possible to uncover the original symbolisations attributed to the constituent phonemes. Thus what in the above bind-pen group is disclosed is the idea of enclosure, of surrounding even, which survives and resides in the subconscious of mankind, reinstalled for each generation as they learn to speak. Of course this goes against the grain of conventional thinking, because we long ago stopped indulging in this kind of analysis, and it is only in the subconscious that the traces of the methodology still survive. It is the poet's blind bran dip. By definition if it is subconscious it is something we are unaware of, so critics will abound. No evolutionary hard wiring is required: the Lithic Hypotheses supercede the genetic hard wiring of Chomskyan and the Massachusets Institute of Technology's (MIT's) neuro-linguistics.

The p consonant certainly seems to get its enclosure meaning from being the thinned version of the phoneme Ba, which is installed in the subconscious as the sound of flesh on flesh from the lips when saying b. P, the thinned version of b which suggests flesh, is thus identified as the thinned version of flesh and so the skin (which surrounds and covers the flesh), leading to surface, lid, roof, cover and then enclosure (a semantic bus). Whereupon - and this illustrates the signature tune or modus operandi of the subconscious mind - the enclosure idea picked up by p feeds back to the prior b. B, as well as flesh, acquires a blocking or bunging function. We may learn from this that in subconscious thinking there are no crisply discriminated categories or pecking orders, as in our waking thinking, but a fuzzier inconsequential relationship of semantic drift. If there is a phonetic contiguity there is a semantic pathway. Meanings flow, travelling in a bus. The neural networks involved with phonetics and semantics evidently mingle. A wide-awake state is needed to separate them and keep them separated.

The late Jacques Derrida's deconstructionism has been regarded as iconoclastic and chaotic, but it was intended as the reverse: as an eye-opener to the richness of interconnected meanings accessible in any text. A text is a phonetic string with associated semantic contents. Derrida launched a broadside caveat against simple deductive thinking. He was clearly aware of the subconscious pot pourri over which our waking rational thinking is carried on a gossamer surface. To be sure rational deduction is not to be sneezed at. Scientific conventions are not contra-indicated. But it does seem Derrida, like Eric Partridge, and perhaps the later Wittgenstein, was half way to understanding Lithic. The Lithic Hypotheses too amount to a "propositional reconstructionism", and in order to reconstruct thinking it is necessary to prick the facade of convention. The way we think is simply the way we think. Thinking is not set in Platonic forms. If a new way demonstrates its utility by providing the stretch to cover the facts as they become known it will be adopted. Admittedly an Einstein is sometimes needed to break the mould, to make a lateral side-step with a new approach rearranging the scenery. But at other times the side step virtually presents itself.

The discovery of burnt bones from seventy thousand years ago, and some snail shells in Western Cape Province in South Africa with holes in and signs of wear from threading, has recently led to a reiteration (with a bit of updating) of some of the old and thoroughly suspect dates of crucial cultural landmarks in the history of man. Because writing began in the last ten thousand years it was guessed speaking should be about four times older. The guess was quite groundless; but as nobody knew any better, the views of the academic establishment were allowed to stand unchallenged. It is in any case no matter of concern. The indications from Lithic of a much longer period of time since our hominid forebears began to speak, say a hundred times longer than the common belief quite recently, for instance, is similarly a matter of no fundamental concern. We have come the way we have come at the pace at which we have come. Since the time scale is anyway very long, even a factor of a hundred is not a principal matter for contention. It may be we brought with us our barbarous mentality even longer than is suggested in these chapters. But there seems no reason to assume it, and there is no call for repentance just because I continue to prefer to relate hominid thinking and the origins of speaking to a far remoter period than academia currently allows. Dating is a modern fetish we do not need to share. The timing of prehistoric change is not critical and the accepted timing of the invention of speech is now getting extended almost from day to day. If it goes on the same they will eventually catch up with my six hundred thousand years since we began to speak. We were hominids then. What a blessing. We are aeons from their sexualityand simplicities.

Whatever one may think of Chomsky, his transformational grammar is self evidently a late construct, irrelevant to any enquiry as to the origins of speaking. The origins are prior. How any transformational grammar might in turn have originated is a quite separate study. The transformational subconscious is certainly one which could take a Lithic performance in its stride, and perhaps vice versa it could be argued a Lithic subconscious might well get up to a bit of transformation later. In any case I suspect our original idioms, still traceable today, will have been involved. They will not be welcome to a wrangler of mathematical bent, heir to a long line of mathematically minded language buffs. But these were his forebears as well as ours, whose thinking I have tried to expose. Words are certainly neither integral nor original and language is learned most readily phoneme by phoneme.

Chapter 16 Conclusions

Writing is the same, and letter by letter is the way to teach it, making use of an idiom the mind has accommodated for hundreds of millennia and many thousands of generations.

Philosophers should take warning from Aristotle. His whole world was one of fantasy. His aether was an insubstantial and so incorruptible element making up all celestial objects, with a natural propensity to move, drawn round the centre of the universe in circles. Air was considered insubstantial. Gases were not yet identified. Wind was evidence of the propensity of the insubstantial to get drawn out, just like other things. The ether was 'ai-tahei-arai', from the Lithic 'that which-vagina-rayed' - and so drawn out just like the male genitalia whenever they encountered these feminine rays - but being celestial the pull for the ether was of course perfectly circular, an eye watering prospect, and windy.

It took two millennia to shake the human mind free from this miasma, during which time, when it proved incorrect, epicycles had been added tier after tier to save the aether from abandon. Aristotle also had the universe composed of four substantial elements, earth, air, fire and water. Earth was massive because it tended to the centre of the earth. With Lithic Ma, in chapter 10, was down, being the opposite of Ish, the flame, which is up (the flame springs upwards); and so in Lithic phonemes ma was earth (inter alia) which is solid and heavy matter and tends downwards, maintaining the pattern of the Lithic dialectic. The old man had grubbed the science out of his subconscious, just like Hegel and Marx who disinterred the dialectic itself somewhat later. Air belonged above the surface of the earth where it sat passive and immobile. It was not going anywhere until tugged, just like the trouserless boys in the age of the Pleistocene. For Aristotle fire went upwards because its home was at the top of the universe. Like our hominid forebears he had spotted the flame leaps upwards unlike solid objects which possessed ma and tended downwards (if dropped for instance). His water belonged on the surface of the earth, hugged by it as it were, the other boy in the family. Our hominid forebears had liquids instinctively lapsing sideways down sloping surfaces diagonally into the lows, which to my way of thinking was a more accurate characterisation than Aristotle's when you think how puddles form and rivers flow; but they were quite closely related. That left fire and earth making up the girls team, as life sources but adding matter only. The boys were claiming the spiritual and structural element, almost as if they were the architects with an element of divinity. They knew nothing, or anyway very little about the birds and the bees, but they had probably divined they contributed some kind of permissive input or know-how by vouchsafing conjugation, seen as an opening process – they had evidently explored the hymen with their grubby fingers.

As a last and capstone work, I have kept Aphrodite as a bon bouche for those who have read the rest of the book all through. Apparently she came ashore riding in an outsize conch shell, after generation from the sea foam (apparently thought of as Zeus's ejaculate) in a particular bay in Cyprus, as I have cause to remember, since some considerable time later I found myself rescuing a soldier being inexorably swept out to sea, without any shell to ride on, from the very same bay. Our very different treatments by Father Neptune was, I believe, due solely to the two sides of the bay, the West side the tide sweeps in and the East side it sweeps out, as must have been known in Ancient Greece but had been forgotten since. I was lucky to discover Aphrodite's secret just in time, and we were washed up on the other side of the bay after an exhausting swim round on the way to Turkey. The boy had cut his foot on a rock and so let his leg hang down as a sail in the current with me thrashing in the opposite direction coastwards. Friends shouted encouragement as we sailed past the Eastern headland on our way out: they would fetch a boat from Larnaca, some fifteen kilometers away. They might as well have asked the

Chapter 16 Conclusions

Turkish coast guards to keep an eye out for us. As hero of the episode I am proud to say I never thought to drop him off and let him sail away to Turkey on his own; but then the water was warm and welcoming just as it was no doubt for Aphrodite when she sailed in – although she apparently stayed dry and alluring aboard her shell.

Aphrodite was the Greek goddess of carnal love, and Lithic analysis can show it. We do not need to follow the etymologists amongst the ancient Greeks who appear to have got the sea foam rubric from the –phro- bit. From Aa-pahei-rau-dai-tai in Lithic elements we may surely read aa, extensive-pahei rau, all the phaluses in arousal- dai, does, -tai, her vagina; or, more loosely "Without cease her vagina is sending every erect phalus its rousing call". With such a performance it is hardly surprising the Greeks unanimously adopted Her as their goddess, and the very exemplar of erotic love. Eros himself, the mischievous putty of arousal, Lithic a-i-rau (s), he-of-all the rays or erections, with his comical minuscule priapism, later airbrushed out altogether so he was given instead a small bow and arrow for the job, was by comparison just hinting. The Lithic Ai-rau(s) for Eros and eroticism at any remove of grammar is easy enough if you understand the sex rays the genitalia were supposed to exchange in olden times, leading to arousal; and are aware the final vowel –u is a completive one: Eros is Ai-rau-s, he of the dual (or reciprocal interacting) rays, with the Greek substantive terminal –s. He was an ever ready (sexual) rayer for all: the sex principle as understood at that time. He was pictured as a cupid, but he was basically a psychosemantic concept arising from the subconscious mind, very much like Lithic language in fact.

Apart from the childishness of the minds which wrapped themselves round these ideas there is some guidance to be gleaned from them on the way we were thinking. First of all, who and where exactly was this potent lady Aphrodite, and how was she able to perform her function in life so omnipresently in everybody´s bed at once, cajoling and inspiring with a single purpose in mind. The answer is of course she was a mental or psychic entity and not a separate personality at all. She was to be found within the subconsciousness of every individual reminded of her. She was eroticism as it presented itself instinctively to each and every hombre. Where the mind was, there she was, potentially anyway. In other words the erotic instinct was in her recognised as mediated by the conscious mind from promptings from elsewhere. She was a straightforward psychic entity as we would say today. The elsewhere was not understood since the self itself was not yet fully isolated from the environment, and so the subconscious was quite readily treated as a separate party, an outsider – in this case the goddess Aphrodite as with other Greek gods, all representing psychic outputs of one kind or another, mostly mischievous and over sexed. There was a time when this was new: Aphrodite was news. She was discovered. The psyche was still largely being lived by natural influences, internal and external alike, without much conscious attention. But now she was recognised and named doing it, labelled for reference and debate. She was the recognition of subconsciousness in an important area, a half way stage on the way to consciousness of our own independent (conscious) selves. Her role was contemporary and perhaps a trifle illiberal by modern day standards. Nowadays these kinds of gods and goddesses are still to be found chiefly in India, with a substantial pantheon. The Lithic language can be seen to have been first of all absolutely explicit as to its function, pathfinding, stark even; but later probably simply repeated parrot fashion without any conscious understanding of its construction. Aphrodite thus marked our early fixation on sex, like so much else in the primitive lexicon. She was living through us, or better we were being lived by her, all the way from our first hominid compilation of the elements of the lexicon, our Lithic Language – just as today we

Chapter 16 Conclusions

are vulnerable to our subconscious promptings which can pull to pieces our consciously constructed personas, leading to "nervous breakdowns" in the modern jargon.

The full and explicit recognition has been sent back down below again, wiped from the slate of conscious attention, as if it were never meant to be brought to the surface in the first place. Freud spotted some of this but unfortunately improvised the semantic contents to suit his personal (drugged) whimsy. But perhaps that is to press the implications in Aphrodite's case too far. What is more likely to my mind is that along with the whole of Lithic language its true nature was submerged over the millennia (represssed much as Freud had it) in a revulsion against the dumb crudity, the sheer animality, of our thought and behaviour at the time our hominid ancestors began to learn to speak. All over the world the species voted for humanity and shucked off their animal origins, and we have been doing it – with notable back slidings on the part of rather too many emotional runts and deviants - ever since. The coarse original semantic contents have thus been tuned out, or at least toned down over the millennia, although vouchsafed astonishing longevity in the subconscious. It is clear the common campus greeting "Hi!" in the States has come a long way from the Ancient Egyptians' glyph of a rutting drake pronounced terhei, or their glyph of a rampant penis, pronounced pa-hei, the whoopee or f...ing piece; and, bless me, this was only a few thousand years ago. The civilised revolution we are living through is as yet a new born babe.

Our humanity comes nevertheless ultimately from those very animal instincts which humans have aspired to outrun. The word defining the human species, in Lithic form "Hai-u-ma´n", "Enjoying-both[sexes]-the earthing, planting, copulating or begetting", marked the consensual conjugation, warm and cuddly together in the heat close around the hearth, which replaced the solitary chase and subjugation of the female in the rest of the animal kingdom, a flipswitch of emotional confrontations between the sexes we are as a species after a myriad generations still in the process of cementing solid. It was the women who for a few hundred millennia sat and worked around the hearth keeping the fire alight while the menfolk hunted unheated, so perhaps it was to be expected the men thought it was the women who were the nymphs, Lithic nai-em-pahei, the drawers out and presentation of their pahei in the warmth when they got back to base. It may indeed require a few more thousand generations before we win through to a uniform genotype enjoining intimate consensual unhurried gentle sexual union enjoyable by both sexes as a matter of course, rather than as an elite achievement. It may not seem much on which to base our humanity at first sight, but on reflection it opens the way of course to a mutual recognition of wants and interests which is the necessary prerequisite for civilised love and affection today. In ending, the derivation of humus makes an apt final run to clear the decks for humanity as above. There have been those who have believed humans identified themselves as the earthlings, the earthy ones. Did this direct Darwin's attention to earth worms, one wonders? Partridge glosses "human" as "the earthy one, the earth born" (sic!). It was one of his less felicitous guesses: it illustrates the propensity of the human mind to accept any nonsense if there appears to be evidence for it – in the absence of the opportunity to refer to all the evidence which Lithic offers. It may seem some way from the earth to copulation, but the fact is the linguistics relates them: they both share a common functionality, the planting of the seed; and for that reason they share the same lithic phoneme, Ma (see chapter 10). Only a little academic slip is needed to serve up rubbish. Etymology without Lithic offers nothing better than a phonetic scrabble game. Almost anything can be fitted to almost anything.

Chapter 16 Conclusions

It may seem presumptuous to pick a whole string of letters (phonemes) from a single word and then attach meanings to every single one of them, since the human mind surely does not fire with that speed and precision: there is something wrong somewhere. But then it has to be said the letters never sprung onto the page of their own accord either. It was the human mind that put them there. Why? It is surely not such a way out idea there could have been reasons for their selection. Word formation goes back a long way. It may even have been single Sapiens' signature tune when first arriving on the scene – before Sapiens Sapiens, who conceitedly fancies it was he who learned to speak, his unique achievement marking him out as uniquely intellectual. If it is true – as I believe it is – that words formed as a secondary process, from the strings of phonemes put together for the combination of their individual meanings, it will have been at a time when the human mind was indeed thinking in terms of these individual meanings. My guess is we spoke a lot slower in those days as we went through the meaning strings like an old priest fingering his beads (beads with no particular meanings, he is probably making them up as he goes). A concomitant of the formalisation of these strings grouped into words was a great saving in ratiocination. When each string had to be analysed to yield its overall meaning, often not immediately obvious for those who had never been sat down to learn their psychosemantic trees, you sometimes even needed a soothsayer for the job, like with "Mene mene tekel upharsin". The Lithic can be read as follows: Mai-nai, mass/amount/weight-protruding/presenting/showing. The repetition indicates plurality, emphasis or both: weighing weighing: you have been weighed in the balance (seven times!). Tekel: compare Hebrew shekel, a weight, from shaqal to weigh from the Lithic elements sha-i-ka-lai, action-which-make-level, action making level. The weighing pans were hanging from the ends of a stick suspended in the middle. It was the balancing action which was indicated, as if judgmental. Upharsin is from the Lithic U-pahei-are-sai'n, un-please-ing-sensed/seen-'one, seen to be displeasing, found wanting.

With words, instead of having to recapitulate the meanings of the gamut of phonemes strung along every time, only the meaning which was the end product needed to be learned in parrot fashion, in place of each of the constituent phonemic meanings and their combinatory indications. The vocabulary is then of word meanings instead of phonemic meanings. But this surprisingly leads not to less meanings, but to more, because the human mind, as it turns out, is quite capable of memorising hundreds of thousands of words and their meanings, not just the few hundred meanings initially provided by the phonemes with which speech was compiled, as it was first spoken. With prestidigitation or phosphorilisation the single word meaning is some fifteen times shorter than the constituent phonemic meanings to construct the word. It is not suggested Tarzan was into this vocabulary, but the pattern is there. Recapitulation is so much easier for us than composition or analysis. Mentally we are copy-cats, or even just parrots. We copy much better than we compose or analyse. The phonemic meanings which had enabled the human mind to break into symbolisation had become restraints, as generation after generation had each added their mickle to the semantic pile. Verbalisation, the reinvention of complex words as simples, was thus a paradigm shift probably greater than any other, perhaps the very marker which in reality distinguishes Sapiens Sapiens from his plain Sapiens predecessor, who jabbered in phonemes. It is clear the old men, the profs of the day, will have resisted the switch as they resist every paradigm switch, labelling the Babel which resulted as a judgment of God upon their contemporaries for their insolence in challenging the pre-existing Divine (Lithic) plan. Had He not spoken to their Adam in the old (unsynthetic) phonetics? Would not these new fangled tricks giving every language

Chapter 16 Conclusions

community a vocabulary of its own, quite outside the dictates of reason, lead to the dissolution of human knowledge, followed by inevitable decline back into savagery, with everyone ignorant of what they were really saying? In practice it proved quite otherwise; but one can not help sympathizing with the Babelites. It was pushing off into deep water without any obvious or proven paddle. Semantics became simply a matter of recollected usage, freeing the mind up, and in due course - well eventually - freed of the ties to phonetic structure it became possible to address the phonetics from a straight-forward technical point of view and represent them in symbols for writing. We have adopted use meanings, adaptable in use. We should not forget the power of untangling what sorts not of itself. It can enable the mind to move forward into areas previously denied to it, as in this case.

Moreover these psychosemantic promptings will today sometimes appear far fetched. Can it really have happened that such trivial indications proved powerful enough pointers to have determined meanings for all time? I believe it can. It seems there were butterflies fluttering over Ecuador long ago in the Stone Age when the human mind was in relative chaos, with little of it operating above the conscious threshold. The original psychosemantic contents I have picked out have survived in the etymological derivations of the languages we use today, not because they were ever determined for all time but just because that is what, when it came to it, just happened to match the comical mental whimsies of the human race. If we could relive the last few hundreds of thousands of years there is no reason to suppose that the same butterflies would be around in Ecuador, or that the history of human thinking would come out precisely the same again, although it might just do it. It is indeed the uniqueness of this human legacy which gives it its principal fascination, a heterogeneous collection of quite disparate original prompts I have named psychosemantic because they were what came naturally from our psychological orientations before conscious consideration had much part to play. The same psychosemantics, which now imprint themselves along with the lexicon on every infant learning to speak, with the Lithic part all below the level of consciousness, can also appear deeply disturbing to those inhabiting well scrubbed environments, scrupulously sweeping any old dust under their carpets. To learn there are all these Lithic creepy crawlies still in residence is not going to be welcome news for them. They will probably prefer to bumble along in their sanitized emporia, with their thirty percent nervous breakdowns at one time or another.

But once you have got used to the idea that there is a subconscious area in the mind which is capable of knowledge of a sort, unsophisticated compared with the hard grafting we have trained ourselves to when we address the world directly and consciously, but nevertheless capable of carrying on a tradition of crude associations sufficient to inform the linguistic record, then you are ipso facto aware that Lithic language is a perpetual accompaniment to rational thinking, just at one remove. In poetic moments I have imagined an unending pie of closely intertwined human bodies stretching back hundreds of thousands of years, miraculously all talking to each other. I have to admit these bodies are naturists, all unclothed and quite unbothered by it, I guess because they symbolise the true nature of their minds, not directly their bodily avatars at all but simply recognising their naked adjacency as the reality of our mental heritage. For the observer there is at first an element of horror in quite so much human flesh so intimately heaped together - a bit like a plague of soldier caterpillars of the Cabbage White butterfly - especially if your imagination starts to play tricks on you and you imagine them all squirming together, like at a weekend Californian flower power party. But it fades when it becomes clear they are

Chapter 16 Conclusions

all alive and well and conversing about anything and everything amongst themselves – as indeed of course they did, though not all at the same time together. As history was really played, Father Time's spotlight lit up a single belt of humanity at a time. But the chain of discourse, that intimate intercourse of ideas, has never been broken. There is no reason to suppose once language started out it ever had to start again from scratch everywhere on earth. No society was ever rendered dumb, although some have suffered capital punishment unless they changed to the victors' tongue. The Egyptian language was lost in this way when the Wahabis rampaged across North Africa masquerading as Moslems. But even Wahabis had Lithic in their subconscious. So Lithic Language is Perpetual Lithic. It is not all that surprising. We have perpetual legs too, though we use them less and less while talking more and more. It is just the legs are not mediated through the mind. After so many years speech has something of the texture of papier-maché, with a fuzzy semantics where the meanings become tinctures made up of surrounding meanings and fade one into the other. That is why you can often read a group of Lithic phonemes in more ways than one, in much the same way that a deaf person – I am now quite deaf, enough to make normal social intercourse quite difficult - can often make sense of a sentence in more ways than one, sometimes leaving him holding the wrong end of the stick entirely. This can not be used as an argument the Lithic meanings attached to phonemes are so general as to make so many meanings available that any assemblage is inconclusive. The psychosemantic trees I have tried to present with the chapters dealing with individual phonemes in turn are actually to some extent misleading because there are innumerable pathways in the mind connecting the semantic contents; and the lines of derivation which I have drawn out are simply one strategem for bringing the linkages into consciousness. However the semantics are by no means limitless. There are necessary patterns.

My vision of a pie of intertwined bodies stretching across time owes something also to the pie of intertwined meanings in the subconscious minds of those bodies stretching across time. The poet's pie is a congealed congeries of pieces forming a semantic mess or mass. The printer's pie is similarly just a collection of pieces with letters on them, put in order to make a text and the frame then tightened around them to hold them in place for printing). As such neither the poet's pie nor the printer's one owe anything to the Lithic etymology of a lidded dish as opposed to an open tart, they are gulls. The congeries of pieces are what lie under the lidded tart. The pie is a classic case in point for fuzzy semantics since simultaneously pai is both pieces and lid, either or both together, which is probably why it won out as the description for the dish. These 'doubles-entendres' or double meanings are common with Lithic derivations, as if they settled arguments in the original naming committees: two pointers counted twice one: when following through the sequence of constituent phonemic meanings, two semantic routes of assemblage were confirmatory and not conflicting.

It will be argued the meanings attributed to phonemes are too multifarious, and their combinations offer such polysemy that the semantic strings chosen as evidence carry no conviction. The semantic contents of the phonemes postulated offer such a wide range of meanings that in every case a reading will always be possible, whether it is veridical or not. The argument has force and must be answered. If warranted, it opens the way to Lithic being a free composition which can all be dismissed as fiction. But there is only one set of universally consistent meanings available to date, those presented in the present work – or perhaps only two, since alternative derivations occur in interpretations, apparently taken as positive confirmation when it came to naming things.

Chapter 16 Conclusions

Critics will then wish to consider, before accepting Lithic, whether the evidences adduced are statistically significant. Statistics are popularly supposed to be the ultimate fabrication, but that is only because statistical theory is so regularly abused. The items adopted for comparison must always be genuine independent variables, so that they must be items with a satisfactory degree of singularity. Establishing the independence of variables is a study in itself, only recently recognised. The whole of philosophy and logic for half a century motored along as if in a trance quite unaware that the idea of independent empirical observations was grossly flawed. It lends tone to the late Arthur Koestler's characterisation, writing at that very time, of the great scientists as sleep walkers. Once established in the academic world you are probably - all unawares - lost in a thicket, mounted on your own achievements, with the truly valid science in second place. In reality observation is subjective at two levels. Nature's signals which it fires at us may be real and their impact "objective", that is to say reflecting accurately the objects whence they come; but the messages we manage to read into these signals are subjective mental-cum-emotional constructs. So for a paradigm or example, with a pinprick the pain is subjective though the actual puncture is objective (which is not the same as our view of it). The subjectivity of the senses is that simple. In chapter 15 the actual prick is Ro (P)for the reality, but the pain is Psi (Ψ) for psychological. But then our psyches go on to inject whimsy, which is Phi (Φ), into every response, often absurdly where ratiocination is involved. Even vision, Psi (Ψ) is a complex mental representation, with its own conventions, of the dance of electromagnetic particles and waves, providing us with a panorama of patterned surfaces for the navigating utility it vouchsafes us. Of course you can introduce further subjective conventions with domains of discourse, symbolic logics and metalanguages, all Pi (Π), to try and insulate the mind from these perceptive misfortunes. But you can not have your cake and eat it: once choiring in these abstract and derivative realms you can not at the same time claim to be directly and objectively observing reality, Ro (P); and you are not. You are subjectively perceiving it.

Statistically it is fair to point out every step in the psychosemantic trees in the chapters on the phonemes, every meaning derived from the original sense has more than one word as exemplar. There are then thousands of complexed meanings and these are for the most part only those prompted by current English usage. World wide there are millions, even an infinity. Each one provides an opportunity of disproof as an independent statistical item. But falsification of the theory does not result from individual cases of misidentification of the evidence but only from wholesale schematic failure, all of the derivations proving false or the majority of them, or there is no subconscious mind, or speech has been intermittent, or a contradictory set of psychosemantic trees is available – not just a rearrangement of the terms but a different set of semantics altogether or none at all. This latter (none at all) is in reality the response already offered by conventional etymologists, but their own word-etymologies which disregard the phonemic meanings are far less falsifiable since they are not universally consistent, they only cover single words, or a few words each, and at a phonetic level only – at which level of course under their rubric anything goes. Moreover since they argue for random word roots that is the same as saying there is no evidence for the etymology other than current word use, regardless of meanings, whereas word structure (prefixes, suffixes and infixes) is common ground between Lithic and anti-Lithic thinking. Under the anti-Lithic random rubric the phonemic semantics can not in any case be prayed in aid, although this is unblushingly contradicted when echoism (onomatopaea) is identified. Or, to put it another way, with prefixes etc the build up of words from phonemic components, some at least single phonemes, is admitted; while from the echoic

Chapter 16 Conclusions

meanings a direct connection of sound and sense is everywhere accepted. Well, Erectus stuck to it.

The fact is the Lithic Hypotheses challenge both the current establishment beliefs, wholly untested, that - first - language roots were originally random, and - second - they have anyway changed so much that they contain nothing of any original structure even if it actually were originally semantically composed in Lithic speak. Both these established views are false. Roots are not semantically random but made up of meaningful phonemes, and the original meanings at the origins of speaking, however long ago it was, can still be traced in the world lexicon today.

The next critique likely to be aimed at Lithic meanings is the opposite of the statistical challenge, on the grounds the meanings are too many to choose from. It is the examples, compared with the number of potential cases, which are not plentiful enough to be significant. With perhaps eight thousand languages to pick from, very many little known, it must be true the number of examples which can be adduced in a single volume represents only an infinitessimal fraction of all potential examples in the world. However that is not the way statistics work. If a significant number of proven independent examples exist, the proof may be extended to all or any of the remainder with a clearcut degree of significance. The degree of significance depends upon the number of truly independent confirmatory instances, and only secondarily upon the size of the population from which they are culled. In any case the population can not be expanded by the critics to include all the languages, the vast majority of which have not been sampled. The only proviso is the sampling must be of genuinely independent variables. This is however a more difficult statistical challenge to rebuff because the statistical computations are too complex to work out. The answer to both challenges therefore is perhaps to issue a challenge on behalf of Lithic in turn. Can the critic put together another scheme as comprehensive, which fits in so many cases, as well? If he can not put up he should shut up. It does not directly prove Lithic is correct, but it does highlight the fact that such a scheme, with such consistency as Lithic, is not easily compiled; so that such a compilation is at least notable and in need of explanation. That is in fact the way I came, overcoming my own original schematophobia. Volume 2 which will deal with a fair span of difficult languages from Basque to Chinese and from Djeribal (a dead North Queensland aboriginal language) to Ancient Egyptian will very much exacerbate the critic's task, if I live long enough to see it all in print.

At the outset (in chapter 1) it was alleged that the whole of the world lexicon, including mankind's finest thoughts, appear to have been initially hammered out on the anvil of our own genitalia. It was, it seems, genital performance which acted, like a cobbler's last, as the formative core shaping humanity's first ratiocination and thence his speech. The source of the metaphors on which Homo Erectus first framed his understanding of the world at large was his own psychological whimsy as he contemplated the fascinations of sex. It was assumed by our semi articulate forebears that the whole of nature followed their own original perceptions; so inevitably they analysed the rest of the world in terms of the ideas they had in their heads; and in a thin crowd there, these were obviously those of their home economy, and first of all their own intimate psychosemantic conceptualisations. The Egyptian rays linked sun, eye, brain and sex together in a universal dialectic, action at a distance, there and back, linked by their teleological missions. Consequently the animal, vegetable and natural worlds all yielded to their own hominid personal understanding of how things went, a version increasingly absurd but by now so firmly imprinted in the human subconscious that it can influence our conscious thinking still. If you have only a limited stock of perceptions they must necessarily be used to cover the whole of your

Chapter 16 Conclusions

experience. In the Stone Age the seven day wonder was the miracle of birth and how it was engineered. Vegetation could be propagated just like animal species. The very first geology buffs had even worked out minerals were spawned from volcanos, giant birth canals, out of the nether world of fire, a match to some extent of the sun which gave birth to light (also from fire) on a daily basis from the fiery empyrean believed to be above the heavenly firmament (of stone). Under this rubric volcanos were vulvas, world ones, like the sun above, not human ones or animal ones or vegetable ones. It was that simple.

It should perhaps be added with some emphasis that our subsequent lucubrations have been devoted to diluting and forgetting, at least to some extent, these original psychosemantic inputs and modifying this original simplistic version of science. It is only our subconscious minds which, individually trained over the aeons by language to think in our old aboriginal ways, have been prompting us to stay within our old subconscious mental ruts. This is where Wayland Smith has picked up his prompts while Scrimshaw man has beavered away to redefine in a much more discriminating mode our perceptions of the real world. This is in fact clearly evidenced by the psychosemantic trees which appear with each of the chapters analysing phonemic meanings. Original motifs, often sexual, have been modified, abstracted and by means of metaphor after metaphor, gulls and buses, removed further and further from our fundamental simplistic orientations. Wayland Smith, meanwhile, has just sung the tune got from within, while Scrimshaw has revised and elaborated the lexicon and carried civilisation forward. Of the two it is Wayland who makes the most comfortable bed fellow, because Scrimshaw is often self absorbed and tending to an element of autism. But we can not do without him. It is he that has brought us down from the trees and it is he who will probably introduce a degree of civilisation now we are walking upright on the ground. Just give him time!

Appendix A is attached, dealing with the academic philosophy of language in order to keep it out of the main body of the book, where it hardly belongs. Logical disputations have since focused on the philosophy of science, which has nevertheless not advanced much in the past eighty years since Karl Popper first wrote[1]. Most if not all of the "Popperian Knights" who made their way up the civil service ladder on the back of his thinking are already in their graves, but his research programme is still largely intact. The arguments have moved towards relativism - a refuge for scoundrels (who would excuse anything) - as realist theories have crumbled. We have some clever gambits like Tarski's metalanguages and Kuhn's paradigm shifts as well as Imre Lakatos' (mental) research programming. I think almost all of this can be rendered somewhat redundant just by my Psi-Phi-Pi-Ro series and my Wallpaper Theory. We are still gripped by Popper's ideas on falsification as the best way of assessing theory, in chapter 15.

I am indebted to Doctor Chalmers for his book "What is this Thing called Science[2] which has taught me my Wallpaper Theory is really "Unrepresentative Realism" in wrangler speak; although I still like my pictorial version of mental activity as sketching on the wallpaper how we imagine the real wall behind better than his wranglers' pie. What is essential for understanding the relationship of all empirical study to the real reality (Kant's ding fur sich) is to separate the two so that the one is not directly related or in contact with the other. This I do by inserting a cognitive level, the wall paper, (which eventually I locate papered inside our own skulls, having made use of all its presentational virtues papered on the wall). All knowledge is virtual knowledge of virtual reality. In these circumstances haven't we done well! I also learned from Dr Chalmers that Latokosian research programmes are descriptions of mental approaches and activities and not expeditionary itineraries as I first imagined – a point Dr Chalmers forgets to mention

Chapter 16 Conclusions

incidentally, so intirely is he taken up within the limitations of his ivory tower and with the wrangling occurring therein. We can all do better, I fancy, just with the expeditionary itineraries. The world is not looking for definitions of truth but for understanding. For that the truth is a handy handrail not to be despised, since it really has no other meaning.

The Oxford University Press report of a symposium on the state of science under the title "Nature's Imagination" edited by John Connell of Jesus College, Cambridge and published in 1995 deserves quotation in full. But here perhaps a short excerpt from the Preface will have to suffice: "Scientific reductionism is a perspective that takes nature and the universe to be deterministic, immutable and non anthropormorphic; a perspective in which all biological and mental events are reducible to properties of matter-energy.....[But] Science itself is conditioned by history". This is of course what historians know as Scientism. It is nowadays the simplistic belief of practical men, who have always taken their ideological environment with a pinch of salt while they got on with their active pursuits; and that includes politicians who these days likely add a whiff at least of dialectical materialism to warrant their otherwise wholly banausic outlook on life. T H Huxley's views were classical Scientism in the nineteenth century, a macho time by any standards. He was in fact a little follower, using Darwin's theories to bludgeon his way to authenticity. It led straight into the massacring civil religions of the twentieth century, the bloodiest on record in all history and probably all prehistory as well. The social history merely reinforces the intellectual descent which set the pace. It was a true intellectual "treason of the clerks". The political puppets just danced to their tune, as ever. Hitler and Stalin are not usually seen as puppets but that is what they were, quick brained but without any understanding of their own. Nazis were actually Socialists, but the socialist intellectuals have dubbed them posthumously reactionaries, and got away with it because German bankers under duress decided to fund them: the treason of the German clerks was compounded by the capitulation of the German financiers. Both, to be fair, were reeling under the traumas of military defeat, which always brings out the worst in anyone, from whining to cheating. The German slate has still to be wiped clean. Perhaps only the fighting SS can be excused, as comrades in arms; and even there, there was monstruous unnecessary brutality. The holocaust SS should all have been put to death and not, as American policy, let off so they would stand up to the Russians, which in the event they never did. Instead the reprieved nazis have plotted to reinstate Hitler's plan for a Thousand Year European Reich under German suzerainty, the Deutschmark renamed the Euro, officially for European peace, but actually, as followers of the black goddess Kali's philosophy of deceit, in a farcical shot at world domination, an ambition as mad as it is outmoded, kept alive by a political elite which has lost its way.

When Huxley took centre stage in an Oxford debate with the Bishop, Darwin and Lyell were horrified, as indeed was my great grandfather who had more than a smidgeon - perhaps not much more - of responsibility for starting this whole vulgar debate off, since he and Charles Lyell (Darwin's mentor) had worked out the relative ages of the sedimentary rocks from the microscopic shells (species) included within them. My great grandfather, a barrister, was a conchologist who had inherited the nucleus of his collection of shells from his father, an Anglican parson and Prebendery of Winchester Cathedral, with a passion for philately (collecting and ordering things). Some at least of Lyell's book (the epochal and scandalous "Principles of Geology" published in 1831) – it made the case for geological evolution over enormous spans of time contradicting quite precisely the literal version of events in the Christian bible - was worked out in the long gallery which extended the whole length of the top floor of Merton Hall, which was filled with two rows

Chapter 16 Conclusions

of double fronted glass cabinets holding thousands of shells, all neatly labelled. I remember them well. They burnt with the Hall round them in 1955. Lyell, a late barrister to earn a living, would weekend working with my great grandfather on the shells, as his book shows, since it notices the Merton Stone, the largest glacial erratic in Great Britain weighing about 25 tons which had been dug up by my farming forebears in the seventeenth century when digging for marl to spread on the land to hold wáter longer – which was later prayed in aid in the eighteenth century by Coke and Townshend, on their heavier north Norfolk soils, enabling their four course Norfolk rotation, which in turn sparked the industrial revolution by over wintering cattle on turnips and much increasing the supply of meat, presenting so many surviving surplus farm workers, sturdy beggars, for employment in the towns. On the European continent they starved, but in Britain they were put into garden sheds because they smelt too rank (soap came later) to have in the house and were found employment by the division of labour – if all you could do was cut out the sole for a shoe then you passed it to the cobblers indoors when it was done, for the more intellectually demanding stitching operation. Cottage industries became manufactures overnight. Great Britain Ltd gained a half century advantage from this quite modest philanthropy. The late Alan (AJP) Taylor taught me this – he famously invented the "Cockup" theory of history - when I studied history under him at Oxford sixty five years ago, after war service.

There is in fact an inclination nowadays amongst philosophers of science to regard Marx and Darwin as fellow workers in the vinyard, confronting religious fuddy duddies with science. This seems to me to be an absurdity. Marx was thinking in the 1830s and found his Left-over ideas then. He was in fact a left-over from eighteenth century philosophy himself; he said as much himself. He had, he felt, driven a coach and horses through the eighteenth century philosophical tradition. He claimed to have stood Hegel's dialectic on its head, where he made it the foundation of his infamous philosophy of "dialectical materialism". This inversion of Hegel's blunder was to prove sufficient to carry the ancient confusion of thought forward for nearly another two hundred years, leading in turn to every kind of intellectual corruption amongst academics and politicians alike, and culminating in Stalinism, Nazism, the Cold War and the decay and collapse of Communist regimes around the world. Darwin did not publish until 1859. He was an offshoot of an entirely different and more recent tradition, a science based upon close biological observation of natural species, starting as it happened with the shells included in sedimentary rocks, by courtesy of Charles Lyell. Philately had come from Linnaeus: he put the flowers in order, identifying species from their flower forms, their sex organs. Shells enabled Charles Lyell (born 1800) to disentangle the sedimentary rock strata of Britain by estimation of their relative ages, judging by the evolution of the forms of the microscopic shells included in them. It was a method no scientist today would countenance because it relied upon the mere assumption that shell forms were getting more convoluted and distorted rather than less, a matter of mere guesswork at the time, with nothing more than what is now recognised as the idea of entropy to go on: live forms became more complex as time went on, while dead forms broke down into even deader less energetic ones. However it produced the right results. It is scientific because it proved to be right.

What was even more surprisng was that Charles Lyell, who published his epoch making book "The Principles of Geology" in 1830-1833, did not possess any shell collection to work on himself. He had consulted a number of European conchologists and been engaged as Secretary of the newly formed Geological Society, but he made

Chapter 16 Conclusions

significant use of my great grandfather's collection of shells finally housed at Merton. They were barristers together in London. As the shells were species the received wisdom that Darwin was prompted by geological evolution in Lyell's book to think of species evolution for himself is false. In 1859 Darwin fibbed about this to excuse his old mentor being sent to Coventry by his fellow dons in dog collars at Cambridge. Darwin had taken Lyell's book with him on his five year round the world cruise in HMS Beagle. The shells are all in there on almost every page. It has recently been republished and I have a copy. Darwin would have had to be a fool to have missed it in 1831.

Darwin feared if he published species evolution disproving a literal reading of the Book of Genesis in the Hebrew bible it would lead to bloody revolution, and scientists might get their heads cut off. It was only some seventy years since Madame Guillotine had been so busy in Paris. He had therefore cautiously prepared a posthumous volume and was only persuaded to publish when young Alfred Russel Wallace wrote to the President of the Linaean Society in 1859 - unsurprisingly it was Charles Lyell – proposing a scheme of species evolution he had worked out for himself, based on his researches in South East Asia. Lyell naturally warned Darwin immediately who immediately prepared a paper from his unpublished major work. Darwin's and Wallace's papers were then read to the Linaean Society and Lyell declared Darwin's the winner. All the recognition Wallace got was the Wallace Line dividing Australian species from the South East Asian ones; but Wallace and Darwin remained on friendly terms. Well you would if there were virtually only the two of you. The media, evidently without reading up the evidence in Lyell's book – they had deadlines to meet even in those sleepy days and had evidently already given up reading books – just copied Darwin's line, so that the fib that he thought of species evolution for himself is in the history books as fact even to this day. None of this has anything to do with linguistics. The Marxist dialectic however has, and it has been finally demolished already in chapter 15 on thinking. Understanding language is the forerunner which should lead to understanding thinking, which is not easy.

Karl von Linné (Linnaeus, 1707-1778), a parson's son in Sweden, had proposed a scheme of identification of plant species by means of their flower structures which he identified as their male and female sex organs. This relatively blameless philately had so incensed the dominies of the Swedish church that they had no hesitation in informing von Linné he would burn in Hell for his blasphemous mischief. It seems silly now, but poor old Karl was shattered by this prognostication, suffered a nervous breakdown and was confined in an asylum until his death three years later. His system of identification of species however lives on, and young ladies in the nineteenth century collected pressed flowers on the excuse they were displaying speciation, but leaving out the sex. The Prebendary's choice of shells in place of flowers may have suggested itself as a slightly more masculine pursuit, or else was prompted, perhaps subconsciously, by the reassurance the moluscae's genitalia were all long gone and even the most censorious episcopal overseer – he had sensibly married Bishop North's daughter - could hardly suspect him of any secret salacious interest in his collection. Had he known of the astonishing genital convolutions involved in two moluscs mating, requiring both participants virtually to turn themselves inside out in slow time and intertwine their organs in the open with a good deal of frothing and slime he likely would never have embarked on his hobby. In those days, one has to remind oneself, there was no geology or biology as we understand them. The discovery of giant bones and shells fossilised in quarries and cliffs was a source of puzzlement, and some of these fossils, it had been suggested, must at one time have belonged to species now extinct and their hard parts somehow preserved in the sediment.

Chapter 16 Conclusions

But there were rival theories such as a provision by the deity to test the faith of the faithful, or else for purposes beyond human comprehension altogether, and therefore best left alone.

The Prebendary's views on the matter are not recorded, but he was a genuine believer and he will have been content to leave these mysteries in God's keeping. He is looking down on me as I write, in a portrait painted in the 1820s. His son, however, armed with legal training to test the evidence, was jointly responsible for a mischief which still haunts the church today.

Now I just ask myself how can it be that I should have uncovered a whole scheme of semantic contents others have overlooked, and so many of them for so long? My wife put an unerring finger on the whole matter on day one when the project was first unfurled: "Why you?" The whole thing narrowly escaped proving a damp squib more than thirty years ago. Doggedness, even bloody mindedness, must count for something; but I think the capacity to hold a great many disparate items in the mind on the whole rather aimlessly, doodling perhaps, convinced in my case most human aiming is usually largely unrewarded (mine anyway), and thus without too much judgmental content - is a great help. Add to that a willingness to be entertained by whatever serendipity threw up, the sheer glee at living and thinking and watching the world go by; and underlying it all a great, almost childish, thirst for understanding alongside a refusal to be fooled. There is also the fact my research programme with languages has been pretty useless all along. Perhaps only a bit of a goof would have wished to go on with it. But then you must remember it was for thirty years and more no more than a hobby for me. I never earned my living by it, and certainly never expected to. I have only been writing consecutively since I was seventy three and able to retire from my businesses. Until then Lithic just took me away from the hard graft of all the business sums, when I was sleeping quite short hours already. My idea of a break was simply to take off into the Stone Age and have a ball. Just ten minutes a night in the company of Eric Partridge would do, and it was as badly needed as the glass of whisky (or two) which generally went with it. It banished business to its proper place so I slept sound, whether pickling onions were selling well or not. At one time I had 1200 ladies peeling one third of all the onions commercially pickled in the United Kingdom, and the calculation of contracted prices in and out as well as the daily wastage from the factories which revealed the gross margin was an only semi-computerised headache I enjoyed alone.

For the man in the street, and of course equally for his sisters, there is a good deal of fun to be had, once the basic Lithic elements have been learnt, in tracing for himself along with his sisters for themselves the Lithic compositions to be found in words of whatever languages they know, released from the constraints of conventional civilised thinking and genuinely back to basics. The audio frequencies are more effortful than the visual but their research is the more rewarding. Even the therapeutic benefits of any such exercise are not to be sneezed at.

Meanwhile there are very serious conclusions to be drawn from our study of Lithic language, because it enables us to see that all our thinking is whimsical like our language and its origins. Knowledge is redefined. Science is not as hard and reliable, identifying relativity for instance, as we thought. We can not know reality, we can only ever sketch it on the wallpaper with which the rather modest windows of our senses provide us. The real wall, behind it, is directly inaccessible to our senses. Nature is in no way determined by our science of it. It has no need of any sums. The sums are our own alone. Nature just does. So finally how does Berty Einstein do? Armed with our study of language, particularly historical etymology properly conceived, that is developing in time by metaphor and an5

Chapter 16 Conclusions

alogy in accordance with the whimsical psychosemantic trees in the preceding chapters, we have the inestimable advantage of understanding that all our ideas are merely mental schema at one remove from reality – which our Berty had still to discover for himself when he started out over a hundred years ago.

His relativity, with a stone dropping from a moving train this time, its trajectory seen from the window of the train and from the embankment, is based upon appearances. He uses the trajectory to identify the relativity of our perception of relationships in space. He then goes on to project the relativity onto time as well, and do his sums on that assumption. It all works swimmingly but it is still not clear if temporal relativity, which is contrary to common sense, is really necessary. What the trick really consists of is to write the maths as if time and space were really equal partners, treating them as equal. Even the equations of uniform motion do this already ($v = u + ft$, $v = \delta s/\delta t = ds/dt$, $s = ut + \frac{1}{2} ft^2$, etc).

The physical explanations he derives from his equations are another thing. We know, from our study of Lithic, they are only the drawings on the wallpaper inside our own heads. We are certainly not going to abandon our everyday assumptions as time goes by. We know taim just means the becomings, tai, the passage of events, Wittgenstein's "the case", what apparently happens. It is all the happenings, the Egyptian "Taun", the world as everything that happens and never mind where, as opposed to the locations we think of when we define the universe in commonly accepted terms. It is really a question of whether you think in terms of an empty space or of the activity of its occupants, because the occupancy then immediately becomes suspect. The Egyptian Taun has really been waiting for Einstein to come along. He got his Nobel Prize for inventing electromagnetic quanta in 1905, and it was this which has given us all the technological spin-offs since then. Everyone these days knows we live in an electromagnetic soup, and indeed are ourselves constituent croutons in it.

The philosophical picture of space-time as a heaving surface came after. But thinking still seems to be independent of these surfaces, as of the foregoing forces, rays and other vehicles we have invented, one after the other, so that the intelligentsia can tell the rest of us how to think. Think Egyptian rays for example, with hands on the ends of the sun's rays pulling up their targets, the vegetation; and our forebears who dreamed them up hunkered around the hearth in their birthday suits. It is as good an image as any, as well as being quite funny – which is more than you can say for the others. What turn out to be relative, depending on the observer's spatial velocity, are not space and time themselves but our measurements of them. Time is not a thing at all but just the omnium gatherum of activity, while space is the omnium gatherum of things – and the mind, incidentally, is just the omnium gatherum of our thinking, another type of activity, this time an invisible one in the brain. But all three patterns are just drawings on the same wallpaper. Simple really! You just need to keep the wallpaper in mind and just keep on refining the drawings, but without for a moment imagining any of them belong in the real world. They don't. They are fanciful sketches of reality, with science an art really. If using them works, that is enough. We should never imagine our thinking is the reality; it is only our ideational methodology for navigating our way around the world in pursuit of our own purposes. The scientific protocols we have invented enable us to sort the wheat from the chaff, that is to tell the formulations which work and are borne out when we try them out in the real world from those which don't. It is quite wrong to think because that is so we have captured a piece of reality. We have just got a good enough protocol for us to be able to use it for the purpose for which we dreamed it up. Both realism and idealism (really much the same) are off limits. Our knowledge is only nominal. The relativity of our thinking has to be borne

Chapter 16 Conclusions

in mind all the time, and particularly when a philosopher comes along with an ideological scheme of things which he thinks determines reality. It doesn't. It is just a new wallpaper design in his head, always at one remove from the real (natural) wall behind his thinking.

Ever since Charles Darwin settled the God business in 1859, first with his wife who was very religious, and then with his book "On The Origin of Species" (a singular process, mark you) we have all been obliged to accept that He works, at least in large part, through the processes of Nature (as we perceive them), so that all our understanding is born of human whimsy out of Mother Nature; and what is more, before we were even hominids we were just animals, and originally even just fishy, since life apparently originated in the deep (although it may have been shallow at the time). Professor Dawkins of Oxford University, England, and others like him, may choose to harangue us to the contrary but I am afraid there will always be a level headed majority who will, reasonably enough, stay with the arts and spirituality and dismiss his rants as the rather wooden-headed single-plank delusions of scientism. Science yes! Scientism no!

NOTES

1. Karl Popper. The Logic of Scientific Discovery. Hutchinson. 1968. (As quoted by Chalmers) "What he [a critic] must do is to formulate an assertion which contradicts our own and give us his instructions for testing it. If he fails to do this we can only ask him to take another and perhaps a more careful look at our experiment [or thesis based on it] and think again.

2. A.F.Chalmers. "What is This Thing Called Science?", Second Edition, Open University Press. Page 60.

APPENDIX A

THE PHILOSOPHY OF LANGUAGE

The philosophy of language is annexed as an appendix only, because it is not directly relevant to the main part of the book. There is the consideration if it were left out altogether it would suggest I knew nothing of it and make it easier for hostile academics to rubbish the main part of the book. I suppose philosophy (from the Greek, meaning knowledge-loving approximately, and used historically for top notch wrangling on any subject) covers the theoretical issues arising with any subject matter: the ultimate nature of language in our case, as well as a critique of our knowledge of it, unkindly put the cat's cradles human whimsy has traced around the study of language to date. The only reasonable approach, it seems to me, is to trace historically the positions struck to date, with commentary. It will not be an overly long study since the nature of language per se has not received a great deal of attention, any more than the nature of thinking, since these too often have been regarded as givens and axiomatic, needing no analysis. Nevertheless I have no doubt that in the search for every kind of understanding a true appreciation of the place of language and its implications for the ways in which we think is absolutely fundamental. That anyway is the perception which lies behind my forty years of hobby study of the origins of speaking. It is just unfortunate that my own homework has borne fruit which is very little related to the academic philosophical contributions to date. All sorts of philosophical schemes have of course held implications for the view you take of language, since philosophy dictates the categories under which thinking proceeds; so in this appendix these implications will be addressed whether they were understood at the time or no.

It was thinking about the philosophy of language, during my philosophical period more than fifty years ago - currently a gaggle of irrelevances easily characterized as cat's cradles - which prompted me to come up front with a title for the book to jolt the potent grave and reverend seigneurs of academe into thinking: "On the Origins of Speaking". But I have reduced the present book to "Lithic Language", with a prompt for what it is about. It is meant to show we have to get down to actual intellectual analysis of meanings themselves, in stark contrast to the school of neurolinguistics trying to reconcile our own experience of cognition with their neurological insights. Their neurobiological perceptions do not address our immediate experience on which alone any analysis of the nature of what it is we are doing when we are speaking should be based. Thought is quite different from its neurology, never mind how tightly interlocked at the biological level they may be. It is no more than a recrudescence of the age old division of the historical and scientific traditions. The historian, currently in relative eclipse, says let us see how it happened; and is less good at making up rules on how it will or should happen in future. The scientist just makes up rules that seem good to him, often based on personal whimsy though sometimes on flashes of insight; but he then goes on to test them to destruction winnowing out all but those with some residual utility for understanding. Forced to study both disciplines, it seems to me the study of language is primarily a matter of history and does not yield its most revealing insights when investigated with a crudely scientific eye trying out pre-ordained schemes, especially those based on the baggage of biology, or even worse of mathematics.

Appendix A Philosophy

This straight away divorces me from a century of linguistics. That is not to deny the close relationship between brain function and mentality. It is merely to reject a common research programme, which really implies a congruence of the two and is palpably absurd. In philosophy it is known as a category error. We are far from the science of everything mathematicians hanker after – with no historical sense whatever. That is a Will-o'-the-wisp fashionable in some quarters, a bit like sitting down to design a single computer programme to do everything under a single magic rubric, which is equally absurd. Software buffs will be aware their programmes are highly specific and run on approximations of digital relationships to reality. Science, even with its simplest and most satisfactory and apparently transparent analyses, suffers from the very same limitations in spite of the fact the human mind is much more flexible than any computer programme and actually "understands" what it is doing - it actually has meaning - though not how it does it. Computers by contrast are just dumb Daleks without understanding, in fact just quick. Before we take leave of the neurobiologists however we should recognize there has been some neat thinking on primitive, that is in scientific terms basic, states of mind from them: the recognition of self as a condition of consciousness for instance, including Julian Keenan's 'mirror test', and some interesting perceptions from Mithen, Cosmides and Tooby, and Gardner and Fodor on the compartmentalization of the mind.

The study of language theory started out as grammar, "the science of letters", more or less as we understand the term today with a bit of literary expertise thrown in. It was a subjective and systematizing interpretation of language as she is spoke by the grammarian, an intellectual. The first on extant record is Pannini in Sanskrit around 500 BC. To the Greeks belongs the honour of recognizing the phonology of language, the choice of sounds to symbolize meanings, as originally derived from echoism, or in Greek onomatopeia which in Lithic is something like "the sounds become the symbols" and in Greek "names making up the words", that is the sounds become the entities, cuckoo for cuckoo and so on. There is no doubt the Egyptians had this beforehand. They were half way to Lithic five thousand years ago. Of course the actual Lithic practice was not so far removed in those days. At one time there were probably more educated Greeks in Egypt than in Greece. As a result half the Greek language comes from Egyptian. The Pharaohs were Akkadian adventurers, Semites farming the native Africans. They got darker over the millennia from concubinage.

The Egyptians believed in natural forces behind every phenomenon. Their hundreds of "gods" were all marked in inscriptions with a pennant blowing in the breeze, a "Natura", which said "Na-", showing, "-Tura", the pull or force. They were exemplars of natural forces. Academic Egyptologists nevertheless still think the pennant or natura is a pointed axe of divinity and call it a neter. The Greeks regarded language as "natural", phusike in Greek, where the "phusi-" was from the Lithic "Pa-hei-u-sai", the action[sai] of the phallus [pahei] when roused [hei]; and the "–ke" was from formed, or in form, forming, equivalent to the English –al. The action prayed in aid was of course to expand and extend, to grow, which the phallus had the trick of doing under your very eyes and in short order. The Greek phusis contrasted, to the Greek mind, with the nominal or conventional like their laws, nomoi, which I read in Lithic as something like 'presenting the thinking', ie laying down the law which is a nominal business rather than inductive.

There was something of the present attempts by scientists to relate linguistics to neurobiology in this. Phusis in Greek was the natural principle of Aristotle's day which informed the animal and vegetable kingdoms, an organic nissus or naturally endowed drive to develop grow and elaborate. The Egyptians used Ka for a very similar concept, like the

Japanese. Probably both got it from the Sumerians, or else perhaps the Japanese got it from the Chinese who had it directly from Eden when the circumpolar ice finally melted and turned Eastern Malaya (Malaya means the Garden Land, so Eastern Malaya is the Garden of Eden) into the South China Sea, whence the Sumerians perforce emigrated. Phusis was a life force, biological, nothing to do with physics in English which concerns the underlying principles which apply to dead nature, the laws of physics and physical chemistry, and only by extension to the organic. It may seem surprising language was not thought of as merely conventional. But language, it was supposed, had always been there as part of the original divine creation of mankind. To claim mankind had made it up smacked of sacrilege. Would the gods have communicated in manspeak? Adam, after all, spoke with God in the Garden of Eden; and the tale was told in Sumer, and merely borrowed by the Akkadian (Semitic) nomads who conquered Sumer (and were then civilized by the Sumerians for their pains) as part of their creation myth.

Adam was not originally a Semite at all, but an Adamite from the Garden of Eden, the Eastern Garden Land, that is to say the land with riverine irrigated paddy now under the South China Sea, flooded when the ice finally++ melted leaving only the mountainous hinterland of "Malaya", the "Garden Land" and dispersing the Adamites to Sumer as well as North to China and probably East across the Pacific Ocean, and north along the coast around the top of the Pacific Ocean as well. This is how Chinese has some roots and words common to Sumerian as well as Malay so that it has even been suggested that the Sumerians were proto-Chinese. But Malays have no eyefold, and no more did Adam or the Sumerians. For the speakers their language was natural but laws were metalanguage and conventional. That left them with the task of getting the law in line with natural justice of course.

Before Plato and Aristotle, Greek skepticism which was originally from Alexandria in Egypt was universally promulgated by the intellectuals. The Greeks attributed this line of thinking to Pyrrhon who was around in 300 BC, and otherwise forgotten. There was also Heraclitus who said you never step twice into the same river: and meant it to apply of course to all our experience of the world, which made apposite judgments hard. Skepticism was the matrix from which Greek philosophy as it is known to us today was born. The skeptics aimed to achieve "ataraxia", literally un-drawn-ness, Greek for a calm resignation in face of the fact the human mind could as happily entertain falsity as truth, there being no way for the mind to distinguish between the two. You only found out when you stepped on the wrong end of the rake. This perception was of course sound, and roughly corresponds with the late Karl Popper's seminal work, "The Logic of Scientific Discovery". He had some equally telling stuff on philosophy, in "The Open Society and its Enemies". He was from the Vienna Circle but wrote in English in England due to Hitler, because he was a Jew. For Pyrrhon ataraxia was his final position, an early academic bumble. Popper never made it to Pyrrhon's base; his world was nearer to a nightmare. He had spotted the present.

So far as I can see, the Greek phusis or biological nissus was not necessarily directed and purposive (teleological), but more like a caterpillar waving about on the end of a twig. Today the accepted version of word origins is nominal (from the Greek nomoi, from Lithic nau-mau-i, showing think-ing) and random, the phonology playing only a misty and minor part in forming meaning, if you have no Lithic. In fact the composition of words from random roots is simply assumed, while linguistics buffs have been busy reforming grammar in accordance with mathematical logic, directing attention away from the semantic contents of individual words and eschewing any relationship between sounds and

Appendix A Philosophy

meanings and finding meaning in sentence structure instead, effectively grammatical rules for linking words and phrases into sentences. This is a radical revision: the grammar may have warranted attention, but the discard of everything else was uncalled for. Having thus confused meaning with grammar, the modern grammarians have then had to redefine meaning to get it out from under grammar again. In reality grammar is a structural matter and parts of speech guide sentence structure (with grammatical rules). Meaning on the other hand is a symbolic matter attaching to words and, in Lithic, to their precursors the semantic contents of phonemes. A prime exemplar of these meanings is the word tiger. The echoic cry "Grrr!" from before speech for when one approached, is transmogrified to Ti-Grrr, Mistress growler, spelt tigre in speech and anglicized to tiger. That covers hundreds of thousands of years of linguistic development, and thus many thousands of generations of speakers – let us say six hundred thousand years of linguistic development and thus probably some thirty thousand generations of speakers passing the word down each to the next generation: a fair sized international football crowd playing Chinese whispers. They will however each have had time for a number of goes – in a lifetime perhaps a hundred or more apiece – so I don't find it hard to believe it. We expect changes, but not the total loss of relationships between phonetic signifiers and the signified which is simply assumed by the "noise" theorists in order quite unreasonably to reinforce their case for randomness.

A nice comparison with the tiger's "Grrr" is the word used by aboriginal speakers of Central Senoi in the jungle of the central spine of Malaya for the bark of a dog "kherrl", which is reported in their creation myth as the cause of the flood when a dog barked at a tree, "mi ikur chok kherrl delong kruing" in their tongue, literally "one tail [of] dog growled at a tree". (Malay too says one tail [of] dog, but pronounces it sa ekor anjing). It would be wrong to claim Adam spoke Malay. He spoke a language quite close to Lithic and Sumerian now lost, but the aboriginal hill tribes of Malaya probably speak a vulgar Adamite which was the original of the Malaysian language family, with many dialects, in total some forty million speakers spread over a vast area with thousands of islands great and small. This was Adam's flood which drove him from Eastern Malaya or the Garden of Eden. I never cracked the thinking behind this myth; but when I recounted it in Senoi, seeking information, my Senoi audience took off into the jungle for fear the whole business might start up again. Perhaps the tree, which is derived from the idea of a form which is "ta-rai", "drawn up" - trees are tall - stood for the head of the vegetable kingdom, and the dog for hunters eating meat. Had the boys been mocking the girls with their digging sticks and their knowledge of agriculture, irrigating rice padi, and this climate change was the watery element's revenge, condemning the girls for hubris? Adam certainly seems to have had it in for Eve, perhaps blaming her for irrigating paddy instead of being content with traditional growing, making God cross so that He said "You want more irrigation, do you, not content with what I send you? Getting other ideas above your station too, I see. What do you want your trews for? Very well. Here is some more water for you. How do you like this?" Anyway Adam shopped her to his God. It suggests he had in mind to keep his own nose clean. To be fair it was a very long time ago. In those days God was apparently taking his garden walks in the cool of the evening. It is hard to know how to think of Him. He must surely have been just a spiritual presence, an incorporeal voice, not really a walker at all.

The Malay for tree is pokok or pohon. Kruing however crops up today in advertisements for garden furniture, said to be made from managed forests (in Borneo, where there are no Senoi) from kruing, a hardwood like teak. It seems clear the entrepreneur enquiring for the name of the timber he was felling (What do you call this one then?) got the answer "It's a tree of course. What do you take me for!" so we are reassured to learn our garden furniture is made of tree, illicitly felled. Soldiers who lived with Senoi tribesmen will be nearly 80 now and will have likely forgotten it all, so garden centres are unlikely to be caught out. "Kherrl" is quite like our growl: the khr- is rasped. The -l in both is in many words for language too, as if the growl was recognized as doggy language of a sort. Does anyone think Senoi is related to English? Or is it a psychosemantic echoism? Kruing is easily Lithicised as Kai-rau-'n, a superlatively grown one; the vowel u is the completive substantive vowel; and Malay pokok meanwhile is a shoot-what-grown-hard (pa-u-kau-kai), with a trunk in fact. Pohon is from pau-kau'n, meaning "shoot-altogether hardened'one", with a trunk too. Trunk is recognized in the Malay language in its metaphorical meaning of the matrix or source or origin also (whence all the branches and leaves spring), and so it is possible the one in the Garden of Eden may have started out metaphorical as a mental root or route rather than a fruit tree. Ma in Lithic can mean drink, eat, but also mental activity (dark and unseen), as well as earth and procreation (earthing and thus planting seed, procreation). Mentri Besar is Prime Minister (Minister First or Big) in Malay. The tree of good and evil could be a misreading. It could have been a source of good and evil and the eating could have been thinking or advising, but it is too remote for correction.

The early medieval church, accepting Greek philosophy in much, challenged the idea of simple realism. Then William of Occam (1288-c1348), as well as his razor, introduced a salutary skepticism into the relation of human knowledge to reality. His razor, "Res non multiplicanda", (concepts should not be multiplied/complicated), resulted from his nominalist philosophy. Words as signifiers were only weakly related to the signified, since a word (name) could not cover every aspect of the signified phenomenon, only pick out its most notable aspect. The connection was shrinking, no longer decreed by nature. With this, of course, phonology was randomised. Language was thoroughly disconnected from the external world, the world of nature – which included noises heard but not human language, a human activity based in the mind. It should not be thought these fourteenth century churchmen lacked perspicacity. On the contrary they were just as fly as any modern senior wrangler; only they were of course rather less well informed. Grammar was actually regarded as a branch of metaphysics in Occam's day – as of course it is, given a modern interpretation of metaphysics as simply outside physics (and biology). We shall see shortly that Ludwig Wittgenstein's final position was not so far from the medieval stance, which in its philosophy probes the lexicon's connection with the real world; and was also much closer to the Lithic Hypotheses than modern neurolinguistics. This is of interest because it suggests it is the neurolinguists rather than the Lithic Hypotheses which are the novel oddities.

Renaissance scholarship, universally seen as a progressive liberal revolution, was actually just as much a rebirth of the old classical philosophy. It was a renaissance solely because in the dark ages civilization had been set back a thousand years by the savagery of the Celtic and Germanic races as they overran Roman civilization. Close to my home, the East Anglian fens were drained and cultivated by the Romanised inhabitants, when East Anglia was the bread basket for Europe as the German invaders burned the crops on the continent. After 650 AD, with the arrival in England of the Saxons, the fens became silted up and provided cover for Hereward the Wake and other local banditi for a thousand years until they were redrained in the seventeenth century by Dutch engineers. On my own home farm in West Norfolk, the buildings now only some three hundred yards East of the

Appendix A Philosophy

Roman farm villa (with pavement discovered in 1870 from crop marks), the forty acre field ("Great Meg"), with the villa on it, (in those days it will have been the whole plough) recently yielded up forty Roman coins dated over three hundred and fifty years, apparently thrown down as libations to the Roman gods to grant a fertile soil and a good crop. I fancy Meg is from the Latin magna, with the translation into the vernacular added. The buildings have moved three hundred yards in 1700 years - averaging between two and three inches a year. For more than half of this time the farming has been in my family. In yields per acre in real financial terms, since the Romans left the farm has not seen the same prosperity again. Boudicca butchered all the workers for siding with civilization, as her savages came romping down Peddars Way alongside which the Romanised Merton Farming Company prospered. Their spirits are said to haunt the Slate Plantation, a few hundred yards south of the villa, where Boudicca's men caught up with them. If there is any Hell she is in it. OK she was raped, but not by anyone in Merton Farming Company.

Grammar schools taught Latin grammar which was the passport to preferment in the church and universities alike. The Romans had taken their philosophy and much else from the Greeks. In the fifteenth and sixteenth centuries the discovery of foreign parts and the exotic languages of the natives which came with the exploitation of the oceans did little to displace Latin grammar. Since these barbarian tongues had no written grammar of their own, the Procrustean categories of Latin grammar were simply superimposed. Indeed the same can be said of the vernaculars of Europe as they came to be written for government purposes. It took a long time for the penny to drop and exotic grammars to be recognized. We were content for twelve hundred years with the grammar laid down by the Latin grammarian Priscian in the sixth century AD – and he had relied largely on the Greek grammarian Dionysus Thrax from seven hundred years earlier still. That was all the philosophy there was in language until just now.

The whole of modern linguistics is virtually confined to the last century and a half. Gottlob Frege (1848-1915) was teaching at Jena University in 1872. His first book in 1879, at 31 years of age, explored the logic of mathematics and distinguished meaning as twofold, sense and reference. Sense was roughly the definition, and reference the thing(s) named. He exemplified his perception with the morning star and the evening star as two senses, with Venus as the reference of both. Lithic might add "Venus" as another definition (The Visitor, like the Egyptian Benu bird), and then the actual planet as the reference of all three. His second book five years later aged thirty six in 1884 argued mathematics was founded on logic, which was developed in language which badly needed tidying up. A precise mathematical symbolism was required in place of the logic based on grammar. Linguistics was heading already for an algebra, from which hard thinking was going to be required to shake it loose. But Frege's teaching was virtually ignored until the following century when it was discovered by Bertrand Russell whose Principia Mathematica (a crib from Newton) in collaboration with Alfred Whitehead, published 1910-1913, fundamentally rehashed grammar as a mathematical exercise by analyzing it in terms of symbolic logic (roughly grammatical terms given mathematical symbols).

The achievement of symbolic logic is analytical; the sign or symbol is external to the mind, a word for instance which may be written on a page and is what it is and not another thing. But it invokes in turn in the mind of the observer an idea, subjective and partial. Meanwhile the logician, in this case Gottlob Frege, had been working on the idea of thinking in terms of the sign or symbol, and he had cleverly come up with another analysis, like this. The sign or symbol (think of a word) has two aspects, namely first of all a "reference" to the actual real thing to which it refers (think of a stone or a star), and also secondly a "sense", a description or definition. He gives examples: Aristotle as 'the pupil of Plato and teacher of Alexander the Great' and also 'the teacher of Alexander the Great who was born in Stegira', with both of these "senses" having the same "reference", the actual bloke, in this case the actual living and breathing Aristotle. There may be a spot of categorical parsimony here. With either sense, or indeed with any sense at all, the reference could, as I see it, be to an idea in the head of the thinker rather than immediately to the actual bloke, only reached in turn by way of the name Aristotle. That idea may then in turn be a sign with sense and reference – with a personal name not much point, but with most nouns at least with Lithic analysis a requirement, since the word structures too started out at least as descriptions. We are certainly close to an infinite regression, or at any rate a lengthy delve into Lithic thinking with meanings analysed through the psychosemantic trees in the chapters on phonemes. Frege's terminology is also in some ways unfortunate. For most of us, sense is close to meaning, while a reference is close to a description like those of Aristotle by way of his lifetime experiences which Frege uses as examples of senses. So we just have to remember parrot fashion that when Frege says sense he is thinking of a description, and when he says reference he is thinking of the actual item he thinks of as being in the real world of things to which a symbol refers, of which it is the symbol. We will stick with Frege while examining his ideas. These senses or definitions are the entrée for Lithic analysis of meanings. Frege's example of choice is geometrical. The intersection of lines a and b and the intersection of lines b and c in the case of a triangle where a, b and c are the lines connecting the vertices of the triangle with the mid points of the opposite sides are two senses of the same reference, the point at which the two senses coincide to define an actual single point. The lines simply intersect at the same point. Got it? It is another case like the morning star and the evening star above. The thinking, satisfactory to a mathematician, is otherwise somewhat trivial: two geometrical constructions do indeed in this case define the same point. Is that sufficient to support a complete explanation of symbolism?

Ferdinand de Saussure (1857-1913), a Swiss academic, whose "Cours de Linguistique Generale" was only published posthumously in 1916, in the middle of world war one – the Swiss don't fight – established structuralism. Structuralism is the idea language is an abstract structure ("langue") as opposed to the actual utterances ("parole"). This effectively meant that instead of the senses (or meanings) of words it was the structure of sentences which needed study: effectively grammar. Structuralism provided much more systematic (ideological) wrangling opportunities than individual meanings and so it won the day as far as intellectual endeavours were concerned, the academics' home ground.

Of course Saussure's thinking was around before. There is always a climate of opinion which principal expositors exploit and are given all the credit for. It saves longer explanations. Wilhelm von Humboldt, a genuine polymath when the scope of human knowledge still allowed such vanities, had hinted at some of it a hundred years before, and Wilhelm Wundt promulgated structuralism too. It was thought that language shaped thought as if it were prior, so that a national language shaped national character. In a trivial sense it does, so a speaker or writer may use a word not entirely congruent with the thought he is trying to express. But a tribesman who has no words for numbers beyond a few does not fail to count for lack of numbers, but on the contrary lacks the numbers because he fails to count. There were those who rejoiced in this linguistic patriotism in those days. It was a time of chauvinistic politics we are still fighting our way out of. For its recipients language no doubt dictated and dictates their thinking to a remarkable degree. But you have to ask how language got the way it did in the first place. Clearly, before

Appendix A Philosophy

language shaped thought, thought shaped language. But once up and running the traffic is both ways, and they tend to be in sync. Brighter folk tend to think their own thoughts anyway, the less bright allow their thinking to be constrained within the compass of the words they know (like Wundt).

Saussure's structural approach was picked up in the United States where the native Indian languages were proving tough cookies. Their grammar was wildly deviant by European standards. The trouble with Saussure was not that he distinguished between the synchronic (structural) approach and the diachronic (historical and semantic) approach, but that he altogether failed to distinguish them. He thereby introduced two completely different subject matters, somewhat after the shape of Aristotle's distinction between form and matter. Grammar, the form, was simply different from the matter, the study of the semantic contents of words and their developments. Once the philosophers staked their claims to revising and improving the grammar there was no holding them. The lexicon went out the window. Any linguist worth his salt was bound to a synchronic study of the system of grammar, most recently with expectations of discovering Chomsky's patterns (transformational grammar, with a basement floor common to all languages in the subconscious mind, where it is supposed to be inborn), even in the primitive languages being discovered, just as they were threatened with extinction around the world. It has been a taxing commitment and by no means a success. Linguistics in the USA has moreover for long been hamstrung by the prevalent empiricist hang-ups amongst scientists, refusing to recognize its meta-physical character; and this refusal still determines the tack of the neurologists based at MIT[1].

What is certain is mathematical thinking has recently demonstrated its ability to reshape language study. That is what modern linguistic philosophy is about. It makes language the tool of theoretical thinking, which you might think would settle the chicken and egg question satisfactorily: the egg preceded the chicken, hatching dinosaurs etc before the chicken was invented. But now it takes a chicken to lay its egg. Now it takes a speaker to contribute a thought. But the thought came before its expression in speech.

In this rather brief history, we have skipped the British colonial judge in India, Sir William Jones, who drew attention to the kinship of Sanskrit and Greek, starting a fashion of comparative linguistics and historical (diachronic, across time) study of language development. Now it is rather dull, but it has bred evolutionary rules - which do not actually apply in practice - for phonetic shunts: from bh to b to p, etc. offering a protocol for blind linguistic change, as if it were a natural process like the evolution of species.

Gottlob Frege (1848-1925) was a significant German mathematician as well as a philosopher and therefore not to be lightly challenged. He was prayed in aid by a succession of mathematically minded logicians tackling language, supposedly without prepossession. Before Frege the Classical philosophers had spent their efforts on categorical thinking, largely Aristotle's syllogisms, never probing behind them. The human mind likes a board with small squares on it. As has been seen in chapter 15, entities (categories) are far from being aboriginal concepts, and carefree entification (categorization) may be a dangerous snare hindering proper discrimination. The bounded category (confused with the unbounded unlocated criterion) separating red from not-red for example, an adjectival concept already invented by the adjectival minds of our hominid forebears, as also evidenced (by recapitulation?) in the mind of the infant exploring his nursery wallpaper (see chapter 15 on thinking), is no good place to start your thinking. The discriminating distinction is prior.

Appendix A Philosophy

Bertrand Russell's Principia Mathematica provided a symbolic grammar. It was a recognition of the influence of language on philosophy and an attempt to sharpen up the language for the job. The Vienna Circle were somewhat similarly engaged at the same time, and classical logic was simultaneously up for review. It was a great time for academic intellectuals and a time for painful readjustment for the churches. There is no doubt that the clarity of thinking was much advanced. Natural language however was reinvented in terms of a logical system of grammar, leaving out traditional semantic examination of the lexicon. The rules of grammar usurped all attention. Finally, with Chomsky, original artificial language was overwritten by a deliberately artificial one, and the understanding and classification of languages, especially those facing extinction, was diverted to analyses of their grammar. Philology has yielded place to linguistics at the same time as philosophy has yielded place to logic. Language study has not been served.

The linguistic stretch which Frege and Russell contrived was a revolt against the eighteenth and early nineteenth century idealist systematisers who can I think now be seen as acting out all unawares the last convulsive death throes of the epistemological stance thrown up by the theologians, in turn founded on Plato and Aristotle, via Tom Aquinas. The systematisers cover a fair spread, from Kant to Marx and even (let it only be whispered) to Darwin. Structuralism and post modern deconstruction are really only a replay. Chomsky is in Kant's post hole. The game has gone to second set because of the math that came in with Frege and Russell, which now has to be filtered out again. Meaning is semantic, and there is little structural about semantics other than the diachronic trees of etymology. Chomsky's synchronic systematization is an imposition and it harks back to Kant's methodology, adding only some psyfi psychology with the subconscious, like Jung's Group Soul carrying ideas from generation to generation for those with the gift to access it. We do better with language as metaphysic in the minds of each generation, with a scientific passage of understanding in the here and now in every case, albeit involving the subconscious minds of the participants via the lexicon and with no magic intergenerational (genetic) transference of the metaphysic. Putting ideas into genetic inheritance via a language organ is not science but magic. Ideas are actions of the brain, and can not be inherited as organic form can. They are not physical entities and can not be passed down in the genes. We are born instinctive beings but not wranglers with the ideas in place for play to commence. The brain provides capacity but does not determine the ideas it generates. The connection between physical function and thought is not understood, and is not to be hypothesized to fit a fancied theory.

What is math? It is a game with simple rules. Reason rules, and consistency counts most. Inconsistency is ruled out, however slightly reason is based (ie merely on linguistic convention). Your sequiturs must resist challenge, but the challenges allowable are only those of logic, a human ability promoted to a superhuman role ruling the universe. Mathematicians equate reason with reality, so that their minds are apt to become trapped in a single closed system. Maths turns out, or rather selects quick brained wranglers, those who make the biggest mistakes. There is a good deal of common sense at the bottom of the bucket like 1+1=2 and 2+2=4 for instance, along with some more difficult equations and transforms, but there is often a good deal of froth at the top where it meets the open air. Radical discoveries often appear at first to overturn conventional rationality, and on reconsideration require redefinition of what it is reasonable to believe. This appendix is on the philosophy of language. It is really beyond its scope to proceed to a philosophy of maths.

Appendix A Philosophy

We need now to undertake a radical analysis of Ludwig Wittgenstein's Tractatus Logico Philosophicus, as a final prolegomena to Lithic, in order to clear away many of the obstacles to thinking about thinking that he left us with. He was born in 1883 of plutocratic parentage in Austria-Hungary and reckoned he had seen through philosophy, announcing the end of it, its questions and answers being compounded of misunderstandings in language and logic - a splendid research programme but perhaps inevitably mishandled in the execution at his time . In aid of all this he produced at length a gnomic document of some 84 pages, Tractatus Logico Philosophicus (A Philosophical Tract on Logic), in which he rather engagingly admitted in his preface it was quite possible nobody would be able to follow unless they happened to have already had the same ideas, or something similar, themselves. There is indeed a nugget here: his schema scores more highly for consistency than relevance to the commonplace reality to which the rest of us have access. That is not to say it is a total misfit, but the fact is it allows itself such a spare frame it would fit almost anything. His genius was to cobble together a whimsy quite unlike other contemporary whimsies while all the time engaged in hard pounding in logical terms. In particular he subordinated language to mathematics, which meant treating it as a branch of logic, rather than the other way around, logic as a branch of language. In this he was encouraged by Bertrand Russell, under whom he studied at Cambridge. This curiosity has spawned Noam Chomsky also. In reality language is language and historically both logic and mathematics have grown out of it. Neither came from dumb hominids after all.

Meditating on Wittgenstein's apothegms, it occurs to me his penultimate view as expressed in his Tractatus was the Stone Age prelinguistic one. He lived, like the Ancient Egyptians also, in a world made up of a succession of pictures or states of play, much like the frames of a cinema film, the same idea we may think which allowed the invention of the cinematograph. These visions he labeled "facts". He was a simple realist, originally from the Vienna school of thinking. He saw his role as clearing up the cat's cradles made up by his contemporaries. That sounds promising. But his minimalist posture made his few statements insufficiently informative. Half way through he changed his mind and never wrote down any clear exposition of his final position.

There is no doubt, since he says so, he had parlayed this world view to one where his pictures were shaped into (treated as) sets of circumstances, which he then chose to further define as "existing in logical space". By now he was fairly far removed from any picture known to the rest of us, whatever value his construct held for him. It is a quirk of the solipsist mind it can make its own leaps of convenience, fancying them as implicit in the nature of things, quite unaware of the subjectivity involved. I doubt if he had heard of Pyrrhon. It was, so far as one can now see, all in aid of making out that the natural world and logic were in some kind of one to one relationship, so that his magisterial logic handling could be made out to entitle him to dispose of the world on his own terms also.

This is of course an absurdity, or more accurately several absurdities one after another. Anyway by this stage he had also departed rather widely from the Lithic perception, which merely parlayed the pictorial scene by using analogy to abstract semantic patterns from the scenery and apply them across the board. The classic Lithic analogy in building vocabulary was by means of these "gulls" or sidestep metaphors. This term is coined for the trick of labeling a character observed in a named phenomenon with the prior name: a gull wing from the shape of the gull's wing, for example, where the gull is named beforehand for it's wailing cry (the same root informing call, gala, gale and gull, all from the two common roots which we can label go-la) and the wing picks up its character from the shape of the gull's wing and the gull's name with it, although the wing is silent and neither calls nor sings. The wing is the wing of the singer but it does not itself sing. Interestingly there is an entrée to syntax here: the analogy is of an abstracted aspect from a substantive symbol (adjective and noun in modern terms).

But that kind of Lithic reasoning falls far short of Wittgenstein's devolution from pictorialisation to propositional representation and then further abstraction to a presentation in a logical space. These transmogrifications are, quite frankly, unwarranted. But senior wranglers are apt to wrangle the way they learned. There is an apostolic succession in academic circles which often keeps the same balls in the air for an inordinately (absurdly) long time. But one man's philosophy is another man's whimsy, and the passage of history has generally justified the whimsiologists (those exposing the whimsies) and not those indulging in them. Thus it is that the pressures nowadays on those proposing to follow through any individual schematism are indeed daunting, and this includes the Lithic Hypotheses in so far as they can be defined as a schematism. That is one reason why the Lithic row to date remains unhoed. The ideology of linguistics has poisoned the wells. We need a new research programme: whimsiology. Yet the instinct to shake out evidence into a form enabling a degree of understanding can not be denied. It must however be done with discretion and a preparedness to tolerate almost any degree of limitation. This is the complete opposite of the wisdom purveyed at staff colleges, and widely practiced in bureaucratic and technical institutions world wide, where the trick is to achieve as structured a scheme of things as possible.

Edward de Bono has made a killing advocating an alternative strategy of thinking sideways, as well as deliberately examining circumstances under different heads or "thinking hats". The latter is to review matters consecutively under radically different aspects, and even other peoples' hats, to discover how the other coons involved may be seeing things. The hats aren't much, but the lateral thinking is clever. It takes us back to Lithic analogy and the gulls again, in place of the common modern game plan of logical consequences. De Bono illustrates the saner side of post modern deconstructionism, much of which is overly relativistic, denying any one version of events as the reality. The truth of course is the world is indeed what it is and not another thing, and the relativist view every text is equally subjective so there can be no ultimate reality is mistaken. It is just we can't directly access reality. Our shots are all off centre.

Wittgenstein's personal habits of mind, it can now be seen, were absurd; but we should admire him nevertheless because he certainly got his mind up and running – as we all can and should – and was prepared to follow his own nose all the way. It may not have been an entire success but it has to be said nobody else's nose will do, so he was not wrong in that. Meanwhile it has also been said he was in school with Adolf Hitler, intellectually a comparative weakling, and his toffee nosed posture may have accounted for Hitler's maniacal anti-Semitism later. This is interesting since Wittgenstein himself eventually came to adopt a position not wholly unlike the Nazi philosopher Oswald Spengler, basing understanding on subjective intuition rather than objective science, a position appealing to those who feel themselves to be geniuses. Wittgenstein's scribblings, when he finally got around to it, incompletely expressed his thinking, leaving generations of professional pickers-over to make their sense of them, inadvertently fortifying his whimsy. The real answer to Wittgenstein is simply to say we do not choose to think in that way. The emperor has no clothes.

Reading Tractatus Logico-Philosophicus, which is a list of definitions, it soon becomes apparent many, indeed most of the words he uses are terms of art. They can not possibly mean for him what they mean for most of us. Here are the first few noted: Paragraph

Appendix A Philosophy

2.0121. "If I can imagine objects combined in states of affairs I can not imagine them excluded from the possibility of such combinations". But surely we can. Even if we might not find such a one we can certainly dream of it. 2.0122. "It is impossible for words to appear in two different roles: by themselves, and in propositions". Has he not come across a dictionary? 3.261."Names cannot be anatomized by means of definitions". Names clearly means something different for him from our general understanding of what names are, which we are quite capable of defining. For instance we give the name carpet to a type of floor covering and we can perfectly easily "anatomize" the name with a definition, for instance a floor covering made of fibres of traditional manufacture with a soft pile. We can go on to describe in complete detail its form of manufacture etc, if we know it. To deny this would be silly. So it is clear "name" for Wittgenstein means something different. What it means to him, it appears, is an atomic meaning which he imagines is the point or base meaning which is in the nature of a point or base term in logic, atomic and therefore incapable of further anatomisation. Just a pun really. A point is the x of mathematics, the exemplar of itemization. It symbolizes one of Wittgenstein's "facts" or prelinguistic 'shots' of the external world, which also is bedrock for Wittgenstein, an axiomatic datum not capable of this further anatomisation. Of course such a one would have no further analysis by definition, since analysis is logical and the 'shot' is prior to logic. This is a rather important matter since it points the way to a fundamental assumption made by Wittgenstein in his Tractatus, namely that reality (the world we live in) is logico-philosophicus, or even in fact logico-mathematicus. This trick he probably picked up from Bertrand Russell, under whom he studied in Cambridge. In fact it could be said he picked up Russell's ball and ran with it. But the construct resulting actually bore little relation to reality, however worthy its credentials as math. Indeed his idea that the 'shots' or frames of external reality are prior to logic sits ill with the conclusion he draws quite soon after that the real world can be defined in logical terms. There is after all no reason why the mathematician's ideas should necessarily have any application to reality. He does not possess any method of distinguishing whimsy with useful relevance to thinking of reality, from any other kind by meditating on the matter. He can only adhere to the hard arbitrament of strict experimental science.

Neither Russell nor Wittgenstein had any historical sense, not a scrap between the two of them. They both lived in a glass universe, elegant, see-through and precise, on mental skate boards since both of them were bright. From these glassy halls they preached their definitive universe made up of neatly interlocking pieces, as if the only world were the world of geometry. Both were somewhat autistic. Autism and egotism, even solipsism, go together. Thus their vulnerability and incompetence in interpersonal relations caused them to construct a carapace for themselves, like the caddis fly worm, but made up of clear-cut intellectual pieces, in which they could choir inviolate and not concern themselves with immeasurable personal exchanges. The result was a determinist ideology like Marxism, which like Marxism their contemporaries could not crack. It was a crystal palace but also a cage with bars made of mathematical tautologies, mental surfaces which bounced you back into the edifice whenever you tried to break out, a hall of mirrors, the biggest mental hephalump trap since the Marxist dialectic (in which the European intelligentsia still wallow and will wallow awhile as yet).

But now we are left astonished Wittgenstein could soliloquize so glibly and self confidently about his flawed presumption, elaborating from one gnomic utterance to the next, pulling in more and more words for his own gloss on them, illustrating in almost every case, like with "name" above, that they were all pieces on his own private chequer

Appendix A Philosophy

board and were being recast to his own Procrustean pattern which he believed was the only true logic. It would still have been a bizarre enterprise had he been right. As it was his life-and-death struggle with his own sea serpents left behind for the senators after his death not wisdom exactly but certainly cats cradles enough to keep them mulling over his rather modest textual contribution in the belief the emperor's clothes must be in there somewhere - in pursuit of Ph Ds and academic tenures. Much of their admiration no doubt was due to the undoubted fact he silenced Bertrand Russell. Anyone who could get the better of Russell, the argument went, must certainly be a senior wrangler.

The reality was he had grasped the wrangler's pressure points (inconsistencies) and worked out the dead ends in wrangling. Russell could not avoid thinking the consequential way he thought. He was a basket case by Edward de Bono's standards. Whatever the weather he sailed a straight course and ran up on the rocks when the terrain confronted him; but he died with his carapace intact on his back. It is the way that mathematicians have. Intellectual integrity is their deity; and the cock crows in vain, they recognize no backsliding. They can even be in a straight (strait) jacket and be quite oblivious of it, such is their megalomania. They have their places at the high tables of the world, and that is sufficient for them. At the court of a million years their seats are puny. A smidgeon of the same time scale sees their every idea dismissed as fatuous and forgotten. It is the fatuity which is the point. They are short on understanding, erudite but erroneous, probably from trying too hard when young. A more liberal education is to be found in the crossword puzzle, by comparison of almost infinite variety. This is not a dismissal of convention as at first may appear, but it is a precautionary skepticism.

To be half way fair, Wittgenstein discovered the absurdity of many of his own ideas and after eight years in retreat, some of it literally in the wilderness, a cottage in North Norway, he returned to Cambridge and lectured for sixteen years several generations of students in his own fashion, without publishing a word. He became finally fascinated by the significance of his own skin, what he owned (within) as contrasted with the alien (without). This was certainly back to basics, what every individual has to work out for himself, even before language. For any individual his skin is his boundary. But in reality it is a boundary with two sides, each of significance and neither negating the other as Wittgenstein was inclined to infer. We have sense organs on both sides reporting to control centre, those looking out sensing the alien while those within sense our own domain. The two activities, "facts" in Wittgenstein's private terminology, have something in common. Wittgenstein's idea the internal senses are immediate and given, by contrast with the external which are derivative and contrived, empirical instead of known a priori, is simply an unthinking extension of Kantian philosophy which Wittgenstein imagined he had long ago driven out into the Gadarene Swine (the philosophers).

His upbringing had been privileged, and liberal where money could buy experience, but astonishingly superficial. He was born in 1883, a year before my father who would be a hundred and twenty nine if alive today. In that time we have seen more independent thinking than in the previous five centuries, and the pace quickens daily. He followed his own father, a committed entrepreneurial achiever. His first adult study was engineering, (a relatively banausic discipline) in England; and he had in fact come only later to classical philosophy, keen to dismember it. His father was an apostate Jew, a man of the world proud of his worldly success, said to be the wealthiest man in Austria in his day, the power of his purse bringing him friendship with the intellectuals as well as the musicians in Vienna. Young Ludwig's philosophy, only lately acquired, seems to have stayed with him in spite of his best efforts to expel it. The total dismantlement of the elaborate structure of

Appendix A Philosophy

an adult weltanschaung, built up in infancy and adolescence layer upon layer, is probably a near impossibility later in life. Certainly it involves a more radical abandonment, even reversal of thinking habits than Wittgenstein was capable of; whence his spiritual turmoil in his wilderness years.

He had cast off from the shores of conventional wisdom and never again found any firm foothold. His posthumous works were posthumous because he never finally adopted any position in his lifetime. He powerfully challenged the sane world of his day but he never replaced it. His life left him in a gaping void, a "néant", which the Lithic Hypotheses must now contribute to bridging over. We can see now that his reliance on contrasting the immediacy and indubitability of internal sensation – he sticks to pain as exemplar most of the time – with the empirical uncertainties of the external senses, seeing and hearing for the most part, but also of course registering a hot and cold environment and the bruising from heavy whacks, is greatly overdone. These latter internal sensations are triggered from the outside but sensed internally, and in that not so far from vision of the other, the outside world, which also – come to think of it - is triggered from the outside but sensed internally, just as pain is.

We can remind ourselves here of the Ancient Egyptians, the earliest thinkers I know much of, whose gallimaufry of there-and-back rays were called into play to explain vision (and much else). A ray went out from the eye and contacted, touched, felt over the panorama, returning with an image of it which it deposited on the iris (the i-rai['s], the irradiated) of the eye for the homunculus behind to view. The eye's action at a distance was thus tamed, and matched with the hand's sensibility of what it touched in a manner these old fogeys found an acceptable explanation. The Egyptians actually drew the all powerful sun's rays with hands on the ends, symbolizing their power to draw the vegetation up with them on their return journey to the sun. Egyptian rays all went there and back like active radar beams, an illusion based on the clear ability of the eye to bring back a picture to the eye, which could actually be seen on the iris; actually a reflection of the light, the eye being in reality a passive sensor and not an emitter at all.

Their language and metaphor may have been crude but they had the business better than Wittgenstein, who was making it up to suit his message to posterity. They kept all their senses internal and reconciled this with messages coming from outside. It would be nice to be able to report they believed in neither the internal nor the external signals they received, but the fact is they appear to have believed in the divine nature of both. Modern science has uncovered bogus sensations, when amputees sense pains or other messages from limbs no longer there, real sensations but misinformative, just as we can mistake what we see. The natures of the respective senses which report internal and external stimuli is not contrapuntal as Wittgenstein wanted them to be to stress the primacy of the emotions like desire and suffering, hope and frustration as the origins of thinking, rather then any calculating (philosophical) thinking. In this of course he was right although he muffed the record. He was grappling with the myriad sottiseries of his day, and he had rumbled many of them.

Wittgenstein's documentation was put into book form ("Philosophical Investigations") posthumously, under the direction of Professor von Wright, a Finnish philosopher of Scottish extraction who inherited Wittgenstein's position at Cambridge. In this his second avatar Wittgenstein had dumped Descartes' ghost in the machine, a dualistic view not evidenced in reality. He argued for a single integral human personality not fully conscious or "knowing its mind". The Lithic language hypothesis quite nicely matches Wittgenstein's belief in the corruption of thinking from the misapprehension of language.

But he insisted internal perceptions (sensed experience), like "I feel a pain", were a priori and not empirical like messages from without. Germans have treated Kant and Hegel like Shakespeare, that is as unchallengeable. Von Wright, who survived into the twenty first century, took Wittgenstein's later sensationalism in his "Philosophical Investigations"one stage further, virtually dumping science for intuition and espousing the radical thinking of Oswald Spengler. Spengler, a runt Nazi philosopher with an outsize grudge for losing the first world war, while employed as a snide secondary school teacher at Blankenburg am Rhein wrote a world history (Der Untergang den Abendlandes, The Decline of the West) in the 1920s, in which he perceived civilizations (cultures) as growths like cabbages and kings, which burgeoned and decayed. He was Hitler's favourite philosopher. The decay stage was Hitler's decadence. His thinking, like all those who see themselves as geniuses, was a tightly textured mix of brilliance and absurdity. It was in rejection of this kind of ideology that Burgess and MacLean, as well as the Keeper of the Queen's pictures, embraced instead the other common insanity of the twentieth century, Marxism, which had a dialectic supposed to trump science. It cost tens of millions of lives learning it did not. But we have now reviewed the intellectual history of the last century and cleared the decks for the study of thinking, without bothering further with academe.

"Philosophical Investigations", published in 1953, some 200 large pages of text in German, discloses thinking which is linear and omnidirectional, with no very elaborate game plan, seeks to tease out the uncertainties in any statements made, so far as I can see in search of a complete logic. He is unaware that by now grown up thinking is a texture, (even a pudding) of ideas, making a texture of words, making a texture of meanings. His stringing of meanings is inadequate. He lived in a single plank world compiled of mathematical thinking, just like Russell and Chomsky, reduced to cat's cradling. His looking was one eyed, without focus. His paragraphs were little individual cobwebs, sketched with fine lines of logic, demonstrating to his own satisfaction his inability to accept any conclusions. He finished up with a view of the world not all that far removed from the state we must have been in before we spoke, when our recollections were in the form of just pictorial "shots" by means of which we were able to resume what was at any time "the case". In this pickle he stuck with the search for certainty with exemplary but inconclusive analyses of what made up the case – in each case. He numbered his intellectual cobwebs consecutively, 1 to 693 in part 1. Part 2 has the pagination all mixed up in my edition, pages 156 to 194 with pages ii to xiv from the preface mixed in to no readily identifiable plan, but fortunately the text carries on regardless, with the pages just wrongly numbered. But the cobwebs are unnumbered in part 2.

To sum up it is probably best to start by just announcing the true nature of language to be a system of symbols by means of which the utterances of mankind are given specific meanings. This at any rate was the opinion of Ferdinand de Saussure (1851-1913), a Swiss academic and professor at the University of Geneva all his working life. He had already produced an original analysis of the use of Indo European vowels while still a student; and that proved his swan song so far as the historical approach was concerned. He graduated to language as a structural system for study either diachronically (historically) in detail, as he had at the outset, picking on the vowel changes, or else synchronically, scientifically he would have said or even logically, emphasizing the systemics. He spent the rest of his life lecturing on this latter aspect of linguistics, the systemics turning out to be the grammar. The historical approach he just dumped.

On the other side of the Atlantic C S Pierce (1839-1914) added his own philosophical analysis of language as the principal sign system of Saussure's "Semiotics", the study of

Appendix A Philosophy

signs and signing. For Pierce a sign was "something which stands to somebody for something". I think we would now prefer to emphasise the relationship is intended to be triadic and say the symbol is a B (the something) connecting A (somebody) to C (another something). Pierce's definition however allows B connecting A to A since he uses 'something' in both cases. The Greek "sum-bol" means thrown or linked together, that is relating things, and the insinuation is the relationship is random, even casual, rather than semantic as in the Lithic Hypothesis. Pierce had three types of signs, which were taken as soundly differentiated for a time and provided student material for generations. With the first type, an icon, the relationship between signifier and signified was one of resemblance, principally a configural representation like the Russian religious ikon, the most straightforward type, painted portraits; but we might put the cuckoo in front of the icon, as a representation by way of a natural echoism. The second type was an index, or indicator, the relationship being by way of a habitual natural association, for example smoke as a sign indicating fire. We might include the cuckoo here also, the call indicating the bird. The ikon or configural representation could of course qualify here by habitual association as well, the visual representation, perhaps only an outline shape, being just as much an indicator as a bird call, but a picture is manufactured, not a work of nature. The third type was much in the majority and was arbitrary and had to be learned, such as most words for things. In fact most words do have to be learned as arbitrary these days. We can however gloss all these types of signs as semantic since they all excite ideas, cuckoos and pictures directly using auditory and visual representations. Indexes like smoke, and cuckoos and outlines if you choose to treat the cuckoo's call as an index of the bird rather than just its auditory representation, and an outline as an indicator of the bloke, all elicit the idea by association with the signifier. Wherever there is smoke there is fire, whenever the cuckoo is heard there is a cuckoo, whenever a good enough icon is presented it is recognized as a representation of the signified. The third type of icon (words for things) appears to have been a Lithic one in disguise, and is therefore conventionally treated as arbitrary.

Meanwhile words, treated as random signifiers, are indeed equally good at evoking the idea. The route is semantic and arises by association, just like on hearing the cuckoo. Note that party A is providing the idea. It is not the signified prompting the signifier nor the signified prompting the sign. The two meet, if they do meet, in somebody's mind (A). We (A) see the smoke (B) and think of the fire (C). We (A) hear the call (B) and think of the cuckoo (C). We (A) say the word (B) and are thinking of the meaning (C). But with the words there is more to be said. Uncovering Lithic reveals hidden semantic links overlooked and forgotten over the millennia. Over the millennia psychosemantics have built semantic structures in the subconscious. I think of them as if they were underwater reefs made up of linked meanings, building all the while and linked by nothing more substantial than the whimsy of the human mind associating analogies, gulls and buses, etc; but for the human mind solid enough material to build an underwater reef. Built into the coral fabric of the reef under the flag of "La" for instance we can find flat and long and line piled on top of slip and slope, lye overlying laut (sea in Malay); and so on across the whole phonemic vocabulary. These structures are ideational fantasies. They are not inheritable. When the mind dies, so do the ideas. Each generation rebuilds them over again afresh, on the underside of the language they learn, and some no doubt learn them better than others. There was no other route to mutual understanding when first we began to speak. Psychosemantic prompts alone gave any hope of mutual comprehension of language. The vocabulary must surely have started out extraordinarily small, and grown slowly with it. The reefs initially were low, but there is a lot of coral in the water now.

Appendix A Philosophy

The whole of linguistics has been railroaded since Saussure and Pierce and sidelined into the study of grammar, so that it now takes a massive effort to recover the missing ground and refocus attention on the semantic contents of the whole of speech and not just the logical relationships of the parts of speech the grammarians have been syncopating for over a century. Over the past century we have virtually dumped the lexicon for a mess of grammatical pottage. The grammarians won't have it; so let us say virtually dumped semantics anyway. Systematising has known no bounds. Every grammarian since Panini with any claim to originality has not only recorded language as spoken but has also been unable to resist refashioning it nearer to his heart's desire, to how he would have wished it to have been (that is to say more uniform). This applies to Professor Chomsky just as much as Panini all those centuries ago. They can not help neglecting the semantics of the lexicon, with ears only for its inflexions.

To some extent the swing to a grammatical focus has been the result of revulsion away from the fanciful etymologies of philologists before the linguistic reformation of the 1900s. Eric Partridge records these as "f/e" or folk etymologies. He was guilty of promulgating a fair number himself, all unawares. Nevertheless he is my hero. But I think of his pies he supposed first made of magpies every time I learn another semantic connection from him, as most days I still do. His mind was completely bereft of any meaning of pai. Both pie and magpie were just happenstance.

The logical positivism which originated in the Vienna Circle, and was still reputable when I was at Oxford only sixty five years ago, reckoned sentence meaning was analytical like logic and mathematics, while traditional semantics was synthetic, a question of the relationship between human thinking and the phenomenal world. This perception rubbished semantics, down grading it to descriptive names, which were taken to be merely conventional anyway, which left etymology just a branch of phonetics. It simultaneously sidelined the historical or diachronic approach, replacing it with the new synchronic science of linguistic analysis in logical terms. It was a first fine caroling of modernism, but it left out most of language in favour of a linguistic algebra which turned out to be a reformed grammar; and when it had to be found a place was consigned to the subconscious because it was not consciously known to speakers. They inherit it and used it but do not know what really goes on down there.

I am endebted to John L Casti's elegant synopsis of linguistic theorising over the past fifty years[2]. What has enabled Noam Chomsky to claim we have an organ capable of passing on hereditary ideas/guidance as to how we should speak is that it appears that "the poverty of stimulus" when youngsters are learning their language can not explain how they learn it so well. The argument is that some further guidance must therefore be helping them; so it must be neurological. Nevertheless the idea that ideas, rather than just instinctive or emotional dispositions, might be heritable seems absurd to many, and certainly to me. So the question for us is where might this tutorial assistance come from, if not from Chomsky's hard wiring of the brain. The answer I believe is twofold, or even threefold. First of all the pattern Chomsky describes is analytical, logical, even mathematical, and quite dubiously relates to the actual development of language. In reality assistance comes from subconscious processing of the data, not inheritance of it. Learning is not a simple or single process. Chomsky himself has described deep structure as not immediately discoverable in the surface structure of language. Lithic language elements similarly are not immediately obvious in the conventional analysis of word structures but nevertheless can be described as a consistent scheme of semantic and phonetic development, once the Lithic psychosemantic patterns are revealed.

Appendix A Philosophy

It has already been suggested in chapter 15 on thinking that the explanation is that processing takes place in the subconscious, which is not immediately apparent when consciously examined. This is very much like Chomsky's transformational grammar, also located in the subconscious. But instead of an unbelievable intellectual cerebral organ, born up-and-running, equipped with linguistic (intellectual) guidance (with thoughts, and quite elaborate thoughts at that), ready to tackle transformational grammar without ever becoming consciously aware of it; in its place the Lithic lexicon itself provides the guidance for the subconscious mind with a Lithic scheme of organization, all the way from the dream world, reinforcing the shallow contacts with the conscious rational part of the mind which human experience provides. The point is the lexicon as it is learned is both the trigger and the source. Youngsters can avail themselves of this muse more than adults in whom it has been drowned out by very much more conscious verbiage acquired from education education education, often misaligned, over many generations. Unlike Kant's high priori or Jung's World Soul or even Freud's overly patterned subconscious, the world lexicon contains all that is required to facilitate learning and it is located in the world we all know and not in any philosophical metaphysical limbo. It provides a guide to meanings. It comes from the semantics of the Lithic elements, which enlighten the subconscious mind, which expands as we learn them. The subconscious mind is learning to speak Lithic while the conscious mind is acquiring the surface language that the child's parents are teaching. This is a pattern of events very similar to Chomsky's subconscious grammatising genius, just with a different medium: the Lithic semantics imprinted in the mind by language. Given the language, entered by parental influences, and the Lithic is picked out of it by the subconscious, pari passu. This accounts for the extra prompts Chomsky was looking for when he lit on the subconscious, and imagined it must be ready made and prepositioned there waiting to boost the inputs from the outside world. We are all simple Neanderthalers under the skin; and it turns out it is this Lithic application, the true science of cognition, which appears to best fit the facts. There really is another way to account for the facts Chomsky uses to validate his transformational grammar. Lithic language has no need initially for any transformational grammar, it just initially enabled us to speak; and the transformational grammarians' glosses on that come aeons after.

There are other things about Chomsky's approach which jar. His famous nonsense sentence "Colourless green ideas sleep furiously" which he used to display his belief that syntactic rules, which are used to form sentences, exist independently of the semantics of the sentence, can also be used to indicate the reverse: namely that his syntactic schemes may be fine but they ignore the actual meanings which comprise sentences made of actual words, rather than algebraic variables. They have nothing to do with knowledge, they can be used (and are used) to construct nonsense sentences just as well as meaningful ones. This is because the meanings actually reside in the words of which the sentences are made up, and only derivatively in the sentences. Sentences and the grammar that goes with them are copied from word structures tidied up by grammarians in accordance with their various schemes, of which Chomsky's is only the latest.

What was really novel about Chomsky's "revolutionary" approach was his understanding the philatelic approach, just collecting languages, was not enough. What was required was new ideas, clear thinking in order to embrace the variety of game plans turning up in exotic tongues. This was fine. It was even true. It involved hard and original thinking. He picked up where symbolic logic left off, that is to say where mathematics led. But mathematical thinking is a minority sport, and always has been. To find mathematical principles hard wired in the brain and inherited for each citizen's self-teach language course was a bridge too far – by far. Lithic primitive language roots demonstrate at least that if Chomsky's grammar is valid it must have come later. It does not fit primitive thinking, of which Chomsky apparently had no direct experience. He is an ivory tower thinker, a true intellectual, politically as well as linguistically. That was the virtue of his approach in linguistics. He freed linguists from the bind they had gotten into when they rejected the semantic content of language – as if we were all Pavlovian dogs. Chomsky however was carrying baggage too. The guidance (I still see it as intellectual, and therefore problematic if also genetic) which he claimed was hard wired was not the one which informed language from the outset, but another set he had compiled from contemporary thinking. He was not afraid of metaphysics, but he was not as good a judge of ideas as he imagined. Sentence structure is peripheral to linguistic performance, not central. It is late, not original. It is derivative, not deeper than or prior to semantic structuring which originates with speaking in the process of word formation.

Chomsky's generative grammar is often designated as "top down" as opposed to the empiricists' school of inductive research which is "bottom up". There is inevitably an element of German high idealism of the materialistic sort in the top down approach, the thinking which has permitted, even encouraged the European totalitarian schools of the past century. So I think the farm boys have it if they can break through the conventional crust and loosen up their thinking. The Sapir-Whorf hypothesis must go too. It comprises two propositions supposedly one implying the other, namely language is prior to thinking, and we think in words; and so, since our words are unique to our language so are our ideas and even our world view. Benjamin Whorf was a fire inspector for an insurance company when he was not writing on language. That is really enough said. His thinking was surface thinking, not deep at all. It may even be his own thinking never did get beyond those insights offered by his vocabulary. In reality thought is pretty obviously prior to its expression, even if vocabulary trammels our minds, as indeed it does.

Chomskyan linguistics, concentrating on transformational grammar at a deep level which is innate, has appealed to the even newer school of cognitive science researching neurolinguistics and claiming computers can think like humans, that thinking is just a dead scheme. It is almost Skinner's revenge on Chomsky: even mental activity like Chomsky's grammar can be clawed back into the empiricists' fold, disregarding John Searle's demurrer[3]. A spin off is computers can be used as models of brain activity. The theory is bunk and computers can not think in any meaningful sense, for which live brain activity is required. James Joyce described the motive of his "Ulysses", the story in the form of a complete flow of self consciousness over twenty four hours in Dublin, in terms of his perception of the "river of unformed analysis flowing inside our hearts". It makes no sense at all in terms of neuroscience, and even less in terms of computers, but it is meaningful all the same. It recognises creativity – with a typical Irish uncritical (hedonistic) acceptance, as if every bubble were of value, to be enjoyed.

At the outset of language it was psychosemantics which prompted the meanings attached to the sounds uttered. This was the origin of the symbolization which introduced linguistic skills. Symbolisation is really a red herring. It was simply a case of recognizing uttered sounds as having meanings, and this came from the psychosemantic (instinctive) realization that imitative sounds were intended to direct your attention to the source imitated. Human whimsy took a liberal view of what the sounds we made were imitating, or anyway indicative of. It was common sense really. Chimpanzees could probably have managed it, if they could make imitative sounds to get the ball in play. If psychic promptings gave us our initial semantic structuring, when did this prompting change to semantics determined by logical considerations? Like much philosophy, this turns out to be a question posed in terms which are bogus. When the change occurred is a misleading question, since it never did. There is right now on an everyday basis the very same mix of subjective whimsy and odd-ball analogy in play as there was when we first began to put meanings to utterances. There is also today some degree of sweet reason superadded, but this is because with a vast lexicon there is the more scope and requirement for good order and logical discipline in the development of the vocabulary. Yet even the basic mathematicological syllogism $1+1=2$ is psychologically inspired. We even know the inspiration, the prehistoric Ts carved on rocks. We sensed items and then we learned to enumerate two. It may be, indeed it is the case that the world performs more or less in accordance with the mathematicological rules we have developed for ourselves over hundreds of thousands of years of trial and error. But the world is not doing the sums. We are. The world's behaviour falls into the patterns we describe (more or less) because it is its own nature to do so. Science describes nature but nature can not follow the argument. Nature is blind and performance based, and outside anything our conscious imagination can tell us, even when it is the nature which is within us. We sketch the nearest simulacrum we can manage using our subjective senses.

When you are picking your way forward trying to discover and frame the terms of procedure in a hypothetical situation such as at the birth of language some six hundred thousand years ago, it actually comes easiest to coin language appropriate to those circumstances, because clearly current prejudicial baggage does not apply. There is a clean slate of possibilities. Psychosemantics is the term hit upon to describe the combination of the unthinking subjective automatic responses of our primitive forebears confronted with their paleolithic environment. Stone Age man in a stone age environment must have reacted, we must assume, as well as he might. At any rate it appears he was able to reach a number of consensual views sufficient to start language off with enough mutual understanding to keep the process and the progress going. The rest was eventual history, after a good deal of prehistory (hundreds of thousands of years) which is missing.

Some at least of the missing bits are recoverable as inclusions in the lexicon, like flies in amber, or indeed like the shell inclusions in sedimentary rocks which with a wild gamble on the evolutionary sequences enabled Sir Charles Lyell (with my great grandfather, 1804-1870, and his shell collection) to spell out the evolutionary tale in scientific terms (Lyell's "Principles of Geology" in 1831) for Charles Darwin to copy in his "On the Origin of Species" in 1859. Species evolution was used to prove geological evolution and not the other way about as appears in the history books, because Darwin prevaricated, in order to save his mentor, Sir Charles, being sent to Coventry by his fellow Cambridge dons in dog collars. In rather the same way the phonemic semantic contents surviving as inclusions in the lexicon are used 146 years later (in 2005 originally) to establish the semantic development of languages all around the world from the original Lithic phonemes given their prehistoric meanings. Mental inclusions guide mental geology. It is a mite more difficult than examining still existent prehistoric microscopic shells; but the story line is the same. World wide, modern languages still carry the patterns which were imprinted on the human mind when first we learned to speak. This does not make the mind immortal, nor hooked into a universal mind; nor even preprogrammed linguistically in any degree by our genes as Chomsky fancies. It is simply that language, like an iceberg, has a large volume concealed below the surface at a deep level in our subconscious minds. When we learn a language with our conscious minds, there are prehistoric roots concealed below the surface of consciousness which are gathered from

Appendix A Philosophy

the words we speak. The Lithic Hypotheses discover these original roots. In mental space they are like the roots of teeth, but of course mental space is a figment.

The Encyclopedia Britannica is a reliable middle of the road compilation recording what is academically correct. In it we find "The great majority of word shapes bear no direct relation to their lexical meanings. If they did languages would be more alike". Both statements are both false and seriously misleading. Words are compositions in the original terms in which we learned to speak, and their phonetic composition is determined by the meanings they carry. That does not make the languages spoken the same because there are innumerable ways of expressing a meaning, and long since we lost the understanding of how we originally composed our words, many millennia of slovening and slurring (as if it made no difference) have blurred somewhat the original configurations. In order to relate word composition to meaning, all you have to manage is an understanding of the Lithic Hypotheses. It still is not easy, because of the whimsicality of the human mind, often quite hard to follow after a few hundreds of thousands of years. But the original structures can most often be recovered, once you know how to open them up again where they have become compressed. Even geological strata compress somewhat in the same timescale, and water spouts up in artesian wells from the pressure of the overburden.

There are always a number of different ways of prompting for meanings, so languages diverge anyway, and we should expect it. The surprise is that most often it turns out any two or more people followed astonishingly similar lines of thought. Psychosemantics is a continual surprise today. But Lithic is veridical, however unwelcome for those with minds already made up with different ideas.

The Britannica quotes Aristotle also: "Speech is the representation of the experiences of the mind". I like this because it recognizes thinking is experienced first, before speech, and because it identifies speech as expressing thought, and not the other way about; and above all because it recognizes thought as something which we experience, by which I mean as something naturally happening to us without necessarily any particular intention on our part. That is half way as I see it to recognizing the subconscious mind's contribution. Aristotle's apothegm is thus for me of an altogether higher order than the two misleading sentences from a modern hack, most likely a professor - of the commonplace. It is even curious the encyclopedia makes such a point of countering a position otherwise unmentioned – perhaps others too have begun to chip away at the randomness of word roots though not as yet in print. Novel ideas are never all that unique, they tend to be in the air; and Chomsky's inherited subconscious grammar has been teasing the linguistic establishment for a number of decades now and must have generated some frictional heat. There is in reality an echoism of one kind or another in every word at coining. But the encyclopedia goes on to suggest the different names for horse in European languages alone proves word formation is arbitrary. It is of course a common presumption if you can not see a connection that there is none. The road to perdition may even be paved with such kinds of presumptions. So it might be worth spending the time to expose the absurdity of the above proposition, demonstrating all the words for horse in all the languages which can readily be called to mind make perfect sense if read in Lithic phonetic elements. OK, you may have to make some adjustments for the slovening of six hundreds of thousands of years.

Horses are unusual in the animal kingdom and have attracted a good deal of human attention and use all round the world. They are renowned for their gameness, spiritedness, strength and speed; and of course they get ridden, when they will even go into battle or confront rioters with you on board. They are intelligent. They are not all Black Beauties

Appendix A Philosophy

(in fact none are), but they are intelligent, even affectionate, way ahead of cows if behind dogs. Anyone handling a stallion, even a Shetland pony, learns to show respect. They strike with their two front hooves which are hard to avoid, if barred from a mare or in defence of a foal, as well as their more casual hoofing with the back feet to discourage pursuit. A cow is a coward easily cowed by comparison, although it wears horns. Now here are the names for horse used by Encyclopedia Britannica to rubbish Lithic, "all unrelated to the animal so named"; "for by far the largest number of words in a language there is no direct association between sound and meaning". There is surely some impatience with what is perceived as time-wasting by mavericks showing here. The author is saying there is more important business: anything in the nature of Lithic should be brushed aside as worthless time wasting. Yet no single mind, at least in the last few thousand years, has ever thought to make any analysis of the sounds involved in framing the semantics. So here goes, on the terrain chosen by the encyclopaedia.

English Horse. It is from Lithic elements Hara-sai, hurrah-active or rejoicing in action. See chapters 7, 12 and 13. He rejoices in action. What animal? Answer: the horse of course. Compare a cow for instance. Young ones will canter. But horses gallop for fun.

German Pferd. It is from Lithic Pa-pahei-dai, goes-with its cock up-does (pa-hei started out as the rampant penis) see chapters 11, 7 and 5. The species is named of course for its boys while still entire.

French Cheval. Compare Spanish Caballo (the Caballiero is the horseman riding it). It is from the Lithic Strong Runner, see chapters 4, 3 and 8. Antelopes may be marginally fleeter but not stronger, and they confine their sprinting to escape from predators.

Latin Equus. It is from the Lithic Ai-Kai-u-s, He is-strong and headstrong-both (u is the dual vowel and -s is the noun ending), literally That which-[has]strengths-dual. See chapter 14 for the vowel meanings and chapter 4 for Kai.

Greek Hippos. It is from Lithic Hei-pau-s, rejoicing-in his legs (-s is the Greek noun ending), a gay galloper. See chapters 7 and 11.

We can add immediately Chinese Ma, see chapter 9 for weighty and firm, and 14 for the reading ma'a, him'a goer (literally that goes). The falling rising tone in Chinese is really distinguishing two consecutive same vowels. It is easiest to pronounce it as such.

Albanian Kale. It is for the chessman too, from the Lithic ka-lai, strong leaper. The knight's move is a leaping one too. See chapters 4 and 8.

Malay kuda. It is from the Lithic Kau-da (like Latin Equus), doubly strong-does or doer, ie in habit. Then pulling a dictionary from the shelf at random:

Hausa Dauki. It is from the lithic Da-u-kai, Does-double-strong. This looks like a similar double strength to the Latin and the Malay horse, strong and headstrong, spirited as well as powerful. There is Arab blood in West African horses. The Ka was the physical and spiritual driving force, in this world and the next, and it came South across the Sahara to the Hausa speakers in northern Nigeria.

The devilling is in the detail, not in the philosophy, mostly ill considered and trifling. Linguistics is first of all etymology. Etymology is as old as philosophy, in fact it must surely be older. It comes from the Greek etymon, coupled with logos. Logos is word and logic, the semantics of words. Etymon is reliably from Lithic ai-tai-maun, as it-born-meant, its original meaning. I believe the Lithic etymon meant simply an original composition or string, and tells us something already: words are complexes and therefore must have constituents, which in my book are the phonemes composing them with the meanings they bring with them. Etymology is the logic of a word's original meaning. It has to be stressed far too many of these old words with proven ancient histories fit the

Appendix A Philosophy

Lithic. It costs nothing and takes no hard thinking to write sentences in an encyclopaedia. They are only well done on well established ground, not when a guess has to be made from long accustomed assumptions. Then the discomfort from the supressed but underlying uncertainty sharpens the expression.

What final conclusion(s) are we left with? Well, not many really! The importance of understanding the Lithic Hypotheses is they disclose the way we have developed our thinking from day one, which is also the way we still do it: it is by metaphor and analogy. Analogical thinking is a process of abstraction of a particular semantic theme from the lexicon and then (with the minor semantic adjustments necessary) attaching it to a phoneme in different circumstances. A new meaning is born and given a phonetic identification. I have described this process as a gull already, from the seagull which is a sea caller giving the meaning of a gull wing which does no calling but merely copies the shape of the seagull's wing in flight as we often see them in pictures of the seaside. With Lithic we do not have to revise our weltanschauung or world outlook. Perhaps we should be rather more persistent in our questioning of the evidence, and not accept the first conclusion that springs to mind – like the idea there is no sense in words per se, so we should not look for any. We should always keep looking. Merely continuing to rehearse what we think we already know is the biggest intellectual sin. That is why professors who only do the teaching don't appeal. Tenures corrupt, and teaching tenures corrupt absolutely. Every day they should disclose something old and something new.

NOTES

1. Massachusetts Institute of Technology is a distinguished scientific institute in Massachusetts, USA, but with a dominating belief in Darwinist evolutionary philosophy, thought to apply across the board, and so even to thinking, which is an activity and not an organism like the brain. The mind is just shorthand for our thinking. Only species can evolve in Darwinian terms. All else just develops one way or another. MIT is Professor Chomsky's home ground.

2. John L Casti. Paradigms Lost. Chapter 4, pages 213-258.

3. Searle, a philosopher, proposed a procedure where Chinese cards are processed by an uncomprehending operator in accordance with a set or dictionary of syntactic rules he has been given without any explanation of the words' meaning. The dictionary of course was compiled by a Chinese speaker taking the semantics on the cards into account, so that the question and answer cards made perfect sense where the language was understood although the operator could not crack it and was going by syntactic rules alone. This scenario takes some hard pounding to think through but the effort is well worth while.

LITHIC LANGUAGE BIBLIOGRAPHY

Legend. OUP = Oxford University Press. CUP = Cambridge University Press. Books are listed under author(s) where given, with title, publisher, edition (where relevant) and date. The subject matter is not always immediately apparent from the title. But space does not allow further guidance here.

Ablay M. Spoken Here. Arrow Books. 2005.
Allegro JM. The Sacred Mushroom & the Cross. Hodder & Stoughton. 1970.
Aitchison J. The Seeds of Speech. Language Origin & Evolution. CUP. 1996.
Anderson SR & Lightfoot DW. The Language Organ. Linguistics as Cognitive Physiology. CUP. 002.
Austin JL. How to do Things with Words. 1962. CUP. 1980.
Ayto J. Dictionary of Word Origins. Bloomsbury Publishing Ltd. 1990.
Baghramian M. Modern Philosophy of Language. JM Dent. 1998.
Baigent M. Ancient Traces. Viking. Penguin Group. 1998.
Baker Mark C. The Atoms of Language. OUP. 2002.
Barkow JH, Cosmides L, Tooby J. The Adapted Mind. OUP. 1992.
Barnhart R. Chambers Dictionary of Etymology. Chambers. 1988.
Barsky RF. Noam Chomsky, A Life of Dissent. ECW Press Council. 1997.
Barthes R. The Semiotic Challenge. Basil Blackwell. 1988.
Baugh AC & Cable T. A History of the English Language. 1951. 3rd Edn. Routledge & Kegan Paul. 1978.
Becker E. The Birth and Death of Meaning. Penguin. 1972.
Bendix EH. The Uses of Linguistics. New York Academy of Sciences Vol 583. 1990.
Berlin I. Against the Current. Essays on the History of Ideas. Random House. 1955.
Berlin I. Karl Marx. Fontana. Harper Collins. 1995.
Berlitz C. Native Tongues. Grenada Publishing Ltd. 1983.
Bermant C & Weitzman M. Ebla. Weidenfeld & Nicolson, Book Club Associates. 1978.
Bermudez JL. Thinking without Words. OUP. 2002.
Bernal Martin. Black Athena. Vol 1. Vintage. 1987.
Bernal Martin. Black Athena. Vol 2. Free Association Books. 1991
Betro MC. Hieroglyphics. Abbeville Press Publishers. 1996.
Bickerton D. Language and Species. University of Chicago Press. 1990.
Black J. George A. Postgate N. A Concise Dictionary of Akkadian. Harrassowitz Verlag Weisbaden. 2000.
Blackmore S. The Meme Machine. OUP. 1999.
Breal M. The Beginnings of Semantics. Stanford University Press. 1991.
Brothers L. Friday's Footprint. How Society Shapes the Human Mind. OUP. 1997.
Brown CM & Hagoort P. The Neurocognition of Language. OUP. 1999. Paperback. 2000.
Bryson B. Mother Tongue. Penguin. 1990.
Budge EAW. Egyptian Language. Routledge & Kegan Paul. 16th Impression.

Bibliography

1978.
Budge EAW. An Egyptian Hieroglyphic Dictionary. 1920. 2 Volumes. Dover Publications. 1978.
Burchfield R. Unlocking the English Language. Faber & Faber. 1989.
Burgess A. Language made Plain. 1964. Flamingo. Fontana Paperbacks. 1975.
Burgess A. A Mouthful of Air. 1998. Hutchinson. Random House UK Ltd 1992.
Burling R. The Talking Ape. How Language Evolved. OUP. 2005.
Byrne R. The Thinking Ape. OUP. 1995.
Calvin WH. How Brains Think. Weidenfeld & Nicholson. 1997.
Cambridge Encyclopedia of the English Language. CUP. 1995. Crystal D.
Cambridge Encyclopedia of the Language Sciences. CUP. 2011. Hogan PC.
Campbell J. Grammatical Man. Allan Lane. 1982.
Casti JL. Paradigms Lost. 1991. Abacus. 2000.
Cavalli-Sforza LL. Genes, People & Languages. Allen Lane. Penguin Press. 2000.
Chafe Wallace. L. Meaning and the Structure of Language. University of Chicago Press. 1970.
Chantrell G. Oxford Dictionary of Word Origins. OUP. 2002.
Chetwin B. The Songlines. Picador, Pan Books, Jonathan Cape. 1988.
Chetwynd T. A Dictionary of Symbols. Granada Publishing. 1982.
Claxton G. Noises from the Dark Room. Harper Collins. 1994.
Chomsky N. Reflections on Language. Random House 1976.
Chomsky N. Language & Responsibility. Harvester Press, Sussex. 1979.
Chomsky N. The Chomsky Reader. Random House. 1988.
Chomsky N. On Nature & Language. CUP. 2002.
Christiansen MH & Kirby S. Language Evolution. OUP. 2003.
Cirlot JE. A Dictionary of Symbols. Routledge & Kegan Paul. 1962.
Cohane JP. The Key. Fontana/Collins. 1973.
Collins D. The Human revolution, from Ape to Artist. 1976. Phaedon Press. BCA. 1976.
Colman AM. Oxford Dictionary of Psychology. OUP. 2001.
Concise Routledge Encyclopedia of Philosophy. Routledge. BCA. 2000.
Corballis MC. The Lopsided Ape. OUP. 1993.
Cowan JG. Myths of the Dreaming. Prism Press, Dorset. 1994.
Crystal D. Linguistics. Pelican. 1971.
Crystal D. Cambridge Encyclopedia of the English Language. CUP. 1995.
Dalby A. Dictionary of Languages. Bloomsbury Publishing plc. 1998.
Davies JP & Hersh R. Descartes' Dream. Penguin. 1986.
Deacon T. The Symbolic Species. The Co-evolution of Language & the Human Brain. Penguin. 1997.
De Grazia A. Homo Schizo. Metron Publications, Princeton. 1983.
Dehaene S. The Number Sense. Penguin. 1997.
Dennett D. Consciousness Explained. Penguin Group. 1993.
Dennett D. Kinds of Minds. Weidenfeld & Nicolson. 1996.
De Santillana G & von Dechend H. Hamlet's Mill. David R Godine. 1977.
Deutscher G. The Unfolding of Language. William Heineman. 2005.
Dixon RMW & Ackenwald AY. The Amazonian Languages. CUP. 1999.
Dixon RMW & Blake BL. Handbook of Australian Languages Vol 5. OUP.

Bibliography

2000.
Doblhofer E. Voices in Stone. Paledin. Granada Publishing. 1973.
Donnald M. A Mind so Rare. WW Norton & Co. 2001.
Dunbar R. Grooming, Gossip and the Origin of Language. Faber & Faber. 1996.
Eco U. The Search for the Perfect Language. Fontana Press. 1995.
Eco U. Serendipities. Language & Lunacy. Weidenfeld & Nicolson. 1999.
Eco U. Kant & the Platypus. Vintage, Random House. 2000.
Encarta. World English Dictionary. Bloomsbury Publishing plc. 1999.
Fischer SR. A History of Language. Reaktion Books, London. 1999.
Flavell L and R. Dictionary of Word Origins. Kyle Cathie Ltd. 1995.
Fodor JA. Concepts. Where Cognitive Science went Wrong. OUP. 1998.
Foley WA. The Papuan Languages of New Guinea. CUP. 1986.
Fontana D. The Secret Language of Symbols. Pavilion Books, London. 1993.
Fontana Dictionary of Modern Thought. Fontana Collins. 1977.
Foucault M. The Archaeology of Knowledge. Tavistock Publications. 1972.
Gaskell MG. The Oxford Handbook of Psycholinguistics. OUP. 2007.
Goossen IW. Navajo Made Easier. Northland Press. 1967.
Gostony C-G. Dictionnaire d'Etymologie Sumerienne et Grammaire Comparee. Editions de Boccaro. Paris. 1975.
Gratzer W. The Undergrowth of Science. OUP. 2000.
Green J. The Slang Thesaurus. Elm Tree Books. 1986.
Greene J. Psycholinguistics. Chomsky and Psychology. Penguin. 1972.
Greenfield S. The Human Brain. Weidenfeld & Nicolson. 1997.
Gregory R L. The Oxford Companion to the Mind. OUP. 1987.
Halliwell JO. Dictionary of Archaic Words. 1850. Bestseller Publications Ltd, London. 1989.
Hart CWM & Pilling AC. The Tiwi of North Australia. Holt Rinehart & Winston. 1978.
Heller I, Humez A & Dror M. The Private Lives of English Words. Routledge & Kegan Paul 1983.
Hendrichson R. QPB Encyclopedia of Word & Phrase Origins. Facts on File Inc. 1997.
Hillian D. Word Lore. W & R Chambers Ltd, Edinburgh. 1984.
Hogan PC. Cambridge Encyclopedia of the Language Sciences. CUP. 2011.
Horgan J. The Undiscovered Mind. Weidenfeld & Nicolson. 1999.
Humphrey N. A History of the Mind. Chatto & Windus. 1992.
Ifrah G. The Universal History of Numbers from Prehistory to the Invention of the Computer. 1994. Harvill Press. 1998.
Jackendoff R. Foundations of Language. OUP. 2002.
Jakobson R & Waugh L. The Sound Shape of Language. Harvester Press. 1979.
Janov A. The Primal Revolution. Abacus. 1978.
Janson T. Speak. A Short history of Languages. OUP. 2002.
Jaynes J. The Origin of Consciousness in the Breakdown of the Bicameral Mind. Penguin. 1976.
Johnson Samuel. Dictionary of the English Language. Times Books. 1983.
Jones S. The Language of the genes. Harper Collins. 1993.
Jones S. In the Blood. God, Genes and Destiny. Harper Collins. 1993.
Jung C. Man & his Symbols. 1964. Picador. Pan Books Ltd. MacMillan. 1978.

Bibliography

Kallir A. Sign and Design. Vernon, Richmond, Surrey. 1961.
Katan NJ. Hieroglyphs. British Museum Publications. 1980.
Katzner K. The Languages of the World. Routledge & Kegan Paul. 1975.
Kenny A. Wittgenstein. Pelican. 1975.
Kenny A. Frege. Penguin Books. OUP. 1995.
Kohn M. A Reason for Everything. Faber & Faber. 2004.
Kovekses Z. Metaphor. OUP. 2002.
Langer SK. An Introduction to Symbolic Logic. Dover Publications. 3rd Edn. 1967.
Lanman CR. A Sanskrit Reader. Harvard University Press. 1884. Motilal Banarsidass 2010.
Leakey L S B and Goodall VM. Unveiling Man's Origins. Methuen & Co. 1970.
Leakey R and Lewin R. Origins. MacDonald & Jane Publishers. BCA. 1977.
Leech G. Semantics. Pelican. 1974. Penguin. 1983.
Lepore L. Smith BC. Oxford Handbook of the Philosophy of Language. Clarendon Press. 2006.
Levy GR The Gate of Horn. Faber & Faber. 1948.
Levy-Bruhl L. How Natives Think. 1926. Princeton University Press. 1985.
Levy-Strauss C. Structural Anthropology. 1963. Penguin Books. 1977.
Lewin R. The Origin of Modern Humans. Scientific American Library. HPHLP NY. 1993.
Lewis CS. Studies in Words. CUP. 2nd Edn. Canto. 1990.
Lewis N. The Book of Babel. Penguin Books. 1994.
Lieberman P. On the Origins of Language. MacMillan. 1975.
Lieberman P. Eve Spoke. Picador. MacMillan Publishers. 1998.
Lockwood WB. A Panorama of Indo European Languages. Hutchinson. 1972.
Loritz D. How the Brain Evolved Language. OUP. 1999.
Lyell C. Principles of Geology. 1830. University of Chicago Press. 1990.
Lyons J. New Horizons in Linguistics. Pelican. 1970.
Lyons J. Chomsky. Fontana. William Collins. 1978.
Lyons J. Language Meaning & Context. Fontana. 1981.
Macdonnell AA. A Practical Sanskrit Dictionary. 1924. OUP. 1976.
MacQueen JG. The Hittites. Thames and Hudson. 1975. Revised Edition. 1996.
MacWhorter J. The Power of Babel. William Heineman. 2001.
Manser MH. Bloomsbury Good Word Guide. 1988. Bloomsbury Publications. 1990.
Matthews PH. Concise Dictionary of Linguistics. OUP. 1997.
Mazar A & Trone A. Voices from the Past. Harvey House Inc. New York. 1967.
Mazonowicz D. Voices from the Stone Age. Allen & Unwin. 1975.
Mengham R. The Descent of Language. Bloomsbury Publishing Ltd. 1993.
Miller G. Language & Speech. W H Freeman. 1981.
Miller G. The Science of Words. Scientific American Library. 1991.
Mithen S. The Prehistory of the Mind. Thames & Hudson. 1996.
Monier-Williams M. Sanskrit English Dictionary. OUP. 1872. 6th Asian Educational Services Edition. New Delhi. 2012.
Moore T & Carling C. Understanding Language: towards a Post Chomskian Linguistics. MacMillan Press Ltd. 1982.
Moore T & Carling C. The Limitations of Language. McMillan Press. 1988.

Bibliography

Nichols J. Linguistic Diversity in Space & Time. University of Chicago. 1992.
Nichols J. Sounds Like Life. The Pasteza Quechoah Language of Ecuador. OUP.
Norrman R. & Haarberg J. Nature and Language. Routledge & Kegan Paul. 1980.
O'Connor JD. Phonetics. 1973. Penguin Books. 1978.
Onions CT. Oxford Dictionary of English Etymology. 1996. OUP 1970.
Oppenheimer S. Eden in the East. Weidenfeld & Nicolson. 1998.
Ostler N. Empires of the Word. Harper Collins. 2005.
Ouaknin Mark-Alain. Mysteries of the Alphabet. The Origins of Writing. New York. Abbeville Press Publishers. 1999.
Oxford English Dictionary on CD.
Oxford Dictionary of Psychology. OUP 2001 Colman AM
Oxford Dictionary of Word Origins. OUP 2002 Chantrell G
Oxford Handbook of the Philosophy of Language. Clarendon Press. 2006 Lepore L Smith BC
Oxford Handbook of Psycholinguistics. OUP 2007 Gaskell GM
Papermac. 1811 Dictionary of the Vulgar Tongue. Digest Bookstore. 1982.
Partridge E. Origins. A Short Etymological Dictionary of Modern English. 1958. Routledge & Kegan Paul. 1978.
Partridge E. A Dictionary of Slang. 1937. Routledge. 8th Edn. 2000.
Partridge E. From Sanskrit to Brazil. Hamish Hamilton. 1951.
Piggott S. The Dawn of Civilisation. Thames & Hudson. 1961.
Pinker S. The Language Instinct. Allen Lane, Penguin Press. 1994.
Pinker S. How the Mind Works. Allen Lane, Penguin Press. 1997.
Pinker S. Words & Rules. Weidenfeld & Nicolson. 1999.
Pinker S. The Blank State. Allen Lane. 2002.
Popper KR. The Logic of Scientific Discovery. Hutchinson & Co. 9th Impression. 1977.
Pribram KH. Brain & Perception. Lawrence Erlbaum Associates. 1991.
Radin P. Primitive Man as Philosopher. 1927. Dover Publications. 1957.
Ravin Y. Lexical Semantics without Thematic Roles. OUP. 1990.
Recoeur P. The Rule of Metaphor. Routledge & Kegan Paul. 1978.
Rees N. Dictionary of Word & Phrase Origins. Cassell. 1996.
Renfrew C. Before Civilisation. Jonathan Cape. 1973.
Renfrew C. Archaeology and Language. Pimlico. Random House. 1987.
Renfrew C. Firth C. Malafouris. The Sapient Mind, OUP. 2009.
Ridley M. The Origins of Virtue. Softback Preview. 1997.
Room A. Dictionary of True Etymologies. Routledge & Kegan Paul. 1987.
Room A. The Cassell Dictionary of Word origins. Cassell. 1999.
Safire W. William Safire on Language. 1980. Avon Books. Hearst Coorporation. 1981.
Samuels ML. Linguistic Evolution. CUP. 1972.
Savage-Rumbaugh S, Shankar SG, Taylor TJ. Apes, Language & the Human Mind. OUP. 1998.
Sayce AH. The Hittites. Religious Tract Society. 1903. Elibron Classics. Adamant Media Corporation. 2005.
Scientific American. Human Communication. Language & its Psychological Bases. 1981.
Searle J. Mind Language & Society. Weidenfeld & Nicolson. 1999.

Bibliography

Shipley JT. Dictionary of Word Origins. Philosophical Library Inc. 1945.
Shlain L. The Alphabet versus the Goddess. Allen Lane. Penguin Press. 1999.
Skeat WW. An Etymological Dictionary of the English Language. 1879-82. OUP.1983.
Slobin D I. Psycholinguistics. Scott Foresman & Co. 1974.
Smith N & Wilson D. Modern Linguistics. The results of Chomsky's Revolution. Pelican. 1979.
Speake J. Dictionary of Foreign Words and Phrases. OUP. 1997.
Spender D. Man Made Language. Routledge & Kegan Paul. 1980.
Springer SP & Deutsch G. Left Brain Right Brain. WH Freeman & Co, San Francisco. 1947.
Stainton RS. Words and Thoughts. Clarendon Press. 2006.
Sternberg RJ & Ben-Zeev T. Complex Cognition. The Psychology of Human Thought. OUP. 2001.
Stevens A. Ariadne's Clue, A Guide to the Symbols of Humankind. Allen Lane. Penguin Press. 1998.
Sturrock J. Structuralism. Paladin Grafton Books. 1986.
Taylor I. Words and Places. 1911. J M Dent. EP Publishing Ltd. 1978.
Taylor JR. Linguistic Categorisation. OUP. 1989.
Todd L. Pidgins and Creoles. Rutledge & Kegan Paul. 1974.
Tolstoy I. The Knowledge & the Power. Reflections on the History of Science. Cannongate Publishing. 1990.
Ungnad A. Akkadian Grammar. Society of Biblical Literature. 1879. 5th Edn. Scholars Press. Atlanta, Georgia. 1992.
Trask R L. Key Concepts in Language & Linguistics. Routledge. 1999.
Urdan L. Dictionary of Differences. Bloomsbury Publishing. 1988.
Van den Hout T. Elements of Hittite. CUP. 2011.
Volk K. A Sumerian Reader. Pontifical Biblical Institute, Rome. 2nd Edition. 1999.
Walker E. Explorations in the Biology of Language. Harvester Press. 1978.
Walsingham Lord T. Fauna Hawaiiensis Vol 1 Pt 5. Microlepidoptera. CUP 1907.
Walsingham Lord J, On The Origins of Speaking. Trafford, Canada. 2006.
Watterson B. Introducing Egyptian Hieroglyphs. Scottish Academic Press. 1981.
Weiner J. Frege. OUP. 1999.
Whitney WD. The Life and Growth of Language. Dover Publications. 1979.
Wills C. Exons, Introns and Talking Genes. OUP. 1992.
Wills C. The Runaway Brain. The Evolution of Human Uniqueness. Harper Collins 1993.
Wilson H. Understanding Hieroglyphs. Michael O'Mara Books Ltd. 1993.
Wittgenstein L. Tractatus Logico Philosophicus. Routledge & Kegan Paul. 1974.
Wittgenstein L. Philosophical Investigations. Blackwell Publishing. 1953. 3rd Edition 2001.
Wray A. The Transition to Language. OUP. 2002.
Yule and Burnell AC. Hobson-Jobson. 1886. 2nd Edition 1903. 3rd Edition 1985. Routledge & Kegan Paul. 1986.

www.ingramcontent.com/pod-product-compliance
Lightning Source LLC
Chambersburg PA
CBHW080410170426
43194CB00015B/2767